Odense University Studies History and Social Sciences
vol. 245

The Amsterdam Treaty

The Amsterdam Treaty:
National Preference Formation, Interstate Bargaining and Outcome

Edited by
Finn Laursen

Odense University Press 2002

© The authors and Odense University Press 2002
Printed by Narayana Press
Cover design by Maria Berenice Lara-Laursen and Unisats ApS
ISBN 87-7838-619-5
ISSN 0078-3307

Odense University Press
Campusvej 55
DK-5230 Odense M
Phone: +45 6615 7999
Fax: +45 6615 8126
E-mail: Press@forlag.sdu.dk
Internet: www.oup.dk

Distribution in the United States and Canada:
International Specialized Book Services
5804 NE Hassalo Street
Portland, OR 97213-3644 USA
Phone: +1-800-944-6190

Table of Contents

List of Contributors	*ix*
Acknowledgements	*xiii*
Preface	*xv*

Chapter 1:
Introduction: Overview of the 1996-97 Intergovernmental
Conference (IGC) and the Treaty of Amsterdam   1
Finn Laursen

Section 1: National Preference Formation

Chapter 2:
Austria: Trailing Behind and Raising the Flag   23
Christine Neuhold

Chapter 3:
Belgium: From Orthodoxy to Pragmatism   43
Bart Kerremans

Chapter 4:
Denmark: The Battle for a Better Treaty   71
Finn Laursen

Chapter 5:
Germany: Safeguarding the EMU and the Interests of the *Länder*   93
Rita Beuter

Chapter 6:
Finland: From Cautious to Hard-Core Member   121
Esko Antola

Chapter 7:
France: A Member State Losing Influence?   139
Florence Deloche-Gaudez

Chapter 8:
Greece: The Difficult Road from Orthodoxy to Neo-Orthodoxy   161
Constantine A. Papadopoulos

Chapter 9:
Ireland: The Politics of Pragmatism?   201
Ben Tonra

Chapter 10:
Italy: From the "Hard Core" to Flexible Integration   225
Laura Corrado

Chapter 11:
Luxembourg: Strong Trends towards 'Communitarized'
Problem-Solving   255
Danielle Bossaert

Chapter 12:
The Netherlands: The Mixed Fruits of Pragmatism   267
Marco Langendoen & Alfred Pijpers

Chapter 13:
Portugal: Preserving Equality and Solidarity among Member States   291
Clotilde Marinho

Chapter 14:
Spain: A "Difficult" Negotiation Partner?   311
Felipe Basabe Lloréns

Chapter 15:
Sweden: Constrained but Constructive?   341
Karl Magnus Johansson & Anna-Carin Svensson

Chapter 16:
The United Kingdom: From Isolation Towards Influence?   359
Edward Best

Section 2: Institutional Actors

Chapter 17:
The European Commission: Seeking the Highest
Possible Realistic Line   381
Mark Gray

Chapter 18:
The European Parliament: Win-Sets of a Less Invited Guest   405
Andreas Maurer

Section 3: Interstate Bargaining

Chapter 19:
First Pillar: The Domestic Politics of Treaty Reform
in Environment and Employment   453
Jonas Tallberg

Chapter 20:
The Common Foreign and Security Policy: Significant
but Modest Changes   473
Simon Duke

Chapter 21:
A New Area of Freedom, Security and Justice:
The Shaping of a Hybrid Compromise   509
Monica den Boer

Chapter 22:
Negotiating Flexible Integration   537
Alexander Stubb

Chapter 23:
Institutions and Procedures: The Limited Reforms   565
Finn Laursen

Section 4: Conclusions

Chapter 24:
Negotiating the Amsterdam Treaty: When Theory Meets Reality   593
Derek Beach

Chapter 25:
Explaining and Evaluating the Amsterdam Treaty:
Some Concluding Remarks   639
Finn Laursen

List of Contributors

Esko Antola	Professor, Jean Monnet Chair, University of Turku, Finland
Felipe Basabe Lloréns	Director General, Fundación Hispano-Portuguesa Rei Afonso Henriques, Zamora, Spain
Derek Beach	Ph.D. student, Department of Political Science, University of Southern Denmark, Odense, Denmark
Edward Best	Professor. Responsible for European Governance and Policy Processes, European Institute of Public Administration, Maastricht, The Netherlands
Rita Beuter	Senior lecturer, European Institute of Public Administration, Maastricht, The Netherlands
Danielle Bossaert	Lecturer, European Institute of Public Administration, Maastricht, The Netherlands
Laura Corrado	Research assistant, European Institute of Public Administration, Maastricht, The Netherlands
Monica den Boer	Associate Professor of Public Administration, Centre for Law, Public Administration and Informatisation, Faculty of Law, Tilburg University, The Netherlands
Florence Deloche-Gaudez	Chargée de mission, Centre européen de Sciences Po, Paris, France
Simon Duke	Associate Professor, European Institute of Public Administration, Maastricht, The Netherlands

Mark Gray	Associate, White & Case LLP, Brussels. Formerly IGC 2000 Unit, European Commission, Brussels
Karl Magnus Johansson	Associate Professor in Political Science and Researcher, Institute of Contemporary History, Södertörn University College, Huddinge, Sweden
Bart Kerremans	Associate Professor in International Relations, Department of Political Science, Katholieke Universiteit Leuven, Belgium
Marco Langendoen	Free lance researcher for the Clingendael Institute, The Hague, The Netherlands
Finn Laursen	Professor of International Politics, Department of Political Science, University of Southern Denmark, Odense, Denmark
Clotilde Marinho	Lecturer, European Institute of Public Administration, Maastricht, The Netherlands
Andreas Maurer	Lecturer, Forschungsinstitut für Politische und Europäische Fragen, Cologne, Germany
Christine Neuhold	Assistant Professor, Department of Political Science, Institute for Advanced Studies, Vienna, Austria
Constantine A. Papadopoulos	Advisor for European Affairs, EFG Eurobank, Athens, Greece. Former diplomat, member of the Greek delegation to the Reflection Group and the 1996-97 Intergovernmental Conference
Alfred Pijpers	Senior Research Fellow, The Netherlands Institute of International Relations 'Clingendael', The Hague. Also attached to the Department of Political Science, Leiden University, The Netherlands.

Alexander Stubb	Adviser, Group of Policy Advisors to the President of the European Commission, Brussels. Professor, College of Europe, Bruges, Belgium
Anna-Carin Svensson	Ph.D., Department of Government, Uppsala University, Sweden
Jonas Tallberg	Research Fellow, Department of Political Science, Lund University, and Swedish Institute of International Affairs, Stockholm, Sweden
Ben Tonra	Deputy Director, Dublin European Institute, University College Dublin, Ireland

Acknowledgments

This book is the outcome of a project which received financial support from the Danish Social Science Research Council. This support is gratefully acknowledged. The editor would also like to acknowledge the co-operation of the European Institute of Public Administration (EIPA), Maastricht, where he worked during the period 1988-95. As will be seen in the List of Contributors, a number of the current scholars at EIPA contributed to this book. Involving a team from EIPA ensured competent contributions, and it made the job of putting a large team together easier. Also thanks to my ex-colleague Sophie Vanhoonacker who took part in and contributed to our meetings without in the end writing a chapter for this book. In many ways, this book can be seen as a sequence to the two books I co-edited with her in Maastricht about the Maastricht Treaty (*The Intergovernmental Conference on Political Union*, 1992, and *The Ratification of the Maastricht Treaty*, 1994, both published in hard cover versions by Nijhoff and in soft cover versions by EIPA).

During this project about the Amsterdam Treaty we had two meetings, where early versions of the chapters were presented. The first took place at the University of Southern Denmark, Odense, 19-20 November 1999, and the second at EIPA, 31 March – 1 April 2000. Most of the chapters were finished during the summer of 2000, but a few in early 2001.

The organiser of the project also wants to thank the Danish Society for European Studies. Some of the members of the Society took an active part in the meeting in Odense in November 1999.

The editor further wants to thank the Department of Political Science at the University of Southern Denmark. The Department's research assistant Steffen Petersen was an invaluable help in connection with the meeting here in November 1999 soon after the organiser (and editor) returned from a year in Japan and moved from Esbjerg to Funen in connection with the university merger that created the new University of Southern Denmark.

During the editorial process Vibeke Pierson, head of the Deartment's secretariat, has been an invaluable help. I am particularly indebted to her for diligent linguistic assistance with this book project.

Finally, I want to thank Stefan Birkebjerg Andersen, the Managing Director of Odense University Press, who accepted this book for publication.

Odense, August 2001.
Finn Laursen

Preface

This book is about the Amsterdam Treaty adopted in 1997 and in force since 1999. The Treaty constitutes a revision of the earlier treaties of the European Communities (EC) and European Union (EU).

When the project started it was organized around analyses of the preferences of the main actors and the bargaining process during the Intergovernmental Conference (IGC) 1996-97, which produced the Amsterdam Treaty. However, beyond such a scheme of preference formation and interstate bargaining no specific theory or approach was imposed on the authors. The contributors were expected to be analytic in the sense of explaining why actor X went into the 1996-97 IGC with certain interests, preferences or positions, and why X made, or did not make, certain formal proposals during the IGC. Actors singled out for studies included all the 15 Member States as well as the European Commission and the European Parliament.

Next, we asked some contributors to analyse specific parts of the negotiations. We selected certain policy areas which, from various perspectives, could be seen as the most significant ones. These areas included changes in the Union's three pillars and the cross-cutting question of 'flexibility':

1. Economic policies in the first pillar, where a new title on employment was introduced and a strengthening of some other policies, including environment, took place,
2. Common Foreign and Security Policy (CFSP) in the second pillar, which *inter alia* saw the introduction of a High Representative for CFSP and the inclusion under the EU's defence dimension of the so-called Petersberg tasks relating to peace keeping, peacemaking and various kinds of humanitarian actions, and
3. Issues falling under cooperation in Justice and Home Affairs (JHA), which used to be under the third pillar of the EU, but which led to the transfer of some policy matters, especially migration and asylum policies, from the third to the first pillar, creating the new Area of Freedom, Security and Justice (AFSJ) under the first pillar. Changes in these areas of JHA also led to the incorporation of the so-called Schengen *acquis* into the EU, i.e. rules following from the abolition of border control within the EU.
4. The question of 'closer cooperation' or 'flexibility', i.e. the possibility that a small group of Member States move ahead of some other members in certain areas.

It was also decided to include a chapter where negotiation theory is confronted with the reality of the Amsterdam IGC negotiations.

In the final chapter. the editor suggests some conclusions from the chapters included in the book and moves beyond questions of explanation to briefly discuss how we can evaluate the Treaty of Amsterdam. How significant was it?

In respect to explanation, it will be suggested that Andrew Moravcsik's framework known as liberal intergovernmentalism constitutes a useful scheme with a number of relevant questions, even if the authors contributing to this book to some extent give answers different from those given by Andrew Moravcsik. On the question of significance, it will be argued that the Amsterdam Treaty, despite its limitations, potentially does contribute to making the EU both more efficient and legitimate. However, the Treaty clearly left the Union in need of further reforms if it is to widen to include most of geographical Europe.

1

Introduction: Overview of the 1996-97 Intergovernmental Conference (IGC) and the Treaty of Amsterdam

Finn Laursen

Background

The Amsterdam Treaty, which was finally negotiated in Amsterdam 16-17 June 1997, resulted from an Intergovernmental Conference (IGC), which had started on 29 March 1996. It was the longest IGC so far in the history of the European Union (EU). Further, the IGC had itself been prepared through the so-called Reflection Group during the second half of 1995.

That such an IGC took place at this point in time was not due to a great wish on the part of the Member States to further deepen integration (Dinan 1999, 169). It took place because the preceding treaty reform resulting in the Maastricht Treaty had included the stipulation in the Treaty's Art. N, that such an IGC should take place in 1996.

Article N specified:

1. The government of any Member State or the Commission may submit to the Council proposals for the amendment of the Treaties on which the Union is founded.
   If the Council, after consulting the European Parliament and, where appropriate, the Commission, delivers an opinion in favour of calling a conference of representatives of the governments of the Member States, the conference shall be convened by the President of the Council for the purpose of determining by common accord the amendments to be made to those Treaties. The European Central Bank shall also be consulted in the case of institutional changes in the monetary area.
   The amendments shall enter into force after being ratified by all the Member States in accordance with their respective constitutional requirements.

2. A conference of representatives of the governments of the Member States shall be convened in 1996 to examine those provisions of this

Treaty for which revision is provided, in accordance with the objectives set out in Articles A and B (Council & Commission 1992, 138).

Agenda Setting

The Treaty also specified some of the agenda points of the future IGC:

- Article N(2): Articles A and B – general principles, including the pillar structure, effectiveness of the mechanisms and the institutions of the Community
- Article 189b(8): scope of the co-decision procedure
- Article J.4(6): security and defence, including role of Western European Union (WEU)
- Article J.10: provisions governing Common Foreign and Security Policy (CFSP)
- Declaration 1: civil protection, energy and tourism
- Declaration 16: hierarchy of Community acts

Thus, unfinished business, and a feeling that further institutional reforms would be required, motivated the decision to call a new IGC relatively soon after Maastricht.

In the end it took a longer time to get Maastricht ratified than foreseen. The treaty finally entered into force in November 1993 (Laursen & Vanhoonacker 1994). The meeting of the European Council in Brussels in December 1993 added the following agenda points for the future IGC:

- role of the European Parliament
- size of the Commission
- weighting of votes in the Council
- efficiency of institutions (European Council 1993)

That the IGC should be prepared by a Reflection Group was decided at the meeting of the European Council on Corfu in June 1994, which also decided that two European Parliament representatives would participate in the work of the group. The Corfu summit further invited the institutions to prepare reports on the functioning of the Maastricht Treaty. The Reflection Group was given the mandate to

> ... examine and elaborate ideas relating to the provisions of the Treaty on European Union for which a revision is foreseen and other possible improvements in a spirit of democracy and openness, on the basis of the

evaluation of the functioning of the treaty as set out in the reports. It will also elaborate options in the perspective of the future enlargement of the Union on the institutional questions set out in the conclusions of the European Council in Brussels and in the Ioannina agreement (weighting of votes, the threshold for qualified majority decisions, number of members of the Commission and any other measure deemed necessary to facilitate the work of the Institutions and guarantee their effective operation in the perspective of enlargement) (European Council 1994).

The Ioannina agreement referred to was concluded in the spring of 1994 in connection with the EU's fourth enlargement. In the EU of 12 Member States, the total number of votes in the Council was 76. Of these a Qualified Majority Vote (QMV) had been established at 54 votes. This meant that a blocking minority consisted of 23 votes. Two big states plus one small state (not including Luxembourg) could thus form a blocking minority. During accession negotiations with the four applicants it was decided to give Austria and Sweden four votes each and Finland and Norway three votes. This would increase the total to 90. It was then proposed, on the basis of an extrapolation, that the new QMV should be 27. The United Kingdom and Spain opposed this. They wanted to keep the blocking minority at 23. The foreign ministers found the compromise at Ioannina in Greece on 26 and 27 March 1994. The blocking minority would be 27 on condition that the Council would try to find a satisfactory solution if a minority between 23 and 27 Member States were against a proposal. In the end Norway did not join, thus, the enlarged EU would have a total of 87 votes and a QMV would be 87. The Ioannina compromise, therefore, came to refer to a situation where Member States representing between 23 and 25 votes opposed a proposal (Laursen 1996, 36). The new members, Austria, Sweden and Finland joined on 1 January 1995. The EU that went through the Amsterdam process thus consisted of 15 Member States.

The European Council at its meeting in June 1993 in Copenhagen had decided to offer membership to the applicant countries from Central and Eastern Europe (CEECs). So part of the context of the Amsterdam process was the future enlargements which might lead to an EU of more than 27 Member States, including 10 CEECs and Cyprus and Malta (Laursen 2001).

Another background was the deteriorating situation in former Yugoslavia, especially in Bosnia-Herzegovina, where EU's efforts to create peace revealed the Union's weakness in respect to the new second pillar of the Maastricht Treaty, the so-called Common Foreign and Security Policy (CFSP). Similarly, questions were asked about the weaknesses of Cooperation in Justice and

Home Affairs (JHA), the Union's third pillar, partly because of the many refugees from former Yugoslavia and other crises areas in the world.

Preparation

During the spring of 1995, the Reflection Group members were appointed (see table 1.1) and the reports of the institutions were presented.

The Reflection Group was chaired by Carlos Westendorp from Spain. It started its work on 2 June 1995 in Messina, Italy, and presented its report to the meeting of the European Council in Madrid in December 1995.

Table 1.1: Members of the Reflection Group.

Austria	Permanent Representative Manfred Scheich
Belgium	Professor Franklin Dehousse
Denmark	Former Secretary General, ambassador Niels Ersbøll
Finland	Former Minister of Defence Ingvar S. Melin
France	Minister of European Affairs Michel Barnier
Germany	State Secretary Dr. Werner Hoyer, Foreign Ministry
Greece	Ambassador Stephanos G. Stathatos
Ireland	Minister of European Affairs Gay Mitchell
Italy	Ambassador Silvio Fagiolo
Luxembourg	Ambassador Joseph Weyland
The Netherlands	State Secretary Michiel Patijn, Foreign Ministry
Portugal	Professor, former Foreign Minister André Goncalves Pereira
Spain	State Secretary Carlos Westendorp, Foreign Ministry
Sweden	State Secretary Gunnar Lund, Foreign Ministry
United Kingdom	Minister of European Affairs David Davis
Commission	Commissioner Marcelino Oreja
European Parliament	Elisabeth Guigou, MEP (French Socialist, former minister of European Affairs) Elmar Brok, MEP (German Christian-Democrat)

Source: Isaksen, Toft and Bødtcher-Hansen (1998), p. 17.

The Cannes meeting of the European Council 26 and 27 June 1995 noted with satisfaction that the work of the Reflection Group had started and suggested that "thoughts should now focus on a number of priorities to enable the Union to respond to its citizens' expectations":

- to analyse the principles, objectives and instruments of the Union, with the new challenges facing Europe;
- to strengthen common foreign and security policy so that it can cope with new international challenges;
- to provide a better response to modern demands as regards internal security, and the fields of justice and home affairs more generally;
- to make the institutions more efficient, democratic and open so that they are able to adjust to the demands of an enlarged Union;
- to strengthen public support for the process of European integration by meeting the need for a form of democracy which is closer to the citizens of Europe, who are concerned about employment and environment questions;
- to put the principle of subsidiarity into practice more effectively (European Council 1995a).

The Reflection Group report recommended that the IGC should concentrate its work on

- making Europe more relevant to its citizens;
- enabling the Union to work better and preparing it for enlargement;
- giving the Union greater capacity for external action (Reflection Group 1995; European Council 1995b, annex 15).

The report had two parts: a 10-page overview and a 50-page summary of the main deliberations. The divisions between the Member States clearly emerged. It often used phrases such as "one of us believes that" and "one of us is opposed to." On some issues, the conclusion might be that "a broad majority of members of the Group favours." It is well know that the minority of one was usually the United Kingdom, which, under the Major Conservative government, opposed further integration (Nugent 1999, 77).

The meeting of the European Council in Madrid in December 1995 received the report from the Reflection Group "with great interest" and concluded that "the guidelines distilled within the Group" constituted "a sound basis for the work of the Conference." It was decided to officially open the IGC in Turin on 29 March 1996. The Madrid summit also laid out the basic procedure:

> The Conference will meet regularly, in principle once a month, at the level of Foreign Affairs Ministers, who will have responsibility for all proceedings; preparations will be conducted by a working party made up of a representative of each Member State's Minister for Foreign Affairs and of the President of the Commission.
> The Secretary-General of the Council will make the necessary arrangements to provide secretarial support for the Conference.

Concerning the European Parliament the Madrid conclusions stated:

> The European Parliament will be closely associated with the work of the Conference so that it is both briefed regularly and in detail on the progress of the discussions and can give its point of view, where it considers this necessary, on all matters under discussion. The detailed arrangements for such association will be determined by the Ministers for Foreign Affairs in line with the provisions which apply to the review of the Treaties.

The Parliament thus was not allowed a full participation despite its full participation in the Reflection Group. Finally, concerning applicant countries and members of the European Free Trade Association (EFTA) the Madrid conclusions stated:

> The representatives of those countries of Central and Eastern Europe which have concluded Europe Agreements, and Malta and Cyprus, will be briefed regularly on the progress of discussions and will be able to put their points of view at meetings with the Presidency of the European Union to be held, in principle, every two months. The European Economic Area and Switzerland will also be briefed (European Council 1995b).

So the applicant countries (minus Turkey) would be able to put forward their points of view. The EEA countries, viz. Norway, Iceland and Lichtenstein, as well as Switzerland, would be briefed.

Prior to the IGC the Member States started putting forward proposals (European Parliament 1996; Griller *et al.* 1996). So did EU institutions and various private organizations.

The European Commission presented its opinion in February 1996 (European Commission 1996). The opinion was organized in three sections. The first section on "A People's Europe" had a first part on the promotion of the European Social model (human rights, rule of law, the social dimension, employment and sustainable development). The second part, "Establishing an area of freedom and security," dealt with Justice and Home Affairs (JHA), including the Schengen Agreement. The Commission suggested that JHA, except judicial cooperation in criminal matters and police cooperation, be transferred to the first pillar of the Union and that the Schengen Agreement be incorporated in the Treaty. A third part on "Simplifying and democratising Europe," *inter alia* suggested the abolition of the cooperation procedure combined with an expanded use of co-decision.

Section two in the Commission opinion was entitled "A Clear Identity on the World Scene." In respect to commercial policy, the Commission called for an updating of the Treaty in respect to services, intellectual property and direct foreign investment, referring to WTO developments. Concerning the Common Foreign and Security Policy (CFSP), the Commission took the view that qualified majority voting (QMV) should be the norm. In respect to the Union's defence identity, the IGC should "allow Union commitments to missions aimed at restoring or keeping peace to be written into the Treaty ('Petersberg' missions)."

The third section in the Commission opinion was entitled "Institutions for the enlarged Europe." Enlargement required an adaptation of the institutions. The European Parliament should be limited to 700 members. Since almost all future new members were relatively small, there was a need to look at voting weights and rules in the Council:

> ... in order to maintain the existing balance, there is justification, when enlargement comes, for either adapting the weighting of votes or introducing a new system which makes a reference both to a majority of the Member States and a majority of the Union's population (Ibid. p. 20).

Further, "in the context of enlargement, the number of [the Commission's] Members should be reduced to one per Member State." Majority voting should become the general rule, and the treaty should organize "closer cooperation" or "flexibility." In this respect the Commission suggested four principles:

(i) compatibility with the objectives of the Union;
(ii) consistency with the institutional framework of the Union;
(iii) opportunity for other Member States which are willing and able to join at any time;
(iv) safeguarding of the single market and the policies accompanying it (Ibid., p. 22).

The IGC started with a meeting of the European Council in Turin on 29 March 1996. The various agenda points were put together in three main groups:

1. A Union closer to its citizens
2. The institutions in a more democratic and efficient Union
3. A strengthened capacity for external action of the Union.

The first group included respect for human rights, democratic values, equality and non-discrimination, JHA issues, the fight against unemployment, a healthy and sustainable environment, and subsidiarity. The second group included simplification of legislative procedures, the scope of co-decision, the composition of the European Parliament, the role of national parliaments, Council voting (weighting of votes, threshold for qualified majority vote, QMV), composition and efficiency of the Commission, functioning of the European Court of Justice and Court of Auditors, and rules to "enable a certain number of Member States to develop a strengthened cooperation." The last point, also know as flexibility, already specified some conditions. It should be "open to all, compatible with [the] Union's objectives, while preserving the *acquis communautaire*, avoiding discrimination and distortions of competition and respecting the single institutional framework." The third group of issues were related to the CFSP, its principles, procedures and structures as well as budgetary provisions. The conference should also study "whether and how the provision for a new specific function could give to the Union the possibility of expressing itself in a more visible and coherent way and with a more perceptible face and voice." Such a new function was popularly known as Mr/Ms CFSP. The Turin Council also called for a clearer definition of the relationship with the Western European Union (WEU) (European Council 1996a).

Conduct of the IGC

While formally the Ministers of Foreign Affairs were responsible for the IGC, "the bulk of the work was done by the Group of Representatives that met regularly for two days a week. Its composition was similar to the Reflection Group, on whose expertise it was thus able to draw" (Petite 1998). (See table 1.2).

Table 1.2: List of IGC Representatives of the Foreign Ministers and Commission President.

Austria	Manfred Scheich, Permanent Representative
Belgium	Philippe de Schoutheete de Tervarant, Permanent Representative
Denmark	Niels Ersbøll, Ambassador, former Secretary-General of the Council
Finland	Antti Satuli, Permanent Representative
France	Michel Barnier, Minister with responsibility for European Affairs
Germany	Werner Hoyer, Minister of State
Greece	Yannis Kranidiotis, MEP, former deputy Minister for European Affairs
Ireland	Noel Dorr, former Secretary of the Department of Foreign Affairs
Italy	Silvio Fagiolo, Minister Plenipotentiary
Luxembourg	Jean-Jacques Kasel, Permanent Representative
The Netherlands	Michiel Patijn, State Secretary
Portugal	Francisco Seixas da Costa, State Secretary
Spain	Javier Elorza-Cavengt, Permanent Representative
Sweden	Gunnar Lund, State Secretary
United Kingdom	Stephen Wall, Permanent Representative
Commission	Marcelino Oreja Aguirre, Commissioner

Source: CONF 3835/96

At the meeting in Florence in June, the European Council noted that the IGC had started its work. It stated that it expected "decisive progress" during the Irish presidency in the second part of the year. It asked the Irish Presidency to prepare "a general outline for a draft revision of the Treaties" for the Dublin meeting in December 1996 (European Council 1996b).

The main achievement of the Irish Presidency was the preparation of the draft requested by the Florence summit.

The draft's main part A was divided into five sections:

1. An Area of Freedom, Security and Justice
2. The Union and the Citizen
3. An Effective and Coherent Foreign Policy
4. The Union's Institutions
5. Enhanced Cooperation – "Flexibility"

There was also a part B on other issues and a part C on simplification of the treaties. Most of this structure was retained by the final Treaty of Amsterdam. However, the draft was still very tentative, suggesting some new treaty texts, but in many cases limiting itself to outline issues or options (CONF 2500/96).

The meeting of the European Council in Dublin 13 and 14 December welcomed the draft from the Presidency, seeing it as "a good basis" for future work. It called for completion of the IGC at Amsterdam in June 1997.

The Dublin summit noted "with approval the particular importance which the Presidency document attaches to the area of Justice and Home Affairs." It called on the IGC

> ... to work to reach agreement on a strengthened capacity for action in relation to visas, asylum, immigration, the crossing of external borders, the fight against drugs and international crime including terrorism, offences against children and trafficking in persons. Europol should have operative powers working in conjunction with the national authorities to this end. These issues are of the most serious concern to citizens in all Member States and the Union must be given the means to act effectively in these areas.

The summit reaffirmed the importance of strengthening the Union's capacity for external action. It also noted the absence of texts in the Irish draft concerning "the issue of flexibility and on certain sensitive institutional questions." On the latter, the European Council stated:

> Institutional issues will be central to the next phase of the negotiations. The Union needs to improve its ability to take decisions and to act. This is already true today and it will be even more necessary as the Union moves to enlarge its membership further. The Union must have comprehensible, transparent and democratic procedures and strong and effective institutions which enjoy legitimacy in the eyes of its citizens (European Council 1996c).

It was then left to the Dutch Presidency to finish the IGC during the first half of 1997.

One reason the IGC had moved slowly during 1996 was the opposition of the British Conservative government to the kind of changes most Member States considered important. It was no secret that it was hoped by many that the upcoming elections in the UK would lead to a change of government.

On 1 May 1997 the Labour Party won the elections. According to the Party Manifesto, Labour would give Britain a leadership role in Europe. The agenda for reform included rapid completion of the single market, high priority for enlargement, urgent reform of the Common Agricultural Policy, greater openness and democracy in EU institutions, Britain's signature of the Social Chapter, but also:

> Retention of the national veto over key matters of national interest, such as taxation, defence and security, immigration, decisions over the budget and treaty changes, while considering the extension of Qualified Majority Voting in limited areas where that is in Britain's interest (UK, Labour 1997).

The new Minister for Europe, Dough Henderson, took part in a meeting of the IGC Working Group of Personal Representatives in Brussels on 5 May 1997.

To prepare the Amsterdam summit scheduled for 16-17 June 1997, the Dutch Presidency decided to call a special summit on 23 May in Noordwijk. It was prepared at a meeting of foreign ministers in the Hague on 20 May. On 14 May 1997, prior to the meeting, the Dutch Presidency tabled a new compilation of texts under discussion, a so-called Non-Paper (SN/2555/97). After the summit in Noordwijk, where the EU leaders had a chance to meet the new British Prime Minister Tony Blair, optimism about Amsterdam increased.

The Non-Paper was followed by a "Consolidated Draft Treaty Texts" on 30 May 1997 (SN 600/97 (C 101)). Finally, the Draft Treaty of Amsterdam was issued on 12 June 1997 (CONF/4000/97).

The Amsterdam summit started 16 June in the morning and went into the early hours of 18 June. After the first day of discussions, the Dutch presidency put forward a working document in the morning of 17 June with suggestions for an overall compromise (CONF/4000/97 ADD.1).

Overview of the Amsterdam Treaty

The draft treaty which eventually emerged in Amsterdam in the morning of 18 June 1997 had the five sections of the Irish presidency draft plus a sixth section on Simplification and Consolidation of the Treaties (CONF/4001/97).

The first section, Freedom, Security and Justice, dealt with fundamental rights and non-discrinimation as well as the Progressive Establishment of an Area of Freedom, Security and Justice (see contribution to this volume by Monica den Boer). "The Union is founded on the principles of liberty, democracy, respect for human rights and fundamental freedoms, and the rule of law, principles which are common to the Member States" (amended Art. F). However, the Union must also "respect the national identities of its Member States." A general non-discrimination clause was added to the treaty, but the main innovation was a system of penalties against Member States that failed to respect the fundamental rights.

The new Area of Freedom, Security and Justice was one "in which the free movement of persons is assured in conjunction with appropriate measures with respect to external border controls, immigration, asylum and the prevention and combating of crime" (CONF/4001/97, p. 11). Basically the treaty moved a number of policy matters from the third pillar to the first pillar over a 5-year transition period during which unanimity would apply. However, the decision to fully apply the Community method for this area after five years would require a unanimous vote in the Council, except for aspects of visa policy, for which QMV already applied (Ibid., p. 20). The Treaty further integrated the Schengen *acquis* into the framework of the European Union, with certain matters relating to free movement eventually to go to the first pillar and other matters relating to police cooperation to the third pillar. The much reduced third pillar, dealing with Police and Judicial Cooperation in Criminal Matters, was improved in various ways, for instance by introducing the new instrument framework decision, which resembles the directive in the first pillar.

Protocols on the UK, Ireland (retaining border controls) and Denmark (only taking part in intergovernmental cooperation) complicated the JHA areas considerably.

The second section, The Union and the Citizen, included a new title on employment and improved articles on social policy, environment, public health and consumer protection (see contribution to this volume by Jonas Tallberg). The employment chapter called for a high level of employment, coordination, guidelines and incentive measures. In respect to social policy, the most important was that the UK now joined. The chapter on environment introduced the concept of sustainable development. Member States were allowed to "introduce national provisions based on new scientific evidence." The Commission must be notified. It will have six months to approve or reject the provisions, but "in the absence of a decision by the Commission within this period the national provisions ... shall be deemed to have been approved" (Art. 100a).

A number of other community policies were also included, some clearly less important than others: Citizenship of the Union, culture, sport, countering fraud affecting the financial interests of the Community, strengthening customs cooperation, outermost regions, island regions, overseas countries and territories, services of general economic interests, public service broadcasting, public credit institutions in Germany, voluntary service activities, animal welfare, trans-European networks and statistics. It was now specified that "Citizenship of the Union shall complement and not replace national citizenship." And the Union should respect and promote the diversity of cultures. The second section also had chapters on subsidiarity, transparency (decisions to be taken "as openly as possible," right of access to documents) and quality of legislation (Ibid., pp. 53-93).

Section three, An Effective and Coherent External Policy, mainly dealt with CFSP. It established a policy planning and early warning unit (Declaration to the Final Act, ibid., p. 111). The Secretary-General of the Council was to become High Representative for CFSP, seconded by the deputy Secretary-General who would be responsible for running the secretariat of the Council (Art. J.8). The third section also introduced a new category of "common strategies" to be decided by the European Council by unanimity. The Council should in principle be able to adopt joint actions, common positions or other decisions on the basis of a common strategy by a special QMV (at least 62 votes in favour, cast by at least 10 members). On this point, however, the treaty included a double safeguard. First a Luxembourg-compromise-type veto:

> If a member of the Council declares that, for important and stated reasons of national policy, it intends to oppose the adoption of a decision to be taken by qualified majority, a vote shall not be taken. The Council may, acting by a qualified majority, request that the matter be referred to the European Council for decision by unanimity (Art. J.13(2)).

Secondly, something known as "constructive abstention" found its way into the treaty:

> When abstaining in a vote, any member of the Council may qualify its abstention by making a formal declaration .... In that case, it shall not be obliged to apply the decision, but shall accept that the decision commits the Union. In a spirit of mutual solidarity, the Member State concerned shall refrain from any action likely to conflict with or impede Union action based on that decision and the other Member States shall respect its position. If the members of the Council qualifying their

abstention in this way represent more than one third of the votes in accordance with Article 148(2) of the TEC, the decision shall not be adopted (Art. J.13).

Finally, the third section added services and intellectual property to the common commercial policy in the first pillar. Contrary to the normal QMV provision of the old Article 113, however, these new areas would require unanimity.

So, confronting the idea of "an effective and coherent external policy" the Member States hesitated and created loopholes (see also contribution to this volume by Simon Duke).

The Irish December draft outline had included the proposal to endow the Union with legal personality. This proposal was not retained in the final treaty.

Section four dealt with institutions. Not much was achieved in this area despite the importance attached to institutional changes at the outset of the IGC. The main institutional winner was the European Parliament. The use of the assent procedure and co-decision procedure was increased. In the end the increase in the use of QMV was much more modest than expected. And the difficult issues of weights of votes and threshold of QMV in the Council and size on the Commission were postponed (see later contribution by the author to this volume).

Finally, the treaty introduced provisions on flexibility (see contribution to this volume by Alexander Stubb). These introduced general clauses in the common provisions of the Treaty on European Union (TEU), clauses specific to the Treaty Establishing the European Community (TEC or first pillar) and specific clauses for JHA (third pillar). The treaty set tight conditions for using the enabling clauses. No similar enabling clause was included in the second pillar. But, as mentioned, this pillar introduced "constructive abstention," a kind of *ad hoc* flexibility.

Ratification

The Amsterdam Treaty was signed in Amsterdam on 2 October 1997. It entered into force on 1 May 1999, the first day of the second month after being ratified by all Member States. Germany was the first to deposit the instrument of ratification on 7 May 1998. France was the last on 30 March 1999. Ratification required referenda in Ireland and Denmark and a constitutional revision in France.

Table 1.3 gives an overview of the ratification processes in the Member States.

Table 1.3: Ratification of the Treaty of Amsterdam.

Member States	Stages of Ratification	Deposit of instruments
Belgium	Senate (4 June 1998), Chamber of Representatives (17 June 1998), French Community (13 June 1998), Walloon Region (15 June 1998), German Speaking Community (30 November 1998), Flemish Region (15 December 1998), Brussels Capital Region (5 February 1999)	19 February 1999
Denmark	Parliament (7 May 1998), referendum (28 May 1998) (55.1%)	24 June 1998
Germany	Bundestag (7 May 1998), Bundesrat (27 May 1998)	7 May 1998
Greece	Parliament (17 February 1999)	23 March 1999
Spain	Congress of Deputies (8 October 1998), Senate (24 November 1998)	5 January 1999
France	Revision of the Constitution (18 January 1999), National Assembly (4 March 1999), Senate (16 March 1999)	30 March 1999
Ireland	Referendum (22 May 1998) (61.27%), Seanad (18 June 1998), Dáil (25 June 1998)	30 July 1998
Italy	Chamber of Deputies (25 March 1998), Senate (3 June 1998)	24 July 1998
Luxembourg	Parliament (9 July 1998)	4 September 1998
The Netherlands	Second Chamber (5 November 1998), First Chamber (22 February 1998)	31 December 1998
Austria	Parliament (special constitutional law, amendment of the Constitution and Treaty of Amsterdam (9 July 1998)	21 July 1998
Portugal	Parliament (6 January 1999)	19 March 1999
Finland	Parliament (15 June 1998)	15 July 1998
Sweden	Parliament (29 April 1998)	15 May 1998
United Kingdom	House of Commons (19 January 1998), House of Lords (11 June 1998)	15 June 1998

Source: European Commission (2000), p. 372.

Bibliography

CONF 2500/96. Conference of the Representatives of the Governments of the Member States, "The European Union Today and Tomorrow. Adapting the European Union for the Benefit of its Peoples and Preparing for the Future. A General Outline for a Draft Revision of the Treaties," Brussels, 5 December.

CONF 3835/96. Conference of the Representatives of the Governments of the Member States, "Presidency Note: Organization of work at the Intergovernmental Conference," Brussels, 29 March.

CONF/4000/97. Conference of the Representatives of the Governments of the Member States, "Draft Treaty of Amsterdam," Brussels, 12 June.

CONF/4000/97 ADD. 1. Conference of the Representatives of the Governments of the Member States, "Working Document. IGC – Presidency suggested overall compromise," Brussels, 17 June.

CONF/4001/97. Conference of the Representatives of the Governments of the Member States, "Draft Treaty of Amsterdam," Brussels, 19 June.

Council of the European Communities and Commission of the European Communities (1992). *Treaty on European Union*, Luxembourg: Office for Official Publications of the European Communities.

Dehousse, Franklin (1997). "Les résultats de la Conférence Intergouvernementale, *Courier Hebdomadaire*, No. 1567-67, pp. 1-53.

Dehousse, Franklin (1999). *Amsterdam: The Making of a Treaty*, London: Kogan Page.

Dehousse, Franklin, Jacques Vandamme & Louis le Hardy de Beaulieu (eds.). *Union européenne: quels défis pour l'an 2000*, Brussels: Presses interuniversitaires européennes.

Devuyst, Youri (1997). "The Treaty of Amsterdam: An Introductory Analysis," *ECSA Review*, Vol. 10, No. 3 (Fall), pp. 6-14.

Devuyst, Youri (1998). "Treaty reform in the European Union: the Amsterdam process," *Journal of European Public Policy*, Vol. 5, No 4 (December), pp. 615-31.

Dinan, Desmond (1999). *Ever Closer Union: An Introduction to European Integration*. Second Edition, Houndsmills: Macmillan Press.

Dony, Marianne (ed.) (1999). *L'Union européenne et le monde après Amsterdam*, Brussels: Editions de l'Université de Bruxelles.

Duff, Andrew (1997). *Reforming the European Union*, London: Federal Trust/ Sweet and Maxwell.

Duff, Andrew (ed.) (1997). *The Treaty of Amsterdam: Text and Commentary*, London: Federal Trust/Sweet and Maxwell.

Edwards, Geoffrey & Alfred Pijpers (eds.) (1997). *The Politics of European Treaty Reform: The 1996 Intergovernmental Conference and Beyond*, London and Washington: Pinter.

European Commission (1995). "Report on the Operation of the Treaty on European Union," SEC(95) final, Brussels, 10 May.

European Commission (1996). *Intergovernmental Conference 1996: Commission Opinion. Reinforcing political union and preparing for enlargement*, Luxembourg: Office for Official Publications of the European Communities.

European Commission (2000). *General Report on the Activities of the European Union 1999*. Luxembourg: Office for Official Publications of the European Communities.

European Council (1993). "Presidency Conclusions, European Council Meeting in Brussels, 10-11 December," *EC Bulletin*, No 12, points 1.2-1.19.

European Council (1994). "European Council at Corfu 24 – 25 June 1994: Presidency Conclusions." Presidency conclusions since Corfu can be downloaded from: http://ue.eu.int/en/Info/eurocouncil/index.htm

European Council (1995a). "Cannes European Council 26 and 27 June 1995: Presidency Conclusions."

European Council (1995b). "Madrid European Council 15 and 16 December 1995: Presidency Conclusions."

European Council (1996a). "Turin European Council 29 March 1996: Presidency Conclusions."

European Council (1996b). "Florence European Council 21 and 22 June 1996: Presidency Conclusions."

European Council (1996c). "Dublin European Council 13 and 14 December 1996: Presidency Conclusions."

European Council (1997). "Amsterdam European Council 16 and 17 June 1997: Presidency Conclusions."

European Parliament, Intergovernmental Conference Task Force (1996). *White Paper on the 1996 Intergovernmental Conference. Volume II: Summary of Positions on the Member States of the European Union with a View to the 1996 Intergovernmental Conference*. http://europa.eu.int/en/agenda/igc-home/eu-doc/parlment/peen2.htm

European Union (1997). *Consolidated Versions of the Treaty on European Union and the Treaty Establishing the European Community*, Luxembourg: Office for Official Publications of the European Communities.

Friis, Lykke (1997). "Amsterdam-Traktaten og udvidelsen mod Øst," *Økonomi og Politik*, Vol. 70, No. 4, pp. 4-17.

Griller, S., D.P. Droutsas, G. Falkner, K. Forgó, Klatzer, Mayer & M. Nentwich (1996). "Regierungskonferenz 1996: Ausgangspositionen," *IEF Working Paper No. 20*, Vienna: Forschungsinstitut für Europafragen.

Griller, S., D.P. Droutsas, G. Falkner, K. Forgó & M. Nentwich (2000). *The Treaty of Amsterdam: Facts, Analysis, Prospects*, Vienna and New York: Springer Verlag.

Isaksen, Susanne, Ole Toft & Jens Bødtcher-Hansen (1998). *En traktat bliver til. Amsterdam-traktaten: Forberedelse, forhandling og resultat*, Copenhagen: Schultz.

Jopp, Mathias, Andreas Maurer & Otto Schmuck (eds.) (1998). *Die Europäische Union nach Amsterdam: Analysen und Stellungnahmen zum neuen EU-Vertrag*, Bonn: Europa Union Verlag.

Junge, Kerstin (1999). *Flexibility, Enhanced Cooperation and the Treaty of Amsterdam*, London: Kogan Page.

Langrish, Sally (1998). "The Treaty of Amsterdam: Selected Highlights," *European Law Review*, Vol. 23, pp. 3-19.

Laursen, Finn (1996). "Regeringskonferencen '96: Institutionernes rolle," *Samfundsøkonomen*, No. 5 (September), pp. 35-41.

Laursen, Finn (1998). "The EU, Neutrals, the CFSP and Defence Policy," *TKI Working Papers on European Integration and Regime Formation* 26/98, Esbjerg: South Jutland University Press.

Laursen, Finn (2001). "EU Enlargement: Interests, Issues and the Need for Institutional Reform," pp. 206-228, in Svein S. Andersen & Kjell A. Eliassen (eds.), *Making Policy in Europe*, 2nd edition, London: SAGE.

Laursen, Finn & Sophie Vanhoonacker (eds.) (1994). *The Ratification of the Maastricht Treaty: Issues, Debates and Future Implications*, Dordrecht: Martinus Nijhoff.

Lodge, Juliet (1998). "Intergovernmental Conferences and European Integration: Negotiating the Amsterdam Treaty," *International Negotiation*, Vol. 3, pp. 345-362.

Lynch, Philip, Nanette Neuwahl & G. Wyn Rees, eds. (2000). *Reforming the European Union – from Maastricht to Amsterdam*, London: Longman.

McDonagh, Bobby (1998). *Original Sin in a Brave New World: An Account of the Negotiation of the Treaty of Amsterdam*, Dublin: Institute of European Affairs.

Manin, Philippe (ed.) (1996). *La révision du traité sur l'Union Européenne: Perspectives et réalités*, Paris: Editions A. Pedone.

Mattera, A. (ed.) (1996). *La Conférence intergouvernementale sur l'Union européenne: répondre aux défis du XXIe siècle*, Paris: Editions Clément Juglar.

Neunreither, Karlheinz & Antje Wiener (eds.) (2000). *European Integration After Amsterdam: Institutional Dynamics and Prospects for Democracy*, Oxford: Oxford University Press.

Nickel, Dietmar & Michel Petite (1998). "Amsterdam and European Institutional Balance: A Panel Discussion," *Jean Monnet Working Papers No. 18/98*, Cambridge, MA.: Harvard Law School. http://www.law.harvard.edu/Programs/JeanMonnet/papers/98/98-18-.html

Nugent, Neill (1999). *The Government and Politics of the European Union*, Fourth Edition, Houndmills: Macmillan.

Petersen, Nikolaj & Finn Laursen (1998). *Amsterdam-traktaten: Baggrund. kommentarer og perspektiver*, Copenhagen: Den Danske Europabevægelse.

Petite, Michel (1997). "Le traité d'Amsterdam: ambition et réalisme," *Revue du Marché Unique Européen*, Vol. 3, pp. 17-52.

Petite, Michel (1998). "The Treaty of Amsterdam," *Jean Monnet Working Papers 98/2*, Cambridge, MA: Harvard Law School.
http://www.law.harvard.edu/Programs/JeanMonnet/papers/98/98-2-01.htm

Reflection Group (1995). "Reflection Group's Report, Messina 2nd June, Brussels 5th December." http://europa.eu.int/en/agenda/igc-home/eu-doc/reflect/final.html.

SN/2555/97. Conference of the Representatives of the Governments of the Member States, "Non Paper (Compilation of Texts under Discussion)," Brussels, 14 May.

SN 600/97 (C 101). Conference of the Representatives of the Governments of the Member States, "Consolidated Draft Treaty Texts," Brussels, 30 May.

Svensson, Anna-Carin (2000). In the Service of the European Union: The Role of the Presidency in Negotiating the Amsterdam Treaty 1995-97. *Acta Universitatis Upsaliensis, Working Paper*, No. 137, Uppsala: Statsvetenskapliga föreningen.

Telò, Mario & Paul Magnette (eds.) (1998). *De Maastricht à Amsterdam: L'Europe et son nouveau traité*, Brussels: Éditions Complexe.

Section 1:

National Preference Formation

2

Austria: Trailing behind and Raising the Flag

Christine Neuhold

Introduction

Austria, being part of the Union's most recent round of enlargement, got off to a flying start with the 1966 Intergovernmental Conference (IGC).[1] Positions which were co-ordinated not only within the Ministries but also with the regions (*Länder*) and the social partners had to be laid down within barely a year's time. The referendum on Austria's accession to the EU was exceptionally positive: 66% of the Austrians voted in favour of EU-membership.[2] The reasons behind this high level of support are manifold and complex, but here only two will be mentioned:

- the main Austrian newspaper "*Kronenzeitung*" (approx. 1.6 million readers daily) argued in favour of Austria's accession to the EU;
- Austria's two main political parties Austrian People's Party (Österreichische Volkspartei – ÖVP) and Austrian Socialist Party (Sozialistische Partei Österreichs – SPÖ) had pushed for EU accession and had linked membership to economic and political benefits.[3]

Particularities of the Austrian Political System and Public Opinion

One of the striking aspects of the Austrian political system is the (theoretically) strong involvement of the *regions* in EU affairs. Based on constitutional provisions, the nine autonomous *Länder* have the possibility of

---

[1] Austria joined the European Union on 1.1.1995.

[2] In Sweden and Finland 52.2% and 57% respectively voted in favour of EU-membership. In Norway 52,5 % of the people spoke out against EU accession.

[3] The former Secretary of State (Brigitte Ederer) proclaimed, for example, that each Austrian would have a 1000 Schillings (approx. 72.9 Euro) surplus in his/her wallet every month. One of the political arguments put forward by the Austrian government was that being a relatively small country, Austria would be favoured as regards to voting powers in the Council. (See H. Dossi, "Die Position Österreichs zur Regierungskonferenz 1996," Conference at the Vienna Rathaus, October 1995).

influencing the EU decision-making process directly.[4] A central aspect of regional participation is the right of the Länder to give a common binding opinion on EU proposals where legislative powers lie within their capacity. The Federation (*Bund*) will then be bound by this opinion during negotiations on European level.[5]

Another aspect that is particular to the Austrian decision-making process is the relatively strong involvement of the *social partners*, i.e. industry and the Trade Unions (at least in the past). It has become common practice for political actors to co-ordinate their positions with these players, although no reference to social partnership is to be found in the Austrian constitution. Within this context, the attempt was made to counterbalance the fact that during the process of European integration – by the transfer of some policy aspects from the national to the European level – the participation rights of the social partners might be circumscribed. In the so-called "Europe agreement" concluded between the Socialist Party and the People's Party in 1994, the social partners were initially even granted *equal* participation rights on EU level in so far as their "own sphere of competence" or other important interests of theirs were affected. Certain participation rights on EU level were subsequently guaranteed to the social partners. The "equal participation" in EU affairs proved to be impossible, however, as this was regarded as a violation of EC-law: only members of the Austrian government are granted speaking and voting rights in European fora (Falkner & Müller 1998, 31).[6]

Since 1945, a *rigid division* of powers between the Austrian Socialist Party (SPÖ) and the Austrian People's Party (ÖVP) largely dominated the Austrian political system. The two parties have ruled Austria since World War II, either in coalition, or what might even be described as a "collusion," with the country's institutions and posts shared out proportionally between the two ruling parties (*International Herald Tribune*, 5-6 Feb., 2000). The role of the opposition was traditionally rather weak. This trend has gradually been reversing since the mid-1980s. Since 1986, a "deconcentration" of the party

---

[4] The involvement of the Länder as regards European decision-making is laid down in the 1994 amendment to the Federal Constitution (Art. 23d).

[5] Although it was feared that a broad interpretation and frequent use of this constitutional provision would cause conflicts between the Länder and the federation, it has not created (major) practical problems, and the Länder have only given a small number of opinions.

[6] The representatives of the social partners have secured observer status in Council working groups and the weekly co-ordination session with an Austrian member of COREPER.

system has occurred, whereby the two bigger parties could only unite two-thirds of the votes, as opposed to more than 90% in the 1970s.[7]

The number of the relevant parties has risen from three since the 1980s to five when the Greens (1986) and the Liberal Forum (1993) became established parties within the Austrian parliament. The main factor contributing to the end to the dominance of SPÖ and ÖVP, however, was the rise of the Freedom Party.[8] The strength of this party increased dramatically, obtaining less than 5% of the votes in 1983 and 21.9% in 1995 (Müller, Plasser & Ulram 1999, 202). In the last elections to the Austrian parliament (3 October 1999) the Freedom Party could boast 27.2% of the vote, marginally more votes than the mainstream Conservatives (ÖVP), subsequently becoming the second strongest party on the Austrian political scene.[9] These election results reflect most pointedly that the traditional loyalties between voters and parties have been dissolved to a considerable extent. The "diversity" of the Austrian political arena was reduced due to the fact that the members of the Liberal Party did not manage to obtain 4% of the vote to take seats in parliament.

The Austrian President, who has the constitutional right to nominate the Federal Chancellor, and subsequently to propose the other members of the government, appointed the head of the SPÖ, Viktor Klima, to take up government negotiations following the recent election.[10] For more than a hundred days, SPÖ and ÖVP negotiated to form a joint government once again. Only when these coalition negotiations failed – *inter alia* due to differing views on distributing the ministerial portfolios and resistance of the unions as regards pension reform – did the ÖVP subsequently form a coalition with the far right-wing Freedom Party under Jörg Haider.[11] This prompted the United States to recall its ambassador to Austria and European governments to begin downgrading relations in protest against Haider's anti-immigration policies (*Financial Times*, 6 march 2000). The (other) 14 EU Member States suspended bilateral relations with the Austrian government due to the

---

[7] The figures are as follows: 1945 - 94.4 %; 1970 - 93.1%; 1983 - 90.8%; 1990 - 74.9%; 1995 - 66.4%. See Müller (1997), p. 224.

[8] Freiheitliche Partei Österreichs.

[9] The SPÖ has 65; the ÖVP and the FPÖ 52 seats each and the Greens 14 members in the national parliament subsequent to the 1999 elections.

[10] Art. 70 of the Austrian Federal Constitution.

[11] Haider resigned as head of the Freedom Party in late February 2000.

inclusion of the Freedom Party.[12] Thus far, however, they have acted on an intergovernmental basis, outside the Treaty framework.

The fact that co-ordination of EU affairs during the 1996 IGC was split between two chief departments – the Federal Chancellery and the Ministry for Foreign Affairs – stems from the fact that both governmental parties wanted to guarantee their involvement on the European level. While the chancellor was at that time from the SPÖ, the Foreign Minister was appointed by the ÖVP. Initially, immediately subsequent to Austria's accession to the EU, both parties aimed at maximising their influence in EU-coordination. The final compromise reached was that intra-Austrian co-ordination fell under the joint direction of the chancellery and the Foreign Ministry, and that the junior minister of the federal Chancellery in charge of EU co-ordination acts as deputy to the foreign minister in the EU General Council (Müller 1999, 7). One should note, however, that this conflict might subside in the future, for since the October 1999 elections, the chancellor comes from the ÖVP and both fora are now controlled by one and the same party.

Public support for Austria's membership in the EU has declined from almost 67% in June 1994 to 60% in March 2000. The figures nevertheless reflect that even after the EU sanctions against Austria took effect, the majority of the population supported their country's accession to the EU (*Profil*, 6 March 2000). A large majority of the Austrian population were strongly in favour of Austrian neutrality; in a July 1999 public opinion poll 74% of the Austrians stated that the concept of neutrality as it exists today should remain unchanged in the future. Only 25% were in favour of abandoning this feature of Austrian Foreign Policy (*Die Presse*, 4 July 1999). The struggle against unemployment and protection of the environment seems to rank high on the agenda of Austrian citizens. When asked in June 1998 what topics should be dealt with under the Austrian presidency 89% responded that these two issues should be tackled with utmost urgency. 82% of the respondents felt that foreign policy issues and transport were the most pressing and only 48% saw EU enlargement as the most topical issue (*Der Standard*, 6.1998). 47% of the Austrian population fear that the level of unemployment will rise subsequent to EU enlargement. Whereas 53% of the Austrians favour Hungary's accession to the EU, only 24% are in favour of Polish membership (*Die Presse*, 1 April 1999). 50% of the Austrian population welcome the enlargement of the EU in general, whereas 45% are hesitant (*Die Presse*, 24 February 1999).

---

[12] This provision was first included in a communiqué issued by the Portuguese Presidency in early February 2000.

Setting the Stage

By entering the EU in January 1995, Austria was immediately faced with one big challenge: the preparation of the ICG. The first position paper (57 pages), "*Guidelines for the Expected Issues of the Intergovernmental Conference 1996*" was put forward on 30 May 1995.[13] A working group composed of members from the Federal chancellery and the Ministry for Foreign Affairs, in co-ordination with the social partners and some representatives of the *Länder*, developed these guidelines. When this document was submitted to the *Länder* themselves, some leaders (Landeshauptleute) protested about not having had enough time to voice their opinions.

Austria submitted its final paper *Austria's Basic Positions* (*Österreichische Grundsatzpositionen*) to the IGC on 26 March 1996, just a few days before the inauguration of the Conference in Turin. This basis for Austrian participation was co-ordinated with all Federal Ministries, the Social partners, the *Länder*, the Federation of Municipalities and the Federation of Cities (Original: Österreichischer Gemeindebund and Österreichischer Städtebund, respectively).[14] No problems arose this time as regards co-ordination of the position, which might also be explained by the fact that the beginning of the IGC coincided with the constitution of the new Austrian government (interview, 30 March 2000).

---

[13] Original title: Leitlinien zu den voraussichtlichen Themen der Regierungskonferenz 1996, hereafter abbreviated to Guidelines.

[14] The second chamber of the national parliament put forward its respective resolution four weeks before the start of the IGC: The government was asked to:
– respect Austria's federal structure and ensure that representation of the interests of the regions in the EU was guaranteed;
– to push for effective implementation of the principle of subsidarity to ensure that decisions are taken as close as possible to the citizen;
– to stand for a co-ordination of European economic and employment policy and to aim for the inclusion of objectives on high levels of employment into the Treaty;
– to improve the Treaty provisions on environment;
– to ensure that the position of small and medium states remained untouched and that the involvement of national Parliaments within the legislative process is strengthened to commit itself to a reform of the institutions, whereby the Union's capacity to act is even guaranteed in an enlarged Union, especially by increasing qualified majority voting, by a simplification of the decision making procedures and by protecting the role of the Commission as the motor of the Community;
– to argue for more effective co-operation in the field of JHA and to commit itself to more communitarisation of these fields to cope with the dangers of international crime, drug trade and terrorism (http://www.parlinkom.gv.at/pd/pk/1998).

Two of the opposition parties, the Greens and Liberal Forum[15] promulgated motions dealing with the IGC, which were, however, to a large extent not taken up by the two parties then in government.[16] The Greens demanded *inter alia* the postponement of the EMU, elimination of solely monetary convergence criteria and their replacement by social and ecological minimum standards. They opposed a communitarisation of the Schengen Agreement and the integration of the WEU into the EU. The Liberal Forum proposed *inter alia* granting EU citizenship to citizens of third states, who have legally resided in an EU Member State for five years. This party also pushed for an extension of parliamentary rights: The EP should be granted a legislative right of initiative and national parliaments should be responsible for dealing with all EU-regulations and directives (http://www.parlinkom.gv.at/pd/pk/1996).

The co-ordination of the Austrian position *during* the IGC differed from the day-to-day political decision-making process. Although meetings were held with the social partners and the *Länder* once a month and also with the respective Ministries, the final decisions were taken by the Federal Chancellery in unison with the Ministry for Foreign Affairs, and the respective parties were not re-consulted. Conversely to the "congenial" decision making-process (as regards European affairs), the room for manoeuvre during the negotiations with the concerned was largely pre-determined by the Austrian position papers, thereby weakening the bargaining position of the Länder, the respective Ministries and the social partners. The day to day decision making process at working group and COREPER level was furthermore characterised by a high degree of formality due to the Presidency, which provided the national delegation with drafts of Treaty texts and Treaty articles, which were subsequently discussed at the national level with the concerned parties. The framework for negotiation was therefore preset within narrow boundaries. More or less intense negotiations took place, however, when laying down the seven proposals Austria put forward during the IGC. These were formulated in close co-operation with the concerned parties: with the Ministry for Social Affairs in the field of social affairs, with the Ministry for the Environment on environmental issues, etc. (Interview, 30 March 2000).

---

[15] As of the elections of October 1999, the Liberal Forum is no longer part of the Austrian national parliament.

[16] At this point only the positions *not* taken up by the parties then in government are mentioned. The Liberals, for example, demanded that the Schengen Agreement be incorporated into the Treaty, a provision that was eventually incorporated into the Austrian basic positions.

Austrian positions

Austria, being a country with a relatively low unemployment rate (4%) and high social standards, vehemently pushed for the inclusion of provisions on *employment* and social policy into the Treaty. In the Basic Positions statement, Austria argued strongly for the inclusion of objectives to attain a high level of employment, for the inclusion of a chapter on employment and for the creation of a supervisory mechanism controlling the endeavours of the Member States in this field (Austrian delegation 1996 (II)).

Austria regarded the inclusion of the provisions on the protocol on social policy into the Treaty as a priority, where the Commission should be obliged to examine all proposals as regards their influence and effects on social- and employment policies.[17] An aspect not yet treated in the *Guidelines* was the question of equal treatment for men and women, where Austria stipulated in the *Basic Positions* that this principle be strengthened and demanded the inclusion of the possibility of *affirmative action* into the Treaty.

A respective working paper was put forward by the Austrian delegation during the IGC, which was eventually replicated almost word-by-word in the Amsterdam Treaty. Another aspect foreseen in the Austrian contribution and eventually included in the Amsterdam Treaty concerned the extension of the principle of equal treatment (which so far had only applied to the principle of equal pay) to working life and employment in general (Austrian delegation 1996b). One has to add, however, that the progress made by the Amsterdam Treaty within the field of equal treatment of men and women derived not solely from the Austrian initiatives within this field, but altso to a great extent from a close co-operation between the Austrian and Swedish delegations, where the respective provisions were drafted by both delegations near the end of the Conference.

Two more Austrian contributions, forwarded during the IGC, dealt with employment policy. In the working paper submitted in April 1996, the necessity of the Union to promote full employment and the obligation of the Member States to present multi-annual reports outlining the national strategies in the field of employment was stressed (Austrian delegation 1996a).

To stress the necessity of the promotion of *full employment* (in the Social Democratic tradition), Austria highlighted this principle in a proposal once again in November 1996. Ultimately, the stipulation was not incorporated into the Amsterdam Treaty itself, but found entry into the Amsterdam European Council conclusions. Another proposal, which was not taken up, was that Member States should submit multi-annual programmes and plan ahead for

---

[17] In the guidelines, Austria still stated that these provisions should fall under the co-decision procedure and that the possibility of extending qualified majority voting in this field should be reviewed during the IGC.

a longer time span. What is foreseen in the Treaty is a leaner version: "each Member State shall provide the Council and the Commission with an annual report."[18] Austria not only supported the notion that the Council should be able to make recommendations to Member States (a possibility now foreseen in the Treaty), but pushed for stronger supervisory measures where the Council would *inter alia* have the possibility to fix deadlines for the implementation of certain measures and in case of non-compliance would make the recommendations public (Austrian delegation 1996g).

As one of the countries boasting the highest environmental standards, within the EU, Austria welcomed any further developments in this area such as including the objective of *"sustainable development"* into the Treaty and the integration of environmental considerations into other policies such as CAP and transport policy. In order not to have to abandon their high environmental standards the possibility of Member States to attain to or to introduce higher environmental standards should be anchored into the Treaty. Although the granting of co-decision rights to the European Parliament (EP) in this field and the extension of majority voting were generally welcomed, it was stipulated for politically sensitive areas such as water resources and environmental planning that unanimity should still be the rule (Austrian Delegation 1996(II). Austria put forward two proposals in the field of environment during the IGC: the first dealing with Article 100A and 30 TEC (ex-36). None of the proposed changes were eventually incorporated into the Treaty, however [19] (Austrian Delegation 1996d). In the latter proposal Austria underlined *inter alia* the necessity that the Commission carry out an assessment of expected environmental implications in *all* its proposals (Austrian Delegation 1996e). A somewhat leaner version was eventually incorporated into the declaration on environmental impact assessments: "The Conference notes that the Commission undertakes to prepare environmental impact assessment studies when making proposals which may have significant environmental implications." Austria, which has no nuclear power plants, and where a high percentage of the population opposes nuclear power, supported the objective of a gradual phasing out of nuclear energy.[20] It was also an

---

[18] Art. 109q TEU.

[19] Austria proposed to complete Art. 36 with stipulations relating to the protection of the environment. It also proposed, *inter alia*, in that Art. 100A (4) the deletion of the provision allowing Member States to maintain national provisions concerning protection of the natural environment or working environments.

[20] The Austrian population spoke out in a public referendum in 1978, when 50.5% voted against the use of nuclear power in Austria. The nuclear power plant in Zwentendorf was subsequently never put into use.

adamant supporter of the introduction of a protocol on improved protection and respect for animals, a provision that is now to be found in the Treaty.

As regards *institutional reform*, Austria welcomed a progressive extension of the participation and controlling powers of the EP, although it stipulated that the democratic legitimacy of the legislative process in the future would also be exerted by the controlling powers of the national parliaments over the representatives of national governments acting in the Council.[21] To this end participation rights of the national parliaments in the European integration process were to be included in the Treaty, where it would be left to the Member States to concretise this principle. The relationship between national parliaments and the EP was to be characterised by co-operation rather than by competition, where forms of co-operation such as the COSAC could be strengthened. The decision-making procedures should be simplified and reduced to 3: co-decision, assent and consultation. Austria welcomed the extension and simplification of the co-decision procedure to clearly defined policy areas.[22] The strengthening of the role of the EP when nominating the Commission President was seen as a possible step.[23] In connection with the composition of - and the electoral system to- the EP, Austria supported the current proportionality of the allocation of seats among the Member States. It stipulated furthermore that this principle should be taken into account when laying down a maximum number of MEPs – before the background of enlargement – (Austrian delegation 1996 (II)).

To increase the efficiency of decision-making within the EU, an extension of the possibility of qualified majority voting was welcomed, but it was highlighted that this had to be examined on a case-by-case basis.[24] The relatively strong position of smaller and medium-sized states in the Council has been from an Austrian point of view (as a relatively small state this comes as no surprise) "an essential feature of the process of European integration" and was to be retained. The fear of larger states being outvoted by smaller and medium-sized states was viewed as unsubstantiated and unfounded (from an Austrian perspective at least). In an enlarged Union, however, precautions

---

[21] National Parliaments are seen as the primary source of democratic legitimacy.

[22] In the guidelines, Austria still stated that a *possible right of initiative* for the EP is seen to have negative consequences for the role of Commission as the "motor" of European integration and has to be examined.

[23] One possible proposal is that the EP could elect members of the Commission on the basis of a list of names proposed by the European Council.

[24] Qualified majority voting, for example, could be introduced in the areas of taxation and some fields of social policy. Unanimity voting, however, is regarded as a necessity in matters such as decisions on own resources and questions in the area of secondary legislation.

should be taken to that end that a minority should not be able to outvote the majority of the EU-population. Austria opposed any lowering of the blocking minority. The rotation system of the presidency should remain unchanged; but the Council Secretariat could be strengthened. Austria did not oppose a reduction in the number of Commissioners, but stated that each Member State should still be able to nominate a member. Being a federal state, Austria welcomed the extension of competences of the Committee of the Regions, where, for example, this body should be consulted by the EP; its consultation rights should be extended and it should be given the possibility to bring charges before the ECJ.[25] As regards the strong role of the social partners in the Austrian political system, Austria values the role of the ECOSOC, where it should receive the status of a community institution and its members should be appointed for a period of 5 years. A stronger involvement of the ECOSOC was to be examined. Austria also welcomed any attempt to strengthen the social dialogue on the European level. The *Länder* have proposed to grant the Committee of the Regions the right of appeal in case of violations of the principle of subsidarity and also to the regions in case of a violation of their competences. These demands were put forward by the Austrian representative within the reflection group, but were turned down by a majority of the other representatives. Nevertheless, Austria committed itself to defend the demands of the Länder within the IGC (Austrian Delegation 1996 (II)).

Walking the tightrope between its *adherence to neutrality* and its membership in the EU, Austria nonetheless stated that coherence exists between its own objectives and those of the CFSP.[26] It welcomed a gradual transition to the communitarisation of foreign policy, where the participation rights of small and medium states and the role of the Community institutions would be safeguarded within the development of CFSP. It supported the concept of creating a planning unit that should be composed of members from the Council Secretariat, the Commission and the Member States. It should be submitted to the control of the General Secretary of the Council and be institutionally anchored in the Council Secretariat.[27] A gradual transition to more majority voting was seen as a necessary precondition to increase the efficiency of decision-making within the CFSP. For politically sensitive topics touching upon national sovereignty, Austria felt that within the field of defence, unanimity should be the rule. The introduction of majority voting should be accompanied by constructive abstention or opting out. Austria

---

[25] The Länder, the Gemeinde- and the Städtebund have been consulted here and were also involved throughout the Conference.

[26] These objectives could be concretised within the IGC.

[27] In the guidelines, it was still stated that it should be examined whether the planning unit should be led by a personality selected by the European Council.

wanted this possibility of a *backdoor* in security issues whenever it felt it could not go along for fear of jeopardising its neutral position. It opposed a model of flexibility where a group of states would have the possibility to take steps in this field in the name of the Union even without a decision of the EU institutions. Although Austria accepted the leading role of the presidency in the preparation of CFSP decisions, it felt that the structural deficits, especially the lack in continuity, could be improved by an enforced co-operation with a reinforced Council Secretariat, with the Commission and a more intensive involvement of other Troika members. The creation of a "Monsieur PESC" was welcomed (with slight hesitancy). Austria stipulated that it greeted the possibility of giving certain states or persons the responsibility for the implementation of CFSP, given that clear framework conditions (transparency, responsibility) were stipulated. In the area of defence and security, Austria underlined that it adheres to the objectives of the TEU, where CFSP encompasses all issues relating to the security of the EU, one aspect of which is the development of a common defence policy.[28] It stipulated (at least on paper) that it would actively participate in this quest. To ensure further convergence of the WEU and EU, Austria stressed that as regards the Petersberg tasks, it would support the fact that the WEU be submitted to guidelines or instructions of the EU (Austrian Delegation 1996 (II)). What is striking is that in the guidelines as well as in the basic positions no reference is made to the concept of neutrality, although the SPÖ, then the main Austrian political party, has adhered to this concept, but as (now former) chancellor Franz Vranitzky stated: "We can do *without* the wording of neutrality, because we are neutral today and we believe that our negotiators in 1996 also know that we are neutral. Within the government one agrees that security policy should not be restricted to defence policy, but that this also incorporates international crime, money laundering, mafia etc." (*Die Presse*, 31 May1995, my translation). The ÖVP opposed the neutral status of Austria, regarding it as an obstacle in the process of constructing a security architecture for Europe. Foreign policy issues have therefore become one of the "hottest potatoes" on the Austrian political agenda and have in the past been characterised by a trade-off between the two political parties.

The topic of *immigration* is one of the most sensitive and most topical debates within the Austrian political arena.[29] In the *guidelines,* Austria stated that it sees the third pillar as one of its main focal points, as the increasing internationalisation of organised crime and the challenges that result from a

---

[28] In the guidelines, Austria still spoke of a common defence policy, which *might in time lead to a common defence.*

[29] Jörg Haider, head of the Freedom Party, led his election campaign in 1999 with slogans such as "schützt Österreich vor Überfremdung" (Protect Austria from foreigners)...

common market without frontiers necessitate the enforced co-operation in the areas of Justice and Home Affairs (JHA). The provisions on JHA should lay down objectives and tasks to ensure the continuity and dynamics within the third pillar. The working levels should be reduced significantly and clear modalities should be stipulated for financing the activities in this area. Austria welcomed an enforced communitarisation of some of the issues within the third pillar, especially in the fields of visa policy, asylum- and immigration policy, control of external borders and customs co-operation. Criminal law, however, should remain within the third pillar. The Commission should have an increased role as the "motor" of co-operation in the fields of Justice and Home Affairs. The possibility of an obligatory competence of the ECJ into the third pillar was to be reviewed. Not only the scope of the information and controlling rights of the EP were to be extended, but also the role of the national parliaments was not to be neglected. The overlapping of competences in the field of Justice and Home Affairs within the three pillars was to be clarified, and the possibility of the incorporation of the Schengen Agreement into the Treaty was to be a goal for the IGC. The possibility of qualified majority voting was to be introduced step by step, especially when it came to organised crime. From an Austrian perspective, the development of modalities of participation within the field of JHA for non EU states such as Switzerland, Liechtenstein, Norway and Iceland, and also for the countries of Eastern and Central Europe was welcomed (Austrian delegation 1996 (II)). To underline its "humanitarian endeavours," Austria also put forward a working paper concerning the accession of the Union to the European Convention on Human Rights, where Member States condemned by the ECJ of violating the convention would be penalised (Austrian Delegation 1996c).

Another Austrian proposal, submitted together with Italy, concerned the question of Union citizenship, and encompassed rather far-reaching proposals, as the right of Union citizens to demand the adaptation of European legislation and their right to participate in trade unions and other associations created on the European level (Austrian delegation and Italian delegation 1996f).[30]

Bargaining within the IGC

This submission of proposals for the IGC together with another Member State, in this case Italy, constituted an exception within the Austrian bargaining strategy. The initiative to submit common proposals in the field of European Citizenship came from Italy, with Italian representatives coming to Vienna to take up negotiations. Austria, being just new to the Union, saw this

---

[30] Regarding European legislation, the proposal must be elaborated in the form of articles and signed by at least a tenth of the European electorate.

Conference as an opportunity to obtain a political profile and therefore submitted its proposals mainly on its own, regarding this path as a possibility to gain political standing especially in the field of environment and employment policies. It should be noted, however, that Austria co-ordinated its positions to a great extent with countries with similar interests, such as Sweden, Finland and Denmark. Near the end of the Conference, negotiations especially in the field of social affairs began to take off subsequent to the elections in France and Great Britain, when it was clear that both countries would be headed by social democratic governments. Austria and Sweden put forward a common draft promoting the equal treatment of men and women, and the proposed changes were incorporated almost word by word into the Treaty.[31]

In the area of CFSP, where the "ice on the Austrian level was very thin,"[32] and where, due to differing views, no common opinion could be formulated on the Austrian level, Austria carefully avoided the submission of a proposal on the European level. In this context, Austria was content to "sail behind other ships," jump on the bandwagon with other neutral countries without having to present too pronounced a position (Interview, 30 March 2000).

Ratification Process of the Amsterdam Treaty

The constitutional committee of the Austrian parliament laid the first step to the ratification of the Amsterdam Treaty on the 7th of May 1998 with the decision of a federal-constitutional law to ratify the Treaty.[33] The constitutional law, passed by a majority of SPÖ and ÖVP, foresaw that for the conclusion of the Amsterdam Treaty an approval of the first and second chamber of parliament is necessary.[34] The path of a special constitutional law was chosen as one wanted to avoid a classification of all the provisions of the Amsterdam Treaty leading to possible constitutional changes. The opposition brought forward *massive legal doubts*. All three opposition parties felt that the way in which the government dealt with constitutional provisions was unclear and even "careless."[35] Despite these claims, the constitutional committee

---

[31] This was not a formal proposal and had no CONF number.

[32] Original: *"Das Eis war auf österreichischer Ebene so dünn."*

[33] Bundesverfassungsgesetz.

[34] More than 50% of the MEPs have to be present and 2/3 of the votes have to be cast.

[35] A member of the Freedom Party spoke of a careless treatment of the constitution *"ein schludriger Umgang mit der Verfassung."* The Greens argued that that by not classifying

proposed to the first chamber of Parliament on 10th June 1998 that the Treaty be ratified, although the decision was to be taken against the votes of the Freedom Party and the Greens. The Freedom Party based its rejection on the grounds that "they could not accept a further loss of sovereignty," and while the Greens argued that the EU's social and environmental standards were being dismantled even further by the Treaty of Amsterdam, whereas the EU was moving closer together in the areas of police and military- co-operation.

The Liberals welcomed the Treaty as "a step in the right direction," especially in the field of CFSP, though no common European defence policy was laid down, and the decision-making procedures in Council and Commission had not been revised before the expected EU-enlargement.[36] The SPÖ and ÖVP cited the progress made by the new Treaty in fields such as employment and social policy, where respective (soft law) provisions were incorporated into the Treaty; the extension of the co-decision rights of the EP; the extended role of the EU in the fight against international crime by integrating the Schengen Agreement into the Treaty and the strengthening of the role of the EU in the area of peace-keeping (Petersberg tasks).

The necessary two-thirds majority of SPÖ, ÖVP and Liberal votes finally approved the Treaty on the 18th of June 1998. The same parties also approved changes of the Federal constitutional law. The motion of the Greens to put the proposal to a referendum was turned down. The second chamber of parliament had already approved the law, with the votes of SPÖ and ÖVP attaining a two-thirds majority and gave its final approval to both the Amsterdam Treaty and the changes of the Federal-constitutional law with the necessary majority at the beginning of June 1998 (http://www.parlinkom.gv.at/pd/pk/1998). Austria subsequently deposited its instrument of ratification on 9 July 1998.

Amsterdam "Leftovers": The Intergovernmental Conference on Institutional Matters

Austria is committed, at least on paper, to a "broad-based and far-reaching review of institutional questions," but in connection with the re-weighting of votes in the Council states that all that can be considered is a *modest adjustment*, even if the five Member States forego their current right to nominate a second Commissioner. In this quest, it stresses that the present

---

constitutional provisions one would lose the insight into what was basic law and what was constitutional law (http://www.parlinkom.gv.at/pd/pk/1998).

[36] The Liberals put forward a resolution in which they stipulated their reservations, but stated that the Treaty should come into force as soon as possible (http://www.parlinkom.gv.at/pd/pk/1998).

qualified majority threshold should not be increased, nor should the blocking minority be reduced. Before the background of enlargement precautions should be taken, however, it is required that the minority should not be able to outvote the majority of the population.

Austria underlines on the one hand that it will continue the "pro-integration stance," which it had already adopted at the last IGC, but it does not welcome an unconditional surrender to the introduction of qualified majority voting in the Council. Objective criteria are needed as regards areas where the unanimity rule is to continue to apply. Consideration in this context might be given to legislative acts of a constitutional character; legislative acts requiring national ratification, derogations from the internal market and the own-resources decision. Furthermore, Austria wants to retain unanimity for areas of special national interest such as water resources and choice of energy resources.

As one of the small Member States, Austria has also "a special interest in seeing the Commission remain a strong and independent Institution," which might sound rather contradictory given the fact that the right of every Member State to appoint at least one member of the Commission is nevertheless regarded as vital. Austria rejects the idea of junior Commissioners, but welcomes administrative reforms, which, however, require no amendments to the Treaties (Austrian Delegation 2000).

Conclusions

For Austria, being one of the youngest members of the Community facing a post Maastricht EU from the very outset, this Intergovernmental Conference was somewhat of a first *"trial round."* Its proposals were carefully prepared and controlled by both sides of the political spectrum: the Federal Chancellery on the one hand and the Ministry for Foreign Affairs on the other.[37] The positions were subsequently co-ordinated with all the major players, although both negotiating parties took the final decisions.[38] The political support for the Austrian final dossier was only partial, however. Both the Liberals and the Greens brought forward motions which were not incorporated.[39] The position papers were refined and in certain areas expanded during the meetings of the

---

[37] These fora are dominated by the SPÖ and ÖVP respectively.

[38] The Federal Ministries, the Social Partners, the Regions (Länder), the Federation of Municipalities and the Federation of Cities.

[39] The Greens, for example, pleaded for the postponement of EMU, and the Liberals wanted to grant union citizenship to citizens of third states who have been residing legally in an EU Member State for 5 years.

Reflection Group, but no substantive changes were made.[40] One of the main priorities for the IGC for Austria – a country with one of the lowest unemployment rates within the EU and relatively high social standards – was the strengthening of the provisions to combat unemployment and the extension of the European social dimension. In this context, it not only pressed for the incorporation of the objective of full employment into the Treaty, but also pushed (by putting forward a proposal) for an elaboration of the Treaty provisions on equal treatment of men and women. The possibility of positive discrimination as one of the new provisions of the Amsterdam Treaty is to be seen as an achievement in this respect. Environmental policy was also high on the Austrian agenda, where the possibility of Member States to attain – or to introduce – higher environmental standards as a specific objective was included in the Treaty of Amsterdam. The policy advances in the first pillar, however, can not only be attributed to Austrian endeavours, but are also due to close co-ordination with the "Nordic" countries who had a leading role in this context.[41] The Austrian engagement for social matters and environment is reflected in the proposals made by Austria during the IGC: of the seven Austrian proposals, two were concerned with environmental issues and two with employment policy and another dealt with the equal treatment of men and women.[42] It might come as a surprise that Austria, as a country faring comparatively well in the field of employment and environment, in unison with countries such as Sweden, Denmark and Finland, should have pressed so strongly for the strengthening of these policies. An explanation which comes to mind is that Austria selected these issue areas, which are high on the agenda of the Austrian people, to raise the flag, to "sell" the Treaty to the wider public.

From an Austrian perspective national parliaments are regarded as the primary source of legitimacy. Nevertheless, the extension of the powers of the EP was welcomed, notably the strengthening of its role when nominating the Commission President. It comes as no surprise that as a relatively small Member State, Austria wanted to maintain its relatively strong voting powers in the Council and did not wish to jeopardise its right to nominate a Commissioner.

In the area of CFSP, Austria, a country with a strong neutralist legacy, held a rather low-key position, trailing behind Sweden, carefully avoiding to put

---

[40] The final position paper contained new provisions on human rights and the equal treatment of men and women.

[41] See chapter by Tallberg in this volume.

[42] The two remaining documents dealt with the accession of the Union to the European Convention on Human Rights Citizenship of the Union (both submitted together with Italy).

forward its own position paper. It welcomed a gradual transition to majority voting, but pleaded for unanimity in especially sensitive areas of national interest such as defence. It tried to create another "backdoor" in security issues by seeking that the introduction of majority voting be accompanied by constructive abstention or opting out. The strengthening of the role for the EU in the peacekeeping sector (Petersberg tasks) was seen to be compatible with the maintenance of its traditional neutral status.

Austria was an adamant promoter of stronger EU involvement in the field of JHA *inter alia* due to its proximity to the countries of Eastern and Central Europe. It welcomed a stronger role for community institutions in this policy field and the incorporation of the Schengen Agreement into the Treaty. Austria supported the reforms of the third pillar, but stated that it would have welcomed a more ambitious solution as regards the responsibility of the ECJ (Bundeskanzleramt 1997, p. 7).

The Treaty was ratified with the majority of what were then the two major parties ÖVP and SPÖ in the national parliament with support of the Liberals, not taking into account the reservations of the Freedom Party and the Greens.[43]

Although Austria's position paper for the IGC 2000 stresses that it welcomes a far-reaching institutional reform, this is not reflected when it comes to substantial issues, which would under certain circumstances entail national sacrifices: The qualified majority and the blocking minority threshold in the Council should remain untouched, unanimity should be upheld for politically sensitive issues such as water resources, and each country should retain its right to nominate a Commissioner. One should also note that Austria's position within the EU has been placed under considerable strain since the October 1999 elections. The other 14 Member States have suspended bilateral relations with the Austrian government, which since the beginning of February includes the Freedom Party.

"The impasse over Austria cast a shadow over the EU's project to reform its internal decision making procedures, which was launched in the first formal session of the 10-month long Intergovernmental Conference (IGC), and its ambitious plans to enlarge the union in eastern and southern Europe" (*Financial Times*, 16 February 2000).

---

[43] This has changed subsequent to the elections taking place in October 1999. The Freedom Party became Austria's second largest party.

Bibliography

Bieber, Roland (1997). "Reformen der Institutionen und Verfahren – Amsterdam kein Meisterstück," *Integration*, 4:97, pp. 236-246.

Bundeskanzleramt (1997). *Der Vertrag von Amsterdam. Das Ergebnis der Regierungskonferenz 1996/97,* Vienna: Bundeskanzleramt, Bundespressedienst, EU-Referat III/1/a.

Dehousse, Renaud (1998). "European Institutional Architecture after the Amsterdam Treaty: Parliamentary System or Regulatory Structure?," *Common Market Law Review,* 35, pp. 595-627.

Duff, Andrew (1997). *The Treaty of Amsterdam: Text and Commentary,* London: Federal Trust.

Falkner, Gerda & Wolfgang C. Müller (1998). *Österreich im europäischen Mehrebenensystem. Konsequenzen der EU-Mitgliedschaft für Politiknetzwerke und Entscheidungsprozesse,* Vienna: Schriftenreihe des Zentrums für Angewandte Politikforschung.

Fischer, Heinz (1997). "Das Parlament," pp. 99-121, in Dachs et al. (ed.), *Handbuch des politischen Systems Österreichs,* Vienna: Manzsche Universitäts- und Verlagsbuchhandlung.

Joop, Mathias, Andreas Maurer & Otto Schmuck (eds.) (1998). *Die Europäische Union nach Amsterdam. Analysen und Stellungnahmen zum neuen EU-Vertrag,* Bonn: Europa Union Verlag.

Leicht, Anton (ed.) (1996). *Regierungskonferenz. Wohin steuert die EU?,* Vienna: Signum-Europa-Bibliothek.

Müller, Wolfgang, C. (1997). "Parteiensystem, Politische Bewegungen," pp. 215-234, in Dachs et al. (ed.), *Handbuch des politischen Systems Österreichs,* Vienna: Manzsche Universitäts- und Verlagsbuchhandlung.

Müller, Wolfgang, C., Fritz Plasser & Peter Ulram (1999). "Schwäche als Vorteil, Stärke als Nachteil. Die Reaktion der Parteien auf den Rückgang der Wählerverbindungen in Österreich," in Peter Mair, Wolfgang Müller & Fritz C. Plasser (eds.), *Parteien auf komplexen Wählermärkten. Reaktionsstrategien politischer Parteien in Westeuropa,* Vienna: Signum Verlag.

Müller, Wolfgang, C. (forthcoming). "EU Co-ordination in Austria: Challenges and Responses," in Kassim Hussein, Guy Peters & Vincent Wrights (eds.), *National EU Coordination,* Houndmills: Macmillan (forthcoming).

Moravcsik, Andrew & Kalypso Nicolaïdis (1999). "Explaining the Treaty of Amsterdam: Interests, Influence, Institutions," *Journal of Common Market Studies,* Vol. 37, No. 1, pp. 59-85.

Nentwich, Michael & Gerda Falkner (1997). "The Treaty of Amsterdam: Towards a New Institutional Balance," *European Integration online Papers* (EIoP) 15:1 (http://eiop.or.at./eiop/texte/015a.htm).

Nickel, Dietmar (1997). "Ein Kommentar zum Amsterdamer Vertrag aus der Sicht des Europäischen Parlaments," *Integration*, Vol. 20, pp. 219-227.

Thun-Hohenstein, Christoph & Franz Cede (1996). *Europarecht. Das Recht der Europäischen Union unter besonderer Berücksichtigung des EU-Beitritts Österreichs*, Vienna: Manzsche Univer-sitäts- und Verlagsbuchhandlung.

Wessels, Wolfgang (1997). "Der Amsterdamer Vertrag – Durch Stückwerksreformen zu einer effizienteren, erweiterten und föderalen Union?," *Integration*, Vol. 3, pp. 117-135.

Austrian Position Papers for the Intergovernmental Conference 1996
Austrian Delegation (1996e). Environment, CONF 3917
Austrian Delegation and Italian Delegation (1996f). Citizenship of the Union – *Submitted together with Italy*, CONF 3941
Austrian Delegation (1996g). Propositions de modifications du traité dans le domaine de l'emploi, CONF 3975
Austrian position paper for the Intergovernmental Conference 2000
Austrian Delegation (2000). Intergovernmental Conference on Institutional matters. Basic principles of Austria's position, CONFER 4712/00
Austrian Delegation 1996 (I). Leitlinien zu den voraussichtlichen Themen der Regierungskonferenz 1996, 30.5.1995
Austrian Delegation 1996 (II). Regierungskonferenz 1996. Österreichische Grundsatzpositionen, 26.3.1996

Austrian proposals and working papers for the Intergovernmental Conference 1996
Austrian Delegation (1996a). Working paper on employment policy, CONF 3840
Austrian Delegation (1996b). Working paper concerning Equal Treatment for Men and Women, CONF 3841
Austrian Delegation (1996c). Working paper concerning Accession of the Union to the European Convention on Human Rights – concerns note no 2 doc. SN 1802/96, CONF 3842
Austrian Delegation (1996d). Environment – Article 100a and Article 36 EC Treaty, CONF 3852

Interviews
Head of Unit, European Integration, Federal Ministry for Foreign Affairs, 30 March 2000, Brussels.
Deputy Head of Unit, European Integration, Federal Chancellery, 30 March 2000, Brussels.

3

Belgium: From Orthodoxy to Pragmatism

Bart Kerremans

Introduction

During almost fifty years of European integration, Belgium has built itself a reputation of being a fervent supporter of European integration in a federal sense. Especially over the last fifteen years – from the Single European Act to the 2000 IGC – Belgium has developed an image as an orthodox federalist member state. Indeed, an analysis of Belgium's policies towards the intergovernmental conferences that have been organized since then – the 1985 IGC that resulted in the Single European Act, the 1991 IGC's that resulted in the Maastricht Treaty, the 1996 IGC, and the ongoing IGC-2000 – shows a continuous support for a European project close to the formation of a kind of European federal state. What Joschka Fischer proposed in his speech at Humboldt University on May 12, 2000 has for fifteen years formed the nucleus of Belgium's approach towards Europe. Indicative (and significant) of this was the first sentence of the official position of the Belgian government on the Intergovernmental Conference of 1996 (Kamer van Volksvertegenwoordigers 1995, 2): "As stated in the Government Program, the construction of the European Union on federal principles is a prior objective of Belgium's foreign policy."[1]

The government presented this position not as a break with the past but as part of a continuous effort to construct a European Union along federal lines. In doing so, the government claimed to follow a tradition in Belgium's policy towards European integration "that always aimed at the securing of welfare and security in Europe by way of the interaction of interests and the pooling of resources."

It may be clear from the outset that with this position, Belgium more or less risked putting itself in the position of an outcast among the Member States, somewhat the antipode of the UK, as it positioned itself until the general elections of May 1, 1997. This position does not mean, however, that the role of Belgium was one of shouting from the fringes while having no impact at all. On the contrary, it seems that in a context where the EU is being confronted with an increasing amount of intergovernmental "reflexes," and where the old federalist ideas are being put on the defensive, a voice in the

---

[1] Original text in Dutch and French. Translation by the author.

opposite direction can act as a counterbalance to these tendencies. This chapter aims at shedding more light on this and assessing what role Belgium played during the 1996 IGC. Before embarking on this endeavor, however, attention will be paid to the arguments on which this orthodox federalist position is based.

The Arguments for Belgium's Orthodox Stance

Although Belgium takes a relatively orthodox stance in favoring a federalist European project, the arguments used by the Belgian government to defend its approach towards the 1996 IGC were largely utilitarian. Otherwise stated, it was not just for the sake of Europe that Belgium took (and takes) such a position, but also for the sake of Belgium itself. However, it is clear that the reasoning used to support this had been strongly influenced by a kind of pro-European federalist ideology. This becomes clear when one delves deeper into the first official position that the Belgian government took towards the 1996 IGC (October 15, 1995). This position was of a more or less general kind. It provided a general overview of the subjects of the 1996 IGC and the Belgian government's position on them. It was a document printed during the preparatory stages of this IGC, as the Reflection Group (under the chairmanship of Carlos Westendorp) was still working on the determination of its agenda. This document was presented to the federal parliament with the purpose of triggering a first parliamentary discussion on the IGC.

The basic assumption of the Belgian government was that as a small country, Belgium depends to a large extent on international cooperation if it wants to maintain a certain grip on its international environment. It is important, however, how such international cooperation is being organized or conceptualized. Traditional intergovernmental cooperation, such is the reasoning, leads either to the lowest common denominator and limits both the scope and depth of such cooperation, or to a "directorate" of the large states (Kamer van Volksvertegenwoordigers 1995, 3). It is only through the "community method" that both problems can be overcome. As the Belgian government has phrased it: "la méthode communautaire permet de concilier efficacité (grâce aux décisions majoritaires) et protection efficace contre les abus de pouvoir."[2]

Instead of the lowest common denominator, more would become possible and feasible than the least cooperative state wants to. Instead of a "*directoire*

---

[2] The government position was written – like all official texts – in both Dutch and French. Because knowledge of the latter is more widespread, we will only quote from the French version.

of large states," the interests of both the large and the small participating states are being protected and warranted. In the European Union, the first is being realized with the application of the qualified majority vote in the Council. The second is made possible by the strong role of the European Commission and by the firm establishment of the rule of law through the strong role of the EC Court of Justice. In addition, by providing a strong system of democratic accountability in the EU itself, the democratic legitimacy of this type of international cooperation can be safeguarded. In other words, a strong role for the European Parliament is a necessary component of this mode of operation.

Remarkable in this position is the high esteem that the Belgian government and parliament have shown for the European Commission, and this quite consistently during the whole 1996 IGC. The reasoning is simple. The Commission is considered to be an independent actor at the Community level, with sufficient expertise of its own to be able to really act independently. "Independent" means in the first place not dependent on the large Member States.

In addition, because of the decision-making rules in the first pillar of the EU, the Commission – according to the Belgian government – has the "key to the efficacy." This is due to the rule that majority decisions are only possible in cases where the Council adopts the Commission proposal. Otherwise, unanimity is required. This rule makes the Commission – an independent and experienced institution, protecting against the power of the large Member States – a key player in the EU decision-making game. It is in Belgium's interest, therefore, that if it agrees to relinquish part of its sovereignty to the EU, to do this to the benefit of such a player, rather than to the benefit of an intergovernmental organization dominated by its large neighbors.

This conception of the role of the European Commission is indicative of Belgium's approach towards integration itself. It is not perceived as being a zero-sum game where the Member States lose what the EU wins. Rather, the Belgian government likes to present integration as a positive-sum, as a win-win situation in which relinquishing sovereignty is equal to winning influence. As it phrased it itself: "L'expérience belge montre que le renoncement formel de souveraineté conduit à une augmentation sensible de l'influence réelle."

This is why the Belgian government put such high stakes in the way in which the EU is being structured and therefore, in the need for real progress in the direction of supranational integration in the 1996 IGC. This is also why Belgium is so concerned about the possible dilution effects of the upcoming enlargements, a concern shared quite insistently by the Belgian federal parliament.

It is important to stress this basic assumption – that relinquishing sovereignty is equal to gaining influence – of Belgium's approach towards European integration in general and towards the 1996 IGC in particular. Two aspects are important here. First, that it helps to understand why Belgium's approach is so radically and consistently different from the approach of Member States such as the UK, Denmark, and Sweden. These countries perceive the process of European integration more as a zero-sum game. Or at least, they do not grant the relinquishing of sovereignty to the EU the benefit of the doubt. And doubts there are!

The Belgian government grants the EU – and especially the Commission – this benefit. And this has been done quite consistently by successive Belgian governments and supported by overwhelming parliamentary majorities (which is remarkable in such an internally divided country).

The statement that relinquishing sovereignty is equal to winning influence may sound unconditional, but it is not. There is an important – albeit largely hypothetical – condition to this approach. The EU has to be structured in a way that it allows pooled sovereignty to be translated into more influence of the EU as a whole. In other words, it is only to the extent that EU decision-making is really "supranationalized" that the Belgian equation between relinquishing sovereignty and gaining influence holds. The 1996 IGC was the first instance in which Belgium was indeed struggling to uphold this principle. Otherwise stated, Belgium was struggling to keep the conditional nature of its basic assumption hypothetical. Indeed, the perspective of the upcoming enlargements is leading to a situation where Belgium's support for European integration will become more and more conditional. In an EU of six or twelve Member States, it was clear (at least for Belgium) that the community method (as it currently stands) was beneficial to the small Members States, as it protected them against the rule of the large ones. In an EU of twenty or twenty-five Member States, it is not at all clear whether this premise will still hold. It is not because that in such an EU, the large Member States will be able to dominate (depending on the outcome of the reforms in the Council's voting system). Rather, it is that Belgium and a number of other Member States that supported European integration in a supranational way will become "minorized." This is not only a problem that Belgium fears for future IGCs, but also for EU decision-making in general. It is the fear of a European integration project restricted to exclusively market-oriented measures. It is the fear of a European Union able to act in order to liberalize trade and to open markets but paralyzed when it comes to creating a European social, environmental, fiscal, and ultimately political space. This makes it understandable why during the 1996 IGC, Belgium evolved into an adamant supporter of the idea of "flexibility," later called "reinforced" or "closer cooperation." A long discussion preceded the adoption of this position. Ultimately, however, the support for such cooperation emerged as an expression of Belgium's growing concerns that the widening of the EU poses a serious, almost unavoidable risk, not just for the EU's deepening but also for its sustainability as a European political project. To put it more concisely, what was at stake in the 1996 IGC was more than just a treaty reform. It was the preservation of a political project that Belgium helped to initiate in the 1950s and that is perceived to be an important if not essential aspect of Belgium's national interests.

The Main Aspects of Belgium's Approach Towards the 1996 IGC

Decision-Making
It is easy to deduce from the above that the Belgian government quite consistently supported the extension of the scope of the application of the "Community method" in the EU. In the 1996 IGC, this was not otherwise. On the contrary, from its start, Belgium was prepared to make this extension a major issue, and to a certain extent, as we shall see, it did.

Already in its October 1995 position, the government stressed the importance of the extension of the scope of qualified majority voting (QMV), the concomitant extension of the European Parliament's powers, the reinforcement of the role of the European Commission and a similar move as far as the Court of Justice's powers were concerned. Related to this position – and especially the QMV's scope – was, of course, the discussion about the reform of the institutions, in the first place the Council (the reweighting of the votes), and the Commission (the number of commissioners).

When talking about the Community method in general, the Belgian position focused on two discussions: the scope of article 113 EC (now article 133 TEC), and third pillar issues. Belgium did not defend the application of the Community method to the second pillar – although it stressed the importance of the QMV here – as that was not considered to be feasible in the first place and necessary in the second.

As far as article 113 EC (now article 133 TEC) was concerned, the application of the Community method focused largely on the scope of this article. Due to a ruling of the EC Court of Justice (advice 1/94), article 113 was not considered to be by definition applicable to all aspects of trade in services and intellectual property rights. One of the issues was therefore, whether a new (fifth) paragraph had to be added to article 113 that would extend its scope to these issues. The Commission brought this issue on the agenda of the IGC. As a matter of fact, it had already brought it up in the discussions of the Reflection Group. From then on, up until the end of the IGC in June 1997, only one Member State supported the Commission in these efforts (Reflection Group, 1995) although others – like Austria (see *Agence Europe* April 14, 1997) – joined the Commission later in the IGC in supporting a compromise related to this issue. That Member State was Belgium (Kerremans, 1998).

In its October 1995 position, the Belgian government presented its support for the inclusion of services and intellectual property rights into article 113 as "exemplary for other areas of external policy." In addition, it referred to the Uruguay Round (a risky endeavor) to show how the negotiating role of the Commission had enhanced the EU's capacity to act as a unified actor in the negotiations with its major trading partners, including on issues such as services and trade-related intellectual property rights (TRIPs). As the government phrased it:

> En matière de relations commerciales extérieures, l'Union a réussi à faire valoir son influence grâce au recours à la méthode communautaire (article 113 du Traité) qui a permis l'union efficace de nos moyens et de nos efforts. Le gouvernement attache par conséquent une importance particulière à ce que la politique économique extérieure de l'Union se poursuivre dans la tradition communautaire et serve également d'exemple pour d'autres domaines de politique extérieure (Kamer van Volksvertegenwoordigers 1995, 16-17).

And explicitly referring to the Uruguay Round, it continues: "Efficacité et cohésion dans les négociations ont été le fruit de la méthode de travail communautaire" (ibid.).

As is well known, France consistently opposed any modification of article 113 in that sense.[3] It even refused to agree with a compromise proposal from the Dutch presidency where the extension of article 113's scope to services and intellectual property rights would be restricted to international negotiations listed in a protocol to the Treaty (and including the GATS- and TRIPs-agreements). The IGC-negotiations on this topic resulted in an agreement that lay somewhere between the Dutch presidency proposal and the French position, far away from what Belgium and the Commission would have liked.[4]

---

[3] France favored a modification of article 113, but only in a way that the Commission's hands would be more tied by the Member States when negotiating trade agreements than is currently the case. The scope of the article had to remain unchanged, however. See document CONF 3882/97 (April 18, 1997).

[4] Indeed, the outcome was that a fifth paragraph has been added to this article that states: "The Council, acting unanimously on a proposal from the Commission and after consulting the European Parliament, may extend the application of paragraphs 1 to 4 to international negotiations and agreements on services and intellectual property insofar as they are not covered by these paragraphs."

For Belgium, the second important issue related to decision-making concerned the third pillar. Not surprisingly, the position here was to extend the Community method as much as possible to issues contained in this pillar. As the October 1995 position phrased it: "Toutes les possibilités de la méthode communautaire doivent être exploitées" (Kamer van Volksvertegenwoordigers 1995, 15).

The reference to "toutes les possibilités" (all possibilities) was to a large extent a reference to article K.9 of the Maastricht Treaty that states:

> The Council, acting unanimously on the initiative of the Commission or a Member State, may decide to apply Article 100c of the Treaty establishing the European Community to action in areas referred to in Article K.1 (1) to (6), and at the same time determine the relevant voting conditions relating to it. It shall recommend the Member States to adopt the decision in accordance with their respective constitutional requirements.

Article K.1 (1) to (6), to which article K.9 referred, consisted of issues dealing with the free movement of persons – i.e., asylum policy, the crossing of the EU's external borders, and immigration policy – on the one hand, and with judicial issues – such as combating drug addiction and fraud, and judicial cooperation in civil matters – on the other hand. Article 100c EC itself dealt with the EU's visa policy.

The possibility under the Maastricht Treaty of the transfer of issues from article K.1 EU to article 100c EC (the so-called "*passerelle*") had not been used, and the first Belgian objective in the 1996 IGC negotiations on third pillar issues was to include this *passerelle* in the new treaty reform. This meant two things. First, the transfer to the first pillar itself, which meant both that these issues would become included in the EC Court of Justice's jurisdiction, and that the European Parliament would acquire an – albeit lightly – stronger role, namely through the consultation procedure, and second, the possible introduction of QMV on all or most of these issues. For the Belgian government, QMV had certainly to be applied to the issues directly related to the free movement of persons.

In addition, Belgium also favored the application of "methods used in the first pillar" to those issues that would remain in the third one, meaning that QMV and a shared right of initiative for the Commission would be provided as much as possible for judicial cooperation in criminal matters on the one hand, and police cooperation for the purposes of preventing and combating terrorism and other crimes such as drug trafficking, on the other.[5]

About one year after Belgium defined its initial position on Justice and Home Affairs, new initiatives were launched to refine this position. The first of these was an initiative in the framework of the Benelux (November 13, 1996), a framework that was quite actively used during the 1996 IGC. The second came at about the same time (November 14, 1996) and was a Belgian proposal on police and judicial cooperation.

The first proposal – dealing with the crossing of external borders, immigration and asylum, protection of the Community's financial interests and penalties for infringements of Community law – referred to issues closely related to the free movement of persons. It was easier, therefore, to reach a consensus on this topic among the Benelux-countries. Central to this consensus was the application of the Community method to these issues. As stated in the explanatory part of the proposal itself:[6]

> If control is to be exercised over migrant flows, the corollary to free movement of persons within the Community must be effective checks at external borders. A common policy covering the conditions of access to the Member States' territory, controls, visas, immigration and asylum is therefore needed.
>
> The current distribution of policy topics between the Community and cooperation lacks coherence. Questions relating to the movement of persons within the internal market and those relating to conditions for entry and residence of third country nationals in Member States' territory are in fact closely linked. In the interests of efficiency, they should therefore be dealt with together under the Community umbrella. This is the purpose of the present proposal.
>
> The communitarization of the rules governing the crossing of external frontiers, immigration and asylum, by using Community instruments, would also make action more effective. It would ensure that citizens were better protected by involving the European Parliament actively in preparing legal texts and would make case-law homogeneous by bringing Court of Justice scrutiny to areas closely affecting the rights of individuals. There should also be special procedures for ensuring that questions in these areas submitted to the Court of Justice of the European Communities are dealt with swiftly.

---

[5] Belgium also favored the inclusion of customs cooperation in the first pillar, despite the fact that it had not been included in the Maastricht Treaty *passerelle* of article K.9.

[6] See document CONF 3909/96 (November 13, 1996), annex, p. 2.

In this memorandum, one can find most of the arguments that Belgium perceives to be essential pleading for the Community method: efficiency, efficacy, democratic legitimacy, and the rule of law. In the case of democratic legitimacy, the proposal contained an "automatic *passerelle*" that was slightly different from the *passerelle* in article K.9 of the Maastricht Treaty. First, the *passerelle* would result in decision-making in which the European Parliament would be involved through the co-decision procedure and not just consultation.

Second, instead of transferring the issues concerned from the third to the first pillar at the moment the *passerelle* would be activated, the transfer would take place immediately. The *passerelle* would then be limited to the use of the QMV in the Council – it would remain unanimous until then – and to the enhancement of the role of the European Parliament (from consultation to co-decision).

The *passerelle* would also be automatic in the sense that QMV and co-decision would be used from January 1, 2003 on without the need for any further decisions in this sense by the Council or the Member States.[7]

The separate Belgian proposal of November 14, 1996 dealt with police and judicial cooperation. The proposal clearly stated that these issues would be dealt with through cooperation among the Member States, not a common policy of the EC, meaning that they would remain part of the third pillar. But at the same time, the proposal contained elements of the first pillar that would be applied to these issues. Among them was QMV in the Council (or a "super" QMV), but only for certain decisions (like multi-annual work programs, framework decisions designed to approximate national laws, and to approximate national practices, and to decisions related to the development of operational joint actions).[8] In addition, the European Court of Justice would start to play a modest role, namely in case of disputes in the context of the third pillar, either between Member States or between a Member State and the Commission. The Court would only be involved in cases where six months of efforts to resolve the issue in the Council would have failed. The Court would

---

[7] For the common policy on visas – more precisely for the determination of the third countries whose nationals must be in possession of a visa when crossing the external borders and for the adoption of a uniform format for visas – QMV would be applied immediately (at the entry into force of the amended Treaty). This was not surprising, given the fact that in the Maastricht Treaty, these policies were already included in the first pillar (article 100C EC).

[8] The proposal also provided for the adoption, through a super QMV, of conventions to be recommended for ratification by the Member States in cases where Member States would not be able to develop a policy based on the approximation of their laws and practices.

also attain the right to issue preliminary rulings on the interpretation of the provisions of the third pillar and of texts adopted as part of it.

In proposing this, Belgium did not stand alone among the Member States. As a matter of fact, both the substance of the Benelux proposal and the separate Belgian proposal on police and judicial cooperation showed up in the positions of many other delegations (among which France, Italy, Greece, Portugal, and Austria).

Original to the Belgian position – compared with the other Member States – was the proposal for a new article K.9 where a new kind of *passerelle* for the remaining issues of the third pillar would be provided for. This proposed provision was more compulsory than that contained in article K.9 of the Maastricht Treaty. The Council would not only get the opportunity to decide unanimously to transfer issues to the first pillar and to recommend the Member States to ratify such a decision, it would be obliged to take a position on such a transfer at least every three years.[9] As stated in the second paragraph of the proposed article:

> Every three years as from the entry into force of this Treaty, the Council, acting unanimously on the basis of a report from the Commission and after consulting the European Parliament, shall decide whether and to what extent the provisions referred to in this Title may be governed by the Community. It shall, where applicable, recommend the Member States to adopt that decision in accordance with their respective constitutional requirements.

The third issue on which Belgium took a position and which was related to the discussion of the "Community method" concerned the cohesion among the three pillars of the EU, a question approached largely from the perspective of the external representation of the Union and from the perspective, therefore, of the second pillar. The government position on the IGC of October 1995 clearly stated "Un objectif du gouvernement belge consiste à rapprocher les pilliers pour finalement les fusionner" (Kamer van Volksvertegenwoordigers 1995, 17).

This position was not a surprise in itself, given the fact that during the 1991 IGC Belgium was the only Member State to support the Dutch proposal for a Union based on a "tree-structure," instead of the current pillar-structure. However, realism and pragmatism caused the Belgian government to refer to this issue only slightly in its position on the 1996 IGC. As a consequence, the

---

[9] The Italian proposal also contained a reference to the *passerelle* in a new article K.9, but did not contain this three-annual obligatory review by the Council. See document CONF 3840/97 (March 6, 1997).

Belgian position focused more on *rapprocher* than on *fusionner*. Typical in this sense was the following part of the October 1995 proposal (ibid. 18):

> Le gouvernement ne s'attend pas à ce qu'au cours de la CIG de 1996, les conceptions des Etats membres soient mûres et que le temps soit venus pour attribuer à la Commission un droit d'initiative exclusive en matière de PESC. Néanmoins, le gouvernement s'efforcera lors de la CIG de renforcer le droit d'initiative de la Commission, notamment par la reprise dans le Traité d'une disposition prévoyant que les propositions de la Commission en matière de PESC soient approuvées à la majorité qualifiée au Conseil.

Otherwise stated, in order to enhance the Commission's role in the second pillar, the government proposed using a model concerning the Commission's role that would come close to the model used in the first pillar. The Commission would not obtain the exclusive right of initiative. But in those cases where the Member States would act on the basis of a Commission proposal, they would be able to adopt a decision by QMV. In proposing such a system – knowing that there was only a slight chance that it would be included in the Treaty amendments – Belgium hoped to create a system in which the sharing of the right of initiative among the Commission and the Member States, would occur in a context where the Commission's right would be more or less preferential.

The Qualified Majority Vote and the Reform of the Council Voting System
The question of the qualified majority vote was one of the most important and sensitive at the 1996 IGC. Two aspects played an essential role here. First, the possible reform of the Council's voting, in preparation for the upcoming enlargements, and second, the question of the QMV's scope.

Whereas Belgium's position was relatively simple and clear on the latter, it took a much more ambivalent stance on the former. Before elaborating on this point, it is important that the questions related to QMV – to be dealt with later – were closely linked to questions on the composition of the European Commission. This was also the case in Belgium's position on these matters, as will become clear. For Belgium, all these questions were interrelated. Modifying the Council's voting – which would inevitably lead to a relative enhancement of the position of the large Member States – could only be accepted if it could go hand in hand with both the reinforcement of the role of the European Commission – making its composition very important – and the extension of the QMV's scope.

Reforming the Council's voting system was not an easy thing to accept, not even for Belgium. Belgium may be an orthodox federalist Member State, but it realized that the reform would inevitably lead to a weakening of its position – one way or the other – in the Council. And it was far from happy with this prospect.

The two possibilities that emerged during the IGC consisted of the reweighting of the votes, and the introduction of a second criterion for adoption of Council decisions (the dual majority principle). On both approaches, different scenarios showed-up in the later stage of the IGC, as Member States and successive presidencies postponed this difficult question until the final stage, realizing then that the necessary concessions could not be made at a level lower than heads of government and state.

As far as Belgium was concerned, it accepted from the outset that a reform would be necessary because of the upcoming enlargement. Similarly, it expressed its understanding for the concern of the large Member States that a reform would have to benefit them in the first place. This was already present in its October 1995 position:

> Bien qu'en pratique, il arrive rarement ou pas du tout qu'un bloc des grands et un bloc des petits s'opposent, le gouvernement comprend la crainte d'un certain nombre de grands Etats members que le poids de leur population ne puisse être neutralisé trop aisément par une "alliance" de quelques petits pays. Cela pourrait en effet entraîner une diminuation de la crédibilité de l'Union dans les grands Etats membres (Kamer van Volksvertegenwoordigers 1995, 38).

The last sentence of this position is particularly important. It expresses – completely concomitant with Belgium's federalist concerns – the opinion that a reform is inevitable because not doing so would reduce the large Member States' preparedness to continue to support European integration.

On the question of how to reform the Council's voting, the government initially left open all options – by mentioning both the reweighting and the dual majority principle – but linked the issue – and more precisely the dual majority principle – to the powers of the European Parliament in a relatively original way, indicating that the risk of the large Member States' population being underrepresented in the EU could be resolved by enhancing the Parliament's powers, since votes in that institution are more closely (or less remotely) related to the size of the population of each of the Member States (ibid. 38).

In making this linkage, the government implicitly (and equivocally) expressed three opinions towards a possible reform. First, that in any way, a reform would not be accepted without a commensurate enhancement of the Parliament's powers (elsewhere, it made a similar linkage between the reform and the Commission's powers). Second, that the reinforcement of the position of the large Members States could be limited in significance because enhancing the Parliament's powers would entail a better representativeness of EU decision-making anyway. Third, that among the two possible options – reweighting or dual majority – Belgium was inclined to prefer the latter. It indicates, therefore, Belgian ambivalence on the voting reform.

This ambivalence remained throughout the IGC although the preference for the dual majority principle gradually became stronger. This became quite clear during the first months of 1996 when the three Benelux countries started to negotiate on a Benelux-position on the IGC. During these talks, it was largely at Belgian insistence that reference was made to the dual majority principle and no reference to the reweighting. As stated in the Benelux-Memorandum of April 30, 1996:

> The Council's effectiveness and working methods are in need of improvement. The three Governments accordingly argue for the use of qualified-majority voting to be expanded. In an enlarged Union, the qualified majority should remain at around 70% of votes. A population yardstick could be used to make certain that the qualified majority represents a majority of the Union's inhabitants (Benelux Memorandum 1996, 15).

The reference to the dual majority was not made in terms of a *conditio sine qua non*, especially at Dutch insistence. But the phrase "a population yardstick *could* be used" without mentioning the other possibility – the reweighting – led the Belgian government to believe that its Benelux-partners had agreed to prefer the dual majority principle just like it did itself. In the context of the Dutch presidency in the final stages of the IGC, this was not considered unimportant. Rather than clarifying positions, however, it ultimately led to misunderstandings. Indeed, from April 1997 on, proposals on the voting reform started to be floated. At the "conclave" of foreign ministers in Noordwijk (April 6, 1997) Italy proposed a reweighting scheme in which the votes of the small and medium-sized Member States (those with currently six votes or less) would remain unchanged but in which the votes of Spain would increase to nine, and those of the Member States that currently hold ten votes (Germany, France, the UK, and Italy) to twelve. The Italians also proposed to set the QMV at 68 votes, which would mean that the blocking minority would remain 26. This proposal led to a confrontation between the small and large Member States that – to quote *Agence Europe* – revealed that the positions were "totally antagonistic." In itself, this was no surprise, as the largely conceptual discussions on the matter in the group of the foreign ministers' representatives (at that time chaired by Michiel Patijn) had indicated precisely the same.

In Noordwijk, however, one of the conclusions of the "conclave" had been that the Dutch presidency had to work out proposals on the two alternatives, the reweighting and the dual majority. On April 24, 1997 it submitted a proposal in that sense to the IGC.[10] It contained a proposal on the dual majority – where a second criterion of ± 60% was proposed (thereby avoiding to take a position in the discussion between 60% and 65%) – and one on the reweighting. For the reweighting, two variants were put forward. In both cases, the relative voting weight of the large Member States would be increased. In variant II, the Dutch closely followed the Italian proposal of April 6 but made a significant change. They gave themselves one vote more than the other Member States that currently have five votes (Belgium, Portugal, and Greece).

In variant I, all the Member States would receive more votes – except Luxembourg – but the large ones would enjoy a larger increase than the others. The result was the following:

– Germany, France, Italy, and the UK: 25 votes each (= +150%)
– Spain: 20 votes (= +150%)
– The Netherlands: 12 votes (= +140%)
– Belgium, Portugal, and Greece: 10 votes each (= +100%)
– Sweden and Austria: each 8 votes (= +100%)
– Denmark, Ireland, and Finland: 6 votes each (= +100%)
– Luxembourg: 3 votes (= +0%)

From a diplomatic perspective, variant I was more attractive, since almost all Member States would receive more votes, though some would receive even more than others. The Dutch proposal left open the question which of the two proposals – dual majority or reweighting – it preferred. In the weeks after the first discussion of the Dutch document – in the foreign ministers' meeting of April 29-30, after which Dutch foreign minister Hans van Mierlo announced that the question had to be arranged by the heads of government "who have perhaps more authority" (*Agence Europe* May 1, 1997) – the Dutch were putting more pressure on the reweighting than on the dual majority.[11] In

---

[10] See document CONF 3888/97.

[11] One of the consequences of this was that the Luxembourg foreign minister Jacques Poos, in an interview published in the Luxembourg newspaper *Tagesblatt*, announced that with 25 votes for the large Member States, three votes for Luxembourg was "totally unacceptable" (*Agence Europe* June 13, 1997). In the same vein, Michiel Patijn, chairman of the group of foreign ministers' representatives, declared to the press that the debate on the reweighting had "raised a confrontation between small and large Member States without precedent in the Community's history" (*Agence Europe* May

Belgium, the government – given the Benelux Memorandum – was convinced that the Dutch were promoting the reweighting scheme for strategic reasons. The Belgians thought that it was clear for the Dutch that the difference between the current Member States with five votes and the Netherlands would never be accepted if France, Italy, and the UK (each 10 votes) maintained the same number of votes as Germany. The Belgians knew, however, that François Mitterrand and Helmut Kohl had made a deal at the Strasbourg European Council of December 1989. It was the summit at which the EC agreed on German reunification in exchange for Kohl's promises on EMU entry (Dinan, 1994: 163). However, Mitterrand and Kohl made another (gentlemen's) agreement in which Germany accepted that except for the European Parliament, no other EC institution would reflect the difference in population between France and the reunified Germany. In other words, France and Germany would always need to have the same number of votes in the Council and seats in the Commission. This is probably why France preferred the reweighting scheme instead of the dual majority, since the latter would indirectly give the Germans a benefit in the Council. The reweighting would guarantee France equal weight with Germany.

The Belgian interpretation of the Dutch presidency's proposal was a relatively complex one. By guessing that the Dutch knew that Belgium would link the difference of its votes with those of the Dutch to an analogous difference between France and Germany, and looking at the Benelux Memorandum, the Belgian government interpreted the Dutch move as an attempt to make the reweighting politically unfeasible and to push the Member States – even the recalcitrant ones like France – to a deal on the dual majority. The Belgians made a mistake, however, as the Dutch were seriously pushing for their variant I and, thus, to have more votes than the Belgians. The question came to the forefront at the Amsterdam Summit, when Belgium insisted on a treatment analogous to France and Germany, which was of course adamantly rejected by Jacques Chirac. Subsequently, the Belgian prime minister became angry at his Dutch counterpart Wim Kok and explained that Belgium would not accept having fewer votes than the Dutch. Dehaene even threatened to leave the meeting, being concerned for the domestic reactions in case he would have accepted the Dutch to have more votes than Belgium. As the debate became hopeless, Helmut Kohl proposed to postpone the decision to another IGC, directly supported by Wim Kok, and Tony Blair, and subsequently by the other participants.

The question of the reweighting made two issues clear: first, that despite its orthodox federalist positions on European integration, the Belgian position towards European integration is primarily determined by its national interests

---

16, 1997).

and by the assessment to what extent European integration serves those interests or not, and second, that animosity (sometimes in an almost folkloristic sense) between countries can feed the domestic debate on certain aspects of the process of European integration. In the case of the Amsterdam Summit, the Belgian prime minister was clearly warned by his advisers that press reports headlined "The Netherlands: 12; Belgium: 10" would not augur well for him, and that his acceptance of the arrangement as proposed by the Dutch presidency would certainly lead to such headlines the day after the Summit.

The Scope of the Qualified Majority Vote
During the IGC, the Belgian government made a clear linkage between the voting reform in the Council and the extension of the scope of the qualified majority vote. The former would only be accepted in exchange for the latter. And whatever the voting reform (or the absence thereof), the Ioannina Agreement of March 1994 had to be repealed.

The extension of the QMV's scope was defended by the government as the only way to preserve the EU's decision-making capacity after its upcoming enlargements, or to create such capacity where it did not already exist, and where it was badly needed. Very sensitive here was Belgium's stance on fiscal provisions and the need to introduce the QMV here. Irritated about the extent to which the unanimity rule had blocked any harmonization in this field and disturbed about what the government saw as a resulting downward fiscal competition, the result was a proposal with relatively radical reforms in that sense. As the government itself motivated its proposal: "Forty years on from the establishment of the European Communities, it has to be said that very little progress has been achieved with fiscal harmonization: on the contrary, tax competition between the Member States has increased."[12]

And it continued:

> Failing such explicit harmonization, i.e. leading to decisions of the Council of Ministers itself, it is clear that the future tendency will increasingly be towards implicit downwards harmonization.
>
> Such a development gives rise to major concern in view, particularly, of its likely adverse effects on tax revenues in all Member States. Furthermore, it is also likely to have a substantial impact on the structure of Member States' tax revenues. Thus, while certain types of income, especially movable income, benefit considerably from this situation, many other types are directly penalized owing to the

---

[12] See document CONF 3864/97 (April 8, 1997).

requirement for the Governments of such States to find essential financial compensation in order to carry out their various tasks. This is the case particularly with income from work, the rising relative cost of which in relation to capital poses a threat to employment and, with that, to social protection funding.

This position was no surprise. Already in the early preparatory stages of the 1996 IGC, the Belgian government had consistently pleaded for reforms that would enable the European Union to help preserve the so-called Rhineland economic model. In such a model, competition has to be reconciled with social justice and, therefore, with the possibility for government – either subnational, national, or European – to intervene in the market. Such intervention has to aim at correcting market inefficiencies or undoing the disproportionate effects of unbridled competition. One of those effects consists of fiscal competition (besides downward pressure on levels of social protection). Among Belgian political elites, a strong consensus in that sense exists, already for years, although some of them reject fiscal harmonization in the EU if it means increasing taxes.

Concomitant with this concern about this perceived downward spiral of fiscal competition, the Belgian government – through its foreign minister – announced a "fiscal offensive" in the IGC, to begin after the end of the summer of 1996. As minister Erik Derycke expressed it: "Because of tax competition in the single market, the Member States have *de facto* lost their fiscal autonomy. This autonomy will only be recovered when tax policy acquires a European dimension, the best remedy for a dual society" (*Agence Europe* August 8, 1996). And he concluded: "The rule of unanimity on fiscal matters must be abolished."

And indeed, this is what the Belgian government proposed in the IGC. It proposed the introduction of the QMV on fiscal matters in three ways. First, by amendments to article 99 (now article 93 TEC) where unanimity applied on provisions concerning the harmonization of "turnover taxes, excise duties and other forms of indirect taxation to the extent that such harmonization is necessary to ensure the establishment and functioning of the internal market" would be replaced by the codecision procedure (including QMV). In addition, a new paragraph on implementing provisions "concerning rates, procedures, and means of control" would be introduced where decisions would be taken by QMV, after consulting the European Parliament. The IGC did not follow Belgium in this matter, however, as article 99 was left unchanged.

Second, the Belgian government proposed to delete the reference to "fiscal provisions" in the second paragraph of article 100A (now article 95 TEC). This would have entailed that fiscal provisions related to the internal market (fiscal barriers) would have been covered by the first paragraph and, hence, by the codecision procedure. But on this matter as well, the IGC did not follow.

Third, the Belgian government proposed a slight change in the second paragraph of article 130S, where it was proposed to delete the second indent. As this indent refers to "provisions of a primarily fiscal nature," a "deletion" would have entailed that such provisions would not have been covered anymore by the unanimity rule of article 130S (2) (now article 175 (2)), but by the codecision procedure as provided by the first paragraph of this article. Here, once again, the IGC refused to follow suit.

The Belgian government not only urged the use of QMV on fiscal matters, it also did so on other issues, thereby favoring the largest possible extension of the QMV's scope. It thereby supported – with one exception – the proposal of the Dutch presidency on the QMV's scope and stressed its application to a number of issues for which it tabled proposals itself.[13] The following table provides an overview of these proposals, the presidency's point of view, and the outcome of the IGC.

Table 3.1: A comparative overview of the positions on the IGC.

Belgian proposal	*Presidency proposal*	*Outcome of the IGC*
Equality between men and women (new article 130Z): article 252 (ex 189B).[14]	No reference to a separate article.	New article 6A (now article 13) with a general reference to non-discrimination (including by sex). Decisions by unanimity, after consulting the EP.
Employment: objectives for an employment policy (new title, article 1 (2)): article 251.	No reference.[15]	No reference.
Employment: recommendations for Member States' policies (new title, article 1 (4)): QMV, consultation of EP.	QMV, consultation of EP.	QMV, consultation of EP.

---

[13] See document CONF 3893/97 (April 30, 1997).

[14] Co-decision procedure.

[15] Irish presidency, document CONF 3906/96.

Belgian proposal	Presidency proposal	Outcome of the IGC
Employment: detailed rules on the multilateral monitoring procedures (new title, article 1 (5)): article 251.	No reference.	No reference.
No reference.	Employment:[16] incentive measures: article 251.	Employment: incentive measures: article 251.
Social protocol (to be integrated in the treaty), article 2 (2): from cooperation procedure to article 251.	Social protocol (to be integrated in the treaty), article 2 (2): from cooperation procedure to article 251.[17]	Social protocol (integrated in the treaty), article 2 (2) (now article 137 (2)): from cooperation procedure to article 251.
Social protocol (to be integrated in the treaty), article 2 (2): from cooperation procedure to article 251.	Social protocol (to be integrated in the treaty), article 2 (3): unanimity, after consulting the EP.	Social protocol (integrated in the treaty), article 2 (3) (now article 137 (2)): unanimity, after consulting the EP.
Universal service: extension of universal service beyond the sectors of telecommunications, postal and transport services and the supply of water and energy (new article): article 251.	No reference.	No reference.

---

[16] Dutch presidency, document CONF 3894/97.

[17] Dutch presidency, document CONF 3895/97.

Belgian proposal	Presidency proposal	Outcome of the IGC
Public service: determination of common principles in a public service charter (new article): article 251.	No reference.	Article 73 (ex 77) on transport: no reference to procedures.

Article 16 (ex 7d) on the enabling of services of general economic interest to fulfil their obligations: no reference to procedures.

Article 86 (ex 90) on the application of competition rules to services of general economic interest: no reference to procedures. |
| Energy (new title, new article 130Q): decisions on actions to be taken under this title: article 251. | No reference to a separate article. | No separate title on energy. Energy dealt with under different provisions relating to TENs (art. 154); environment (art. 175, where the Council acts by unanimity, after consulting the EP). |
| Public health (new article 129bis): decisions on measures relating to procedures, quality, and safety regarding health data and substances of human origin, in particular organs, blood, and blood derivatives: article 251. | Public health (extended article 129 (4)):[18] measures setting minimum protection levels in the veterinary and phytosanitary fields and in respect of quality and safety of organs and substances of human origin, blood, and blood derivatives: article 251. | Public health (extended article 129 (4)): measures setting high standards of quality and safety of organs and substances of human origin, blood, and blood derivatives: article 251. |

---

[18] Dutch presidency, document CONF 3868/97 & CONF 3897/97.

Belgian proposal	Presidency proposal	Outcome of the IGC
Tax provisions (article 93, ex 99): Adoption of provisions (and principles) for the harmonization of legislation concerning turnover taxes, excise duties and other forms of indirect taxation to the extent that such harmonization is necessary to ensure the establishment and the functioning of the internal market: article 251.	Tax provisions (article 93, ex 99): Adoption of provisions (and principles) for the harmonization of legislation concerning turnover taxes, excise duties and other forms of indirect taxation to the extent that such harmonization is necessary to ensure the establishment and the functioning of the internal market: QMV.[19]	Tax provisions (article 93, ex 99): Adoption of provisions for the harmonization of legislation concerning turnover taxes, excise duties and other forms of indirect taxation to the extent that such harmonization is necessary to ensure the establishment and the functioning of the internal market: Unanimity, after consulting the EP.
Tax provisions (article 93, ex 99): Adoption of implementing provisions concerning rates, procedures and means of control: QMV, after consulting the EP.	Tax provisions (article 93, ex 99): Adoption of implementing provisions concerning rates, procedures and means of control: no inclusion in the treaty.	No reference.
Tax provisions, exclusion of fiscal provisions from article 95, ex 100A (article 95 (2), ex 100A (2)).	No reference to 100A (2), now 95 (2).	No reference to 100A (2), now 95 (2).
Environment (article 175 (2), ex 130S (2)): Decisions on provisions primarily of a fiscal nature: article 251.[20]	Environment (article 175 (2), ex 130S (2)): Decisions on provisions primarily of a fiscal nature: QMV, after consulting the EP.	Environment (article 175 (2), ex 130S (2)): Decisions on provisions primarily of a fiscal nature: Unanimity, after consulting the EP.

Source: Compiled by the author.

---

[19] The role of the EP was not made explicit. Significant however was that article 99 (now 93) was not included in the presidency's list of treaty provisions where the procedure of article 251 would be applied.

[20] The Belgian proposal for this amendment removed the first indent (provisions primarily of a fiscal nature) from ex article 130S (2). This means that such provisions would not be excluded anymore from the scope of ex article 130S (1).

The only exception to this general stance on the extension of the QMV's scope was Belgium's position on article 128 dealing with culture. This was a little bit awkward, as it somewhat weakened the principled nature of Belgium's position in favor of the QMV. Moreover, the position was made even more awkward because article 128 (5) TEC not only contained the unanimity requirement but the combination of this requirement with the codecision procedure. Internally, it was an insurmountable obstacle to overcome, however, because of – just like during the 1991 IGC's – opposition by the Flemish government. As on some issues related to the IGC, the federal Belgian government could take a position only after accord from its subnational counterparts – which means that Belgium's position on these was determined internally by consensus (see Kerremans, 1999). The Flemish government succeeded in sticking to its concern that a European cultural policy should not lead to any threat to the cultural specificity of, and the cultural diversity inside the Member States. The only way to avoid this – so was the opinion – was to preserve the capacity of each of the Member States to veto any move in the opposite direction.[21]

The 1996 IGC became a disappointment for the Belgians as far as the QMV's extension was concerned. To a certain extent, this disappointment was predictable, as it was clear from the outset that most Member States did not support such a liberal extension. In addition, in the run-up to the Amsterdam Summit, the German government – from which the Belgians expected most support on QMV – expressed its reservations about the extension of the QMV's scope to issues with direct budgetary consequences for the Member States. After the group's meeting of May 5-6, 1997, the German member of the group of foreign ministers' representatives indicated that the (Dutch) presidency's latest proposal on the QMV's scope[22] contained a number of treaty provisions "of considerable financial importance, like taxation, social policy, the structural funds, and research policy." He indicated that it was necessary for Germany "to very carefully examine, on a case by case basis, whether our financial interests are not best guaranteed through unanimity." In addition, he linked the extension of the scope to the reform of the Council's

---

[21] In the same vein and on request of the Flemish government, Belgium proposed to make a more explicit reference to cultural diversity in article F (1) TEU and in article 128 (4) TEC. In addition, it proposed to stress the language rights of EU nationals by amending article 8 TEC in that sense, and to stress cultural specificity in article 92 (3), point d TEC. Of all these proposals, only the amendment to article 128 (4) was accepted, but in a slightly weaker form than that proposed. Instead of adding to the sentence "The Community shall take cultural aspects into account in its action under other provisions of this Treaty" to the sentence "to preserve the diversity of cultures and opinions," was added: "to respect and to promote the diversity of its cultures."

[22] See document CONF 3893/97.

voting in a very significant way. Indeed, he said that "the large Member States, and *in particular the net contributors*, will be prepared to renounce unanimity and the possibility of a veto that this comprises only if, when voting through a qualified majority, they may influence a decision in a way that corresponds to their weight." This was a significant way of presenting the case because of the reference to the "net contributors." Indeed, this implicitly expresses the concern that the QMV's extension may not only be detrimental to the large Member States as such – if the voting reform would fail to grant them a voting weight "that corresponds to their [demographic] weight" – but to net contributing states as well. This is significant, since this may indicate that even a reform of the Council's voting may not be sufficient to alleviate these concerns, making the QMV's scope extension even more problematic.

For the Belgian government, German public utterances of this kind should have indicated that their hope to extend the QMV's scope was running into big trouble. Perhaps it did. However, Belgian reactions after the Amsterdam Summit – and especially their finger pointing at Helmut Kohl – gave the impression that they were more or less surprised by Kohl's reluctance in Amsterdam to accept a full-blown application of the QMV on issues of the first pillar. The Belgians blamed the German *Länder*, and especially Edmund Stoiber, Bavarian minister-president, for having made a (successful) last-ditch effort – by calling Kohl at the summit – to convince him not to agree with a too liberal extension of the QMV's scope. For the Belgians, the only alternative left was to find large-state partners to support an explicit linkage between the QMV's scope, the future reform of the Council's voting, and of the Commission's composition – the "institutional triangle" as Michel Barnier, former French European Affairs minister called it in his November 1996 speech to the European Delegation of the French Assemblée nationale – thereby creating what later became the third "leftover" of Amsterdam (Thijs 2000, 7).

Indeed, the linkage between the three issues of the institutional triangle was made in a Joint Declaration of France, Italy, and Belgium, attached to the Amsterdam Treaty, containing the following:[23]

> Belgium, France and Italy observe that, on the basis of the results of the Intergovernmental Conference, the Treaty of Amsterdam does not meet the need, reaffirmed at the Madrid European Council, for substantial progress towards reinforcing the institutions.

---

[23] See "Declaration by Belgium, France and Italy on the Protocol on the Institutions with the Prospect of Enlargement of the European Union," Declaration n° 6 attached to the Amsterdam Treaty.

Those countries consider that such reinforcement is an indispensable condition for the conclusion of the first accession negotiations. They are determined to give the fullest effect appropriate to the Protocol as regards the composition of the Commission and the weighting of votes and consider that a significant extension of recourse to qualified majority voting forms part of the relevant factors which should be taken into account.

The Composition of the European Commission
It has already been indicated above. The Belgian government felt it essential that the European Commission should continue to play an important role in EU decision-making, especially in the first pillar. The government defended this position using two arguments. The first referred to the fact that the Commission was (and is) seen as a protector of European Union interests and, therefore, as a counterbalance – even a safeguard – against possible dominance by a large Member State.

The second argument states that in a system of qualified majority, the Commission can act as a protector against what James Madison would have called the "tyranny of the majority." Indeed, this is why the introduction of the QMV would have to go hand in hand with both the granting to or preservation of the Commission's exclusive right of initiative and the linkage of the Commission initiatives to the Council's voting requirements. This clearly is a reference to article 250 (1) TEC (ex 189A (1)) which states that: "Where, in pursuance of this Treaty, the Council acts on a proposal from the Commission, unanimity shall be required for an act constituting an amendment to that proposal, subject to Article 251(4) and (5)."

The Belgian government defended this linkage in its October 1995 position:

> Pour le gouvernement belge, la majorité qualifiée est un élément essentiel d'une construction démocratique. La Belgique accepte qu'une majorité ait une opinion divergente sur la définition de l'intérêt commun, à condition que cet intérêt commun et la minorité soient protégés par une institution commune, notamment la Commission européenne (Kamer van Volksvertegen-woordigers 1995, 37).

By stressing however, the central role of the Commission, the question of the Commission's composition also became more important. And here the Belgian government took a position that is somewhat incompatible with its orthodox federalist position on other issues. It defended the principle that the Commission should be composed of at least one national from each Member State. The government defended this position with the argument of legitimacy.

It claimed that if the Commission would not contain a national from each Member State, its legitimacy would be negatively affected, and therefore, its capacity to defend forcefully and credibly the European Union's interests against the large Member States or against a possible "tyrannical" majority. It was only later in the IGC that Belgium declared its willingness "give up *its* commissioner" in exchange for a "strengthening of the first pillar" (*Agence Europe* May 1, 1997, italics added). In practical terms, however, this meant that Belgium supported the point of view of most – if not all – small Member States that the number of commissioners had to be reduced to twenty, one national for each member state, and that further reform had to be postponed until EU membership would have exceeded twenty Member States.

Closer Cooperation
When Karl Lamers and Wolfgang Schäuble issued their September 1994 paper on flexibility, not many Belgian officials and politicians were convinced that their approach towards European integration was the best one. On the contrary, many criticisms were expressed.

Gradually but steadily, however, the Belgian government became convinced that one way or the other, flexibility was a possible way out of future difficulties in an enlarged Union. Moreover, Belgium transformed itself from an initially recalcitrant opponent into an enthusiastic supporter of this approach. When it issued its first position on the 1996 IGC – the October 1995 document – it was still weighing the pros and cons of the idea. Although it expressed support for flexibility in this document, it did so without enthusiasm – more as a last resort – and without a clear view as to how to materialize this idea. Quite rapidly, however, ideas became clearer, as did convictions. Already in the Benelux Memorandum, closer cooperation was elevated in status to one of the Benelux's priorities for the IGC.[24]

In the October 1995 document, Belgian concerns with flexibility (differentiated integration) were visible in the numerous conditions that it wanted to attach to it. Many of these conditions were later included in the Benelux Memorandum and in the Amsterdam Treaty, not because Belgium as such proposed them, but because several Member States did.[25] These conditions referred to the rejection of a "Europe à la carte," the compatibility of differentiated integration with the objectives of the Treaty on European Union, its use as a last resort, its accessibility to all Member States that do not

---

[24] See document CONF 3844/96.

[25] As a matter of fact, widespread support for the differentiated integration existed among the six founding Members States, the Commission, and Finland. In particular, France, Germany, Belgium, and Luxembourg supported its applicability to the first pillar as well.

initially join (or can join, because they were not EU members yet), the preservation of the *acquis communautaire* and of the proper working of the internal market, the preservation of the single institutional framework of the EU, and a leading role for the European Commission. On this last aspect, the Belgian position gave a stronger role to the Commission than did the Benelux Memorandum. Whereas the latter stated that the Commission had to play a leading role "in applying the criteria and arrangements for differentiation," the Belgian position stated that the Commission had "to hold the key to differentiation," adding that "as independent institution and protector of the community interest, she is the only one in the position to assess in which cases and on the basis of what criteria differentiation is justified." And it concluded: "The Commission proposes, the Council decides by QMV."[26]

In the subsequent discussions on how the differentiated integration had to be applied, Belgium (together with France, Germany, and Luxembourg) belonged to the Member States that supported its applicability to the first pillar as well. Of the Benelux countries, the Netherlands had more reservations here because it doubted whether it could be applied in the EC (the Dutch saw fertile ground for flexibility in the third pillar).[27] In addition, Belgium, the Commission, and Austria were the only ones to initially support the idea that nothing in the EU could be *a priori* excluded from its application – as a discussion was going on on the use of a positive or negative list to define the flexibility's scope – but that precise conditions and criteria were needed in order to apply it.

As far as decision-making on the start of differentiated integration was concerned, Belgium was among the countries that supported the QMV (together with the Commission, Italy, France, Germany, Luxembourg, and Spain, with only hesitant support from Finland, the Netherlands, and Austria). With the exception of the UK, all Member States quite rapidly supported the principle that in the first pillar, the Commission should have the exclusive right of initiative "to trigger" differentiated integration.

The outcome of all these discussions is well known, and Belgium is not very happy about it. It applauds the inclusion of the differentiated integration – diplomatically called "closer cooperation" – but believes that the IGC compromise was a bad one as it reflects the lowest common denominator of the conditions set by the Member States, rather than a seriously workable way of operating. Indeed, the long list of conditions in both the EU and the EC Treaties, and the "last resort unanimity rule" make it almost impossible to

---

[26] Kamer van Volksvertegenwoordigers (1995, 32-33, translation by the author).

[27] During the IGC ministerial discussions on differentiated integration, the Benelux countries normally worked with one spokesman for the three countries.

begin the differentiated or closer cooperation.[28] That is why Belgium perceives those conditions and criteria as one of its priorities for the 2000 IGC.

Conclusion

Despite efforts to hide its disappointments, it was difficult for the Belgian government to give the impression that it was satisfied with the outcome of the 1996 IGC. The conflict with its Benelux-partner, the Netherlands, was especially painful, and although Belgium was happy – even to a certain extent proud – that it had succeeded in attaching a joint declaration on the QMV's scope to the Amsterdam treaty, it realized that the big battle was yet to come.

Indeed, Belgium actually faces a double battle, largely as a consequence of the 1996 IGC. In the first place, it must deal with its position as a small Member State in the EU and with the fact that institutional reforms will probably be more beneficial for its larger counterparts. It is certain that Belgium will have to – once again – assess the balance between the extent to which it relinquishes its own potential influence in the EU due to the upcoming institutional reforms, and the extent to which the QMV's scope has been extended and the European Commission's role enhanced. Unlike the 1996 IGC, it will be difficult to refuse to accept a reform of the Council voting in case the QMV's scope extension is considered to be insufficient. In other words, during the 1996 IGC, Belgium could more or less escape the dilemma. In the 2000 IGC, this will be more difficult, if not impossible.

The second "confrontation" will be even more difficult. It will be Belgium's struggle to uphold its orthodox federalist stances on European integration, while recognizing that these stances may be detrimental to Belgium's national interests in an enlarged EU. A less conditioned closer cooperation may provide an escape route, but only partially and to a limited extent. In other words, the Belgians will have to decide whether their principles of the past will be suitable and sustainable in the enlarged EU of the future. The probable outcome will be that Belgian orthodox federalist principles will give way to a large dose of pragmatism and possibly even to Euro-skepticism.

---

[28] See article 43 TEU & article 11 TEC. Although the Council can decide by QMV, a Member State can – for important and stated reasons of national policy – express its intention to oppose the granting of the authorization, after which the Council – acting by QMV – can refer the question to the European Council (or rather, the Council meeting in the composition of the Heads of State or Government), for decision by unanimity.

Bibliography

Dinan, D. (1994). *Ever Closer Union: An Introduction to the European Community*, London, Macmillan.

Kamer van Volksvertegenwoordigers – Chambre des Représentants (1995). *Beleidsnota van de Regering aan het Parlement betreffende de Intergouvernementele Conferentie van 1996 – Note de politique du Gouvernement au Parlement concernant la Conférence Intergouvernementale de 1996*, Document 146/1 – 95/96.

Kerremans, B. (1998). "Le systéme économique international et l'Union européenne après Amsterdam: vers une politique commerciale extérieure plus cohérente," pp. 175-197, in F. Dehousse, J. Vandamme, L. Hardy de Beaulieu (eds.), *L'Europe et les grands défis de l'an 2000*, Bruxelles: Presses Interuniversitaires Europeennes.

Kerremans, B. (1999). "Regieren im Mehrebenensystem und Bundesstaatlichkeit: Zur Mitwirkung der subnationalen Ebene Belgians im Rat der EU und an der Regierungskonferenz 1996/97," pp. 479-509, in *Jahrbuch des Föderalismus 2000: Föderalismus, Subsidiarität und Regionen in Europa*, Tübingen, Europäisches Zentrum für Föderalismus Forschung, Baden-Baden: Nomos Verlagsgesellschaft.

Thijs, S. (2000). "Het Belgisch Europabeleid in de kering?," *Demokritos*, No. 1, pp. 1-28.

4

Denmark: The Battle for a Better Treaty

Finn Laursen

Introduction

The Danish political establishment went into the 1996 Intergovernmental Conference (IGC) with some nervousness. Its fear was a repetition of the 1992 referendum where a small majority of the Danish electorate voted against a Treaty, which had wide support in the political establishment including the Parliament. Given this fear, the Danish government worked very hard to influence the new treaty along lines that were expected to be popular among the Danish voters and to avoid developments that could be hard to sell in Denmark. In this chapter we shall outline the Danish contributions to the 1996-97 IGC and see how the ensuing Amsterdam Treaty was received in Denmark, by the government, the political parties and the electorate.

Parties and Public Opinion[1]

Attitudes to European integration in Denmark are very complex. A majority of the Danish people support economic integration in Europe as long as it does not affect Danish autonomy too much. Denmark joined the EEC in 1973 after a referendum in October 1972 where 63.4 percent of the Danish people supported membership. The Single European Act (SEA) was ratified after being supported by 56.2 percent of the Danish people it in a referendum on 27 February 1986. But the Maastricht Treaty was first voted down by a narrow majority of 50.7 percent on 2 June 1992. When it was accepted in a second referendum on 18 May 1993 by 56.7 percent of the electorate Denmark had secured four exemptions at the Edinburgh summit in December 1992 (Laursen 1994). One of these dealt with Economic and Monetary Union (EMU), where Denmark decided not to take part in the third phase.

The three other exemptions dealt with Citizenship of the Union, Justice and Home Affairs (JHA) co-operation and defence policy. Denmark would not join the Western European Union (WEU) and only take part in

---

[1] Parts of this paper have relied on earlier writings by the author, especially Laursen, forthcoming.

intergovernmental JHA co-operation. The four areas of exemptions were those where a deepening of integration was taking the process closer to the traditional symbols of the nation state: citizenship, money and defence.

The hesitancy of the Danish public should be contrasted with an economic and political elite who are much more pro-integration. 141 members of the Danish parliament voted in favour of membership in 1972, against 34 "no" votes. In 1992 and 1993 there were quite large majorities in the Parliament, too. The only exception from the rule was January 1986, when the opposition denied the Liberal-Conservative government a majority in favour of the SEA. However, after a referendum, where a majority of the people supported the SEA, a substantial majority of MPs voted for the treaty.

On 12 May 1992, the *Folketing* authorised ratification of the Maastricht Treaty with 130 votes in favour, with only 25 voting against (23 members were absent and a Faroese member abstained). After the four Edinburgh exemptions had been accepted by Denmark's partners, prior to the second referendum in 1993, 154 members of the Folketing voted for ratification of the Maastricht Treaty as supplemented with the four exemptions. The Treaty was now supported by the new government coalition of Social Democrats, Social-Liberals, Centre Democrats and the Christian People's Party as well as the Liberals and Conservatives, which in the meantime had gone into opposition. An important difference compared with 1992 was the support from the Socialist People's Party, which had been actively involved in reaching the so-called national compromise, which became the basis for the Edinburgh exemptions. (Three MPs from the People's Socialists also voted against the Treaty in 1993). The Progress Party remained opposed, but the total number of "no" votes was only 16 (including also one Social-Liberal MP).

At the elections to the *Folketing* in September 1994, a new radical left-wing party, the Red-Green Alliance or the Unity List, opposing European integration, entered the Parliament.

The next election to the *Folketing* took place on 11 March 1998 just prior to the referendum on the Amsterdam Treaty. In the new *Folketing,* the following parties opposed the Amsterdam Treaty: Socialist People's Party, Danish People's Party, the Unity List (Red-Green Alliance) and the Progress Party. The Socialist People's Party, however, was split on the issue. The Danish People's Party was a splinter group from the Progress Party.

At the latest election to the European Parliament in June 1999 the June Movement gained 16.1 percent, the People's Movement against the EC Union 7.3 percent and the Danish People's Party 5.8 percent of the votes. The anti-EU vote thus remained very large. The Social Democrats received 36 percent

Table 4.1: Parliamentary Representation of Danish Parties and Groups.

	European Parliament Election 10 June 1999		Folketing Election March 1998		European Parliament Election 9 June 1994		Folketing Election 21 September 1994	
Seats won in the election and % of the total votes in Denmark	Seats	% of vote	Seats	% of vote	Seats	% of vote	Seats	% of vote
Social Democrats	3	16.5	63	36.0	3	15.8	62	34.6
Liberal Party	5	23.4	42	24.0	4	19.0	42	23.3
Conservative Party	1	8.5	16	8.9	3	17.7	27	15.0
Socialist People's Party	1	7.1	13	7.5	1	8.6	13	7.3
Danish People's Party	1	5.8	13	7.4	NP			
Centre Democrats	0	3.5	8	4.3	0	0.9	5	2.8
Social-Liberal Party	1	9.1	7	3.9	1	8.5	8	4.6
Red-Green Alliance	NP		5	2.7	NP		6	3.1
Christian People's Party	0	2.0	4	2.5	0	1.1	0	1.9
Progress Party	0	0.7	4	2.4	0	2.9	11	6.4
June Movement	3	10.1	NP		2	15.2	NP	
People's Movement against the EC Union	1	7.3	NP		2	10.3	NP	
*Greenland**			2				2	
*Faroe Islands**			2				2	
Total number of seats	16		179		16		179	

NP: did not participate
* Greenland and the Faroe Islands have home rule and are not members of the European Union.

Source Ministry of Foreign Affairs, "Political Parties in Denmark" http://www.um.dk/english/danmark/ om_danmark/partier/, and "The referendum in Denmark on 28 May 1998 on the ratification of the Amsterdam Treaty," http://www.um.dk/english/udenrigspolitik/europa/vurderinguk/. "Europa-Parlamentsvalget den 10. juni 1999," http://www.im.dk/ev1999/evland.htm.

of the votes at the Folketing election in March 1998 but could only muster 16.5 percent in the EP election in June 1999.[2]

The hesitancy of the Danish public has in many ways made Denmark a "minimalist" state in European integration. Danish EU-policy is domestic-politics driven. Pro-integration parties fear retribution at the polls if they become too pro-European.

Whereas Denmark's original reasons for joining the EEC were based on the interests of Danish agriculture and industry there is now, however, increasingly an agenda of issues where Denmark actively seeks European solutions, viz. the environment, consumer protection, social policy and employment. Since the beginning of 1993, Denmark has had Social Democratic-led governments, which have actively sought to give the EU a more "progressive" face in the hope of making the two-level game between the domestic constituents and the European partners easier. This has also included support for increased transparency in EU decision-making and support for subsidiarity – or nearness – as it is usually translated into Danish.

The basic attitudes of the established political parties have not changed fundamentally in recent years. The Liberal Party and the smaller Centre Democrats remain the most pro-integration parties. The current government parties, the Social Democrats and Social Liberals, are in favour of integration, but have minority factions that are sceptical. These two parties remained committed to the four Edinburgh exemptions through the Amsterdam process. The integration of the Schengen *acquis* into the Union by the Amsterdam Treaty has created some pressures on the JHA exemption, and the new British attitude to a common European defence policy from 1998 has created some pressure on the Danish policy on European defence. A referendum on Danish participation in the euro called on 28 September 2000 ended with a no vote. Thus, it will probably take some time before a government decides to call another referendum.

The Conservative Party is also pro-integration, but less so than the Liberal Party. It is the small parties on both the left and the right wing that have tried to exploit the public's scepticism by advocating anti-integration policies. These small parties have sometimes been very successful in setting the agenda of the Danish EU debate.

---

[2] The latest Danish election statistics can be found on the web site of the Ministry of the Interior: www.im.dk.

The Maastricht Court Case

The Danish debate in connection with the Amsterdam Treaty was affected by a legal challenge to the Maastricht Treaty. A group of individuals started proceedings at the High Court in Copenhagen against the Prime Minister, arguing that the Maastricht Treaty violated the Danish constitution.

The Parliament is normally considered supreme in Danish politics. The Danish courts have tried to stay away from politics. In line with this, the High Court first dismissed the case. When the Danish Supreme Court on 12 August 1996 decided to look into an appeal it was therefore a surprise to many. The Court delivered its judgement on 6 April 1998:

> Neither the additional powers that have been delegated to the Council in pursuance of Article 235 of the EC Treaty, nor the law-making activities [of] the Court of Justice can be regarded as incompatible with the demand for specification in sect. 20 (1) of the [Danish] Constitution.[3]

The Danish Constitution allows the transfer of powers to international organisations "to such an extent as shall be provided by statute." In Danish the term is *"i nærmere bestemt omfang,"* which means that the transfer must be specified. The appellants had pleaded that this condition had not been met (Rasmussen 1999).

The Court went far in deferring to politics:

> It must be considered to be assumed in the Constitution that no transfer of powers can take place to such an extent that Denmark can no longer be considered an independent state. The determination of the limits to this transfer must rely almost exclusively on considerations of a political nature.[4]

Afterwards the Prime Minister stated that he was "satisfied that the matter [had] been closed with a clear and unanimous decision." [5]

---

[3] Text of The Danish Supreme Court's Judgement of 6th April 1998 at: http://www.um.dk/udenrigspolitik/europa/domeng/. The Danish version, "Udskrift af Højesterets Dombog. Højesterets Dom af 6. April 1998," is also available from the EU Information of the *Folketing*.

[4] Loc. cit.

[5] Press release at http:/www.um.dk/udenrigspolitik/europa/domeng/prerel.html.

Policy-Making Mechanisms

The most direct "lesson" of the problems of getting the Maastricht Treaty ratified was an increased Danish emphasis on policies that could make the whole integration process more legitimate. This led to more emphasis on environment policy, consumer protection, social policy and employment policy as well as openness, nearness, etc. Indeed, the trauma from 1992 affected the way the Amsterdam Treaty negotiations were prepared in Denmark

Institutionally, the Maastricht Treaty's two new pillars had required some adaptations, involving the Foreign Affairs and Legal Affairs Committees of the Parliament in CFSP and JHA matters. Similarly, there has been an effort to involve the functionally specialised committees in the Parliament earlier and to a greater extent in first pillar legislation.

In connection with the Amsterdam Treaty negotiations a special mechanism was established for preparation of Danish policy. All interested ministries were represented in the "EC Committee in special session" (*EF-udvalget i særlig samling*) at the level of head of office (*kontorchef*) and chaired by the Head of the Northern division in the Ministry of Foreign Affairs. Above this was the Summit Committee (*Topmødeudvalget*), in which all interested ministries were represented by the Heads of Department (*departementschef*). The interesting thing was that this committee was chaired by the Head of Department from the Prime Minister's Office. This meant a somewhat weakened position of the Ministry of Foreign Affairs. About half the ministers took part in the government's own Summit Committee (*Regeringens topmødeudvalg*).[6] All in all, this lead to a broader involvement in policy preparation compared with the 1991 IGC, which negotiated the Maastricht Treaty. The purpose was to capture as many of the domestic implications as possibly and avoid the problems of the Maastricht Treaty ratification. Prime Minister Poul Nyrup Rasmussen's personal interest may also help explain the greater involvement by the Prime Minister and his Office (Petersen 1998).

The government's interest in central control is clear. It wants to control the politically sensitive aspects of the EU decision-making process. Since even technical details, such as which food additives are allowed or prohibited, can become political issues, getting input from experts and affected interests is important. An elaborate system of co-ordination has been set up to ensure

---

[6] Foreign Ministry, "Den danske beslutningsprocedure i EU-sager," (Copenhagen August 1997) gives the following group of participants: Prime Minister (chairman), and Ministers of Economy, Finance, Foreign Affairs, Environment and Energy, Business and Industry, Justice, and Food, Agriculture and Fisheries.

these relevant inputs. The central role normally played by the Foreign Ministry can be explained by Denmark's efforts to get as much influence in Brussels as possible. Thus, there are both consensus and efficiency considerations behind the established co-ordination mechanisms.

The Government's Main Priorities

The government's main priorities for the IGC were debated by the Folketing on 12 December 1995. First of all, the government sought achievements concerning enlargement, employment, environment and openness (Danish Government 1995; Denmark, Foreign Ministry 1996, 14-17).

According to the government, the superior goal of the IGC was to create the basis for an enlargement of the EU with Central and Eastern European Countries (CEECs). This goal required certain changes, including institutional adaptations. It was considered important that an enlarged EU should remain effective. Denmark wanted each Member State to retain a Commissioner. Support was expressed for a double majority in the Council and extended use of qualified majority in the first pillar. In the second pillar, Denmark could support some kind of "consensus minus one" (or "consensus minus two") when joint actions are adopted. In respect to the Presidency, Denmark could support a group presidency. Beyond that there were no concrete proposals for institutional adaptations.

With 17 million people unemployed in Europe, the question of employment was seen as the biggest issue in Europe. Although the EU could not solve this issue, the IGC should help create a framework, which would make it easier for the Member States to solve the problem. Some of the more concrete proposals later put forward at the IGC were already mentioned at this time before the IGC even got started.

Environmental problems do not respect national borders. Effective measures require international co-operation. Denmark wanted environmental co-operation within the EU strengthened. This was particularly important in connection with future enlargements given the environmental problems in the CEECs after forty years of environmental failures under Communism.

The fourth main priority mentioned by the government prior to the start of the IGC was that of openness. The government claimed to be in the front of the battle for greater openness in the EU. The IGC should take further steps in this area.

Concerning CFSP and JHA co-operation, the Danish government wanted these to remain intergovernmental co-operation.

The parliamentary debate finished with the adoption of a resolution (*motiveret dagsorden*) where the Parliament accepted the proposed priorities as basis for the IGC negotiations. The Danish exemptions from 1993 could only be changed through a referendum. The Parliament also expected to be continuously informed about the progress of the negotiations (Isaksen *et al.* 1998, 32).

Danish Contributions to the IGC

Denmark made seven formal proposals during the IGC. They dealt with employment, environment, openness, consumer protection, fraud, subsidiarity and national parliaments, and the role of national parliaments in relation to cooperation on JHA.[7]

The proposal concerning employment stressed that employment should have a more prominent place in the new treaty. There ought to be a separate chapter on employment, strengthening the goal of a high level of employment as a common task that requires a co-ordinated effort. Denmark also proposed annual reports on employment policies, adoption of recommendations to Member States and incentive measures as well as the establishment of an advisory employment committee. Employment, however, should primarily remain a national responsibility (CONF 3864/96 of 8 July 1996).

Environmental policy is domestically very sensitive in Denmark. It was therefore natural that the Danish government sought improvements here, too. Denmark worked for four main objectives: (1) introduction in the Treaty of the objective of sustainable development – with reference to the Rio Conference, (2) integration of environmental considerations in other policies, e.g. agriculture and transport, (3) assuring that the internal market can be realised while respecting the environment, and (4) that certain environmental taxes can be adopted by a qualified majority. In respect to the internal market, Denmark wanted a more precise formulation of the so-called environmental guarantee (Art. 100A par. 4). On the last point, Denmark had to fight until the last moment in Amsterdam in June 1997 (CONF 3904/96 of 16 September 1996). The battle was about fine linguistic nuances, "scientific facts" vs. "scientific evidence." In the end it was stipulated that a Member State can "introduce national provisions based on new scientific evidence relating to the protection of the environment or the working environment on grounds of a problem specific to that Member State arising after the adoption of [a] harmonisation measure" (quoted from Duff 1997, 75). The Commission

---

[7] Danish versions of the proposals were made available on the Foreign Ministry's web site: www.um.dk. Six of them were also published in the leaflet *Tæt på det åbne Europa* (Foreign Ministry March 1997). The seventh proposal on national parliaments and JHA cooperation was made in May 1997 (CONF/3915/97).

would have six months to approve or reject such national measures. In the absence of a decision by the Commission, the national provision would be deemed approved.

Denmark also wanted increased openness in the EU. The Danish proposal had four points: (1) Incorporation in the treaty of the principle of openness, (2) incorporation in the treaty of right of access to documents, (3) holding of open Council meetings when the Council deals with legislation for the first time as well as the last time and publication of voting results, and (4) publication of all proposals and adopted acts within JHA (CONF 3905/96 of 16 September 1996).

Concerning the fight against fraud, the Danish proposal also had four main parts: (1) Incorporation in the treaty of the principle of sound management of the Community's means, (2) authority to adopt measures against fraud by a qualified majority (3) enabling the Commission to act swiftly against fraud, and (4) intensified co-operation between the Commission, the member states and the Court of Auditors (CONF 3981/96 of 13 November 1996).

The Danish government further sought a strengthening of the Union's consumer policy. Denmark suggested: (1) consumer protection should be mentioned as a separate objective for the EU, (2) there must be adequate information for consumers, including labelling, and (3) consumer organisations should be more involved directly in co-operation about legislation (CONF 3980/96 of 13 November 1996).

The Danish proposal to the IGC concerning subsidiarity and the role of national parliaments, linking the two, would create the foundation for an agreement between the European Parliament, the Council and the Commission on national parliaments' access to information on EU and Commission proposals. A declaration should make the content of the agreement more precise. National parliaments should be heard more and be given longer time limits to respond to proposed legislation. The agreement should include more systematic use of green and white papers with the objective of getting the views of national parliaments before important legislation is proposed (CONF/3982/96 of 13 November 1996).

The Danish proposal concerning the role of national parliaments in relation to cooperation on JHA was put forward late in the negotiations. It referred to the earlier Danish proposal on subsidiarity and the role of national parliaments and noted that the section in the Irish Draft Treaty of December 1996 included a section that would strengthen the role of national parliaments. Denmark now said that "a number of special conditions apply to the role of national parliaments in relation to cooperation on justice and home affairs." So, "in parallel with the development and strengthening of cooperation on justice and home affairs ... it is necessary to establish a better framework for the involvement of national parliaments to ensure the democratic supervision of cooperative efforts." Referring to proposals from France and the UK, Denmark proposed the establishment of a special committee for JHA comprising representatives from national parliaments. This committee should *inter alia* be kept informed of developments and be offered an opportunity to present its opinion on JHA proposals (CONF/3915/97 of 16 May 1997). In the end the thrust of these Danish proposals fared well at the IGC. However, Denmark also went into the IGC wanting to retain the Danish exemptions from the Edinburgh agreement in December 1992. Here, Denmark approached the Conference with a low profile from the outset. In the end, the Danish exemptions were secured, in various way.

Since the 1996-7 IGC did not deal with EMU directly, the Danish exemption was not affected.

Concerning citizenship of the Union, the new Treaty now includes the stipulation that "Citizenship of the Union shall complement and not replace national citizenship (amended article 8A par. 2)." This means that the Danish reservation in respect to citizenship of the Union in reality has become part of the Treaty (Denmark, Foreign Ministry 1998, 11).

More at risk were the Danish exemptions in respect to defence policy and JHA co-operation. These were central issues on the IGC agenda.

With respect to defence, however, Denmark could on the whole hide behind the UK and the EU "neutrals," Ireland, Sweden, Finland and Austria (Laursen 1998). Although the language of the second pillar changed a fair amount the real changes were relatively minor. The Petersberg tasks of "humanitarian and rescue tasks, peacekeeping tasks and tasks of combat forces in crisis management, including peacemaking," were written into the treaty (Art. J.7) following a Swedish-Finnish proposal. The Western European Union was not merged with EU on this occasion, but the possibility remained open for the future: "The Union shall ... foster closer institutional relations with the WEU with a view to the possibility of the integration of the WEU into the Union, should the European Council so decide" (quoted from Duff 1997, 114).

Since many Member States wanted to move part of the third pillar to the first pillar to make this co-operation more efficient, it was in reality the Danish exemption in respect to JHA co-operation that turned out to create the greatest problem for Denmark. As the determination of the dominant actors to move major parts of the third pillar to the first pillar became clear, Denmark had to seek a special protocol to retain the Danish exemption. The whole move was further complicated by the decision to integrate the Schengen *acquis* into the treaty.

Denmark's decision to accede to the Schengen Convention was confirmed by the *Folketing* on 10 June 1997 without much debate shortly before the

Amsterdam summit. In the end, this became an important point in the public debate on the Amsterdam treaty.

A protocol on the "Position of Denmark" was included in the final agreement at the time of the negotiations in Amsterdam in mid-June 1997. The protocol states clearly that "Denmark shall not take part in the adoption by the Council of proposed measures pursuant to Title IIIa of the Treaty establishing the European Community" i.e., the newly transferred parts of JHA, mainly asylum and immigration policy. No new measures, provisions or decisions of the Court of Justice interpreting these measures and provisions "shall be binding upon or applicable in Denmark." However, Denmark continues to take part in visa policy, which had already been included in the EC pillar at the time of Maastricht.

Concerning Schengen, Art. 5 of the protocol stated: "Denmark shall decide within a period of 6 months after the Council has decided on a proposal or initiative to build upon the Schengen *acquis* under the provisions of Title IIIa of the [TEC], whether it will implement this decision in its national law. If it decides to do so, this decision will create an obligation under international law between Denmark and the other Member States ..." Further, "If Denmark decides not to implement a decision of the Council ... the European Union will consider appropriate measures to be taken" (quoted from Duff 1997, 29-30).

Incidentally, the Danish protocol also mentioned the defence exemption: "Denmark does not participate in the elaboration and implementation of decisions and actions of the Union which have defence implications." But it also added that Denmark would "not prevent the development of closer cooperation between Member States in this area."

After this, the Danish government could go home and claim that the Edinburgh exemptions were respected by the new Treaty (Petersen & Laursen 1998, 58-60; Denmark, Foreign Ministry 1998a).

The Ratification Debate

After the negotiation finished in Amsterdam in June 1997, the Danish government went far in stressing the Danish imprint on the Treaty as well as the notion that the Treaty was preparing the Eastern enlargement of the EU, expected to be one factor that could help sell the Treaty to the Danish public.

When the *Folketing* opened in October 1997, the Prime Minister claimed to have learned from the Maastricht referenda:

> We have learned, and we have listened. The Danes are not against being a part of Europe. Europe may also be a part of Denmark, but only a part.

For the government, therefore, it was decisive to reach a result in Amsterdam, on which the Danish people can recognise the values that society in Denmark is built. We succeeded, we succeeded.[8]

He went on to give three reasons why the Danes should vote "yes" for the Treaty:

1. The Amsterdam Treaty was the basis for widening the EU to include the Central and Eastern European Countries (CEECs), a precondition for a peaceful Europe.
2. The Amsterdam Treaty was simply better than the Maastricht Treaty in respect to the Danish central values (*mærkesager*): democracy, human rights, better co-operation about the environment and employment.
3. The four Danish exemptions were intact and secure.

He explained the EU as an association, but not an association where there should be co-operation about everything. Co-operation should be limited to the necessary.

How did the political parties receive the treaty? The *Folketing* had a first reading on 21 October 1997 of the Bill to ratify the Amsterdam Treaty. Due to the parliamentary election on 11 March 1998 however, the new Parliament had to start the parliamentary proceedings again. Another first reading therefore took place on 1 April 1998 (*Folketingets Forhandlinger*, no. 2, 1997-98 (2. session), pp. 181-233).

Jacob Buksti, representing the Social Democrats, said the treaty was better. It had Danish imprints. The treaty would allow for an eastern enlargement process to start. Thus, it was a peace project. And the Danish exemptions had been retained. To those who said that the EU was interfering in too many things he said that it was not the EU but the world that interfered. The EU was a means to get influence. "The paradox is that it is only through participation in the Community that we can retain our autonomy" (Ibid, p. 184, author's translation).

Charlotte Antonsen, representing the Liberal Party, stressed that the treaty was a precondition for enlargement. She saw various improvements in the treaty, including more openness, more influence for the European Parliament and more QMV in the Council, but, overall, the changes were said to be minor. The issue was really whether Denmark wanted to continue to take part in the co-operation in which Denmark had taken part since 1973. During the

---

[8] Author's translation from the Danish text which can be found on the internet site of the *Folketing*: www.folketinget.dk.

debate she also said that the Liberal Party wanted to get rid of the Danish exemptions as soon as possible.

The spokesperson for the Conservative party was Lene Espersen. She too supported the treaty, arguing that it was a better treaty and a precondition of enlargement. She further claimed that it was cementing a Europe of nation-states (*fædrelandenes Europa*). Although that sounded slightly Gaulist she also approvingly cited Jean Monnet about unifying peoples, not countries. The treaty would make the EU more effective, simple and flexible. This was necessary for enlargement. The treaty was also better because it would allow for solutions of problems considered important by the citizens such as environment and consumer protection. She also said that it was important to get a common refugee and asylum policy, and she stressed that Denmark had already accepted the Schengen agreement. Concerning CFSP she said it would be strengthened. At the same time "constructive abstention" allowed for respect of national sovereignty.

The Socialist People's Party was represented by its leader Holger K. Nielsen who argued against the treaty. For security reasons he was in favour of enlargement. But in an EU with more than 25 members the old goals could not be maintained. The old goal of Schuman, Monnet and Spinelli was federalism. Economic integration would be expected to lead to political integration. In order to get the CEECs into the EU it was necessary to abandon these old federalist goals. This indeed, had been the message from the Danish people on 2 June 1992, and this attitude was the underlying reason for the Danish exemptions. Looking at the Amsterdam Treaty he argued that it implied more union especially in respect to JHA, by moving much of this to the First pillar. He also argued that the mentioning of enlargement with five CEECs in the protocol to the treaty would create a new social division line in Europe. A "no" to the treaty should be used for new negotiations. The treaty was not good enough.

Kristian Thulesen Dahl from the Danish People's Party also expressed opposition to the treaty. The EU, he claimed, was getting more and more centralistic and bureaucratic. The Amsterdam Treaty would lead to more central regulation of more areas with more QMV. The European Parliament would also get more power. The question was, therefore, whether Denmark should transfer more sovereignty to the EU system. JHA was singled out as a special problem. The new construction would create a situation where the Danish parliament would have to decide whether to accept the rules adopted by the other members through supranational co-operation. The party was against the Schengen agreement, which was now been incorporated into the treaty. Abolishment of frontier controls would lead to increased criminal activity across borders.

Arne Melchior, Centre Democrat, argued that there were three clear advantages of a "yes." First, taking part in the EU gives access to information. Second, it gives influence on decisions. Especially small countries have an interest in being present at the table. Third, Denmark can set a good example. It can be hoped that other countries will follow sound Danish ideas, methods, organisational forms, attitudes of solidarity, etc. But in reality the main reason to say "yes" to the treaty was to avoid a new world war in Europe. Issues should be solved at the negotiating table, not on the battle fields. Old-fashioned sovereignty had become outdated.

Elisabeth Arnold spoke on behalf of the Social Liberal Party. Her argument focused upon enlargement, improvements in respect to fundamental rights, employment, environment, openness as well as the retention of the Danish exemptions. She admitted that not so much had happened in respect to institutional changes as her party had hoped.

The spokesman of the Unity List was Keld Albrechtsen who claimed that the Danish protocol on JHA was a clear circumvention of the Danish exemption. It would allow Denmark, on an ad hoc basis, to take part in supranational co-operation, he claimed. Saying yes on 28 May would mean a further deepening of integration. Concerning enlargement he noted that a new treaty would be necessary to take in more than five CEECs. This would lead to a changed distribution of power in the Union unfavourable to the smaller states. Flexibility was seen as a way to circumvent treaty changes. The development of the Union could thus proceed without involving the people, he claimed. He also claimed that the Union was getting tremendous powers in the area of defence policy. He foresaw the possibility that the EU might have to intervene in Africa to defend French interests. Looking at JHA he claimed the exact opposite of treaty opponents in the Danish People's Party: the treaty would create a Fortress Europe by closing external borders and establishing police co-operation with massive surveillance. Incorporating Schengen in the Union would make it extremely difficult for CEECs to join.

Also speaking against the Amsterdam Treaty was Kim Behnke representing the Progress Party. The treaty would mean more union, less freedom. 20 areas would move to QMV. Incorporating Schengen was also a mistake. It was not correct to argue that the treaty was necessary for the CEECs. Their problem could be solved through free trade. The new employment chapter would create possibilities of EU interference in Denmark. The EU should not deal with defence. The party was in favour of European co-operation, but not the kind of co-operation found in the Amsterdam treaty.

Jann Sjursen represented the Christian People's Party. The party supported the ratification of the Amsterdam Treaty. The enlargement perspective was important. It was therefore regrettable that the IGC had not solved the institutional issues. However, the party was satisfied that it had been agreed that each Member State would have a commissioner in the future. Another important argument for the party was that the four Danish exemptions had not been affected; indeed, they had been strengthened. The third major argument was the improvements in the treaty in respect to subsidiarity, flexibility, environment and role of national parliaments. The increased role of the European Parliament, on the other hand, worried the party. It was taking the EU in the direction of a federal state, not a Europe of nations as wanted by the Christian People's Party. Oddly enough, it was argued that an increased role of the European Parliament meant an increased democratic deficit. It would be more difficult for the Danish Parliament to influence events, it was argued.

Steen Gade spoke as a private member of the Socialist People's Party. He was in favour of ratification. He gave three reasons. One, leaving the EU was not an alternative. Second, only the EU could get Europe to "hang together" after the end of the Cold War. Third, there was a great need for supranational decisions in the world. Many problems e.g., environmental problems, could not be solved nationally. Supranational, binding legal rules and majority decisions were necessary. He also mentioned the specific improvements in the Amsterdam Treaty and said that a Danish no would be seen as a nationalistic decision in the rest of Europe.

Another private member, who was very active during the debate, was Frank Dahlgaard from the Conservative Party. He broke the party line by being against the Amsterdam Treaty. The treaty was too much union for him.

Finally, the Minister of Foreign Affairs Niels Helveg Petersen spoke. He repeated some of the well known arguments of the government including preparation for enlargement. He also mentioned that Denmark actively had supported the idea of a double majority in the Council. There had to be a qualified majority, but this majority should also represent at least half of the citizens in the EU, he said. He argued that enlargement did not necessarily mean less influence. When Finland, Sweden and Austria had joined the EU, Denmark did get a reduced share of the votes, but Denmark also got new allies and friends. In respect to Schengen he emphasised that the Nordic Passport Union had been retained because Norway and Iceland had got agreements with the Schengen group.

The Parliament then decided to send the Bill to the European Affairs Committee, which issued a short report on 24 April (*Folketinget,* European Affairs Committee 1998a). A short second reading in the Parliament took place on 30 April 1998 (*Folketingets Forhandlinger, no. 5, 1997-98 (2nd session)*, pp. 951-954).

The Amsterdam Treaty was accepted by 92 votes after the third reading on 7 May 1998 in the Parliament (Social Democrats, Liberals, Conservatives, Centre-Democrats, Social Liberals and Christian People's Party) against 22 votes (Socialist People's Party, Danish People's Party, the Unity List, the

Progress Party and one Conservative MP, Frank Dahlgaard). Four members of the Socialist People's Party indicated afterwards that they would have voted for the Treaty, had they been present, saying that it was a mistake that they had not been present (*Folketingets Forhandlinger*, no. 6, 1997-98 (2nd session), p. 1275).

The Referendum

To the extent that the Amsterdam Treaty meant a transfer of new powers to the EU, the Danish Constitution's article 20 would apply. But did such a transfer actually take place? After examining the Treaty, the Ministry of Justice concluded that such a transfer of new powers to the EU took place in three areas, viz. articles 6A, 129A and 236. These concerned "appropriate action to combat discrimination based on sex, racial or ethnic origin, religion or belief, disability, age or sexual orientation (new Article 6A), which was found to go beyond already existing stipulations concerning non-discrimination. In respect to consumer policy, it was the extension of contributions to protect the interests of consumers to include the words "to organise themselves in order to safeguard their interests" (from amended Article 129A). Finally, it was concluded that the new possibility of suspending the voting rights of a Member State (Article 236) breaching the principles of democracy, respect of human rights and fundamental freedoms, and the rule of law, would require the application of Article 20 of the Danish Constitution (Denmark, Ministry of Justice 1998).

Article 20 required a five-sixths' majority in the *Folketing* or an ordinary majority decision in the *Folketing* followed by a decisive referendum. Given the fact that there was no five-sixths majority in the Parliament, the referendum was necessary for Danish ratification.

Interestingly enough the three areas singled out by the Ministry of Justice were in no way central issues during the referendum debate.

The referendum result on 28 May 1998 was a "yes" vote of 55.1 percent. The turnout was 74.8 percent, lower than earlier EU referenda.[9] Maybe the Treaty did not spark the imagination of the Danes? Or maybe they were a little weary after the two Maastricht referenda.

---

[9] As reported in the Danish press, e.g. *Jyllands-Posten*, 30 May, 1998.

Denmark's Post-Amsterdam Situation

In November 1998 the European Affairs Committee put forward a draft report concerning greater openness in Danish EU decision-making (*Folketinget*, European Affairs Committee 1998b). The main proposals were to increase further the involvement of the specialised committees (*fagudvalg*) of the *Folketing* at an early stage, to open some meetings of the European Affairs Committee to the public, and to invite Danish MEPs to some meetings of the European Affairs Committee.

According to press reports, the Prime Minister decided after the Supreme Court case about the Maastricht Treaty to seek to make the decision-making more democratic. Some EU legislation concerning food additives, where the otherwise environmental and consumer friendly European Parliament did not ask for high levels of protection, had also inspired the proposals. Getting the Parliament's expertise involved early and creating a stronger link to the European Parliament was seen as a way to improve EU legislation. Further, a public debate on important proposals should take place, it was argued. The government would be asked to present such proposals to open meetings of the European Affairs Committee as soon as possible after being made by the Commission (Bostrup & Andersen 1998).

The Amsterdam Treaty also influenced the way of thinking in Copenhagen in respect to the role of the Danish members of the European Parliament. Because of the increased use of the co-decision procedure the role of the EP would increase. The government therefore started regular meetings with the Danish MEPs in the summer of 1998. The proposal from the European Affairs Committee would give MEPs access to open meetings of the committee in the future with a right to speak. These open meetings, however, would not take decisions. Decisions, including mandates for negotiations to the government, would still be taken in closed meetings.

On 19 February 1999, the European Affairs Committee issued its report on greater openness in the Danish EU decision making process (*Folketinget*, European Affairs Committee 1999). The government had agreed to the parts that affected its involvement. The general lines of the draft proposal from November 1988 were confirmed. Since 1 March 1999, when the report entered into force, it has become possible to have open meetings in the European Affairs Committee including the presence of Danish MEPs. MEPs can also send proposals to the other standing committees of the *Folketing*, and the efforts to involve these specialised parliamentary committees early in the process are reinforced.

The integration of the Schengen *acquis* and the movement of some JHA matters to the first pillar under the Amsterdam Treaty seem now to be starting to put pressure on the Danish system, however, no institutional adaptation has taken place yet.

Concluding Remarks

Danish policy-makers drew certain lessons from the Maastricht debacle (Laursen 1997). They tried actively to avoid a repetition of the 1992 referendum by working to influence the treaty in certain directions while at the same time retaining the Danish exemptions from 1993.

Domestically more openness and earlier debate in connection with the Amsterdam process was sought. Also, the Prime Minister played a very active role in the process. This led to some adaptations in the long established policy co-ordination system that usually allows Denmark to speak with one voice in Brussels. In general this system allows for a fair amount of democratic control of EU policy in Denmark.

The domestic politics of EU policy in Denmark has occasionally made Denmark a difficult partner in the EU. At the same time, however, the Danish system of co-ordination has made Denmark good at implementing EU legislation. The early involvement of interest organisations and administrative agencies that have to implement legislation has made this part of the process a success story.

Where the Danish system sometimes fails, it can be argued, is its lack of success in communicating the rationale of the continued process of integration in Europe to the citizens in a convincing way. Trying to give the EU a more "progressive" face has become part of the government's strategy to create more legitimacy for the process.

The Danish exemptions increasingly restrict the government. The fact that the referendum on Danish participation in the euro on 28 September 2000 ended with a no vote implies that the government will have to try to live with these exemptions for some time to come.

It can be concluded that the Danish political leadership is still struggling with a not-so-permissive consensus among the Danish public when it comes to European integration (Laursen 1994b). Or, put differently, the quest for legitimacy remains somewhat illusory (Nehring 1998).

Bibliography

Bostrup, Jens & Nina Vinther Andersen (1998). "Folketinget vil tage magt fra regeringen," *Politiken,* 31 December, p. 6, 1 section.

Danish Government (1995). "Basis for Negotiations. Open Europe: The 1996 Intergovernmental Conference," SN 522/95 (REFLEX 23), 11 December.

Denmark, Foreign Ministry (1995). *Dagsorden for Europa. Sammendrag*, Copenhagen, August.

Denmark, Foreign Ministry (1996). *På vej mod det åbne Europa*, Copenhagen, November.

Denmark, Foreign Ministry (1997a). *Tæt på det åbne Europa*, Copenhagen, March.

Denmark, Foreign Ministry (1997b). *Det åbne Europa.* Copenhagen, July.

Denmark, Foreign Ministry (1997c). *Amsterdam-traktaten og miljøet*, Copenhagen, December.

Denmark, Foreign Ministry (1997d). *Amsterdam-traktaten og åbenheden*, Copenhagen, December.

Denmark, Foreign Ministry (n.d.). *Amsterdam-traktaten – kort fortalt*, Copenhagen.

Denmark, Foreing Ministry (1998a). *Amsterdam-traktaten og Danmark – de danske forbehold*, Copenhagen, February.

Denmark, Foreign Ministry (1998b). *Amsterdam-traktaten og nærheden*, Copenhagen, February.

Denmark, Foreign Ministry (1998c). *Amsterdam-traktaten og den fælles udenrigs- og sikkerhedspolitik*, Copenhagen, March.

Denmark, Foreign Ministry (1998d). *Amsterdam-traktaten og udvidelsen*, Copenhagen, March.

Denmark, Foreign Ministry (1998e). *Amsterdam-traktaten: Særtryk af lovforslag L 1 vedrørende Danmarks ratifikation af Amsterdam-traktaten, fremsat for Folketinget den 26. marts 1998*, Copenhagen.

Denmark, Foreign Ministry (1998f). *Amsterdam-traktaten og beskæftigelsen*, May.

Denmark, Ministry of Justice (1998). "Justitsministeriets redegørelse for visse forfatningsretlige spørgsmål i forbindelse med Danmarks ratifikation af Amsterdam-traktaten," http://www.um.dk/udenrigspolitik/europa...am/forfatn_ret_sp/.

Duff, Andrew (ed.) (1997). *The Treaty of Amsterdam: Text and Commentary*, London: Federal Trust/Sweet and Maxwell Ltd.

Folketinget, European Affairs Committee (1998a). "Til lovforslag nr. L," Folketinget 1997-98 (2. samling), Betænkning afgivet af Europaudvalget den 24. april 1998.

Folketinget, European Affairs Committee (1998). "Udkast til beretning fra Europaudvalget om større åbenhed i den danske EU-beslutningsproces m.v.," Alm. del – bilag 225, 26. november.

Folketinget, European Affairs Committee (1999). "Beretning om større åbenhed i den danske EU-beslutningsproces m.v.," Beretning afgivet af Europaudvalget den 19. februar.

Friis, Lykke (1998). "Denmark's Fifth EU-Referendum: In Denmark nichts Neues?" *Working Papers,* No. 13, Copenhagen: Danish Institute of International Affairs.

Friis, Lykke (1999). "EU and Legitimacy – the Challenge of Compatibility: A Danish Case Study," *Cooperation and Conflict,* Vol. 34, No. 3 (September), pp. 43-71.

Isaksen, Susanne, Ole Toft & Jens Bødtcher-Hansen (1998). *En traktat bliver til. Amsterdam-traktaten: Forberedelse, forhandling og resultat,* Copenhagen: Schultz.

Laursen, Finn (1992). "Denmark and European Political Union," pp. 63-78, in Finn Laursen & Sophie Vanhoonacker (eds.), *The Intergovernmental Conference on Political Union,* Dordrecht: Martinus Nijhoff.

Laursen, Finn (1994a). "Denmark and the Ratification of the Maastricht Treaty," pp. 61-86, in Finn Laursen & Sophie Vanhoonacker (eds.), *The Ratification of the Maastricht Treaty,* Dordrecht: Martinus Nijhoff.

Laursen, Finn (1994b). "The Not-So-Permissive Consensus: Thoughts on the Maastricht Treaty and the Future of European Integration," pp. 295-317, in Laursen and Vanhoonacker (eds.), *The Ratification of the Maastricht Treaty,* Dordrecht: Martinus Nijhoff.

Laursen, Finn (1995). "Parliamentary Bodies Specializing in European Union Affairs: Denmark and the Europe Committee of the *Folketing,*" pp. 43-60, in Finn Laursen & Spyros A. Pappas (eds.), *The Changing Role of Parliaments in the European Union,* Maastricht: European Institute of Public Administration.

Laursen, Finn (1997). "The Lessons of Maastricht," pp. 59-73, in Geoffrey Edwards & Alfred Pijpers (eds.), *The Politics of European Treaty Reform: The 1996 Intergovernmental Conference and Beyond,* London: Pinter.

Laursen, Finn (1998). "The EU "Neutrals," the CFSP and Defence Policy," *TKI Working Papers on European Integration and Regime Formation,* No. 26, Esbjerg: South Jutland University Press.

Laursen, Finn (forthcoming). "Denmark: In Pursuit of Influence and Legitimacy," in Wolfgang Wessels, A. Maurer & J. Mittag (eds.), *Fifteen into One? The European Union and the Member States,* Manchester: Manchester University Press.

Nehring, Niels-Jørgen (1998). "The Illusory Quest for Legitimacy: Danish Procedures for Policy Making on the EU and the Impact of a Critical Public," pp. 60-81, in Georg Sørensen & Hans-Henrik Holm (eds.), *And Now What? International Politics After the Cold War: Essays in Honour of Nikolaj Petersen*, Aarhus: Politica.

Petersen, Nikolaj (1997). "The Nordic Trio and the Future of the EU," pp. 159-187, in Geoffrey Edwards & Alfred Pijpers (eds.), *The Politics of Treaty Reform: The 1996 Intergovernmental Conference and Beyond*, London: Pinter.

Petersen, Nikolaj (1998). "Denmark, the IGC 1996 and the Future of the European Union," pp. 43-59, in Bertel Heurlin & Hans Mouritzen (eds.), *Danish Foreign Policy Yearbook 1998*, Copenhagen: Danish Institute of International Affairs,.

Petersen, Nikolaj (1999). "The Danish Referendum on the Treaty of Amsterdam," pp. 101-122, in Bertel Heurlin & Hans Mouritzen (eds.), *Danish Foreign Policy Yearbook 1999*, Copenhagen: Danish Institute of International Affairs.

Petersen, Nikolaj & Finn Laursen (1998). *Amsterdam-traktaten: Baggrund, kommentarer og perspektiver*, Copenhagen: Den Danske Europabevægelse.

Rasmussen, Hjalte (1999). "Folketing, EF/EU og grundlovens § 20," pp. 371-412, in Ole Stig Andersen et al. (eds.), *Folketingets festskrift i anledning af grundlovens 150-års-jubilæum den 5. juni 1999,* Copenhagen: Folketingets Præsidium.

5

Germany: Safeguarding the EMU and the Interests of the Länder

Rita Beuter

Introduction

In contrast to the ratification of the Treaty on European Union (TEU), when Germany ratified as the last Member State, its ratification of the Amsterdam Treaty was quick and uncontroversial. Germany became the first Member State to ratify the Treaty on 27 March 1998. This paper will address, first, the preparation of the IGC by different actors, including the German Länder. Second, it will examine German preferences and specific proposals during the IGC leading up to the Amsterdam Summit. Reactions on the Amsterdam outcome by the German political establishment and German public opinion on European integration issues will be dealt with in the third part. Furthermore, it will tackle the ratification process by examining the debate in the *Bundestag* and the position of the German upper house, the *Bundesrat*. Finally, the chapter will try to give some explanations as to Germany's reluctant attitude towards further integration at Amsterdam.

One should recall that with the ratification of the Maastricht Treaty, the role of the *Bundestag* and of the *Bundesrat* was strengthened in matters of European affairs, on the one hand by inserting Article 23 in the German Constitution, and on the other hand by the judgement of the German Constitutional Court of 12 October 1993. Article 23 on the realization of the European Union states, *inter alia*, that the transfer of sovereign powers requires the consent of the *Bundesrat*, and also lays down the obligation that the government informs the *Bundestag* and the *Bundesrat* in good time on matters related to the European Union. The German Constitutional Court in its judgement, clearly pointed to the need for stronger national democratic control over EC decision-making. It specified that as long as democratic control cannot be exercised at the Community level, it is the task of national parliaments to ensure democratic control.

Preparing for the IGC- Position of Parties and the Government[1]

Following German unification in 1990 the German government's stated objective in the Intergovernmental Conference (IGC) on political union was the creation of federal structures in the EC, which would be able to accommodate a united Germany and address the new demands on the post-Cold-War era. The German objective at Maastricht was that monetary union and political union had to be linked and accomplished simultaneously. The shortcomings of the Treaty on European Union (TEU) and the difficult ratification process in Germany did not, however, question Germany's commitment to the European integration process. Consensus among all political forces in Germany was that there was no alternative to the European integration process and a united Germany had to be anchored in the European system (Beuter 1993). Outside Germany questions were raised as to the continuity of Germany's European policy (Anderson & Goodman 1993), the limits and possibilities of Germany's diplomacy in the EU and whether a united Germany might become more assertive (Bulmer & Paterson 1996).

Towards the mid-1990s, the German government's main approach at the same time deepened and widened. In September 1994, the CDU/CSU Parliamentary Group in Germany put forward proposals for the future process of European integration in the light of the forthcoming enlargement. The document, entitled "Reflections on European Policy" dealt with three main issues: the current situation in the EU; Germany's interests in Europe; and proposals for the future. This paper actually opened the debate on the reform of the European Union. Fears of a degeneration of the EU and problematic developments in the EU were the driving force behind the paper. Critical factors concerned: the over-extension of the EU's institutions; the growing differentiation of interests and socio-economic development; different perceptions of internal and external priorities; profound structural economic change (unemployment, economic crisis); the rise of regressive nationalism (migration, return to nation-state); challenges and weaknesses of national governments and parliaments in the light of these economic problems and questions of when and how to expand the European Union to Eastern Europe (CDU-CSU 1994). Concerning Germany's interest, the paper stipulated that, to prevent the drifting apart of Europe, it will be necessary to create a security system with Germany, to establish a stable order for the Eastern part of the Continent and therefore integrate Eastern Europe into the West European system, and to set up a comprehensive partnership with Russia. In order to achieve stability in Europe, enlargement to Eastern Europe and the deepening of integration would need to occur simultaneously. Proposals for reform included:

---

[1] This section draws on Beuter, 1997.

reform of EU institutions, a strengthening of the EU's hard core, intensification of Franco-German relations, improvement of the Union's capacity to act in the foreign and security policy and enlargement to the East.

These proposals have triggered a lively debate, mainly on the controversial issues of a hard-core but also on the institutional development towards a federal state, and on Franco-German relations. The "hard-core idea" irritated not only those Member States not mentioned as belonging to the core, but in Germany too, the Social Democrats and the Foreign Minister, Klaus Kinkel, distanced themselves from this idea, and Klaus Kinkel emphasized that the document had not been sanctioned by the government. A day before the CDU/CSU paper was released, French Prime Minister, Edouard Balladur, proposed in an interview with *Le Figaro* that Europe should develop along the lines of three concentric circles whereby France and Germany would be part of the inner core surrounded by other Member States in the second circle and the East European countries being part of the outer circle. With both proposals, the discussion on "flexibility" or "enhanced cooperation" had been opened. On institutional reform, the CDU/CSU paper advocated the development of a quasi constitution, which would clarify the competence at various levels and define fundamental values. This quasi-constitution should be oriented towards a federal state enshrining the subsidiarity principle and its clear definition. All existing institutions were to be reformed. The European Commission should develop into a European government answerable to a European Parliament with full legislative powers together with the Council, which would develop into a second chamber. These federalist ideas were shared neither by France nor the UK. In the French parliament support had been given to the idea of a second parliamentary chamber at European level, composed of members of national parliaments.[2] According to Edouard Balladur, democratic control should be exerted by national parliaments. There were also French fears that Germany might acquire far greater power than it had in the past with the enlargement towards Austria and the Scandinavian countries as well as towards Eastern Europe. Therefore, France demanded that an Eastern enlargement would need to be balanced by a new initiative towards the Mediterranean countries.

The objectives of the German government as regards European policy and the IGC were detailed in the coalition agreement between the CDU/CSU/FDP on 11 November 1994. The prime aim of the coalition's European policy was seen in the stabilization of the EU by a consequent application of the EU Treaty and the EU's further internal and external development. Two main policy orientations were highlighted. First, the traditional French-German cooperation and,

---

[2] See the speech by the President of the European Parliament Klaus Hänsch on "Relations between the EP and National Parliaments," *Agence Europe, Europe Documents*, No. 1920, 27 January 1995.

secondly, the realization of Economic and Monetary Union (EMU) according to the letter of the Treaty and the strict interpretation of the convergence criteria. The coalition agreement stressed that the EU should have the capacity to act and react quickly in foreign and security matters. Accordingly, a strengthened Common Foreign and Security Policy (CFSP) had to entail: majority voting; stabilization of neighbouring regions, namely, Central and Eastern Europe; enhanced operative capabilities of the Western European Union (WEU); development of an autonomous European security and defence identity with the WEU becoming the European pillar of the Atlantic Alliance and the defence component of the EU. Four main priorities were identified for improved cooperation in Justice and Home Affairs: the application of the Schengen agreement and the external borders accord; a strengthening of Europol towards a European police office; common asylum and immigration policy combined with a just distribution of refugees among Member States. Both the CFSP and cooperation in Justice and Home Affairs were to be integrated into the Community framework. On flexibility, the government's position was that all Member countries should equally be able to participate in the deepening of the European integration process, yet this should not be hampered by the veto of a single member country. It was acknowledged that the *Bundesländer* will participate in the preparation of the German position for the IGC and the German representation at the IGC conference. The Bundestag and the *Bundesrat* would receive information on drafts of EU legislation in due time. According to the coalition agreement, the strict application and concretization of the subsidiarity principle – a clear distinction of tasks, competences of the EU and the Member States; checking of legislation whether it corresponds to the subsidiarity principle (tourism, catastrophe protection); and a precision of the subsidiarity principle (Article 3b) concerning the burden of proof – had to be defended at the IGC. Guiding principles of Germany's European policy would be solidarity in the context of a fair financial burden-sharing and budgetary discipline.

The coalition accord defined the broad guidelines of the Federal Government's European policy but did not go into detail as to the required institutional reforms for the 1996 IGC. In February 1995 Foreign Minister Klaus Kinkel called for majority voting in all respects. This was also supported by Wolfgang Schäuble from the CDU in an interview with the *Financial Times*, on 25 March 1995, saying that EU decision-making procedures should be made more effective by extending majority voting and by eliminating the right of veto. According to Schäuble, co-decision was required for the European Parliament.

In the summer of 1995, the Executive Committee of the CDU/CSU Parliamentary Group released two discussion papers in preparation of the IGC. One, according to which the key objective of the 1996 IGC should be to make the Union capable of more effective action in the field of foreign and security policy, (CDU/CSU Parliamentary Group, 1995) and the other entitled "Further

Development of the Community Foundations of Justice and Home Affairs Policy at the Intergovernmental Conference in 1996" (CDU/CSU Parliamentary Group 1995a). Similar to the coalition agreement, but more detailed and more far-reaching proposals were made for CFSP and the defence policy. Qualified majority voting (with a double majority) was to be applied for foreign and security policy decisions which have no military implications. For decisions with military implications, the German proposal advocated "flexibility," with a possibility of abstaining, instead of exercising a veto, but all countries would need to finance military operations. A common European defence policy and defence were to form an integral component of the CFSP, whereby all EU members would become NATO members and membership of NATO would be linked to EU membership. Furthermore, the IGC was to fix a timetable for the integration of the WEU into the EU to ensure the irreversibility of a common defence policy. Detailed proposals were additionally made on the establishment of the fully operational capability of the WEU, the organizational link between the EU and the WEU, the transatlantic alliance, and the harmonization of Member States' policies on arms exports.

The second paper of the Executive Committee of the CDU/CSU Parliamentary Group (CDU/CSU, Parliamentary Group (1995a) proposed, besides the integration of some policies of the third pillar into the Community framework, to closely align criminal law and procedures among Member States and to develop a constitutional Community.

Also during the summer of 1995, the opposition in Germany came forward with several proposals to the Committee on the Affairs of the European Union of the German Bundestag.[3] This Committee, representing members from different parties, was set up during the Maastricht negotiations under the name EC Committee with the idea of reducing the democratic deficit in Germany, i.e. European integration decisions were not to be solely left to the government. The federal Government's chief negotiator Werner Hoyer, Minister of State, from the Federal Office reported to the Committee on progress, first in the Reflection Group and later on in the process of the IGC negotiations. The intensive involvement of the EU Committee facilitated that the Amsterdam Treaty received the wide parliamentary support in the subsequent process of ratification in the German *Bundestag*.

In December 1995, the EU Committee endorsed the German governments negotiation guidelines certain initiatives of the opposition were rejected in the Committee and later in the Bundestag.[4] The Social Democratic Party (SPD) requested the government to ensure the inclusion of a basic catalogue of

---

[3] Deutscher Bundestag, *WiB Heft* 12/28 June 1995.

[4] Deutscher Bundestag, *WiB Heft* 23/13 December 1995.

fundamental rights in the Treaty and equality between men and women as a fundamental right. They also supported a common electoral system in the EU, the integration of the Social Protocol and the Social Charter in the Treaty and the objective of the protection of the environment should be guaranteed. Further cooperation in Justice and Home Affairs, as well as the fight against xenophobia and racism was to be tackled. The rights of the European Parliament should be strengthened and majority voting should become the rule. *Bündnis 90*/the Greens emphasized that the key problem of the EU was to overcome the democratic deficit and that only a democratic, ecological, social and civilian Europe would be able to gain credibility. The development towards a Political Union should not end in a new European "superstate," on the contrary, stronger democratic control of the EU would need to be ensured. Any concept of a "Core Europe" should be rejected and similarly to the SPD, support should be given to the insertion of a catalogue of fundamental rights (including the European Convention on Human Rights) in the Treaty and an anti-discrimination clause. *Bündnis 90*/the Greens demanded that the realization of the Internal Market should be explicitly linked to the objective of an ecological union. The Party of Democratic Socialism (PDS) supporting the integration of human rights, emphasized in addition that the right of asylum should be guaranteed in all Member States of the Union. They also called for a fundamental democratic reform process, transparency and openness as well as for an enhanced role of the European Parliament in the legislative process and by granting it the right of initiative.

In their joint letter of 6 December 1995 addressed to Felipe Gonzalez (Madrid Summit) President Chirac and Chancellor Kohl identified the five challenges that the EU and the Member States faced in the medium-term as follows: the revision of the TEU, the realization of EMU, preparation of negotiations for accession, the definition of the financing arrangements beyond 1999 and an active political dialogue with Russia, Ukraine, Turkey and the Mediterranean countries. Their agreement on the IGC was that it should be short and concentrate on four priority areas: CFSP (to be visible, efficient, coherent and the relationship between WEU and EU to be detailed); common approach for asylum and immigration and stronger cooperation to fight terrorism; extension of majority voting in the Council (revision of voting system); to tackle the democratic deficit and closeness to citizens and the desirability of including a flexibility clause. This joint letter gave a broad orientation but was rather vague on the details and hid the different perceptions of France and Germany in specific issues. It actually ignored the main issue of the IGC – a common vision on institutional reforms. During the seminar of the German and French Foreign Ministers, in Freiburg on 27 February 1996, "guidelines" were adopted for the CFSP, which called for more efficiency, coherence, continuity, solidarity and visibility of the CFSP.

Only in March 1996, were the German government's objectives for the IGC mapped out.[5] According to the German government, the conference should not be overloaded, but should concentrate on essential issues. The right balance would be required between progress in the European integration process and unrealistically high expectations. In this context, the IGC was mentioned as a step towards further integration but not as a finality of the integration process. According to the document, the basis for the German position was, the coalition agreement and the Kohl/Chirac letter of 6 December 1995. Five objectives were identified:

- *Common Foreign and Security Policy*: based on the joint German/French guidelines, the specific proposals were: creation of an analysis and planning unit; appointment of a Secretary-General of the Council of Ministers; extension of qualified majority voting but the application of unanimity in certain areas, i.e. for operational capabilities; the European Council should lay down guidelines for the WE, which would be integrated into the EU in the medium-term; inclusion of a "political solidarity clause" in the Treaty; incorporation of the "Peterburg tasks" in the TEN and the development of a common armaments policy.
- *Justice and Home Affairs*: in order to fight international crime and drug trafficking at EU level it was proposed that police cooperation be strengthened, the long-term objective being the creation of a European police office with operative competences; harmonization of criminal and judicial civil norms; communitarisation of visa policy, right of asylum, customs cooperation and immigration policy; extension of tasks to include the fight against xenophobia, racism and fraud at the expense of the EU budget; enforcement of the role of the Commission, European Court of Justice and the European Parliament.
- *Subsidiarity, closeness to citizens, democracy and transparency*: concretizing the subsidiarity principle in a protocol to the Treaty; transparency in decision-making; more access to documents and openness; strengthening of the European Parliament in the legislative process; strengthening of the rights of the individual citizen through protection of fundamental rights at EU level and enhancement of the union citizenship in the Treaty.
- *Institutional reforms*: more qualified majority voting (QMV) in the Council; introduction of a double majority, representing a sufficient majority of population; a guarantee of the participation of a large Member State in the Presidency's Troika; limitation of the number of Commissioners and limitation of the number of MEPs to 700.

---

[5] Deutsche Ziele für die Regierungskonferenz, Das auswärtige Amt informiert, Bonn, 26. March 1996.

- *Flexibility*: flexibility should be introduced along the Kohl/Chirac proposal with "no veto" and "no hard-core."

In a speech on his position with regard to European policy in March 1995, Jacques Chirac stated that "the Franco-German relationship is without equivalent as it is the foundation for peace and prosperity on our continent; our two countries play an irreplaceable driving role in European construction.... I would, however, like to stress that I shall give priority to tackling with Chancellor Kohl, the need for a common Franco-German approach on the 1996 Intergovernmental Conference" (*Agence Europe* 23 March 1995). Yet it took quite some time until some joint French-German guidelines or positions were put forward. During the period leading to the opening of the IGC in March 1996, France and Germany developed some guidelines on foreign and security policy, made proposals on flexibility, underlined the importance of extending qualified majority voting (QMV), and stressed a common approach on asylum and immigration. The lack of joint French-German proposals on institutional reform, the vagueness of some proposals, hiding the different perceptions, and the long-drawn-out common positions, can be explained by several factors. First, strained French-German relations resulting from the Schäuble/Lamers paper from 1994 and the French government's decision in the mid-1990s to test nuclear weapons in the South Pacific. Second, there were different perceptions, interests and preferences. Janning notes, "With symbolic politics largely exhausted, a lack of strategic consensus between Paris and Bonn may become a problem... there is hardly an area on which the concepts, interests, perceptions and actions are as convergent as seems necessary for ideal partnership" (Janning 1996, 41). For example, for Germany enlargement to the East was the top priority, whereas France was concerned about the EU's balance of power tilting to the North and East. Moreover, the asymmetry of the Franco-German economic relationship (Szukala and Wessels 1997), was exemplified with Germany's preoccupation with EMU and stability, whereas France was haunted by having to cope with unemployment. In September 1995, German Finance Minister Theo Waigel made proposals on a Stability Pact and repeatedly stressed that there was no room for interpreting the deficit criteria. The German President of the *Bundesbank* noted France's shortcomings in terms of budgetary discipline and price stability criteria. Third, uncertainties in French-German relations have also been explained by the exchange of professional personnel in French politics and administration. According to Vernet, the new professionals surrounding President Chirac were newcomers to French-German relations (Vernet 1998). According to Vernet, an example of this was the unilateral French decision to restructure its army which provoked French-German tensions during the IGC in 1996.

Preparing for the IGC – The Position of the *Länder*

By the end of the 1980s, the *Länder* called for constitutional changes which would assert that their participation in internal decision-making on EC affairs is laid down in the German Basic Law and that the transfer of sovereign powers to the EC is subject to the approval of the Bundesrat. This needs to be seen in the context of the reduction of powers as perceived by the *Länder* first, through the increasing transfer of *Länder* competences to the EC level and, second, by the dilution of their constitutional right to participate in policy-making at the federal level. A major new article, Article 23, on the realization of the European Union, was inserted in the German Constitution arising from the ratification of the Maastricht Treaty and the demands of the *Länder*. According to this article, the transfer of sovereign powers requires the consent of the *Bundesrat*, if provisions of the German Basic Law are affected, a two-third's majority of the *Bundestag* and the *Bundesrat* are required. The participation of the *Bundesrat* and the rights of the *Länder* in matters related to the European Union has been laid down in a specific law.[6] In case issues falling under the sole responsibility of the *Länder* are discussed in the Council of Ministers, Article 23(6) allows a *Länder* representative with ministerial rank to replace a Government Minister. The powers of the *Länder* have also been strengthened through other constitutional changes, among the more significant ones are Article 50 and 52 of the Basic Law relating to the participation of the *Bundesrat* in matters concerning the European Union and the establishment of a European Chamber whose decisions count as the decisions of the *Bundesrat*. The European Chamber, which is composed of the European ministers of the *Länder*, has been very active in the preparation of the IGC 1996. These constitutional changes have definitely strengthened the role of the Länder and had significant implications for the IGC negotiations.

In case of the IGC 1996, Bavaria and Rhineland-Palatinate were nominated as the representatives for the *Bundesrat*. They could participate at all levels of the negotiations as observers. This system would ensure a permanent feedback from the *Länder* during the negotiation phase (Piepenschneider, 1997). Due to the majority of the SPD governed *Länder* in the *Bundesrat*, the representative from Rhineland-Palatinate was the senior negotiating partner. At an early stage already in March 1995, the *Bundesrat* put its position concerning the *Länder*'s demands for the IGC on paper (*Bundesrat*, 1995). During the same month, Bavaria, too, delivered its own position paper on Bavarian objectives for the IGC 1996. In its decision of March 1995, the *Bundesrat* explicitly stated that the European Parliament should play the role

---

[6] Gesetz über die Zusammenarbeit von Bund und Ländern in Angelegenheiten der Europäischen Union vom 12. März 1993, *Bundesgesetzblatt*, No. 9, 19 March 1993.

of co-legislator in all cases where the Council decides with a majority, and that it was in favour of extending qualified majority voting. The *Bundesrat* also suggested that major areas of the second and third pillar should be integrated into the Community framework and that it would like to have the question of a catalogue of fundamental rights examined.

The decision from the *Bundesrat* was further elaborated and concretized in a later decision entitled "Demands of the Länder for the IGC 1996" from 15 December 1995 (*Bundesrat* 1995a).[7] It is argued that a clear deepening of the European integration process through institutional reforms and through a clear division of competences is required in order to achieve closeness to citizens, enable the European Union to act and to improve democratic legitimacy. Moreover, the implementation of the subsidiarity principle was to be improved and regional participation to be strengthened. The *Länder* also requested that the European Union should receive additional competences in the field of Justice and Home Affairs and should be able to play a more active role in foreign and security policy. These reforms were indispensable in order to start early accession negotiations with the Central and East European countries. It was pointed out by the *Länder* that in the light of the launching of EMU, a "balanced Political Union" should be achieved, defined as encompassing Foreign and Security Affairs, Justice and Home Affairs as well as environmental and social questions. This "balanced Political Union" would form a counterweight to economic and monetary affairs. However, the *Länder* stated that the Treaty articles on EMU were not to be reopened and that they would resist any softening of the convergence criteria.

The detailed demands of the Länder and the proposed formulation of specific Treaty articles were put forward under four main headings: first, subsidiarity and improved division of competences, second, strengthening of the closeness to citizens, third, improvement of regional participation and, fourth, a strengthening of the capacity to act and democracy.

The *Länder* demanded in particular:

- *Concerning subsidiarity and improved division of competences:* a precise formulation of the subsidiarity principle and a clear division of powers between the EU, the Member States and the regions with a listing of exclusive competences of the EU. A precise formulation of competences in specific areas falling under the competence of the *Länder* in Germany, such as vocational training, research and development, etc. A division of

---

[7] This decision was prepared by the Europaministerkonferenz in Berlin of 14 and 15 September 1995, with the objective to achieve consensus among the Länder in order to successfully implement their interests. Decision: "Demands of the Europe Ministers and Senators for the IGC'96," 11. Europaministerkonferenz in Berlin, 14 to 15 September 1995.

competences according to the subsidiarity principle: exclusive competences for the Member States and the regions in the area of energy, tourism, town and country planning; limitation of competences in trade policy – elimination of Article 115, which had become obsolete; additional competences for the European Union in Justice and Home Affairs: communitarization of asylum and visa policy and essential parts of immigration policy, however, aliens law should remain a competence of the Member States; a strengthening of Europol, Schengen and parts of cooperation in Justice to be communitarized. In addition, the social protocol should be incorporated in the Treaty.

- *As regards closeness to citizens, specific proposals were made with a view to:* improve fundamental rights towards the development of a catalogue of basic rights in the long-term; better participation of consumer and environmental organizations; achieve an environmentally friendly and socially acceptable transport policy; establish environmental principles and the principle of sustainable development; include local self-determination in the Treaty; respect of the constitutional status of religious communities; improve integration of municipalities and regions.
- *improvement of regional participation*: several detailed proposals were made concerning the strengthening of the Committee of the Regions, in particular, right of complaint for the Committee and for the regions, extension of consultation, etc.
- *strengthening of the capacity to act and democracy*: reducing the decision-making procedures to three: the assent procedure, a simplified co-decision procedure and consultation; extension of the codecision procedure to those areas where qualified majority applies; right of complaint for national parliaments before the European Court of Justice; common European election procedure for the European Parliament; qualified majority voting to become the rule in the Council of Ministers and introduction of a double majority in which account would be taken of both the states and their population. The unanimity principle should only be applied in a few sensitive areas. The number of Commissioners should be limited, the role of the Commission in the second and third pillar should be enlarged, by extending the right of own initiative. Moreover the role of the Commission President should be strengthened and the Commissioners should be approved by the European Parliament. According to the *Länder*, considerable improvement was also required in the procedure and structures of intergovernmental cooperation in the third pillar. Specific proposals were made concerning the setting-up of an independent European Restrictive Practices Office and the application of German as a working language in the institutions.

As will be seen below, most of the *Länder's* demands were included in the official proposals by the German government.

Positions and Proposals during the IGC

During the IGC negotiations, the Federal Experts Committee on Foreign and Security Policy of the CDU launched in September 1996 some additional ideas on the further development of the CFSP.[8] The CDU urged a more significant role for the European Commission, proposed an EU foreign policy troika and sought ways of binding the EU's neutral members into a common defence structure. It rejected the French idea of appointing a single high representative and called instead for a new troika, comprising the chairman of the General Affairs Council, a Council Secretary General responsible for foreign affairs and the EU foreign affairs Commissioner. A step by step integration of the WEU, and a protocol to the EU Treaty on Article V of the WEU, would enable neutral EU States to participate in humanitarian, peace keeping and peace enforcing action while preserving their neutrality (*Financial Times* 17 September 1996). In the course of the IGC, Germany, France, Italy, Spain and Belgium prepared a joint proposal on the relations between the EU and the Western European Union (WEU).[9]

While referring to the Kohl/Chirac letter of 6 December 1995, the Foreign Ministers of France and Germany forwarded a discussion paper on "Enhanced cooperation with a view to a further deepening of European integration" on 22 October 1996.[10] It stated that "A general clause should be inserted in the Treaty, offering those States that are willing and able the possibility of developing closer cooperation, while maintaining the Union's single institutional framework." The paper advocated common principles for closer cooperation in all three pillars and for a differentiated approach in each pillar

---

[8] The decision of the CDU is entitled "Further development of the CFSP of the European Union in the IGC 1996."

[9] *Agence Europe* 14 March, 1997. Some of the common issues to be included were the gradual integration of the WE into the EU; insertion of deadlines for the different phases; first phase would consist of better cooperation between EU and WE; second phase would comprise the merger of institutions (with a single Parliament, Council, Secretariat); final phase to offer assistance and common defence in case that a Member States would be attacked. The proposal further included "flexibility."

[10] Joint France and German Proposal by Foreign Minister Klaus Kinkel and Foreign Minister Hervé de Charette to the Intergovernmental Conference on the Revision of the Maastricht Treaty on "Enhanced Cooperation" *Agence Europe, Europe Documents,* No. 2009, 29 October 1996.

(specific provisions). It proposed the insertion of a general clause in Title I under the common provisions (to be added as CI). No Member State should be able to veto closer cooperation between groups of EU countries and closer cooperation would apply in areas requiring unanimity. In the EC Treaty closer cooperation should not apply to the internal market, regulations on related matters or existing common policies. It was proposed to draw up a list with possible areas where closer cooperation could apply. The closer cooperation clause specific to the CFSP, should specifically apply to defence matters. The clause specific to Justice and Home Affairs could apply to all areas of Title VI of the TEU, while some areas were to be transferred to the first pillar. McDonagh mentions that it took Germany and France a rather long time to flesh out their ideas on the issue of flexibility, which first came up in the joint Kohl/Chirac letter (McDonagh 1998).

Official Proposals for the IGC

As will be seen below, the official proposals submitted by the German government have been strongly influenced by the specific interests of the German *Länder*. Germany put forward 28 proposals in the course of 1996/97. Most of the proposals derive from the specific Länder demands and others reflect some narrow interests from certain organizations (churches, the German sport association, etc). In terms of overall policy, the more significant proposals concern those on the principle of subsidiarity, several proposals on security and defence matters, including the joint proposal with Belgium, France, Italy, Luxembourg and Spain, the joint Franco-German proposal on closer cooperation as well as the environmental and police cooperation proposal.

The official German proposals included the following:

- *European Restrictive Practices Office* (CONF 3855/96, 22 May 1996). To establish a European competition office modeled along the lines of the German Cartels Office which would guarantee effective enforcement of the competition rules. This would, however, imply that the enforcement of competition rules would be moved away from the Commission. Germany also proposed the possibility of appealing to the European Court of Justice and the Court of First Instance with regard to decisions of the European Restrictive Practices Office.
- *Application of the principle of subsidiarity* (CONF 3897/96, 30 August 1996). Germany submitted a draft Subsidiarity Protocol to the TEU with the purpose of defining the criteria as regards the second paragraph of

Article 3b of the TEC and of safeguarding the consistent application of this principle by all EU institutions. However, the German draft text was not met with approval by the other Member States. The Presidency came up with an alternative proposal which would not change the wording of Article 3b (definition) and which would follow the Edinburgh conclusions concerning implementation (CONF 3944/96, 8 October 1996). The comments (CONF 3953/96 15 October 1996) by the German delegation on the Presidency's proposal relate mainly to the German request to include a definite description of the Community's exclusive competence, a concretization of the efficiency criteria, an obligation to justify Community financing, a time limit for application of Community law in specific cases and Member State competence for the administration of Community law. *Subsidiarity Protocol* (CONF 3851/97, 20 March 1997), this draft proposal provided comments on the draft of the Irish Presidency proposal. Further amendments were made to the Presidency's proposal for a protocol on subsidiarity (CONF 3909/97, 13 May 1997).

- *Communitarization of Customs Cooperation.* There were two proposals on this matter (CONF 3938/96, 2 October 1996), (CONF 3807/97, 29 January 1997). The German delegation recommended that cooperation of customs administrations to be moved from the third pillar to the first pillar in order to guarantee the application of customs rules, to achieve simplification and an increase of efficiency.
- *Closer Cooperation* (CONF 3955/96, 18 October 1996), this joint Franco-German proposal suggested inserting into Title I of the TEU a general clause on closer cooperation, dealing with the fundamental principles of its application, the institutional framework and accession. It also suggested including specific clauses as to the fields of application, right of initiative and financing concerning the EC Treaty, concerning the CFSP (in addition: practical implementation, decision-making) and concerning Justice and Home Affairs.
- Detailed proposals were submitted on *Environmental policy* (CONF 3966/96 25 October 1996) and on *External economic relations* (CONF 3912/97 13 May 1997). Germany included a list of exceptions to the protocol of Article 113(5) as a complement to the Dutch Presidency's text. This is a listing of numerous areas and cases in which Article 113(5) would not apply. Germany also suggested having a Declaration attached regarding the promotion of trade which clarified that the promotion of and financing of foreign trade do not fall under the Community's exclusive competence for trade policy.
- *Security and Defence* (CONF 3972/96 30 October 1996) proposals dealt with a new formulation of Article J.4 paragraph 1 to 3 of the TEU and the decision-making procedure for the launch of military operation. The joint

proposal from Belgium, France, Italy, Luxembourg, Spain and Germany *Security and Defence Aspects* (CONF 3855/97 24 March 1997) proposed changes to Article J.4 of the TEU. Concerning Article J.4.1, a common security and defence policy was to include the Petersberg tasks and an armaments policy. The latter was not included in the Presidency proposal. Concerning Article J.4.2 it was proposed to integrate the Western European Union (WEU) progressively into the EU. The details were to be defined in a Protocol annexed to the Treaty. The decision-making procedure J.4(4) would be that of the overall CFSP. This joint proposal went much further than the one proposed by the Dutch Presidency. It was also proposed to include a *Solidarity clause in the CFSP* (CONF 3971/96 30 October 1996).

- *Justice and Home Affairs – Police cooperation* (CONF 3910/97 13 May 1997). This proposal examined the Presidency proposal concerning the new Articles K.1 and K.2 of the TEU, particularly concerning the strengthening of Europol.

- Some specific proposals were made on *Statistics* (CONF 3939/96 2 October 1996), on *Religious communities – fundamental rights* (CONF 3952/96 15 October 1996), to amend Article F of the TEU concerning the respect of the constitutional status of religious communities in the Member States. As Duff put it, " the Declaration on the status of the church was generated by the German government which had come under pressure from its conservative church elements ... to maintain the enhanced status of Christianity in particular against the American importation of the Church of Scientology"(Duff 1997,10). On *Local self-government* (CONF 3967/96 30 October 1996) proposals were made for additions to Article F(1)TEU concerning the self-government of local authorities. Concerning *Animal protection* (CONF 3983/96 14 November 1996) it was suggested to revise Article 3 with a view to improve animal protection. As regards *Town and country planning policy* (CONF 3911/97 13 May 1997) the proposal for an additional protocol was made which would lay down specifically the competence of the Member States in this area. *System of property ownership – public credit institutions* (CONF 3926/97 29 May 1997) This was a proposal for a protocol on Article 222 TEC, which would provide protection for public credit institutions. As Devuyst put it, the Declaration on public credit institutions in Germany was explicitly intended to limit the Commission's margin of interpretation in the area of state aid (Devuyst 1998). The joint British-German proposal on *Direct taxation* (CONF 3922/97 27 May 1997) demanded a protocol relating to direct taxation clarifying the principle of prohibition of discrimination on grounds of nationality and tax matters. Inspired by the German Sport Association, *Sport* (CONF 3927/97, 29 May 1997) was put on the agenda, whereby

Germany suggested the inclusion of a declaration on sport and its social significance.
- Institutional proposals forwarded by the German delegation concerned the *European Parliament* (CONF 3960/96 22 October 1996), pushing for a uniform electoral procedure, the *Court of First Instance* (CONF 3962/96 22 October 1996) with amendments to Article 168a (1) and (2) of the TEC. It was proposed to extend the competence of the CFI to give preliminary rulings. Proposals were made concerning the *European Court of Auditors* (CONF 3844/97 10 March 1997) and the *Committee of the Regions* (CONF 3984/96 14 November 1996) by extending the consultation of the Committee of the Regions in the decision-making process and for specific policies, i.e. environment and vocational training. The proposal on the *Statute of officials and other servants of the European Communities* (CONF 3906/97 12 May 1997) suggested changes to the procedure for staff regulations of officials of the European Communities and the conditions of employment of other servants.

During the IGC, the *Bundesrat* developed further its position. Based on the initiative from the Saarland, (governed by the Social Democrats), employment reforms were to be put on the agenda of the IGC. In this decision of the *Bundesrat* of 8 November 1996 (*Bundesrat* 1996) the German government is pressured to give up its resistance to the proposed Treaty changes on employment. The *Bundesrat* demanded the insertion of a new title on employment, development of basic guidelines by the Council on employment and a better coordination of employment policy. The competence for employment policy should remain with the Member States, but the coordination function of the EU should be strengthened. At the Europe Minister's Conference on 27 February 1997, the *Länder* supported in general the proposals on employment policy by the Irish Presidency, but strongly rejected the Irish proposal about including EU employment programmes with financial implications. The *Länder* also deplored the lack of progress on essential institutional matters in the Irish draft and that some specific *Länder* interests were not covered sufficiently.[11]

---

[11] 15. Europaministerkonferenz in Bonn (Brandenburg), 27 February 1997. In order to avoid unnecessary administrative costs for economic operators, particularly small and medium-sized businesses, the Länder proposed that EU statistics should be limited.

Towards Amsterdam

There were early indications that a major breakthrough might not be achieved in Amsterdam. In a speech to the Irish Parliament in October 1996, Chancellor Kohl spoke about important decisions such as EMU, the enlargement of the EU and the IGC which would influence the 21st century. The Chancellor indicated, however, that the results of the IGC might be insufficient, and in that case a Maastricht III would be required (*Handelsblatt* 4 October 1996). In the spring of 1997, he also confirmed his candidacy as chancellor for the new general elections, introducing the Euro and NATO enlargement. German chief negotiator, Werner Hoyer, noted in the spring of 1997 that Germany faced a tremendous credibility problem with respect to QMV and raised the question of whether Germany contributed to the deepening of the European integration process or was more and more pulling back whenever sensitive issues arose.[12] He also deplored the lack of political will to solve other sensitive institutional questions. Under the Dutch Presidency, the link was made concerning the reweighting of Council votes and the composition of the Commission, according to which Germany would have 25 votes in the Council and would give up one Commissioner. Yet "President Chirac refused an entirely new dual majority system, ... whereby a proposal would need a (two-thirds) majority of member states representing at least a (two-thirds majority) of the EU's population. Such a new voting system would give Germany a greater weight in Council voting than France, thus eliminating a symbol of formal equality between France and Germany" (Devuyst 1998, 628).

In the spring 1997, the domestic economic situation was difficult. By then, the EMU debate had reached its peak in Germany, and record unemployment levels threatened Germany's participation in the Euro. Finance Minister Waigel insisted on a strict interpretation of the convergence criteria, a "landing on the dot" of 3 percent of the budget deficit criteria. Due to the decisions of the *Bundestag* and *Bundesrat* on the TEN and the Constitutional Court's verdict from October 1993, Edmund Stoiber from the CSU (part of the coalition government), Prime Minister of Bavaria, demanded a strict interpretation of the criteria, alternatively, a "controlled delay" would be necessary. The Social Democrats announced that they would reject the government's tax reform bill in the *Bundesrat* (SPD-controlled).

On 1 June 1997, Alain Juppé's right-wing government was defeated by Lionel Jospin's left-wing coalition. This caused a shift in French economic

---

[12] "Europas Zukunft – Stand und Perspektiven der Regierungskonferenz zur Reform des Vertrages von Maastricht," Rede im Historischen Rathaus zu Köln am Europatag, 5 May 1997.

priorities, as Jospin had won the elections on the basis of the fight against unemployment. According to German officials, a suspicion arose in Germany, that the Socialist-led coalition had abandoned all intentions of meeting the deficit target of 3 per cent in 1997 (*Financial Times* 26 June 1997). At Amsterdam, almost the entire first day was devoted to the Stability Pact (Devuyst, 1998) and French-German tensions were smoothed by the Resolution on "the Stability and Growth Pact." As Andrew Duff notes, "... the shock election of a socialist-communist government in France on 1 June scuppered the usual Franco-German joint formulation of positions before meetings of the European Council" (Duff 1997 p.155).

Yet as Duff further remarks, "The biggest surprise at Amsterdam was that Helmut Kohl pulled back from traditional German positions on QMV. Led by Bavaria, the *Länder* governments, which compose the SPD-led *Bundesrat*, were anxious to protect their prerogatives over areas of domestic legislation, particularly concerning the environment and immigration," and "... the Germans insisted against the wishes of the presidency and the Commission on retaining a veto on the introduction of QMV in the field of immigration and asylum in five years time" (Duff 1997, 155-156).

Reactions on the Results of the Amsterdam Summit

On 27 June 1997, chancellor Kohl mentioned in the Bundestag,[13] the successful conclusion of the Amsterdam Summit, the prospects for enlargement and the strong signal emerging from Amsterdam that the "Euro is on its way." Kohl emphasized the significance of the Stability and Growth Pact and the conviction that the third phase of EMU will start on time, with the strict application of convergence criteria. Turning to the employment chapter and the resolution on Growth and Employment, he stressed that this would neither imply new EU competences nor additional financial transfers to the EU. He also noted that some specific German objectives were achieved, such as the protocols on the subsidiarity principle and on the system of broadcasting and the declaration on public credit institutions in Germany. Considerable progress could be achieved in the field of Justice and Home Affairs. However, as he pointed out, Germany had to safeguard its national interest by insisting on unanimity for immigration and asylum, as Germany alone had to cope with more asylum seekers than all of the other Member States put together. He also reiterated that Germany was able to block

---

[13] Regierungserklärung von Bundeskanzler Dr. Helmut Kohl vor dem Deutschen Bundestag zu den Ergebnissen des Europäischen Rates von Amsterdam (Auszüge), (Jopp, Maurer & Schmuck 1998, Dokument 2.1.).

uncontrolled access by third country nationals to the German social system and labour market. According to him, positions in these fields were greatly coordinated with the Länder. He was more critical of the results achieved in the foreign and security policy, which were not entirely in line with German objectives. As to institutional reforms, he indicated that some progress was achieved by limiting the number of Commissioners to 20, under the condition that a linkage is made with the weighting of votes in the Council to guarantee a representative balance. According to him, the extension of QMV was, as expected, difficult, due to concrete differences in national interest. He pointed out that Germany had to defend its own national interest for example in industrial policy, handicrafts ordinance and for free movement of migrant workers.

The Christian Democrats supported the Amsterdam results and stressed that the subsidiarity principle should be applied vigorously in practice, meaning that a renationalization could not be excluded in case that certain EU provisions did not correspond to the principle (Jopp, Maurer & Schmuck 1998, Dokument 2.2). In future, the development of a catalogue of competences would be required. Fair burden-sharing in asylum policy should be ensured and the exploitation of the German welfare system by third country nationals prevented.

Edmund Stoiber from the CSU and Minister President from Bavaria stated that the Amsterdam Treaty upgraded the *Länder* as a "Counterweight to Communitarization" (Jopp, Maurer & Schmuck 1998, Dokument 2.3). He vehemently turned against the employment chapter and employment oriented stability policy, which he perceived as a great danger to the Euro. He deplored that Amsterdam could not achieve a division of competences. Stoiber was extremely critical of the new Article concerning the right of residence for third country nationals and emphasized that despite his pressure he could not achieve a stricter formulation, but that Chancellor Kohl at least had managed to achieve unanimity. He also reiterated that he was particularly grateful to Foreign Minister Kinkel and Chancellor Kohl who succeeded in having a Declaration attached, specifying that Member States have the right to determine the modalities and preconditions for immigration.

The Liberals in Germany stressed the great success of the German negotiation team in concluding the stability pact (Jopp, Maurer, Schmuck, 1998, Dokument 2.4). They were, however, disappointed by the limited achievements concerning institutional reforms.

For the opposition in Germany, particularly the Social Democrats, the inclusion of the employment chapter was the most positive outcome of Amsterdam (Jopp, Maurer & Schmuck 1998, Dokument 2.5).

The SPD welcomed the extension of co-decision, the subsidiarity protocol and the establishment of a planning and analysis unit for the CFSP, but criticized particularly the decision-making and instruments of the CFSP as "intergovernmentalist." Chancellor Kohl was blamed for the limited institutional results achieved. With regard to asylum and immigration, the SPD criticized the German government's insistence on unanimity. Because of the lack of democratic control by the European Parliament in case of unanimity decisions in the Council, the SPD requested that during the ratification process, the *Bundestag* and the *Bundesrat* should ensure that appropriate internal procedures were established, which would guarantee the *Bundestag*'s prior approval for unanimity decisions and for the new "framework decisions." Moreover, the SPD deplored the lack of a Charter of fundamental rights.

For the *Bündnis 90*/the Greens, Amsterdam led to an increase of the democratic deficit due to the lack of co-decision for the European Parliament in the field of Justice and Home Affairs and CFSP (Jopp, Maurer & Schmuck 1998, Dokument 2.6). The government was criticized for the discrepancy between its integration rhetoric and its blocking of QMV for structural funds, immigration and asylum and for trying to undermine the employment chapter. Concern was expressed about the future developments in the field of defence, but, fortunately, according to *Bündnis 90*/the Greens, the German proposals on the integration of the WEU into the EU had been watered down. The PDS heavily criticized the European policy of the government as "undemocratic" and "neoliberal" (Jopp, Maurer & Schmuck 1998, Dokument 2.7). The outcome of Amsterdam was further rejected on the grounds of "the militarization of the EU" and an increase of the democratic deficit.

Public Opinion and Debate

Opinion polls conducted in the autumn of 1997 on the question "If a referendum on the Treaty of Amsterdam was organised in Germany, do you think you would vote for or against it?," made clear that only 19% in Germany would vote in favour, 12% against, whereas 69% indicated that they did not know what they would vote. These percentages hardly differ from the answers given in other EU Member States (European Commission, 1998). Asked about specific policy areas in the spring of 1997, 52% in Germany supported Europe-wide action to combat unemployment, 74% were for EU action to combat drugs trafficking, 53% were in favour of an immigration policy, and 55% for EU-wide rules for political asylum (European Commission, 1998). Considerable support was indicated for democratic processes[14] with 75% in

---

[14] On the question whether the President and members of the European Commission should have the support of a majority in the European Parliament and whether the

favour of the Commission being supported by the European Parliament and 52% for equal legislative powers for the Parliament in taxation and expenditure. Strong support was also indicated for cooperation with developing countries (76%), a common foreign policy was supported by 71% and a common defence policy by 60%. This is in strong contrast to the answers given on the question concerning a single European currency, where confidence in Germany had dropped considerable in the spring of 1997, with 32% of the German respondents in favour and 54% against. Opposition to a single currency (60% of the Germans were against) was at its highest in Germany in the summer of 1993, the time of the series of Constitutional Court cases against the Maastricht Treaty pending at the Constitutional Court. During the mid-1990s, opposition to EMU weakened in Germany, however, in the spring of 1997 compared to autumn 1996 a marked drop in confidence occurred (-19 points in net scores). Overall in Europe an increasingly negative sentiment could be observed towards the Euro during this period. In Germany it was very pronounced. Despite drastic cuts in social spending during 1996, indicators pointed in the direction that Germany might not be able to meet the budget deficit criteria of 3%. Unemployment reached a peak of 4.5 million in the beginning of 1997 and proposals in March by the German Finance Minster Theo Waigel for further cuts in social welfare in order to meet the budget deficit criteria, were strongly opposed by the Social Democrats and the trade unions. The full focus of the German media, industry and politicians was on the Euro. On the one hand, there was the position of Theo Waigel that a strict interpretation of the deficit criteria was required, on the other hand, Foreign Minister Kinkel indicated "scope for interpretation" and Gerhard Schröder from the Social Democrats, Prime Minister of Lower Saxony, was in favour of postponement. Others argued that both a punctual start of EMU by 1 January 1999 and a strict fulfillment of the criteria could not be achieved simultaneously.

Support for European integration was at its lowest in Germany in 1996/1997. In the spring of 1997 only 36% considered EU membership a "good thing," whereas in the period 1994/1995 between 50 and 60% where in favour of membership. This skeptical attitude was also reflected in the answers on the benefits from European Union membership (European Commission 1998). It should, however, be noted that from the end of 1997 and onwards German support for European integration increased. Similarly, a downtrend in support for EU membership could be observed in other EU countries, however, the one in Germany was most striking. Economic recession, unemployment and the BSE crises were some of the explanations

---

European Parliament should have equal rights with the Council of Ministers in taxation and expenditure.

provided by Eurobarometer. I would argue, however, that in the case of Germany, the Euro debate had a decisively negative influence on public opinion. The Amsterdam Treaty itself has not been discussed in the media, attention in the course of 1997 and 1998 shifted towards Germany's contribution to the EU budget, Agenda 2000 and the quest for "burden-sharing."

Ratification of the Amsterdam Treaty

Ratification requirements are laid down in Article 23 (1) in combination with the provisions of paragraph (2) of Article 79 of the German Basic Law. This implies that the Act concerning the Treaty of Amsterdam required the approval of two thirds of the members of the *Bundestag* and two thirds of the votes from the *Bundesrat*.

The *Bundestag* ratified the Treaty on 5 March 1998 on the recommendation of the European Union Committee with 561 members of Parliament in favour, 34 members against and 50 abstentions. CDU/CSU, the FDP and SPD had previously announced their support, the PDS voted against and the *Bündnis 90*/the Greens abstained. It was argued that abstention was necessary due to the wrong political objectives of the Treaty and due to the German government's blockade policy in the course of the negotiations. However, *Bündnis* 90/the Greens pointed out that they did not question at all the binding of Germany in the European integration process.[15] The chairperson of the European Union Committee, Norbert Wieczorek (SPD), and his deputy from the CDU/CSU pointed out that the *Bundestag* was involved in the consultation process right from the beginning in contrast to the negotiations of the Maastricht Treaty. As stated earlier, the participation and role of the *Bundestag* and the *Bundesrat* in matters related to the European Union is guaranteed by the German constitution. Article 45 of the Basic Law provides for the setting-up of a European Union Committee by the German Bundestag.

The recommendation of the European Union Committee[16] based on a common text of the CDU/CSU, SPD and FDP fractions to the *Bundestag* was to accept the draft law by the German government. It was, however, pointed out that unfortunately, no agreement had been reached on the charter of fundamental rights. Progress would also be needed with regard to the free movement of persons, external border control, asylum, immigration and the fight against crime. The inclusion of the employment chapter was considered

---

[15] Deutscher Bundestag, *WIB Heft* 4,10 March 1998.

[16] Deutscher Bundestag, *WIB* 17 February 1998.

to be decisive for the approval of the Social Democratic Party. The Liberals deplored the limited reforms but found that the Treaty pointed into the right direction.

The four proposals[17] by the *Bündnis 90*/the Greens, and the proposal by the PDS to renegotiate the Treaty, did not find a majority in the Bundestag. The proposals from the *Bündnis 90*/the Greens related mainly to the lack of democratic reforms, the increase of democratic deficit and criticized the government for emphasizing the wrong issues during the negotiations. The PDS rejected the Treaty and demanded a renegotiation of the Treaty[18] and a referendum on the European Union.

The *Bundesrat* approved the Act on the Treaty of Amsterdam on 27 March 1998 with all votes from the German *Länder*. The *Bundesrat* welcomed the Treaty of Amsterdam and expressed that the result of the negotiations reflected major interests of the German *Länder*, mainly the strengthening of the subsidiarity principle and of the Committee of the Regions.[19] The *Bundesrat* made a listing of positive and negative results for the *Länder*.[20] On the positive side was notably the subsidiarity protocol and particularly the insertion of two clauses, the "necessity clause" for the Community to act and the "improvement clause." The Declaration on the subsidiarity clause, that the responsibility of implementation of Community law lies with the responsibilities of Member States according to their constitutional set-up and the common Declaration by Germany, Austria, Belgium regarding the application of the subsidiarity principle for the sub-national level, were also perceived as a major success. Positively evaluated was the strengthening of the Committee of the Regions, however, the *Länder* regretted that its right of complaint to the European Court of Justice could not be achieved. The Protocol on broadcasting, concerning financial support by Member States to public broadcasting was welcomed, as was the Declaration on public credit institutions concerning the role of cooperative banks and their contribution to society.

According to the *Bundesrat*, the *Länder* could not achieve the right of local self-determination in the Treaty and a division of competences. The new legislative act "framework decision" for the approximation of national laws in the third pillar would require internal German adjustments.

---

[17] Deutscher Bundestag, *DIP*, 13/7823, 13/7824, 13/7825, 13/7822.

[18] Deutscher Bundestag, *DIP*, 13/9379.

[19] Pressemitteilungen, Bundesrat 58/1998 of 27 March 1998.

[20] Deutscher Bundestag, *DIP*, 13/9339.

With regard to the policy issues and main results of the Amsterdam Treaty, the *Bundesrat* in its opinion, was positive towards a strengthening of social policy and the coordination of employment policy. The *Bundesrat* underlined that regarding employment policy, the primary competences would remain at the national level and that the employment chapter did imply some additional financial commitments. The Stability and Growth Pact was appreciated, so was the inclusion of the social protocol, the extension of co-decision to the social chapter and the fight against social exclusion. Along the same line was the evaluation of the environmental policy, namely the integration of environmental policy in other policies, the concept of sustainable development and co-decision in the field of environment. The strengthening of fundamental rights with the new phrasing of Article 6 (previously F) was seen as a success. However, the lack of a catalogue of fundamental rights was considered a major failure. According to the *Bundesrat*, the issue will be put on the agenda of the next IGC and acts of the institutions should also be checked concerning fundamental rights. The limited reforms of the CFSP were also mentioned and that the government's objective of integrating the WEU into the EU could not be achieved. According to the *Bundesrat*, considerable progress was made in Justice and Home Affairs, particularly with visa, asylum, immigration, protection of external borders, cooperation in civil law and customs cooperation being communitarized. The German wish for unanimity in immigration policy had been secured. The strengthening of Europol and the integration of the Schengen *acquis* were seen as a success, however, regarding the former it was stated that the exclusive executive power remains within the powers of the *Länder*. The *Bundesrat* also welcomed the phrasing of the new Article 63 (4) on the right of residence for third country nationals where, according to Germany's wish, the formulation "including access to employment" had been taken out. Extension of co-decision and the strengthened role of the European Parliament were perceived as a major success. The *Bundesrat* in its decision paints an overall positive picture of the results of the Amsterdam Treaty for the German *Länder*: "small but positive steps." The German government was requested to contribute quickly to the solution of the open institutional questions. Under the condition that certain internal adjustments were made, the Bundesrat approved the law on the Amsterdam Treaty. Internal adjustments were required, as the Amsterdam Treaty introduced a new instrument, "the framework decision," for police and judicial cooperation in criminal matters, similar to a directive. The "framework decision" is binding on the Member States as to the result, but leaves to the national authorities the choice of form and methods (new Article 34 (2b). According to the *Bundesrat*, its participation in the legislative process was required as far as its powers were affected. "Framework decisions" could affect the powers of the *Bundesrat*. The law concerning the cooperation between the *Bund* and the *Länder* for European Union affairs of 12 March 1993 had to be changed, so that the powers of the *Länder* were not undermined.[21]

How to Explain the Amsterdam Outcome?

At the time of the Maastricht negotiations, Chancellor Kohl assisted the Dutch Presidency in finding solutions to open questions and acted as an arbiter between the different parties (van Wijnbergen, 1992). This time, Kohl did not play the role of a mediator, but was blamed for pushing for an institutional *status quo* and for a lack of political will. There are various explanations.

First, I would agree with Duff, that Kohl was "…preoccupied with the single currency project and unable to forge either a coherent or progressive German policy on institutional questions" (Duff 1997, p.155). As stated earlier, when explaining the results of Amsterdam in the *Bundestag*, he mentioned first that the Euro was on its way. The entire German public debate in the autumn of 1996 and spring of 1997 focused on the belief that the Euro and EMU could not fail. Moravcsik/Nicolaïdis further note (1999) "In *Germany,* nearly all commentators agree, Chancellor Helmut Kohl's decision in the final weeks of the negotiations to support only modest institutional reforms, rather than the more radical proposals Germany had earlier backed, stemmed from his last-minute concern about domestic political opposition, particularly given the concurrent movement forward on EMU. This was combined with his understanding – shared by all participants we questioned – that a similar agreement could be feasible at any time over the next eight to ten years." (Moravcsik/Nicolaïdis, 1999, p. 68).

A second explanation is the weakness of the French-German axis. Already prior to the start of the IGC there was a lack of common perceptions and concepts by the "French-German tandem" particularly on institutional reform. During the meetings of the Reflection Group in the summer of 1995, McDonagh remarks "there was no sense of an agenda being driven from any particular direction. At that stage, for example, I had no sense of a clear overall Franco-German approach which in the past has often acted as a "motor" for the development of the European Union" (McDonagh 1998, 37). During the IGC, French-German tensions were also provoked by the unilateral French decision to restructure its army. Except for the leading role played by Foreign Ministers de Charette and Kinkel in pushing closer cooperation, the

---

[21] As a result of the Amsterdam Treaty, and to clarify the powers between Bund and Länder, additional changes to the law were also required concerning Article 308, concerning research policy, etc. Bundesrat 784/97.

Franco-German couple failed to provide leadership (Devuyst 1998). At the Extraordinary Nordwijk European Council, Germany – with the agreement of France – took the initiative to push for institutional *status quo* instead of adaptation (*Agence Europe* 26-27 May 1997). The Franco-German axis, which in the past was the "motor" for the European integration process, ended in a "crisis" as expressed by Laurent Fabius, Socialist President of the Parliament in July 1997 at a Conference organized by the Friedrich Ebert Foundation (*Handelsblatt* 1 July 1997). The "crisis in French-German relations" was, according to Fabius due to different philosophies – the fight against unemployment versus criteria for EMU, and French-German relations were additionally hampered by the co-habitation between a Gaulist President and a Socialist Prime Minister.

Third, the federal system in Germany and the strengthened participation of the *Bundestag* and particularly of the *Bundesrat* in European Union affairs with the change of the German Basic Law and the verdict of the Constitutional Court in 1993. It became apparent that with the Amsterdam negotiations, the *Länder* have become a force to be reckoned with. At an early stage, the detailed position of the *Länder* was put on paper and most of the *Länder* demands were integrated into the government's position, with one major exception, the *Bundesrat*'s request that the German government should give up its resistance to the proposed *Länder* Treaty changes on employment. In the end, Kohl had to accept the employment provisions under pressure from the other Member States and the *Bundesrat,* despite strong criticism from Bavaria. Outside Germany, everybody was taken by surprise with Kohl's turnaround with regard to the free movement of individuals, asylum and immigration. As the German *Länder* share responsibility for immigration with the federal Government and bear the financial costs of immigration, Kohl was pressured to insist on unanimity. Although Edmund Stoiber from Bavaria was the most outspoken on this issue, I would argue that there was agreement in the *Bundesrat*, due to the fact that Germany took most of the refugees who sought asylum in the EU and the *Länder* had to pay for it. I would also argue that the *Länder* blocked majority voting in those areas which fall under their powers and those with financial implications. Devuyst (1998) calls this the *Länder*'s challenge to the Community method which forced Chancellor Helmut Kohl into adopting a very reluctant attitude towards further European integration. Additionally, one could also say that in the light of the next general elections and the downturn in public confidence in European Union matters, Kohl decided for a more pragmatic approach.

Bibliography

Anderson, Jeffrey J. & John B. Goodman (1993). "Mars or Minerva? A United Germany in a Post-Cold War Europe," pp. 23-62, in Robert O. Keohane, Joseph S. Nye & Stanley Hoffmann (eds.), *After the Cold War International Institutions and State Strategies in Europe, 1989-1991*, Cambridge MA: Harvard University Press.

Bayerische Staatskanzlei (1998). *Subsidiaritätsliste: Beispiele für Subsidiaritätsverstösse und Kompetenzüberschreitungen der EG*, 31.08.

Beuter, Rita (1994). "Germany and the Ratification of the Maastricht," pp. 87-113, in Finn Laursen & Sophie Vanhoonacker (eds.), *The Ratification of the Maastricht Treaty: Issues, Debates and Future Implications*, Dordrecht: Martinus Nijhoff.

Beuter, Rita, (1997). "State Strategies after the End of the Cold War: The Case of Germany," *TKI Working Papers on European Integration and Regime Formation*, No. 28, Esbjerg: South Jutland University Press.

Bulmer, Simon & William E. Patterson (1996). "Germany in the European Union: Gentle Giant or Emergent Leader?," *International Affairs*, Vol. 72, No. 1, January, pp. 9-32.

Bundesrat (1995). *Decision of the Bundesrat for the Preparation of the IGC 1996*, 31 March, No. 169/95.

Bundesrat (1995a). *Decision of the Bundesrat "Demands of the Länder for the IGC 1996,"* 15 December, No. 667/95.

Bundesrat (1996). *Decision of the Bundesrat for Employment Reforms through the IGC 1996*, 8 November, No. 813/96.

CDU/CSU, Parliamentary Group (1994). "Reflections on European Policy," *Agence Europe, Europe Documents*, No. 1895/96, 7 September.

CDU/CSU, Parliamentary Group (1995). "A European Union Capable of More Effective Action in the Field of Foreign and Security Policy," *Pressedienst CDU/CSU*, 13 June.

CDU/CSU, Parliamentary Group (1995a). "Expansion of the Rule of Law at EU Level," *Pressedienst CDU/CSU*, 13 June.

Devuyst, Youri (1998). "Treaty Reform in the European Union: The Amsterdam Process," *Journal of European Public Policy*, vol. 5, no. 4, pp. 615-631.

Duff, Andrew, ed. (1997). *The Treaty of Amsterdam: Text and Commentary*, London: Federal Trust/Sweet and Maxwell Ltd.

European Commission (1997). *Eurobarometer*, Brussels: October, No. 47.

European Commission (1998). *Eurobarometer*, Brussels: March, No. 48.

Hennes, Michael (1997). "The Future of Europe: Monetary or Political Union," *Aussenpolitik,* Vol. 48, No. 1, pp. 11-21.

Hoffmann, Stanley (1997). "Back to Euro-Pessimism?," *Foreign Affairs* Vol. 76, No. 1, January/February, pp. 139-145.

Janning, Josef (1996). "A German Europe – a European Germany? On the debate over German's Foreign Policy," *International Affairs,* Vol. 72, No. 1, pp. 33-41.

Janning, Josef (1996a). "La politique européenne de l'Allemagne entre désir et réalité," *Politique Étrangère,* No. 1, spring, pp. 23-36.

Jopp, Mathias, Andreas Maurer & Otto Schmuck, eds. (1998). *Die Europäische Union nach Amsterdam: Analysen und Stellungnahmen zum neuen EU-Vertrag.* Bonn: Europa Union Verlag, Institut für Europäische Politik.

McDonagh, Bobby (1998). *Original Sin in a Brave New World: An Account of the Negotiation of the Treaty of Amsterdam.* Dublin: Institute of European Affairs.

Moravcsik, Andrew & Kalypso Nicolaïdis (1999) "Explaining the Treaty of Amsterdam: Interests, Influence, Institutions," *Journal of Common Market Studies*, Vol. 37, No. 1, pp. 59-85.

Müller, Christian (1998). "Aus dem Tritt geraten: Belastungen des deutsch-französischen Tandems," *Internationale Politik,* Vol. 53, No. 9, pp. 7-12.

Piepenschneider, Melanie (1997). "Deutschland," pp. 59-68, in Rudolf Hrbek (ed.), *Die Reform der Europäischen Union.* Baden-Baden: Nomos Verlagsgesellschaft.

Schmidt, Peter (1996). "German Security Policy in the Framework of the EU, WEU and NATO," *Aussenpolitik,* Vol. 47, No. 3, pp. 211-222.

Szukala, Andrea & Wolfgang Wessels (1997). "The Franco-German Tandem," pp. 74-99, in Geoffrey Edwards & Alfred Pijpers (eds.), *The Politics of European Treaty Reform: The 1996 Intergovernmental Conference and Beyond.* London: Pinter.

Van Wijnbergen, Christa (1992). "The Federal Republic of Germany," pp. 49-61, in Finn Laursen & Sophie Vanhoonacker (eds.), *The Intergovernmental Conference on Political Union.* Maastricht: European Institute of Public Administration.

Vernet, Daniel (1998). "Ungewissheiten in der Europe-Politik: Neue deutsch-französische Entscheidungsträger," *Internationale Politik,* Vol. 53, No. 9, pp. 1-6.

6

Finland: From Cautious to Hard-Core Member

Esko Antola

Introduction

Finland joined the European Union on January 1st 1995. By that time, the work of the Reflection Group had already opened the process of the Intergovernmental Conference (IGC). In March 1995, the parliamentary election brought to power a new Social Democrat – Conservative coalition government supported by three smaller parties. The "Rainbow Coalition" included both the Greens and the Left Union, former communists, as the core of the party. It also included the traditional balancer, the Swedish Party, which represents the interests of the Swedish speaking minority in Finland.

The General election marked a shift in political power in the country. The Center-Conservative coalition of 1991-95 lost the election. It took the decision to apply for membership of the European Community in 1992. This coalition, headed by a Prime Minister from the Center Party, also negotiated the accession.[1] The leading coalition member, the Center Party, gained large support from the rural population and the agricultural sector. Its rank and file were largely in opposition to the EU Membership mainly for reasons of farming and foreign policy. In spite of considerable political difficulties, the Prime Minister was able to convince his own party to support the Membership, but lost the Parliamentary election in March 1995.

The new government, headed by a Social Democrat Prime Minister, was considerably more pro-European in its attitude.[2] The Government, in its April 1995 work programme, made a promise that "the preparations in Finland for the IGC shall be based on open public debate and on the involvement of the

---

[1] The Center-Conservative Government took office in May 1991 after a General Election. It was headed by Mr. Esko Aho, Chairman of the Center Party. In February 1992, the Parliament voted in favour of the Government's Proposal to apply for Membership in the European Community. Accession negotiations were opened in February 1993 and the Accession Treaty was signed in Corfu in June 1994. In a referendum in October, 57 per cent of the Finns voted in favour of Membership.

[2] Mr. Paavo Lipponen, the Chairmnan of the Social Democratic Party, an early supporter of the Finnish EU Membership, was nominated as the Prime Minister in April 1995.

Parliament." This promise set the guideline for preparation throughout the process.

However, the first steps in drafting the Finnish policy on the IGC were taken already in autumn 1994, before Finland was even a Member of the European Union. A small group of experts in the Ministry for Foreign Affairs was nominated to make preparations. An early departure was motivated by the need to get a flying start for membership in the European Union. Finland faced a wide range of new issues without experience in the functioning of the European Community, let alone in the Maastricht Treaty. Public opinion was still overtaken by the referendum on Membership in October 1994. There was not much public interest in the IGC. Various opinion polls also indicated that Finns saw the European Union rather distant, although their basic attitude was positive as such. The Government wished to draw interest into the issues of the IGC by incorporating a wide range of civil society organisations into the preparatory work.

How the Strategy was Drafted

A distinctive feature in the Finnish approach to the IGC was a commitment to make the preparations of the national objectives as transparent as possible. A very comprehensive organisation was set up involving not only different ministries and interest groups but also the civil society and the Parliament. In the end, however, the drafting of the national positions was in the hands of a very small group of diplomats and civil servants. In practice, the key players were the members of the negotiation team nominated at September 21st, 1995. It was headed by the Foreign Minister.

As the first step, the new Government of Finland established three working groups of top civil servants even before Finland was a Member of the Union. The working groups focused on the CFSP, on economic matters and on institutional questions. At the top of preparatory organisation was a high-level Steering Group under the chairmanship of the Under Secretary for Foreign Affairs and the chairmen of the three working groups, plus special aides of the ministers as its members. The working group also assisted the nominated representative of the Finish Government in the Reflection Group.[3] The Group issued a memorandum on the Finnish positions in September 1995.

Its mandate lasted until the Madrid European Council in 1995. It was followed by a much wider planning organisation. The planning and conduct of the Finnish strategy in the IGC was based on three components. The first

---

[3] The Finnish representative was Mr. Ingvar Melin, former Cabinet Member and former MP.

element consisted of Cabinet Members and high level civil servants. This component was of key importance because it represented the expertise that was gained during the accession negotiations. The policy preparation was in the hands of most experienced civil servants from the top of the bureaucracy. Ultimately, the group was very small and proved to be in a key position in drafting the strategy.

At the top of the structure was the Ministerial Committee which was chaired by the Prime Minister. The Committee has chief responsibility in deciding on the Finnish EU policy in general as well. In the Ministerial Committee, final positions of Finland for the IGC were decided in the presence of competent cabinet members. Below the EU Ministerial Committee was the *Committee for EU Affairs*. It was also a permanent part of the co-ordination of the EU affairs in general and consisted of high-level representatives from all ministries, the Prime Minister's Office, the Office of the President, Bank of Finland, Provincial Government of Aland Islands and the Office of Chancellor of Justice. The Committee is responsible for co-ordinating the work of ministries in EU affairs and during the IGC covered also its topics. It discusses wide-scale horizontal matters but also resolves the issues, which have not been finalised in sections.

The involvement of the civil society was the second component of the mechanism. Most important civil society organisations were represented in the twenty working groups. Also, a large consultative body under the chairmanship of the Prime Minister was established. It consisted of over 60 members, mostly from the civil society organisations. The main purpose of that body was to convey information and to invite debate on the issues of the IGC. Its main function was clearly to serve as a platform of discussion and it conveyed the IGC topics into the civil society more than it channelled civil society views into the IGC process.

The third component in drafting the strategy consisted of the parliamentary scrutiny. The Parliament was involved in the process throughout the negotiations. This procedure followed the overall pattern of the Parliament's involvement in EU matters. It is an established part of decision-making in EU policy in general. Under the relevant Parliament Act, the Prime Minister must convey to the Parliament information on the European Council meetings both before and after the meeting. In similar fashion ministers must report to the Parliament on their voting behaviour in Council meetings.

The Parliament also has the right to receive all the information required in order to assess the relevance and importance of issues discussed before Parliament draws its conclusions. In addition, Parliament has the right to require that the statements of its relevant committees serve as guidelines to the representatives of Finland in EU decision-making. On the basis of its internal rules, two Parliamentary Committees have a special role in the scrutiny. The

Grand Committee serves as the major body in this process. In matters of CFSP, it is again the Foreign Affairs Committee who is the competent authority.

Finland's Objectives at the IGC?

The Position of the Finnish Government

Keeping the European Union as an association of independent states was the fundamental premise of Finland through the negotiation process. This was highlighted in numerous official statements. This concept was introduced in a Memorandum of the High Level Steering Group in early September 1995 (*Memorandum* 1995). The Memorandum states the basic premise of the Finnish Government:

> It is Finland's basic premise that the European Union will continue to be developed as an association of independent states, to which the members have transferred competencies that can be exercised jointly in working towards the agreed goals. Finland's objective is a Union that efficiently ensures the welfare and common values of its citizens while also working for the development of the international community towards stability, co-operation and security (Memorandum 1995, 2).

Government Members echoed this fundamental starting point in their deliberations. It was on some occasions made more explicit by stressing that Finland was not in favour of a federalist Europe (Niinistö 1995).

The Memorandum also stressed that the objectives as well as the timetable of the IGC must be defined jointly. Also, the equality of the Member States to take part in the decision-making process was stressed. The decisions in the IGC should also safeguard the achievements that the Union has gained. The Prime Minister's Report in May1995 emphasised four issues as the main aims of the Finnish Government. Focus was on: keeping the European Union as an intergovernmental institution, the need to bring the European Union closer to the citizen, the need to improve efficiency of the Union and the support to measures adding transparency and democracy in the Union (Prime Minister's Report 1995).

From the outset, the main objective of the Finnish Government was that the Union should be developed into an efficient instrument in ensuring welfare and common values of its citizens. Finland emphasised that the Union should become strong enough so as to make a contribution to the development of the international community towards stability, co-operation and security. These elements were also outlined in a Government report on the future of Europe

(*Finland and the Future of Europe* 1996). The report argued that it is in the best interest of Finland to consolidate the European Union as a strong union of all its Member States. The Report argued: "It is Finland's goal to promote all efforts to strengthen and advance the fundamental values underpinning the fabric of Europe: democracy, welfare, tolerance and civil rights" (*Finland and the Future of Europe* 1996, 8-9).

Concrete aims and national aspirations were made public in the opening document for the negotiation strategy presented by the Government to the Parliament on February 27, 1996 (VNS 1/96 vp. :Finland's Points of Departure 1996). The starting premise of the Finnish Government was to see the future of the European Union as an association of independent states. This basic aim is in line with the Government's premises that the European Union should be developed "as a strong association of states in which the Member States have shared power in order to use it to achieve the objectives that they have collectively approved." (VNS 1/96 vp., 9.) Finland also stressed that the objectives and the timetable of the Conference must be defined collectively and respecting the equal rights and obligations of the Member States. Finland favoured a limited agenda of the IGC with a focus on amendments that would make the Union capable of coping with challenges of future.

The Government of Finland committed itself to support improving the capability of the European Union to promote stable economic development, environmental protection and employment. The Government also declared its support for the development of the CFSP in a manner that enables it to promote its objectives actively and respond to crises that threaten stability and security. From the very beginning, openness was also an important topic on the Finnish agenda. The focus of the Report is clearly on questions dealing with the citizen and the European Union. Of eight concrete proposals made to the Conference, six had their focus on issues close to citizens.

Finland was also supportive of the idea of flexible integration, brought up in the final report of the Reflection Group. The Government Report was in favour of including the topic on the agenda of the IGC and subscribed to the general conditions outlined by the Group (VNS 1/96 vp., 9-10).

Citizens and the Union
The section "Citizens and the Union" covered the promotion of European values, free movement, employment, social dimension, environmental matters, transparency and subsidiarity. The value section stressed the importance of the protection of fundamental rights. Finland was committed to advancing the idea of the accession of the Community to the European Convention on Human Rights. The Government Report saw this as the best solution but did not exclude other options as the idea of a European Union Bill of Rights. However, the Government was supportive of the extension of elements of the

citizenship of the Union and of the idea of the inclusion of new rights (VNS 1/96 vp, 13-14).

The Government Report discussed at length the question of the Third Pillar. Justice and Home Affairs clearly had a high preference in the Finnish views. The initial position was that the co-operation had not progressed as expected (VNS 1/96 vp., 15). The Report pointed both to the problems in decision-making and in the competencies. Therefore, the Finnish Government concluded that the Communitarisation of the Third Pillar should be accepted. In the Government's view, more decisions should be taken by qualified-majority voting and more powers given to the Commission in initiating in all issues in this field. The Finnish Government was also prepared to extend the power of jurisdiction of the Court of Justice in this field (VNS 1/96 vp, 16).

From the very beginning in its negotiating objectives, the Finnish Government supported strengthening the employment commitment to be added to the treaties. Later on in the process, Finland supported the successful Swedish proposal on the employment chapter. Added to the wish that the social protocol be inserted into the treaty and that the idea of sustainable development also be added to the Treaty objectives aligned Finland with Sweden. It also allowed the Government, in its final account of the Amsterdam process, to state that most of the issues it wanted to promote were actually incorporated into the Amsterdam Treaty.

Institutional Matters

In institutional matters, Finland was less focused. Two complementary explanations can be given. First, during its initial year of membership, Finland had not gained much experience on the institutional side of the Union. It was much easier to show interest and even concrete ideas in soft elements of integration, which are also politically less sensitive issues for a new Member State. On the other hand, the Finnish Government was on the move in institutional matters and was quite flexible. Although the founding principle of the strategy stressed the European Union as an association of independent states, during the Amsterdam process Finland begun to show more understanding of ideas concerning stronger institutions.

This shift was partly a result of a learning process. Finnish civil servants became more experienced with European institutions and began to see them from an insider's perspective. On the other hand, Finland quite early in its Membership started to align with the other small states. The small state perspective emerged quite early and marked a gradually increasing distance from the two other Nordic countries. An important factor in shaping Finnish positions in institutional matters was her willingness to meet the criteria of the Economic and Monetary Union. Early membership in the EMU became a major goal of the Government. This goal shaped the attitude of the Government more favourably towards the idea of flexibility.

The starting point in the institutional matters was that the institutional balance should be maintained unchanged (VNS 1/96 vp., 23). The pursuit of democracy, efficiency and the interests of small Member States motivated this attitude. The argument fits well into the general philosophical view of the European Union as an association between independent states. As a new Member with limited experience in the work of EU institutions, Finland established a cautious and restrained approach to institutional changes. On the other hand, the Finnish strategy during the negotiation process proved to be flexible and even active.

More detailed aims were drawn from these premises. Finland was of the opinion that the position of the *European Parliament* should be improved in the legislative process in the interest of reducing democratic deficit, but "the Union's character as an association of states should be preserved" (VNS 1/96 vp, 24). Two implications were drawn: Finland rejected proposals to strengthen the position of the Parliament in the Treaty-amending procedure, and it was not supportive of ideas to enhance the Parliament's powers to decide over own resources.

As to the role of the national parliaments, the Government of Finland initially expressed views that their role as such is important but that the improvement of their position is mainly an element of the dimensions of transparency. More effective participation of national parliaments in decision-making would strengthen the democratic character of the Union. The possibilities to improve the position of national Parliaments should be improved at the national level (VNS 1/96 vp, 32).

In the same spirit, Finland was in favour of maintaining the autonomous position of the European Commission in relation to the Member States. The key role of the Commission must be maintained and its central role in the first pillar retained. Finland was in favour of strengthening surveillance and supervision of the Commission. The Government was also initially in favour of increasing the influence of the Commission in the Third Pillar but did not see the need to alter the Commission's position substantially in foreign and security policy. As to the composition of the Commission, Finland favoured the existing system. In sum, Finland was among the Member States that supported the strengthening of the Commission and maintaining its composition and the nomination procedure untouched (VNS 1/96 vp, 24-26).

In reforming the Council of Ministers the starting point of the Finnish Government was very clear. The fundamental opinion was that the Council should remain as the central decision-making body, with equality of the Member States as the founding principle (VNS 1/96 vp, 27). In the same spirit, Finland saw no need to change the weighting of votes, at least before the future enlargement. However, through the Conference, Finland supported the expansion of the use of the QMV. Finland stood opposed to any changes in the rotating Presidency.

The same cautious reform line was maintained in reactions to the Reflection Group proposals concerning other institutions. Finland showed sympathy to ideas that the Court of Justice competence should be considered in the Third Pillar but opposed its extension to the Second Pillar. On the other hand, from the very beginning, Finland supported the strengthening of the competence of the Court of Auditors as part of her strong support to strengthening the supervisory powers in the Community (VNS 1/96 vp, 29-31). Finland saw no reason to make Treaty changes concerning the Committee of Regions or the Economic and Social Committee.

External Relations

No doubt the main achievement of Finland in the IGC was the inclusion of the Petersperg tasks in the competence of the Common Foreign and Security Policy. The solution was based largely on the joint proposal by Finland and Sweden. When applying for Membership in the EU, Finland emphasised that accession would not essentially change her basic foreign policy line. At the same time, a wide understanding prevailed that Membership in the European Union would gradually call for new interpretations of the policy of neutrality. By joining the European Union, taking part in Foreign Policy co-ordination was also seen as a possibility for wider participation in world affairs. As vital interests in other policy areas pointed to the merits of Membership, the costs of taking part in previously encapsulated areas of "high politics" constituted a problem, albeit a tolerable problem.

With accession, Finland accepted without reservations the principles of the CFSP. Events in the European security arena convinced the Finnish Government that the strengthening of the capacities of the European Union in the field of Common Foreign and Security policy would serve the security policy interests of Finland as well. This was expressed in the IGC process by Finland's interest in attempts to improve the crisis management capabilities of the EU. Finland contributed jointly with Sweden a Memorandum on the IGC and Defence Dimension in October 1996 (CONF/394/96).

The core of the Memorandum is the idea of merging the so-called Petersberg tasks of the Western European Union into the capacity of the European Union. The proposal has at least three motivations. An obvious national interest of both former neutral countries was that the CFSP constitutes for them the main security policy forum. Strengthening of the capacities of the EU in crisis management enhances the security of the two countries. They both have closed the option of NATO membership, at least in the current conditions, preferring security through the EU.

Two other motivations can be seen. First, as non-members to the WEU, they faced the possibility of being excluded from European crises management operations under the WEU management. This would again contradict their traditional roles as "Great Powers of Peace-Keeping." Participation in peacekeeping operations has been an important element of the international identity of both countries. Finally, there was also an element of compromise making between those Members of the EU which aimed at a rapid merger of the WEU into the EU and those who were not ready for such a move.

The joint Finnish-Swedish proposal was incorporated into the Treaty of Amsterdam in the form of article 17. This guarantees that all Member States of the European Union, independent of their respective national security policy arrangements, have the right to take part in crisis management operations of the EU. This is perhaps the greatest impact Finland and Sweden have made in the European Union during the first five years of their Membership. It is also an important achievement against the background of their different strategies as Member States. Despite their differing strategies with respect to the EMU, Finland and Sweden have proven to be able to co-operate in other issues.

During the IGC, Finland moved to support the establishment of the High Representative. Initially Finland was skeptical of the idea on the grounds that such a system could make the question of responsibilities even more complicated than in the Maastricht arrangement. Finland was in favour of strengthening the visibility of the CFSP, but through the Presidency. From the very beginning, Finland also supported the establishment of a monitoring and evaluation unit in the Council Secretariat but expressed reservations about the extension of QMW in implementation (VNS 1/96 vp, 30-40). A similar tone was also presented in the issue of the legal personality.

Reactions of the Parliament
The general procedure of scrutiny in EU matters was applied in the IGC as well. The Government informed the Parliament eleven times during the process through either general reports on its objectives or on more detailed questions. The detailed reports were partially drafted at the Parliament's request. The Amsterdam Treaty ratification proposal was introduced by a major report of 392 pages (HE 245/1997 vp).

The reports were addressed to the Parliament as a whole. Parliament also gave its opinion and reaction to each of them. According to the rules of Parliament, the practical work was carried out in three relevant Committees (The Grand Committee, the Constitutional Committee and the Foreign Affairs Committee). The Committees organised expert hearings as part of their report drafting. Reports were presented to the Assembly for final adoption.

Table 6.1: The Parliamentary scrutiny in the IGC process.

May 1995	Prime Minister's Report of Government's general preparedness to the IGC
Sept 1995	Prime Minister's Announcement
February 1996	Government Report on its objectives in the IGC
Autumn 1966	Report on Legal Personality
	Report on extension of QMV and co-decision procedure
	Report on 3rd Pillar issues
	Report on external economic relations
Spring 1997	Report on QMV
	Report on Legal Personality
	Report on Environmental Taxation
January 1998	Government Proposal for the Ratification of the Amsterdam Treaty

In addition to the Government reports, the Minister for Foreign Affairs explained the IGC objectives of the Government before the Grand Committee of the Parliament prior to each ministerial meeting of the IGC. The Prime Minister informed the Grand Committee before and after every European Council meeting. This procedure is based on the rules of procedure of the Parliament in EU affairs as a constitutional requirement. The normal scrutiny procedure was applied in the IGC matters to keep the Parliament informed.

Parliament's view was basically in harmony with the Government's Reports. However, particularly in issues concerning "Citizens and the Union," the views expressed by the Parliamentary Committees differed from the Government's initial proposals. A good example is the question of the citizen's rights. In its reaction to the Government's Report, the Foreign Affairs Committee of the Parliament required that Finland should set as her aim the accession of the Community to the European Convention on Human Rights (UaVM7/1996 vp, 8). Both the Constitutional Committee and the Grand Committee of the Parliament took the same position (UaVM7/1996 vp, 25 and 33). The Parliament Committees even saw the European Union Bill of Rights as a harmful development with regard to the evolution of national norms of the Member States and in terms of the advance of the universal system of human rights. In Third Pillar issues as well, the Parliament basically agreed with the Government view but called for a more detailed report by the Government. The Government subsequently prepared such a report.

On institutional issues, the Parliament requested special reports and further clarification of the Government's positions. It also demanded that the Parliament should have the possibility to review national positions during the IGC. Special reports were demanded on the institutional matters on qualified majority voting, on legal personality of the Union as well as on co-decision procedure. The Parliament thus kept the Government abreast of institutional matters. One is tempted to conclude that the Government might have been more willing to support the strengthening of the institutions but that Parliament was much more concerned about the inter-governmental nature of the Union.

In Parliament's view, its own position could be ensured only if the intergovernmental nature of the Union was to be preserved. The Foreign Affairs Committee, for instance, stressed that decision-making powers in matters concerning the legal order, founding principles and financing of the Union must remain with the Member States and their Parliaments (UaVM7/1996 vp, 12). The Constitutional Committee and the General Committee shared this basic approach. The Parliament thus strongly supported the Government's basic view that the European Union should remain as an association of independent states.

In questions related to the institutional balance of the European Union, the Parliamentary Committees were strongly in favour of maintaining the balance. The Foreign Affairs Committee, for instance, opposed the idea of institutionalising co-operation between national Parliaments and the European Parliament in enhancing subsidiarity, which it saw in principle as a positive development. The Foreign Affairs Committee supported the extension of the codecision procedure to all matters under the qualified majority rule and thus supported the strengthening of the position of the European Parliament. The Finnish Parliament was very strict, however, in demanding that it must be consulted before the Government decides on its own approach to the extension of qualified majority voting (UaVM7/1996 vp, 13).

The Parliament also expressed strong opinions in the CFSP issues. The Foreign Affairs Committee, for instance, required that the decisions in the IGC not be in contradiction with the Finnish policy of military non-alignment. Finland should, however, provide a constructive input to the further development of the CFSP in its intergovernmental form (UaVM7/1996 vp, 17). The Committee also expressed its disapproval as to the establishment of the position of the High Representative.

Perhaps the most restrictive view expressed by the Parliament concerned the possibility of a common defence policy. The Foreign Affairs Committee required that as a militarily non-aligned country Finland take part in the military crisis management only if it retains its right to sovereign decision-making in matters that concern its own security. Furthermore, the equality between the Member States in decision-making in crisis management must be preserved, argues the Report (UaVM7/1996 vp, 20).

What Finland Proposed to the IGC?

As a new Member with limited experience in the workings of EU institutions, Finland was not in a position to be very active in making official proposals. The IGC 1996 was primarily a learning process and an adaptation period. The modest role may also be explained through the traditional role that Finland played in international relations before the Membership, a role characterised by mediation and compromise making rather than by outspoken activity in public diplomacy. In this tradition, Finland also lent her active support to proposals made by other Members. Perhaps the best example of this role was the support given by Finland to the Swedish activities in compelling the employment chapter.

Due to the lack of experience of the work of European institutions, Finland focused her rather modest activity on making proposals concerning the soft side of integration. The Government of Finland presented eight official proposals to the IGC as shown in Table 6.2.

Table 6.2: Finnish proposals to the IGC.

Simplification of Budget Procedures	CONF 3963/969
Environmental elements of the Internal Market	CONF 3969/96
Strengthening of the position of the consumers	CONF 3968/96
Strengthening of the legal protection of Individuals in the 3rd pillar	CONF 3923/97
Transparency	CONF 3865/97
Social policy and equality between women and men	CONF 3907/97
Civil Protection	CONF 3923/97
On the improvement of the crisis management capabilities of the EU (jointly with Sweden)	CONF 3946/96

The core interest in the proposals was the advancement of the position of the European citizen. The focus is in line with the initial areas of preferences as expressed in Government reports prior to the opening of negotiations. Many of the items are very wide and likely to remain on the agenda of future institutional reforms as well. A good example in this respect is transparency.

The Finnish priorities included concrete topics as well. A good example is the proposal concerning the improvement of budgetary procedures (CONF 3963/969). Government had already given considerable weight to the issue in its Report to the Parliament. The content of the proposal was rather technical, reflecting the generally low political profile that Finland assumed. Finland initially wanted to avoid a debate about her own resources in the IGC but wanted to focus on the budgetary procedure (VNS 1/96 vp, 35). The proposal was drafted in the same spirit.

Transparency
No doubt the politically most important proposal concerned the advancement of transparency. Issues of transparency were stressed in the national debate, and particularly in parliamentary debates. Transparency was also stressed by the time of the Accession. For that purpose, the Finnish Government issued a Declaration in which it declared its commitment to continue its practice of openness. Special emphasis was given to access to public documents. Finland regarded the openness of public documents as an element of legally and politically democratic society.

The commitment to transparency was further highlighted by a report from the Ministry of Justice. The report, published in June 1995, listed ways of improving transparency. The suggestions included two main items: adding to the Treaty an article securing public access to documents and strengthening its implementation by a Council Regulation. The basic line of the Ministry of Justice Report was that Union citizenship should include the right of access to information on actions and documents of the European Union. The right of access should be extended to all institutions with the exception of the Court of Justice.

Improving transparency was high on the Finnish agenda from the very beginning of the process of the IGC. In the Finnish view, the issue was intimately linked not only with direct or indirect democracy in practise but also with making the Union more democratic (*Memorandum* 1995, 5). Adding transparency thus served two purposes: it helped to improve the practice of democracy in the existing institutional framework but at the same time served as a key principle in making the Union more democratic as a political system (VNS 1/96 vp, 19). In its Report to Parliament, the Finnish Government confirmed its aims by a demand that the new Treaty include an article on public access to documents to be implemented by a Council Regulation at a later stage (VNS 1/96 vp, 20).

Along these lines, the Government of Finland submitted a proposal to the Conference on Transparency (CONF/3865/97). The proposal contained an addition to the proposed new article 192a. The article confirms the right to every citizen of the Union, or any natural or legal person residing or having its registered office in a Member State, of access to documents of the European Parliament, Council and Commission documents. Right of access may be restricted only on the grounds of essential private or public interest. The proposal also contains a statement of general principles and conditions set by the Council before January 1st, 2001. In addition to a new article, the Finnish proposal also contains a Declaration relating the public access to documents.

The final result was that in the Treaty of Amsterdam, improvements were achieved in the field of transparency. Article 1 was modified to include a wording on transparency. Of particular relevance is the inclusion of a new article (255) that confirms the principle of public access. New elements of transparency no doubt reflect the Finnish initial aims and give credence to the conclusion of the Government that "The Finnish input in breakthrough of the acceptance of the principle of transparency can be regarded even as essential" (Hallituksen esitys 1997, 27).

Environmental questions were also high on the Finnish agenda from the very beginning of the negotiation process. The initial aim was to introduce the principle of sustainable development into the Treaty. This aim was achieved, although the idea was not a Finnish novelty. In principle, Finland supported the strengthening of the competence of the Community in environmental matters both by extending the QMV into this area and by simplifying the decision-making procedure. In the spirit of the Nordic tradition, the possibility to maintain higher environmental standards was to be strengthened. Finland submitted to the Conference a proposal for environmental aspects of the internal market (CONF 3969/96).

As in environmental matters, Finland aimed at strengthening the Union powers in non-discrimination and equality. In the same spirit, the Government argued that the stronger role of the Union in these matters should not prevent Member States from issuing regulations that go further (VNS 1/96 vp., 14). A proposal to advance the Finnish position was presented at the Conference (CONF 3907/97). Other Finnish proposals reflect the interest of improving the powers of the Union in matters that are close to European citizens.

Conclusions

In its proposal to the Parliament for the ratification of the Treaty of Amsterdam, the Government summarised the final result by arguing that Finnish aims were generally achieved (HE 245/1997 vp, 15). This is a general conclusion that all Governments drew as a conclusion from the IGC process.

A more qualified conclusion was that particularly on issues where a special Finnish proposal was submitted to the Conference, the final text either follows the Finnish proposal to a great extent or is at least close to the Finnish line. The Report mentions all the Finnish proposals as examples of success. The report also mentions issues where the results were not quite satisfactory from the Finnish point of view. Such is the case, for instance, concerning the competence of the Union in external economic relations, where Finland expected more progress. Finland would also have preferred to extend the use of QMW in a wider range of issues than what was agreed upon. Furthermore, Finland was uncomfortable with the decision-making procedures introduced in Home and Justice affairs.

In his final account of the results of the IGC, the Finnish Prime Minister argued that the EU is now closer to its citizens, more effective in its external relations and has better institutional prerequisites for effective decision-making. However, he also regretted that in some areas the achievements were not far- reaching enough. He particularly cites external economic relations, where the accomplishments were not as extensive as Finland had hoped. In general, the Prime Minister expressed his satisfaction with the success that the Finnish initiatives had received (Lipponen 1997).

The Prime Minister also echoed the general Finnish argument that Finland was ultimately successful if measured against her background as a new and small Member State. In his introductory speech to the Parliament at the opening of the ratification process, the Prime Minister argued that the Finnish strategy was based on a "constructive approach" which enhanced the image of Finland as a Member State actively contributing to the development of the European Union (Lipponen 1998).

The ratification process in the Parliament was smooth. In the final voting of the Parliament in June 1998, 110 votes were cast in favour of the ratification and only 4 against it. Changes made to the Treaty stayed within the limits of general political acceptability. If the political interest in the IGC issues was not very high in the early stages of the process because of the fatigue about the EU issues, the ratification stage was taken over by the closeness of the EMU debate. The EU agenda was dominated by the final stages of the national debate on that issue. The low political intensity of the issue is also seen in the exceptionally high number of MPs, 85, not being present for the final voting which was taken at the end of the political season.

Changes made to the Maastricht Treaty were not regarded as profound enough to evoke the constitutional issue. According to Finnish law, the Constitutional Committee of the Parliament decides the constitutional acceptability of changes. The Committee concluded that there was no need for a constitutional procedure, thus simplifying the ratification procedure. The Parliamentary scrutiny and the incorporation of the civil society and interest groups into the planning process without doubt helped the ratification process as well. Continuous reporting from the Government to the Parliament worked to the same end. The wide political coalition in Government gave no leverage to the opposition even to challenge constitutional requirements.

Altogether, 11 out of 13 parliamentary committees gave their reports to the Foreign Affairs Committee, which delivered its own report on the Treaty (UaVM 8/ 1998 vp). The report followed the general positive evaluation presented in the Government's evaluation. The report concludes that the Government had paid due attention to the Parliament's viewpoints and that the final result in the Amsterdam Treaty is satisfactory. The Foreign Affairs Committee hailed the progress made in the areas of transparency, openness and European citizenship. It noted as well that the Treaty entailed only a modest deepening of integration. On the contrary, the Report is rather critical towards the provisions of flexible integration. The Parliament saw that these provisions may actually complicate the work of the institutions.

The Report devoted a special attention to article 17 of the Treaty. It referred to the argument previously presented by the Constitutional Committee that from the constitutional perspective, decisions of the European Council on the creation of common defence were binding without national ratification. The report also envisaged that decisions on the issue should require a new inter-governmental conference. In general, the Parliament tood a positive view towards strengthening the actor capabilities of the Union in the CFSP but regretted that progress in strengthening the capacity of the Union in external economic relations was not achieved.

The Finnish strategy was both cautious and flexible. Flexibility showed itself in two ways. First, Finland was quite adaptable in institutional matters, where the strategy initially was cautious and where the level of ambition was low. The Finnish strategy focused mainly on issues of low politics such as gender equality, consumer protection and environment but when pushed to take a view on matters of high politics, the flexibility appeared. The Government was able to keep the initially fundamental aims in institutional affairs but showed compliance in potentially difficult national areas like the CFSP. Secondly, Finland was flexible on issues which emerged during the negotiation process and on which no strong national opinions were presented in the early stages of negotiations. Enhanced co-operation and the inclusion of Home and Justice affairs into the First Pillar serve as good examples. A final assessment of Finland's success should be seen in terms of setting a profile of a new Member State rather than any concrete achievements on specific issues.

Profile rather than concrete achievements dominate the accomplishments of Finland. It is probable, although empirical evidence is hard to present, that during the process of the IGC, Finland moved from its initial cautious and reserved position towards the mainstream of the Member States. At the end of the IGC, Finland was less inter-governmentalist than in the opening stage. A logical explanation to this is that at the same time Finland had deliberately moved towards the EMU and into the "hard core" of the European Union. The thrust to the EMU core had an impact on the IGC policy of the country as well.

The effort to reach the core of the European Union distanced Finland from her traditional reference group, the Nordic Group. As a consequence, Finland moved closer to the traditional small states in the EU. Elements of a small-state identity emerged during the IGC process. The decisive question was probably the attitude towards the introduction of the principle of flexibility, which divided the Member States into two groups: into probable members of the federal core and the probable candidates of exclusion (Moravcik & Nicolaïdis 1998, 20). On this question at least, Finland moved toward the positions of Members which supported the idea of flexibility.

Bibliography

Finland and the Future of Europe (1996). Future Report of the Government of Finland to Parliament. Part 1, *Prime Minister's Office, Publication Series*, 4.

HE 245/1997 vp, *Hallituksen esitys Eduskunnalle Euroopan unionista tehdyn sopimuksen, Euroopan yhteisöjen perustamissopimusten ja niihin liitettyjen tiettyjen asiakirjojen muuttamisesta tehdyn Amsterdamin sopimuksen eräiden määräysten hyväksymisestä.*

Lipponen, Paavo (1997). *The Enlargement of the EU after the IGC*, speech delivered at Helsingin Sanomat Europe– seminar, October 9th.

Lipponen, Paavo (1998). *Introduction to the Ratification of the Treaty of Amsterdam to the Parliament*, February 12.

Memorandum Concerning Finnish Points of View with Regard to the 1996 Intergovernmental Conference 1995 of the European Union, Ministry for Foreign Affairs, September 18, 1995.

Moravcsik, Andrew & Kalypso Nicolaïdis (1998). "Federal Ideals and Constitutional Realities in the Amsterdam Treaty," *Journal of Common Market Studies*, vol. 36, Annual Review, pp. 13-38.

Niinistö, Sauli, Minister of Justice (1995). *Finnish Positions at the 1996 IGC*, speech given to the seminar Finland and the 1996 IGC, October 4th.

Prime Minister's Report to the Grand Committee and the Committee of Foreign Affairs of the Parliament, May 31, 1995.

UaVM 7/1996 vp. *Eduskunnan ulkoasiainvaliokunnan mietintö 1/96 valtioneuvoston selonteosta "Suomen lähtökohdat ja tavoitteet Euroopan Unionin vuoden 1996 hallitusten välisessä konferenssissa."*

UaVM 8/1998 vp. *Eduskunnan ulkoasiainvaliokunnan mietintö 8/98 hallituksen esityksestä Eduskunnalle Euroopan unionista tehdyn sopimuksen, Euroopan yhteisöjen perustamissopimusten ja niihin liitettyjen tiettyjen asiakirjojen muuttamisesta tehdyn Amsterdamin sopimuksen eräiden määräysten hyväksymisestä.*

VNS 1/96 vp. *Finland's Points of Departure and Objectives at the 1996 Intergovernmental Conference. Report to the Parliament by the Council of State, February 27, 1996 (English translation).*

7

France: A Member State Losing Influence?

Florence Deloche-Gaudez

Introduction

In France, the Treaty of Amsterdam, concluded in June 1997 after an Intergovernmental Conference of over one year, was perceived as a failure at the time. Looking at press reports is convincing enough: after the Amsterdam European Council, *Le Monde* ran the headline: "Echec des Quinze au sommet d'Amsterdam sur la réforme des institutions européennes" ["Failure of the Fifteen in the Amsterdam summit on EU-reform"]; a few months later, when the Treaty was signed, *Le Figaro* recalled that "the institutional headache remained unsettled" and *Libération* plainly wrote that "the new European Treaty was hopeless" (*Le Monde* 1997; *Le Figaro* 1997; *Libération* 1997). Admittedly, government representatives had failed to agree on the institutional reform viewed by French leaders as crucial in the perspective of EU enlargement to the East. More broadly, France did not appear as much of an influential actor in the Intergovernmental Conference (IGC) (Moravcsik & Nicolaïdis 1999; Beach contribution to this volume).

In these circumstances, the French authorities were tempted to put the blame on others: Germany was considered as having "betrayed" on the night of 17th June; small states had refused to give up their former privileges; the original community spirit had been lost, especially since the last enlargement; finally, in no way could anyone do more than "one thing at a time" in the European Union and priority had been given to implementing the EMU.[1] Some of these arguments were not actually unfounded. However, in this chapter we will examine whether it was not rather on account of the substance of its positions and attitude during the negotiations that France found it difficult to carry weight on the result of the 1996-1997 Intergovernmental Conference (IGC). As European integration deepened, was it not getting increasingly difficult to reconcile its commitment to the European construction and to French sovereignty? Did France, before and during the negotiations, make certain it held positions which could generate "advocacy coalitions" which would include in particular Germany and the small states?

---

[1] This latter argument was, for instance, put forward by Raymond Barre and Jacques Delors in a forum published in *Le Monde* dated 2 October 1997 ("Au-delà de l'euro").

In response to these questions, I will argue that French positions were not coherent enough, often isolated and too scattered.

Preparation of the ICG: the Difficulties of Acting as Custodian of Both French and European Temples

The limitations of the French positions do not seem to have been due to lack of preparation. Prior to the ICG, officials in charge at the time had actually considered the positions they would advocate. These, nevertheless, presented contradictions which undermined them from the start.

Originally, the attitude of the French representative in the Reflection Group set up at European level in June 1995 under the chairmanship of Carlos Westendorp from Spain may substantiate the assumption of insufficient preparation (Menon 1997). However, the French may have been cautious then for another reason. Mr Michel Barnier, who represented France, had just been appointed as deputy minister for European affairs following Jacques Chirac's victory in the May 1995 presidential elections. It is quite likely that he did not want to commit himself until clear positions had been determined by the new government. It was not until November 1995 that "guidelines" were discussed and finalized during an interministerial meeting chaired by Alain Juppé, the former foreign affairs minister who had become Prime Minister. This internal document, published in *Le Figaro*, was even passed on to a number of majority as well as opposition political leaders whom the President of the Republic met for discussion (*Le Figaro* 1996; *Le Monde* 1996b; Juppé 1996). Finally, in March 1996, two weeks before the opening of the IGC in Turin, a debate was held in the *Assemblée nationale* on French positions. Michel Barnier summarized these under three priorities: reforming the Union's institutions towards its enlargement; bringing the Union closer to its citizens; evolving a common foreign and security policy worthy of the name (Barnier 1996a).

At a more administrative level, at the end of 1995, the new foreign affairs minister, Hervé de Charette and the deputy minister for European affairs, Michel Barnier, set up a restricted "negotiating team" gathering officials from the departments involved together with members of their "cabinets" and associating the French permanent representative in Brussels, Pierre de Boissieu. In the Quai d'Orsay, an interministerial IGC preparation and follow-up group was also set up including the members of the negotiating group as well as the President of the Republic's and the Prime Minister's advisers, Mr Menat and Mr Cadet respectively, together with representatives from other ministries (*Le Monde* 1996a). At the beginning of 1996, Hervé de Charette also asked Pierre Lepetit to join his staff and to devote himself to the IGC issue. Finally, regarding the other European policy issues, interministerial meetings continued to be held, both at the SGCI (*Secrétariat Général du Comité Interministériel*),[2] in particular to prepare French positions on technical issues, and at the Hôtel Matignon, under the chairmanship of the Prime Minister or of members of his staff, to finetune more specifically political options.

However commendable this preparation work may have been, it was not devoid of contradictions which weakened its impact. The French seemed to be torn between, on the one hand, their desire to promote continuation of the European construction and, on the other, their determination to preserve the "sovereignty" of France. Many French officials sincerely wished that the European construction, which France had largely contributed to promote and for which they felt responsible, should be continued. This "custodian" attitude actually accounts for the fears the enlargement of the Union generates in France. The French dread that this may lead to a "watering down" of European integration, as it may be impossible to continue implementing, deciding and funding common policies in a Union of 25 or 30 Member States. This was why they insisted that institutional reforms should be carried out prior to an enlargement. At the same time, the French were reluctant to strengthen the supranational institutions and procedures which an enlarged Union would actually need in order to operate smoothly. As aptly summarized by MEP Jean-Louis Bourlanges, France wants "a strong Europe" but "with weak institutions" (Jean-Louis Bourlanges 1995). Until then, the French had managed to reconcile such conflicting views through their leadership in Europe: especially with the support of the "Franco-German axis," they had been able to influence European developments according to their preferred options, particularly through assigning decision-making authority to intergovernmental bodies (Menon 1996). Today, the increase in the number of Member States together with the extension of Community powers force them to decide one way or the other: it is getting less and less realistic to advocate decision-making procedures that should be effective while remaining under national governments' control.

The positions finalized by France on the eve of the Intergovernmental Conference highlighted this contradiction. It is, for instance, quite typical that in the same paragraph of the "guidelines" defined in 1995, the French should have successively expressed support for an extension of qualified majority voting and then for the continuation of the Luxembourg Compromise achieved

---

[2] The SGCI is the administrative structure in charge of co-ordinating French position on Community matters.

by France in 1966.³ It was therefore explained that in "an enlarged Europe the existence of a consensus [rule] was often a blocking factor" and at the same time that "it was self-evident that any Member State could validly invoke a very important national interest justifying the vote should be postponed and negotiations continued" (*Le Figaro* 1996).

Similarly in the second pillar, France wanted to "give a face to the Union," and went on to explain that the current six-month term for the presidency "led to depriving the Union of the strong image it imperatively needed to assert itself on the international scene" (*Le Figaro*, 1996). The French then suggested that the European Council should designate a High Representative for the Union with a multi-annual term of office. He would have a leadership and representation role in the CFSP field and be entrusted with any other task the European Council or Council might decide. This was quite typical of the French ambiguity: calling upon a "strong" personality who would nevertheless be controlled by governments and would ideally ... be French (the name of the former President of the Republic Valéry Giscard d'Estaing was mentioned)! (Moravcsik & Nicolaïdis 1999). And yet, there was an alternative solution: giving this role to the commissioner in charge of external affairs. This would have had the advantage of bringing together the political and economic external policies of the Union and giving a clearer image of the European external policy which would then have covered not only statements made by the Fifteen under the CFSP but also decisions taken on common commercial policy or humanitarian assistance. However, the drawback of such a solution for France, as admittedly for other Member States, was that it would have given more power to a supranational institution in a field connected to "high politics."

Last, in the third pillar, according to the deputy minister for European affairs, Michel Barnier, France was "prepared to take the necessary steps forward to further enhance actions by the Fifteen against terrorism, international crime, drug trafficking, uncontrolled immigration, laundering of dirty money..." (Barnier 1996a). More specifically he argued that it was a way to meet the daily concerns of the Europeans and to increase the legitimacy of European integration. On the occasion of a debate on the Schengen Convention on 26 March 1996, before the reputed conservative *Sénat*, he even stood for some degree of "communitarisation" of the third pillar on the basis

---

³ The Luxembourg Compromise of January 1966 stipulates that "where in the case of decisions which may be taken by a majority vote on a proposal from the Commission, very important interests of one or more partners are at stake, the members of the Council will endeavour, within a reasonable time, to reach solutions which can be adopted by all the members of the Council." The compromise specifies that for the French delegation, where very important interests are at stake, the discussion "must be continued until unanimous agreement is reached."

of pragmatic reasoning: the third pillar did not work well and it was probably necessary to import some of the methods of the first pillar which "had proved their worth" such as qualified majority voting (Barnier 1996b). At the same time, however, the French "guidelines" did not consider bringing in the initiative monopoly of the Commission although it was a key element of the Community method (*Le Figaro* 1996).

Such French contradictions reflected diverging views in the political establishment itself. On European issues, the dividing line does not run between the right and the left of the political spectrum, but between proponents and opponents of the European construction within each party. This is particularly relevant for Jacques Chirac's gaullist party, the *Rassemblement Pour la République* (RPR), as clearly shown during the ratification of the Maastricht Treaty. Discussions prior to the opening of the 1996 IGC, in particular those which were held in the *Assemblée nationale*, further illustrated that split. The deputy minister for European affairs, Michel Barnier, future representative of France in the Group of Representatives, seemed favourable towards increased European integration (Barnier, 1996a). Others, however, such as the RPR member of parliament, Pierre Mazeaud, voiced a traditional fear – that Europe should lead to "complete relinquishment" of sovereignty (*Les Echos* 1996). As for Prime Minister Alain Juppé, he went on to stand up for French positions, trying at the same time to reassure some members of parliament by recalling the existence of the Luxembourg Compromise (Juppé 1996).

ICG Negotiations: Positions Which Turn Out to Be Too Incoherent, Isolated and Scattered

In the course of the IGC which was held from March 1996 to June 1997, a number of French positions remained too incoherent to carry conviction. In addition, France was often isolated, both phenomena not being completely disconnected. Hence, the French only had some success with a number of "crucial points" they stuck to through to the end of the talks.

Positions Which Were Too Incoherent
The incoherence of French positions was patent with respect to the composition of the Commission and the weighting of votes in the Council. It was, therefore, not surprising that the French did not manage to impose their views on these two issues. Some provisions relating to closer cooperation, which might erroneously lead to the belief that France was unable to act upon the course of that negotiation, were in actual fact further evidence of French ambiguity.

In accordance with the first "guidelines" already mentioned which advocated a reduction in the number of commissioners so as to "restore its full capacity of initiative and decision," France tabled a written contribution during the negotiations proposing "a Commission with 10 members, which would be raised to 12 should there be over 20 Member States." To guarantee a "principle of equality between Member States," the French also put forward a "formula for rotation between Member States" (CONF 3852/97). This position, defended by Michel Barnier in particular, revealed a genuine concern that collegial management should prevail in an institution in charge of a key mission – that of furthering the common interest from the beginning of the decision-making process. As a matter of fact, in the course of negotiations, to prove it was a real source of concern to them, French representatives did not hesitate to waive having a French commissioner in the first Commission which would be set up on such basis.

However, this proposal did not get through for several reasons. First, the other large Member States were not prepared to accept similar concessions, and the small states continued to fear that a restricted Commission would mainly include nationals from the large Member States. Above all, the suspicion in which the French simultaneously held the Commission led to some doubt about their genuine intentions. Without referring to the past, within the IGC itself, France took stands which could lead to the belief that in fact it tried to weaken the Commission. In particular, the French refused to increase its role in each of the three pillars. As we have already explained, giving the office of High Representative to one of the commissioners could have been considered. And yet, it is quite understandable that France should have refused to extend the role of the Commission in the sensitive field of foreign policy, especially as its proposal had been negatively received in other Member States.

However, French negotiators also refused to increase the powers of the Commission in one of its traditional areas of authority: the common commercial policy. With the support of a majority of Member States, the Commission actually argued in favour of an extension of its competences to services and intellectual property to meet the developments of world trade (Petite 1997). In one of its contributions to the IGC's work, France, on the contrary, tabled a new wording for former Article 113 which not only made no mention of services or intellectual property but also listed several measures intended to better control the Commission in the course of trade negotiations (CONF/3882/97).

The experience of the then Prime Minister, Alain Juppé, could explain this very firm French posture. In the course of the previous GATT negotiations, he was foreign affairs minister and had secured that his European partners would support the French request for renegotiating the Blair House agreement on farming issues. In his view, this agreement was mostly due to the Commission being poorly controlled by the Council and, after a memorable confrontation, Alain Juppé had managed to impose on the commissioner in charge of the negotiations, Leon Brittan, that he should stick to a negotiating mandate (*Le Figaro* 17 December 1993; *Le Monde* 22 September 1993; *Libération* 15 December 1993). It is now understandable why the French contribution called for a "strict respect" of the Council's Directives by the Commission (CONF/3882/97). At the end of the negotiations, Alain Juppé's resignation as Prime Minister in the wake of the socialist victory in the May 1997 elections could therefore explain the weakening of French resistance to an extension of Community powers. However, the French concession in this respect should not be overestimated. The concern of the French negotiating team was to avoid the immediate attribution of new powers to the Commission in the field of services or intellectual property and the decision as such which was finally accepted corresponded in principle to the ultimate French stand.[4]

More concisely, as we have already indicated, French representatives expressed "far-reaching ambitions" with respect to the third pillar and, more concretely, considered introducing Community procedures for more effective action. French positions actually included introducing qualified majority voting for the adoption of measures relating to the free movement of persons (visas, asylum, immigration) – on condition, however, that the decision to remove controls at internal borders would be taken unanimously. No mention, however, was made of any possible extrapolation of the proposition monopoly the Commission enjoys in the first pillar: it was merely conceded a co-initiative right shared with Member States. Finally, in the eyes of the French, the European Court of Justice could not have authority over any measure involving public law and order[5] (Chirac & Kohl 1996; CONF/3824/97; Petite 1997).

More generally, as regards the Court of Justice, the French written contribution to the work of the IGC yet again reflected the image of a country, which, whatever the discourse, was in fact reluctant to increase the powers of supranational authorities (CONF/3853/97). Consequently, the French advocated the introduction of a new article which would have enabled Member States to modify any act the Court did not interpret in accordance with their views. Contrary to what had happened for the third pillar, this proposal did not actually get through.

---

[4] Subparagraph 5 of former Article 113, subsequently 133, stipulates that "the Council, acting unanimously (…), may extend the application of paragraphs 1 to 4 to international negotiations and agreements on services and intellectual property."

[5] Article 68 of the Amsterdam Treaty gave them satisfaction in this respect.

Another example of the lack of French consistency is that of the new weighting of votes in the Council. Even though no written contribution had been submitted on the issue, it was high on the list of priorities for France and it turned out to be the stumbling block for the institutional "package" at the Amsterdam European Council. In June 1996, at the end of the Florence European Council, the President of the Republic had the opportunity to specify the position of France on this issue. For him qualified majority voting could be extended only on two conditions: the continuation of the Luxembourg Compromise and the reweighting of votes (Chirac 1996b). The French applied the following argument: in the perspective of the accession of small applicant countries from Central and Eastern Europe, the over-representation small Member States enjoy in the distribution of votes in the Council might well lead to qualified majorities which would represent only a small number of Europeans; circumstances that could undermine the legitimacy of decisions taken under such a procedure. At the same time, the French refusal of the dual majority system brought some doubt as to the sincerity of the French reasoning. According to the double majority system, a decision is actually adopted if it receives a majority of the votes in the Council while at the same time representing a majority of the inhabitants of the Union. The French emphasized the "risks of blockage" of decisions if new population criteria were applied (Chirac 1997). However, the French leaders most likely refused the system because it disrupted the parity between France and Germany, each country currently having 10 votes in the Council. It was then getting very difficult to explain to the small states that they should accept the granting of additional votes to states with a larger population than their own, and at the same time refuse to give more weight to a country with a larger population than one's own.

To get back to the link between the qualified majority and the Luxembourg Compromise as reiterated by France on many occasions, it accounts for some of the final provisions relating to closer cooperation. From the start of the IGC, France wished that in an enlarged Europe, Member States having the "capacity and willingness" to develop "closer forms of cooperation" between them should be entitled do so without having to wait for other countries (*Le Figaro* 1996). This concern was shared by Germany. In their first joint letter dated December 1995, Chirac and Kohl underlined that the "temporary difficulties of one of the partners in proceeding forward" should not "impede the action and progress potential of the Union" (Chirac & Kohl 1995). A year later, foreign affairs ministers Hervé de Charette and Klaus Kinkel drafted a joint letter devoted to the issue (de Charette & Kinkel 1996). Such positions no doubt contributed to the issue being placed on the agenda of the IGC. However, difficulties appeared when it came to defining the modalities for triggering potential, reinforced cooperation. France and Germany wished that no state could have a right of veto, while countries which might stay out of such cooperation, such as Great Britain, were favourable to unanimous decision-making. Consequently, the final provisions – triggering reinforced cooperation with a qualified majority but with a sort of Luxembourg Compromise veto – may lead one to think that France and Germany did not manage to influence the negotiations (Beach, contribution to this volume). But it could also be considered that the reassertion of the spirit of the Luxembourg compromise was satisfactory to the French. The final compromise could therefore have been approved by President Jacques Chirac and the new British Prime Minister, Tony Blair, during their meeting in Paris shortly before the Amsterdam European Council. The French President probably expressed his opposition to any form of unanimity, the "very negation" of the principle of enhanced cooperation, as he explained during the Amsterdam European Council (Chirac 1997). However, the two men agreed that the trigger mechanism for flexibility should be qualified majority with a so-called emergency brake similar to the Luxembourg Compromise. Consequently, it was not surprising that both delegations supported this wording during the final negotiation phase.

To conclude on the issue of enhanced cooperation, it should be noted that the subtraction of the second pillar from the mechanism of closer cooperation might again have been a reflection of French hesitation. According to some officials, whom we interviewed in the SGCI, French leaders would in fact have dreaded any setting up, in the context of the second pillar, of cooperation which might have eluded them or run counter to France's choices. This example clearly shows that beyond the discourse on sovereignty, the contradictions of France's European policy could also be explained by its fear of being unable to influence Community decisions. Hence the determination to preserve instruments which allow opposing decisions such as use of the veto right or reference to the Compromise of Luxembourg.

Positions Which Were Too Isolated
Not only has France not always put forward coherent positions, but it has also often found itself isolated. Germany, and the small states in particular, did not always share its views.

First, at key moments in negotiations, Germany's support was lacking. And yet, there were many Franco-German documents and meetings: the French President and the German Chancellor wrote two joint letters (Chirac & Kohl 1995; 1996), the French and the Germans presented a joint contribution to the work of the IGC on closer cooperation (CONF/3955/96), joint press conferences were held (for instance on 22 October 1996 by Michel Barnier and Mr Hoyer, or again, on 22 January 1997 by Hervé de Charette and Klaus Kinkel) and even joint articles were published (*Financial Times* 1996). According to the diplomats we interviewed, the French genuinely played the game of Franco-German "concertation" even though the lack of interministerial coordination in Germany and subsequent divergences between the Chancellery and the German foreign affairs ministry did not always make things easy. Thus, from the outset, the French could have ruled out associating with other partners, sometimes more akin to their views, so much so that some observers were subsequently quite critical (Bourlanges 1997).

All the same, on account of the content of some of their positions, in particular on institutional issues, the French did not really promote a genuine Franco-German understanding. To begin with, as already explained, France steadily opposed the dual majority system called for by Germany.

In addition, the French determination that national parliaments should play a greater role in the European decision-making process was not approved by the Germans. Germany already considered the European Parliament as a source of popular legitimacy and the increasing of its powers as the means to strengthen the democratic legitimacy of the Union. Conversely, French leaders have traditionally been hostile to the European Parliament believing that the legitimacy of the Union would be promoted by a greater involvement of the representatives of each nation. This suspicious attitude towards the European Parliament is probably due to the fact that it is a supranational institution which they feel they cannot control. The drawback was that it isolated France unreasonably. On the one hand, while it is true that Members of the European Parliament have at times expressed a degree of hostility towards France, they can equally support French positions, for instance on social issues. On the other hand, if the French feel they do not have enough influence on the work of the European Parliament, this is due to the fact that French MEPs are scattered among too many political groups and therefore do not carry enough weight within each of them (*Le Monde* 20 July 1994).

As was the case for the role of the Commission in trade negotiations, personal experience may have played a part, too. The fact that Jacques Chirac had had to present the results of the French presidency in July 1995 to the boos of MEPs up in arms against the resumption of French nuclear tests certainly did not prompt him to reappraise the traditional mistrust in which France held them. In any event, the French proposed the creation of a "high parliamentary council" which would consist of members of national parliaments and would assess the respect of the principle of subsidiarity, in particular for the third pillar (*Le Figaro* 1996).

No Franco-German position could be achieved on this proposal. In their joint letter dated 6 December 1995, Jacques Chirac and Helmut Kohl reasserted in a conventional mode the need to "strengthen the democratic anchorage of a Union which would be closer to its citizens." The subsequent proposals seemed to be the mere juxtaposition of two antagonistic views instead of the result of common thinking: the text advocated both "a closer association of the European Parliament to the responsibilities for European construction" and "a stronger involvement of national parliaments" (Chirac & Kohl 1995). A year later, in a new and more detailed letter by the two leaders, proposals relating to parliaments still appeared to present two different visions (Chirac & Kohl 1996). Actually, as soon as the IGC opened, the divergence appeared clearly: the French foreign affairs minister, Hervé de Charette, allied for the occasion with his British counterpart but contrary to his German colleague Klaus Kinkel, refused any participation of Parliament's representatives in the negotiating sessions on the grounds that it was an intergovernmental conference that is, a conference between governments (*Le Monde*, 1996c). However, Hervé de Charette could not prevent that exchanges of views regularly took place outside the formal negotiating forum.

And yet, in the Amsterdam European Council which concluded the IGC, the French President spoke in favour of an extension of the co-decision procedure which put the European Parliament on a footing with the Council of ministers. During his press conference at the end of the Amsterdam European Council, he even called this development "a major innovation which France highly values" (Chirac 1997). There could be several reasons for this new approach: first, the change of government in France brought Elisabeth Guigou to office as minister of justice, whereas she had previously been one of the European Parliament's representatives in the IGC. Confronted with her staunch claims that more power should be given to the European Parliament, the President of the Republic could have accepted the principle considering that in any event it was an issue of "secondary" importance (Moravcsik & Nicolaïdis 1999). In addition, the French President could be all the more flexible as the French had otherwise been successful on the issue of the seat of the European Parliament and, to a lesser degree, on that of national parliaments.

To get back to Franco-German "concertation," announcing a few days before the Amsterdam European Council that France wished to modify the stability pact demanded by Germany for implementation of the euro was not necessarily the best way to secure support from Germany during the final negotiations on institutional questions. In actual fact, during his election campaign for legislative elections, the future socialist Prime Minister Lionel Jospin had denounced the prevalence of monetary and financial concerns, with the stability pact as a symbol, and called for greater consideration of social issues, in particular unemployment, from those involved in the European Union. On 9 June 1997, during a Council of ministers, far from leaving such campaign talk aside, the new finance minister, Dominique Strauss-Kahn, cast some doubt as to whether France would sign the pact in the absence of compensations in the social field. While recalling that France in December 1996 had approved the pact in the Dublin European Council, the gaullist President did not really go against the demands of the new government, although of the opposite political colour, as he himself had called for "a European social model" in March 1996 (Chirac, 1996a). Finally, in the Amsterdam European Council, the French succeeded in getting a resolution on growth and employment adopted (resolution taking up the stability pact as well as a resolution on employment); it was also decided to insert a chapter on employment in the Amsterdam Treaty. For the Germans, the main objective had been met: even though the title had become "stability and growth pact," the stability pact remained unchanged and the new resolutions did not lead to any additional expenditure. All the same, they did not feel any particular urge to support the French in the last round of negotiations.

France should not be held entirely responsible for the misunderstanding between France and Germany, as evidenced by the qualified majority voting question in the context of the third pillar. Germany favoured an extension of qualified majority voting on some issues and it benefited from French support. However, in the Amsterdam European Council, Chancellor Helmut Kohl suddenly back-pedalled. He was obviously anxious to avoid a clash with the *Länder* and curb their attacks on his European policy by protecting their authority in this field (Dehousse 1997; Petite 1997). More generally, the Germans did not seem to attach as much importance as the French to institutional reform. Chancellor Kohl's priority was the implementation of the single currency which admittedly was quite a complex issue in Germany. Along with others, he may have considered that in the future there would be time to carry out an institutional reform which, in any event, did not appear in a favourable light (Moravcsik & Nicolaïdis 1999).

Not only did France not enjoy the support of Germany, but its institutional proposals triggered opposition from the small states. As had happened with Germany, France did not deliberately cut itself off from the small states. However, it underestimated the fact that its proposals required a lot of concessions on their part: the extension of qualified majority meant that in a growing number of cases they would have to give up the equal treatment offered by the unanimity procedure; in the event of a vote, a new weighting of votes would have lowered their relative weight too; last, they feared that a smaller number of commissioners would mean that commissioners from small Member States would go first (the others always managing to have a representative in the house). It should be added that this opposition from small countries was all the more likely to appear as, contrary in particular to Germany, France generally does not have enough consideration for these small states. In actual fact, regarding the question of the Commission, in the informal Noordwijk Council, in May 1997, it was Helmut Kohl who suggested a reassuring compromise for the small countries: retaining the current number of 20 commissioners (*Le Monde* 25/26 May 1997). Admittedly, it was a satisfying gesture for his foreign affairs minister, Klaus

Kinkel, who favoured keeping two German commissioners. At the same time, however, the Chancellor showed a sound understanding of the fears of the small countries, not merely for the occasion. Isolated from both its privileged partner and small countries, France finally accepted this compromise. [6]

Similarly, the French project of a High Representative for the CFSP came up against opposition both from Germany, at any rate from Klaus Kinkel, and from the small states, although for different reasons (Colloque 1998). The former feared that an excessively strong personality might overshadow the foreign affairs ministers of the Member States. The latter feared that he might deprive them of the impact the rotating presidency of the Union gave them on the international scene. In these circumstances, it was difficult for the French to go against the will of the majority of Member States – in other words against the idea that the position of High Representative should be held by a civil servant, the General Secretary of the Council.

And yet, still in the second pillar, the example of "common strategies" demonstrated that when acting together, the French and the Germans remain quite influential. Pursuant to a compromise adopted by the two countries, the Treaty set up a new instrument, the common strategy, which allowed the introduction of more qualified majority voting in a field still widely governed by unanimity (Colloque 1998; Dehousse 1999; Duke contribution to this volume).

Positions Which Were Too Scattered
Short of putting forward coherent proposals which other partners may share, an ultimate way to get the upper hand in Community negotiation is to focus on a few priorities. The drawback with such a strategy is that it necessarily means cutting down on one's claims. Again, France did not make the choices which could have produced institutional reform. At the end of the negotiations, the "hard points" in the French positions seemed to include the location of the European Parliament in Strasbourg, the situation of overseas departments (DOM) and the recognition of the French idea of a "public service" more than institutional issues. On each of these three points, the French did all they could to be successful. First, they systematically tabled specific written proposals (CONF/3902/97; CONF/3964/96; CONF/3911/96). Then they looked for allies among participants in the IGC. As regards public services, they drew support from the Commission; the French commissioners in particular took care that in the Commission's Opinion on the IGC, access of citizens to "general interest services" should be listed under the common values of all European societies (*Les Echos* 29 February 1996). For overseas

---

[6] In his press conference, Chirac talked of a proposal "that was made by Chancellor Kohl and myself," but it does not seem to be the case.

departments, the French joined with Spain and Portugal to draft a joint contribution on ultra-peripheric regions (CONF/2501/96).

Thus, it was not surprising that the French were satisfied with the outcome of these issues. A protocol of the Amsterdam Treaty took up the decision on the location of the seats of the institutions as approved in December 1992 by the Edinburgh European Council. It clearly specified that "the European Parliament shall have its seat in Strasbourg where the 12 periods of monthly plenary sessions, including the budget session, shall be held." As regards overseas departments (DOM), France, as well as Spain and Portugal achieved that the provisions of the Treaty as such, and no longer a Declaration as in the Maastricht Treaty, should acknowledge the difficult situation of some outermost regions, including the DOM. As called for by French negotiators, it is even by a qualified majority that the Council may take "specific measures" to help these regions (new Article 299 of the Amsterdam Treaty). Finally, with regard to public services, even though the provisions of the Treaty do not exactly follow the wording of their proposal, they were satisfactory to French officials (new Article 16; Chirac 1997).

In turning the institutional issue into a key issue, France also achieved that a protocol on the role of national parliaments in the European Union should be included. Admittedly, there was no longer any mention of a high parliamentary council and the protocol was limited to the recognition of the role that the Conference of European Affairs Committees (COSAC) might have. In particular, it may send contributions to the European Parliament relating to the implementation of the subsidiarity principle and the setting up of an Area of Freedom, Security and Justice. These contributions are no more binding on the European Parliament than on the national parliaments. However, considering the isolation of France on the issue, it was actually difficult to achieve anything more. Moreover, the protocol deals with the information of national parliaments. In particular, it sets a six-week delay between the day a proposal from the Commission is submitted to Council and the day it is put on the Council's agenda so that members of national parliaments have ample time to consider it.

It was also, so it would seem, on account of the insistence of the French President in the Amsterdam European Council that it was accepted that the Secretary General-High Representative and the Deputy Secretary General should be two different persons, with separate functions, the latter taking up the administrative tasks of the former (Chirac 1997). Thus, the French hoped to preserve the spirit of their proposal, in other words that the representative of the Union on the international scene should be "a personality with actual stature" (CONF/3863/96). Since then, the appointment of Mr Solana to this office has apparently met their concerns about the matter.

For the French negotiators, it was obviously impossible to devote as much time and energy to all the matters addressed and the list of this type of "gains" is inevitably limited. So the reweighting of votes, which appeared as a "hard point" for the French at the end of the negotiations, remained unsettled. Likewise, the change of government, shortly before the Amsterdam European Council, may have weakened the position of France. It resulted in drawing the attention of the French away from institutional reform. In the European Union, one cannot possibly wage war on all fronts and Lionel Jospin chose employment. As for Jacques Chirac, it was not difficult to imagine that just after this unexpected setback he simply had other things on his mind.

Another problem with this strategy is that it encourages all the delegations to do the same, each of them wanting to go back home with a "Christmas present" of their own. So, it would seem that the relatively low profile of the provisions on defence might well have been due to the intransigent attitude of Tony Blair on the issue in the Amsterdam European Council (Colloque, 1998). While the French are traditionally in favour of creating a European defence as such, the British Prime Minister, in actual fact with the agreement of the Dutch presidency, successfully opposed any provision which might have strengthened the WEU and weakened NATO (Dehousse 1999; Petite 1997). As compared with the Maastricht Treaty, the Treaty of Amsterdam even specifies that some Member States "see their common defence realised in NATO" (new Article 17).

Ratification of the Treaty of Amsterdam : Still Regrets

As we have already indicated, the result of the IGC, the Treaty of Amsterdam, was criticized in France. Afterwards, however, the ratification of the Treaty was conducted without any particular problem, especially in comparison with the ratification of the Treaty of Maastricht. It should be added that the French leaders carefully avoided holding a referendum and selected, as authorized by the French constitution, the parliamentary route.

The French constitutional revision preceding the ratification of the Treaty nevertheless gave renewed evidence of the divisions of the French Right regarding Europe and increased the power of control of the French parliament on European matters. The *Conseil constitutionnel* had in fact considered that the possibility offered by the Treaty of Amsterdam of delegating, within five years, national authority on immigration, visas and asylum demanded that the constitution should be revised. On the occasion of the insertion of a new Article in the Constitution authorizing transfers of powers with regard to the "free movement of persons" and "connected issues," some Gaullist members of parliament tried to challenge France's commitments. So, the RPR tabled an amendment subordinating the changeover to qualified majority, as made possible for such questions within five years by the Amsterdam Treaty, to the voting of a law. The former foreign affairs minister Hervé de Charette, member of a centre-right party favourable to European integration, the UDF, sharply criticized this attempt at "two step ratification" which, in any event, did not get through. (*Le Monde* 26 November 1998; 19 January 1999). On the other hand, parliament secured the possibility of voting resolutions on texts falling under the second and third pillars, while previously they could only do so on economic and monetary questions. Admittedly, such resolutions are still not binding on the government, but they generate parliamentary debates on European issues and give parliament the chance to express its views.

The ratification process itself was interesting as it showed that although it had not succeeded in Amsterdam, the declared institutional priority stated by the French representatives actually corresponded to the concerns of French political circles. In December 1997, during a debate in the *Assemblée nationale*, the opposition member of parliament, Valéry Giscard d'Estaing, former President of the Republic, suggested that the ratification of the Treaty of Amsterdam should include an article specifying that the French parliament would not approve the joining of new members until "substantial progress had been made towards the strengthening of the institutions" (*Journal officiel* 1997). The members of parliament supported the idea: the law of 23 March 1999 enabling ratification of the Treaty, as adopted by the *Assemblée nationale* and *the Sénat*, exceptionally includes a second article which expresses the "determination" of the French Republic "to witness, beyond the provisions of the treaty of Amsterdam, substantial progress towards reform of the EU institutions in order for the Union to become more democratic and more effective, before the first accession negotiations" (*Journal officiel* 1999). This is the object of the new Intergovernmental Conference which has opened in February 2000.

Has France Learnt the Lesson From Amsterdam?

The holding of this new Intergovernmental Conference offers an opportunity to examine whether France has been able to draw the lessons from Amsterdam. At first sight, it does not seem to be the case. Admittedly, according to the wishes of France, so as to make sure the questions considered are settled, this Intergovernmental Conference only addresses institutional issues. More specifically, the issues are the three "leftovers" from Amsterdam: size and composition of the Commission, weighting of votes in the Council, possible extension of qualified majority voting in the Council, and the question of closer cooperation. However, the French continued to argue in favour of a ceiling on the number of commissioners, which is still opposed by small Member States, and the weighting of votes remains a French priority which is not shared by all (La Lettre 2000).

Upon reflection, in relation to Amsterdam, the French position has somehow changed. Asking for a number of commissioners lower than the number of Member States may this time be mainly a tactical element – the idea being to prompt small Member States to accept a new weighting of votes while in return keeping their commissioner. Knowing the opposition met by the French position, the present-day deputy minister in charge of European affairs, Pierre Moscovici, publicly considered that the formula of one commissioner per country may prevail, but specified that this could not be "without compensation" (Moscovici 2000a). While increased hierarchy in the college is no doubt one such compensation, it is probably not the only one (Moscovici 2000b). Moreover, if France continues to reject the double majority voting system, it could nevertheless secure support from Germany in accepting, in the perspective of weighting of the votes, that France and Germany should be "uncoupled." By indicating, during the Franco-German summit in Mayence in June 2000, that the weighting of votes "would certainly not be a problem between us," the French President actually seemed to indicate that France could accept that Germany should hold more votes than itself (Chirac 2000; *Le Figaro* 9 June 2000; *Libération* 9 June 2000).

Thus, while France seems partly to have drawn some lessons from Amsterdam, it nevertheless has to reckon with a new element: holding the presidency during the latter semester of 2000. Although it may appear as an opportunity to act upon the course of negotiations, it entails a number of constraints. French representatives will have as a priority task to secure compromises acceptable to all rather than put forward national claims.

More generally speaking, one may wonder whether the positions of France really serve its long term interest. Such interest is actually based on lasting European integration on which it could have an impact. In this perspective, priority should be given to preserving the decision-making capacity of an enlarged Europe and consequently to limit the scope of unanimity which gives a right of veto to each Member State. Admittedly, the French say they are in favour of an extension of qualified majority. Before the *Assemblée nationale*, Pierre Moscovici considered that it was "probably the most important" of the three issues left over from Amsterdam and that qualified majority "should be recognized as the general principle for all common policies," the IGC being then limited to defining exceptions to it (Moscovici 2000a). However, as in the course of negotiations, each delegation, including the French, has in turn objections to put forward, the extension of qualified majority may well remain fairly limited in scope.

A majority decision-making process involving an increasing number of actors is obviously difficult to control. But is it really through asking for reweighting of votes, through getting a few additional votes that France might be in a position to maintain control? Would it not be better to work towards developing strategies of influence based first on conviction and on the constitution of "advocacy coalitions" rather than attempting to use power strategies requiring veto rights and Luxembourg Compromise? The former are more novel for a Member State which, so far, has managed to impose its options, and more demanding in so far as they imply acting as much upstream as possible, developing precise and convincing arguments and looking for the support of other actors. However, these strategies are much better suited to the present-day fluid type of Community decision-making (Deloche-Gaudez, 1998).

Conclusion

In conclusion, one should not go from one extreme to another. While the difficulty France had in influencing IGC negotiations cannot merely be accounted for by exogenous factors, it cannot entirely be brought back to errors of its own. In fact, a number of participants did not consider institutional reform as a priority task and in emphasizing such issues, French leaders were doomed to fail (Dehousse 1999).

Moreover, the loss of influence of France should not be exaggerated. Apart from the reweighting of votes, its demands were in fact met on the items it considered essential. With regard to the first pillar, it managed to avoid the extension of qualified majority where it did not want it; in particular, the Commission was not given any immediate authority in the field of a common trade policy; the French idea of public service has been acknowledged and the French overseas departments will be able to benefit from specific measures. As regards the second pillar, even if its impact was then uncertain, the French project of a High Representative for the CFSP was finally accepted; subsequent to the Franco-German initiative, a new instrument was created: the common strategies which introduce a limited dose of qualified majority, in keeping with French wishes. The French also secured that part of the third pillar should be transferred onto the first while avoiding a complete "communitarisation" of issues relating to the free movement of persons. Even on institutional issues, the French achieved that the European Parliament would stay in Strasbourg and got a protocol mentioning the role of national parliaments on European questions. Lastly, the Treaty does include a clause enabling closer cooperation; the conditions relative to their triggering have admittedly been "toughened" in the course of negotiations, however, this does not necessarily displease the French.

Nevertheless, it remains that especially in relation to the past, France may seem in a weaker position to influence the development of European integration as evidenced by its inability to get through an institutional reform while it had presented it as a preliminary to the enlargement of the Union. It would in fact seem that the French did not really give themselves the means to succeed on this issue. Persisting in making no clear choice between effective and government controlled institutions, while the prospect of enlargement requires a clear option in favour of a more supranational Europe, they did not have enough credibility. In a Union which already has a large number of actors, on whom it is more and more difficult to impose one's views, it is on the contrary essential to be able to convince and draw support on the basis of consistent arguments. The French would be more influential if they accepted unambiguously to give up a set form of control of the European decision-making process.

Bibliography

Unless otherwise indicated, statements by French leaders (including Franco-German documents) can be accessed through the data base available on the foreign affairs ministry's site (http://www.doc.diplomatie.fr/BASIS/epic/www/doc/SF).

Barnier, Michel (1996a). Débat à l'Assemblée nationale sur la CIG. Discours du ministre délégué aux affaires européenne, M. Michel Barnier. Déclaration du gouvernement, Paris, 13 Mars.

Barnier, Michel (1996b). Convention Schengen – Intervention du ministre délégué aux affaires européennes, M. Michel Barnier au Sénat, 26 March.

Bourlanges, Jean-Louis (1995). "La redoutable contradiction française." *Le Figaro*, 26 June.

Bourlanges, Jean-Louis (1997). "Les trois erreurs d'Amsterdam," *Libération*, 3-4 August.

de Charette, Hervé & Klaus Kinkel (1996). Lettre conjointe du ministre des affaires étrangères, M. Hervé de Charette et du ministre allemand des affaires étrangères, M. Klaus Kinkel, adressée au président du Conseil des ministre des l'Union européenne, M. Dick Spring, 17 October.

Chirac, Jacques (1996a). "Pour un modèle social européen," *Libération*, 25 March.

Chirac, Jacques (1996b). Conseil européen de Florence. Conférence de presse du président de la République, M. Jacques Chirac, 22 June.

Chirac, Jacques (1997). Conseil européen. Point de presse conjoint du Président de la République, M. Jacques Chirac, et du premier ministre, M. Lionel Jospin, 18 June.

Chirac, Jacques (2000). Conseil franco-allemand de défense et de sécurité. Conférence de presse conjointe du Président de la République, M. Jacques Chirac, du premier ministre, M. Lionel Jospin, et du chancelier allemand, M. Gerhard Schroeder, 09 June.

Chirac, Jacques & Helmut Kohl (1995). "Lettre commune du Président de la République, M. Jacques Chirac, et du Chancelier de la République fédérale d'Allemagne, M. Helmut Kohl, au président de l'Union européenne, M. Felipe Gonzalez," 06 December.

Chirac, Jacques & Helmut Kohl (1996). Sommet franco-allemand de Nuremberg. Lettre commune du président de la République, M. Jacques Chirac, et du chancelier allemand, M. Helmut Kohl, au président de Conseil européen, M. John Bruton, 09 December.

Colloque sur le traité d'Amsterdam (1998). *Réalités et perspectives*, Paris, La Sorbonne, 27-28 February.

Dehousse, Franklin (1997). "Les résultats de la Conférence intergouvernementale," *Courrier hebdomadaire*, Centre de recherche et d'information socio-politiques, n° 1565-1566.

Dehousse, Franklin (1999). *The making of a Treaty*, London: Kogan Page.

Deloche-Gaudez, Florence (1998). *La politique de la Communauté européenne à l'égard des pays d'Europe centrale et orientale de juin 1988 à juin 1993. Une réflexion sur le caractère pluraliste de la construction européenne*, Thèse de doctorat, Paris: Institut d'Etudes Politiques de Paris.

Financial Times (1996). "Europa – Klaus Kinkel and Hervé de Charrette. A duty to be demanding." *Financial Times*, 29 March.

Journal officiel (1997). "Compte rendu intégral de la séance du mardi 2 décembre 1997," *Journal Officiel* (Débats parlementaires – Assemblée nationale) n° 86, 2 December, p. 6761.

Journal officiel (1999). "Loi n° 99-229 du 23 mars 1999 autorisant la ratification du traité d'Amsterdam," *Journal Officiel* (Lois et Décrets) n° 71, 25 March, p. 4463.

Juppé, Alain (1996). Débat à l'Assemblée nationale sur le CIG. Discours du premier ministre, M. Alain Juppé, 13 March.

La Lettre (2000). La lettre du gouvernement du 24 février 2000 (disponible sur le site http://www.diplomatie.fr/europe/politique/fiches/lettregvt.html).

La Serre, Françoise (de) & Christian Lequesne (eds.) (1998). *Quelle Union pour quelle Europe?* Editions Complexe.

Le Figaro (1996). "Le texte confidentiel qui fixe les grandes orientations de la France pour la conférence intergouvernementale de 1996," *Le Figaro*, 20 February.

Le Figaro (1997). "Le casse-tête institutionnel reste entier," *Le Figaro*, 2 October.

Le Monde (1996a). "Michel Barnier a été chargé, pour la France, du suivi des négociations sur les institutions européennes," *Le Monde*, 7 February.

Le Monde (1996b). "Les principaux points de la position française," *Le Monde*, 21 February.

Le Monde (1996c). "Paris et Bonn s'opposent sur les modalités de la conférence intergouvernementale de Turin qui s'ouvrira le 29 mars," *Le Monde*, 12 March.

Le Monde (1997). "Echec des Quinze au sommet d'Amsterdam sur le réforme des institutions européennes," *Le Monde*, 19 June.

Les Echos (1995). "CIG: la France favorable à une extension des votes à la majorité qualifiée," *Les Echos*, 6 December.

Les Echos (1996). "La majorité gênée par la remontée des anti-Maastricht au sein du RPR," *Les Echos*, 14 March.

Menon, Anand (1996). "France and the IGC of 1996," *Journal of European Public Policy*, June, p. 231-252.

Moravcsik, Andrew & Kalypso Nicolaïdis (1999). "Explaining the Treaty of Amsterdam: Interests, Influence, Institutions," *Journal of Common Market Studies*, Vol. 37, No. 1, p. 59-85.

Moscovici, Pierre (2000a). Forum sur les priorités de la présidence française de l'Union européenne. Intervention du ministre délégué chargé des affaires européennes, M. Pierre Moscovici, 28 March.

Moscovici, Pierre (2000b). Discours du ministre délégué chargé des affaires européennes, M. Pierre Moscovici, devant le Conseil économique et social, 28 June.

Petite, Michel (1997). "Le traité d'Amsterdam: ambition et réalisme," *Revue du marché Unique Européen*, Vol. 3, p. 17-52.

8

Greece: The Difficult Road from Orthodoxy to Neo-Orthodoxy

Constantine A. Papadopoulos[1]

Introduction

Greece came to the negotiating table at the 1996 IGC with a relatively ambitious set of goals: *first*, to help achieve positive and equitable results with respect to the objectives which compelled the Maastricht Treaty negotiators to include a specific commitment to the convening of a new IGC in 1996, *viz.*, the need to introduce institutional and other reforms, especially in view of the Union's future enlargement to the East and South, and to clarify the state of play with respect to European security and defence; *second*, to support and encourage reforms in the direction of greater democratic legitimacy and accountability of the Union, as well as a stronger social character, all with a view to bringing it closer to the citizen; and, *third*, to promote certain issues closer to Greece's specific national interests which nonetheless had a strong pro-"European" character, particularly in the areas of foreign policy, defence, the "new" policies, and others.

A common theme underlying Greece's positions was a general belief in the virtues of European integration, and the benefits that can be derived from a strengthening of the supra-national, "communitarian," features of the European construct.

The Policy-Making Process and Elaboration of Positions

The Greek delegation's positions at the IGC were the outcome of a multi-layered process of policy-elaboration and policy-making. This process involved not only formal and "active" procedures (preparation of position papers, consultation between the Foreign Ministry and other government departments and non-governmental organisations, debates in Parliament both at plenary and committee level), but also wider informal and "passive" elements, *viz.* of a historical, geostrategic and cultural nature. However,

---

[1] The views expressed in this chapter are the author's alone and do not necessarily reflect the views of the Hellenic Ministry of Foreign Affairs or EFG Eurobank.

ultimate responsibility for the negotiations lay with the Foreign Ministry, its political leadership and the latter's representatives.

At the most macroscopic level, Greece's positions were, and are, influenced by its geostrategic position in southeastern Europe. In this sense, Greece occupies a unique position among the Union's fifteen Member States, being not only the sole Member State without a common border with any other Member State, but also located in the most turbulent corner of the continent. This, of course, has a fundamental impact on how Greece perceives the questions of: security and defence; solidarity among Member States, both political and economic; the EU construct's cohesion, robustness and resilience, especially in view of the buffeting it may experience from the outside (migratory waves, instability on its borders, enlargement itself). This is particularly relevant when compared with Member States that not only are more prosperous, but also, for mainly geographical reasons, view the EU – at least in recent years – primarily as an economic proposition, linked above all to their prosperity, rather than as intimately linked to their political and economic security, as Greece does.

The Greek stance was, and is, also influenced by her historical experiences with EC/EU membership since 1981. These consist of a history of relations now ambivalent and tense, now close and constructive, which were due to changes in government and changes in party philosophy (where Pasok is concerned), experiences whose overall balance is now deemed unambiguously positive by both main political parties. This is mentioned in order to substantiate the view that the Greek stance would not have been significantly different, if at all, had the party in power during the negotiations been New Democracy, rather than Pasok. The domestic political implications of European integration are no longer considered deep enough in Greece to justify a "Left" *vs.* "Right" approach, neither to the general direction nor to the specifics of European integration between the two main political parties in Greece. This phenomenon is likely to be reinforced by the broader tendency to convergence between "Left" and "Right" ideology in domestic European politics. In sum, throughout the nineties both main political parties on the whole supported the principle of greater integration in a "communitarian" direction. By derogation to this general principle, however, they did on occasion entertain reservations in connection with specific issues perceived to have an asymmetrical importance for Greece. These issues, whether economic, institutional, or foreign-policy-related, required special attention within the workings of an organisation which, by common consent of its members, in principle tended to attach greater priority to the interests of the whole (however defined) than to those of its parts.[2] Greece's slow progress in meeting the Maastricht EMU convergence criteria in the mid-nineties also amplified this latter effect, creating, as it did, a sense of insecurity whenever proposals were forthcoming that were perceived as capable of leaving Greece out of the future running (see below the section on "flexibility").

At a narrower level, Greece's positions were influenced by the historical conjecture in which the IGC took place. This included such factors as the disaffection with European integration observed among large sections of Europe's public opinions (and to a lesser extent perhaps also in Greece); the loss of inspiration of the Paris-Bonn axis; the deliberately low-profile role of the Santer European Commission; the emerging tendency, rooted in fears of the possible consequences of the future enlargement, of Member States wishing to aim at, above all, the preservation, protection or even strengthening of their national prerogatives, specificities and privileges at the forthcoming IGC, rather than to promote grand visions; and the emergence of a potential new divide between large and small Member States, prompted by institutional proposals put forward by some Member States in the name of "efficiency" in view of enlargement. Given this particular climate, Greece, through her positions at the IGC, could claim to be upholding traditional pro-European values and policy approaches, even as some Member States were gradually transforming the way the latter would henceforth have to be interpreted and understood.

Finally, the country's representatives to the IGC process (which included the deliberations of the Reflection Group, a Greek initiative proposed during the Greek Presidency in the first half of 1994), each brought their own sensitivities, knowledge and experience to the day-to-day proceedings of the IGC, thus colouring Greece's stance on a number of issues that emerged in the course of the negotiations.[3]

---

[2] This statement makes a dinstinction between the "whole" and the "parts," not between "large" and "small," or "more" and "less" influential states. To this extent, it is not inconsistent with the other view which regards supranational structures as more protective of the interests of *small* countries than is the case in classical international organisations.

[3] Greece was represented by three consecutive negotiators during the IGC "process." Ambassador (ret.) Stephanos Stathatos was in charge throughout the deliberations of the Reflection Group. The late Yiannos Kranidiotis, at the time MEP, represented Greece at the IGC from March 1996 until January 1997. The MFA's Secretary-General for European Affairs Stelios Perrakis led the team from January 1997 to the end of the negotiations in June 1997. In addition to their wide experience, they each brought specific expertise on matters of foreign policy and defence, institutional issues, and fundamental and social rights. Overall responsibility for the negotiations in the closing months of the IGC was in the hands of the (then) Alternate Minister of Foreign Affairs

The Five Main Chapters of the Negotiations

The Union and the Citizen

One of the main challenges facing European governments was to regain the confidence of citizens and to encourage their support for European integration and its institutions.

In this context, Greece set as one of its main goals the development of "Citizen's Europe and the Social Area," by means of specific policies and actions, with a view to addressing Europe's social problems, including unemployment, social and economic cohesion and real convergence.

Employment
The position Greece took on the issue of whether or not to include a new chapter ("Title") on Employment classed her from early on among the most supportive of new provisions on employment. This position was primarily motivated by the perceived need to redress the balance in the treaty between monetary goals (EMU) and economic goals of direct concern and relevance to the citizen. It was not the result of a serious national unemployment problem – at the time, the unemployment rate was still below the EU average. The primary motivation was one of principle, based on the need to bolster the goals of growth, cohesion, high employment and social protection – notwithstanding that for Greece an ambitious EC employment policy risked shifting attention from the support of regions lagging behind in development, of which policies the country is a prime beneficiary, to regions suffering from unemployment, which is a different proposition and likely to benefit other countries more. For their part, the government's economic policy-makers initially expressed doubts as to whether the setting of ambitious goals in the area of employment would be entirely reconcilable with efforts to meet the Maastricht convergence criteria then under way, or with efforts to introduce, with sufficient smoothness, the necessary reforms in Greece's relatively rigid labour laws.

In the end, the fact that the new provisions on employment were to be linked to, and consistent with, the general economic guidelines, rather than become a part of social policy or, indeed, structural/regional policy, and the fact that the related surveillance mechanism would not be too intrusive, leaving prime responsibility of the issue in the hands of national governments, left all quarters in the government entirely satisfied with the end result.

(now Foreign Minister) George Papandreou.

Social Policy
As mentioned already, Greece was a fervent supporter of proposals to reinforce the EU's "social" character. Thus, it was in favour of the new legal bases for the promotion of equality of opportunity and treatment of men and women at work, as well as for the fight against social exclusion. At this point, it should be mentioned that, in Greece, not only non-governmental organisations active in the field, but also the government itself relies to a considerable extent on the additional discipline imposed by EC regulations and the EC enforcement system in order to see social, environmental and other policies actually implemented, as opposed to simply enacted.[4]

Greece also supported enriching the objectives of social policy through an explicit reference to fundamental social rights, which is now also part of the main body of the treaty. This was achieved thanks to the U.K.'s rescinding its opt-out from the Social Protocol, thus also allowing a lifting of the Union's hitherto observed reluctance to make full use of its provisions.

Environment
The inclusion of the notion of "sustainable development" as one of the main objectives of the Union; the integration of environmental protection in all sectoral policies; and the balance achieved between the needs of the Single Market and those regarding the environment in the framework of the new article 100 A.4, were all deemed a net gain for the Union and were therefore supported by the Greek delegation.

Public Health and Consumer Protection
Likewise, Greece endorsed the amplified and improved articles in the above two areas.

Other Community Policies
Greece was unsuccessful in promoting the adoption of a new Title on Tourism, even though this had explicitly been mentioned as a possibility in the Treaty on European Union.[5] Notwithstanding the risk that an EU-wide policy

---

[4] Some aspects of Greek environmental policy (*e.g.*, rubbish dumps) are decentralised to local government. The latter on certain occasions has obstructed implementation of the rules. In the first case of a Member State being ordered to pay a fine for failing to comply with a Court order, the Greek government, on 4 July 2000, was ordered to pay a 20,000 euro fine per day for failing to halt the discharge of dangerous waste into a river in Crete. The failure was due to the local municipality's opposition to the location of new waste-disposal facilities. Hopefully, government pressure resulting from the size of the fine will lead eventually to the lifting of local objections.

[5] The Greek memorandum did not speak of a transfer of competences to the Community, but rather of a coordinating and facilitating role, respecting subsidiarity.

on tourism might increase costs at the national level, *e.g.*, through the imposition of higher, harmonised standards, particularly among smaller hoteliers (the prospect of additional Community funds for the Greek tourist industry had been discounted in view of the prevailing budgetary climate), it was felt that bringing tourism within the competences of the Community was "good" European policy. In particular, it was seen as encouraging Community action to promote competitiveness, employment and stronger cultural links in an area of great and growing economic and cultural importance across Europe, hitherto largely, and surprisingly, ignored by the Community.[6] Furthermore, these initiatives were backed by certain professional organisations that were keen to see the introduction of a degree of planning and coordination in Greek tourist policy *via* the European route, given that their petitions (so they claimed) with the government were going essentially unanswered.

Likewise, Greece was unsuccessful in her efforts to introduce new articles on civil defence and energy. In the former case, such an article would have provided for an assistance mechanism for Member States hit by natural or man-made disasters, as well as acted as an expression of solidarity between Member States, a visible way for the Union to come closer to its citizens.[7] In the case of energy, a new article would have stressed such notions as "security of supplies," energy conservation, the use of renewable sources of energy, as well as associated energy with the goals of cohesion and protection of the environment. These proposals fell foul of the prevailing climate which on the whole was averse to extending Community competences, in particular through the introduction of new legal bases.

Like most Member States, Greece was in favour of new provisions to counter fraud affecting the financial interests of the Community, provided this did not run counter to the primacy of national criminal law and the national administration of justice, concerns reflected in the article eventually adopted.

On the question of outlying regions, Greece ultimately had to concur with *demandeurs* France, Spain and Portugal, if only for the sake of consistency, given her demands for a strengthening of the central article on cohesion (article 130a) through inclusion of an explicit reference to the islands.[8] In this, Greece obtained satisfaction, thus gaining some assurance that the problems

---

[6] To take one statistic, the tourist industry's contribution to EU GDP is three times larger than agriculture's.

[7] Today, Community action is limited to assisting, on an *ad hoc* basis, in the coordination of the interventions of national civil protection teams.

[8] Greece submitted a memorandum to the conference dated 22 May 1996.

of these very fragile regions would not be ignored, were a major overhaul of regional policy to be contemplated some time in the future[9].

On the question of public services, Greece concurred with the proposals emanating from the Commission, the Parliament and France. The Greek delegation judged the new article to be supportive of the goals of social and territorial cohesion in the Member States, as well as germane to government notions of the proper role of government in the case of market failure (to take one example, the provision of basic public services to isolated and sparsely populated islands lying on the periphery of the country).

Greece also submitted memoranda on "Youth" and "Culture" (with a view, in the latter case, to enshrining the principle of the "cultural equality" of Member States, which should be taken into account in the elaboration of the Union's policies). Neither of them was retained by the Conference.

European Citizenship
On this score, it proved difficult to agree to new rights or to a widening of existing ones. This was due mainly to the fact that the relevant discussions were overshadowed by the corresponding discussions on fundamental rights, which applied to *all* individuals, and not just European citizens.

Subsidiarity
On the question of subsidiarity, Greece felt that the issue had been exhausted at Maastricht and the subsequent summits at Birmingham and Edinburgh. A new debate on the subject invited the prospect of a reopening of the discussion on the scope of future, as well as current, Community competences, if not at the IGC itself, at least at some point down the road, with the lead being taken by Member States favouring their curtailment. To this prospect, Greece was averse, ever fearful of a "repatriation of competences" to the capitals, particularly, though not exclusively, in the spheres of regional and agricultural policy. In the event, the lead was taken by countries, such as Germany and Austria, with strong regional/provincial constituencies that presumably sought a reinforcement of their presence and role in EU legal texts. Eventually, this issue – internal to Member States, and therefore *a priori* outside the scope of the IGC's remit – gave its place to a codification of earlier notions about the respective roles of the Community and Member States; in the process, subsidiarity gained the status of an unambiguous legal concept. Given Greece's general confidence in the system of EC law, this posed no particular problems in principle.

---

[9] A new Declaration was also annexed to the revised treaty, acknowledging the special status of island regions, and providing also for the possibility of special measures being taken in their favour.

Transparency

As the issue of transparency was connected to the broader one of how to associate the citizen more closely with the work of the Union's institutions, Greece was generally favourable to new provisions in this direction, especially if they did not compromise the effectiveness of negotiations within the institutions. In the event, the new provisions on transparency limited themselves essentially to the right to access to documents of the Parliament, the Council and the Commission. An added gain was the new provision giving citizens the right to a reply in their own language to letters addressed to the institutions and bodies of the EU. Presumably, this would also act as a bulwark against possible future attempts to limit the number of official languages.

The Quality of Community Legislation and the Simplification and Codification of the Treaties

Greece went along with the mainstream, not having any serious problems with the current state of affairs. Therefore, it was willing to accept any proposal which made the EU's work on the whole more accessible to the citizen.

Freedom, Security and Justice

As one of the most discussed chapters during the Conference, this subject drew its importance from a perception that citizens were demanding more and better action from their governments and the Union in response to the fallout from the growing internationalisation of migratory flows and modern forms of criminal activity, and the uncertainties and insecurity generated by the latter. However, there was a strong sense that a beefed-up security chapter would require, as a counterpoint, a greater preoccupation with the questions of freedom and fundamental rights. This was very much the Greek government's position too.

Fundamental Rights and Non-Discrimination

Greece's preferred approach was for Member States to inscribe a full catalogue of Fundamental Rights in the opening chapters of the Treaty itself. This was basically a matter of principle, deriving from Greece's desire to consolidate a conception of the European Union as a real union of democratic states. Such a conception required a charter commensurate with its ambitions and history.[10] However, given the complexities inherent in such an enterprise,

---

[10] Although this option was not retained by the conference, it was subsequently brought back into the debate. A new charter of fundamental rights is already being negotiated

a second-best solution would have been to see the EU becoming a party to the European Convention on Human Rights. However, even this posed difficulties for many Member States, whereupon Greece settled for the, admittedly astute, compromise solution, proposed by the Irish Presidency, consisting in rendering explicit the Court's competence to pronounce on Community (as distinct from EU) action possibly impinging on matters falling under the ambit of the European Convention.

A matter in which Greece expressed reservations long into the negotiations was that of a sanctions mechanism against Member States that failed to respect fundamental rights. The reasoning behind this position was relatively simple. While it was never made very explicit, the rationale for such a mechanism was the alleged risk of infractions in one or more of the *future* Member States. Greece considered that the mere existence of an *ex post facto* sanctions mechanism held the danger of incumbent Member States unconsciously relaxing the criteria by which applicant countries' candidacies would be judged – when what really was required by the applicants was incontrovertible *ex ante* evidence that they were in a position to guarantee, now and *ad finem*, the highest degree of protection of fundamental rights and democratic freedoms. Still, as Greece found herself almost alone in holding this position, and being unable to argue convincingly that it was *inconceivable* that any Member State, future *or* present, would ever breach the rules, it went along with the relatively mild sanctions regime finally adopted.

Greece supported a general clause on non-discrimination based on sex, racial or ethnic origin, religion or belief, disability, age or sexual orientation. Less satisfactory, from Greece's point of view, was the fact that the ensuing article had no direct effect, allowing only for secondary legislation, which furthermore required unanimity and only simple consultation with the European Parliament. The main reason why countries were reluctant to be more malleable/accommodating was the fact that a rigorous pursuit of these goals, in particular with regard to disability or age, could open a Pandora's box of social-policy measures entailing, for their successful application, prohibitive economic and/or fiscal costs.

Finally, Greece achieved a notable success in the speedy acceptance, by the conference, of the contents of its memorandum on the protection of individuals with regard to the processing and free movement of personal data, and the inclusion of a new article to that effect providing for a new independent supervisory body for monitoring the application of new Community acts on the matter.

---

for adoption in view of the next revision of the treaties.

Progressive Establishment of an Area of Freedom, Security and Justice
Greece is the main southeastern gateway into the EU. It is the only Member State sharing borders solely with non-EU states; it has an extensive coastline difficult to police (a frequent destination of illegal migrants, and often the site of actual engagements between the Coast Guard and foreign criminal mobs); and it plays host to a very substantial number of economic immigrants.[11] As such, Greece has a strong vested interest in an effective coordination of policies at EU-level, irrespective of the fact that the main burden for effective action lies, and will continue to lie, with the national authorities.[12] An equally strong motive was the desire to see more effective action at the EU's *external* borders. This had both direct appeal, insofar as Greece stood to gain from any eventual sharing of technical expertise and application of common standards, and indirect appeal, in the sense of reinforcing the notion of EU interest and involvement in the common external borders, something which hopefully would reverberate positively also in the discussions on the future shape of CFSP.

Disappointment with the results of the policies based on the Maastricht Treaty's Third Pillar led Greece to support proposals for the substantial communitarisation of the Third Pillar, and the incorporation of the Schengen *acquis* into the Treaty. Despite a certain reticence, initially, regarding the acceptability of QMV, especially in matters of penal and police cooperation, Greece became a supporter of majority voting even under the revised Third Pillar. (In the First Pillar, QMV posed no particular problems, and was in harmony with Greece's general philosophy regarding "Community" matters.) This was deemed necessary, not only to enhance the effectiveness of decision-making, but also to weaken the general case for a "flexibility" clause. (The possibility of a national veto could prompt the other 14 to resort to a "flexible" approach, if such an approach were allowed by the new treaty, thus entirely bypassing the dissatisfied Member State.)

Given the unexpectedly successful results of the Conference in the area of Freedom, Security and Justice, the Greek delegation could well claim to have achieved the great majority of its aims in this area.

---

[11] Reliable figures are hard to come by. An attempt, in 1998, to issue provisional work permits to illegal immigrants produced 370,000 applications. Estimates, therefore, range from 400,000 to double that figure, *i.e.*, between 3.8 and 7.6 per cent of the total population of 10.5 million. This includes both legal and illegal immigrants.

[12] It is the internationalisation of criminal activities that brings about the need for more coordination between national police and judicial authorities. In an area without borders, the perpetrators of criminal acts often find it easier to escape the arm of the law than those agents, who are entrusted with the role of enforcing it, find it possible to extend its actual reach.

An Effective and Coherent External Policy

Common Foreign and Security Policy
Greece attached great importance to a strengthening of the EU's Common Foreign and Security Policy, both for reasons of European principle, and for reasons of national security. In its Memorandum, submitted to partners and EU institutions in January 1996,[13] the Greek government emphasised that "the EU needs more means and better-defined goals in order to face with effect the new situation that has emerged on our continent, and beyond, after the end of the Cold War."[14]

The Greek government was of the view that the success or failure of the CFSP depended first and foremost on the willingness of countries to cooperate, to arrive at common positions and to pursue common actions, *i.e.* on the political will to *make use* of the treaty provisions already in place. Moreover, it noted that in some important cases of common interest (Bosnia-Herzegovina, Turkey), certain Member States had not availed themselves of the scope afforded by the CFSP, and on several occasions had acted in concert outside the Union's framework, in *ad hoc* "contact groups," leaving other EU members without an effective voice.

However, institutional arrangements and treaty language could also make a difference, it was felt. Thus, the broad Greek position during the IGC could be described as revolving around three main themes, which combined the two abovementioned elements (*viz.*, political will and accommodating institutions):

(a) the need for a clarification of general principles and goals with a view to a gradual framing of common fundamental interests[15];
(b) the development of practical measures of an institutional and procedural character contributing, among others, to a greater "communitarisation" of the current CFSP framework (endowing the EU with a legal personality; better coordination between CFSP and the Commission's

---

[13] Ministry of Foreign Affairs, *Toward a Democratic European Union with Political and Social Content*, Athens 1996.

[14] *Ibid.*, p. 26.

[15] Contributing to conflict-prevention and stability, especially in the countries of Central and Eastern Europe, the Balkans and the Mediterranean basin; the peaceful resolution of differences; the respect of international law; the promotion of human rights and democratic freedoms, are some of the principles that should be embodied in the revised treaty.

external relations departments; a more active consultative role for the European Parliament; possibly a role for the Court of Justice); and

(c) the affirmation of common values, to be expressed in the new treaty by way of an explicit recognition of the solidarity existing between Member States, and a mutual commitment to protect the territorial integrity and external borders of the Union.

Like other Member States, Greece had to make an evaluation of the Union's CFSP as conducted since the entry into force of the Maastricht Treaty, an exercise inevitably permeated by the Yugoslavian experience. However, unlike the other Member States, Greece also faced security problems that were entirely specific to her.

To fully understand the Greek position with respect to the common foreign, security and defence policy at the IGC, a little background history is necessary.

Greece's Insecure External Borders

Greece is in an entirely unique position among EU Member States. It is the only country whose internationally recognised borders are contested by a neighbouring country, *viz.*, Turkey, a NATO ally. This dispute has followed a path of escalation. It has its origins in Turkey's ceding, in 1973, large areas of the Aegean Sea for petroleum exploration and exploitation. In so doing, Turkey in effect challenged the right of Greek islands to a continental shelf, as provided for by the Law of the Sea.[16] The following year, and quick on the heels of her successful military operation in Cyprus, Turkey, *via* a NOTAM, demanded that all flights east of a North-South line running through the centre of the Aegean Sea be subjected to the control of Turkish civil aviation authorities (to which the Greek government responded by closing, for

---

[16] In November 1973 the Turkish government formally ceded to the (Turkish) State Petroleum Company large tracts of the Aegean Sea for exploitation. These areas encircled Greek islands in the eastern Aegean and included parts of the Greek continental shelf. Despite Greek remonstrations, Turkey proceeded to expand the areas covered by the concessions. Greece claims that islands are entitled to their own continental shelf, according to the 1958 Geneva Convention which constitutes a codification of customary law; therefore Turkey's non-signing of the convention (and the subsequent Treaty on the Law of the Sea signed on 10 December 1982) does not diminish the validity of its rules. Consequently, the dividing line should be the median line between the islands and the Asia Minor coast (not the median line between the Greek mainland and the Asia Minor land mass, which would divide the Aegean in two, as argued by Turkey).

security reasons, all air corridors between Greece and Turkey).[17] In January 1975 Turkey, invoking the Chicago Convention, announced the non-recognition of Greece's ten-mile airspace, arguing that this is inconsistent with territorial waters of 6 nautical miles, as is the case in Greece, and therefore illegal under international law – notwithstanding (a) that for the preceding forty-four years Turkey had accepted without any objections this state of affairs, which is based on a Greek law dating from 1931, and (b) that Greece voluntarily has refrained from using its right, established in the 1982 Treaty on the Law of the Sea, to extend her territorial waters to 12 nautical miles. In fact, Turkey has announced that an extension of Greek territorial waters in the Aegean Sea from 6 to 12 n.m. would be considered a *casus belli*. Following the Imia/Kardak incident in January 1996 in the Dodecanese (southeastern Aegean Sea),[18] Turkey began enunciating claims about the alleged "undetermined" status of an unspecified, but large (possibly around 150), number of Aegean isles and islets, most but not all uninhabited, disputing some of the reach of the international agreement of 1947 by which Italy ceded the Dodecanese to Greece (annexed by Italy from Turkey in 1912).[19]

To this day, the Turkish aim behind proposals for a Greek-Turkish dialogue to resolve "pending" bilateral issues is the redefinition of the *status quo* in the Aegean. Greece replies that it is inconceivable to embark on discussions on the subject of her sovereign rights – with the exception of the continental shelf issue, which is a proper matter for bilateral negotiations and, eventually, adjudication by the International Court of Justice. To this suggestion, Turkey has not yet responded positively, as it considers *all* "outstanding" issues (Cyprus is not considered one by Turkey in this context) as not only eligible for bilateral negotiations, but also capable of resolution in the form of a "package deal."

Greece's Efforts to "Re-invent" the WEU's Article V
This state of affairs largely explains why Greece was the only country at the IGC to pursue the insertion, in the new treaty, of an article on the

---

[17] The Turkish NOTAM was rescinded in 1980. This change of heart did not extend, however, to the claims themselves, *viz.*, that, for security reasons, the area of responsibility of the Istanbul FIR should cover the whole eastern half of the Aegean.

[18] At the end of January 1996, a Turkish commando landed for a few hours on an adjacent island, forcing the Greek Navy to set sail for the region. The crisis was defused following Washington's intervention in both Athens and Ankara.

[19] Turkey recognised Italian sovereignty over the Dodecanese only years later, when it signed the Treaty of Lausanne on 24 July 1923. However, since 1996 Turkey has claimed that because earlier agreements did not mention by name every single islet and rock of the Dodecanese, their present status is "ambiguous."

"inviolability" of the EU's external borders, backed by a "solidarity and mutual assistance clause."

The argument was couched in open "European" terms, but also with complete regard for transatlantic links: an explicit defence role for the EU would respond to the logic of Maastricht; by allowing better coordination between the various instruments of crisis management (political, economic, humanitarian, as well as military) available for effective action by the Union in crisis situations, it would lend credibility to the CFSP; and, last but not least, it would reflect real solidarity amongst Europeans, hitherto essentially confined to the economic sphere.[20]

The Greek initiative, first formulated in the Reflection Group, was acknowledged in the group's final report, but only after persistent efforts on the part of the Greek representative, who faced considerable resistance owing to Greece's isolation on the matter.[21] The same line was pursued later at the IGC itself, and a memorandum to this effect was submitted to the conference on 6 June 1996.

Other Member States with a similar interest in enhancing the EU's security and defence dimension argued that the issue of territorial defence should be examined in the context of the future status of EU-WEU relations. But for Greece, this bypassed the crux of the matter: six months prior to completing negotiations to join the WEU as a full member (in November 1992), Greece saw the WEU (at Petersberg in June 1992) change its "constitution" and abrogate its mutual defence commitments in the special case of a dispute between a full member (*e.g.*, Greece) and an associate member (*e.g.*, Turkey). Of course, from a political point of view, this was the price to pay for the decision taken in the early nineties to make full WEU membership available only to EU NATO members (rather than, as the British, Dutch and others had hoped, to all European countries of NATO). From a technical point of view, this was required to maintain consistency with the relationships binding

---

[20] In the case of Greece, a common defence at EU level would enable the government to reduce military expenditures – in *per capita* terms, the highest among the European allies – and therefore prove an economic boon as well. This would be seen also to reinforce the Union's goals on cohesion (given that, indirectly, lower military expenditures would imply a higher developmental impact for incoming Community structural and cohesion funds).

[21] The report contained the following (generous) reference: "In this context, the idea that the IGC examines the possibility of including in the revised Treaty a provision on mutual assistance for the defence of the external borders of the Union has been put forward by some members." This statement was included in the first section of the report, which was more in the nature of a "political" statement from the Group as a whole, rather than the second section whose purpose was to list, without much comment, the views of members. Only the European Parliament held similar views.

Greece 175

countries within NATO (NATO membership being, of course, a prerequisite for full and associate WEU membership). And NATO was not about to change its fundamental character: nearly ten years earlier, Greece had proposed to her NATO allies that the Alliance assume formal responsibilities in the area of dispute-resolution involving two NATO allies, a proposal that the NATO countries turned down without any discussion.

Greece's efforts to "re-invent" article V and involve the EU *per se* in the subject of territorial-defence commitments without proper regard to the actual state of the negotiations concerning the future status of the WEU – a European organisation that had already been entrusted with this vital task, and to which, tellingly, only two out of three EU members belonged – were somewhat unrealistic. The future outlook for the WEU (the Brussels Treaty would expire in 1998 anyway) could in theory, of course, include its formal dissolution, the incorporation of its objectives, tasks and organisational structure into the EU, and a renegotiation of its commitments *vis-à-vis* both full and associate members (including special arrangements for EU members averse to sharing Article V obligations). However, given the whole history of the post-war period in the area of defence – on which Turkey's relations with the West were founded – it was highly unlikely that this country's or any other non-EU NATO member's, status or rights would be downgraded in any future redesigning of Europe's security and defence architecture.

The course of the actual discussions, at the IGC, on the future of EU-WEU relations corroborates this view. The choices essentially came down to one of either of the following possibilities: first, annexing a protocol to the new Treaty of Amsterdam providing for the incorporation, in stages, of the WEU into the EU, to which subscription by the four neutrals and Denmark would – in the final analysis – be optional,[22] and, second, incorporating only the

---

[22] As the WEU's *Contribution to the European Intergovernmental Conference of 1996* adopted by the WEU Council of Ministers at Madrid on 14 November 1995 explained, there were three choices: (a) the first choice consisted essentially in preserving the *status quo*, with the WEU remaining an autonomous organisation, but with closer ties to the EU; (b) the second option, reflecting the "majority view" of WEU members, advocated the "gradual integration" of the WEU into the EU with "the purpose of achieving greater coherence than at present of European action in the security and defence field," while bolstering the ESDI and fostering further collaboration between the WEU, EU and NATO. This objective could be met through a "flexible and juridically non-binding formula" (Paras. 59-75). This option did not specify whether it applied only to the ten WEU members of the EU or to the fifteen EU members, hence the use of the term "flexible"; (c) the third option posited integration of the WEU into the EU, noting that, "for this integration to provide further added value, the operational capabilities necessary for these kinds of actions should be made available, both through arrangements for the use of NATO assets and capabilities, including CJTF, and through the development of complementary EU capabilities" (Paras. 76-98). This option

"Petersberg tasks" (see below) into the new treaty, applicable to all EU Member States.[23] The first option would have the effect of ultimately bringing within the Union framework the whole WEU *acquis*, including Article V and the Petersberg Declaration,[24] which (a) determined the WEU's new tasks in the areas of humanitarian missions, peacekeeping operations and crisis management,[25] and (b) defined relations between members and associate members.[26] However, on the EU side this would have direct effect only on the signatories of the protocol. The second option entailed the continued autonomous existence of the WEU, but with the EU, at "15," "availing itself" of the WEU to carry out the "Petersberg tasks;" henceforth the latter would be brought fully within the ambit of the Union's concerns in the common foreign and security policy sphere. In the process, the WEU would become politically and operationally subordinate to the EU in respect of operations of this sort (though not in respect of Article V responsibilities). (We shall return to this issue below.)

If there was any discussion about the status of associate WEU members in the medium term, it was conducted implicitly in the framework of discussions for a protocol providing for enhanced cooperation between the EU and the WEU ("within a year from the entry into force of this protocol"); the latter necessarily took the current status of associate members for granted. Parallel discussions within the WEU at the time, and, above all, Nato's diversification into "non-article 5" tasks decided at the Berlin NATO ministerial meeting in June 1996, reinforce the impression that the dynamics under way tended to favour an enhanced role for associate WEU (*i.e.* European non-EU Nato) Member States, not their marginalisation.

The Option of an EU-WEU Merger
Greece's objectives with respect to the protection of the *Union's* external borders did not prevent her also openly supporting the option of a gradual EU-

---

suggested that, ideally, all fifteen Member States should be involved, however, without precluding the possibility of selective opt-outs.

[23] A third view, that of Germany, supported bringing a NATO article 5-type provision into the treaty. However, this proposal did not specify which organisation would be responsible for enforcing it. Also, it did not explain the future relationship between the EU and the WEU associate members.

[24] Western European Union Council of Ministers, *Petersberg Declaration*, Bonn, 19 June 1992.

[25] Part II, paragraph 4 of the Declaration.

[26] Part III of the Declaration.

WEU merger. (Hence the Greek representatives' surprise upon realising that Greece had not been invited to co-sponsor a paper submitted in March 1997, to the Conference, by Belgium, France, Germany, Italy, Luxembourg and Spain proposing a protocol setting out a timetable for the full integration of the WEU and EU).

Thus, notwithstanding the knowledge that it did not directly respond to her narrow national concerns, Greece shared the majority view that a defence protocol would arm the Union with a potent weapon in its efforts to project a credible and effective common foreign policy.[27] In the interim, Greece supported the conclusion of a legally or politically binding agreement whereby the WEU would undertake to carry out the EU's decisions and actions.

The merger option was debated at length, both in the conference room and at the representatives' private dinners. Throughout the conference, the four neutral/non-aligned countries, plus the UK and Denmark, remained adamant in their rejection of it – these countries had been warning about this since the days of the Reflection Group).[28] However, this did not mean there was not any progress between Maastricht and Amsterdam.

The Petersberg Tasks

Greece's actual contribution to the evolving security dimension of the EU was of a somewhat different, but ultimately more relevant, nature. Aware of the manifold difficulties associated with the mutual-assistance-clause proposal, the Greek delegation proposed to the Reflection Group – as a fallback position – that the EU assume competence to undertake "Petersberg missions," *without* waiting for the prior incorporation of the WEU into the EU. Everyone agreed that the new international situation posed new challenges to the security of the Union and its Member States. At a time when the fear was not of an all-out attack against a Member State but, rather, of local crises and conflicts, it was clear that, at least in theory, the Petersberg tasks had acquired a new prominence. Furthermore, already by the early nineties, the notion was increasingly taking hold among WEU countries that, although the implementation of the collective defence commitments embodied both in Article 5 of the Washington Treaty and Article V of the modified Brussels Treaty would in practice continue to be assured within the framework of NATO, Europe needed to forge its own common security arrangements in order to

---

[27] Supporters of this view acknowledged at the same time that the WEU would have to develop further its operational capabilities.

[28] See paragraph 168 of the *Report of the Reflection Group*, Brussels, 5 December 1995. For the neutrals, even a presumption that the EU was turning into a military-defence organisation was deemed unacceptable, for it would certainly be met with implacable opposition at home.

deal with threats which by their very nature were unlikely to be – or *should not* be, to avoid overstraining the commitment of the North American allies – addressed by NATO. Therefore, the Common European Defence should be seen as complementary to the Atlantic Alliance and not as antithetical to it.[29] For all these reasons, Greece argued that, independently of the need to include a mutual defence guarantee in the new treaty on grounds of European solidarity, the "Petersberg operations" should be incorporated in the revised treaty both to reflect the changed nature of security in the new geopolitical environment in which the EU had to operate, and to take advantage of the wider membership of the Union compared with the WEU (the EU including countries that, though experienced in the conduct of peace-keeping and humanitarian missions, were not about to join the WEU, given their well-known unwillingness to assume collective-defence obligations).

The assessment in Athens was that, ultimately, this proposal was highly likely to strike a chord with all fifteen partners. And it did not have to confront the very different philosophies and attitudes existing among the "15" regarding the question of a common defence. Its acceptance would still be of considerable merit to Greece, however, considering that these problems were all taking place at her doorstep. Still, the latter would give rise to a paradox: the EU would be taking on responsibilities for restoring stability *outside* the Union's borders, but not inside them, were the Union to be subjected to an external attack or exposed to destabilising forces of foreign provenance. However, in the long run this very paradox could lead to internal pressures to resolve it, thereby leading to reforms in the defence domain in tune with the original Greek objectives.

In the event, this proposal eventually was backed, at the IGC, by all fifteen delegations:[30] for those wishing the integration of the WEU into the EU, this

---

[29] To the objection that the "15" would be arming themselves with mutual defence commitments against NATO members Turkey, Norway and Iceland, one could counterargue that this was precisely what had existed throughout most of the post-war period, from the early 1950s to 1992, *i.e.*, until the Petersberg Declaration removed WEU members' obligation to act collectively in case of an attack from a non-WEU NATO ally.

[30] By the time the Reflection Group completed its work in early December 1995, it appeared that the proposal had received very wide backing, including, crucially, from the neutral/non-aligned members (see repeated references to this possibility in the Group's final report of 5 December 1995: Part I, section III, and Part II, paragraphs 168, 173 and 176). Only the British continued to be opposed to it. Still, the German and French governments felt the need to repeat its merits publicly in two joint statements. The first was a letter dated 6 December 1995 from President Jacques Chirac and Chancellor Helmut Kohl. The second was the common guidelines for the preparation of the 1996 IGC issued at the end of the Franco-German ministerial meeting held in

scheme, if adopted, would enable the EU to address its most pressing and relevant security concerns, while avoiding the enormous political, institutional and legal complications of an outright merger; for those objecting to a formal defence role for the EU as being incompatible with their own neutral or non-aligned tradition, it brought them back into the game, by offering them the means to play a constructive part in the shaping of the new security architecture, to which part, furthermore, they would bring to bear their peacekeeping tradition and experience;[31] for those afraid that a too high European profile in defence matters risked undermining the transatlantic relationship and NATO, the proposal, by leaving the WEU's Article V outside the discussion, left the hard core of that relationship unaffected, *viz.*, the "hard defence" commitments, as embodied in Nato's Article 5.

This was a historical moment, in that, for the first time in its history, the Union was expanding the scope of its competences into the military and quasi-military field. Subsequent initiatives, such as the Franco-British plan, announced with considerable fanfare in December 1998 at St.-Malo in France, "calling" on the EU to develop credible, autonomous military forces, and the Helsinki European Council's decision, in December 1999, to develop a rapid-reaction capability, all have their direct origins in the decisions taken at Amsterdam.

The Principle of the Inviolability of the Common External Borders
As the conference proceeded, it became increasingly obvious that the Union would not end up assuming collective defence responsibilities on behalf of its members. The Greek delegation endeavoured, therefore, to enshrine in the

---

Freiburg on 27 February 1996 between Klaus Kinkel and his French counterpart, Hervé de Charette. Both ministers, as part of their agenda-setting ideas, proposed, among other things, that the European Council should lay down guidelines for security and defence on the basis of which the WEU could, at the request of the EU, undertake actions on the latter's behalf. This would include the WEU's 1992 Petersberg missions, which should be incorporated in the TEU.

The Italian Presidency, which launched the IGC at Turin in March 1996, considered that the Conference should give priority, among other things, to "beginning at once the process of introducing the Petersberg tasks into the Treaty" (see its *Position of the Italian Government on the Intergovernmental Conference for the Revision of the Treaties*, Rome, 18.3.1996, CONF/3839/96).

[31] A joint Finnish-Swedish memorandum submitted to the conference in April 1996, setting out these countries' position in the new emerging European security structure, helped greatly to tip the balance in favour of the proposal. By effectively undercutting the original British position that it was an illusion to think that one could be absolutely certain that "Petersberg" operations could not spill over into Article V-type military engagements, Finland and Sweden made a major contribution to the debate, not least by eventually inducing a change of heart among the British.

new treaty the *principle* of the inviolability of the Union's external borders and its territorial integrity. Simple affirmation of the principle on its own had no military implications, as long as the Union was not explicitly endowed with the legal and military means to enforce it. The principle itself is encountered in many states' constitutions, and has an existence which is quite independent of that of another principle, that of states' right to self-defence.

This proposal was first put to the Foreign Ministers in a letter addressed from Athens to the fourteen capitals, followed up by a memorandum for a revision of Article J.1 (on the CFSP's goals), submitted to the conference on 29 October1996. The letter argued the need for a proclamation in the revised treaty by which the Union would commit itself to bringing to bear all the powers at its disposal (*viz.*, commercial, humanitarian, diplomatic, political – but not military, since at this point it had none) in defence of the principle of the inviolability of the EU's common external borders.[32] The memorandum, for its part, proposed specific language. The effect of this proposal would have been not only to strengthen the content of the Maastricht Treaty's article outlining the goals of the CFSP, but also to introduce the concept of the "common external borders" in the 2nd Pillar, oddly missing in the relevant chapter of the Treaty on European Union.

Even this relatively inoffensive proposal encountered considerable resistance from the other delegations. In the event, (new) Article J.1 §1 third indent was somewhat extended, to include the words "including those on external borders"[33] (not *common* external borders"), which added little or nothing of substance to the relevant passage in the Maastricht Treaty.

Solidarity Clause
As mentioned earlier, Greece had proposed, since the days of the Reflection Group, the insertion of a "solidarity clause" in the new treaty. The aim was to render explicit the solidarity a Member State could expect from its partners in the event of a foreign policy crisis affecting primarily that Member State but not the others. Such a clause would commit Member States to stand by their

---

[32] The Greek delegation submitted a detailed memorandum to this effect on 6 June 1996, followed by a letter from the Greek Minister of Foreign Affairs addressed to his European colleagues confirming these views. A written proposal containing specific language for a revision of Article J.1 (on the CFSP's goals) was submitted to the conference on 29 October1996.

[33] The relevant passage of the new article reads thus:
"The Union shall define and implement a common foreign and security policy covering all areas of foreign and security policy, the objectives of which shall be: (…) to preserve peace and strengthen international security, in accordance with the principles of the United Nations Charter, as well as the principles of the Helsinki Final Act and the objectives of the Paris Charter, *including those on external borders* (…)" (our italics).

partner in his hour of need, or at least refrain from differentiating themselves openly, thereby lending substance to the Union's avowed desire to present a common front *vis-à-vis* the outside world. Not least, a solidarity clause – it was suggested – would make Greece more accommodating on the question of introducing QMV in the CFSP.

This proposal had its origins in Greece's comparatively numerous, and difficult, experiences in the foreign policy domain, especially in matters which from a Greek point of view were considered of prime national importance, such as relations with Turkey and FYROM. In these areas, she often found herself having to struggle hard to persuade her partners why her views were the correct ones. True, in terms of strategic perceptions and final positions, there has never been a serious rift between Greece and her partners in the foreign policy domain – in fact, solidarity has always been forthcoming whenever the Union undertook to elaborate an official, and therefore principled, stand (a fact that the more cynical observers attribute to the existence of the national veto in the 2nd Pillar). Nonetheless, differences have frequently emerged with respect to tactics. This, in conjunction with the phenomenon of isolated attacks from individual European politicians, including politicians in government positions, has at times led Greece to feel insufficiently understood and supported by her partners, and therefore psychologically isolated. Arguably, the only other country to have been through an analogous (though not as traumatic) experience was the United Kingdom in the case of the 1982 Falkland crisis.

Some of the large countries immediately countered the Greek proposal by suggesting the introduction of the concept of "diplomatic solidarity" or "political solidarity" in the new treaty. The added nuance, or "precision," clearly watered down the original thrust of the Greek proposal for it appeared to exclude the display of solidarity through other means, *viz.*, economic or military, *e.g.* withholding aid or other forms of assistance from the offending third country, or even activating the EU's links with the WEU. The version adopted in the treaty (Article J.1 §2) spoke of the need for Member States to "support the Union's external and security policy actively and unreservedly in a spirit of loyalty and mutual solidarity," but also to "work together to enhance and develop their mutual political solidarity." Member States were also urged to "refrain from any action which is contrary to the interests of the Union or likely to impair its effectiveness as a cohesive force in international relations." In themselves, these exhortations were perfectly reasonable; however, they completely side-stepped Greece's original concerns, calling as they did for countries to keep rank, theoretically even in those cases where the issue in hand was of much greater importance to them than to the majority of Member States.

Institutional Issues

Another "big" issue in the CFSP chapter was that of the institutional provisions and decision-making arrangements.

Once again, Greece was faced with a classic dilemma. On the one hand, Greece was in favour of a more effective and cohesive CFSP that would enable Europe, and Greece as an integral part of Europe, to play a more constructive and beneficial role in the world. Endowing the EU with a more effective foreign and security policy apparatus should also, among other things, tend to place limits on the observed phenomenon of some large countries undertaking common foreign-policy initiatives in Europe outside the Union framework, without involving their partners. On the other hand, the notion of a more effective CFSP was usually associated with more majority voting. Given that some of Greece's foreign policy concerns were related to matters considered of vital national interest, majority voting risked finding Greece overruled in the Council, which could trigger both a crisis at home and a crisis between Greece and her EU partners.

Greece, of course, was not alone in entertaining reservations with regard to the prospect of a substantial extension of QMV in the Second Pillar – which as time went by became more and more the focus of the discussions.[34] Foreign policy is an area where there is hardly any experience, in any country, of being outvoted in a collective decision-making body, yet still having to implement the ensuing common decision. However, rather than taking a negative stance and declaring her outright opposition to QMV, Greece stated that her general approach to decision-making would depend, first, on the objectives that would be included in the CFSP and, second, on the introduction of certain "communitarian" elements in the general system of CFSP (*e.g.*, better checks and balances from a stronger presence of the institutions). If this were the case, Greece would temper her insistence on the safeguards usually associated with intergovernmental procedures.

After a global assessment,[35] the Greek delegation decided to support the proposed two-tier system, which would consist in the European Council deciding unanimously on the general guidelines and common strategies, and the Council deciding on the implementing decisions by QMV. This would have to be accompanied by the following four elements. First, a solidarity clause, which would allay some of the fears of isolation. Second, a "vital national interest" clause (Greece was not alone on this), which would safeguard her national interests in the most sensitive of cases. Third, the

---

[34] The main advocates of this view were the French (who introduced the notion of the two-tier system of decision-making – see below) and the Germans.

[35] This included developments with respect to such matters as "Mr. CFSP," the legal personality of the Union, etc.

possibility of "constructive abstention." Fourth, Greece insisted on a detailed definition of the objectives, scope, means, conditions and duration of the common strategies and joint actions, so that a change of circumstances would be reflected quickly in the Union's response and Member States would not be obliged to comply with implementing decisions based on out-of-date common strategies.

In the end, the two safeguard mechanisms – the "vital interest" clause and "constructive abstention" – and the suitably well-defined scope of the common strategies and joint actions proved effective in curbing Greece's, and other Member States', initial reticence, thus opening the way for adoption of the new, and no doubt more efficient, decision-making mechanism.

Finally, there was the question of whether or not the EU needed to introduce a Mr or Mrs PESC (from the French acronym for CFSP) in order to give the Union's foreign and security policy a distinct "face." The original Greek position was one of scepticism: one more function, *i.e.* one additional to the Presidency and the Commission, risked multiplying rather than reducing the Union's "voices" that could speak competently on matters of foreign policy.[36]

Furthermore, given Greece's broad predilection in favour of a convergence between pillars, there was a perception that potential new problems of coordination might emerge between, on the one hand, the intergovernmental activities embodied in Mr/Mrs PESC and, on the other, Community powers in EU foreign policy (which included not only a number of important topics – trade, aid, humanitarian assistance, etc. – but also a network of delegations, answerable to the Commission, representing the EU around the world). Greece favoured the option of the Presidency-Commission "tandem."

Lastly, it would be necessary to ensure that the person chosen to occupy the new position – should the idea be finally adopted – would be capable of expressing with sensitivity the Member States' collective views. The latter would have to be defined not merely as the outcome of a least-common-denominator calculation (broadly speaking, the current approach, upon which the IGC was aiming to improve), nor a "broad majority" view (probably dominated by the big countries), but as a subtle and sensitive synthesis of *all* countries' views. Whereas, from the Greek point of view, the Commission had, over the years, refined its ability to do this, the new post of Mr/Mrs CFSP, being intergovernmental in nature, had yet to build such a "European" culture, something that could take a long time, depending also on the personalities chosen to fill the post.

---

[36] As the President of the Commission, M. Jacques Santer, put it before the European Parliament (13.12.1995): "Plutôt que d'accroître la visibilité, (this personality) accroîtra la confusion et les conflits de compétences."

Greece ended in accepting the proposal for a High Representative, accountable to the Council and working together, in his capacity as Secretary-General, with the new policy planning and early warning unit within the Council General Secretariat. The fact that: 1) the High Representative was to be accountable to the Council (and not report to the European Council[37]), *i.e.* would be a part of the Community's institutional framework, and not a relatively autonomous "high personality;" 2) that final responsibility for the CFSP lay with the Presidency; and 3) that the new CFSP unit, of which he would be in charge, appeared to be well-equipped to become a centre of "European" diplomacy (drawing also personnel from the Commission, the Member States and the WEU), gave hopes that the new arrangements would prove superior to those in existence until then.

Conclusion
The final results of the IGC as regards the CFSP chapter reflect only to a relative degree the hopes and objectives of Greece. Of course, ambitions were set high also in order to widen the terms of the debate in directions consistent with Greek goals, thus energising the debate in this area. In this, the Greek delegations to the Reflection Group and the IGC proper were highly successful, in that they probably took the discussion further than otherwise would have been the case. All in all, in some important respects the Greek contribution made a difference to the final text, in particular as regards the inclusion of the "Petersberg tasks," even if it was achieved at the price of sidelining questions of common defence. Greater progress in this would have been proof of the existence of greater solidarity between the Member States, both in the eyes of the Union's citizens themselves and the outside world.

External Economic Relations
Greece was fully aware of, and to a large extent agreed with, the arguments of those who supported an extention of Article 113 to the "new" areas of services, intellectual property and investment. There was only one sticking point: Greece was loath to surrender her sovereignty in the area of shipping. Being the largest maritime power in the world (in terms of ownership),[38] Greece felt that if it allowed the Commission to have the final say in the WTO

---

[37] From the Greek point of view, the drawbacks, such as they were, of the Mr/Mrs PESC proposal would have been even more pronounced in the alternative version proposed in the course of the IGC, which would have consisted in appointing a High Representative who would be above the Council, and more closely associated with the members and work of the European Council.

[38] Greek ships accounted in early 2000 for 15.32 per cent of total world gross tonnage (57 per cent of EU gross tonnage).

trade-liberalisation negotiations, it would lose control over the shape of the negotiations as well as the final outcome. Shipping would become just another bargaining chip in the service of achieving a positive *global* outcome. In this model, the distribution of losses and gains for the EC side is indeterminate, *ex ante*, and the Commission has ultimate discretion on this score. Previous experience in the Uruguay Round suggested that Greece would be better off if she, rather than the Commision, retained, at least in principle, the final say in matters pertaining to shipping.

The effects of the Greek dilemma on the negotiations were muted by the existence of even stronger objections coming from other countries. These objections, at least in some cases, derived from relative dissatisfaction with the conducting of the negotiations by the Commission during the Uruguay Round (especially France), while in other cases it was a matter of principle as regards the ceding of sovereignty (the UK and Denmark). In the event, the conference made practically no changes to Article 113. Still, for Greece the dilemma does not seem likely to be resolved soon, given the asymmetrical importance for Greece of this single sector. And the issue is not likely to disappear any time soon: after all, thanks to a new Amsterdam Treaty provision, extension of the application of Article 113 to cover services and intellectual property does not require a new IGC, but can be decided by the Council, acting unanimously, on a proposal from the Commission. In all likelihood, the Commission will press anew for changes in the run-up to the next negotiating round.

The Union's Institutions

In many ways, the reform of the institutions was seen by the Greek government as the heart of the matter: the aim was not only to enhance the democratic legitimacy of the institutions, but also to reinforce the efficiency of the institutional apparatus as a whole, especially in the light of future enlargement. *A priori*, this dual goal was not seen as potentially devoid of contradictions or internal tensions, and it would be necessary to ensure that, in the process of making the Union's institutions stronger, more accountable and more efficient, individual Member States did not lose their ability to maintain their influence and preserve their individuality, regardless of their size.

In the event, Greece shared the common view that the conference was much more successful on the first score than the second: while efforts to enhance the democratic legitimacy of the institutions could lean on decades of democratic experience in the western countries, providing broadly-accepted guiding principles, the question of appropriate criteria by which to judge the efficiency of the Union's institutions proved more complex and open to disparate views – as the conference amply discovered.

The main principles guiding the Greek delegation's positions were the need to preserve the inter-institutional balance, to maintain or enhance the effectiveness of the individual institutions, as well as to improve the *modus operandi* between them. From the Greek perspective, the ensuing gains would be even greater if in parallel the conference succeeded in communitarising certain facets or policies of the Second and Third Pillars, thus blurring the existing relatively rigid distinctions between the pillars. Another fundamental principle that would have to be respected was the equal status of Member States.

However, the Greek delegation was soon to discover that no matter how "orthodox" its views in defence of forty years of institutional achievements, the European debate had already begun shifting to new ground. The trigger for this change was, of course, the prospect of the Union's enlargement to include up to a dozen new Member States, all European to be sure, but having lived through radically different political, economic and social experiences in the 20th century.[39]

The institutional chapter could be said to be more important than the sum of its parts. In retrospect, the failure of the conference to make much progress in this area is not surprising. All that is required to explain the limited results (limited at least in comparison with the original ambitions of most) is that one interprets the negotiations less as a technocratic attempt to "streamline" the functioning of the Union's institutions,[40] and more as a political attempt to recast the balance of power within the Union by affording a more prominent position to the Union's more powerful and influential nations in the new, enlarging Europe, allowing them to influence more readily the future agenda of European integration. This much is clear. More controversial is the extent to which the means proposed to achieve this result – reallocating the votes in the Council in favour of the large countries, and, especially, introducing the highly ambiguous new concept of "flexibility" – will end up being supportive of the long-term goal of an "ever closer Union," as claimed by the protagonists of this approach, or will, instead, lead at least to the possibility

---

[39] The debate was effectively set off in September 1994 with the publication of the German CDU/CSU paper entitled *Reflections on European Policy*, by Karl Lamers and Wolfgang Schäuble, which argued in no uncertain terms that integration needed to be taken forward by a "core group" of five or six countries; the rest would follow at different speeds, depending on their ability.

[40] Which, as never ceases to be repeated, essentially is based on a model devised forty years ago for six Member States.

of a Europe of first-class and second-class members, as feared by those who felt more at risk by the new proposals.

The European Parliament
Greece's predilection for the Community model, as it has grown through application of the treaties and historical experience, is best exemplified by the stance she took in the debate on the future powers of the European Parliament.

The objective here was to increase the powers of the Parliament as the central means for reducing the "democratic deficit." This very important goal – whose significance has yet to be fully appreciated by the wider public – was largely achieved thanks to the following reforms:[41]

a) preservation of the assent procedure for all important decisions, including its extension to one new treaty provision and four existing ones;
b) virtual generalisation of the co-decision procedure in the First Pillar, including its extension to fourteen existing treaty provisions, eight new articles, as well as the articles resulting from the transposition into the treaty of the agreement on social policy. Greece, along with Germany, Belgium and Luxembourg, supported from the start the extension of co-decision to all legislative acts subject to QMV in the Council;
c) simplification of the co-decision procedure, with abolition of the "third reading."

As regards the proposals for placing a ceiling on the maximum number of parliamentarians, Greece could support the proposal, provided the numbers allotted to each Member State would preclude neither an adequate representation of the national political spectrum, nor an adequate representation of all European peoples. Greece accepted the number of 700.

However, Greece saw another of its proposals rejected, a memorandum which argued for the institution of European political parties. By raising the awareness of citizens on European issues in a common, cross-border way, this proposal would also have gone some way toward "de-nationalising" the EP elections and placing European issues closer to the centre of politics in Member States. Finally, the view, supported by Greece, that the European Parliament ought to provide its assent for any modification of the treaties was not endorsed by the conference.

---

[41] Greece submitted a memorandum on the role of the European Parliament to the conference on 30 May 1996.

The National Parliaments

On the matter of the democratic legitimacy of the Union's institutional arrangements, Greece, like most Member States, was pulled by two opposite forces: on the one hand, a general desire to improve the involvement and participation of citizens in European politics and European affairs; on the other, the need to maintain the institutional balance, including an efficient allocation of roles and responsibilities consistent with modern views of subsidiarity. At a more concrete and practical level, the question posed by some, notably France, was how to implicate national parliaments better in the preparation of Community initiatives. This was seen as necessary in order to minimise the risk of rejection at the later stage of transposition into national legislation. It concerned particularly the area of Justice and Home Affairs (whether or not the latter would be "communitarised" to some degree), where the Community would be called upon to treat sensitive matters that traditionally had fallen within the prerogatives of national parliaments.

In terms of enhancing the role of national parliaments in the European institutional structure, there was, in the event, little the conference could add to the provisions already in existence in the Treaties without upsetting the logic of current arrangements. Certain proposals, such as the submission of Green Papers by the Commission, the occasional presence of Commissioners in the national parliaments, intensifying contacts and exchanges of information between the national and the European Parliament all could go ahead, it was asserted, without treaty revision. Repeated French proposals for creating something akin to a new body to represent national parliaments ("Haut conseil consultatif") were consistently rejected by the fourteen other delegations on the grounds that this risked blurring the distinction between legislation at the national level and legislation at the Community level. The Greek delegation agreed with the view taken by the European Parliament itself, *viz.*, that such a new body would weaken the role of the Parliament, being also reminiscent of the time, 15 years ago, when European parliamentarians were appointed by their national parliaments. The conference had to content itself with a tightening of the provisions relating to the timely informing of parliaments on the activities of the Union, and an explicit reference to the (non-binding) contributions that the COSAC (the Conference of European Affairs Committees) could make to the legislative activities of the Union (notably in the areas of Justice and Home Affairs and subsidiarity).

The Council

The issue of the efficient working of the Council came up frequently both during the work of the Reflection Group and the IGC. Most of the more practical solutions, it was felt, could proceed without any treaty change, for what they required, above all, was more self-discipline, and greater compliance with the well-known demands of Council work, on the part of its members.

However, other issues were infinitely more controversial, *viz.*, the extension of the use of qualified-majority voting (QMV), and the re-weighting of the votes.

a) The extension of the use of QMV
One of the articles of faith that emerged before and during the IGC (propounded mainly by the Commission, the Parliament and several Member States) was that it was time to do away with unanimity in the Council in the first pillar, except in the exceptional case of constitutional-type decisions. Under a system of unanimity, the chances of blockage in the Council increased exponentially as a function of the number of members. In a system comprising, say, 28 members, the chances of a single state exercising its right of veto are, *ceteris paribus*, almost infinitely greater than in a system with, say, two members.[42] Generalising the use of QMV would, therefore, in this view, be a pre-requisite for more efficient decision-making in an enlarged Council.

Other countries admitted that QMV was no panacea. Indeed, how fair was it to say that current problems were really due to the continuing use of unanimity? After all, the Single Market programme, the heart of the 1st pillar, had long ago introduced QMV as the rule. Most other articles of a non-constitutional nature in the Community pillar were subject to QMV, including most on EMU, and if they were not, it was for a reason: they impinged on states' cherished fiscal sovereignty. In other cases, such as the research framework-programme, unanimity was related to the distribution of substantial pecuniary resources to Member States; here, experience suggested that the existence of unanimity had not prevented the achievement of outcomes that – though perhaps not perfect (however that term is defined) – were to the satisfaction of the great majority, without offending anyone in particular. As for the second and third pillars, unanimity was the result of

---

[42] In a system with two members, where each had a 50-50 chance of using a veto, the chances of a positive outcome are one in four (there is a one-in-four chance for each of the following outcomes: (a) member A veto-ing the proposal – member B veto-ing the proposal; (b) member A veto-ing the proposal – member B voting in favour; (c) member A voting in favour – member B vetoing; (d) member A voting in favour – member B voting in favour). In other words, in a two-member system, the chances of a positive outcome are $(1/2)^2$, or one in four. In a system of 28 members, the corresponding chances are $(1/2)^{28}$, *i.e.*, one in 268,435,456. Of course, this figure is reduced if the chances of any country vetoing a proposal are considerably less than 50-50, which is a more realistic assumption.

Member States' (unanimous) decision to place the relevant provisions within an intergovernmental framework, and, in this sense, was no accident.

Greece belonged to this second group of countries. It did not believe that unanimity in the fields of culture, industrial policy or the professions was at the root of the Council's problems. Nonetheless, the Greek delegation declared itself open to discuss, on a case-by-case basis, the extension of QMV to these and other areas (*e.g.*, the soon-to-be communitarised areas from the Justice and Home Affairs chapter). This was for two reasons: first, the need to play a constructive part in the negotiations, bearing in mind the general thrust of the discussions, and, second, in order to undercut arguments that "enhanced cooperation" was the only way to ensure the future progress of European integration, as claimed by some (see below). Although QMV and "flexibility" are not the same thing, in theory they have in common an ability to expedite decisions in the Council, albeit with different effects on those who are outvoted.[43]

Although Greece had no objection to the application of QMV in the new provisions adopted in the first pillar (such as employment guidelines, public health, customs cooperation, etc.), it was in fact one of the last to accept switching to QMV in the other first-pillar areas where unanimity traditionally held sway. Nonetheless, the Greek delegation made a substantial effort at Amsterdam, and finally accepted to lift most of its objections, only to find at the last minute Chancellor Kohl refusing, for his own domestic reasons, to oblige his partners.

b) The weighting of the votes

Perhaps for the first time in the history of European integration, this most controversial of issues introduced an element of suspicion among Member States. The arguments put forward by the large countries were deemed unconvincing by the small ones, who consequently wondered how certain large countries' insistence on increasing their relative voting power ultimately fitted into their wider strategy on institutional reform, even as crucial elements were still missing from the overall picture (see, *e.g.*, the debate on "flexibility," discussed below).

Thus, the claim that the legitimacy of Council votes was going to be "eroded" due to the accession of "over-represented" small states made sense only if population were the sole criterion by which to judge the legitimacy of Council decisions, which by definition cannot be the case in a body

---

[43] In the case of QMV, the outvoted member is obliged to implement the decision; in the case of "flexibility," the outvoted member sees the other Member States and the institutions of the Community proceed with an action which he not only voted against, but from which he is excluded.

representing *states*. The novel tendency of large countries to couch the argument in terms of the interests of "large" states *vs.* "small" states misrepresented the consequences of enlargement, as seen from any individual small country's point of view. Even as small incumbent states were preparing to see their relative voting power diminish in the Council, in line with expanding membership, they were additionally being asked to actually give up votes to compensate for other small countries' joining the Union, irrespective of the fact that there was no reason to presume that a "small-country voting bloc" was ever likely to emerge. There is no *a priori* reason why a small country should ally itself with another small country on any particular vote merely because it is *small*, rather than, say, a country in its geographical proximity, a country with a similar standard of living, a country with similar sectoral and economic interests, etc., etc.

Furthermore, even in the extremely unlikely case where, in a Union of 27, the smaller countries "ganged up" on the larger countries (as argued above, a scenario so far-fetched that merely to invoke it in itself raised suspicions, however unfounded, that the converse may actually occur one day), under the current system they would still be unable to outvote the four largest current members (who would retain, between them, their blocking-minority power). The inference was, therefore, that today's four or five largest countries wished to maintain their blocking rights merely *à trois* – three countries blocking the wishes of twenty-four. Moreover, if a qualified majority heavily composed of small-country votes did materialise, Commission statistics showed that even in the most extreme case it would still represent over half the Union's total population (in fact, 50.2 per cent, admittedly less than the 58.3 per cent that is the minimum obtainable today under the current system).

On the other hand, in a Union of 28 (where the 28th member was a small country – when in fact today the 28th candidate is Turkey), it would be conceivable, under the current system, that certain decisions were passed representing less than half the EU population. In this case, it would make sense to introduce a population criterion, in order to disallow the vote. Generalising from this train of thought, a second, population, criterion would make sense if countries agreed to maintain a certain population threshold for voting in general (*e.g.*, 60 per cent, or 55 per cent). In all other cases, the extrapolation of the present system to a Union of 27 Member States preserved the basic democratic majority (50+ per cent) rule both in terms of votes (in fact, 70-71 per cent of votes) and population. In fact, the large countries' claim that a redistribution of votes was necessary in the name of proper democratic representativeness jarred somewhat with their parallel insistence that a relatively high population threshold be maintained at the same time. (However, the latter did reinforce their case for a redistribution of votes).

Greece, by contrast, could have envisaged a lowering of the population threshold closer to 51 per cent, as that was what democratic rules suggested.[44]

Greece supported the "dual-majority" solution in the knowledge that in the vast majority of cases the population criterion would be easily satisfied (as long as the population threshold was not set too high, or higher than at present). However, even if the Greek delegation felt satisfied that it, and other smaller-country delegations, had won the argument on both "constitutional" and common-sense grounds, it would still have to confront the age-old negotiating conundrum of having to trade apples for pears for a solution acceptable to all, in the institutional chapter, to emerge in the end.

The Commission
The question of the number of Commissioners, an issue deemed by many as the key to the necessary reform of the Commission, sooner or later became directly linked with that of the distribution of votes in the Council (which, incidentally, became directly linked with the question of QMV, at least as far as some of the big-country delegations were concerned). If large countries were going to give up their second commissioner (apples), they would have to be compensated in the Council with more votes (pears).

In the meantime, the conference agreed to reinforce the post of president of the Commission (see other chapters in this volume), in part by making his selection by the European Council subject to the approval, by absolute majority, of Parliament. Greece supported this approach, seeing it as strengthening the institution as a whole. (In fact, Greece, along with Austria, had gone a step further and advocated the election of the Commission

---

[44] To be sure, under the current system, one vote from, say, Ireland represents 1.2 million Irishmen, whereas one vote from France or Britain represents about 5.7 million Frenchmen or Britons. However, this huge discrepancy has been more or less the case since 1973. The solution to this problem – to the extent that *enlargement* was somehow deemed to exacerbate it – would be to envisage a bold reorganisation of the Parliament along national population lines. This would be more in tune with standard bi-cameral models, whose relevance in the EU context inevitably increased following the IGC's decision to grant the Parliament the status of co-legislator on practically all legislative matters (under the first pillar). This was never proposed, however. If anything, increasing the powers of the Parliament – provided this was accompanied by a redistribution of seats reflecting more closely the distribution of populations – ought to lead the Council more in the direction of a one-state, one-vote system, not the opposite. (This argument is on more shaky ground when applied to decision-making in the Council in matters falling under the second and third pillars).

And the argument that a "small" redistribution of votes in favour of the large countries could be shown to leave unaffected practically every Council decision of the past, could be seen to work both ways.

President by Parliament on the basis of a list prepared in advance by the European Council.)

Generally speaking, Greece's position was motivated by its traditional view of the Commission as guarantor of the interests of smaller Member States and as bulwark to any tendency for big countries to form a *"directoire."*

On the thorny question of the number of Commissioners, Greece supported an extrapolation of the present system. Greece did not concur with those countries that argued that the College was in danger of becoming too big, unwieldy and inefficient with enlargement. After all, most national governments consisted of cabinets of over 35 members. The Greek delegation listened with interest to the French plea for a small, management-board-type Commission consisting of fewer members than states. However, no matter how sympathetic it was in theory to this or any other proposal, Klaus Kinkel's sudden insistence on a permanent German presence in the Commission – in contrast with the spirit of the discussions, where delegations appeared, at least, willing to explore different avenues for an equitable sharing of the burden of personnel-cutting – caused the Greek delegation to revert to its original stance, rejecting in the process such notions as "junior Commissioner," "Commissioner without portfolio," or permanent and rotating members of the Commission. The Greek view was that Greece, perhaps more than most countries, could not dispense with its representation in this most important of institutions, given also its relative under-representation in the higher ranks of the Commission's and other Community institutions' services.[45] If the large countries wanted to give up their second commissioner, this was their affair. Of course, the issue is not closed, and these ideas are being revisited in the run-up to the next enlargement, after which the rule "one commissioner per Member State" will apply for as long as the Member States do not exceed twenty – provided an agreement has been reached on the weighting of the votes in the Council.

The Court of Justice
The IGC extended considerably the competences of the European Court of Justice (ECJ), in line with Greece's original desires. It should be mentioned that Greece's trust in the work of the ECJ is deeply entrenched.[46]

---

[45] The situation has probably improved in the last few years, especially if one looks at statistics aggregating all grade A staff and not just at the A1 and A2 ranks.

[46] Apart from Greece's support for the CoJ as a driving force of European integration, the Court has taken a number of very important decisions, favourable to the Greek cause, in areas which impinge on Greece's vital national interests. These include decisions on the illegality of Turkish-Cypriot exports imported into the EC that are unaccompanied by official Republic of Cyprus documents, as well as a landmark ruling, favourable to

The competences of the Court were enlarged and better specified with respect to the protection of fundamental rights. The same essentially applied to matters falling under the new 1st-pillar chapter on Freedom, Security and Justice. The Court's competences were widened also in the 3rd pillar, according to certain modalities (see elsewhere in this volume). All of these measures had the support of the Greek delegation.

Finally, the conference maintained the principle of "one country-one judge," an important matter especially from the point of view of the small Member States.

Other Institutional Issues
a) Court of Auditors: Greece supported the Court's right of appeal to the Court of Justice for the purpose of protecting its prerogatives; Greece accepted also the extension of the Court's powers to bodies managing Community funds within Member States, in liaison with the competent national authorities.
b) Committee of the Regions: Greece, having recently adopted a system of direct elections at prefecture level, on the whole supported any measures, administrative or substantive, which enhanced the role, stature or autonomy of the Committee, believing it to be a useful link between citizens, the regions and the Union.
c) Economic and Social Committee: For Greece, supporting the extension of the domains in which the ESC will henceforth have to be consulted (including the new provisions on employment, certain social matters and public health), was a natural concomitant of its efforts to raise the social profile of the Union, as well as deepen its democratic character.

Flexibility

Without the slightest doubt, the question of "flexibility," or "enhanced cooperation," was the most controversial of the conference, judged from the Greek perspective. "Flexibility" was seen as more than a simple innovation designed to facilitate the Union's future work. It was perceived as a sign of the times: an attempt by the Union's most advanced and committed members to no longer countenance or accommodate the Union's awkward or obstreperous members. The "core" was finally turning the tables on those countries which in the past had forced a breaching of the hitherto sacrosanct principle of "unicity" and abused the understanding of their partners, either by demanding

---

Greece, on the then Greek trade embargo of the Former Yugoslav Republic of Macedonia.

opt-outs (EMU, the social protocol, citizenship), or by forcing them to form, against their will, new formal associations outside the framework of the treaties (Schengen), or both. It was potentially also a powerful instrument in the hands of those who were not prepared to see any obstructionism or dragging-of-feet, either on the part of the less capable or laggard members of the current Union, or the future members from Central and Eastern Europe.

Hence, the enormous amount of soul-searching that went on within the Greek delegation. With only the most speculative of views about the possible uses of "flexibility" at its disposal, the Greek delegation had to make an assessment of its pros and cons from the peculiar perspective of a country which, after all, economically was one of the least developed of the EU, yet needed the EU more than most to push through necessary domestic reforms. "Flexibility" also held out the danger of major problems in foreign policy, given Greece's particular difficulties with her neighbours. Generally speaking, it was felt that "flexibility" in the first pillar was difficult to conceive of, given the constraints of the single market, competition rules, and exclusivity in Community competence in the most important areas. If one wandered into the higher theoretical debate on wholesale political and economic union, it was unclear to what extent these could be pursued without prior, unanimously approved, treaty changes. The possibility of this seemed far less likely in respect of "political union" than of subsequent stages of EMU (see below). In the second pillar, "flexibility," inappropriately and uncarefully pursued, could lead to tension and conflict between partners.[47] The third pillar looked, from the Greek angle, like the most inoffensive area for deepening cooperation through "flexible" policies involving less than the full membership of EU partners.

The fact that the proponents of "flexibility" were coy about its potential uses certainly made Greece much more sceptical and uneasy than would otherwise have been the case. Their inability, or unwillingness, to provide concrete examples during the conference[48] can be interpreted in at least three

---

[47] Notwithstanding this, and in order not to be branded as a wholly negative player by her partners, Greece declared her support for a "flexibility" clause in the second pillar on the understanding that it would be used to promote the cause of a greater defence role for the EU in the future. However, given a chance to change her mind – which was offered when the UK took the lead at the European summit at Amsterdam and proposed that the enabling clause in the second pillar be dropped in favour of the notion of "constructive abstention" – Greece quickly concurred.

[48] An attempt was nonetheless made by the deputy French representative, who mentioned the possibility of some central continental countries being interested in cooperating more closely in the area of riverways management. It was never explained why other countries, presumed indifferent to the initiative, should object and veto such a Community initiative.

ways: first, an understanding that, at present, there was not much scope for application of "flexibility" in practice; second, even if there were such scope, *e.g.*, a defence protocol in the second pillar, announcing *ex ante*, *i.e.* prior to the actual introduction of a "flexibility" clause, an intention to seek closer cooperation in precisely such an area, notwithstanding the perfectly well-known objections of the presumed future non-participants,[49] would only end up provoking a major crisis among partners (not to mention sealing the fate of any "flexibility" clause at the IGC); third, proponents of "flexibility" were more interested in the long term,[50] and therefore at this stage could only delineate the necessary pre-conditions for future integration, *i.e.*, the method, rather than spell out in which areas integration would proceed, *i.e.*, the substance.

Still, for Greece, the perfect candidate for "flexibility" in the short to medium term appeared to be EMU, with hints from Paris that the EMU countries should go further and set up their own, informal, forum to discuss wider economic-policy issues. With a "flexibility" clause in place, this "informal" forum (which of course was immediately set up once EMU was inaugurated) could well become a "formal" one, with Greece, a prospective "out," being unable to influence developments prior to joining the single currency. Indeed, this possibility led to a new train of thought within the Greek delegation. What if the EMU "in" countries decided to integrate further in certain economic areas and in so doing redefined the terms of future EMU membership beyond what had been agreed by all at Maastricht? Clearly, there was a danger in this type of "vertical flexibility" whereby, once the original group of countries was given the go-ahead to proceed along "flexible" lines under certain pre-specified terms, they went on to gradually modify, improve or "deepen" their common policy – this would only be natural and consistent with historical experience – thereby making the terms of entry for the unconsulted "outs" even more difficult to attain.

So, difficult choices had to be made as to the exact tactics one would need to employ. Whereas one could always veto an unacceptable proposal, *e.g.*, on the question of Council votes, in the final analysis, one could revert to the system already in place – "flexibility" was an entirely new concept[51] which

---

[49] Austria, Finland, Ireland, Sweden plus the UK and Denmark.

[50] A period beginning, say, after the next fifteen years, *i.e.* after the new CEEC members' transitional periods had run out.

[51] Some experts consider the Maastricht Treaty's EMU chapter and Social Protocol as the first cases of "flexibility." This is no doubt true. But there was a crucial difference between the ultimately consensual approach that underlay the admittance (however reluctantly on the part of the "Ten") of the British and Danish opt-outs in 1991, and the thrust of the discussions at the 1996-97 IGC, which was to do away with unanimity and

one could not readily dismiss, for it looked like the shape of things to come. From an *ad hoc* aberration associated with the behaviour of the Union's most reluctant members, it was being upgraded to a central principle of European integration. Indeed, one was constantly reminded that the choice was not between "flexibility" and no "flexibility," but between "flexibility" within the treaty (where one had at least a sporting chance to influence the outcome and to secure one's participation), and "flexibility" outside the treaty, where one was potentially ignored altogether.

Greece naturally aligned herself with the more "traditional" members, of whom there were not few. In this vein, Greece reminded her partners of the virtues of "transitional periods" (as an alternative to "flexibility"). Greece submitted a memorandum (CONF 3866 1997) on the eve of the ministerial meeting of 25 March 1997 whose main aim was to render the clauses on "flexibility" as concordant as possible with Community "orthodoxy." Thus, among other things, the aim of the Greek paper was to restore the Commission's exclusive power of initiative (in the first pillar) in matters of "enhanced cooperation," confirm its role as arbiter of the consistency of individual "flexible" policies with the spirit and letter of the Treaties, promote "inclusiveness" by facilitating as much as possible easy entry for "out" countries aspiring to become "ins," and confirm the principle of "solidarity" of the "ins" with the "outs."[52] The defining issue, of course, was whether one accepted the "QMV trigger" for launching a policy of "enhanced cooperation" (the proponents), or whether one insisted on unanimity (the sceptics). Greece, of course, supported the latter option. Greece maintained this position until the end, despite the fact that most of her fellow sceptics, one-by-one, began lifting their objections as the negotiations approached their climax and as the conditions attached appeared to ensure broad consistency with the spirit of European integration. This probably reduced the influence of the Greek contribution, no doubt perceived by the other delegations as reflecting an excessively "defensive" outlook. In the end, Greece also agreed to the trigger by QMV, having secured first, however, certain conditions which, she felt, ensured by and large that "flexibility," when applied, would not fundamentally undermine the cohesiveness of the Union, rupture the single institutional framework or impede disordinately the later accession of the "pre-ins." These included the principle that the Commission would not be sidelined by

---

introduce QMV, thus enabling some countries to proceed with closer cooperation *over the heads* of the "outs."

[52] Another original Greek proposal was to insert a clause to the effect that rejection of a "flexible" proposal in the Council would preclude the interested countries from pursuing it outside the institutional framework. The conference did not retain the proposal.

member-state initiatives;[53] "flexible" policies would not affect the *acquis communautaire*; "enhanced cooperation" would be used only as a last resort; it would encompass only a majority of Member States;[54] it would not prevent easy access by late-comers, under terms ultimately set by the Commission rather than the "in" countries; finally, and perhaps most importantly, countries reserved the right to prevent a particular policy of "enhanced cooperation" from going ahead if they felt it affected their fundamental national interests, the famous "emergency brake."

As an afterthought, it should be recalled that no attempt has yet been made to implement the hard-fought, and much-vaunted, provisions on "closer cooperation." Surprisingly, what discussion there was after Amsterdam about the practical aspects of "flexibility" revolved almost exclusively around the possibility of relaxing to various degrees the enabling conditions to make the concept more "operational." To the sceptics, the "core" countries' eagerness to reopen the debate on the implementing framework – despite the fact that it had never been tested – merely reinforced their fears of potential mismanagement[55] and potential tendencies to exclusiveness – the apparently necessary price to pay for combining effectively, in the coming years, "deepening" with "widening."

Conclusions

As suggested in the Introduction, Greece looked to the 1996 Intergovernmental Conference as an opportunity to complete the revision of the Treaties begun at Maastricht. Despite the previous IGC's great success in the sphere of economic and monetary policy, and in laying down the basic framework for a more coherent foreign policy and a more effective policy in the areas of Justice and Home Affairs, it was felt that it would now be

---

[53] Other countries, such as Austria, Belgium, Italy and Portugal, were of the same view.

[54] Admittedly, Greece had hoped for a much higher proportion, *viz.*, at least two-thirds.

[55] For example, reducing the number of potential participants to one-third of the membership, as advocated by some countries and the Commission itself during the Nice IGC, opens up the theoretical possibility of two or three subgroups competing to pursue similar policies whose mutual consistency *a priori* cannot be taken for granted. In addition to the question of consistency, subgroups will have a vested interest in hurrying and submitting their proposals (however well thought-out) to the Commission as soon as possible, so that if a question of inconsistency were to arise, it would affect the later applicants, not them. Finally, one may also question the capacity of the Union's institutions to cope with the complexities of managing concurrent policies for small subgroups of members.

necessary to enrich the Treaty on European Union with new provisions emphasising fundamental rights and the social dimension of the European Union; to strengthen the democratic character of the Union's institutions, while at the same time improving their efficiency; to endow the Union with the means to actually conduct a common foreign and security policy reflecting European values, but also European responsibilities in the world, commensurate with its economic power, including the means to ensure the territorial integrity of its Member States; to adopt new policies in areas that were becoming increasingly important to the European economy and the European citizen; and to devise effective policies to lend a sense of greater security to the citizen.

Such an ambitious agenda no doubt provided material for more than one IGC. Nonetheless, Greece could claim that the final results, achieved both by working together with her partners and through proposals of her own, were in many respects to the Government's satisfaction: the new role of the Parliament, thanks mainly to the practical generalisation of co-decision in legislative matters; the very substantial communitarisation of provisions relating to Justice and Home Affairs; the new Title on employment and the references to fundamental rights, social rights and non-discrimination; new references to the islands and the protection of personal data, to name some of the most important. In the 2nd pillar, the inclusion of the "Petersberg Tasks" in the Treaty was a major step toward conferring on the Union a much stronger role in security affairs – albeit at the price of sidelining questions of Europe's common defence. On the more controversial matters brought up by the debate on institutional reform, Greece had the satisfaction, through working with other partners, of being able to mute some of the more unpalatable, and arguably "un-European," propositions, as regards mainly the weighting of the votes in the Council and "flexibility." Of course, the institutional chapter was not closed at Amsterdam, and the subsequent Treaty of Nice produced a set of results which, judged in terms of the Amsterdam debate, are certainly not uncontroversial.

Still, with Greece's subsequent acceptance into the Eurozone and easing of tensions with its neighbours to the East and North (achieved to a significant degree through constructive use of her status as the sole Balkan member of the EU), Greece is now justifiably in a position to project a more confident self. Given the formidable challenges that lie ahead, this should stand Greece in good stead as the country strives to make its own positive contribution to the construction of the new Europe.

9

Ireland: The Politics of Pragmatism?

Ben Tonra

Irish Attitudes

Pragmatism rather than any political or ideological commitment frames the traditional picture of Irish attitudes towards European integration. Ireland's entry to the then European Communities in 1973 was presented and popularly understood in terms of quantifiable economic benefits (Maher 1987; Hederman-O'Brien 1983). The scale and political significance of these economic transfers (amounting to a total of more than 30 billion euro in the period 1973-1999) was significant. So too was the Foreign Direct Investment attracted to Ireland by virtue of its EC membership and its highly developed system of state aids and other investment incentives (O'Malley 1981). Economic self-interest thereby defined an early and broad domestic consensus in favour of membership (Coakley 1983).

That consensus was reflected in Irish policy objectives towards the European Communities. These included the development of a treaty-based and substantial regional/cohesion policy (O'Donnell 1991) – an early precursor of "fiscal federalism" – and the maximisation of budgetary transfers through the Common Agricultural Policy (Conway 1991). This latter objective entailed defence of CAP market intervention mechanisms as well as support for structural policies designed to improve the competitive position of Irish agricultural producers. Irish policy makers, determined to maximise the inflow of overseas capital through Foreign Direct Intervention, were also anxious to minimise the direct and indirect costs arising from the Communities' regulatory regime. Such costs were deemed to have an adverse impact on overseas, particularly North American, multinational investment and to weaken the competitive position of domestic industry. Due to its political sensitivity, policy makers were also anxious to ensure that developments within the framework of foreign policy co-operation (EPC and later CFSP) were not seen by a domestic audience as threatening Irish neutrality (Laffan 1991).

In more recent years, "Europe" is seen as having provided the foundations and the blueprint for Ireland's economic success (NESC 1999). First, regional, structural, social and cohesion funds developed Ireland's physical and human capital base and thereby helped to establish the necessary conditions for Ireland's recently spectacular economic growth. Second, the European social model of "partnership" between the state, employers, trade unions and other interest groups provided the political framework within which from the late 1980s, national development programmes could be agreed and resources directed toward shared goals of growth and prosperity. Finally, the macroeconomic template imposed by Economic and Monetary Union (together with a hard-won domestic economic consensus) imposed a crucial discipline on national finances and established a policy focus on competitiveness, low inflation growth and labour market flexibility. With economic growth rates at more than twice the OECD average in the 1990s and expectations of continued growth at above 6 per cent per annum well into the next decade (ESRI 2000), the Union is seen to have been good for Ireland.

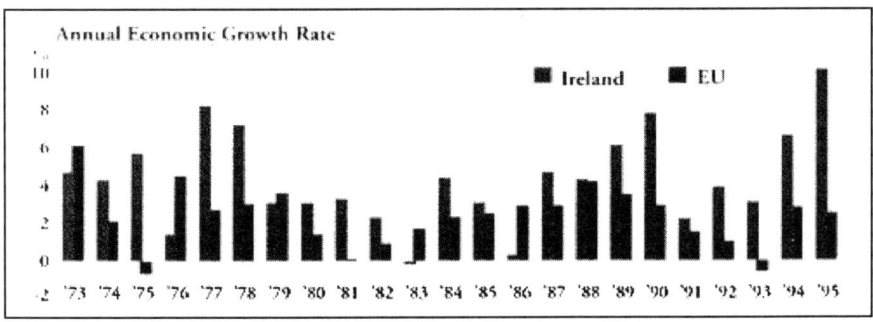

Source: Department of Foreign Affairs http://www.irlgov.ie/iveagh/eu/facts.html

At a political level, Irish interest and commitment to Europe is predicated upon its successful, low-key, non-confrontational exploitation of short and medium-term opportunities. The approach of successive Irish governments has been to position the state at the rhetorical core of the integrative process (presenting Ireland as a "good European") while aggressively prosecuting the state's short term material interests. In the main this has meant Irish governments sailing in the wake of larger partners with shared interests and only rarely darting out from behind that political cover to pursue specific interests. It is, according to a memorandum presented to a key cabinet subcommittee in 1996 "very much in our interests to be *seen* to be amongst those that are willing to contemplate further steps in the process of integration" (original emphasis). Moreover such perceptions were "an important element in the pursuit of our interests in the Union" (Memorandum 1996).

The traditional picture thus far painted does not, however, include the perspective of seismic change that the Union now faces. Ireland's economic success has removed most of the state from the category of Objective 1 less-developed regions and it now raises the very real prospect of Ireland becoming a net contributor to the Union budget. The significance of this psychological change should not be underestimated as it marks a shift from what was once pejoratively characterised as a "begging bowl" mentality toward that of a more assertive and self-confident strategist (*The Irish Times* 6 May 1998; Laffan & O'Donnell 1998). The domestic political repercussions of this change are as yet unclear although "future referendums (on EU treaty change) may reveal more in the way of membership costs than benefits" (Keatinge 1994, 170).

Enlargement poses its own challenges to Ireland's positive engagement with Europe (NESC 1997). The scale and scope of institutional reform that has been proposed to accommodate enlargement challenges many of the most dearly held Irish assumptions about institutional balance. Enlargement's impact on major policy portfolios such as agriculture is also significant, accompanied as it is by – from an Irish perspective – the unwelcome redesign of basic policy mechanisms. The movement towards a European defence and security capacity touches upon a neuralgic point in Ireland's relationship with Europe. Irish policy elites are acutely conscious of the political costs of "opting out" of any agreed defence/security structures and the implications of Ireland's marginalisation from a new core policy area. At the same time, they are aware of the fact that any treaty reform package that entails – or which may be characterised as entailing - the "loss" of Irish neutrality, risks rejection in a popular referendum.

Ireland and Amsterdam

The Irish Government's ambitions for the 1996 Intergovernmental Conference (IGC) were coloured by the fact that it held the Council presidency in the second half of that year and delicate negotiations on the launch of Economic and Monetary Union had yet to be concluded. Therefore, its most immediate priority was the successful conduct and conclusion of its presidency – including the submission of a general outline of a draft for treaty reform as requested by the 1996 Florence summit. Moreover, that task was complicated by the fact of Ireland's unique relationship with the United Kingdom (see Gillespie 1996). Through its presidency, the Irish Government was most anxious to avoid the marginalisation of the British in the IGC negotiations. The beleaguered administration of Prime Minister John Major was fighting its own (largely unsuccessful) battles against Conservative Party Eurosceptics. As a result, the Irish Government was determined to avoid worsening an already difficult relationship between Britain and its European partners which would force unwelcome choices between Ireland's core bilateral relationship and its European ambitions (Halligan 1997, 183).

As regards the presidency itself, Irish Governments have traditionally seen these 6 monthly periods in the chair of the Council of Ministers as an opportunity to generate valuable political capital. Indeed, in the words of a former Taoiseach, Garret FitzGerald "It is through successful handling of the heavy responsibilities involved in Community presidencies that small countries can make their most significant contributions to the European Union.... this is particularly important (to Ireland), because (Ireland is) one of the major beneficiaries of Community budget transfers while contributing nothing to its defence and security" (*Irish Times* 4 May 1996). At a domestic level too, the Government hoped to generate some political advantage – attempting to characterise its presidency as being concerned with the pursuit of "peaceful Europe, secure jobs, sound money and safe streets" (*The Irish Times* 24 June 1996).

In general terms, Irish ambitions for the IGC were consistent with those that had gone before and which continue to underscore Ireland's relationship with the Union. These are: to maintain a position at the core of the integrative project, to preserve, protect and defend existing institutional balances that are deemed to be sympathetic to Irish and small state interests and to ensure that developments in the field of security and defence may be presented to a domestic audience as involving no threat to Irish neutrality. The Irish determination to position the state as close as possible to the rhetorical core of the integrative project reflects the belief that as a small state in an enlarging Union, political proximity to the decision-making centre maximises influence therein. The greatest perceived danger for Irish policy makers is, therefore, the threat posed by a serious deterioration in Britain's relationship with the rest of the Union.

For the authors of a major report outlining the issues, options and implications for Ireland in the 1996 IGC, the most "malign scenario" for Ireland at the IGC was one in which British euro-tensions came to be insurmountable and could only be reconciled by creating a two-tier, or variable geometry Union. In such a case, Irish policy makers would have to make difficult and costly choices (IEA 1995). Therefore, a key function of the Irish Presidency was to ensure that Britain was kept on board – even as Britain's European partners held their breath for what was a seen as a near inevitable change of government in the weeks preceding the final IGC summit. According to Garret FitzGerald this meant that "...in the presidency we must be concerned not only with protecting our interests but also with finding ways...to conciliate differences between the British and the rest." (*The Irish Times* 16 March 1996). A report to a cabinet subcommittee illustrates the practical difficulties of having to make choices between Britain and Europe. In the case of integrating the Schengen provisions on passport-free movement for example, Ireland was faced with "the stark prospect of either the loss of the

Common Travel Area (with the UK) or relegation from the core of the Union" (Memorandum 1996).

This function – from the perspective of Dublin – was also seen to be of strategic interest to Ireland's European partners. Based upon their shared history and the depth of contemporary relationships, it was assumed that the Irish were best placed to understand the British and that they had a greater comparative capacity for dealing with them. The Irish, it was thought, could explain the British to the continentals and the continentals to the British. According to one former Taoiseach "We should not be surprised at these expectations of our capacity to understand and get on with the British. The manner in which successive Irish governments have dealt with Britain over Northern Ireland during the past quarter of a century commands considerable respect on the Continent." (*The Irish Times* 4 May 1996)

On institutional reform, the position of the Irish Government towards the IGC was formally laid out in a Government White Paper published in March 1996 (Government of Ireland 1996). The Irish position, however, had been established sometime earlier and again reflected well-established lines in Irish policy. Speaking on 22 May 1995 the Tánaiste (Deputy Prime Minister) and Foreign Minister, Dick Spring TD, argued that the key issue vis-à-vis institutional reform was the defence of "balance" both between and within the EU's institutions. The existing balance was deemed to be "delicate," "fair and effective" and reflective of a "reasonable equilibrium" between the Member States. The Minister insisted that while the Government remained open to proposals for change, the "onus, however, will be on any member state presenting proposals for reform of the system to demonstrate that their proposals would in reality result in a more efficient system" (Spring 1995). The core of the Government's position was that "Ireland's interests are best served through strong central institutions in the European Union, within which we can play a full role and ensure that our voice is heard." The Commission was "central" to this analysis and only its exclusive right to initiate legislation had "...ensured that the competing national interests of the member states...are reconciled in texts prepared by an independent institution which reflects the common interest" (*The Irish Times* 23 May 1995).

On security and defence the government's White Paper insisted that Ireland supported the principle of a more effective Common Foreign and Security Policy and was willing to consider proposals in that regard. At the same time, however, the government indicated that it would accept only limited engagement in the so-called "Petersberg Tasks" of the Western European Union insisting that "The Government do not intend that Ireland will be involved in tasks of combat forces in crisis management" (Government of Ireland 1996, 140). The three-party coalition government also committed itself to the holding of a popular referendum in the event that anything agreed in the context of the 1996 IGC would entail a reversal in Ireland's non-membership of any military alliance (the Government's own definition of "neutrality"). According to the Tánaiste this would "...ensure that Ireland's policy of military neutrality will remain unchanged unless the people themselves decide otherwise" (*Irish Times* 19 October, 1995).

The IGC Agenda

If we move beyond the "big ticket" items in the Irish negotiating basket, we can take a closer look at some of the detailed Irish opening positions on issues and assess the strategies designed to achieve negotiating objectives. As regards issues under Pillar One of the European Union, the Irish approach was characterised as being one which would "enable us to demonstrate our positive and constructive position" (Memorandum 1996). The Government's strategy was reactive rather than proactive. It would limit itself to responding to proposals from other Member States or from the Presidency and would make its own proposals in a limited number of areas only when "it may prove useful, in the first place from the domestic point of view" (Memorandum 1996). These areas were ultimately specified as being employment and the fight against drugs.

On employment the Irish objective was to achieve a separate treaty chapter dedicated to this issue, written in clear and precise terms, but avoiding any additional fiscal expenditure or any commitment to "full employment." It was also deemed important from a political point of view that the Government be seen by the domestic electorate to be active on this issue. The Irish Congress of Trade Unions – a key constituency in referenda battles – had earlier indicated that its support for further treaty change would be conditional on a tough, specific and detailed chapter on employment (*The Irish Times* 15 May 1996). Indeed, the only specific proposal for treaty change discussed at an early stage by the Government's Ministers and Secretaries Group – the cabinet subcommittee tasked with co-ordinating Ireland's input to the IGC – was a draft chapter on employment which, it was proposed, would be tabled at the IGC by the Tánaiste and Minister for Foreign Affairs.

Faced with a domestic crisis in the proliferation of drugs and drug trafficking in Ireland, the Government was also anxious to underline the utility of a European framework in tackling an issue that was clearly of cross-border significance. Drugs, according to the Irish member of the IGC Reflection Group was an issue that the EU had failed to come to terms with and was an example of "...how everyday issues of concern to the citizen are not being tackled in a sufficiently co-ordinated way in Brussels." (*The Irish Times* 25 September 1995). Government proposals sought to remove ambiguities in the Treaty over members' commitment to customs co-operation and to provide for higher levels of co-operation on a range of activities such as communications infrastructures, the adequacy of port and airport search facilities, and administrative co-ordination.

Far from the shores of domestic political interest, the issue of "flexibility" within the Union also exercised the attention of Irish negotiators. In the light of perceived British obstructionism and further waves of enlargement, proposals to allow the creation of a "core" of member states pursuing deeper integration within the EU treaty framework were proliferating. In that context there was an absolute Irish determination to clip the wings of such proposals so that such an option could operate only in a limited number of circumstances and only under the tightest institutional control. The Irish concern was to avoid the formalisation of any "variable geometry" or "multi-speed" Union that would force unwelcome choices upon Irish decision-makers. In their earliest contributions to this debate, the Irish negotiating team insisted that any proposal to employ a "flexibility clause" would have to be initiated by the Commission. It would also have to be framed in an inclusive way so that any use of the EU's institutions and legal framework would always start with a collective decision of the 15. This was another part of a broad cross-party consensus on the EU's institutional framework. The previous government's junior minister handling the EU portfolio had already rejected models of variable geometry. He had insisted that "Ireland was not interested in being in any slow lane or outer circle of the European Union," and that arguments based on existing treaty-based opt-outs (on EMU and Social Policy for example) should not be allowed to "elevate regrettable exceptions to the status of orthodoxy." (*The Irish Times* 23 September 1994).

On other institutional issues the Irish position was predictable. At its core rested the assertion that "there is merit in sticking to the existing institutional arrangement and continuing with the process of incremental change" rather than embarking upon any radical reform of institutional structures (IEA 1995, xiii). The Irish were especially anxious to defend the Commission's sole right of legislative initiative and its centrality to the policy process – the Commission being defined by the Taoiseach, John Bruton, as being at the "heart of integration" (*The Irish Times* 6 December 1995). Irish policy makers insisted that a strong Commission was the best advocate of small state interests and the best insurance against the development of a large state *directoire*. There was therefore a determination to maintain the right of Irish Governments to nominate one member of the Commission – and consequent opposition to any proposal for "senior" and "junior" Commissioners. The Government consistently made it clear that it was "not prepared to compromise on the right to a full Commissioner" (Memorandum 1996). According to the Tánaiste this did not cut across the effectiveness of the

Commission since: "No member state attaches greater importance than Ireland to an effective and independent Commission…(but) the right of all member states to nominate a full member of the Commission is not only compatible with that objective, but necessary for the effectiveness of the Commission." The issue, according to Irish sources, was simply "non-negotiable" (*The Irish Times* 1 May 1995).

As regards the Parliament, the Irish position was far less full-blooded. Even though Irish popular support of the Parliament as an institution was exceptionally high – with 63 per cent saying it served their interest well or very well (*The Irish Times* 28 November 1995) – Irish Government reservations in giving more power to the Parliament remained. These doubts were rooted in the belief that as an institution the Parliament was – in the words of the Taoiseach – "somewhat disengaged from European opinion." (*The Irish Times* 30 March 1995). In their deliberations therefore, senior civil servants argued that an extension in the use of the co-decision procedure might best be considered on a "case by case basis." Ireland might then support a general extension in its use *except* in case of the CAP or the Common Commercial Policy and only so long as it was not automatically linked to the use of QMV within the Council. A reapportionment of seats in a Parliament limited to 700 members was also acceptable with the proviso that smaller Member States were left with an unspecified "adequate level of representation." (Memorandum 1996).

As regards the Council, the Irish Government adopted a utilitarian approach that might best be characterised as supporting proposed extensions to QMV where such extension looked most likely to occur. In that way there would be "a certain advantage in Ireland having been seen to have taken a positive view" (Memorandum 1996). Four specific proposals for the extension of QMV had explicit Irish support. These were in the areas of transport, culture, research and the environment. Irish policy makers opposed any use of QMV as regards fiscal matters or treaty change and had reservations in the area of social policy so long as the UK maintained its opt-out on such provisions. Government Departments were asked to review treaty provisions relevant to their own areas of responsibility and were requested to "justify in detail" where they felt unanimity in Council voting should be retained. If such justification was not forthcoming – or not found to be credible – the Irish would maintain "an open mind" on QMV's extension in that field.

The weight of national votes in the Council was not in itself deemed to be of vital Irish interest but it was seen in the context of other institutional proposals. The Government was concerned that any radical shift in voting weights might be perceived as resulting in the marginalisation of Ireland within the Council. This perception would be exacerbated if such a development were to be linked with any substantial loss in parliamentary seats and proposals that would result in the loss of an "Irish" seat at the Commission. In more general terms, there was also some concern expressed by Irish negotiators about the central position of the European Council being won at the expense of the General Affairs Council.

As regards Pillar Two issues, the Irish Government – addressing itself to the domestic audience – translated proposals in this area as being simply a European extension to Ireland's existing peacekeeping duties exercised through the UN. With the single reservation on the use of combat forces in support of crisis management operations, Irish policy makers endorsed proposals for a more effective Common Foreign and Security Policy. The Government did, however, oppose suggestions that the WEU be formally merged into the EU. That opposition emerged, however, within the context of substantial opposition from several other Member States and, in particular, the opposition of the British Government – in both its Conservative and Labour formulations. While the Government remained concerned that any move towards a common defence would require an Irish "opt out" and a consequent step away from the main parlour of European integration, they were even more alert to domestic political opposition. In the event, senior Government figures argued that the Amsterdam Treaty entailed an indefinite delay to the merger project and that it had instituted a "double lock" on the future development of a Common Defence. This had been achieved through the new treaty's demand that a unanimous decision of the European Council would first be necessary and the stipulation that any such a decision would have to respect national constitutional requirements (*The Irish Times* 19 June 1997).

Issues in Pillar Three exercised considerable Irish attention, dealing as it did with issues of political sensitivity. At the same time, the Government identified several areas in which a high profile was deemed to be desirable.

The proposed integration of the Schengen *acquis* on passport-free movement was one problematic area for Irish policy makers since – as noted above – it encapsulated the dilemma that forced a choice between Ireland's closest neighbour and its European partners. The strategy adopted was comparatively striking in so far as it entailed marshalling Irish arguments against the principle of integration. The Irish Government initially insisted, for example, that the Schengen states had yet to prove their case for Union-wide "added value" resulting from the integration of the Schengen *acquis*. In the certain expectation, however, that they would lose this argument, the subsequent approach was agreed to be that of trying to "mitigate the damage that (Schengen's) incorporation on a variable geometry basis will do to our interests" (Memorandum 1996). The core of those interests was to maintain the Common Travel Area with the United Kingdom and only then to "explore" how far Ireland could go – in both rhetorical and practical ways – moving towards indicating its support for the Schengen model. According to the Tánaiste, such a model would need to facilitate Irish participation in the Schengen arrangements to the maximum extent desired by the Irish Government (*The Irish Times* 9 May 1997).

The Government also identified action against drug trafficking as a central political objective in Pillar Three negotiations and for its presidency overall. It hoped to see the protection of the Union's external frontiers defined at least in part by the fight against drugs and aspired to seeing an identifiable package of measures emerging from the IGC which might be presented to a domestic audience as a concrete Irish contribution to the new treaty. This came to be reflected in Irish support for additional measures in the realm of cross-border co-operation in criminal matters.

The longest single section in the final Irish Presidency draft on possible treaty amendments was concerned with Justice and Home Affairs issues, consisting mainly of Irish-drafted amendments. These proposals listed areas in which Member States might cooperate to greater effect and where they might develop common action. They included all forms of police co-operation; the combating of drug trafficking; preventing the trafficking of persons and offences against children; preventing racism and xenophobia and judicial co-operation. The Irish Presidency also suggested setting 1 January 2001 as a target date for the completion of the development of the EU as "an area of freedom, security and justice." This would have involved setting target dates for new rules governing the crossing of the EU's external borders; drawing up common visa rules; setting out common asylum and immigration rules and providing for more coherent action against illegal drugs.

Alliances With Other Players

As indicated above, coalitions are a crucial feature of the Irish approach to the Union in general and the 1996 IGC in particular. One interesting aspect of this ambition to participate in coalition building is an Irish determination to avoid exposure as a close partner of the United Kingdom. On many key issues Irish and British interests are comparatively close. Nonetheless, there does appear to be an abiding ambition to distinguish publicly the Irish position from that of the UK – regardless of the substantive proximity of their positions. On the integration of the Schengen *acquis*, for example, it was argued within government that "our approach should be seen to be quite distinct from that adopted by the UK" while Ireland's very conservative position on flexibility had to be presented in such a way "which does not put us in a UK camp" (Memorandum 1996).

At the same time however, there does appear to be significant, if informal, co-ordination between the two governments on which of them has the strongest negotiating position and/or arguments in a portfolio where both share a similar position. On the issue of flexibility, for example, there was understood to have been significant British satisfaction taken from the fact that the Irish delegation was making the running on this issue within the IGC. While the antipathy to "flexibility" was shared, the Irish could frame their arguments from a perceived position as a "good European" and their opposition could not be dismissed – as might that of the British – as simply being anti-European obstructionism. Similarly, the Irish, feeling themselves rather exposed on defence and security issues, were more than happy to sail in the wake of British objections to an EU/WEU merger. The British could construct their arguments from a committed "NATO-first" perspective. This was seen in Dublin as being more powerful than the arguments to be put forward by a country that might best be seen as being semi-detached from the mainstream of European security debates (*The Irish Times* 2 May 1997).

In many portfolios there are other well-established Irish partnerships. These include alliances with the French on protection of the CAP, with the so-called "cohesion four" on redistributive policies and often with Austria, Finland and Sweden on issues of security and defence. With the Dutch, Belgians and Luxembourgers the Irish share perspectives on defence of the "Community-method" in decision making, in opposition to the development of a large state *directoire*, on the rights and role of smaller states and on the defence of the Commission's political and legislative prerogatives. The Irish have also shared, from time to time, positions with the UK and Germany on free trade and competitiveness issues. The fluidity of such alliances and cross-interest brokerage that ensues in the kinds of package deals constructed within IGCs is quite important to a smaller player such as Ireland – friend to all at some time and enemy of none all of the time.

Domestic Actors in the Irish European Drama

The key Irish actors in this European drama are to be found in the Executive. Three major departments of state determined the broad lines of Ireland's strategy towards the 1996 IGC: the Department of the Taoiseach, the Department of Finance and the Department of Foreign Affairs. While most day to day management of Ireland's relationship with the Union is left in the hands of the "line" departments such as Agriculture, Enterprise and

Employment, Environment etc, the key co-ordination function rests in the hands of the Department of Foreign Affairs.

Strategic management, however, is largely an ad hoc affair. At various points in Ireland's membership of the Union, cabinet subcommittees and ministerial task forces have been established to meet specific challenges whether that be the 1992 Single Market project or the 1996 IGC. These subcommittees – including the most senior of them, the Ministers and Secretaries Group – meet on an irregular basis and then only in response to specific issues. In the meantime, a cadre of senior experts liase informally through a comparatively open and "light" civil service bureaucracy and only slightly more formally through the Irish Permanent Representation (PermRep) in Brussels and interdepartmental channels of communication. This is presented by Irish officials as being at least in part a comparative advantage that they do not have the same competitive pressures between "great departments of state" (Tonra 1994).

The Oireachtas (parliament) plays only a peripheral policy role on EU issues. Irish parliamentary committees are limited in power and poorly resourced. Moreover, the nature of Ireland's political system is such that, for all intents and purposes, parliament is a servant of the Executive. Apart from offering an arena for set-piece engagements between government and opposition on key IGC issues, the only significant contribution of the Oireachtas to the IGC debate was a report – drafted by academic consultants – on some of the main IGC issues. Among other things, the report called for a referendum if there were to be any significant impact on Irish neutrality arising from reform of the Union's Common Foreign and Security Policy (CFSP). It also argued for the establishment of a European DNA bank for genetic finger printing to assist police forces throughout Europe, and demanded the inclusion of a quantifiable employment target for the treaty and for a special emphasis upon the rights of citizens to a clean and healthy environment. Its central point on the institutional development of the Union was to demand that Ireland, and other small states retain the right to nominate a European Commissioner (*The Irish Times* 2 May 1997).

One key additional domestic actor has been found, however, in the Irish courts. The ambition of the Irish Government in 1986 to ratify the Single European Act through a parliamentary vote was thwarted only when the High Court, and subsequently the Supreme Court, were called upon to intervene. The Supreme Court ultimately ruled (Crotty 1987) that while large parts of the SEA might be said to have flowed naturally from the popular decision to join the Communities in 1973, aspects of the SEA – particularly the provisions on European Political Co-operation (i.e. foreign policy co-operation) – required popular assent.

Subsequently, the courts have intervened to delimit further the rights of Government in pursuing constitutional change – and by an implication not lost upon activists – of the terms of Irish membership of the European Union. The courts have ruled, for example, that it is inappropriate for Government to spend public monies in support of a particular referendum outcome (McKenna 1996). While Ministers and the Government may campaign in a referendum, they must do so without recourse to the public purse – leaving the weight of a referendum campaign upon the shoulders of the political parties and/or campaigning groups. At the same time the courts have also determined that during referenda, "free" time on the State-run broadcasting networks cannot be allocated proportionally on the basis of party political support in parliament but more equally between advocates and opponents of a particular constitutional change (Coughlan 1998). The first of these rulings prompted the Government in 1998 to establish a non-partisan Referendum Commission whose role it is to issue information on the arguments for and against proposals in constitutional referenda. This meant that the Government could avoid the prospect of having to fund publicly what they saw to be a plethora of small, unaccountable, aggressive and anti-establishment political advocacy groups.

The court cases noted above have been taken – at considerable financial risk – by members of this very same small, poorly funded but often well-networked lobby of activists and organisations that are critical of or opposed to Irish membership of the European Union. Populated largely by left-wing activists, members of the Green movement, some trade unionists and some conservative/nationalist organisations, this lobby has employed the courts as a bulwark against the ambitions of the Executive, the overwhelming majority of parliamentary opinion and all of the formal "social partners." While the electoral support of formal political parties within this broad anti-EU coalition would rest below a collective 5-7 per cent in general elections, their arguments in opposition to further EU integration and treaty amendment win between 30 and 40 per cent support in constitutional referenda campaigns on EU treaty change.

Their key arguments in opposition to the Amsterdam Treaty and previously both Maastricht and the SEA, revolve around a loss of sovereignty, a loss of national identity and independence, the threatened imposition of liberal social mores and associated legislation and, crucially, the threat posed to Irish neutrality (Noonan 1992). This latter issue is especially potent and a number of issues are employed to bring it to public attention. These range from the creation of a conscripted European Army, through to the installation of nuclear weapons bases and the loss of a "moral" and "active" and "independent" Irish foreign policy.

For their part, the mainstream social and political organisations in civil society are supportive of both membership of the Union and its further development and integration. Differences do, of course, arise. During the Amsterdam Treaty negotiations, for example, the Irish Congress of Trade Unions threatened to withhold its support for the treaty in any subsequent referendum campaign unless a dedicated, detailed and effective chapter on employment was to be found within it (*The Irish Times* 15 May 1996). Similarly, a range of interest groups and NGOs participated actively in various debates surrounding specific proposals arising from the IGC talks. These included organisations of disabled citizens, adult literacy campaigners, women's groups, youth organisations, groups campaigning against poverty, the unemployed, trade unions and the traditional large sectoral interest groups. While many of these organisations were critical of the final outcome of the treaty – and most complained that the treaty provisions in "their" areas were too timid – very few campaigned actively against the treaty. Most were critically supportive while the larger and well-funded "social partners" actively campaigned in support of the treaty.

For its part, public opinion towards European integration in Ireland appears to be positive but shallow. A brief review of referenda results is indicative of how support has ebbed over time as the integrative threshold has been pushed higher in subsequent rounds of treaty change.

Table 9.1: Irish EC/EU Referenda.

	Votes in Favour	*Votes Against*	*Turn-out*
1972 Membership	83.1	16.9	70.9
1989 SEA	69.9	30.1	43.9
1992 Maastricht	69.1	30.9	57.3
1998 Amsterdam	61.7	38.3	54.9

At the same time, in regular Eurobarometer polls Irish support for EU membership is consistently high with only 8 per cent of the electorate expressing outright opposition to EU membership and a consistent 70 to 80 per cent supporting Irish membership on the basis that it has brought specified benefits to Ireland (Sinnott 1995). This proportion of support reached an all-time high in a 1997 Eurobarometer survey which registered a massive 93 per cent support level among the Irish electorate for further European integration (*The Irish Times* 26 February 1997). On the issues before the IGC, the Irish were among those most sympathetic to the ending of national vetoes in EU decision making, with 46 per cent in favour and 28 per cent against while a larger majority still (56 per cent) favoured sharing more sovereignty with other EU member (*The Irish Times* 28 November 1996). Electors also sought the development of new priority policy areas such as the fight against drugs and international crime - with 27 per cent ranking that at the top of their agenda and 24 per cent arguing that unemployment should be the main EU priority (*The Irish Times* 26 February 1997).

While support may be high, it would appear also to be shallow. Knowledge of the EU is comparatively low. In the autumn of 1995 – in advance of a much-publicised Irish Presidency of the Council of Ministers, less than 25 per cent of people in Ireland had even heard of the IGC (*The Irish Times* 28 November 1995). This had risen to only 34 per cent by the end of the Presidency (*The Irish Times* 26 February 1997). This lack of knowledge was greatest in working class areas where recognition of the EU and its institutions was at its lowest and support for integration was also comparatively weak (Sinnott 1995).

Faced with this "soft" level of support, the Government sought to engage various means for strengthening Irish understanding and linkages to the European project. In a major Government-sponsored report a "Task Force on Communicating Europe" was drawn together and asked to report on ways and means of engaging Irish public attention towards Irish membership of the EU. The final report specified a number of routes towards that end – most of which entailed the "education" of the Irish electorate and its young people on the European Union and improving their access to European information sources (Government of Ireland 1995).

The Ratification Process

The Irish constitution makes no provision for the ratification of treaties by any means other than parliamentary assent. However, the Supreme Court judgement in the Crotty case (Crotty 1987) ruled that the state could not assign, prejudice or compromise the sovereignty of the state except by reference to the people through a referendum amending the constitution. From that date no Government has sought to challenge the assumption that formal constitutional authorisation is required for any substantive amendment of the EU treaties.

In the case of the ratification of the Amsterdam Treaty two controversies arose. The first related to the shape of the amendment and the second to its timing. Initially the Government proposed, on advice from the Attorney General, that a single paragraph amendment to the constitution would authorise the ratification of the treaty and enable the Government to exercise its discretion in pursuing further integration in unspecified areas where this was provided for within the treaty. Mainstream opposition parties immediately objected, claiming that any attempt to issue the Government with a "blank cheque" would raise popular suspicions and endanger the treaty's ratification (*The Irish Times* 30 January 1998). In the event, the Government revised its proposal so that it specified in a second paragraph, those elements within the treaty that provided for further integration and granted the Government explicit authorisation to pursue same – subject to parliamentary approval.

Arguments were then raised about the timing of the referendum. The terms of the 1998 Northern Ireland peace agreement, signed at Belfast on April 10, required a host of implementing legislation which itself implied changes to respective constitutional provisions. In the Republic of Ireland this also entailed, inter alia, the amendment of key constitutional articles on the definition of the state and the removal of a constitutional claim to jurisdiction over Northern Ireland. Arguing that there were direct and indirect linkages between the proposed EU treaty change and the political settlement in Northern Ireland, the Government made a case for holding both referenda on the same date. Senior officials also raised the practical benefits of holding both votes at the same time. In the event, the Government indicated its intention to present both referenda to the electorate on the same day – May 22, 1999. Critics and opponents of the Amsterdam Treaty complained that this decision was based in a desire to "railroad" the Amsterdam Treaty through on the back of a popular settlement to the conflict in Northern Ireland (Mansergh 1999).

The campaign on the Amsterdam Treaty was undoubtedly "lost" within a much broader debate surrounding the prospects for peace in Northern Ireland arising from the Belfast agreement. While the five largest parties in the state all campaigned in favour of ratification of both proposals, the public does not appear to have been engaged in the debate on EU treaty reform. Just 10 days prior to polling day, more than half of the electorate insisted that it did not have enough information to judge the merits or demerits of the treaty (*The Irish Times* 16 May 1998). One month previously, more than 2/3rds of the electorate claimed never even to have heard of the treaty (*The Irish Times* 12 April, 1998). This was despite the expenditure of more than 6 million euro by the Referendum Commission in its own information campaign covering both issues. More than one third of those voting against the treaty explained their vote in terms of a lack of information on the issues.

The tenor of the debate that did exist followed predictable lines. The major political parties, the "social partners" (most trade unions, the employers' organisations and sectoral interest groups) all advocated a "yes" vote to the Amsterdam Treaty. A "No" vote, it was threatened, would endanger Irish prosperity and jobs, would leave Ireland in a state of political limbo vis-á-vis the rest of Europe, would indicate a lack of confidence in Ireland's future and would lose Ireland the added benefits (economic and social) contained in the treaty. Opponents concentrated upon what they saw as the threats posed to Irish sovereignty and neutrality. The implications of agreements on a European defence policy were seen to pave the way for the creation of a European army and Irish adhesion to a nuclear-armed military alliance without further reference to the public through a referendum 1999; Gilland 1999).

Passage of the referendum by 38 to 62 per cent of the valid poll masks some interesting features. First, opposition to the Amsterdam Treaty was highest among the skilled and unskilled working classes, among the young, among women, and in densely populated inner city urban areas. Support was greatest in rural areas, among larger farmers and the professional classes, among those over 65 years of age and among men (Mansergh 1999). Second, the ratio of popular support to opposition was wholly unreflected in parliament where ratification there was opposed by less than a handful of parliamentary deputies. Third, while a lack of information was cited by a large proportion of "no" voters there was certainly no lack of printed material and broadcast time devoted to the subject. The question as to whether referenda are a suitable mechanism for ratification of complex packages of treaty change emerged as a point of debate in the aftermath of the referendum.

The Amsterdam "Leftovers" and IGC 2000

In its approach to IGC 2000, the position of the Irish Government was again firmly rooted in a rhetorical dedication to traditional European ideals coupled with a pragmatic set of short-term negotiating goals.

The Taoiseach, presenting his analysis of the IGC's agenda, was careful to underline Ireland's commitment to the enlargement project and to acknowledge that this process would bring change to the Union. He argued that enlargement was "not narrowly confined to money and markets" but entailed a wider commitment to "freedom, security and prosperity" across the European continent (Ahern 2000). He did, however, raise the rhetorical question as to the possible extent of enlargement – where do the boundaries of the future Union lie? He argued that the process cannot continue indefinitely and that it is now necessary to consider "other forms of association" and how these might be structured so as to create an interlocking and mutually reinforcing network of relationships across the Eurasian continent and southwards towards Africa.

IGC 2000 was presented by the Taoiseach as being a crucial step in the Union's adaptation of itself so as to be ready for enlargement. For the Irish Government, the agenda was broken down into two elements: the Amsterdam "leftovers" (the extended use of QMV, reweighting votes in the Council of Ministers and the number of Commissioners) and a "parallel track" of initiatives including the Charter of Fundamental Rights and the further development of the Union's security and defence capacity.

The overall Irish approach continued to be minimalist, driven at least in part by an emerging ambition not to have to hold a referendum on the next round of treaty change. According to the Minister for Foreign Affairs, Brian Cowan, if the agenda could be confined to the Amsterdam "leftovers" then a referendum would not necessarily be required (*The Irish Times* 4 July 2000). This reflected earlier comments of the Taoiseach, Bertie Ahern when he insisted that while he had no "fear" of a referendum and would welcome a debate on EU institutional matters, his belief was that the limited agenda of IGC 2000 would not address issues requiring constitutional change (*The Irish Times* 13 December 1999). The Government argued, for example, that the proposed Charter of Fundamental Rights was agreed as a political declaration and that any attempt to recast it within the context of treaty change would "inevitably complicate and delay the whole IGC process."

As regards progress in security and defence, the Irish position was again cautious; support for progress in this area was duly noted, alongside the Irish contribution to it. Crucially, however, that support was explicitly contextualised within that which had already been agreed at Amsterdam. Thus, the Taoiseach argued that since the Amsterdam provisions had been in place less than 12 months, it was both premature and speculative to consider further treaty change in this area. Interestingly, however, the Taoiseach lay a clear marker against ambitions to incorporate an Article V-type mutual security guarantee in the treaties. This, he insisted, "is not a road which the Irish people are prepared to travel" and that this fact was "...a matter which our Partners should bear in mind in the context of any proposals to widen the IGC agenda."

On what was presented as the core of the IGC negotiations – the so-called Amsterdam leftovers – the Government was very explicit in setting forth its position and relied again on arguments about delicate and innovative institutional balances which must be "passed on to future generations." Based in research which shows that national publics see "their" Commissioner as a key legitimator of the Union's political and decision making system, the Taoiseach unambiguously drew a line under the right of future Irish Governments to nominate a member of the Commission and dismissed suggestions about rotation, or senior and junior Commissioners. This was a right that he could not "envisage" any Government relinquishing (Ahern 2000).

On both the extension of QMV and the reweighting of votes in the Council, the position of the Irish Government was the same as before. The Irish were "open to any well founded case" for the extended use of QMV except in the area of taxation and "other areas of core national interest." In Irish eyes, the case for reweighting Council votes remained unproven and risked upsetting yet another "delicate" balance. However, in the context of a quid pro quo for the loss of the larger states' second Commission nomination, the Irish Government was open to considering a dual majority system that was easily explained to the public and obviated the necessity of negotiating new, politically sensitive weights among the Member States (Ahern 2000).

The Irish Government was also anxious to forestall assumptions that the treaties' provisions on "flexibility" might be loosened within this round of IGC negotiations. According to the Taoiseach since the existing provisions had yet to be tested and no deficiencies could yet be identified, "the case for wider and easier use remain unproven" and that "the case for radical change has yet to be made."

Conclusions

It is clear from the above analysis that the main lines of Irish policy towards the European Union and its constitutional/treaty development are well established and have been applied with almost identical rigour across at least two phases of treaty change (the IGC 1996 and IGC 2000). In many ways these lines of policy are unsurprising – a commitment to the defence of the central institutions and in particular the Commission, a determination to protect the various institutional "balances" which are seen as having been sympathetic and supportive to Irish policy interests, a dedication to coalition formation in support of policy objectives in treaty negotiations and a determination to stay as close as possible to the political centre of the integrative project. What is perhaps more interesting in the specific case of the Amsterdam Treaty negotiations are the more uniquely "Irish" elements in this overall approach – the highly utilitarian dedication to the rhetoric of integration, the ambivalence towards coalition formation with the United Kingdom, the difficulty with security and defence, the strength (and weaknesses) in popular support for the European project and the efforts made to engage the attention of the Irish public more directly with the European Union.

In the final Amsterdam Treaty all key Irish policy objectives were achieved. Even though several key institutional decisions were left over to another IGC, the Irish clearly marked the ground that their right to nominate a member of the Commission was, from their perspective, unassailable. Blockage of the proposed EU/WEU merger was also a point of satisfaction – with most of the headway having made by the new British administration. On flexibility, as noted above, the Irish made a significant input to debates and argued in the aftermath that they had been significant players in ensuring that the scope for flexibility would be limited and set firmly into an all-EU institutional context. On Schengen the Irish managed to square their crucial circle of matching a British opt-out on passport-free travel while ensuring that the framework to that opt-out was distinctive from the UK's and structured in a more integrationist-friendly way. There was also some success on the policy issues prioritised by the Irish in their Presidency and subsequent IGC negotiations. As well as the new treaty chapter on employment – which closely reflected the earlier Irish draft – the new treaty also included new measures in the fight against crime which, the Taoiseach claimed, "the Irish presidency put a lot of work into." Finally, as the result of a late Belgian proposal, the Irish also claimed the unexpected victory of a new right of citizens to correspond with the Union's institutions, and get a reply, in the 12 treaty languages (as opposed to Official Languages) which included Irish (*The Irish Times* 17 June 1997).

At the rhetorical level the Taoiseach, Mr Bruton made all the right noises. The extension of qualified majority voting agreed was, he insisted, "modest" and he gravely expressed his disappointment that it had not been more significant. Moreover, he averred that he was "…particularly disappointed at the quarter from which the opposition to that has come," in a direct reference to the German Chancellor, Dr Helmut Kohl. Significantly, Mr. Bruton accused those who framed the Maastricht Treaty of bearing some responsibility for the lack of progress on key issues at Amsterdam. "At Maastricht they set up a number of issues to be dealt with (in 1996), and they probably knew it could not be done. That's a lesson people can learn from this: if you say you can't deal with a problem now and you decide to let four years elapse before dealing with it, those years will elapse and you'll have to face it then anyway" (*The Irish Times* 17 June 1997).

Ireland's experience in the European Union has been a case study in success. Ireland has changed much as a result of EU membership and has contributed to change within the EU and the Irish electorate has given strong support to the country's participation in the further evolution of European integration. Conscious of its political and economic advantages for Ireland, successive Irish Governments have shown a strong commitment to the integration process. As the Government's White Paper on Foreign Policy states, "Ireland has been a full participant in the process of European integration for a generation. We have benefited enormously from membership of the European Union, and have at the same time contributed comprehensively to the Union's development. Irish people increasingly see the European Union not simply as an organisation to which Ireland belongs, but as an integral part of our future. We see ourselves, increasingly, as Europeans. Ireland's membership of the European Union has always been about more than free trade and financial transfers, important as these may be. The period of our membership of the Union has coincided with an increase in national self-confidence, a strengthening of our identity and an increase in our international profile."

Bibliography

Ahern, Bertie (2000). *Ireland and the EU: Future Prospects*, address by the Taoiseach, Mr. Bertie Ahern T.D., to the Institute of European Affairs, Dublin, 21st March.

Barrett, Gavin (ed.) (1996). *Justice Cooperation in the European Union*, Dublin: Institute of European Affairs.

Coakley, John & Michael Gallagher (eds.) (1996). *Politics in the Republic of Ireland*, Dublin: PSAI Press.

Coakley, John (1983). "The European Dimension in Irish Public Opinion 1972-1982", pp. 43-67, in David Coombes (ed.), *Ireland and the European Communities: Ten Years of Membership*, Dublin: Gill and Macmillan.

Conway, Andy (1991). "Agricultural Policy," pp. 42-59, in Patrick Keatinge (ed.), *Ireland and EC Membership Evaluated*, London: Pinter.

Coombes, David (ed.) (1983). *Ireland and the European Communities: Ten Years of Membership*, Dublin: Gill and Macmillan.

Coughlan v The Broadcasting Complaints Commission and Radio Telefis Eireann and the Attorney General (Notice Party), High Court, 24 April 1998.

Crotty, William & David E. Schmitt (eds.) (1998). *Ireland and the Politics of Change*, New York: Longman.

Crotty v An Taoiseach and the other members of the Government of Ireland, Ireland and the Attorney General, Supreme Court, [1987] ILRM 400, 9 April.

Drudy, P.J. & Dermot McAleese (eds.)(1984), *Ireland and the European Community*, Irish Studies 3, Cambridge: Cambridge University Press.

ESRI (2000). *Quarterly Economic Commentary*, June 2000, Dublin: ESRI.

Gilland, Karin (1999). "Referenda in the Republic of Ireland," *Electoral Studies*, Vol. 18, No. 3, pp. 430-438.

Gillespie, Paul (ed.) (1996). *Britain's European Question: The Issues for Ireland*, Dublin: Institute of European Affairs.

Government of Ireland (1996). *Challenges and Opportunities Abroad: White Paper on Foreign Policy*, Dublin: Department of Foreign Affairs.

Government of Ireland, Communicating Europe (1995). *Report of the Communicating Europe Task Force*, Dublin: Communicating Europe Task Force.

Government of Ireland (1971). *The Accession of Ireland to the European Communities: White Paper*, Dublin: Department of Foreign Affairs.

Hederman-O'Brien, Miriam (1983). *The Road to Europe: Irish Attitudes 1948-1961*, Dublin: Institute of Public Administration.

Institute of European Affairs (1995). *The 1996 Intergovernmental Conference: Issues, Implications and Options for Ireland*, Dublin: Institute of European Affairs.

Keatinge, Patrick (ed.) (1992). *Maastricht and Ireland: What the Treaty Means*, Dublin: Institute of European Affairs.

Keatinge, Patrick (ed.) (1991). *Ireland and EC Membership Evaluated*, London: Pinter.

Keatinge, Patrick (ed.) (1991). *Political Union*, Studies in European Union No.1, Dublin: Institute of European Affairs.

Keogh, Dermot (ed.) (1989). *Ireland and the Challenge of European Integration*, Cork: Hibernian University Press.

Laffan, Brigid & Rory O'Donnell (1998). "Ireland and the Growth of International Governance," pp. 156-177, in William Crotty & David E. Schmitt (eds.), *Ireland and the Politics of Change*, New York: Longman.

Laffan, Brigid (ed.) (1996). *Constitution-Building in the European Union*, Dublin: Institute of European Affairs.

Laffan, Brigid (1991). "Sovereignty and National Identity," pp. 187-189, in Patrick Keatinge (ed.), *Ireland and EC Membership Evaluated*, London: Pinter.

Laver, Michael; Michael Gallagher, Michael Marsh, Robert Singh, & Ben Tonra (1995). *Electing the President of the European Commission*, Trinity Blue Papers in Public Policy No.1, Dublin: Department of Political Science.

Maher, D.J. (1984). *The Tortuous Path: Ireland's Accession Negotiations to the European Communities*. Dublin: Institute for Public Administration.

Maguire, John & Joe Noonan (1992). *Maastricht and Neutrality: Ireland's Neutrality and the Future of Europe*, Cork: People First/Meitheal.

Mansergh, Lucy (1999). "Two Referendums and the Referendum Commission: The 1998 Experience," *Irish Political Studies*, Vol.14, pp.123-131.

McKenna v An Taoiseach Supreme Court, [1996] 1 ILRM 81.

Memorandum (1996). Unpublished official *memorandum* tabled to cabinet subcommittee on Irish negotiating strategy in advance of the 1996 Intergovernmental conference. Dated 19 April 1996.

National Economic and Social Council (1999). *Opportunities, Challenges and Capacities for Choice: Overview, Conclusions and Recommendations*, NESC 104, Dublin: National Economic and Social Council.

National Economic and Social Council (1997). *European Union: Integration and Enlargement*, NESC 101, Dublin: National Economic and Social Council.

National Economic and Social Council (1989). *Ireland in the European Community; Performance, Prospects and Strategy*, NESC 88, Dublin: National Economic and Social Council.

O'Donnell, Rory (ed.) (1991). *Economic and Monetary Union*, Studies in European Union No. 2, Dublin: Institute of European Affairs.

O'Donnell, Rory (1991). "Regional Policy," pp. 60-75, in Patrick Keatinge (ed.), *Ireland and EC Membership Evaluated*, London: Pinter.

O'Malley, E. (1981). *Industrial Policy and Development: A Survey of the literature from the Early 1960s*, Dublin: National Economic and Social Council.

Sharp, Paul (1990). *Irish Foreign Policy and the European Community*, Dartmouth: Aldershot.

Spring, Dick (1995). *Speech* to IBEC Kerry Regional Conference on Ireland's EU Presidency Priorities, Tralee.

Tonra. Ben (ed.) (1997). *Amsterdam: What the Treaty Means*, Dublin: Institute of European Affairs.

Tonra, Ben (1996). "Die irishe Präsidentschaft der europäischen Union: Flexibilität und Phantasie," in *Integration*, No. 3, pp. 133-145, Bonn: Institut für Europäische Politik.

Tonra, Ben (1994). "Ireland in European Political Co-operation: The Victory of Substance over Form," *Irish Political Studies*, PSAI Press, Vol. 9, pp. 99-118.

10

Italy: From the "Hard Core" to Flexible Integration

Laura Corrado

Italy and European Integration

Of the six founding members of the European Communities, Italy can undoubtedly be considered as the one most in favour of and committed to the process of European integration. Historically, this enthusiastic support for the creation of a European Community – not only as an economic, but also and above all a political entity[1] – can be explained by the need to rebuild international credibility, heavily compromised by twenty years of fascism and a humiliating defeat in the Second World War. The Italian political class – similar to the German one – realised that a strong commitment in favour of European unification, together with participation in the Atlantic Alliance, was the only possible foreign policy option for Italy in a bi-polar context (Martial, 1996). The further developments of European integration, from the launch of the common market initiative to the signature of the Single European Act and of the Treaty of Maastricht, have constantly received the support of the Italian political *élite*. If criticism was made, it rather tended to stress the insufficient progress achieved in the direction of a closer integration aimed at the creation of a European political and, eventually, federal entity.

At the basis of this attitude, there has always been a diffused conviction, in the political class, of a substantial convergence between the national and the general European interests (Pistone 1991; Bonvicini 1997). Such a convergence touches upon different aspects. From an economic point of view, Italy has undoubtedly benefited from the expansion brought about by the single market[2], as well as from the Community funds in favour of its poorest

---

[1] In the early 1950s, during the discussions for the creation of a European Defence Community (EDC), the Italian Government presented a memorandum – based on a paper by Altiero Spinelli – to add a political dimension to the proposed defence Community (Olivi, 1993).

[2] Italy experienced a remarkably high annual GDP growth during the 1960s (5.22% in 1961-65 and 6.22% in 1966-70) and, to a lesser extent, in the 1970s (2.78% in 1971-75 and 4.46% in 1976-80). Economic growth started to decelerate in the 1980s (1.51% in 1981-85 and 2.97% in 1986-90) and the gap with the other EU economies widened

regions, although they often remain unspent (Cecchini 1997). However, the economic factor is neither the only nor the primary one. More important is probably the perception of Europe as an "anchor" to cling on to in order to be able to overcome internal deficiencies and problems. The need for Italy to "keep up" with Europe and its standards (in every field, from the strictly economic criteria to environmental or health requirements) has often been perceived – and more particularly, in the last few years – as a modernising factor, i.e. the positive input without which crucial internal reforms and changes would have never been achieved, or at least not so quickly. A clear example illustrating this is the budget reform started in 1992 in order to comply with the Maastricht economic criteria and be part of the group of countries entering the third stage of the Economic and Monetary Union (EMU) from the 1 January 1999. The reform process suddenly accelerated in the autumn of 1996, with the levy of a so-called "Euro-tax" (or "contribution for Europe"), a tax designed specifically to reduce the 1997 deficit in time for EMU qualification, which was accepted with a certain resignation by the majority of the population as the inevitable price to pay for "getting Italy into Europe" (*European Voice* 17 November 1996). With the Maastricht target in the horizon, Italy amazingly managed to reduce its public deficit from 10.5% in 1991 to 6.8% in 1996 and 2.7% in 1997 (OECD 1992; Prodi 1999).

If we take a look at the "Eurobarometer" opinion polls, we can see that the same "enthusiastic" support and pro-European attitude has generally been shared also by the majority of Italian citizens.[3] Such a support, even if it has encountered slight variations throughout the years, has always been above the Community average and never below 60%.[4] On 18 June 1989 (the same day of elections to the European Parliament), a consultative referendum was called, asking the Italian citizens whether they were in favour of the transformation of the Community into a Union, with a Government responsible before the European Parliament, giving the latter also a sort of "mandate" to draft a European Constitution. The referendum had the only effect of being a general opinion poll, showing that a very large majority of Italians (88.1%) were in favour of a "federal" evolution of the Community (Cartabia 1998). Interestingly, but not surprisingly considering the very considerable political fragmentation and governmental instability at the

---

during the 1990s (1.16% in 1991-98) when Italian growth lagged behind the EU average (European Commission 1999).

[3] According to the last issue of *Eurobarometer* (n° 52, April 2000), 60% of the Italians support EU membership, 66% support joint EU decision-making (the highest score amongst EU members), and 85% are in favour of the Euro.

[4] *Ibidem*, p. 36.

national level – Italian citizens are at the same time the least satisfied with the way democracy works in their own country, Italy being the only EU country where less than half its population (27% in Autumn 1999)[5] declare to be satisfied with it, against an EU average of 56%. We could even argue that Italians are as positively disposed towards European integration as they are dissatisfied with their national political system.

On the eve of the 1996 Intergovernmental Conference (IGC), support for the EU was particularly high: 86% of the Italians declared themselves in favour of European integration (the highest score amongst EU members), 74% supported EU membership, 75% were in favour of a Common European Foreign Policy, and 75% favoured a single currency.[6] However, in spite of the fact that Italy would hold the Presidency during the first stage of the IGC for the reform of the Maastricht Treaty, awareness of the IGC amongst Italian citizens was one of the lowest (21%, against 56% in Denmark, for example). The forthcoming IGC was evidently considered by public opinion as a marginal item on the broader European agenda, which was rather dominated by the discussions on the single currency and on whether Italy would or would not be part of the "Euroclub" from the beginning. It should be pointed out that, although the discussions about the monetary union were not formally part of the negotiations for the revision of the Treaties, the parallel debate around the single currency (i.e., which countries should enter the third stage, the "Stability Pact" and the sanctions in case of excessive deficits) certainly had an impact on the IGC, and especially on those Member States risking exclusion. As far as Italy was concerned, it is undeniable that its schizophrenic position on flexibility, for instance, was greatly influenced by its fear of being excluded from the monetary "hard core."

However, in spite of the impressive scores mentioned above, there has been a growing contradiction between such a strong pro-European attitude and the day-to-day, actual participation of Italy in the EU decision-making and activities. In particular, the role played by Italy in the process of European integration has steadily diminished since the mid-1980s – somehow paralleling the slowing down of the economy – leading to its progressive marginalisation (Bonvicini 1997). A weak participation in the decision-making phase (and thus, only a limited influence on the shaping of Community policies), delays in the implementation of Community law (CNR 1998), as well as serious difficulties in the utilisation of Community funding are the elements characterising the Italian European policy of the last two decades. The causes of this situation are numerous, but they originate

---

[5] *Ibidem*, p. 13. This figure was slightly higher (34 %) in the spring of the same year (see *Eurobarometer* n° 51, July 1999).

[6] *Eurobarometer* n° 44, April 1996, respectively pp. 14, 15, 43 and 44.

primarily in the instability of the political system (57 Governments since 1946!) and in the lack of appropriate administrative structures able to ensure both the coordination in the definition of national positions and the efficient implementation of Community law (Franchini 1992; CNEL 1996; Cecchini 1997).

The Post-Maastricht Debate

Both during the preparations of the 1991 IGCs on Monetary and Political Union (Italy held the EU Presidency in the second half of 1990) and during the successive negotiations, did the Italian Government insist on the need to strengthen the political pillar of the Union, which was seen as a necessary counterweight and complement to the set up of the EMU pillar (Cangelosi & Grassi 1996). This partly reflected the fear that the focus on EMU and the excessive stress on strict monetary and economic criteria would be very unfavourable to a country such as Italy, whose economic situation was rather critical at the time[7]. However, the results eventually reached on Political Union were not so much influenced by Italy, in spite of the good start provided during the Presidency in the second half of 1990. *De facto* Italy did not do battle to affirm its "federal" ambitions (e.g., extension of the EP competences, a strengthening of the Commission powers, general recourse to qualified majority), reflecting the absence of a real national debate on Italy's European – and in general, foreign – policy and, consequently, a lack of clear objectives, unless particularly sensitive issues (like EMU) were at stake (Neri Gualdesi 1993). On the contrary, Italy's behaviour was somewhat ambiguous. Although, generally speaking, its positions were very close to those of the traditionally pro-integration Member States such as the Benelux countries, Germany[8] and, to a lesser extent, France, it did not refrain from seeking occasional alliances with the UK, in particular on foreign policy and defence issues. The Anglo-Italian Declaration on European Security and Defence of 4 October 1991[9] – which considerably stressed the role to be played by the

---

[7] In 1991, the inflation rate was 6.2% (3.5 above the average of the three best performing countries), the long-term interest rate was 13.1% (3.5% above the average of the three best performing countries), the ratio deficit/GDP was 10.5% and the ratio debt/GDP 102.9% (the parameters set up in Maastricht were 3% and 60% respectively) (OECD 1992).

[8] See for instance the *Joint De Michelis-Genscher Declaration* of April 1991 on the role of the EP (AE, 11 April 1991).

[9] The text can be found in *Agence Europe - Documents*, n°1735, 5 October 1991.

Atlantic Alliance in the development of a European identity in the field of defence, revealing the Italian difficulty in choosing between the European and Atlanticist option[10] – was received with some surprise, if not irritation, from the other Member States (Cangelosi & Grassi 1996; Missiroli 1997). It is also interesting to note that Italy, in spite of its traditionally advanced positions on the (federal) evolution of the EU, did not support the draft Treaty put forward by the Dutch Presidency in September 1991 proposing a unitary structure for the Community,[11] as opposed to the three-pillar structure envisaged in the previous Luxembourg Presidency draft.[12] The reason given by the Italian Government was that the Dutch proposal was not realistic and that no other Member State was ready to support it, however, there was probably also the fear that it could jeopardise a possible agreement with the UK on the link between the EU and WEU (Neri Gualdesi 1993). Concerning the ratification, Italy was the only country where no serious parliamentary debate on the Maastricht Treaty took place. The ratification procedure was indeed relatively quick[13] and the implications of the new Treaty were not thoroughly discussed within the Parliament (at least not prior to the ratification)[14], since it was decided to give a strong signal reaffirming Italy's commitment to European integration, especially taking into account the difficulties encountered by other Member States (Camera dei deputati 1994). Therefore, both at the political and at the public opinion level, few Italians seemed to realise, at the time of its ratification, what Maastricht really meant and implied. Even discussions on the convergence criteria for EMU – a very "hot" issue for Italy – became particularly acute only a little over one year later, during the short-lived centre-right Berlusconi Government (May-December 1994), when the Minister for Foreign Affairs, Antonio Martino, a member of the Euro-sceptics "Bruges Group," repeatedly criticised the Maastricht criteria and the whole

---

[10] It has also to be kept in mind that Italy refused the invitation from France and Germany to take part in the "Eurocorps" – set up in May 1992, but already announced in October 1991 – seen at the time as a potential threat to the Atlantic orientation, which still characterised Italian foreign policy (Aliboni 1993).

[11] *Agence Europe - Documents*, n° 1734, 3.10.91.

[12] *Agence Europe - Documents*, n° 1722/1723, 5.7.91.

[13] The Treaty was approved by the *Senato* on 17 September 1992 and by the *Camera* a few weeks later, on 29 October. The ratification law (n° 454/92) entered into force on 3 November 1992.

[14] A parliamentary enquiry to analyse in detail the implications of the Maastricht Treaty, both at Community and national level, took place just afterwards and was concluded on 20 October 1993 (Camera dei deputati 1994).

strategy to pursue monetary unification,[15] as well as European social policy (*Agence Europe* 15 March 1994 and 17 May 1994). This was probably the first time the other Member States (and the Commission) had serious doubts not only about Italy's willingness to join the single currency, but also about its firm commitment to the European integration process (Cangelosi & Grassi). Some comments in the press went even further, speaking of the possible creation of a "Rome-London axis" (*Agence Europe* 26 May 1994; *Sunday Times* 22 May 1994).

In September 1994, another major debate was sparked off by the controversial document presented by the two *Bundestag* parliamentary groups CDU/CSU (Schäuble and Lamers' paper) on the need for a "hard core" of States – Germany, France and Benelux were mentioned, i.e. the founding members except for Italy – which would be the forerunners of new initiatives aimed at deepening European integration, in order to avoid the EU "becoming a loosely knit grouping of States restricted to certain economic aspects and composed of various sub-groupings."[16] Although it did not represent the official position of the German Government, the document had a considerable impact on countries like Italy which, for the reasons analysed above, already felt the risk of becoming more and more a part of a "second category Europe." Criticism of the document was publicly expressed by the Prime Minister Berlusconi, then in office, who declared that ideas about a core potentially risked "breaking down the European integration process" and were "incompatible with the Maastricht Treaty" (*Agence Europe* 5/6 September 1994).

The 1996/1997 IGC

Launching the IGC: The Italian Presidency

If in 1990, Italy had the responsibility for preparing the mandate of the two parallel IGCs on monetary and on political Union, this time the Italian Presidency coincided with the first stage of the 1996/1997 IGC, launched in Turin on 29 March 1996. It coincided also with a difficult domestic political

---

[15] Martino, during the discussion of parliamentary resolutions prior to the Amsterdam European Council, on 11 June 1997, even admitted that if the Berlusconi Government had lasted longer, he would have asked for the modification of the EU monetary strategy to be included into the new Treaty (Camera dei Deputati 1998).

[16] The full text of the paper, "Reflections on European Policy", can be found in *Agence Europe-Documents*, n° 1895/96 of 7 September 1994.

crisis that started well before the Presidency[17] and, in spite of attempts to avoid a political vacuum during such an important international commitment,[18] it exploded shortly after the beginning of the term, with the Prime Minister, Lamberto Dini, resigning on 12 January 1996 (*European Voice* 4 January 1996; *Economist* 27 January 1996). The situation became worse when, after a failed attempt to create a new Government without dissolving the Parliament, the President of the Republic called for a general election for the 21st of April. This meant that a new Government would not take office – in the most optimistic scenario – before the end of May. In the meantime, the Dini Government would hold office as a caretaker, thus being in an even weaker position than before.

It is obvious that the political turmoil at home and not having a working Government for most of the term of the Presidency created several problems. Criticism concerned both the practical, organisational aspects, e.g., chaotic handling of the meetings, sudden changes in the dates (*European Voice* 18 January 1996 and 7 March 1996) and the lack of political impetus and leadership (Attinà 1996; Svensson 2000).[19] However, as far as the IGC was concerned, in spite of the difficult domestic situation work progressed relatively smoothly under the direction of Silvio Fagiolo, senior Foreign Ministry official who had also been the Italian representative to the Reflection Group, and whose experience in Community affairs ensured continuity.[20] Paradoxically, the traditional weakness of the coordination system for European Affairs within the Prime Minister office, and the predominant role

---

[17] The Berlusconi Government, which had collapsed in December 1994 due to the withdrawal of support from the Northern League Party, had been replaced by a "technocratic Government" led by Lamberto Dini – former Treasury Minister in the previous Government – with the limited mandate of achieving fundamental budget and pension reforms. However, not being the result of an election and thus not backed by a solid parliamentary majority, the Government margin of action was extremely limited and it was on the edge of a crisis almost on a daily basis. This situation protracted for one year, until it was ready to explode just before the beginning of the Italian Presidency of the Union and the launch of the 1996 IGC.

[18] The Italian newspaper "Corriere della Sera" even suggested to ask for a postponement of the Italian Presidency, in order to allow for national political elections without disrupting the EU term (AE 4 November 1995).

[19] See for example, Italy's failure in concluding the Euromediterranean agreements – clearly very important for its own national interests – with Egypt, Jordan and Lebanon.

[20] Fagiolo had also been involved in the Italian Presidency during the second half of 1990 and in the preparation of the 1990/1991 IGC, being the author of the draft approved at the Rome Summit in October 1990 which formally launched the process for the review of the Treaties.

played by the Ministry for Foreign Affairs, was in this case fortunate.[21] More difficult to assess is whether the Italian Presidency had a substantial influence in shaping the IGC discussions. In this respect, besides the domestic crisis two other important external constraints have to be kept in mind: the timing of the Conference itself (which was to be concluded only more than one year later) and the British open policy of non-cooperation, particularly acute between March and June 1996 because of the "mad cow" crisis (*Economist* 25 May 1996; *European Voice* 17, 20 and 22 June 1996), which risked paralysing any progress of the Conference until the British elections of May 1997 (McDonagh 1998).

The Italian views on the IGC were presented by the Government and discussed before the Parliament (*Camera dei deputati* and *Senato*) on several occasions: a first statement on foreign policy guidelines was issued on 23 February 1995, followed by a statement on 23 May 1995,[22] which provided the platform for the Italian representative to the Reflection Group. Finally, the Italian official position on the IGC, as well as the programme for the forthcoming Presidency, were presented to the *Camera dei deputati* and thoroughly debated on 5 to 7 December 1995, leading to the adoption of several resolutions (*Camera dei deputati* 1996). Although the resolutions were not legally binding for the Government, they were politically important, since they demonstrated a substantial unity of views amongst all the parties on Italy's approach to the IGC,[23] thus providing an indirect assurance that Italy's European priorities would remain the same even in case of a change in Government. The official position was detailed and presented to the Conference in the programmatic document of 18 March 1996 ("Position of the Italian Government on the IGC," CONF/3839/96), in which Italy's pro-European commitment was reaffirmed, as well as "its vision of a continually

---

[21] Until the early 1980s, the main coordinating body for Community Affairs was the Ministry for Foreign Affairs. In 1981 a *Department for Community Affairs* (became in 1987 *Department for the Coordination of Community Policies*) was set up within the Prime Minister Office, in an attempt to improve inter-ministerial coordination. Furthermore, since 1980 a Minister for Community Policies (without *portfolio*) is usually – but not always – appointed, with a delegation from the Prime Minister to deal with EU issues. However, in respect of Community affairs, both the Department and the Minister were never given the means nor the power to exert a real coordination, which is therefore still weak (Franchini 1992; Cartabia 1998).

[22] See: European Parliament – Intergovernmental Conference Task Force, *White Paper on the 1996 IGC – Vol. II – Summary of positions of the Member States of the European Union with a View to the 1996 IGC*.

[23] A motion containing a critical reference to the Maastricht Treaty and EMU criteria, called for by former Foreign Minister Martino, was eventually withdrawn (AE 9 December 1995).

evolving integration process aimed at creating a federal structure which fully respects the historical and cultural identities of all its components." The priorities listed followed the structure of the Reflection Group Report, which had highlighted the following three main issues: bringing Europe closer to its citizens; enabling the Union to function better and preparing it for enlargement; endowing the Union with a greater capacity for external action.

For the launch of the IGC at the Turin European Council on 29 March 1996, the Italian Presidency tried to draw up a "pragmatic but ambitious" agenda, through a series of preparatory bilateral meetings with all Member States.[24] This approach attracted some criticism and accusations of repeating the exercise of the Reflection Group, without allowing for a real start of discussions (*European Voice* 7 March 1996). The Turin Conclusions (Council of the European Union 1997) eventually outlined a broad mandate for the IGC, centred around the three main themes mentioned above, with some more specific issues highlighted,[25] such as the fight against unemployment (defined as "the priority task"), Justice and Home Affairs and, in the area of Common Foreign and Security Policy (CFSP), the definition of relations between the EU and WEU "taking into account in particular the deadline of the Brussels Treaty in 1998." It was also confirmed that flexibility was part of the IGC agenda, although the wording was still rather cautious: the Conference was invited to examine "whether and how to introduce rules either of a general nature or in specific areas in order to enable a certain number of Member States to develop strengthened cooperation." From April onwards, the Presidency started to circulate notes (*"fiches"*) on a certain number of issues (30 in total) sometimes even trying to produce a draft Treaty text (e.g., on citizenship or on certain aspects of JHA). In the meantime, on the domestic plan, the outcome of the general elections of 21 April had lead to the formation of a centre-left Government headed by Romano Prodi, with Lamberto Dini – former Prime Minister – appointed as Foreign Minister. The new Government confirmed since its appointment Italy's pro-European orientation, thus ensuring the continuity of its European policy, especially with regard to the efforts required to comply with the EMU criteria (*European Voice* 25 April 1996 and 23 May 1996; *Economist* 27 April 1996).

During the last two months of its term, the Italian Presidency tried to force the pace of negotiations by presenting "summary notes" on the three main topics to be considered by the Conference – relations with the citizens

---

[24] However, in order to avoid any preventive negotiation of the mandate, Fagiolo did not hand out any paper containing the Italian proposals to the delegations (Svensson 2000).

[25] They also contained some typical "hobby horses," such as the status of outermost regions and overseas territories or the compatibility between competition and the principle of universal access to essential services.

(CONF/3848/96), institutions (CONF/3849/96) and external action (CONF/3850/96), which were discussed both at the level of Representatives and of Ministers (an informal conclave was held in Rome on 17 June). The three summary notes eventually became the "Progress Report" presented by the Presidency to the Florence European Council (21 to 22 June 1996) under its responsibility, which had no "claim to be exhaustive" and did not "commit delegations as to the future discussions" (Council of the European Union 1997). Some tentative draft articles were also annexed to the Report.[26] The report identified those few issues in which a broad consensus existed or was possible (i.e., human rights, certain aspects of Justice and Home Affairs cooperation and of CFSP), "open options" (e.g., employment, where a "cautious" and, alternatively, a "more ambitious" approaches were proposed) and those which needed to be discussed further and had to be left for the final stages of the conference (e.g., most of the institutional issues). The section devoted to Common Foreign and Security Policy is probably the area which the Italian Presidency attempted to further emphasise:[27] for instance, by insisting on the need to insert a constructive abstention clause (and, in some cases, for closer cooperation), as a remedy to the "rigidity and even paralysis in the decision-making process." Furthermore, the Report stressed the importance of security and defence issues for the EU (including the relations EU-WEU), recommending to give a "more thorough consideration" to the implications of the conclusions of the NATO's North Atlantic Council meeting on 3 June 1996, which set the objective of developing a European Security and Defence Identity within the Alliance" and provided for the possibility of WEU-led operations including NATO resources. The report also acknowledged a general consensus on two less controversial issues: the establishment of a "stronger policy planning and alarming system," and the appointment of a CFSP High Representative.

Negotiating Amsterdam: Strategy and Alliances
Besides the contributions presented during the term at the helm of the EU, Italy put forward several proposals both during the Irish and the Dutch Presidency, concerning the most important issues covered by the IGC: citizenship and human rights, CFSP, flexibility, Justice and Home Affairs

---

[26] Fagiolo admitted later on that the first idea – then abandoned due to lack of time and support – was to already produce a draft treaty for the Florence Summit (EV 1 August 1996).

[27] See also the intervention of the Minister for Foreign Affairs Dini before the European Parliament, plenary session in Brussels, 3 July 1996 (www.esteri.it/archivi).

cooperation and institutional reforms.[28] Other issues in the Treaty, such as the inclusion of new policies (i.e., civil protection and tourism), more stringent provisions on environment, transparency or the introduction of a hierarchy in Community acts, though mentioned in the Italian position paper of 18 March 1996 (CONF/3839/96), were not formalised afterwards.

Before going into the details of the different proposals, it is worth pointing out that the negotiations that lead to the Amsterdam Treaty took place in a very different context, compared to Maastricht. If during the negotiations of the Maastricht Treaty, Italy seemed to swing between trying to follow the Franco-German tandem and, at the same time, leaning towards the British diplomacy (on defence issues), in 1996 these two options were less practicable. On the one hand, the Franco-German motor appeared not to work as effectively as before[29] and, on the other, the particularly negative attitude of Britain towards any progress in European integration did not leave very much margin for a possible alliance, even on specific issues.[30] Furthermore, the relations with Germany were made difficult by the polemics concerning Italy's economic situation and its participation in the single currency, which Germany – and especially its Finance Minister Theo Waigel – initially opposed, fearing a weakening of the "Eurozone" linked to the Italian participation (*European Voice* 10 April 1997). Nor was there a concrete possibility of forming a Southern block: with France, divergences and difficulties had started even before the launch of the Conference;[31] concerning

---

[28] In the last stage of the Conference, Italy also presented two other proposals (which will not be analysed here), concerning: the inclusion in the Treaty of a new Title on energy (CONF/3905/97) and the attribution to the Commission of regulatory powers to sanction the infringement of the internal market rules (CONF/3913/97).

[29] The only joint Franco-German proposal presented at the Amsterdam IGC was the one on flexibility (CONF/3955/96), on which, anyway, the two countries had different interpretations.

[30] It is nevertheless interesting to note the *Joint Anglo-Italian Declaration on the WEU* (in view of the respective Presidencies of the EU and WEU in the first half of 1998), made at the bilateral summit of Florence on 6 December 1995 (AE 8 December 1995). The declaration stressed the importance of developing closer institutional and operational links between the EU and WEU, as well as to reach effective agreements between the WEU and NATO for the use of the latter's assets in WEU-led operations.

[31] On 24 to 25 November 1995, following the open criticism by Italy of France's nuclear tests in the Pacific, Chirac had cancelled the planned Franco-Italian Summit in Naples (AE 20 November 1995). Divergences had emerged also at the launch of the IGC on the role and participation of the European Parliament to the Conference's work (AE 11 March 1996).

Spain, the Italian-Spanish Summit of Valencia in September 1996[32] had clearly showed Aznar's determination to take Spain into the "hard core" of the Union, both economically and politically, thus refusing the idea of any Southern axis and giving instead priority to the relations with Germany and France.

The first proposal put forward by Italy was a joint contribution with Austria on human rights and citizenship presented on 3 October 1996 during the Irish Presidency (CONF/3941/96). The Progress Report presented in Florence by the Italian Presidency already contained some "consolidated positions" in this area, such as the insertion of certain fundamental principles in the Treaty, including the principle of non-discrimination and the possibility of sanctioning Member States that do not comply with these rights. The proposal of October 1996 went further, providing for: the possibility of the Union acceding to the European Convention on Human Rights (ECHR); the extension of the notion of citizenship, also including the right of association in political parties and trade unions at the European level, as well as the possibility of the citizens (representing 1/10 of the electorate of at least three Member States) proposing draft legislation[33] and – of the citizens of a Member State residing in another State – taking part in municipal referenda. The proposal even codified the right of every citizen to receive an education taking into account the "common heritage" of European civilisation, as well as to learn another EU language different from the mother tongue. A paragraph also referred to the need of respecting the constitutional status of churches and other religious associations "as an expression of the identity and of the culture of the Member States."[34] A further contribution in this area was presented by the Italian Government on 27 February 1997, concerning the abolition of the death penalty (CONF/3832/97). The document proposed to either insert a sentence in the new article on the basic principles on which the Union is founded ("Member States [...] undertake to respect the right not to be subjected to the death penalty or to other cruel, inhuman or degrading punishment") or to make a

---

[32] During the Summit, Italian Prime Minister Prodi had tried to convince Aznar to ask jointly for a derogation (or at least for a "flexible" interpretation) of the EMU parameters. The Spanish refusal – together with criticism on the Commission's part – pushed the Italian Government to present a correction to the draft budget for 1997, almost doubling the initial figures proposed, from 32,500 billion lire to 62,500 billion lire (including the "contribution for Europe," which amounted to almost 13,000 billion) (EV 11 July 1996, 17 October 1996 and 7 November 1996).

[33] The draft article proposed reflects a similar provision (Art. 71) of the Italian Constitution.

[34] Cf. *Declaration n°11 concerning the status of the churches and non-confessional organisations,* annexed to the Treaty of Amsterdam.

declaration, to be annexed to the Treaty, referring to Protocol n° 6 of the ECHR on the abolition of the death penalty.[35]

Another very sensitive issue under the heading "the Union and the citizen" was the question of employment. Although Italy did not present any formal proposals, it was very much in favour of the inclusion in the Treaty of a new Title on employment establishing the commitment of the Member States to better coordinate their labour policies (CONF/3836/96). This was undoubtedly linked to the fact of being one of the EU countries with the highest unemployment rate: 11.6% in 1996 and 11.7% in 1997 (ISTAT 1998). During its Presidency, Italy therefore encouraged the linkage between EMU and an active EU policy to combat unemployment (Fagiolo 1996), supporting the Commission's initiatives aimed at elaborating a European Employment Pact (*Agence Europe* 8 January 1996; 30 March 1996; 18 April 1996). Furthermore, at the ministerial meeting in Nordvijk on 6 to 7 April 1997, Italian Under-Secretary of State Fassino stressed: the need to put employment and monetary policy on the same level (by giving the new Committee on employment a rank equal to that of the Monetary Committee); the explicit mention in the Treaty of the Union's priorities in the field of employment (training, preventive action against long-term unemployment, greater flexibility and non-inflationary growth); and finally, the inclusion of economic and social rights in the Treaty (*Agence Europe* 7 April 1997).

On the Common Foreign and Security Policy, since its first statements on foreign policy matters, including a Joint Statement with Germany on 15 July 1995[36] (*Agence Europe* 17 July 1995), Italy stressed the need to improve and strengthen the Second Pillar of the EU, in order to give the Union a stronger external identity. It is not difficult to understand why developments in this area were particularly important for Italy: the weak and limited CFSP that emerged from the Maastricht Treaty had not prevented the formation of *de facto* foreign policy "*directoires*," from which Italy had often been excluded, as in the case of the "Contact Group" for Bosnia in 1994, in spite of the geographical proximity and the relevant Italian interests in the Balkans (Missiroli 1997). Therefore, already during its term at the helm of the EU,

---

[35] Cf. *Declaration n °1 concerning the abolition of the death penalty*, annexed to the Treaty of Amsterdam.

[36] The two Foreign Ministers (Kinkel and Agnelli) agreed that the IGC should be the opportunity for "a substantial deepening of the integration process." Concerning CFSP, the need for extending qualified majority voting and strengthening the Union's analysis and planning capabilities was stressed. On security issues, it was agreed to develop the security and defence dimensions of the Union, while fully safeguarding the Transatlantic ties and strengthening the role of the WEU, which should be placed under the direction of the European Council (its integration in the EU remaining a long-term goal).

Italy had tried to insist on the importance of making progress in this area, especially in the most problematic ones, i.e. decision-making and defence. The contribution put forward on 25 October 1996 (CONF/3965/96) was quite comprehensive, dealing both with "soft" and "hard" security issues.

On decision making, it was proposed to extend qualified majority voting to all Council decisions taken on the basis of the guidelines and framework previously adopted by the European Council (excluding decisions on the defence area). On questions decided by unanimity, Italy was in favour of introducing a mechanism of constructive abstention, but without granting any possibility of veto to the Member States abstaining. This approach would eliminate "the need for a flexibility clause specifically for foreign policy" (see the proposal on flexibility, CONF/3801/97). The only exception concerned the security and defence field, where flexibility seemed justified "given the objective differences in Member States' situations" (CONF/3965/96). The reference here was obviously to the WEU: Member States should be "authorised to develop, through the institutions, procedures and mechanisms of this Treaty, closer collaboration in the area of security and defence – including cooperation on armaments – based on their common membership of WEU." The authorisation would be granted by the Council by qualified majority at the request of the States concerned, which should in any event "include the Member States of the Union which are also Members of the WEU." Thus, flexibility in the area of defence would become an obligation for WEU members and an opportunity for the non-Members (Stubb 1998).

On the role of the WEU, the proposal provided that the EU "shall have recourse" to the WEU, which is "an integral part of its development with the prospect of an eventual integration," to elaborate and implement decisions and actions having defence implications. Two alternatives were proposed: a Protocol specifying the timetable and stages of WEU integration into the EU, or an amendment to the existing Art. J.4 TEU (providing for a future revision of the Treaty in 2002, on the basis of the progress made and experience gained). At a later stage of the Conference, during the Dutch Presidency, Italy joined five other Member States (France, Germany, Spain, Belgium and Luxembourg) in signing a proposal for a three-stage integration of the WEU into the EU, presented at the Rome Conclave on 24 March 1997 (CONF/3855/97). Although some argued that this proposal came too late and that the proposing Member States were in general not too "serious" about it (Stubb 1998), in the case of Italy, there was a real political will to develop the Union's defence dimension,[37] in parallel and in addition to the "soft military

---

[37] Italy had already presented a proposal on the merger EU-WEU during the Maastricht IGC, namely at the informal meeting of Foreign Affairs in Asolo on 6 October 1990 (Aliboni 1993).

dimension" represented by the inclusion of the Petersberg Tasks (which Italy also supported). The dichotomy European vs. Atlantic defence, which had a major influence on the Italian position during the Maastricht negotiations, seemed to be overcome in Amsterdam, mainly due to the positive evolution of NATO's stance on the development of a European Security and Defence Identity (ESDI).[38]

In May 1997, a third proposal on CFSP was presented jointly with the Spanish delegation (CONF/3908/97), concerning the modification of Articles J.2.(3) and J.5.(4) on the representation within international organisations. The proposal aimed at strengthening the obligation for the Member States participating in international conferences to "keep the other Member States fully informed" and to concert with them on their position. Those Member States also being permanent members of the United Nations Security Council should, in particular, "represent the Union in this organ in matters coming within the common foreign and security policy." This undoubtedly reflected the concern about ensuring a coherent and consistent external representation of the Union, but it also echoed – at least in the case of Italy – the parallel debate (and controversy) concerning the membership of the UN Security Council[39] (Dini 1997b).

The Italian proposal on flexibility was presented at the beginning of the Dutch Presidency, on 15 January 1997 (CONF/3801/97), and helped to keep the debate on the issue alive. The paper followed the "1+3 enabling clause model," i.e. a general enabling clause plus specific provisions concerning the different pillars. As discussed above, one of Italy's main preoccupations concerning flexibility was to avoid or at least minimise the fears of exclusion and marginalisation (the risk that Italy would not participate in the third stage of EMU was still very acute at the time). On the other hand, as one of the founding and more pro-integrationist EU members, Italy was also very keen on being part of the *avant-garde* of Member States promoting and deepening

---

[38] During the 1994 Brussels Summit and the 1996 Berlin Summit, the Alliance leaders had confirmed that the emergence of ESDI would strengthen the European pillar of the Alliance, enabling the European Allies to take greater responsibility for their common security and defence while reinforcing the Transatlantic links.

[39] The Italian proposal for the reform of the UN Security Council suggests adding other 8/10 non-permanent seats to the existing ones, subdivided amongst the different geographic groups and attributed on a rotational basis (for the full text see: http://www.italyun.org/sc.html). The proposal aims at avoiding at any cost the marginalisation of Italy within the UN – taking also into account the fact that since January 1998, Italy has become the 5th largest contributor to the UN budget – which might happen if other proposals, and in particular the so-called "quick fix" attributing two new permanent seats to Germany and Japan (supported among others by the United States), would prevail.

European integration, especially in view of the enlargement. This resulted in an approach which was in principle favourable to flexibility/enhanced cooperation in all three pillars, bearing in mind that it ought to be "the exception and not the rule, not used by a minority to forge ahead while the rest look on; rather it should be the means for avoiding a minority stopping differentiated initiatives from proceeding in a restricted framework with the agreement of the majority" (CONF/3801/97). This approach was already clear from the wording used: "differentiated integration," as opposed to enhanced/closer cooperation (for instance, in the Franco-German proposal). Thus, the Italian proposal contained a series of strict rules[40] and conditions in the enabling clause, which would limit and frame the recourse to it, especially within the First Pillar: flexibility was to be a last resort measure; the Commission would be the one to decide whether and when to trigger flexibility; core policies (citizenship, the four freedoms, CAP and fishery policy, competition, common commercial policy and economic and social cohesion) would be excluded; non-participating States would have the possibility of joining the initiative at any time.

The proposal significantly differed from the Franco-German one (CONF/3955/96) on the role of the Commission which, in the latter, was not to be the judge of the "desirability" of the "closer cooperation projects put forward by Member States," but was only given the right to express a "formal opinion (assent) on their compatibility with the conditions set in the general clause," which "would serve as the basis for the Council's decision" on them. Furthermore, the Franco-German proposal was also quite strict on the later accession of the non-participating Member States, which would have the possibility of joining the forerunners provided that they would "demonstrate [their] ability" in fulfilling all the obligations required by the cooperation, "including the common *acquis* developed under closer cooperation."

A further proposal put forward at a late stage of the Conference (6 March 1997) concerned a key issue for Italy: the realisation of a European Area of Freedom, Security and Justice. Since the beginning of the Conference, Italy had stressed the importance of reforming this area, by bringing issues such as immigration, asylum, control at external borders and customs cooperation into the Community competence, and by strengthening the existing instruments in the areas that were to remain part of intergovernmental cooperation. It is obvious that a country like Italy, with its 8,000 kilometres of maritime frontiers, and thus highly exposed to illegal immigration, tended to favour a common European approach and responsibility on these issues. Furthermore, this would also represent an incentive to reform national legislation and

---

[40] A list of conditions for flexibility had already been included in the Reflection Group report, mainly based on the Spanish position paper on the IGC (Stubb 1998).

improve administrative structures dealing with immigration and asylum issues. This is what happened, for instance, with its participation in the Schengen Convention,[41] whose constraints obliged Italy – excluded in a first stage from its implementation because of non-compliance with the conditions and requirements laid down in the Convention itself[42] – to adopt important and necessary legislation in the field of data protection and immigration (Corrado 1997). This could also help explain why Italy was very much in favour of the integration of the Schengen system into the EU Treaties[43] as a form of enhanced cooperation, which was seen as a way to diminish the risks of exclusion which would certainly be higher in a totally intergovernmental framework where no clauses and guarantees for non-participating States can be foreseen.

Concerning the content of the proposal, Italy wanted a complete communitarisation of the policies directly linked to the free movement of persons (immigration, asylum and external borders): exclusive right of initiative of the Commission, full competence to the ECJ and automatic application of the co-decision procedure after a transitional period of three years (in which unanimity and simple consultation would apply). For the subjects not transferred to the Community Pillar (police and judicial cooperation in criminal matters), the decision-making mechanism would be similar to the one proposed in the area of CFSP: the Council would adopt pluri-annual working plans unanimously and, on that basis, it would adopt single pieces of legislation by qualified majority (which would then become the rule). Every Member State would, nevertheless, maintain the possibility of applying national provisions "on grounds of public policy or the protection of the principles of its legal order and as far as is strictly necessary."

On institutional questions, the position of Italy was not univocal: if, on issues such as the extension of QMV and of the EP powers, Italy's views were very advanced and close to those of the Benelux countries, on other issues, i.e.

---

[41] The Schengen Convention on the abolition of border controls of persons was signed on 15 June 1990 between France, Germany and the Benelux countries (Italy joined in November of the same year).

[42] The Convention, after some delays, entered into force on 26 March 1995 for the 5 founding members plus Spain and Portugal (which joined one year later than Italy, in 1991). Italy was able to apply the Convention only from 1 October 1997.

[43] In the Progress Report presented to the Florence European Council, the Italian Presidency presented an "Outline Draft Schengen Protocol," authorising the Schengen Contracting parties to incorporate "the instruments constituting the Schengen *acquis* into the European Union framework." The details of the integration (decision-making, competence of the ECJ, conditions of participation of non-Schengen MS) were left open.

the composition of the Commission and the re-weighting of votes within the Council, its position was very much influenced by its status of "big country." A detailed proposal was presented in April 1997, in the midst of the Dutch Presidency (CONF/3863/97). Since its first documents and statements on the issue, the Italian Government stressed the need to preserve the right balance between the institutions and between the Member States, at the same time enabling – a soon enlarged – Union to function efficiently and effectively. This meant that the generalised recourse to qualified majority voting – excluding only "constitutional or quasi-constitutional" provisions and articles concerning derogations from internal market rules – had to go hand in hand with a re-weighting of Council votes in favour of the large Member States,[44] in such a way that decisions taken by qualified majority would always represent at least 60% of the population of the Union. In its statement of 23 May 1995 on the size of the Commission, the Italian Government did not "consider that a reduction in the number of Commissioners would increase the supranational nature of the institution," and proposed a system whereby "although the number of Commissioners would not be reduced below the number of Member States, provisions would be made for the large Member States to have a deputy Commissioner instead of two Commissioners as at present" (European Parliament 1996). This early position evolved throughout the negotiations and, in the formal proposal of 7 April 1997, the following two alternative options were proposed: either to fix the number of members at 15 while specifying that "the number of members of the Commission having the nationality of the same State shall not be more than one;" or, "should a more gradual process of Commission adjustment be desired," to fix a higher maximum number of Commissioners (20), which would, however, remain unchanged also after the number of Member States would exceed 20. Although this aspect was not included in the formal proposal on institutions, Italy also favoured an extension of the legislative powers of the European Parliament, which would be linked to the introduction of a hierarchy of Community acts (see the general position document, CONF/3839/96).

Outcome and Ratification

In the words of the Italian Prime Minister Prodi, immediately after the Amsterdam European Council of 16/17 June 1997, the new Treaty was "good" and "serious," allowing for progress to be made. However, it was "certainly

---

[44] According to the proposal, the four big countries would be given two additional votes (from 10 to 12) and Spain one vote (from 8 to 9), thereby increasing the qualified majority from 62 to 68 votes.

not the Treaty [Italy] would have liked," the outcome being below Italy's expectations, especially concerning the extension of qualified majority voting and institutional issues in general, one of the three key areas to be reformed (*Agence Europe* 19 June 1997). In the Italian Government's view, the Treaty of Amsterdam could be accepted in spite of its shortcomings, bearing in mind, however, that it had to be considered as a stage in a process not completely achieved (Dini 1997a).

It is in this perspective that Italy decided to join (together with France) the Belgian initiative to add to the new Treaty a *Declaration on the Protocol on the institutions with the prospect of enlargement of the European Union*.[45] In the Declaration, the three above-mentioned countries observed that "the Treaty of Amsterdam does not meet the need [...] for substantial progress towards reinforcing the institutions." Therefore, since they considered that "such reinforcement is an indispensable condition for the conclusion of the first accession negotiations," they were determined to give the fullest appropriate effect to the Protocol on institutions[46] "as regards the composition of the Commission and the weighting of votes [within the Council]" and considered that "a significant extension of recourse to qualified majority voting forms part of the relevant factors which should be taken into account." The declaration opened the door to the possibility of calling another IGC before enlargement, even in the perspective that only one new country would join (*European Voice* 3 July 1997).

The position of Italy on institutional reforms has been substantially confirmed in the position paper issued for the ongoing IGC on institutional reforms (CONF/4717/00), although in the new document more emphasis is put on the linkage between the "sacrifice" of a Commissioner by the four large countries (interestingly, Spain seems completely forgotten here) and the need to re-balance the weighting of votes within the Council in favour of the latter, especially in view of the accession of small/medium countries.[47] On the composition of the Commission, the possibility of having fewer Commissioners than Member States – and thus, of a Commission without an Italian

---

[45] *Declaration (n° 6) by Belgium, France and Italy* (of which the Conference took note), annexed to the Treaty of Amsterdam.

[46] *Protocol (n° 7) on the institutions with the prospect of enlargement of the European Union*, annexed to the Treaty of Amsterdam.

[47] In a speech before the Committees for Foreign and European Affairs of the *Senato* on 10 February 2000, explaining the Italian position on the ongoing IGC, the Minister for Foreign Affairs Dini affirmed that it would be unthinkable that, in an enlarged Union, a decision could be taken in spite of the opposition of 3 or 4 "big countries" http://www.esteri.it/attivita/italiae/.

member – is (theoretically) reaffirmed. However, since at the same time it is recognised that "it is impossible for some Member States to envisage surrendering their claims to a post of Commissioner," this seems to be more a rhetoric position than a genuine one, also taking into account that the same document considers that "the principle of one judge per Member State should be upheld," in order to maintain the principle of "the representation of all judicial systems within the Union's courts."

Another issue, where the result was not considered too satisfactory, concerned the provisions on the Common Foreign and Security Policy. Despite some undeniable progress in this area (i.e., inclusion of Petersberg tasks in the Treaty, appointment of a High Representative for CFSP, set up of an early warning and policy planning unit), the key questions remained unsolved in Amsterdam and the ultimate objective of strengthening the Second Pillar unachieved. The decisions on the relations EU-WEU were considered as "particularly unsatisfactory" (Dini 1997a), since the outcome – the fostering of institutional relations between the two, leaving open the possibility of integration "should the European Council so decide" unanimously – was ultimately very different from what was proposed in the Joint Protocol of 24 March 1997 and also in the Italian proposal on CFSP. The unsatisfactory outcome was to a great extent probably due to a lack of support from the two major players, France and Germany. Particularly disappointing was also the abandoning of the possibility of a closer cooperation in the defence and security area, which Italy had strongly supported, but which was not supported by the Dutch chief negotiator, Patijn, in the final, decisive stage of the Conference (Stubb 1998).

Although at the time of its presentation, the Italian blueprint for applying the principle of flexibility was considered as the most likely to be taken as a basis for the final formula (*European Voice* 5 February 1997), the Amsterdam provisions on flexibility can be considered only partly satisfactory, from an Italian point of view. If, on the one hand, the Italian approach of giving a pivotal role to the Commission – the guardian of the Treaties – in triggering closer cooperation was accepted, together with the granting of authorisation by qualified majority, on the other, flexibility was totally excluded from the Second Pillar and, similarly as in the case of constructive abstention, every Member State has now the right to oppose the granting of an authorisation by qualified majority "for important and stated reasons of national policy" (see the new Art. 40 TEU and Art. 11 TEC). It is worth pointing out that Italy is one of the countries currently favouring the inclusion of flexibility in the scope of the ongoing IGC, since "the Amsterdam provisions on closer cooperation appear quite inadequate for an enlarged Europe"[48] (CONF/4717/2000).

More satisfactory was the outcome concerning the Third Pillar and its partial communitarisation (including the incorporation of the Schengen *acquis* into the EU), although the Italian proposal went further on certain aspects, providing for a shorter transitional period (three years instead of five) before moving to co-decision in the new communitarised areas and for a more extensive use of qualified majority voting in the areas remaining under the Third Pillar. A partial deception was instead another chapter of the relations between the citizens and the Union, i.e. human rights and citizenship, where the Italian (and Austrian) proposal was very, perhaps too, advanced, claiming the inclusion of economic and social rights and the accession of the EU to the European Convention on Human Rights (ECHR). Nevertheless, the possibility of sanctions against Member States infringing fundamental principles was eventually agreed upon, although the new Art. 7 TEC requires a unanimous deliberation by the Council, whereas the Italian-Austrian document proposed qualified majority voting.

Criticism of this half-satisfactory result came also from the Italian Parliament, where a parliamentary enquiry on the reform of the Maastricht Treaty was convened on 12 September 1996 to follow the IGC negotiations (*Camera dei deputati* 1999). The conclusive document of the enquiry (4 May 1999) highlighted some "missed objectives" of the new Treaty (due, according to the document, to the limits of the intergovernmental method): the completion of institutional reforms; the strengthening of the CFSP; the deepening of relations between the EU and WEU; the coordination between monetary and employment policies.[49] However, as it occurred with the Maastricht Treaty, the ratification process was neither long nor difficult. In this respect, it has to be kept in mind that although its involvement in European affairs has undoubtedly increased since the end of the 1980s,[50] the

---

[48] In the new proposal, Italy reaffirms the need to introduce flexibility in security and defence and calls for the review of the provision giving a veto right to non-participating Member States, as well as for the lowering of the threshold of minimum participating countries.

[49] Interestingly, an entire chapter of the parliamentary enquiry was devoted to the "political and institutional reflections on the single currency," an issue that – although not part of the IGC mandate – developed in parallel to the IGC work and became progressively more and more important. It has to be recalled that, following the decision of the Brussels European Council of 2/3 May 1998, Italy was eventually included amongst the countries entering the third stage of EMU on 1 January 1999.

[50] In particular, the so-called "law La Pergola" (n°86/89), which introduced the mechanism of the annual *legge comunitaria* for the transposition of Community law, gave the

Italian Parliament does not have the same role and influence than, for instance, the Danish or the Dutch one have in determining their country's foreign and European policy (Norton 1996; Cartabia 1998). In case of international agreements, the Italian Constitution provides that all treaties having important political or financial implications have to be ratified by the Parliament (no special majority is required). Thus, Parliament has the formal right, although it has never used it, to reject a treaty whose content it does not approve.

Both the *Camera* and the *Senato* approved two resolutions (in March 1997) affirming that they would not ratify the new Treaty without a positive judgement from the European Parliament[51], trying in this way to place the institution in a pivotal position in the IGC (*European Voice* 26 March 1997). The initiative – backed by the Government which, at the time of the Presidency, had insisted on a greater involvement of the EP in the work of the Conference – was of course not a legal pre-condition for the ratification of the Treaty by Italy, but an attempt to launch a strong political signal. Following the issuing of a critical but overall positive opinion from the EP on the Amsterdam Treaty on 19 November 1997[52] – recommending its ratification by the Member States – the ratification bill was presented by the Government to the *Camera* on 29 January 1998 and approved two months later, on 25 March. Once approved also by the *Senato* (on 3 June), the ratification law (n° 209/98) entered into force on 16 June 1998. However, both Houses of Parliament expressed their criticism *vis-à-vis* the new Treaty with a resolution (*ordine del giorno*), approved at the same time as the ratification bill, committing the Government to: re-open the reform process, especially what concerns institutional reforms, in view of the enlargement of the Union; propose co-decision mechanisms, thus with the involvement of the EP, for the future reforms of the Treaty; support the strengthening of political union, in parallel with EMU; and, finally, re-launch the Euro-Mediterranean partnership (*Camera dei deputati* 1999).

Parliament more responsibilities in the implementation stage. It also committed the Government to inform and send to the *Camera* and *Senato* all Community legislation and acts.

[51] A similar initiative was taken in respect of the Maastricht Treaty by the Italian Parliament and the Belgian House of Representatives.

[52] CONF/4007/97 – C4-0538/97, OJ C 371 , 8.12.97, p. 99.

Conclusions

The negotiations leading to a new Treaty, especially at the European Union level, are obviously a very complex process, in which several factors are involved and play a role in determining the final outcome. It is, therefore, always difficult to measure and assess the role played by an individual actor in such negotiations. If it is true that "Governments with attractive and effective unilateral policies tend to be sceptical of co-operation, while governments able to achieve policy goals only by altering the pattern of externalities imposed by the policies of foreign government policy tend to favour it" (Moravcsik & Nikolaïdis 1999), Italy can certainly be included in the latter group. The benefits of European integration, especially in terms of external input needed to make Italy progress towards economic and political reforms, are clear to – almost – any Italian political leader. Without any doubt, both in Maastricht and in Amsterdam, the Italian Government was one of the most 'integrationist' actors, pushing for a thorough reform of the Union and its institutions, as well as for its strengthening, especially with regards to the external dimension.

This does not mean, however, that the Italian action has always been consistent and effective in pursuing the aim mentioned above. The basic reason lies in the traditional domestic political instability and the consequent lack of political leadership, which has constantly affected – and still does – the external action of every Italian Government, greatly reducing its influence on the international and European stage, in spite of its not negligible economic weight.[53]

It has to be acknowledged that, once the political turmoil of the first months of 1996 was overcome, the Prodi Government, that took office on 17 May 1996 (until 9 October 1998), was one of the most stable, at least by Italian standards, and committed (to the process of economic and political reforms) of recent years. However, as we have tried to highlight, during the whole negotiating process leading to the Treaty of Amsterdam most of the energies of the Italian Government were absorbed by the efforts needed to "get Italy into Europe," that is to comply with EMU criteria and be part of the "Eurozone" as of 1 January 1999. This occurred because the participation in the single currency, besides its economic implications, was perceived as a necessary step in order to re-acquire international credibility, jeopardised by

---

[53] In 1996, Italy's total GDP (expressed in billions of dollars, at April 2000 prices and exchange rates) was equal to 1228,8. To have a comparative view, in the same year the total GDP of France was 1554,4, Spain 608,8, the UK 1177,3 and Greece 124,4 (OECD 2000).

years of political instability, corruption scandals[54] and economic non-discipline: an exclusion from the monetary hard core would have had repercussions going far beyond the economic plan, increasing the risk of exclusion and marginalisation also in other fields, first of all in foreign policy (Bonvicini 1997).

This also helps explain the particular attention given to the debate on the concept of flexibility, where due to the threats of potential "hard cores" excluding Italy, the Italian position evolved from a very defensive attitude to a "cautious support" (provided that certain conditions and guarantees would be included), perhaps because of a growing awareness that "it would maybe be better to temporarily have a Europe without Italy than an Italy permanently outside of Europe"[55] (Fagiolo 1996).

---

[54] It has to be kept in mind that the *Mani Pulite* ("Clean Hands") operation, which started in 1992 with a series of judicial investigations, had uncovered massive political corruption (*Tangentopoli*), forcing an entire generation of post-war politicians out of office.

[55] Translation from Italian by the Author.

Annex

Proposals Presented During the IGC

- CONF/3839/96 (General) Position on the IGC for the Reform of the Treaties
- CONF/3941/96 Fundamental Rights and Citizenship (with A)
- CONF/3965/96 Common Foreign and Security Policy
- CONF/3801/97 Flexibility
- CONF/3832/97 Fundamental Rights – Abolition of Death Penalty
- CONF/3840/97 Third Pillar
- CONF/3855/97 Protocol on EU-WEU integration (with B, F, D, L, S)
- CONF/3863/97 Institutions
- CONF/3908/97 CFSP- Representation in International Organisations (with S)
- CONF/3905/97 Energy
- CONF/3913/97 Internal Market

Italian Presidency:

- CONF/3801/96 Note n°1: Citizenship
- CONF/3802/96 Note n°2: Fundamental rights
- CONF/3803/96 Note n°3: JHA (objectives and scope for action)
- CONF/3804/96 Note n°4: JHA (decision-making and instruments)
- CONF/3805/96 Note n°5: JHA (jurisdictional control)
- CONF/3806/96 Note n°6: Employment
- CONF/3807/96 Note n°7: Environment
- CONF/3808/96 Note n°8: Community policies
- CONF/3809/96 Note n°9: Subsidiarity
- CONF/3810/96 Note n°10: Transparency
- CONF/3811/96 Note n°11: European Parliament (composition/electoral procedure)
- CONF/3812/96 Note n°12: European Parliament (legislative function)
- CONF/3813/96 Note n°13: European Parliament (non-legislative functions)
- CONF/3814/96 Note n°14: Role of the national parliaments
- CONF/3815/96 Note n°15: Qualified-majority voting and unanimity
- CONF/3816/96 Note n°16: Qualified majority threshold/Weighting of votes
- CONF/3817/96 Note n°17: Functioning of the Council
- CONF/3818/96 Note n°18: Commission (membership/powers)
- CONF/3819/96 Note n°19: Court of Justice

- CONF/3820/96 Note n°20: Other institutions and bodies
- CONF/3821/96 Note n°21: Enhanced Cooperation/Flexibility
- CONF/3822/96 Note n°22: External Economic Relations
- CONF/3823/96 Note n°23: CFSP (objectives/conception/preparation of decisions)
- CONF/3824/96 Note n°24: CFSP (decision-making procedures)
- CONF/3825/96 Note n°25: CFSP (implementation/operation/solidarity)
- CONF/3826/96 Note n°26: Financing the CFSP (and JHA)
- CONF/382796 Note n°27: CFSP – Legal personality for the EU
- CONF/3828/96 Note n°28: Common Defence Policy and Common Defence
- CONF/3828/96 Note n°29: Security and Defence – Relations with WEU
- CONF/3830/96 Note n°30: Security and Defence (armaments)
- CONF/3835/96 Presidency Note (organisation of works)
- CONF/3836/96 Presidency Note (calendar of works)
- CONF/3843/96 Questions for discussions (2nd meeting at ministerial level)
- CONF/3847/96 Topics for discussions (3rd meeting at ministerial level)
- CONF/3848/96 Note from the Presidency ("A Union Closer to Its Citizens")
- CONF/3849/96 Note from the Presidency ("Institutions")
- CONF/3850/96 Note from the Presidency ("Strengthened External Action Capability")
- CONF/3860/96 Presidency Report to the Florence European Council
- CONF/3862/96 Note for Ministers' Conclave

Bibliography

Aliboni, Roberto (1993). "Il dibattito sulla politica europea di sicurezza e difesa," Part II, Section II, pp. 142-154, in Istituto Affari Internazionali, *L'Italia nella politica internazionale – Anno Ventesimo*, Rome: SIPI.

Attinà, Fulvio (1996)."Italy's EU Presidency," *ECSA Review*, Fall, pp. 9-14.

Bonvicini, Gianni et al. (1997)."Il costo della non partecipazione ad alcune politiche dell'Unione Europea. Analisi e proposte," Part I, Chapter 1, pp. 11-35, in G. Bonvicini et al. (eds.), *Italia senza Europa? Il costo della non partecipazione alle politiche dell'Unione Europea*, Milano: FrancoAngeli.

Camera dei Deputati – Commissione Speciale per le Politiche Comunitarie (1994). *Indagine conoscitiva sui problemi connessi all'attuazione del Trattato di Maastricht*, Roma.

Camera dei Deputati – Commissione III (1996). *La Conferenza Intergovernativa. Scheda e documentazione di base*, Roma.

Camera dei Deputati – Servizio Studi (1997). *La Conferenza Intergovernativa. Documentazione di base*, Roma.

Camera dei Deputati – Servizio Rapporti Comunitari e Internazionali (1998). *Ratifica del Trattato di Amsterdam. A.C. 4500*, Roma.

Camera dei Deputati – Commissione III (Affari Esteri e Comunitari) (1999). *Indagine conoscitiva sulla revisione del Trattato di Maastricht anche in vista dell'allargamento dell'Unione europea. Documento conclusivo*, 4 May.

Cangelosi, Antonio & Vittorio Grassi (1996). *Dalle Comunità all'Unione. Il Trattato di Maastricht e la Conferenza intergovernativa del 1996*, Milano: FrancoAngeli.

Cartabia, Marta (1998). "L'ordinamento italiano e la Comunità europea," Chapter 4, pp. 111-158, in B. Beutler et al. (eds.), *L'Unione europea*, Bologna: Il Mulino (Italian edition).

Cechhini, Paolo (1997). "L'Italia e le politiche comunitarie: una debolezza strutturale," Part IV, Chapter 8, pp. 213-229, in G. Bonvicini et al. (eds.), *Italia senza Europa? Il costo della non partecipazione alle politiche dell'Unione Europea*, Milano: FrancoAngeli.

CNEL – Documenti (1996). *La Presidenza Italiana dell'Unione Europea e la Conferenza Intergovernativa per la Revisione dei Trattati*, Rome: CNEL.

Consiglio Nazionale Delle Ricerche (CNR) (1998). Istituto di Studi Giuridici sulla Comunità Internazionale, Acts of the Colloquium "La partecipazione dell'Italia all'Unione europea e la nuova disciplina della Legge Comunitaria," *Iter Legis*, May-August, pp. 61-120.

Corrado, Laura (1997). "L'attuazione della Convenzione di Schengen in Italia," *Affari Esteri*, n° 116, October, pp. 847-860.

Council of The European Union – General Secretariat (1996). *1996 Intergovernmental Conference. Reflection Group Report and other References for Documentary Purposes*, Luxembourg: OPOCE.

Council of The European Union – General Secretariat (1997). *Intergovernmental Conference on the Revision of the Treaties. Italian Presidency (collected texts)*, Luxembourg: OPOCE.

Dinì, Lamberto (1997a). "I risultati del Consiglio europeo di Amsterdam: luci ed ombre," *Relazioni internazionali*, n° 39, July-August, pp. 11-16.

Dini, Lamberto (1997b). "L'Italia e l'ONU," *Vita Italiana (nuova serie)*, pp. 14-20.

European Commission – DG for Economic and Financial Affairs 1999). "Italy's Slow Growth in the 1990s: Facts, Explanations and Prospects," *European Economy. Reports and Studies*, n° 5, Brussels.

European Parliament – Intergovernmental Conference Task Force (1996). *White Paper on the 1996 IGC – Vol. II – Summary of positions of the Member States of the European Union with a View to the 1996 IGC*, Luxembourg.

Fagiolo, Silvio (1996). "L'Unione Europea e la revisione del Trattato di Maastricht," *Affari Esteri*, n°111, July, pp. 501-507.

Francioni, Francesco (1992). *Italy and EC Membership Evaluated*, London: Pinter.

Franchini, Claudio (1992). *Amministrazione italiana e amministrazione comunitaria*, Padova: CEDAM.

Istituto Nazionale di Statistica (ISTAT) (1998). *L'Italia in cifre*, Roma.

Martial, Enrico (1992). "Italy and Political Union," pp. 139-153, in F. Laursen & S. Vanhoonacker, *The Intergovernmental Conference on Political Union: Institutional Reforms, New Policies and International Identity of the European Community*, Maastricht: EIPA.

McDonagh, Bobby (1998). *Original Sin in a Brave New World. An Account of the Negotiation of the Treaty of Amsterdam*, Dublin: Institute of European Affairs.

Merlini, Cesare (1997). "Maastricht riveduto e corretto," *Mondo Economico*, March, pp. 4-6.

Missiroli, Antonio (1997). "La Pesc e la politica estera italiana: vincoli, problemi e scenari," Part II, Chapter 2, pp. 37-61, in G. Bonvicini et al. (eds.), *Italia senza Europa? Il costo della non partecipazione alle politiche dell'Unione Europea*, Milano: FrancoAngeli.

Moravcsik, Andrew & Kalypso Nicolaïdis (1999). "Explaining the Treaty of Amsterdam: Interests, Influence, Institutions," *Journal of Common Market Studies*, vol. 37, n° 1, March, pp. 59-85.

Neri Gualdesi, Marinella (1993). "La politica dell'integrazione e il dibattito sull' Unione europea," Part II, Section I, pp. 114-141, in Istituto Affari Internazionali, *L'Italia nella politica internazionale – Anno Ventesimo*, Roma: SIPI.

Norton, Philip (1996). *National Parliaments and the European Union*, London: Frank Cass.

OECD (1992). *Economic Surveys (Italy)*, Paris.

OECD (2000). *Main Economic Indicators*, Paris, April.

Olivi, Bino (1993). *L'Europa difficile*, Bologna: Il Mulino.

Papisca, Antonio (1985). "La Presidence du Conseil des Ministres des Communautés européennes: rapport national sur l'Italie," Chapter 8, pp. 163-186, in C.O. Nuallain (ed.), *The Presidency of the European Council of Ministers. Impact and Implications for National Governments*, London: Croom Helm.

Pistone, Sergio (1991). "L'Italia e l'integrazione europea," *L'Italia e l'Europa*, n° 28/29, pp. 167-192.

Prodi, Romano (1998). *Un'idea dell'Europa*, Bologna: Il Mulino.

Quadrio Curzio, Alberto (1996). *Noi, l'economia e l'Europa*, Bologna: Il Mulino.

Secchi, Carlo & Dario Velo (eds.) (1997). *La Conferenza intergovernativa europea del 1996*, Bari: Cacucci.

Stubb, Alexander C.G. (1998). *Flexible Integration and the Amsterdam Treaty: Negotiating Differentiation in the 1996-97 IGC*, (Thesis submitted for the Degree of Doctor of Philosophy), London: London School of Economics and Political Science.

Svensson, Anna-Carin (2000). *In the Service of the European Union. The Role of the Presidency in Negotiating the Amsterdam Treaty 1995-1997*, (Thesis submitted for the Degree of Doctor of Philosophy), Uppsala: Uppsala University.

11

Luxembourg: Strong Trends towards "Communitarised" Problem-Solving

Danielle Bossaert

In the smallest EU Member State Luxembourg[1] the progress made in Amsterdam was welcomed as a necessary step towards continuing integration, which however should still be further deepened (*Chambre des Députés*, no. 14/97-98, p. 3303 et seq.). The Grand Duchy's strong preference for solutions at EU level, particularly concerning the internal market and the second and third pillars (*Aide-mémoire* 1996, 6, 8-12), clearly reflects Luxembourg's highly positive attitude towards the European integration process. For instance, membership of the European Union was never a point of discussion. The attitude of the founding member Luxembourg towards the EU is characterised by broad consensus, among the public, political parties as well as interest groups, on the government's pro-integrationist course. In contrast to most other Member States, EU policies are not subject to energy-consuming domestic disputes. With regard to the major issues such as the accession of Luxembourg to the Economic and Monetary Union, the institutional reform, the maintaining of unanimity voting in fiscal matters, the further "communitarisation" of the Common Foreign and Security Policy as well as in the field of Justice and Home Affairs, there was general agreement among the large parties and according to public opinion: these issues are nearly completely uncontroversial. This uncomplicated attitude is, for example, illustrated by the fact that the ratification of the Amsterdam Treaty passed by unnoticed.

This highly positive attitude of the founding member Luxembourg towards European integration is based on the conviction that its national economic and security interests can best be safeguarded in a supranational community and that there are no real alternatives with regard to active and committed cooperation in the EU. Membership of the EU is seen as vital to the prosperity and security of the country. What is also important in this respect is that the Community particularly offers a small state like Luxembourg - whose independence was repeatedly threatened by Belgian, German and French attempts at annexation during its more than 150 years of existence - many advantages that can help overcome the vulnerability linked to small size.

---

[1] Luxembourg has a population of about 435,000 inhabitants, 34% of whom are foreigners (mostly from EU Member States).

Especially the EU's supranational architecture, which guarantees an optimal representation of small states in the decision-making processes, contributes to the strengthening of Luxembourg's national autonomy. The former Minister of Foreign Affairs of Luxembourg, Jacques Poos, expressed this idea in the following words: "As a full member of the EU and hence co-decision-maker in a community uniting its reconciled larger neighbours, Luxembourg found its sovereignty and its capacity to make itself heard in the international arena, reinforced to an unprecedented extent" (*European Voice* 12-18 June 1997). Moreover, the principle of equal status for all Member States ensures that the Grand Duchy has influence disproportionate to its size and its political weight. An example: While Luxembourg is now represented as a full and equal Member State within the European Central Bank, its position was not so clear in the Belgian-Luxembourg Economic Union, as is illustrated by the fact that in 1982 Belgium devaluated the franc before even having consulted Luxembourg. In this light, it seems quite understandable that the ideas that "equal status must be maintained for all Member States" and the "equal footing as regards participation and involvement in the decision-making processes [...] and institutions" were sacred principles for the smallest Member State throughout the Intergovernmental Conference of 1996. These principles could not be touched upon.

Another important factor, which is determining for the formulation of Luxembourg's national interests, is its heavy dependence on exports and imports from abroad, mainly from other EU Member States. Since the early 19th century, Luxembourg is used to enjoying the economic advantages of being integrated into larger areas such as the German *Zollverein* or the Belgian-Luxembourg Economic Union (BLWU). The great dependence on a large internal market which operates as smoothly as possible also explains why the completion of the internal market was an important item for Luxembourg on the IGC agenda (*Aide-mémoire* 1996, 6-7).

Over the past few decades, Luxembourg has been able to develop into the richest Member State within the EU with the highest gross national product and the lowest unemployment rate. This extremely favourable economic development as well as its domestic stability have favoured a European policy which particularly stands out on account of factors such as continuity, deep commitment, and reliability. Moreover, the pursuance of this rectilinear, pro-integrationist course is also made easier by the fact that Luxembourg is a centralist, unitarian state with no regional or intermediate levels of government and consequently no powerful regional players. This is of course an important factor which gave considerable leeway to the national government during the IGC. In this sense and without exception, European policy is formulated, decided on and implemented centrally. Furthermore, the role of the national executive in the forming of preferences is strengthened by the rather weak role of the parliament in the EU decision-making process. The opinions of the parliament are not binding on the government and the parliamentary scrutiny during Intergovernmental Conferences mainly involves being regularly informed by the government. In contrast to the rather complex, fragmented and often time-consuming decision-making processes in some larger Member States, Luxembourg is characterised by its fairly quick, informal, ad-hoc and flexible decision-making and coordination mechanisms. These mechanisms are also characterised by the informal and personal relations of the small state as well as the high-speed communication channels within small networks. Another characteristic of the Luxembourg political system is the consensus-oriented decision-finding structures which attach great importance to consultation and provision of information to interest groups, employees' organisations, etc. Of course, this permanent consultation and negotiation between the various socio-political actors also favours the finding of compromises that are acceptable to all actors involved. So, European policy is also defined in close and constant interaction between politicians, interest groups and the officials concerned.

Furthermore, in a small state such as Luxembourg the search for acceptable unanimous political solutions is facilitated by the fact that the number of political and economic key decision-makers is very limited, that they know each other very well on a personal level and that they are highly motivated to find appropriate solutions in order to safeguard national interests. A typical characteristic of small size which should also be considered is the fact that in contrast to large countries such as Germany and France, the debate on vital domestic interests is far less controversial. The advantage is of course that in certain areas, Luxembourg may be more prepared to compromise and can often act as a mediator between conflicting interests.

Luxembourg's Positions, Interests and Preferences
For the 1996/97 IGC, Luxembourg presented its national positions both in a national memorandum and in a joint Benelux memorandum together with its two partners Belgium and the Netherlands. Even before the official start of the Conference, at the Benelux Summit in June 1995, the three Heads of Government underlined their firm commitment to "intensify their contacts," to "coordinate their points of view" in order to take "initiatives, where possible" and to "play a leading role again" (*Agence Europe* 8 June 1995). For Luxembourg, this close cooperation and coordination with Belgium and the Netherlands was an important means to strengthen the visibility of its positions and to better defend its national interests. So, for many of the other small EU Member States – such as Denmark, Portugal, Ireland and Greece, as well as the three "newcomers" Finland, Sweden and Austria, which had had no experience with IGCs so far – the Benelux was an "essential" interlocutor,

mainly where it concerned the second and third pillars (Goy 1998, 64). However, this strengthened dialogue with Belgium and the Netherlands should not be considered as an exclusive relationship since at the same time, depending on the issue, Luxembourg also maintained bilateral consultations and relations with other Member States. The so-called "Benelux reflex" was mainly characterised by the fact that whenever one of the three countries expressed its opinion, it usually did so in the name of the Benelux and mainly with regard to topics such as the completion of the internal market, the development of a minimum level of social rights, better integration of environmental policies into other policy areas, integration of the social protocol into the Treaty, introduction of new measures regarding employment policy, further "communitarisation" of the second and third pillars, gradual integration of the WEU into the Union, incorporation of the Schengen Agreements into the Treaty, maintaining the strong role of the Community institutions (Commission, Parliament, Court of Justice) as important allies for small Member States, introduction of a flexibility clause, extension of the co-decision procedure to all policy areas where the Council votes by qualified majority, strengthening of the EU institutions and decision-making processes, etc. However, despite this close cooperation of the Benelux throughout the negotiation process, it is also important to consider the limits of this "coalition," which became apparent at the very end of the Conference in Amsterdam, when the Dutch Presidency proposed a modification of the current weighting system in the Council favouring the large Member States, without first having consulted its other two partners. Another issue, on which the three Benelux countries held different views, concerned qualified-majority voting. While for the Netherlands, QMV should become a rule with certain exceptions and Belgium wanted to extend it to fiscal matters, Luxembourg was not in favour of giving up its national sovereignty regarding this issue.

During the IGC 1996, one of the most sensitive issues for Luxembourg was the potential reform of the institutional structure. Particularly all questions linked to the reduction of the size of the Commission, the re-weighting of the voting system in the Council and other changes related to the Presidency of the Council and the size of the Parliament, turned out to be quite a challenge to the smallest Member State (*Chambre des Députés*, no. 14/97-98, pp. 3310-11). For instance, a thorough institutional reform would be a major concern especially for the smaller Member States, which in comparison to the larger and more populous Member States have a very comfortable position in the EU decision-making process. During the 1996/1997 IGC, one of the government's priorities was to ensure representation of all Member States in each institution and representation of all the main political forces of a Member State in the directly elected European institutions (*Aide-mémoire* 1996, 14-15). At the 2000 IGC, this topic is still a high priority for Luxembourg, all the more so since attempts were made in the run-up to the institutional reform to reduce the disproportionately strong influence of small states. So, Luxembourg was not prepared to give up "its seat" in the European Commission or its right to the rotating Presidency of the Council. The main reason was that losing the Commission seat would mean that Luxembourg would no longer be represented in this institution which as the guardian of the Community interests, besides the European Court of Justice (ECJ), is an important ally of the small states against too great an influence of the large states. Furthermore, the abolition of the "Luxembourg Commissioner post" would certainly have a negative effect on the pro-European attitude of Luxembourg.

Another highly sensitive matter for Luxembourg was the extension of QMV to certain areas, such as for example new accessions, Treaty reform, European citizenship and, above all, taxation. The great concern about the tax issue and more particularly the introduction of a capital gains tax in all EU Member States, is closely linked to the highly vulnerable economic structure of the Grand Duchy where the finance sector is most important.[2] In this light, it is understandable that Luxembourg has to treat this issue with the greatest care.

During the IGC of 1996/1997, the pro-integrationist course of Luxembourg was expressed very clearly in its constructive proposals concerning the second and third pillars. With regard to the second pillar, Luxembourg was strongly in favour of extending QMV and strengthening the decision-making and implementation processes. It also supported farther-reaching measures such as the establishment of a policy-planning and early-warning unit within the Council Secretariat, the incorporation of the so-called Petersberg tasks into the Treaties, the progressive merging of the EU and the WEU and the attribution of legal personality to the Union (*Aide-mémoire* 1996, 8-10). Of course, this pro-active attitude should also be seen in the light of the large dependence of the smallest Member State on an efficient community of solidarity in security and military matters. And this great need for security is even more understandable when we consider that Luxembourg's existence as a state was challenged by its immediate neighbours more than once in the course of its history.

During the Intergovernmental Conference, Luxembourg assumed the same pro-integrationist attitude towards the third pillar. It was in favour of integrating the Schengen Agreement into the Treaty, of extending the competence of the Court of Justice of the EC and of extending QMV to the fields of asylum and immigration policy, the policy on nationals of third

---

[2] Between 1970 and 1997 the number of banks rose from 37 to 215, while the overall balance increased from 236 to 20,838 billion Luxembourg francs.

countries, combating drug addiction, combating fraud of international dimensions, and cooperation in customs affairs (*Aide-mémoire* 1996, 10-12).

Besides a further deepening of the second and third pillars, as well as the completion of the internal market, Luxembourg also gave high priority to the strengthening of the social dimension of the EU, a demand which to a certain extent also reflects the domestic focus of the Christian Social government of Jean-Claude Juncker. In this context, he repeatedly expressed his support - during the European Council as well as during the reform negotiations in 1996 and 1997 - for the introduction of social minimum standards such as for instance a minimum wage at EU level. During the Luxembourg Presidency in the second half of 1997, he also played an active role at the employment summit in the matter of the implementation of a coordinated labour market policy at EU level. How important the social issue is to Luxembourg also becomes clear considering that one of the thirteen senior officials at the Luxembourg Permanent Representation to the EU exclusively deals with employment and social affairs.

Other important topics on the Luxembourg agenda included more symbolic issues, such as the striving for a more integrated and democratic Europe based on greater solidarity, the proposal to include the protection of human rights and fundamental freedoms in the Treaty, equality between men and women, measures to combat racism and xenophobia, and the reaffirmation of solidarity between small and large Member States (*Aide-mémoire* 1996, 13).

A major concern of the Luxembourg government with regard to the enlargement, which was also reflected in its positions on the 1996/97 IGC, is that the EU - as Prime Minister Jean-Claude Juncker recently put it - might develop into an advanced free trade area (*Luxemburger Wort* 1 November 1999) and that this would result in a weakening of the Community institutions. The main examples put forward regarding this risk to the integration process are the opting out by the United Kingdom in the field of social policy and the EMU, and the opting out of Denmark as regards the EMU. Accordingly, Luxembourg's position paper is strongly against a Europe *à la carte*, without however ruling out that some Member States can go forward faster than others (*Aide-mémoire* 1996, 12). The thought behind these considerations is mainly that the pace of integration cannot be set by the "slower states," i.e. the countries least keen on integration.

Negotiating Within the IGC: Strategies of Success
States that have a small population and carry only little economic and political weight are also weak countries in so far that, unlike large countries, they cannot assert their interests through power politics, for instance by using their demographic or economic power. This rule also applies in the Council of the EU, where Luxembourg has 2 votes (Germany has 10) which very rarely are

decisive for the adoption or rejection of a decision. However, on the other hand, its position is made stronger by the fact that within the EU there are no permanent alliances and that in order to successfully push through their proposals in the Council, the large states to a certain extent need the smaller states that have fewer votes. The result of this minor importance is that generally speaking and where possible, Luxembourg tries to compensate for this weakness by means of specific qualities such as for instance sophisticated negotiation skills, useful mediation activities, closer coordination with other Member States and great commitment. At the Intergovernmental Conference of 1996/97 it benefited from the fact that in the most important committees it could rely on competent negotiators who have many years of experience in European circles and, therefore, are most familiar with the rules there. Another element that may also have a positive effect during negotiations is the considerable language skills of the negotiators and the fact that Luxembourg, being a very small and economically open country with very long borders, has strong affinities with two key players in European integration, Germany and France.

A good example of how to optimise negotiation skills was set by Jean-Jacques Kasel, the long-standing ambassador of Luxembourg to the European Union, whom Philippe de Schoutheete de Tervarent described as a terrible negotiator and an old *"routinier"* in European affairs. His strengths were that he was very well acquainted with the dossiers, that he was perfectly aware of the weak and strong points of the other EU negotiators, that he intervened very often during the negotiations and that he made himself useful by putting forward interesting ideas and proposals. In this sense, the Luxembourg concerns were sometimes taken more seriously than those of, for example, Portugal and Austria (Goy 1998, 62). During the 1996/1997 Intergovernmental Conference, Luxembourg could rely on competent and experienced negotiators, not only at European level but also at national level, and due to their high degree of commitment this contributed to the fact that Luxembourg, though being the smallest Member State, was respected and heard. A good example in this context is Jean-Claude Juncker, the Luxembourg Prime Minister (since 1995), who has already had 16 years of experience in government and in European affairs and who, through his multifunctional positions,[3] has a deep insight into European politics and decision-making processes. His influence is closely linked to the fact that his European counterparts consider him a prestigious personality who can be consulted in the case of very technical dossiers when divergent interests threaten to block progress. Another Luxembourg politician with almost 20 years of experience

---

[3] During the previous legislative period, from 1994 to 1999, Jean-Claude Juncker was at the same time Minister of Employment, Minister of Finance and Prime Minister.

in EU affairs is the former Minister of Foreign Affairs, Jacques Poos, who committed himself to safeguarding the institutional privileges of the small Member States, and who has thus to a certain extent become the "leader" of the smaller Member States in defending the right of small Member States to have their own commissioner. In this way, he was also able to gain the respect of the large Member States that wanted to consult him on this matter (Goy 1998, 63).

According to the information provided by a senior official at the Permanent Representation of the Grand Duchy of Luxembourg, other aspects which strengthen Luxembourg's position during negotiations, are, on the one hand, the short and unbureaucratic communication channels within the small-scale administrative machinery and, consequently, the quick response possibilities of the negotiators that may be required in the case of difficult decisions, and, on the other hand, the extensive horizontal expertise of officials. Due to the small size of the central administration, the Luxembourg civil servants are often fairly competent generalists, who have to deal with a wide variety of subject areas. And this wide knowledge can of course be an advantage in that it gives them a good overview of the broader context of the issues dealt with.

Outcome and Ratification

When comparing the results achieved in Amsterdam with the Luxembourg positions, one can see that in some respects the latter were more ambitious than the changes incorporated into the new Treaty. During the debates on the ratification of the Amsterdam Treaty in the *Chambre des députés*, the *Chambre* particularly welcomed the progress in the social field such as the inclusion of the social protocol in the Treaty, the establishment of a planning and analytical unit for the second pillar, the incorporation of the Petersberg Tasks and the Schengen Agreement into the Treaty and the preservation of the present structure which is based on the principle of equality of all states (*Chambre des Députés* no. 1497-98, pp. 3303-75). During the negotiations Luxembourg had indeed the highest priority to all these topics, which means that Amsterdam can certainly be called a success for the Grand Duchy, also when considering that Luxembourg had been able to get its way in sensitive matters that directly affected its national interests. For instance, unanimity will still be required when tax issues are voted on, the principle of the rotating Presidency will also be maintained for the time being and in the future Luxembourg will, just as all other Member States, be represented as a full member, i.e. with one Commissioner in the Commission, and it will also be represented by 6 members in the European Parliament. Finally, other proposals of Luxembourg were also included in the new Treaty, such as closer involvement of national parliaments in EU decision-making process and priority to fundamental rights such as equality between men and women, as well as the wish to include references to a more effective fight against racism and xenophobia. However, it is also interesting to note that in some areas, such as the "communitarisation" of the second and third pillars, Luxembourg's proposals went beyond the result achieved. Luxembourg's wish to grant the EU legal personality was not included in the Treaty either. However, despite some, mostly insignificant criticism, the Amsterdam Treaty met with widespread approval in the smallest Member State. Following Germany, Denmark and Sweden and after an uncontroversial discussion in the national parliament in July 1998, it was adopted by 55 votes with four abstentions and 59 members present. Due to the great importance of this Treaty, the Luxembourg Constitution stipulates that three fourths of the members of parliament must be present and that a two-thirds majority is needed for ratification. This process presented no problem, since Article 49a of the Luxembourg Constitution stipulates that competences reserved for legislative, executive and judiciary powers can be temporarily transferred by treaty to institutions under international law.

Preparing for the IGC of 2000

At the IGC of 2000, Luxembourg's views on the institutional reform have proved remarkably stable (*Aide-mémoire* 2000, 1-8). The attitude and approach of the new government coalition (since June 1999) between the Christian Socials (CSV) and the Democrats (DP) are hardly different from those of the former coalition between the Christian Socials (CSV) and the Socialists (LSAP). The new government shows the same determination in aiming to maintain the principle of equal representation of all Member States in all institutions and to improve the functioning of the EU institutions, in order to do everything possible to prevent the EU from developing, to use Jean-Claude Juncker's words, into an "advanced free trade area" (*Luxemburger Wort* 12 September 1999). Not least for this reason, has Luxembourg supported a broader reform mandate than originally provided for in the Amsterdam Treaty.[4]

The sensitivities are again very similar to those during the last negotiations on reform: the smallest Member State is still resolutely keeping to each state's right to supply a commissioner and not to be represented in the Commission as just a "junior partner" with fewer decision-making powers or by a Commissioner without portfolio. To Luxembourg this would be unacceptable in view of the crucial role which the Commission plays, for instance, as a mediator between different national interests. On the other hand, it shows great willingness to reform where it concerns the reorganisation of the weighting of votes

---

[4] According to the government, all institutions should undergo a review in order to continue to guarantee an efficient functioning of the EU after the enlargement.

in the Council of Ministers, as it is in favour of a double majority whereby, when decisions are to be taken, both a majority of states and a majority of the population represented by them would be required. As regards voting methods, Luxembourg still insists on maintaining the unanimity rule in certain areas.[5]

This time, too, the government coordinated its positions beforehand in a joint memorandum with both of its Benelux partners, Belgium and the Netherlands, which is very similar to the Dehaene report on institutional reform. A key point in this memorandum is the strengthening of the flexibility clause,[6] a demand Luxembourg puts far more emphasis on this time than four years earlier. This setting of priorities mainly results from the view held by the government that the veto right of other Member States can in no way deter the states that are willing and able to integrate, from pushing the EU deepening process forward even after the enlargement by 12 states.

Also this time, as at the 1996/97 IGC, Luxembourg as the smallest Member State insists on maintaining the equality of all Member States as a fundamental principle of the Treaties. This attitude is of course all the more understandable since especially this year, topics will be dealt with which could restrict in particular the rights of the small Member States which are now well represented in the EU institutions and decision-making process. The small Member States' fear of a threatening loss of influence is not completely unfounded, particularly when one considers that in the present Commission, important portfolios (enlargement, budget, external relations, trade policy) are held by the large Member States and that small Member States had already been excluded from important decisions about the second pillar, as illustrated for example by the Kosovo contact group, which was only composed of the four large EU Member States (*Agence Europe*, 10 February 1999).[7] Also at this IGC, in view of the topicality of the subjects for all small Member States, Luxembourg will probably not be isolated in its views on institutional reform. However, at the same time, the gap between the "small" and the "large"

---

[5] In the case of Treaty amendments, inclusion of new Member States, institutional issues, tax issues, sources of income, certain matters concerning social security, questions involving military obligations.

[6] The proposal of the 3 Benelux countries states that irrespective of the total number of EU Member States, eight Member States can decide between themselves to take farther-reaching integration measures, without another state being able to veto this decision.

[7] The Kosovo contact group, for example, was only composed of the four large EU Member States. In this context, the Belgian Minister of Foreign Affairs, at a meeting with journalists, condemned the tendency of "big" countries to form "directorates" and refused to accept that "small" countries were simply being used as "cannon fodder."

threatens to become bigger and become a central issue in the consultations on reform.

Bibliography

Aide-mémoire du gouvernement luxembourgeois sur la Conférence intergouvernementale de 1996, Luxembourg.

Aide-mémoire du gouvernement luxembourgeois sur la Conférence intergouvernementale de 2000, Luxembourg.

Chambre des Députés (1998). Compte rendu des séances publiques, No. 14/97-98, 59th session séance, Luxembourg.

Goy, Christine (1998). *Le Grand-Duché de Luxembourg face aux débats institutionnels de la CIG de 1996 liés à la grande Europe,* Mémoire, College of Europe 1997-1998.

Hoscheit, Jean-Marc (1992). "Administrative adaptation in the context of regional integration: Luxembourg and the European Community," pp. 265-283, in Randall Baker (ed.), *Public administration in small and island states*, West Hartford: Kumarian Press.

Interview with Prime Minister Jean-Claude Juncker about the EU summit in Helsinki, Luxemburger Wort, 12 September 1999, p. 2, at http://www.wort.lu/waktu/1999120914105.htm.

McDonagh, Bobby (1998). *Original Sin in a Brave New World. An account of the negotiation of the Treaty of Amsterdam,* Dublin: Institute of European Affairs.

Mémorandum de la Belgique, des Pays-Bas et du Luxembourg en vue de la CIG, 8 March 1996.

Moravscik, Andrew & Kalypso Nicolaïdes (1999). "Explaining the Treaty of Amsterdam: Interests, Influence, Institutions," *Journal of Common Market Studies*, Vol. 37, No. 1 (March) pp. 59-85.

Weides, Robert (1999). "L'économie luxembourgeoise au XXe siècle – un bilan rapide," *Luxemburger Wort*, 1 July, p. 6, at http://www.isp.lu/dossiersecofin/.

12

The Netherlands: The Mixed Fruits of Pragmatism

Marco Langendoen & Alfred Pijpers

Dutch EU Approach in the 1990s[1]

While in the first decades of its existence, the European Community was just one sector of Dutch foreign policy (though a very important one), over the years it developed into the main framework for nearly all Dutch external relations, as well as for considerable parts of its domestic politics. The three pillars of the EU leave hardly an area of national policy untouched. Most aspects of the Dutch external relations are now to a large extent conceived and implemented through the widening EU-CFSP-prism. And, though the nature of EU policies and their degree of domestic penetration can vary considerably, the whole European complex has more or less reshaped the Netherlands from a country with active sectoral EC policies such as trade or agriculture, into a part of a federalising system. Federal thinking, however, is no longer very popular.

Because of the steady involvement of so many departments, subnational authorities, regions, and interest groups in the European political process, Dutch views on European integration have become more heterogeneous. Other domestic voices make themselves heard in Brussels alongside traditional departments and lobbies, sometimes in open conflict with the "federal" orthodoxy of the Foreign Ministry. The Ministries of Social Affairs, Home Affairs, or Justice, for instance, prefer intergovernmental forms of co-operation in their fields, with the fall-back position of a veto, rather than using the full Community method (Van Schendelen 1995, 64). The Prime Minister, too, sees the role of intergovernmentalism in and around the European Council in a more favourable light than does the Foreign Ministry.

The decline of the federal orthodoxy is partly related to the fact that, since the early 1990s, the Netherlands has turned from being a net recipient of Community funds into a net payer. From 1970 until 1991, the Dutch received

---

* The first paragraphs have been drawn from: Alfred Pijpers and Sophie Vanhoonacker, "The position of the Benelux Countries," in: Geoffrey Edwards and Alfred Pijpers (eds.), *The Politics of European Treaty Reform, The 1996 Intergovernmental Conference and Beyond*, (London / Washington: Pinter 1997).

on average 2 billion guilder (about 1 billion ecu) each year (apart, that is, from the overall benefits of the common market). Beginning with the implementation of the Delors I package, this has changed. Under the Delors II package and the McSharry reforms, The Hague, in 1994 and 1995, was annually paying a net contribution of about 4 billion guilder (2 billion ecu). At the time of the IGC 1996, the Dutch belonged to the foremost net payers in the EU, both as a percentage of GNP and in per capita terms. This development caused the Ministry of Finance to complain, not only about the size of the contribution, but also about the ways in which money was spent in Brussels. An in-depth review of the cohesion policies and of the way the structural funds are operating was called for, in terms akin to the principle of *juste retour*, so fiercely rejected in the 1970s by the Dutch government. Hence, we meet the paradox that while the EU was becoming more federal in several respects (EMU, subsidiarity, citizenship, the idea of a common defence, or increasing administrative interdependence), Dutch perspectives, as reflected in government departments, political parties, and public opinion, were less so. Dutch "supranationalism" in the early EC years was, essentially, confined to the Community method, and not necessarily to radical ideas of political union. It seems that the Dutch were only in favour of a "European Union" so long as the concept remained vague and ill-defined.

Though enlargement as such has never been a controversial element in Dutch foreign policy, the widening to include Eastern and Southern European countries called for a new philosophy. The government was holding the view that, in order to avoid chaos in the former orbit of the Soviet Union, "the only possible solution is to integrate the countries of Central and Eastern Europe into western economic and political structures" (Ministry of Foreign Affairs 1994, 3). It realised, however, that a number of obstacles needed to be cleared before the road to membership would be open: "The institutional adjustment of the Union is not the least of these obstacles. It is therefore of great importance to find a balance between on the one hand the wish to bring forward the moment at which the countries of Central and Eastern Europe accede, and, on the other, attempting to ensure that the existing Union maintains its cohesion and decisiveness" (Ministry of Foreign Affairs 1994, 3).

To find this balance, the Dutch government used a number of guidelines which aptly summarise some Dutch core interests on the eve of the 1996 IGC: (i) achieving a stable security policy, socio-economic development, and democratic stability in Central and Eastern Europe; (ii) maintaining the active participation of Germany in the European integration process and in the joint European and Atlantic security structure; (iii) maintaining the internal market and the common legal order and thus a European Union that is capable of decisive action; (iv) achieving the aforementioned objectives at acceptable cost (Ministry of Foreign Affairs 1994, 5).

Preparations and Priorities for the 1996 IGC

The preparations for the IGC by the Dutch government were thorough. Already in November 1994, it sent the first of a series of four white papers about the IGC 1996 to the parliament.[1] During the spring of 1996, other papers followed which laid down the priorities of the Ministries that were involved in the IGC. All of these papers were discussed rather extensively in the parliament and the media. A remarkable fact was that the four IGC-papers were translated into English, French and German in order to inform the other Member States adequately about the Dutch priorities and interests. From these documents the following picture emerges as to the principal preferences and viewpoints (though not final positions) of the Dutch government.

One basic feature stands out: the Dutch attitude towards further treaty reform was cautious and middle-of-the-road. The government emphasised that the objectives of the EU did not need to be adapted or supplemented with new policy areas. Deepening was only called for in the sense of institutional improvements. Most if not all Dutch documents and advisory reports were, in a striking way, empty of any reference to the need, or the possibility, for creating a true federal EU in the near or not so near future. At the 1991 IGC on Political Union, the Dutch government had still been prepared to launch outspoken federal concepts – including the ill-fated "tree structure" presented by the Dutch Presidency in September 1991 (Wester 1992, 172-5; Van Hulten: n.d.; Penders & Kwast 1992, 253-70) – for a new Union treaty with strong support from all the large fractions in the Second Chamber, opposition parties included. By 1995, the government's proposals implicitly or explicitly acknowledged the pillar structure to be the most realistic option for the near future, though its view was also that the role of the EC institutions should be expanded, especially in the second and third pillars. Communitarian decision-making in the first pillar "remained sacrosanct" in the view of the government (Ministry of Foreign Affairs 1995, 22).

The Foreign Ministry in The Hague and its advisory bodies tended to regard the IGC mainly as a means of consolidating the *acquis communautaire* and *acquis politique* in the context of broadening Union membership, with the

---

[1] The four papers dealt respectively with the issues of enlargement, Common Foreign and Security Policy, co-operation on Justice and Home Affairs and institutional reform (Ministry of Foreign Affairs 1996).

internal market and its functionally related policy areas (including monetary unification, co-operation in the fields of Justice and Home Affairs, the social chapter) as its most essential elements. If the IGC would contribute to preserving the core elements of the EU under the trying circumstances of further enlargement, chronic instability and crises in the immediate external environment of the EU, and the impact of a globalising economy, then it could already be considered a success.

Institutional Matters
The Dutch shared the general consensus that the application of a simple extrapolation model for the institutional set-up of a further enlarged Union should be rejected. It was felt that "the accession of the EFTA countries had already stretched the extrapolation model to the limit," and that a continued application of this model "would cause the decision-making machinery to grind to a halt" (Ministry of Foreign Affairs 1994, 19-20). The voting weight per Member State, the number of Commissioners and MEPs, had to be established in a different way than before, and so would the procedures necessary to obtain a qualified majority. These changes were to avoid a situation in the foreseeable future where a group of small countries, representing only a minority of the population in the EU, would be able to overrule all larger Member States under the existing QMV procedures. The Netherlands and other small states encountered here the dilemma between a proper national representation in the EU institutions, and the necessity to streamline decision-making.

The overall approach of the government was to maintain the principle of disproportionality[2] (which gives the small countries a larger share in terms of institutional representation as compared to the large ones), but to mitigate it. This approach appeared in a number of suggestions made by the Dutch government on issues such as decision-making in the Council, voting weights, the rotation of the Council Presidency, or the number of national representatives in Commission, EP and Court.

The government was of the opinion that all decision-making in the first pillar, in principle, should be on the basis of QMV, except for fiscal matters, "own resources," and for decisions with a constitutional character such as treaty revision, enlargement, and the number of languages used in the Union (Ministry of Foreign Affairs 1994, 13). The Dutch government rejected the

---

[2] A joint Benelux memorandum, presented to the Lisbon meeting of the European Council in June 1992, stated that: "the basic idea which should be endorsed is that in the Commission, the Council, and the European Parliament the larger countries will have to accept some over-representation of the smaller Member States" (Bal 1994, 112).

further application after the IGC of the Ioannina Agreement, which, though establishing the threshold for a blocking minority at 26 votes, had stipulated that if 23 to 25 votes were to be cast against a certain measure, the Presidency should continue consultations, without taking the issue under consideration to a vote. The threshold for a blocking minority in the Council should remain at 30 per cent of the total amount of votes.

The Hague also expressed itself in favour of introducing a double key for QMV: one reflecting the present number of votes per Member State, and an additional key stipulating that the majority should also represent at least 50 per cent of the total EU population. Such a double key formula had the advantage of maintaining the principle of disproportionality, but it made it more acceptable to the larger states. The Netherlands, with its comparatively large population, would not itself be badly off. However, the government was reluctant to mitigate the idea of disproportionality by simply giving the large members more votes. Such a move might lead to new calculations among the four big states, with the potential of friction between them.

A similar compromise formula was conceived for a better functioning of the EU Council Presidency. In the existing arrangement, adopted by the European Council in December 1993, the former alphabetical order was substituted by a rotation scheme of successive troikas, each with a large Member State taking part. The scheme was rather gratifying for the Netherlands, appointed an "honorary" large state to take on the troika with Luxembourg and Ireland during the first half of 1997. Yet the government realised that in a Union with 20 and more members (when a Member State might occupy the Presidency only once each decade) other measures were called for, such as extending each presidential term to one year, dividing tasks between "internal" and "external" presidencies, to opt for an elected President, or a team presidency. The Dutch government itself favoured a team presidency in which tasks were divided between the members of a troika serving a term of one year (Ministry of Foreign Affairs 1994, 15).

A more sensitive point concerned the composition of the Commission. According to most analysts, a ceiling had already been reached with twenty Commissioners. A college of more members could hardly work effectively, and made it difficult to create a relevant portfolio for each of the Commissioners. At the same time, the Dutch government was well aware of the importance of the role of the Commission in the EU. It remained of the opinion that each Member State ought to be represented in the Commission, preferably with one Commissioner (Ministry of Foreign Affairs 1994, 16). At the beginning of the IGC debate, the government was still fairly flexible on the point, it was not wholly opposed, for instance, to small states having fewer Commissioners than the large members, on the strict condition that all members would, in principle, be prepared to forsake their right to a seat in the Commission. This possible concession was dropped after domestic pressure and discussions within the Benelux framework.

Common Foreign and Security Policy

The pragmatic approach of the Dutch government was also reflected in its proposals for the second pillar. The Hague accepted that there had been several "significant weaknesses" in the operation of the CFSP (Ministry of Foreign Affairs 1995, 16): divisiveness over Bosnia and Rwanda; slow decision-making and insufficient joint analysis; difficulties of consistency between the first and second pillars; and lack of democratic control. It did not, however, see any need to reformulate CFSP objectives as listed in Article J.1.2. of the Treaty on European Union: "The existing wording allows sufficient scope, and experience to date with the CFSP gives no grounds for reformulation" (Ministry of Foreign Affairs 1995, 16).

The problems with the CFSP were seen not as technical but political. Some procedures, however, could be improved. The "capacity for analysis" or the ways policies were prepared could be strengthened, through, for instance, a better staffing of the CFSP unit, or even the creation of a new unit halfway between the Council and the Commission, and possibly headed by a "Secretary-General of its own." The Hague has also traditionally favoured the strong involvement of the Commission in the CFSP, which could be extended "to include preparations for decision-making." Similarly, the Article J.3 procedure could be improved, and the government agreed with the German idea of allowing the adoption of joint actions by QMV. However, a true communitarisation of the CFSP was regarded as only "an option for the long term" (Ministry of Foreign Affairs 1995, 17, 18, 20); the lessons of Black Monday had been learnt.

The Dutch were aware of the necessity of further developing a common defence policy. To this end they favoured the future integration of the WEU in the EU, not by establishing a new, fourth pillar in the EU treaty, but through the incorporation of the WEU into the second pillar. This incorporation would have the advantage of "smoothing the transition from CFSP to common defence policy," while preserving the single institutional framework of the EU better than a separate fourth pillar (Ministry of Foreign Affairs 1995, 29). It was recognised that this had to be a gradual process which could only be completed in the long run, given the differences between EU, WEU and NATO membership in the wider Europe. In the meantime, an "Atlantic contract" should bridge the possible gap between NATO and EU membership (Ministry of Foreign Affairs 1995, 32, 26).

Multiple Speed

The Dutch government has always tried to ban "inner circles," "directorates" or other informal clubs outside the regular channels for decision-making and consultation in the EU (Voorhoeve 1979, 187-8). Such tendencies were regarded as undermining the legal order of the Community and likely to lead to a hegemony of the large states. Gradually, however, it occurred to the Dutch that even though the classical concept of a "directorate" should remain taboo, certain forms of differentiated integration were unavoidable in a Union of more than fifteen members, with considerable economic and monetary divergencies, and different strategic interests. The government, though, was of the opinion that differentiated forms of integration should remain the exception, and that such forms, in whatever variant, should not detract from the single institutional framework of the EU (Ministry of Foreign Affairs 1994, 17). Each variant should also be compatible with the following criteria: "(i) differentiated integration had to be compatible with the objectives of the TEU; (ii) each Member State should be free to participate if it could and wanted to meet the requirements for the fast track; (iii) differentiated integration should not undermine the Community legal order or, in principle, impair the cohesion of the internal market; (iv) Member States which elected to opt out should not be allowed to oppose the formation of a leading group which did meet the above-mentioned criteria" (Ministry of Foreign Affairs 1994, 23-4).

Though these criteria would seem to allow for a variety of modes of integration, it transpired that the only form the Dutch government believed met all the criteria was multiple speed integration, whereby the policy objective is the same for all Member States, though the speed at which they are achieved may vary. Multiple speed integration was not an end in itself, but a means to an end: "it enables a core group, or rather a leading group of Member States to proceed with further co-operation and integration," or to achieve "gradual convergence when new Member States join the EU" (Ministry of Foreign Affairs 1994, 22).

The government was less enthusiastic about the concept of variable geometry, whereby not just the speed, but also the integration objectives may vary among the Member States. Variable geometry should, it held, be avoided in the Community sphere, since "allowing our objectives to diverge will only encourage disintegration" and might easily undermine the Community legal order. For the second and third pillar, however, The Hague "would not exclude the option of variable geometry altogether." This was perhaps clear already from the Dutch participation in Schengen and in several forms of European military co-operation. Needless to say, the Dutch resisted any form of opting-in or opting-out at will. As the government stated, European integration "cannot survive a Europe à la carte" (Ministry of Foreign Affairs 1994, 23).

The Domestic Background

When the first steps towards a discussion on the issues of the 1996 Intergovernmental Conference were taken, the Dutch government was faced with increasing scepticism about further transfers of policy fields to the European level. As mentioned earlier, the Netherlands had changed from a very pro-European Member State into a more moderate proponent of integration. The decline in support for European integration was visible in the parliament, but there were also indications that it had become part of a more general attitude in the Netherlands. The government was therefore less secure about domestic support for further integration in the negotiations with the other Member States. Moreover, there was a growing awareness that the far-going decisions, as laid down in the Maastricht treaty, had been taken without serious domestic reflection in the Netherlands. It was only after the Madrid summit in December 1995, where 1 January 1999 was confirmed as the starting date for the Euro, that the pros and cons of the Economic and Monetary Union were publicly discussed among the Dutch intellectuals and in the media (Rozemond 1997, 117-8). Despite the good intentions of the government, a general debate about the main issues of the IGC 1996 did not evolve either. Instead, the discussion remained largely limited to the government, the parliament and the advisory councils of the government.

Political Parties and Advisory Councils
During the preparations for the IGC 1996, it seemed that parliamentary support for European integration had declined. Especially the conservative liberal VVD, one of the parties of the government coalition, made it clear that it was not much in favour of allowing further transfers of sovereignty to the European level. Disagreement between the VVD and the other coalition parties, the Social Democratic PvdA and the Liberal Democratic D66, is therefore one of the explanations for the modest goals the Dutch government had set for itself at the IGC.[3] When a joint memorandum of the Benelux

---

[3] Kwast-van Duursen, in 1996, feared even problems for the Dutch position at the IGC: "The disagreements in the cabinet and between the PvdA, D66 and the VVD are likely to cause problems in the next few months. For the first time since the beginning of European integration there is no longer a consensus on the Dutch position." (Kwast-van Duursen 1996, 60).

countries contained proposals with a more *communautaire* character, the VVD strongly criticised the government and disputed the status of the document.[4] The Liberal Democratic D66, the smallest party in the government coalition and an explicit proponent of a federal Europe, admitted that the atmosphere in Europe and in the Netherlands at the time of the IGC did not leave room to treat the federal ideal still as a realistic aspiration.[5]

The reverse development of the decline in support for European integration was that the Dutch discussion about Europe became more influenced by national interests, such as the need for the Netherlands to maintain its influence in the European institutions as a relatively small Member State and the wish to restrict the Dutch financial contribution to the EU. The Socio-Economic Council[6] criticised the nature of the discussion about the Dutch contribution to the EU-budget. It stated that it is "incorrect, and even misleading" to equate the costs and benefits of European integration with the balance of incomings from and outgoings to the EU-budget. The Council itself did not have objections against a net-payer status for the Netherlands, provided that this status would be compensated by high quality policies in the EU (Socio-Economic Council 1995, 54-5, 80). With regard to the position of small Member States, the Socio-Economic Council accepted that a pragmatic approach was necessary and that the representation of these states had to be brought more in line with their populations (Advisory Council on Peace and Security 1995, 33-4). The Advisory Council on Peace and Security argued in a similar way that the main interests of the Netherlands are the economic advantages of the internal market and the maintenance of a *communitarian* decision-making structure, which could serve as a counterbalance against larger Member States (Advisory Council on Peace and Security 1995, 8).

With regard to the reform of the European Commission, none of the Dutch political parties appeared to be willing to give up the Dutch Commissioner. However, a definite position could wait until the actual enlargement of the EU. The Socio-Economic Council supported the view that the Dutch Commissioner should not easily be given up. For the long term, when effective control by the European Parliament would be guaranteed, the

---

[4] Plenary debate, Second Chamber of Parliament, 9 April 1996, *Handelingen 1995/96*, no. 23, 4543.

[5] Plenary debate, Second Chamber of Parliament, 19 June 1996, *Handelingen 1995/96*, no. 34, p. 6221 et seq. See Tellegen 1995.

[6] The Socio-Economic Council is the government's official advisory council and is composed of representatives from employers, trade unions and independent experts.

Council proposed the idea of "regional" or "group" commissioners (Socio-Economic Council 1995, 80).

During the preparatory debates in Parliament, controversy between the political parties existed on a number of specific issues on the IGC agenda. With respect to the second pillar, the VVD dissented from the majority in parliament – including the other coalition parties – by opposing the introduction of majority decision-making in the second pillar. According to the VVD, majority voting in the field of Common Foreign and Security Policy would in practice only take place at the expense of small countries such as the Netherlands, since large Member States would not give up their possibility of using a veto. According to the VVD, the true reason for the deadlock in the second pillar was not the decision-making procedure, but the absence of a common idea about European security. The VVD was supported in this position by a small minority in parliament, including the small right-wing Christian parties (SGP, GPV and RPF) which usually held a eurosceptic viewpoint.

Another point of disagreement over the second pillar was the future of the WEU. The PvdA and the largest opposition party, the Christian democratic CDA, favoured the integration of the WEU in the EU. The VVD, with a more Atlantic outlook, was against this idea and even disputed the continuance of the WEU as an organisation. The Advisory Council on Peace and Security supported the integration of the WEU in the second pillar and suggested taking a decision at the IGC on a time-table that would complete the formal integration in 1998 (Advisory Council on Peace and Security 1995, 28-32).

Concerning the incorporation of provisions for employment in the Treaty, the VVD and the CDA did not support the government's efforts to incorporate a separate article in the Treaty. This issue also caused controversy. The VVD argued that Treaty articles do not create more employment and considered social and employment policies as not being a desirable task for the European Union (Weisglas 1997, 130).[7] While the CDA accepted the incorporation of the Social Protocol in the Treaty, the VVD wanted to abolish this Protocol. Between the VVD and the other government parties, therefore, a fundamental difference of opinion existed about the division of competence between the European and the national level in the field of social and employment policy.

---

[7] See also a statement by Frits Bolkestein, Plenary Debate, Second Chamber of Parliament, 19 June 1996, *Handelingen 1995/96*, no. 34, p. 6229 et seq.

There was widespread support in Parliament and in the advisory councils for the enlargement project.[8] Enlargement was seen as a good opportunity for institutional reform of the EU. According to all major political parties, the role of the European Parliament had to be strengthened, at least by giving it the right of co-decision for decisions that are taken by majority in the Council. A motion was adopted which requested the government to make efforts to ensure that the expenditures in the second and third pillar were made subject to control by the European Parliament by marking them compulsory.[9] Moreover, all parties agreed that decision-making in the Council should be more transparent and that there should be a right for citizens to have access to European documents. These positions marked a continuance of the traditional Dutch support for further democratisation of the European institutional framework.

The concept of differentiated integration received relatively much attention from politicians and advisory bodies. Both the government parties and the main opposition party CDA considered two or more levels of speed as inevitable in an enlarged Union, but differed slightly on the extent to which differentiation was acceptable. The largest government party PvdA emphasised that different levels of speed were only acceptable as an instrument; the final goal should remain the parallel development of all Member States. The PvdA rejected permanent core groups, but also temporary core groups were seen as a threat to the internal market. New opt-outs, similar to the situation of the UK with the Social Protocol, had to be avoided. The political parties agreed that an *à la carte* situation should be avoided and that the internal market should not be negatively affected.

The Scientific Council for Government Policy and the Advisory Council on Peace and Security had a notable difference of opinion on the subject of flexibility. The Scientific Council supported the idea of a single core group and considered, under certain circumstances, variable geometry as a possible solution. It argued that the objections against variable geometry "pale somewhat when measured against the risk that a postponement of EMU is likely to lead to the abandonment of the idea and, thus, to a dilution of the internal market and possibly of European integration itself" (Scientific Council for Government Policy 1995, 114). The Advisory Council on Peace and Security, on the other hand, emphasized the risks of differentiation for the cohesion of the EU. Differentiation should only apply to policy fields where it is inevitable. According to the Advisory Council, the concept of different

---

[8] Plenary Debate, Second Chamber of Parliament, 14 February 1995, *Handelingen 1994/95*, no. 18.

[9] Motion no. 19, Second Chamber of Parliament, doc 24609, *Handelingen 96/97*, p. 5707.

levels of speed should therefore remain limited to the Economic and Monetary Union and the development of a European military capacity (Advisory Council on Peace and Security 1995, 24 et seq.).

The pillar of Justice and Home Affairs constituted a sensitive issue in the Netherlands, especially because of the dispute with France about the liberal Dutch drugs policy. Since there is no efficient control by the European Parliament, the Dutch Second Chamber of Parliament insisted on a right of assent for all draft decisions in the third pillar, similar to the Danish model of parliamentary control on European issues. Although the political parties were hesitant to introduce common policies in the field of drugs and crime, most parties supported the communitarisation of the visa and asylum policy.

Public Opinion and the IGC

The attitude of the Dutch citizens towards European integration in the period before the IGC 1996 was not entirely clear. The low turn-out in the Netherlands (36%) at the European Parliament elections in 1994 came as an unpleasant surprise to many politicians. Some surveys also pointed in the direction of a growing scepticism towards Europe, but the striking differences between the outcomes of various opinion polls showed that much depends on the wording of the questions. For example, while in one Eurobarometer study 72% of the Dutch respondents declared their support for a European government responsible to the European Parliament,[10] another survey carried out in the same period resulted in a percentage of 76% of the respondents being opposed to a European Union that would become a United States of Europe, with the Netherlands as one of the federal states (Kapteyn & Schijf 1996).

The reaction of the general Dutch public to the European policy of the government could probably better be characterised by a lack of interest in and knowledge of European issues, rather than by a widespread dissatisfaction with Europe. As was also mentioned above, the debate about the IGC still remained limited to the political elite and the advisory councils. In the autumn of 1995, only 22% of the Dutch respondents to a Eurobarometer survey was aware of the IGC 1996.[11] The awareness increased when the Netherlands held the EU presidency in the first half of 1997: 82% of the Dutch had at that time heard or read about their country's presidency.[12] In the same poll, 66% of the

---

[10] *Eurobarometer 45*, December 1996 (fieldwork: February-May 1996), European Commission.

[11] *Eurobarometer 44*, Autumn 1995, European Commission.

[12] *Eurobarometer 47*, October 1997 (fieldwork: February-June 1997), European Commission.

Dutch declared to feel not very well or not at all informed about the European Union against 33% who felt quite well or very well informed. The general support for EU membership remained high. Although the percentage had slightly dropped from 80% in the autumn of 1995, in the months prior to the Amsterdam summit 72% considered the Netherlands' EU membership a good thing.[13]

The Role of the Dutch EU Presidency

From the very start of the Presidency, the Dutch government emphasised that the position of the Netherlands in the negotiations should have a pragmatic character, hereby allowing some disregard for specific Dutch wishes and preferences. The government was determined to prevent a repetition of "Black Monday," especially because the IGC 1996 was scheduled to be concluded again during the Dutch EC/EU Presidency.

The deliberate mission of the Dutch government to act in the interest of the European "collective," together with its solid preparatory work, has clearly contributed to the relatively smooth performance of the Presidency. However, this policy also led to domestic criticism and confusion. The government was for example, criticised by Dutch parliamentarians because it was unclear whether the Dutch priorities represented the position of the Netherlands or its position as President during the IGC. One member of parliament observed for instance that the Netherlands as President appeared to be willing to give up its own commissioner in the future, while at the same time it was opposed to the idea as a Member State.[14] Criticism of the Dutch presidency came also from several Dutch members of the European Parliament. Their main grievance was that the programme of the Dutch presidency was neither innovative nor ambitious enough (Werts 1997, 453). This criticism gave support for the observation that a political distance existed between the Dutch members of the European Parliament and their colleagues in The Hague.[15]

---

[13] *Eurobarometer 44*, Autumn 1995, and *Eurobarometer 47*, October 1997. The same question was asked in the survey by Kapteyn and Schijf and resulted in the same percentage of 72% (Kapteyn & Schijf 1996).

[14] MP Van den Bos (D66), Plenary Debate, Second Chamber of Parliament, 21 May 1997, *Handelingen 1996/97*, no. 29, p. 5667.

[15] Another illustration of this situation is the fact that the ELDR-group in the European Parliament, in which the VVD participates, was explicitly in favour of the integration of the WEU in the EU, while at the same time the VVD had clearly declared in the Dutch parliament to be against this development (ELDR 1995).

A first concrete result of the Dutch presidency was the "Addendum to the Dublin II-concept" which was presented on 20 March 1997, one day before the special remembrance meeting of the 40 year-old EEC Treaty in Rome. Not a new blue-print this time, but only a supplement to an earlier Irish draft. The Irish and Dutch "Dublin" proposals were only an enumeration and identification of problem areas, rather than a true interim treaty. In the spring of 1997, there appeared to be agreement among the Member States with respect to several issues on the IGC agenda. These included the integration of the Schengen Agreement into the Treaty of Amsterdam, the appointment of a High Commissioner for the CFSP, the introduction of new forms of differentiated integration, and the inclusion of provisions against discrimination on the basis of sex, race, religion, disability, age or homosexuality.

On the other hand, serious discord persisted on different major topics, such as institutional reform and the integration of the WEU in the European Union. An extra scheduled summit in Noordwijk on 23 May 1997 brought little change in the deadlock. The meeting was undoubtedly useful for "exploring the political will," as Dutch Prime Minister Kok stated, and to get acquainted with the new British Prime Minister Blair, but it produced hardly any progress regarding the IGC. The United Kingdom was willing to sign the Social Protocol, but remained opposed to any deepening of the European social policy. Moreover, like his conservative predecessors, Blair refused to create a role for the European Court of Justice in Europol affairs, and was against the integration of the WEU in the European Union. Another point of disagreement in Noordwijk, especially between France and Germany, was the contents of a new chapter on employment in the Treaty. Progress on institutional reform was mixed. While the Member States now agreed on the preferred size of the European Commission (twenty members at a maximum), the negotiations on the reweighting of votes in the Council seemed to stagnate.

The unexpected elections in France in early June caused a complication in the Dutch schedule. The newly elected socialist Prime Minister Jospin demanded a revision of the Stability Pact for the EMU, a document that had already been approved in Dublin and which had to be officially signed in Amsterdam. This French demand not only represented a serious threat to the EMU, but also created an inconvenient burden at the last stage of the IGC. The Dutch Finance Minister Zalm managed, due to German support, to prevent a crisis over the EMU. The question dominated, however, the agenda on the first day of the summit in Amsterdam (16-17 June 1997) and reduced the negotiation time that was already short in itself.

The Treaty of Amsterdam: Outcome and Ratification

Outcome
In the early morning of 18 June 1997, the heads of government and presidents of the fifteen Member States succeeded, after laborious deliberations, in reaching a settlement about a concept-treaty of Amsterdam. The Dutch government could only be satisfied that its main goal, "an IGC with a result," was reached at the Amsterdam summit. The fact that there was eventually a treaty did not mean, however, that the result met the expectations. Even when it is taken into consideration that the Dutch government had followed a pragmatic policy and had explicitly warned against raising expectations too high, the final outcome of the IGC was considered as very moderate. The ambition to reform the institutions in order to prepare the European Union for the coming enlargement of a wide range of new Member States from Central, Eastern and Southern Europe had not been realised. The main reason for this "Protocol of Failure," as a British expert has called it (Duff 1997), was the contrast between the interests of the large and small Member States.

The final proposal of the Dutch Presidency on institutional reform was based on the realisation that most of the small Member States refused from the outset of the negotiations to give up their own Commissioner. In order to keep the Commission at a size that enabled it to remain effective, the larger Member States had to give up one of their two Commissioners. They could be compensated for this loss by increasing their voting weight in the Council. This proposal, however, was rejected by some small countries. Especially Belgium was unwilling to revise the voting weights in the Council in favour of the large Member States as long as this revision was not accompanied by a substantial expansion of the application of qualified majority voting. Moreover, and this was the consequence of an unpractical strategy of the Dutch Presidency, the Belgian Prime Minister Dehaene was annoyed about the Dutch intention to set the future Dutch voting weight in the Council at a higher level than the voting weight of Belgium. Since the foundation of the Community the Netherlands and Belgium had been at the same level, a situation that has promoted the relationship between the two countries in both the EU and the Benelux. Some larger Member States had problems with the proposal as well. France was against the proposal of the Presidency to take the size of the population of the Member States into consideration for determining a majority in the Council. For France, this meant that the disparity with Germany would be emphasised too much. Spain, which had been awarded a double representation in the Commission at its accession in 1986, refused to give up its second Commissioner unless it would be adequately (i.e. equal to Germany, France, the United Kingdom and Italy) compensated in the Council. Thus, the impasse in the institutional reform question that had come to the surface already in Noordwijk had now become complete and the suggestion of the German Chancellor to postpone the question to a next IGC was readily accepted.

Nor was much progress made in the second pillar. The Member States and the European institutions had explicitly declared to aim at strengthening the external capacity of the European Union. However, the effect of the procedural changes in Title V about the Common Foreign and Security Policy that were decided on in Amsterdam is limited. The ambition of the Dutch Presidency to integrate the WEU in the European Union was not realised either. Especially the United Kingdom made problems in this respect. The British ambassador in The Hague had informed the Dutch presidency in early June 1997 that the European Union should not become a defence organisation and that there could never been a subordination of the WEU to the EU, or integration in the EU.

Despite the meagre result of the Amsterdam summit in several policy fields, there were also a number of decisions that were assessed positively in the Netherlands. For example, "drastic surgeries" have been applied in the co-operation on Justice and Home Affairs (Boer 1997), including the transfer of some legal instruments related to asylum, immigration, visa and external borders to a new title in the first pillar. After a transitional period, this title will be fully subjected to the communitarian regime. The Treaty of Schengen was also incorporated in the Treaty of Amsterdam. Finally, the third pillar would only deal with the police and judicial co-operation in criminal cases. A remarkable aspect of these measures is that the Dutch proposals that had been defeated in September 1991, now became partly realised after all. Other positive decisions taken in Amsterdam that met Dutch approval included the anti-discrimination provisions, the combat of fraud, employment, the integration of the Social Protocol, flexible integration and the right to co-decision for the European Parliament. On balance, a considerable part of the Dutch IGC priorities, or at least the priorities of the Dutch Presidency, was realised in the Treaty of Amsterdam (see Annex 1).

The Reaction to the Treaty of Amsterdam in the Parliament and the Media
The first parliamentary debate about the Treaty of Amsterdam took place already on the 18th of June 1997.[16] The official text of the treaty, which had only been concluded the night before, was not yet available to the members

---

[16] Plenary Debate, Second Chamber of Parliament, 18 June 1997, *Handelingen 1995/96*, no. 33, p. 6519-6564.

of parliament. The debate could therefore not be more than a very general evaluation of the final results of the summit.

The government did not meet serious difficulties in parliament while defending the treaty. The parties of the government coalition extensively praised the negotiation skills of the government representatives in their role as president. PvdA-leader Wallage admitted that the final treaty only constituted a moderate result, but this was in his opinion the consequence of the lack of willingness of the other Member States and not of the Dutch presidency. D66 regretted that the integration process had been slowed down, but it could live with the overall outcome of the summit. The extension of majority voting and the institutional reforms showed, according to D66, "a meagre result." The VVD, after earlier criticism in which its leader Bolkestein had even threatened to vote against the treaty, now concluded that the positive points of the treaty outweighed the negative ones. Bolkestein declared in the debate that his party was happy to see that the possibility of a veto in the second pillar remained and that no decision had been taken to integrate the WEU in the EU. The party remained opposed to the protocol on employment policy, but took comfort in the perception that the protocol would mean nothing in practice. Moreover, in the view of the VVD politicians, the successful conclusion of the stability pact compensated for their dissatisfaction with the decisions about employment policy.

The opposition parties were, not surprisingly, less positive about the results. The CDA called the treaty "a tiny one" and emphasised that Europe had not been made stronger and more efficient. The IGC had, according to the CDA, put a heavy burden on the enlargement negotiations. The Green Left party noted that the Treaty did not meet the goals set by the Member States prior to the IGC. With a view to the enlargement project, Green Left considered it "very sad" that no agreement had been reached about sufficient institutional reforms. Most sceptical was the small right-wing Christian party GPV, which remarked that the process of European integration had reached its final limits. With respect to the third pillar, the parliament regretted the fact that the aspects which were brought under the community pillar were still subject to unanimity decision-making.

The comments in the daily newspapers largely reflected the atmosphere of the political parties in parliament. The government was complimented upon its performance as president. It was true that the final result was moderate, but the fact that there was a treaty could already be called a success. *NRC Handelsblad* argued that it was not only political rhetoric when Helmut Kohl had called the summit a success, since the road to a single European currency and to enlargement was still open.[17] The *Volkskrant* wrote that the most important conclusion from the Amsterdam summit was probably that the expectations of the Member States about the integration of Europe had now been put at a somewhat lower level than in the years before.[18]

A survey among a number of civil servants in Dutch ministries who contributed to the presidency indicated that the overall result of the presidency was positively assessed by the bureaucracy as well. Although the researchers noted that the level of success is not easy to define in this context, nearly all respondents considered the Dutch presidency as successful (Clingendael 1998).

Ratification
The ratification of the Treaty of Amsterdam, in November 1998, was carried through by a large majority in the parliament. Except for Green Left, the small Christian parties and the small Socialist Party, all parties voted in favour of the ratification.[19] There were, however, some additional critical notes about the final treaty text. There was widespread disapproval of the complex formulation that had made the treaty rather unreadable. It astonished the parties in parliament that the government had accepted that the European Parliament would meet at least twelve times a year in Strasbourg. The CDA called this "unbelievable" and pointed to the fact that this was in clear contradiction to the government policy to restrict the Dutch expenditures to Europe. A further point of criticism was the continuing lack of democratic accountability in Europe. A motion was adopted that asked for more openness of the legislative meetings of the Council.[20] Another motion requested the government to strongly object to the increase of the informal meetings of the Council which, according to the PvdA, started to disturb the balance between the European institutions. Green Left proposed a new procedure for the approval of treaty changes in which the national parliaments would get an opportunity to be consulted about the draft treaty, after which a second summit of the Member State governments could decide about the final version. Various parties expressed their concern about some legal aspects of the Schengen *acquis*, but a motion of the GPV which asked the government

---

[17] Versterkt fundament, in: *NRC Handelsblad*, 18 June 1996.

[18] Europese krampen, in: *de Volkskrant*, 19 June 1996.

[19] Plenary Debate, Second Chamber of Parliament, 3 November 1998, *Handelingen 1998/99*, no. 19, p. 1145-1200.

[20] Motion no. 19 (25922), *Handelingen 1998/99*, no. 21.

to postpone the ratification of the treaty until this point could be clarified was rejected by a large majority in parliament.[21]

The pragmatic approach of the Dutch presidency was undoubtedly helpful in concluding a long road of preparations for the 1996-IGC, which started already with the Treaty of Maastricht. It is also interesting to note that many of the items which were inserted in the final text, reflected collective viewpoints, rather than national priorities. The Dutch presidency was in this regard more the instrument of a European process, than of specific Dutch interests or preferences.

---

[21] Motion no. 18 (25922), *Handelingen 1998/99*, no. 21.

Annex 1   Dutch IGC Priorities and the Treaty of Amsterdam

Dutch priorities*	Treaty of Amsterdam Realised		
	yes	no	partly
I. Principles			
• strengthening the fundamental rights in the EU Treaty	x		
• enshrining the right of public access to government information in the EU Treaty	x		
• simplifying the EU Treaty			x
• improving the application of the subsidiarity principle, on the basis of better argued proposals from the Commission	x		
• efforts to improve the quality of EC legislation	x		
• furnishing the Treaty with criteria and provisions which will make multi-speed integration possible on a selective basis	x		
• clarification of the environmental provisions aimed at integrating environmental policy more closely to other policy areas	x		
• maintaining the equal status of the EU languages	x		
II. Institutions			
European Parliament			
• reducing the number of decision-making mechanisms to three (consultation, co-decision-making, assent)	x		
• simplifying the co-decision procedure, and applying it to more areas	x		
Council			
• maintaining and, where possible, extending qualified majority voting in the field of the internal market			x
• using caution when it comes to re-weighting votes; possible adoption of the double-key option		x	
Commission			
• leaving its current powers and prerogatives intact	x		
• increasing its effectiveness			x
• increasing its duty of accountability to the EP	x		
• increasing the personal accountability by making it possible to dismiss individual Commissioners			x
• simplifying the committee procedures			x
• retaining a Dutch Commissioner	x		
Court of Justice			
• leaving the Court's prerogatives intact, and extending them to the sphere of JHA co-operation	x		
Court of Auditors			
• affording it the right of appeal to the Court of Justice	x		

Dutch priorities*	Treaty of Amsterdam Realised		
	yes	no	partly
III. Internal market			
• strengthening the anti-fraud instruments	x		
• conditional preference for a Treaty provision on employment	x		
• opposing the introduction of such new Community policy areas such as energy, tourism and civil defence	x		
• opposing the new exceptions to freedom of movement in the area of public service utilities	x		
• incorporating the Social Protocol in the Treaty	x		
IV. Common Foreign and Security Policy			
• establishing a planning and analysis unit, to which member states, Council Secretariat and Commission would contribute experience; not a new institution with the right of initiative	x		
• extending decision-making by majority voting: possible variants to be decided on later		x	
• opposing the appointment of a "Mr/Ms CFSP" with a high political profile; in any event, such an official must be subordinate to the General Affairs Council	x		
• gradually integrating the WEU into the EU, and to this end improving co-operation between them			x
V. Co-operation in the field of Justice and Home Affairs			
• strenghtening the role of the Court of Justice, the Commission and the European Parliament			x
• increasing the scope for a Community approach to visa and asylum policy	x		
• incorporating the Schengen *acquis* into the Union	x		
• lowering the threshold of the bridging clause ("passerelle"), i.e. making it easier for JHA policy areas to be transferred to the EC legal order	x		

* As formulated by the Dutch government in the paper *The Netherlands and Europe – Priorities Spring 1996*, The Hague: Ministry of Foreign Affairs, March 1996, pp. 16-18.

Bibliography

Advisory Council on Peace and Security (Adviesraad Vrede en Veiligheid) (1995). *Een nieuwe uitdaging – Europa 1996* (A new challenge – Europe 1996), The Hague: SDU, Report No. 17.

Bal, L.J. a.o. (1994). "Institutionele hervorming van de Europese Unie," *Internationale Spectator*, Vol. 48.

Boer, Monica den (1997). "Hollen of stilstaan? Justitie en Binnenlandse Zaken in het nieuwe Verdrag van Amsterdam," *Nederlands Juristenblad (NJB)*, 3 October.

Clingendael Institute (1998). *Het Nederlands Raadsvoorzitterschap geëvalueerd*, The Hague, February.

Duff, Andrew (1997). *The Treaty of Amsterdam*, London: Sweet & Maxwell/Federal Trust.

European Liberal, Democrat and Reform Party European Parliament (1995). *Proposals on the 1996 Intergovernmental Conference*, April 1995.

Hulten, Michiel van (n.d.). *The Short Life and Sudden Death of the Dutch Draft Treaty Towards European Union*, mimeo.

Kapteyn, Paul & Bert Schijf (1996). *Europa: ja, nee, geen mening – Europese gezindheid in Nederland*, Amsterdam: Het Spinhuis.

Kwast-van Duursen, Marja (1996). "The Dutch debate: a shifting policy on Europe," pp. 46-60, in A.C.G. Stubb, L. Cohen-Tanugi, S. Fagiolo & M. Kwast-van Duursen (eds.), *The 1996 IGC – National debates (1) Finland, France, Italy and the Netherlands*, London: the Royal Institute of International Affairs, Discussion Paper 66.

Ministry of Foreign Affairs (1994). *Enlargement of the European Union: Possibilities and Problems*, The Hague (first IGC memorandum of the Dutch government).

Ministry of Foreign Affairs (1995). *European Foreign, Security and Defence Policy: Towards Stronger External Action by the European Union*, The Hague (Second IGC memorandum of the Dutch government).

Ministry of Foreign Affairs (1996). *The Netherlands and Europe – Priorities Spring 1996*, The Hague, March 1996.

Penders, Jean & Maria Kwast (1992). "The Netherlands and political union," pp. 253-270, in Alfred Pijpers (ed.), *The European Community at the Crossroads,* Dordrecht: Martinus Nijhoff.

Rozemond, S. (1997). "Wijsheid vooraf en onwijsheid achteraf," *Internationale Spectator*, March.

Schendelen, M.P.C.M. van (1995). *Gelijkhebben of Winnen: Nederlandse belangenbehartiging in de Europese Unie*, Amsterdam: Amsterdam University Press.

Scientific Council for Government Policy (Wetenschappelijke Raad voor het Regeringsbeleid) (1995). *Stability and Security in Europe – the changing foreign policy arena*, Report No. 48.

Socio-Economic Council (Sociaal Economische Raad) (1995). *Uitbreiding en verdere ontwikkeling EU* (Enlargement and further development EU), Advisory report No. 9, 19 May.

Tellegen, Jan Willem (1995). "Nieuwe wegen, de Intergouvernementele Conferentie 1996," *Idee* (Magazine of the scientific bureau of D66), No. 3, July.

Voorhoeve, J.J.C. (1979). *Peace, Profits, and Principles: A Study of Dutch Foreign Policy*, The Hague: Martinus Nijhoff.

Weisglas, Frans (1997). "Nederland dit keer geen gidsland," pp. 129-132, in Menno Wolters & Rogier Kuin (eds.), *Het Verdrag van Maastricht op de schop – de Intergouvernementele Conferentie in vogelvlucht*, Zutphen: Walburg Pers.

Werts, Jan (1997). "IGC van 1997 moest als nachtkaars uitgaan – Minimalistische houding Kabinet garantie voor goede afloop," *Internationale Spectator*, September.

Wester, Robert (1992). "The Netherlands," pp. 163-176, in Finn Laursen & Sophie Vanhoonacker (eds.), *The Intergovernmental Conference on Political Union*, Maastricht: European Institute of Public Administration.

13

Portugal: Preserving Equality and Solidarity among Member States

Clotilde Marinho

Introduction

Portugal prepared and entered the negotiations for the 1996-97 IGC with apprehension. The context was not favorable for small and medium Member States and in particular for those having a development rate below the Union average.

Among the Portuguese concerns were first of all, the large Member States' preferences for a profound institutional reform announcing a battle for greater control over policy making which could have serious and irreversible consequences for the already limited Portuguese influence at EU level.

Second, and even though the enlargement was seen as the most important imperative of Europe, the Portuguese were well aware of its risks for cohesion countries. In particular, the position of Portugal was delicate since it had been estimated that it would be the only country where it would have a negative impact (Martins 1999). It was strongly felt as unfair that those countries, which were not benefiting from the enlargement, would be the ones to finance it, in the name of "financial subsidiarity" (ibid.).

Third, the question of whether Portugal from the beginning would take part in the third phase of Economic and Monetary Union, which has been the main priority of the national European policy, was still open. The uncertainty regarding the inclusion in the most advanced group, while proposals for the establishment of a hard core were divulged, was a major concern. Portugal feared being pushed to a position at the periphery, a situation that would be worsened by its geographic position and economic dependence. Above all, the setting up of a hard core was perceived as rather dangerous for the European Union itself, and could lead to its disintegration.

In this situation it is easy to understand the extreme attention and caution devoted to a revision of the Treaty. Portugal, a country that did not have in the past positions of voluntarism prepared for this negotiation, determined to struggle for the relative power in the EU. If one wanted to encapsulate a complex negotiation strategy in a few key words, certainly those that were mentioned by the former Secretary of State would be appropriate. Portugal strove for confidence among Member States, solidarity and efficiency (Assembleia da Republica 1995, 275).

Portugal and the European Union

Impact of Membership

After fifteen years of membership, the assessment of the balance of the costs and benefits for Portugal has normally been positive. As it has often been underlined (e.g. Silva Lopes 1993) the accession contributed to the consolidation of democracy and political stability, which was the most important objective of Portugal's membership application. Also, it had a positive impact on the substantial economic and social improvements since 1985, although there have been periods of not very good economic results. The transfers received from Structural Funds contributed to this performance with visible effects on the creation of infrastructures and on professional training (even if the net flow of the funds has been below that of other cohesion countries). Moreover, accession contributed to the modernization of the public administration and strengthened the national position in the international scene.

Despite the overall positive evaluation, negative effects have been pointed out in some areas, which remain problematic areas: agriculture, certain industries such as textiles, and fisheries. Another area of concern remains the participation in the Economic and Monetary Union, precisely the most important priority of the Portuguese European policy in the last years. Similarly to previous strategic options, such as participation in the Schengen group, or more recently, the participation in peacekeeping missions, this priority reflects the fundamental national strategy of belonging to the hard core and avoiding the risk of marginalization. However, it has been reiterated by many that participation in the EMU may condemn, at least in its present monetary orientation, the development and economic convergence process in course (Louçã 1998).

Political Parties and Public Opinion

To this predominantly favorable assessment corresponds a positive attitude of the main political parties represented in the Parliament, and of the public opinion, towards European integration.

In broad terms, the position of the political parties towards European integration has remained unchanged since accession, with the exception of the Christian Democrats. The main political parties, the Socialists and the Social Democrats, are very much pro-European and have no explicit policy differences regarding EU policy. Some specific divergences, as the one regarding the support of the employment chapter during the 1996-97 IGC, which will be mentioned below, only confirm the existence of a rather integrated and consensual approach. Both parties have naturally supported the Amsterdam Treaty. Also the Christian Democrats favored the Treaty, returning to the old path of support for European integration, which was abandoned in 1992 when unexpectedly it joined the ranks of the Maastricht opponents.

The political parties opposed to the ratification of the Amsterdam Treaty were the small parties on the left: the Communists, previously also opposed to membership and the Maastricht Treaty, and the Greens.

Table 13.1: Parliamentary representation of Portuguese political parties and coalitions.

	Seats in the national Parliament Since 1995 to 1999	Seats in the national Parliament after October 1999 elections	Seats in the European Parliament after 1999 elections
Socialist Party (PS)	112	115	12 Party of European Socialists
Social Democrats (PSD)	88	81	9 European People's Party and European Democrats
Popular Party (CDS-PP)	15	15	1 Union for the Europe of Nations
Democratic Unitary Coalition(CDU); Communist Party (PCP) and Greens	15	17	2 European United left/Nordic Green Left
Left Bloc (BE)		2	

The Socialist Party (PS) is a moderate, social-democratic party and is a member of the Socialist group in the European Parliament. The Social Democratic Party (PSD) is a social liberal party. PSD is currently a member of the European People's Party in the European Parliament, having left the Liberal, Democratic and Reformist group of the European Parliament. The Popular Party (CDS-PP) are the Christian Democrats, which joined the Union for the Europe of Nations after having been expelled from the European People's Party due to its position regarding the Treaty of Maastricht. The Communist Party is a member of the European United left/Nordic Green Left.

Although the citizens continue to be badly informed and lack knowledge on the Treaty (Fraga 1999) and European integration, the majority remains supportive of the EU (Eurobarometer July 1999). The perception by an overwhelming majority that the country benefits from membership certainly contributes to this generalized support. In the absence of a referendum, which was attempted but was blocked, there was a specific campaign to clarify the content of the Treaty. Universities and various organizations held several debates and seminars in which the government and the parliament participated. Yet, in general, only the elite and academics attended (Fraga 1999). The population remains quite indifferent and apathetic as in the past.The attention devoted to the Treaty by the media was far from extensive. Issues such as the Euro or Agenda 2000 did, however, get a considerably wider coverage.

Evolution of National Preferences: A Quiet Revolution?
There has been a stepwise evolution of the Portuguese position towards European integration since accession (Durão Barroso 1998). Initially, Portugal adopted a low profile at the European level and quite often it joined discretely the most reticent positions regarding political integration. Gradually, Portugal became acquainted with Europe and has been moving from a passive, sometimes reluctant position, to a stronger identification with the pro-integrationists.

The most important change relates to the swing from an Atlanticist tradition towards a more continental approach, which was reflected in the support, during the 1996-97 IGC, of the integration of the WEU into the European Union. The alignment with the United Kingdom, the old ally, has been diluting and Portuguese positions tend to be closer to the European mainstream.

The relationship with Spain, the powerful neighbor, also evolved. As a result from the participation of both countries in the same international organizations, the interests of both countries converge very often (ibid.). Nevertheless, it has been avoided to empower Spain as the exclusive representative of the interest of the Iberian Peninsula, which could lead to Portugal being underrepresented at the European and international levels. Moreover, it could lead to inequalities and unfavorable effects in terms of investment and trade, e.g. concentration of investment of multinationals in Spain, marginally spreading to Portugal (Medeiros Ferreira 1993). Besides, there have been sensitive questions shadowing the relation between the two countries, e.g. water resource problems.

The progressive continentalization of the foreign policy and the commitment to political union have been compensated with a reiterated emphasis on the African dimension and the Portuguese ability to act as mediator in this region as well as in other Portuguese speaking regions, e.g. Brazil. The reaffirmation of this specific Portuguese vocation, perceived also as an enrichment for the EU, has also been visible with the summit EU-Africa during the Portuguese Presidency.

Underlying this movement towards the center, meaning towards the core European players leading the European integration process, has been the fundamental strategy of avoiding any kind of periphery status. Aware of the Portuguese particular geographic position at the western fringe, its special social conditions and its economic dependence, the main concern of the political leaders, has been to avoid the establishment of a core group, or at least to ensure participation in it. This concern has also been very much omnipresent during the negotiations of the Amsterdam Treaty and was shared by both the government and the opposition.

The gradual change of the behavioural pattern into a more convicted European partner has started with the former government and has been cemented by the new government. However, it has also been accompanied by some disenchantment openly voiced by the government on the recent course of events and tendencies at the EU level, in particular with the stronger emphasis on national interests and the lack of a spirit of solidarity which inspired European integration in the past (Seixas da Costa 1997). Criticism has also been voiced in respect to the European Commission, which was no longer seen as the old ally of small and medium Member States as the Delors Commission. On the contrary, it was accused of giving in to pressures from the most powerful Member States and of taking into account solely the interests of the majority while ignoring marginal and minority interests (*Público* 16 May 1996).

Portuguese Position in the IGC: Objectives and Contributions

There were two governments involved in the preparation and the negotiations of the Amsterdam Treaty. The Social Democrats initiated the preparations for the IGC and appointed the Portuguese representative in the Reflection group. After the elections in 1995, the Socialists took over. This change in government did not lead to a shift in the Portuguese position in the 1996-97 IGC. As mentioned earlier, the two parties have similar policy orientations regarding the European Union. The only significant difference was the emphasis on employment, dear to the new government.

Portugal presented and published for the first time a document in March 1996, which defined the main lines of its position towards the IGC. This document was both a negotiation mandate and a public compromise, which would provide the general public with information about the main questions on the agenda during the Conference.

The main objectives announced in that document were to ensure that European integration continued to develop in a gradual and pragmatic way and that:

- the principle of equality between Member States continued to be respected as well as the different cultures and the fundamental rights;
- the basic institutional balance was preserved;
- the political and economic solidarity remained as a guiding principle and was complemented with social solidarity;
- the principle of sufficiency of means was guaranteed.

The first allies sought by the Portuguese were the European citizens. As stated in the document and often reiterated by political leaders, the final result of the negotiations had to be accepted by the public opinion, in some Member States even by referendum. Such collective acceptance, it was often stated, would probably not occur, should the final result create divisions between the Member States.

The main motto of the Portuguese negotiators, which was also reflected in the document, was to ensure that Portugal's relative influence in the European project and the ability to safeguard its specific interests would not be reduced.

This most important preoccupation was very clearly expressed in the Portuguese reservations regarding possible fundamental changes to the European architecture, institutional reforms and reinforced cooperation.

First of all, Portugal opposed *"constitutional" changes* such as abolition of the unanimity rule for revision of the treaties or the possibility of the entry into force of the Treaty without ratification or signature by all Member States.

Secondly, on *institutional issues* Portugal rejected changes, which would condemn small and medium countries to a secondary status. It strongly defended the continuing rotation of the presidency, maintenance of the principles underlying the weighting of votes in the Council as well as of one Commissioner per Member State and the equality of status for all national languages.

This position was rather defensive and successful to a certain extent. The alliance with other small and medium Member States (Ireland, Luxembourg and the Nordic countries) permitted resistance to the pressure from the larger Member States, which was weakened by lack of coordination between the Germans and the French in the final stages of the negotiation. However, it was argued that it would have been preferable that the positions had been clearly presented at an earlier stage to permit a peaceful discussion and a solution rather than to postpone it as part of a linkage, considered negative, between Commission composition and reweighting of votes (Seixas da Costa 1997).

Portugal supported other institutional improvements, which would permit a better functioning of the institutions without affecting the current institutional balance. It favored the increased role of the Commission in the second and third pillars, the Court of Justice competence in the third pillar as achieved. It moreover supported the reduction of the number of procedures; the extension of qualified majority voting and the simplification and extension of co-decision, in spite of the awareness that reinforcing the power of the European Parliament means reinforcing the power of the most densely populated Member States. This support was weighted carefully since, as implied, the European Parliament increasingly represents important national interests. It also represents an evolution in the Portuguese attitude towards the European Parliament, which was very reticent in the past. Furthermore, Portugal favored the increased involvement of national parliaments.

Finally, the Portuguese negotiators were firmly opposed to *flexibility and reinforced cooperation*. Since it was a very sensitive question for the Portuguese and as it was felt to be unavoidable, it deserved careful consideration and the most pro-active involvement. Portugal presented the first proposal, outlining in detail clear and strict rules for enhanced cooperation, which was close to the provisions finally agreed upon, e.g. respect for the single institutional framework and the *acquis communautaire*, last resort, openness to other Member States, initiative by the Commission. Besides Portugal, together with the United Kingdom, Greece and Sweden (*Agence Europe* 16 April 1997) insisted on the unanimous decision for triggering the enhanced cooperation. In the end, Portugal succeeded at least to include a safety valve consisting in the possibility of a Member State opposing the decision for important national reasons. However, from the preliminary set of conditions that were proposed by Portugal, it failed to convince the others of the need for an impact assessment and follow-up measures to avoid distortions resulting from enhanced cooperation.

The above main motto also determined the government's firm opposition to any effort to dilute the policies of the Union. It opposed a negative and restrictive concept of subsidiarity, which would result in the stand-still of the integration process or, which would be even worse, try to transfer to the national level any Community policies such as social and economic cohesion in the name of the ingenious concept of "financial subsidiarity" (Martins 1999). Contrary to the position of net contributors, Portugal defended the deepening and extension of the Union policies.

The most important issues in this respect were the development of a European social dimension, the further elaboration of citizenship and the consecration of a special status for the outermost regions.

In relation to the *social dimension*, Portugal took the view that concrete provisions against unemployment and social exclusion, while preserving the social and economic cohesion, should accompany economic and monetary progress. Although Portugal has not been greatly affected by unemployment, the government defended the development of a European strategy to tackle this problem at the European level as an integral part of a social policy which would able to respond to the challenges of technological changes. This strategy, which was not shared by the opposition, certainly took into account the serious problems of social exclusion, with which Portugal is confronted (Silva 1998). The inclusion of the chapter on employment, made possible at the last minute by the attitude of the new French government, would be further developed during the Portuguese Presidency at the Lisbon Summit.

Portugal stressed the importance of *citizenship* favoring the inclusion of a European Citizenship Charter, clear provisions on human rights and the accession of the Union to the European Comvention on Human Rights (ECHR). A proposal on a European Citizenship Bill was made. Such Charter would list all the rights, including economic and social rights, deriving from the European citizenship, which go behind the rights emerging from national citizenship. The purpose was to provide citizens a clear picture of the advantages and added value of European citizenship. However, the proposal did not receive the support of other Member States (Seixas da Costa 1998). In respect to human rights, the treaty results were lower than the Portuguese ambitions. Nevertheless, the Portuguese negotiators saw introduced in the Treaty the mechanism for sanctions of Member States violating human rights, proposed by Portugal (ibid.).

On the *outermost regions*, the government presented and defended very successfully a joint proposal with Spain and France, with financial implications. On the other hand, the reinforcement of Community action on tourism, or even the creation of a specific Title, defended by the Mediterranean countries, France and Ireland stumbled on firm opposition from the United Kingdom, Germany and the Netherlands. Also progress in other fields, such as energy and civil protection, did not gain the support of the other Member States (ibid.). Other Portuguese proposals, which were successful, related to the protection of religious institutions and specificity of sport structures (ibid.). Moreover, Portugal would support the most progressive positions in areas such as the environment, health and consumer protection. It supported the French proposal on the services of general interest, and with Belgium and Sweden secured the protection of the public service of broadcasting (ibid.).

In the area of *CFSP* Portugal was again concerned with reforms endangering the principle of equality between Member States, namely the abandonment of the rotation of the Presidency or the creation of some kind of directory. This was an important issue for Portugal whose foreign policy has not always been on the same wavelength as some of the "large" countries, e.g. on East Timor. Portugal was cautious regarding ideas such as Mr. CFSP and the alert mechanism or the positive abstention, conditioning support to several restrictions. It had difficulties in accepting the qualified majority voting for decisions implementing common strategies and succeeded in including a safeguard clause for vital interest. Portugal even defended the absolute parity among Member States (One State one vote) in the case of qualified majority voting. There was some evolution on the Portuguese position regarding WEU integration in the EU. While initially favoring such integration in the long term, it joined, at a later stage, the six Member States (Belgium, Luxembourg, France, Germany, Spain, and Italy) which proposed a stepwise integration of this body. However, the proposal did not gather the support of the other Member States which was regretted in the end (Seixas da Costa 1998).

The Portuguese position was most open and flexible in the area of *Justice and Home Affairs* (*Público* December 1996). It favored the partial (and eventually progressive) communitarisation of the third pillar, in particular in respect to asylum and immigration and eventually external borders. The wide support for more ambitious improvements was probably not anticipated, but the Portuguese had no major problems going along with it. But Portugal wanted to maintain a non-exclusive right of initiative for the Commission. Moreover, Portugal successfully demanded the inclusion of three interpretative declarations: Member States' external policy considerations have to be taken into account in the implementation of the visa policy; Member States can introduce limitations on the free movement of persons for security reasons which may be grounded in external policy; the possibility of special regimes in the immigration policies. Furthermore, Portugal supported the improvement of the cooperation in the third pillar, e.g. use of binding legal instruments, streamlining of working structures, increased role of the European Parliament, the Commission, and the Court of Justice and national Parliaments.

From this overview on the main lines of the Portuguese position, it can be remarked that the Portuguese did their homework and prepared carefully a consistent and coherent position. Nevertheless, it was also a dynamic position, evolving during the negotiation process, e.g. on CFSP and JHA. Aware of their limited influence on the European scene, the Portuguese negotiators defined few, clear and specific priorities which were defended persistently and, in the end, quite successfully. The two formal proposals which fared well at the IGC, on flexibility and outermost regions, gave expression to the two main principles which inspired the negotiation strategy: equality and solidarity. The priorities and contributions strongly emphasized the defense of national interests. However, the Portuguese position was not exclusively inward looking, and there was a genuine effort to support and initiate constructive proposals pursuing the European interest, e.g. citizenship or employment. Obviously, this was not a purely altruistic approach, but it was based on the assumption that pursuing the European interest is also a way of pursuing national interests in a globalized world. In any case, it reveals the Portuguese ambition to show a truly European spirit and a more active involvement in the European project.

The Parliament and the Amsterdam Treaty: Follow-up and Ratification of the Treaty

Follow up of the 1996 IGC Preparations and Negotiations
Compared to what happened during the negotiations of the Maastricht Treaty the national parliament followed much more closely the whole process during the 1996 Conference. This is undoubtedly a sign of the post-Maastricht times. On the other hand, this increased involvement was also a reaction to the CDU/CSU report in September 1994 (the Lamers paper) which had a strong impact on the Portuguese political elite. The Parliament responded rapidly, on 29 December 1994, to this paper, presenting a report with a resolution on the main guidelines for the amendment of the treaties. For the Parliament it was essential to safeguard the Portuguese language, to preserve the principle of equality of States and the non-exclusion from the hard core. The same concerns were discussed in the debates held in the Parliament and the Committee on European Affairs from June 1995 onwards with the government and members of the regional parliaments, representatives of the civil society (management confederations and labor unions), NGO's, associations and universities.

The Ratification Process
According to the Portuguese Constitution, Treaties are negotiated by the Government, approved by the Parliament and ratified by the President.

On 6 January 1999, the Portuguese Parliament approved the Amsterdam Treaty by an overwhelming majority with 205 votes in favor and 24 votes against. Both the Socialists (122) and the Social Democrats (88) supported the Treaty. The members of the Christian Democrats were divided, only the Bureau Group voted in favor (5), the others voted against (9). Also the Communist Party (PCP) (13) and the Greens (2) opposed the Treaty.

This result came as no surprise. It was very similar to the outcome of the voting on the Maastricht Treaty (200 in favor, 21 against) and it reflected once more the wide consensus in the Portuguese political establishment regarding European integration. As in the past, the two main political parties (the Socialists and the Social Democrats) remained faithful to their strongly pro-

European attitudes. Equally faithful to their previous standing on EU matters were the Communists and the Greens who opposed the Treaty. The only new element was the division among the Christian Democrats. Contrary to what happened in 1992, the official party line was supportive of the Treaty as a result of a change in leadership. With a new Bureau and a more pro–European leader, Paulo Portas, the party could have returned to the good old times, prior to Maastricht, of the pro-integration attitude. However, breaking the party line, nine members, including the ex-leader, Manuel Monteiro, voted against the Treaty, reflecting the internal division in the parliamentary group between those supporting the current leader and the ex-leader. The ex-leader would make a plenary intervention which concentrated the attention, in particular the media attention, during the debate (Fraga 1999).

During the plenary debate leading to the approval of ratification of the Amsterdam Treaty, the favorite issues included, not surprisingly, the institutional reform.[1] Everyone basically shared the opinion that the reform was minimalist and agreed that it was partially positive for Portugal and the Union since changes endangering the present institutional balance and the relative power of the Member States were avoided. The new status for the outermost regions, relevant for the Autonomous Regions of Madeira and Azores, was much praised as well as the provisions on flexibility and reinforced cooperation subject to clear rules and a set of strict preliminary conditions. Another issue very much focused upon was the reinforced role of the national parliaments.[2] Furthermore, the improvements of CFSP and the communitarisation of some third pillar issues were highlighted. The discussion on the chapter on employment which was related with the question of structural funds and agenda 2000, was the most critical. The support of the government to social and employment policies was not welcomed by the main opposition party, which claimed that the government did not defend the national interest in the best way.

In the view of the government, as expressed by the Prime Minister, António Guterres:

> "The Amsterdam Treaty represents a step, perhaps not as daring as many would wish but a safe step in the right way of reinforcement of

---

[1] Prior to the debate, the Committee on European Affairs issued a report on the Treaty of Amsterdam and requested other five specialized committees to issue reports too. Also on this report the institutional issues deserve particular attention.

[2] Both the improvements resulting from the Amsterdam Treaty and those resulting from the revision of the Constitution in 1997 were mentioned. In particular Articles 161 and 112 (9) which reinforce the role of the Parliament in European affairs.

the political, economic and social integration of Europe which provides Europe with an enhanced capacity to intervene at world level."[3]

Both his speech and the opening speech by Jaime Gama, the Minister of Foreign Affairs, highlighted the virtues but also the flaws of the Treaty. It was argued that the objectives set by the government for the reform had been achieved. In particular, the results in the areas of employment and social policy, including the provisions on social exclusion, Justice and Home Affairs and outermost regions, were stressed. On the issue of the institutional reform, the positive improvements on the functioning of the institutions and role of the national parliaments were highlighted. The government also assessed positively the lack of solutions to the questions of the composition of the Commission and weighting of votes in the Council. Moreover, it was signaled that the strict drafting of the flexibility clause and reinforced cooperation reflected the Portuguese position and proposal on the issue. On the other hand, the government was discontent with the limited progress achieved on the CFSP and citizenship. Although it welcomed the improvements in those areas, it regretted that it was not possible to agree on the WEU integration in the EU, nor to include in the Treaty a list of fundamental rights, including social and economic rights. It argued, however, that the foundations of an "ethical pillar" were laid down, in particular by providing for the possibility of sanctioning States which would not respect human rights.

Durão Barroso, representing the main opposition party, the Social Democrats, welcomed roughly the same positive aspects, including institutional matters. However, he considered that overall the Treaty lacked major substantive reforms, did not respond to the European ambitions, and reflected lack of leadership and strategic vision. The important criticism to the government's strategy was the support given to the employment chapter. In his view, this emphasis on the employment issue leading to the setting of the unemployment criteria for granting structural funds, was contrary to the national interest since Portugal does not have a high unemployment rate. Moreover, it also had negative consequences for the negotiation block of the cohesion countries and would be damaging for the future negotiation on the Agenda 2000.

Also supporting the Treaty and welcoming the minor institutional reforms introduced was Luis Queiró representing the Christian Democrats. He argued it was a better Treaty than Maastricht, since it was the return to a gradual approach and the rejection of the federalism. He mentioned as positive aspects among others the flexibility clause which permits each country to decide how far it wants to integrate, the transparency provisions, and the maintenance of

---

[3] Author's translation.

the official languages, the improved role of the national parliaments and the subsidiary principle.

With a divergent opinion and speaking against the Treaty, contrary to the party line, was Manuel Monteiro, the ex-leader of the Christian Democrats. He argued that the Treaty was the follow-up of the Maastricht Treaty and therefore continued on the federalist course. The federalist nature of the Union was visible, he argued, in the power of the Agriculture Commissioner (he was referring to the embargo on export of Portuguese meat) and in recent declarations of the President of the Central Bank (who stated that Member States not complying with provisions agreed upon would be punished).

The leader of the Communist Party, Carlos Carvalhas, argued against the Treaty, against the Euro and requested renegotiations of the stability pact. He strongly defended the principle of social and economic cohesion. Moreover, he pointed out the need to reduce the democratic deficit by means of improving the role of national parliaments and the European Parliament, reducing the power of the Commission and safeguarding the right of veto in the Council. Finally, he stressed that national cultures should be respected.

Also against the Treaty spoke Isabel Castro representing the Greens. The Treaty, she claimed, introduced new restrictions to the freedom of movement, denied the right of asylum and reinforced the powers of the police. Moreover, it did not change the stability pact and did not provide adequate solutions to the problems of employment, exclusion and social rights. Finally, it did not change the old concept of security based on NATO and left unadressed in practice the environmental problems.

All the opposition parties voiced criticism against the government for having failed to call for a referendum on the Treaty. The prospects for the organization of a referendum seemed at a certain point to be very concrete. In the end however, as explained in the following section, the idea was abandoned.

The Referendum Saga

Already during the debate on the Maastricht Treaty, the Christian Democrats proposed holding a referendum. This idea was fated to fail. The government, at the time the Social Democrats, did not favor it and argued that the referendum was unconstitutional (although this was a controversial issue). Also the Socialists' official position was against the referendum, while the Communists, initially opposing it, would change their position during the debate. However, this question divided internally the political parties and several opinion leaders made public their support for the referendum.

Although without any immediate consequences this idea was not completely abandoned.

After the legislative elections of 1995, and the subsequent change of Government, the four main parties were in favor of the referendum in general as well as the referendum on the new Treaty. In 1997 the Constitution was amended to permit a referendum "of issues of relevant national interest which must be the subject of international agreement (...)."[4] With the constitutional reservations removed, the government and the three opposition parties presented draft texts for the referendum question on the Treaty of Amsterdam. By agreement between the Socialists and Social Democrats the following question was approved on 29 June 1998 by the Parliament:

> "Do you agree with the continuation of Portugal's participation in the European Union construction in the framework of the Amsterdam Treaty?"[5]

Following the compulsory request by the President to the Constitutional Court for examination of the referendum proposal's compliance with the Constitution, the proposal was blocked. The Constitutional Court, in its judgement of 29 July 1998 (8 judges voted in favor and 5 against) considered that the question was not formulated in an objective, clear and precise manner, to which it would be possible to answer with a simple yes or no.[6] In broad terms, the Court took the view that it would be difficult for the average citizen to understand what would be the result of a negative answer to the referendum question, even with the referendum campaign.

After this decision on unconstitutionality, the President vetoed the proposal and sent it back to the Parliament. The Parliament could then either have changed the question or confirmed it by a majority of two thirds of its members. None of these options were used. There were two main reasons that could explain this. The first was related to the conviction that the Amsterdam Treaty had not the same importance as the Maastricht Treaty and in view of the limited reach of the reforms, the citizens' consultation was not that essential. The second derived from the repercussions of the results of the first referendum held in Portugal on 28 June 1998 on a more liberal abortion law. After a quite heated campaign of both sides, the abstention was 68.1% (the "no" won with 50.9%). The low turnout was quite evidently a disappointment

---

[4] Article155 (5) of the Portuguese Constitution. Available at http://www.parlamento.pt/leis/constituicao_ingles/crp_uk.htm

[5] Author's translation.

[6] Therefore, the question proposed violated Article 115 (6) of the Constitution.

for politicians, who became apprehensive regarding the use of the referendum in the future, and in particular on the Treaty of Amsterdam. The second referendum on the creation of the Regions was held on 8 November 1998 and the turnout confirmed the public indifference towards national politics: abstention 51.7%; against 63.5%; in favor 36.5%.

The outcome of the two referendums confirmed the huge gap existing between the political elite and academics and the rest of the population. The lesson to be learned by the politicians was that any referendum to be held in Portugal in the future, including on European integration, has to be carefully prepared. An investment has to be made to come closer to public concerns and needs, to educate and involve the population in order to achieve its effective participation in public choices.

Portugal and the Outlook for the Next IGC

With Portugal in the Euro and after a successful negotiation of Agenda 2000, some of the worries of the Portuguese political leaders disappeared in the post-Amsterdam situation. Still, even ignoring the ghost of the potential creation of a hard core from which Portugal would be excluded, the aim of the next IGC, exclusively devoted to the unsolved institutional issues, is a difficult political debate for the Portuguese. For that reason, it was no surprise that Portugal supported a broader agenda for the IGC, which could, besides the institutional issues, focus on the deepening of the security and defense policies (*Público* 11 November 1999).

The government has not yet produced any documents on the national position at the next IGC, although Portugal, holding the Presidency, had to keep the necessary openness to conduct the initial negotiations. Nevertheless, the Portuguese position has been revealed occasionally by the political leaders, and their declarations indicate that the attitude towards the institutional reforms remains the same as it was formulated during the 1996 IGC. Already during the parliamentary debates on the ratification of the Amsterdam Treaty, Guterres firmly reiterated the Portuguese position on institutional reforms. He stated that Portugal would be among those countries who want more democracy, more transparency and more efficiency, and against those who want to take advantage of the debate to reinforce their position and power in the Union framework.

The reasons behind this position, the vulnerability of the Portuguese situation at the European level and the apprehensions of the political leaders towards recent developments and tendencies have been publicly exposed.

It has been stressed that already currently Portugal has a limited power in the Council which is particularly damaging since Portuguese interests are rarely reflected in the position of the majority, in particular since the last enlargement. Moreover, the weakness of the Commission has been pointed out, accused of serving the interests of the strongest. This is felt to be even more serious when combined with the modest Portuguese representation at high level in the Commission. In fact, there were recently several conflicts and tensions with the Commission which did not exist in the past. Members of the government have also openly denounced the clear determination of some Member States to reinforce their relative power in the Union, in the name of efficiency or transparency (Seixas da Costa 1999). The changes proposed, it has been argued, aimed to increase the dominance by those countries already dominating the decision-making process and the budgetary management, and to avoid the future possibility of a creation of blocking minorities by less developed countries. Moreover, it was added, they also aimed at ensuring that decisions in the CFSP and JHA areas reflected their interests, when the unanimity would be set aside in the future (ibid.).

It is, therefore, to be expected that the Portuguese will continue to strongly resist the reforms, although some evolution in position has already been disclosed. In more concrete terms, Portugal defends the extension of qualified majority voting, though with limitations in certain vital issues, such as the revision of the treaties or budgetary decisions. It reiterates the need for a slight correction in the weighting of votes, showing some sympathy towards a system of double majority (Seixas da Costa 1999). Contrary to previous positions, it appeared that in respect to the number of Commissioners some flexibility could be expected. The Minister of Foreign Affairs stated that should it be agreed upon that the number of Commissioners should be less than the number of Member States, Portugal would be committed to guarantee the access on the same conditions to the seats for all Member States (*Público* 11 November 1999).

Conclusions

In the 1996 IGC, Portugal had its own national agenda to defend, which was to ensure that its own relative ability to influence the EU decision-making and to safeguard its particular interests would not be reduced. In addition, the Portuguese also tried to pass through their own ideas of Europe and to assume a constructive role in the whole process. More than in the past, the Portuguese presented formal and informal proposals and ideas, which echoed differently on the other side of the negotiation table. While some proposals would be quite successful and effective, such as the one on flexibility or on the outermost regions others, for example on a Bill of rights, would fail to be met by sympathy by many other Member States. In the end, however it can be concluded that the outcome was positive for Portugal.

Changes in domestic politics did not determine a shift in the national position, the only relevant substantive difference being the support by the Socialist government to the employment chapter. The Portuguese position remained essentially stable prior and during to negotiations, however some evolution towards the support of more progressive proposals occurred in the areas of CFSP and JHA.

The involvement, information and discussion in the Parliament increased considerably during the 1996 ICG and started already in the initial phases of the preparation, which is a quite positive feature. This certainly contributed to a smooth ratification process. The main political parties welcomed the compromise reached in Amsterdam, while the small political parties on the left opposed it, which reflected the traditional attitudes of the Portuguese political parties towards European integration. The only novelty worth mentioning relates to the Christian Democrats, who, at least partially, recovered their former pro-European attitude after the turn during the Maastricht ratification, when they joined the rank of the skeptical parties.

Public opinion, however, remained outside the process despite the expectations created around a referendum that was never held. Clearly, it was not enough to remove constitutional reservations to make use of the referendum. There is a wide gap between the elite and the citizens, which needs to be addressed before any possible consultation in the future. To overcome the disinterest, politicians have to build bridges and touch the lives of the population.

The negotiations of the Amsterdam Treaty mirrored the slow evolution of Portuguese European policy towards a more integrationist approach. The political leaders sought to replace the image of the good pupil, mostly passive and sometimes reluctant, of the initial years by a profile of convicted and actively involved Europeans. This gradual movement initiated almost imperceptible during Maastricht, continued and was even slightly accentuated by the change in government. The changes are most visible in the area of CFSP but also for example in the more favorable attitude towards the European Parliament or the support to the employment chapter.

The open question is whether and when Portugal will join the ranks of the federalists, favoring the emergence of a democratic political power at the European level. This is not a rhetorical question. Some influential people questioned whether the alternative for countries like Portugal was not to opt for a federalist scheme in which the power of every Member State, irrespective of size and its political or economic influence, would be reduced (Lucas Pires 1997). They called for a far-reaching institutional reform towards a federation or a confederation. This quantum leap towards integration, opposed both by those favoring the creation of a directoire and those defending the sovereignty of Member States, is regarded as the way to ensure a minimum of solidarity and parity among States as well as more democracy at the European level. In this context, the creation of a Second Chamber, a kind of Senate with representatives of Member States is also advocated (Medeiros Ferreira 1998). Even members of the government seemed to back up the need for a major reform and for a comprehensive reflection on the future Union and its institutional framework. The actual model, in which intergovernmental features are progressively abandoned without being replaced by schemes of a more federal nature, is perceived as an ideal ground for the arising of directories and denial of solidarity (Seixas da Costa 1999). Therefore, it would not be strange, should the reluctant Member State of the past turn into an enthusiastic federalist. This is however futurology…

Bibliography

Assembleia da República, Comissão de Assuntos Europeus (1995). *Acompanhamento Parlamentar da Revisão do Tratado da União Europeia na Conferência Intergovernamental de 1996,* Vol. I, Lisbon.

Assembleia da República, Comissão de Assuntos Europeus (1995). *Acompanhamento Parlamentar da Revisão do Tratado da União Europeia na Conferência Intergovernamental de 1996,* Vol. II, Lisbon.

Assembleia da República, Comissão de Assuntos Europeus (1999). *Amsterdão um Novo Tratado para a Europa. O Processo de Aprovação para Ratificação do Tratado de Amsterdão,* Lisbon.

Corkill, David (1999). "Portugal's 1998 Referendums," *West European Politics,* Vol. 22, No. 2, pp.186-192.

Covas, António (1996). *A revisão do Tratado da União Europeia: Contributos para a Conferência Intergovernamental de 1996,* Oeiras: Celta.

Durão Barroso, José Manuel (1998). "Portugal e a Europa: à Procura de um Novo Equilíbrio," pp. 99-115, in *Portugal na Transição do Milénio,* Lisbon: Fim de Século.

Fraga, Ana (1999). *The ratification of the Amsterdam Treaty in Portugal,* paper presented at the seminar on the ratification of the Amsterdam treaty, Florence: IUE.

Louçã, Francisco (1998). "Integração Europeia e Moeda única: Algumas das Mentiras que os Nossos Banqueiros nos tem Contado," pp. 193-201, *Portugal na Transição do Milénio,* Lisbon: Fim de Século.

Pires, Lucas (1997). "Amesterdão: Maastricht 2 ou só 1,5," pp. 116-123, in *Europa Novas Fronteiras,* No. 2. (November), Lisbon: Centro de Informação Jacques Delors.

Marinho, Clotilde (1994). "Portugal and the Ratification of the Maastricht Treaty," pp. 231-240, in Finn Laursen & Sophie Vanhoonacker (eds.), *The Ratification of the Maastricht Treaty. Issues, Debates and Future Implications,* Maastricht: European Institute of Public Administration.

Martins, Vítor (1999). "O Quinto Alargamento da União Europeia," pp. 41-48, in *Europa Novas Fronteiras,* No. 2., Vol. 6 (December), Lisbon: Centro de Informação Jacques Delors.

Medeiros Ferreira (1993). "Political Costs and Benefits for Portugal Arising from Membership of the European Community," pp. 173-181, in José da Silva Lopes (ed.), *Portugal and EC Membership Evaluated,* London: Pinter.

Medeiros Ferreira (1998). "As Democracias do Ocidente na Transição para o Século XXI," pp. 119-131, in *Portugal na Transição do Milénio,* Lisbon: Fim de Século.

Ministry of Foreign Affairs (1996). *Portugal e a Conferência Intergovernamental para a revisão do Tratado da União Europeia*, Lisbon, March.

Seixas da Costa, Francisco (1997). "A Perspectiva Portuguesa da Negociação do Tratado de Amsterdão," pp. 22-30, in *Europa Novas Fronteiras,* No. 2. (November), Lisbon: Centro de Informação Jacques Delors.

Seixas da Costa, Francisco (1998). "Portugal e o Desafio Europeu," pp. 15-28, in *Nação e Defesa,* No. 85, Serie 2, Lisbon: Instituto de Defesa Nacional.

Seixas da Costa, Francisco (1998). "O Tratado de Amsterdão e a Segurança Comum Europeia," pp. 12-17, in *Europa Novas Fronteiras,* No. 3. (June), Lisbon: Centro de Informação Jacques Delors.

Seixas da Costa, Francisco (1998). "Para uma Cidadania de Novo Tipo," pp. 31-35, in *Europa Novas Fronteiras,* No. 4. (December), Lisbon: Centro de Informação Jacques Delors.

Seixas da Costa, Francisco (1999). "Uma Reforma Indespensável?," pp. 4-10, in *Europa Novas Fronteiras,* No. 5. (June), Lisbon: Centro de Informação Jacques Delors.

Silva Lopes, José da (ed.) (1993). *Portugal and EC Membership Evaluated*, London: Pinter.

Silva, Manuela (1998). "Integração e Exclusão Social: Portugal e as Duas Europas da Europa," pp. 273-287, in *Portugal na Transição do Milénio*, Lisbon: Fim de Século.

14

Spain: A "Difficult" Negotiation Partner?

Felipe Basabe Lloréns

Spain and European Integration: Domestic Determinants of National Preference

Broad Social and Political Consensus on Pro-European Commitment as a Consequence of Historic Isolation and Conditions of Accession to the European Communities

Attitudes towards European integration in Spain are rather stable and easy to evaluate; no major differences can be ascertained among the main political parties and societal actors, partly due to the historic and political context of accession (Bassols 1995). Spain's entry into the European Communities in 1986 was the result of a long political process and the fulfilment of a historical aspiration for the Spanish society (Ramirez Jimenez 1996). For most internal and external observers, Spain's incorporation to the EC constituted the final step of a transition process to democracy. Accession to the EC was supported at that time almost unanimously by all political parties and societal actors (Moreno Juste 1998). This broad social and political consensus has presided over the negotiation and ratification processes of the later Treaty reforms and is still to be found at the basis of most of the present features of Spanish public attitudes towards the process of European integration (Almarcha Barbado 1993; Burgorgue-Larsen 1995; Barbé 1999).

The broad support for European integration mentioned above has, nevertheless, experienced a relative decline in the past years – 1995 onwards – due to political conflicts on certain specific issues (fisheries, industrial reconversion, reform of olive oil CMO) (Morata 1998; Barbé 1999, 73, 85) and the arising of interests groups – still on a minor scale – and dissenting opinions within some of the national political parties (People's Party, United Left) contrary to further developments in the process (VV.AA. 1992; Alvarez-Miranda Navarro 1994). However, the perception of the general public and political elites still confirms a very positive attitude and integrationist approach to European issues, which have traditionally been considered as "state policy" not subject to down-to-earth political debate (Cienfuegos Mateo 1996; Cienfuegos Mateo 1997; Barbé 1998; Barbé 1999, 31). Both Presidents, González and Aznar, have publicly declared that "the most precious asset Spain has with regard to EU negotiations is the general consensus among the political parties on the necessity and success of the process of European integration."[1] The 1999 EC budgetary reform and the future enlargement to the Central and Eastern European candidate countries will necessarily be a crucial test for such consensus (Comisión Mixta 1999).

Economic and Social Background: the Need of Economic Development and Modernisation Process of Uncompetitive Sectors
Spain's membership of the EC/EU has had a direct impact on the consolidation of the democratic functioning of its political system (Burgorgue-Larsen 1997; Newton & Donaghy 1997), the acceleration of economic development (Martin 1997) and the modernisation of public administration structures and procedures (Dastis 1995; Morata 1998a), and as such is perceived by the public opinion, despite the lack of knowledge of the actual functioning of the system. The set-up of various internal policies – particularly environment, regional development, consumer protection, immigration policy – has taken place in a parallel way to the national implementation of the respective Community policies (Morata 1996; Morata 1998a). Another direct consequence of Spain's accession to the EC/EU has been the dynamisation of its civil society, leading to a massive creation of interest groups, professional associations and coordination structures both at national, regional and local level in all economic and activity sectors (García 1990; Baena del Alcazar 1992). Spain's role in the international arena has also been considerably enhanced in the past years, partly due to its accession to the EU (Gillespie *et al.* 1995). Its traditional connections with Latin America and the Arabic world have not decreased but changed its nature, mostly because of Spain's economic development and its compliance with EC legislation.

Dynamics of Political Parties at Domestic Level
The results in the 1989, 1994 and 1999 European Parliament elections tend to reflect similar results to those in domestic elections (Almarcha Barbado 1993; Moreno Juste 1998). The alternative massive predominance of the Spanish Socialists' Party (PSOE) and the People's Party (PP) has barely been changed by the electoral presence at EU level of the United Left (Izquierda Unida) – which temporarily borrowed Socialist votes in 1994 – and changing coalitions among the "nationalist" regional parties in order to achieve the election of at least one seat which shall later rotate among the parties' coalition members. In any case, the relevance of the "nationalist" parties, especially the Catalonian, Basque and Canarian ones is enormously reduced at EU level, due

---

[1] In fact, the political use of the case of alleged corruption in EC flax subsidies within the Spanish Ministry of Agriculture, under the former mandate of the current Vice-President of the European Commission, Ms. Loyola de Palacio, during the 1999 EP electoral campaign and the Commissioners' EP individual *audits,* has constituted a major exception, which was heavily criticised by most political actors and national press.

to the single national constituency used for EP elections, compared to their actual preeminent role at national level.[2]

Political Parties	1999 EP Elections			1994 EP Elections		
	% Votes	Seats	Groups	%Votes	Seats	Groups
People's Party – PP	39.74%	27	27 PPE	40.12%	28	28 PPE
Socialist Party – PSOE	35.32%	24	24 PSE	30.79%	22	22 PSE
United Left – IU	5.77%	4	4 IUE	13.44%	9	9 IUE
CiU (CDC +UDC) Catalonian centre-right	4.43%	3	1 PPE + 2 ELDR	4.66%	3	1 PPE + 2 ELDR
C.E. (CC/ PA/UV/PAR) Canarian/Aragones/Valencian /Andalusian Centre	3.20%	2	1 ELDR + 1 V-ALE			
C.N. (PNV/EA/ERC/UM) Basque/Catalonian/Balearic "Radical" Nationalists	2.90%	2	2 V-ALE	2.82%	2	1 PPE + 1 CRE
BNG (Galician nationalists)	1.65%	1	1 V-ALE	0.75%		
EH (Basque Independentists)	1.45%	1	NI	0.97%		

In any case, it can be concluded that Spanish EU policy is definitely not domestic-politics driven (Morata 1996; Moreno Juste 1998). The established political parties have not fundamentally changed their political lines towards EU issues, with the exception of the Basque Nationalist Party (PNV) which, within the context of the current Basque "peace process," has recently been obliged to abandon the European People's Party. The main differences with regard to international politics among the Spanish political parties mainly concern Cuba and, to a lesser extent, other Latin-American and Mediterranean specific relationships (Barbé 1999, 121). Finally, the appointment of Mr. Javier Solana as Secretary-General of NATO, apart from its repercussions for domestic politics, helped dilute traditional reticences and misconceptions within the Spanish left-wing parties towards NATO and other military alliances.

---

[2] See the controversial Judgment 28/91 of 14 February of the Spanish Constitutional Court denying the abolition of the single electoral constituency for the whole Spanish territory d manded by the Basque Regional Parliament.

Territorial Distribution of Power: Increasing Asymmetric "Regionalisation" and Relevance of "Nationalist" Parties

Spain's gradual incorporation to the process of European integration has followed a parallel process to its internal territorial redistribution of power – progressive transfer and acquisition of powers from the central State by the regions (*Comunidades Autónomas*) – and reorganisation of its administrative structure and decision-making procedures, hence facilitating its adaptations to the EC/EU decision-making process (Morata 1996; Burgorgue-Larsen 1997; Newton & Donaghy 1997; Arias Martín 1998). During its fourteen years of membership of the EC/EU, Spain has contributed relevantly to the process of European integration with important initiatives, such as the European citizenship, the development of the notion of economic and social cohesion and, together with Germany and Belgium, the creation of the Committee of the Regions, and has also played an active role arising from its well balanced integrationist approach (VV.AA. 1994; Molina del Pozo 1996; CEOE 1996; Elorza Cavengt 1997).

The arising of the "nationalist" regional parties, especially the Catalonian (CiU), Basque (PNV) and Canarian (CC) ones, onto the main national political stage from 1993 to 2000 has somewhat changed a great deal within Spanish politics, due to the "moderating" role played by these parties and their continuous demands of a territorial nature. Though it was commonly accepted that no national Government would be constituted without the participation or agreement of one or various "nationalist" parties, the 2000 general election granting absolute majority to Aznar's party will inevitably lessen the political influence and decision power of "nationalists" at national level. The dramatic ongoing Basque "peace process," and the surprising results of the 1999 Catalonian regional elections, had already *de facto* weakened the political influence of the "nationalist" parties.

Constitutional Provisions and Institutional Set-up Regarding the Role of the Government and Parliament in International Affairs

The Spanish Constitution of 1978 grants the Government most powers vis-à-vis the conduct of international relations and the negotiation of international agreements (Pérez Tremps 1994; Mangas Martín 1997); there is hardly any role for the Parliament (*Cortes*) in such issues, apart from the ratification procedures of international treaties[3] and the *ex post* control of international negotiations conducted by the Executive (Closa 1996; Cienfuegos Mateo 1997). The predominant role in international negotiations is therefore assumed by the Ministry of Foreign Affairs, though the dynamics of European integration are increasingly granting larger protagonism to other sectorial

---

[3] Arts. 93, 94 and 96 of the 1978 Spanish Constitution.

Ministries, to the President's Office, and to the Permanent Representation in Brussels acting as the Ministry's long-distance direct agent. There are no constitutional powers whatsoever granted to the Autonomous Communities in strict "international affairs" issues (Mangas Martín 1997), though the EU decision-making-process has indirectly provoked and allowed their, still incipient, participation in the process (M.A.P. 1995; Morata 1996; Arias Martín 1998). The set-up of such participation and coordination mechanisms vis-à-vis the definition of the Spanish national negotiation positions is the main demand to the Central Government unanimously shared by all "nationalist" parties and, in some cases, regional Governments (Comisión Mixta 1998).

Personalities and Ideological Ascriptions: Content and Style of González vs. Aznar's Leadership
President Aznar came to power in 1996 with two major handicaps at European level, both linked to his relative lack of extensive experience in these areas: the fact that some months later he practically became the only head of Government in the EU belonging to a conservative political party and the permanent memory of President González's role in and influence on the EU negotiations (Moderne & Bon 1993). In fact, the 1996 IGC was the first major international dossier and negotiation handled by his Government which necessarily implied the search for continuity of the previous negotiation positions and strategies (Arias Salgado 1995). The Treaty of Amsterdam was to mean for Aznar vis-à-vis the Spanish public opinion what the Treaty of Maastricht at its moment meant for González, and became a permanent source of internal comparison, especially after Aznar's controversial declarations in 1992 after the Edinburgh European Council on González's negotiating abilities (Molina del Pozo 1996; Moreno Juste 1998; Barbé 1999, 112, 140).

The fact that the Spanish political elite – long before the actual negotiations for accession started (Bassols 1995) – and the general public, despite its lack of in-depth knowledge of the actual functioning and consequences of EC membership – shared the same illusion and common aspiration has clearly facilitated both the adaptation of internal structures and from time to time the adoption of unpopular decisions. The EC/EU dimension has been present throughout the past fourteen years as an important element of all Spanish major national processes and challenges: economic transformation, social change, regional conflicts (CEOE 1996; Molina del Pozo 1996; Barbé 1997a). In 1995, President González justified the extension of his Government's term in office and his refusal to call a general election with reference to the need of political stability to assume the Presidency of the Council of the EU in the second semester of that year (Barbé 1999, 99). A distinctive feature of the Spanish political elite dealing with international affairs, both in the last

Socialist Government and the present Conservative, is its previous professional experience and personal connection with the process of European integration and/or the European institutions[4] (e.g., Westendorp; Matutes; De Miguel; Atienza; De Palacio; Oreja).

Strategic Evolution on the Basis of Economic Success and Administrative Restructuring: from Idealism to Pragmatism

Spain's political priorities with regard to EU policy making have to some extent evolved from the first years of membership of the EC to the present situation. The internal process of modernisation of the administrative and productive structures, and the enhancement of a regionally-balanced economic development, initially centred the attention and priorities of the Spanish political elite in the period prior to the adoption of the Treaty on European Union (Moderne & Bon 1993; Almarcha Barbado 1993; Dastis 1995). Traditionally, Spain adopted "integrationist" negotiating positions and tried to cope in the first years with the requirements imposed during the long transitional periods leading to its full participation in all Community policies (Barbé 1998). Obviously, all matters related to the definition of a regional development policy at European level were the focus of Spain's political priorities, as well as the subsequent management of the Structural Funds (Ordoñez Solis 1997). Agricultural and fisheries issues were also high-ranking among Spanish priorities – no doubt due to the enormous and painful restructuring processes undergone by some Spanish agricultural sectors – within the general preoccupation for Spain's full accession to the Single Market.

The implementation of the Treaty of Maastricht, together with the end of most of the transitional periods in 1991 and 1993 for certain economic sectors and the natural adjustment of the Spanish administration to the uses and practices of the EC/EU decision-making process, have caused the extension and diversification of Spain's political priorities in the EU (Barbé 1998). Agriculture and fisheries continue to be one of the highest ranking areas – especially the fisheries issues following the conflicts with Canada (1993), Morocco (1995), the enlargement negotiations with Norway and the foreseeably complex negotiations on a new fisheries agreement with Morocco, as well as those matters related to regional development policy, particularly the Structural Funds, the Cohesion Fund, and social and economic cohesion. The pursuit of a special status for the Canary Islands and its tax regime is to be explained in terms of the support granted to the Conservative Government by the Canarian "nationalist" parties. At the same time, the process leading to

---

[4] A political trend which has been somewhat altered with the recent nomination of Mr. Josep Piqué and his new team at the Spanish Ministry of Foreign Affairs (May 2000).

the creation of the Economic and Monetary Union has been the main focus of Spain's attention (Martín 1997), especially since President Aznar came to power, including Spain's entry into the third stage of EMU as the main issue of his electoral programme and the fundamental motivation for his parliamentary alliance with the "nationalist" parties (Barbé 1999, 113).

Another aspect which has immediately attracted Spain's political interest is the cooperation in the fields of Justice and Home Affairs, especially issues related to immigration, external borders control and police cooperation in the fight against terrorism and drug trafficking (M. Interior 1997; Gosalbo Bono 1998). The Spanish Ministries of Home Affairs and Justice, traditionally reluctant to international cooperation, have developed a new dynamic approach to these issues and even held leading positions and presented initiatives at European level in this field. Spain's activity within the Common Foreign and Security Policy has been less relevant, its efforts concentrated on the relationships with the Mediterranean countries and Latin America (Gillespie et al. 1995).

Finally, Spain played an important role in the 1990-91 Intergovernmental Conferences where, due to its special position within the EC/EU institutional structure, it showed its interest in institutional issues, and in those related with the deepening of the contents of European citizenship and the fight against unemployment. This particular interest in institutional issues was also reflected in the negotiations which concluded with the adoption of the so-called "Ioaninna Compromise" in 1994 (VV.AA. 1994). Spain has always defended the principle of subsidiarity as a means to improve Community action, not so much for the devolution of powers to the Member States, and its exclusive application to the EC-Member States relationships, nor within the internal structure of the States themselves. Obviously, this view has been traditionally contested by the regional Governments, especially in those Autonomous Communities with "nationalist" parties in power (Morata 1996; Arias Martín 1998). Traditionally, Spain has also assumed a major role in budgetary negotiations as a leader of the so-called "cohesion countries." It could be stated in general terms that Spain has evolved from adapting its internal structures and interests to the EC/EU decision-making process to strengthening its negotiating positions with a view to a wider and stronger defence of its national interests (Barbé 1997a).

Other Historic, Geographic and Demographic Determinants of National Preference

Finally, other determinants of the Spanish national positions vis-à-vis the process of European integration not to be overlooked are: its cultural and historic ties with certain world geographic areas, namely Latin America and the Islamic countries, especially in the Mediterranean region, ties that clearly influence its positions in Second and Third Pillar issues, as well as its demands and expectations vis-à-vis the enlargement process towards the Central and Eastern European countries (Gillespie *et al.* 1995; Ramirez Jimenez 1996); its strategic geographic position in Southern Europe between the Mediterranean and Atlantic Ocean as a springboard both towards Northern Africa and Latin America makes Spain assume the role of "bridge" and "gatekeeper" with regard to migratory movements from those two areas; the activity of the terrorist pro-independentist Basque group ETA and its subsidiary political representation at regional level, clearly influence most Spanish positions in terms of police and judicial cooperation in criminal affairs, as well as the Gibraltar issue with regard to external borders control and other specific areas linked to the fulfilment of the Single Market (M. Interior 1997); and, finally, the country's demographic composition and structure which, in institutional terms, places Spain as a unique case of "medium-sized" country between the large and smaller EU Member States.

National Preference: Spanish Interests and Negotiation Positions During the 1996-97 IGC

Spain played a relevant and high-profile role in most phases of the 1996-97 Intergovernmental Conference. Its traditional "integrationist" approach in previous IGCs was this time more moderate; the Spanish delegation acted in clear defence of its national interests in several negotiation dossiers (Elorza Cavengt 1997a; VV.AA. 1998,35). In fact, despite its official position, the Spanish delegation did not in practice envisage enlargement to the CEECs as the all-embracing common objective justifying the reform, nor did the Spanish public opinion. The Spanish negotiation positions during the different IGC phases were not affected by the change of political parties at national government level because of the broad consensus in these fields, the maintenance of the same negotiating team at technical level centred around the Permanent Representation staff (VV.AA. 1998, 45) and the referral to the *Cortes* Resolution on the 1996 IGC (Comisión Mixta 1995)[5]. For the first time in an IGC, the Spanish delegation relied upon a complete parliamentary text agreed by all Spanish political parties within the Joint Commission Congress-Senate for the European Union – which acted to a certain extent as a

---

[5] *Dictamen de la Comisión Mixta para la Unión Europea en relación con el Informe elaborado por la Ponencia sobre consecuencias para España de la ampliación de la Unión Europea y reformas institucionales (Conferencia Intergubernamental, 1996)* of 21 December 1995 (Boletín Oficial de las Cortes Generales Serie A, Nº82, of 29 December 1995, pp. 1-28).

"negotiation mandate," plus two specific legislative proposals on the status of the Canary Islands (29 October 1996) and child protection (9 April 1997). The serious impact on the Spanish political elite caused by the Lammers/Schäuble Report of 1994, especially its "variable geometry" scheme and the proposal for a massive transfer of policy areas to qualified majority voting (QMV) at a later stage, is to be found at the basis of the *Cortes* Resolution and most of the later Spanish negotiating positions (Elorza Cavengt 1997a; VV.AA. 1998, 331; Barbé 1999, 80).

The document *"Bases para una reflexión"*[6] prepared by the Spanish Government on 2 March 1995 and made public during its 1995 Presidency of the Council, together with the initiatives undertaken by Carlos Westendorp as Chairman of the Reflection Group, whose nomination implied the first diplomatic conflict with France during the Corfu European Council, helped to define the IGC agenda and general framework for the development of the negotiations, in accordance with some of the Spanish proposals (Boixareu Carrera 1996; VV.AA. 1998, 39; Oreja Aguirre & Fonseca Morillo 1998).

Spain's priorities with regard to the revision of the Maastricht Treaty were made public in October 1996, some months after the accession of the People's Party (PP) to power, and followed the general consensus among the major political parties as contained in the *Cortes* Resolution of 21 December 1995. Continuity presided both over the content of the proposals and the nomination of the non-political members of the negotiating team of the new Spanish conservative government with regard to those of the previous Socialist government (Barbé 1999, 118). Internal debate only arose with regard to the so-called "asylum protocol" (VV.AA. 1998, 87; Barbé 1999, 132). Spain presented twenty-nine official written proposals,[7] three of them jointly with other Member States. Ten of them were finally incorporated into the new text of the Treaty and adopted with minor changes. Other nine proposals were tabled during the last stage of the negotiations without having been officially codified (VV.AA 1998, 45, 57).[8]

The main Spanish proposals (M.A.E. 1995b; Barbé 1997b), apart from the maintenance of the clear separation between the IGC negotiations and the EMU process (VV.AA. 1998, 42), were: support to the incorporation of a new Chapter on Employment; the creation of an Area of Freedom, Security and Justice, together with the reinforcement of the role of Europol and judicial

---

[6] Ministerio de Asuntos Exteriores (Ministry of Foreign Affairs), *La Conferencia Intergubernamental de 1996: Bases para una reflexión*, Madrid, 2 March 1995.

[7] See "Annex: Spanish proposals for the 1996 IGC negotiations," at the end of this Chapter.

[8] See Annex, as in Footnote 7 *supra*.

cooperation at a European level, and – what constituted the most controversial issue for the Spanish general public and media – the prohibition of the admissibility of political asylum requests by EU nationals. These three proposals were to be understood within the framework of the fight against the Basque terrorist group ETA in its international dimension (M. Interior 1997; Gosalbo Bono 1998; VV.AA. 1998, 61, 73, 103); the reinforcement of the Committee of the Regions (together with Germany, Austria and Belgium) (VV.AA. 1998, 315); the simplification of the co-decision procedure; the establishment of an effective common security and defence policy by means of the prospective integration of the WEU within the EU (VV.AA. 1998, 223); the justiciability of the European Convention on Human Rights before the European Court of Justice (VV.AA. 1998, 291); the reinforcement of the principle of equal treatment between men and women; the encouragement and coordination of voluntary organisations; and the creation of a permanent statute for the ultra-peripheric and island regions (Canary Islands) (VV.AA. 1998, 155). The Declaration on the protection of the family failed to gain overall support from other Member States.

With regard to the institutional issues, Spain never presented any written proposal either on the weighting of votes in the Council or on the number of members of the Commission (VV.AA. 1998, 251, 271). Its oral proposals of a tactical nature in this sense defended a "final number of Commissioners smaller to that of Member States" – one permanent Commissioner for each large Member State, rotation for the rest – necessarily linked to the re-weighting of the votes within the Council. Spain ended up having to block the final result of the Conference at the last minute, due to the conviction that its national interests were not being sufficiently safeguarded with the final text adopted on institutional reform, therefore calling for a redrafting of the so-called "institutional protocol" (Oreja Aguirre & Fonseca Morillo 1998; VV.AA. 1998, 47). Spain was not ready to accept the refusal to one of its Commissioners without parallel compensation within the Council voting system. The "Ioannina compromise" was therefore extended in its enforcement period, and Spain accepted the insertion of a political Declaration stating that its particular case would be taken into account at the moment of further institutional reform following future enlargement of the Union. The plenary debate at the Spanish Congress of Deputies, following the intervention of President Aznar to explain the results of the Amsterdam summit, precisely focused on this institutional dossier, as well as on the results achieved with the insertion of the controversial "asylum protocol" (Congreso de los Diputados 1997).

Finally, Spain clearly rejected certain proposals by other Member States which would have affected its national interests, especially those of a wider notion of the principle of "flexibility"and the re-drafting of the conditions of application of the principle of subsidiarity (VV.AA. 1998, 163, 331). At the same time, certain attempts to reduce the powers of the European Court of Justice and the European Commission (VV.AA. 1998, 52, 291) or to reinforce the role of national Parliaments within the EU decision-making process (VV.AA. 1998, 321) were also attacked by the Spanish delegation. On the other hand, Spain defended the extension of qualified majority voting exclusively to certain specific areas, with a total rejection of such extension in the cases of management of the Structural Funds, social protection and management of water resources (VV.AA. 1998, 54). The Spanish delegation also managed to avoid any reference in the new Treaty to the so called "quota hopping" fisheries issue defended by the United Kingdom and the inclusion of any provision which might negatively influence Spanish claims in the Gibraltar issue (Elorza Cavengt 1997a).

The Spanish negotiation positions and national interests, though not so proactively expressed as in the Maastricht negotiations, were clearly focused on the institutional issues, the reluctance to the extension of qualified majority voting to certain areas, the limitation of the inclusion of the concept of flexibility within the Treaty and the creation of a European Area of Freedom, Security and Justice with the reinforcement of police and judicial cooperation in criminal matters.

Bargaining Within the 1996-97 IGC: Spanish Negotiation Strategies and Alliances With Other National and Supranational Actors

In general terms, it could be stated that Spain's negotiation strategies and methods during the 1996 Intergovernmental Conference have been rather similar and in keeping with those used during the Maastricht negotiations, with the exception of an increased presence and decisive intervention of the President of the Government and his private Cabinet (Barbé 1999, 130). This continuity is mainly due to the fact that the components of the Spanish negotiating team at technical level have been practically the same in both Conferences and even during the different phases of the 1996 IGC, despite the change of political parties at national Government level, as was the case with other national delegations. The negotiating team was always under the direction of the Spanish Permanent Representative, Mr. Javier Elorza Cavengt[9], who acted both as a Spanish member of the Reflection Group and

---

[9] At the time of adding final remarks to this Chapter, Ambassador Elorza Cavengt has recently assumed the direction of the Spanish Embassy in Paris and been replaced by Ambassador Francisco Javier Conde at the Permanent Representation of Spain before

Representative of the Spanish Government at the later stages of the negotiation process.

On the other hand, the economic and political context – radically influenced by the situation of economic crisis and high unemployment rates at EU level, the triumph of Mr. Blair and Mr. Jospin in their respective national elections, and the lack of a main negotiating goal and general model shared by all Member States (Bullain 1996) – inevitably led to continuous changes in the negotiation strategies, imprecise definition of national positions and a recurrent mixed use of tactical and subtantive proposals, in a more dynamic and open negotiation process than that of Maastricht (VV.AA. 1998, 45).

The traditional alliance of Spain with the Franco-German axe, which had helped to define at a very early stage some of the common negotiating positions vis-à-vis the likely results of the Conference, did not function so effectively as on previous occasions. The reasons were internal problems and contradictions within the German delegation, the lack of an effective dialogue between Kohl and Aznar's administrations, and, particularly, the radical change in some of the French positions after Jospin's election, which were publicly recriminated by Aznar some days before the Amsterdam European Council, especially with regard to institutional issues and the transfer of certain areas to QMV. Spain actually lost major allies in some of the most relevant negotiation issues due to the results of the British and French elections. In any case, Spain was forced to use in the 1996 IGC a wider range of negotiation alliances – some of them with non-traditional EU allies, such as the Nordic countries or the United Kingdom – than on previous occasions and experienced traumatic conflicts with regard to specific issues (asylum protocol, subsidiarity, "quota-hopping," Schengen) with national delegations with which other dossiers were perfectly jointly prepared and negotiated (VV.AA. 1998, 45; Barbé 1999, 130, 132). On the other hand, to a very large extent, Spain could not play its traditional role as leader of the "cohesion countries" (Martín 1997).

The negotiation on the so called "asylum protocol," particularly important vis-à-vis the Spanish internal political debate, provoked a serious conflict with Belgium, resulting in the final inclusion in the Treaty of a Declaration by Belgium on the issue, and to a lesser extent, with Ireland, as well as with the French, Dutch, Swedish, Finnish and Austrian delegations. The extreme visibility and general public debate arisen by ACNUR and Amnesty International's (AI) comments on the Spanish proposal to suppress "political asylum" for EU nationals put the protocol at the forefront of the follow-up of the negotiations by the Spanish public opinion and, much to the regret of the Spanish negotiation delegation, obliged Aznar to come back home with a

---

the EU. See A. Ortega, "El hombre que sabía demasiado," El País 26 June 2000, p.10.

"necessary victory," which tied the hands of the Spanish negotiators, as recognised by Elorza himself (Elorza Cavengt 1997a), with regard to other issues.

Once the negotiation itself was concluded, a second serious argument arose with the British delegation with regard to the "quota-hopping" dossier (VV.AA. 1998, 56). The argument arose over a letter sent to the Spanish Minister of Foreign Affairs by the Commission Secretary General, Mr. David Williamson (19 June 1997), which was very negatively interpreted and agressively rejected by the Spanish Government – and the drafting of the final text of the Schengen Protocol (26 June 1997). The final text required unanimity voting (and not QMV, as alleged by the British delegation) for the later participation and acceptance by the United Kingdom and Ireland in decisions adopted within the Schengen framework. This latter issue was vital for the Spanish delegation because of its "Gibraltar repercussions" (M. Interior 1997).

Spain acted jointly with Germany, France, Italy, Belgium and Luxembourg on defence and CFSP issues, against some of the British counter-proposals aiming at reducing the scope of the defence provisions within the Treaty. This negotiation was particularly delicate for Spain, as it did not wish to interfere with the parallel ongoing negotiations for its full integration within the military structure of NATO (Arias Salgado 1995; Barbé 1999, 126). Spain acted very effectively together with France and Portugal for the inclusion of a special statute for ultra-peripheric and island regions in the Treaties, as well as with the Austrian and Swedish delegations vis-à-vis the strengthening of the provisions on the principle of equal treatment for men and women. Denmark and the United Kingdom were unexpected last minute allies in the refusal of the transfer of certain policy areas to QMV. In fact, Spain used its only major tactical proposal linked to this QMV negotiation, that of the strict defence of the principle of sufficiency of financial means, in order to indirectly reject the abandoning of unanimity voting in certain policy areas (Social Security, Structural Funds, Environment).

The German, Austrian and British delegations proposed for different reasons a redefinition of the principle of subsidiarity; the Spanish Government, at a high internal political price – the rejection of the proposals in a similar direction by most Autonomous Communities and the "nationalist" parties –, which later bitterly arose within the parliamentary debates on the ratification process of the Treaty of Amsterdam (Congreso de los Diputados 1997), defended the continuity of the "Maastricht subsidiarity formula." The Spanish delegation also had to assume the defence of bullfighting as a tradition of national cultural identity against the proposals by the United Kingdom, Germany, Austria and the Nordic delegations; and was obliged to draw back its proposal for a "family protection" provision, which had been heavily publicised by certain national media. Spain firmly opposed what was defined as *"regressive proposals"* by some national delegations, namely the British attempt to reduce the powers of the European Court of Justice and the German suggestion to create an independent Competition Agency at European level.

However, it was the "flexibility" dossier and the institutional issues which put most pressure on Spain's negotiation strategies within the 1996 IGC (VV.AA. 1998, 50, 331). With regard to "flexibility," Spain fought for the strictest possible drafting of the principle, for fear of the "multi-speed Europe" concept which hid behind the Franco-German proposal (supported by the Italian and some Benelux delegations) (Barbé 1999, 80). Spain initially joined the opposing group constituted by the United Kingdom, Ireland, Greece, Portugal and the three Nordic countries. At a second stage it followed the alternative proposal defended together with Portugal, Ireland and Sweden which required not only unanimity voting for the application of reinforced cooperation schemes, as demanded by the United Kingdom, Denmark and Greece, but also a preliminary set of conditions. Much of this negotiation was agreed in parallel with the Nordic demands for greater flexibility of Internal Market rules vis-à-vis environmental requirements.

Finally, the negotiation on the institutional issues was the most dramatic and risky one for Spain, mainly due to its special, weak position within the EU institutional structure in terms of representation within the Commission and the Council. The failure of the previously agreed alliance with France, and the negotiation tactics used by the Dutch Presidency in this dossier, forced the Spanish delegation to finally block the global negotiation and the final agreement of the Conference by means of the agressive play of a "national" card. The last minute meeting between Aznar, Kohl, Kok and Dehaene resulted in amendments to the final drafting of the so-called "institutional protocol" (Oreja Aguirre & Fonseca Morillo 1998). The protocol postponed the institutional reform, and the inclusion of a Declaration which recalled the special interests and compensations required by Spain for the loss of its second Commissioner (Elorza Cavengt 1997a). This extremely delicate agreement was at the core of the national ratification debate and placed the Spanish delegation in an awkward position vis-à-vis the next Intergovernmental Conference for institutional reform (García Santos 1997; Barbé 1999, 171), especially taking into account the reduced number of possible trade-offs due to the limited agenda scope initially agreed.

The Ratification Process of the Amsterdam Treaty in Spain

The Treaty of Amsterdam was fully ratified by the Spanish Parliament on 16 December 1998 after a long procedure in both Chambers[10] which, contrary to some fears by the Government, did not provoke major political controversies (Congreso de los Diputados 1998; Mangas Martín 1999). In fact, the whole ratification process had an extremely low profile and was dealt with by the Government and the Cortes with a high degree of technicality, which clearly hindered a broad political debate (Donaire Villa 1998). Most of the parliamentary proceedings were parallel to the ratification of the agreements leading to Spain's full participation within the military structure of NATO and the accession of the first new Central and Eastern European States, which somewhat diluted the relevance of the Amsterdam ratification vis-à-vis the public opinion and even the parliamentary forces (Barbé 1999, 172). In comparison with the ratification of the Maastricht Treaty, this was simple, fast and free of unexpected legal or political problems (Donaire Villa, 1998; Mangas Martín 1999).

President Aznar presented the results of the Amsterdam negotiations to the Plenary Session of the Spanish *Cortes* on 25 June 1997. Aznar opted for an

---

[10] The whole series of parliamentary documents related with the process of ratification of the Treaty of Amsterdam are published in the Boletín Oficial de las Cortes Generales (BOCG) as follows: Proyecto de Ley Orgánica 121/000116 (BOCG Congreso de los Diputados Serie A Núm. 117-1, of 26 May 1998); Ampliación del plazo de enmiendas (BOCG Congreso de los Diputados Serie A Núm. 117-2, of 10 June 1998); Debate de totalidad (Diario de Sesiones del Congreso de los Diputados, Pleno y Diputación Permanente, Núm. 171, of 18 June 1998); Enmiendas (BOCG Congreso de los Diputados Serie A Núm. 117-3, of 22 June 1998); Ratificación de la Ponencia (Diario de Sesiones del Congreso de los Diputados, Pleno y Diputación Permanente, Núm. 492, of 24 June 1998); Informe de la Ponencia (BOCG Congreso de los Diputados Serie A Núm. 117-4, of 22 September 1998); Debate del Dictamen de la Comisión (Diario de Sesiones del Congreso de los Diputados, Pleno y Diputación Permanente, Núm. 514, of 23 September 1998); Dictamen de la Comisión (BOCG Congreso de los Diputados Serie A Núm. 117-5, of 30 September 1998); Debate del Dictamen de Comisión (Diario de Sesiones del Congreso de los Diputados, Pleno y Diputación Permanente, Núm. 184, of 1 October 1998); Aprobación por el Pleno (BOCG Congreso de los Diputados Serie A Núm. 117-6, of 8 October 1998); Proyecto de Ley Orgánica 621/000103 (BOCG Senado Serie II Núm. 103(a), of 9 October 1998); Propuestas de veto (BOCG Senado Serie II Núm. 103(b), of 26 October 1998); Enmiendas (BOCG Senado Serie II Núm. 103(c), of 26 October 1998); Informe de la Ponencia (BOCG Senado Serie II Núm. 103(d), of 6 November 1998); Debate del Dictamen de Comisión (Diario de Sesiones del Senado Núm. 358, of 12 November 1998); Dictamen de la Comisión (BOCG Senado Serie II Núm. 103(e), of 18 November 1998); Debate de totalidad (Diario de Sesiones del Senado Núm. 107, of 24 November 1998); Texto aprobado por el Senado (BOCG Senado Serie II Núm. 103(f), of 1 December 1998).

extremely technical intervention, which made the ensuing debate focus basically on the political aspects of the "asylum protocol," the special statute agreed for the Canary Islands and the final solution agreed for the institutional problem. While no major discrepancies arose with regard to both issues – though some criticised Aznar for an exaggeratedly positive presentation of the results "addressed to the internal public opinion consumption" (Barbé 1999, 132), the "nationalist" parties insisted that the results obtained were poor with regard to the redefinition of the subsidiarity principle and, once again, demanded the creation of effective coordination and representation institutional mechanisms for their interests in the EC/EU decision-making process.[11]

The later parliamentary debates at Committee or Plenary level connected with the ratification process took place on four occasions: 10 March 1998, 10 June 1998, 1 October 1998 and 16 December 1998. In these debates, special attention was paid to different issues than those initially expected, namely the modalities and problems derived from the inclusion of a new Chapter on Employment within the Treaties and again the "nationalist" demand for new regional coordination and representative institutional mechanisms; this was due to the controversial role played by President Aznar during the Luxembourg extraordinary European Council on Employment (November 1997), which gave rise to harsh criticisms from the Spanish Trade Unions and the Socialist Party (Barbé 1999, 134). Throughout the whole ratification process, only three special *"parliamentary motions"* were addressed to the Government, namely with regard to the maintenance of the Cohesion Fund (PP 8 October 1997), the principle of subsidiarity (EA 29 October 1997) and the role of the Autonomous Communities in the EC/EU decision-making process (IU 10 March 1998).

While the Spanish press occasionally paid attention to the developments of the ratification process in other Member States – especially the Danish referendum, the French constitutional reform and the German reactions to the Treaty – and the *Cortes* themselves demanded information from their French and Italian colleagues on their respective ratification processes (Donaire Villa 1998), most of the Spanish parliamentary debates were exclusively centered on an issue absolutely separate to the process of ratification itself, which was the need for increased participation and representation of the Regions vis-à-vis the definition of the Spanish negotiating positions at EU level. In fact, the only amendments proposed to the draft proposal for an Organic Law of ratification

---

[11] See "Informe de la Ponencia de la Comisión General de las Comunidades Autónomas sobre papel y funciones de los entes territoriales en el futuro de la Unión Europea" (543/000010), Boletín Oficial de las Cortes Generales, Senado, VI Legislatura, Serie I, Núm. 360, pp. 1-21.

tabled by the Government came in this sense from the Basque "nationalist" parties (PNV and EA) and the United Left (IU) and merely included the redrafting of the Preamble of the Organic Law, not its substantive content.[12] These amendments to the text of the internal Organic Law of ratification were globally rejected. However, due to a procedural error by the PP parliamentary Group, they resulted in a so called *"proposición no de ley"* (non-binding parliamentary legislative proposal), which had to be accepted by the People's Party despite its lack of future legal effects (10 March 1998).

The Spanish Ratification Act of the Treaty of Amsterdam, published in the Official Journal of 17 December 1998,[13] was passed with the practical unanimity of votes from all political parties, except for some abstentions by the Basque "nationalist" MPs and IU members. The Act includes a short Preamble and a single substantive article, together with an additional provision accepting the automatic jurisdictional competence of the European Court of Justice vis-à-vis preliminary rulings in the field of judicial and police cooperation in criminal matters (Gosalbo Bono 1998), though the questions or demands for a preliminary ruling are restricted to courts or tribunals against whose decisions there is no judicial remedy under national law. This latter point seems to be rather contradictory with the actual negotiation positions defended by the Spanish delegation during the IGC (Elorza Cavengt 1997a; VV.AA. 1998, 291).

The Spanish Post-Amsterdam Debate: Preparing for the Subsequent IGC 2000

The nomination of Javier Solana as Mr. PESC and his role in the Kosovo crisis had a major impact on the national public opinion in Spain's post-Amsterdam political scenario; this paradoxically influenced the peculiar process of strengthening the internal and external political position of President Aznar. A minor process of internal reform of the administrative structures (mainly at the Ministry of Foreign Affairs, but also within the Parliament) dealing with EU affairs was motivated on the changes involved by the Amsterdam Treaty (Basabe Lloréns, forthcoming). While the Socialist Party stresses the Spanish Government's loss of influence on the international position, the apathy which presides over the traditional German-Spanish

---

[12] Boletín Oficial de las Cortes Generales, Congreso de los Diputados, VI Legislatura, Serie A, Núm. 117-3, pp. 73-76.

[13] Boletín Oficial del Estado, 17 December 1998, p.1ss.

diplomatic relationships[14] and the less "integrationist" approach to EU issues to that of the González era, it seems quite evident, at least from a quantitative point of view, that Aznar's Government continues to play a rather active role in the European arena (Barbé 1999, 168). With the exception of the momentary crisis related to the alleged corruption scandal in EC flax subsidies under De Palacio's ministerial mandate, the People's Party and the Government have been keen on playing an active role in adopting EU initiatives in issues related to Home and Judicial Affairs and other economic areas, assuming a certain protagonism during the Tampere and Lisbon European Councils within the framework of the new cooperation "tandem Aznar-Blair," as well as with the joint proposal with France (26 October 1998) for the creation of a Council of Defence Ministers, together with a reduced military structure, at EU level, to compensate for the previous Franco-German and Italo-Anglo initiatives in these fields.

Spain played a high profile role in the negotiation processes concerning the EC budgetary reform (Barbé 1999, 143); not so much until the present moment in what concerns the accession of new Member States (Comisión Mixta 1999). The reasons why Spain assumed the role of major actor in such negotiations were that Spain was, at that time, the only large EU state with a Conservative political party in power – no doubt Aznar's leadership within the European People's Party had been strongly reinforced in the previous months, and that Spain felt obliged to lead the position and interests of the so called "cohesion countries" vis-à-vis the proposals of the Northern countries for budgetary reform.

Aznar achieved a major internal political success with the entry of Spain into the third phase of the Economic and Monetary Union (Martín 1997). This was one of the major points of the electoral programme of the PP on which Aznar placed, at a certain time, most of its political energies and weight. The result has been accompanied by good economic results regarding inflation rates, employment growth, public deficit and interest rates – though the inflation percentages have dangerously risen in the last months. The effective performance of Aznar's economic team of advisors, the relative lack of internal social tensions – apart from the new scenario created by the complex Basque "peace process" which polarises the current political national debate, the new role to be played within the European Conservative political parties (especially with regard to the Austrian ÖVP crisis) and their leaders, the experience accumulated in the European and international arenas in the last four years, together with the absolute majority obtained in the 2000 general

---

[14] After the controversy arisen by former Ambassador Wegener's declarations to the national press and Schröder-Aznar's confrontation during the Berlin European Council negotiations.

elections are the main foundations of Aznar's internal solid position vis-à-vis the EU negotiation processes. The coordinating role of the "cohesion countries" was strongly reinforced by means of close contacts with the Portuguese and Greek Governments.

Spain could have been one of the Member States to have its national interests most negatively affected by the results of the 1999 EC budgetary reform. The management and effectiveness of the Structural Funds in the Spanish economy have only started to develop its full effect in the last years (CEOE 1996; Molina del Pozo 1996; Elorza Cavengt 1997a; Martín 1997). Coordination, both vertical and horizontal, among the different administrative levels with regard to EU affairs, still needs reinforcing and global improvement (Ordoñez Solís 1997). The Spanish Government believes in the need to extend as long as possible its present status as a net recipient state in financial terms in order to further reduce the economic gap between its regions and with regard to other Member States. The renationalisation of the traditionally "integrationist" Spanish policy towards the process of European integration seems unavoidable, at least in the short term, given the current European political scenario (Barbé 1999, 176).

Spain's reticence vis-à-vis the enlargement of the EU towards Central and Eastern Europe is mostly motivated by its financial and institutional repercussions. Recent contacts at the highest political level between the Spanish Government and certain Governments of candidate countries (Poland, Hungary, the Czech Republic) confirm this impression. The access of Spanish economic actors to such new markets is limited and unlikely to result in greater expansion, and historical and cultural links with such countries are not very close either. Spain shall be in the position to condition the enlargement to the maintenance of a certain *status quo* within the present institutional and financial set-up of the EU (Comisión Mixta 1999; Barbé 1999, 148).

The Spanish Government has not adopted any official position or internal document at the present moment with regard to the next IGC for institutional reform, though its strong interests and delicate role to play in such a Conference seem obvious, taking into account the results of the institutional dossier at the Amsterdam European Council. The initial negative reactions to the *Dehaene Report* have caused some Spanish media[15] to timidly start a debate on the suitability of such an aggressive national approach, taking into account the extreme relevance of the EU institutional dossier for Spain and the negative consequences to be derived from such an *"anti-integrationist tone."* The political reaction of the Spanish Government has insisted at the first stages of negotiation on the rejection of an increase in the presidentialist character of the European Commission against its collegial nature, as well as

---

[15] El Pais, 24 October 1999 and 23 June 2000.

on the possibility of the division of the Treaty into two texts of different nature which could be respectively reformed by unanimity and qualified majority voting.

Spain's expected positions vis-à-vis the IGC 2000 are inevitably centred around the idea of a minimalist Conference (the "mini-reform") strictly limited to institutional issues, including to a minimum extent, the possibility of a facilitation of the "flexibility" rules and extension of qualified majority voting to new policy areas. In any case, the defence of the initial Spanish positions vis-à-vis the 2000 IGC seems to be very influenced by the scarce *"marge de manoeuvre"* left by the brief scope of the negotiation agenda with a limited number of trade-offs; the precedent of the Amsterdam "institutional protocol" should in any case set a legal basis for the Spanish demands of respect and comprehension regarding its particular institutional situation within the EC/EU politico-administrative system.

Conclusions: Lessons Learned from Maastricht to Amsterdam

Without any doubt, the Spanish policy-makers drew lessons from the Maastricht negotiations and its controversial process of ratification within the Member States. They actively tried to avoid the interrelation between the EMU process and the IGC, the adoption of various "regressive proposals" and the systematic use of country exemptions during the actual negotiations. They were also aware of the need to defend certain national interests to the required extent in order to facilitate the later ratification of the Treaty and the global acceptance by the Spanish public opinion (VV.AA. 1998; Barbé 1999). The Amsterdam ratification process in other Member States – especially Denmark, France, Germany, Italy and Belgium – was carefully monitored by the Spanish policy-makers. Taking into account the applicability of the notion of "permissive consensus" to the Spanish case, the high degree of technicality in the public debates tends to be used by the political elite to divert the attention from the substantive contents of the process. At the same time, policy-makers are aware of the need to exploit certain specific "close-to-the-citizen" issues to justify the success of the Spanish negotiators for "internal political consumption" purposes.

Nevertheless, a new negotiation style, more in terms of form than substance (Barbé 1999, 171), and the tactical defence of a wider catalogue of national priorities, have characterised the Spanish position at the Amsterdam negotiations in comparison to that of Maastricht. The increasing protagonism acquired by the Spanish Permanent Representative to the EU, Mr. Elorza, together with the further involvement of the President's Cabinet in the negotiations, are signs of a more personalised and high politics negotiating strategy and have led to some adaptations in the internal policy-coordination system (decrease in the role of the Ministry of Foreign Affairs...) (Basabe Lloréns, forthcoming). Aznar has managed to differentiate himself from the tactics and style of the González era, which had a deep impact on the Spanish public opinion and the national public Administration.

For the first time, the Spanish *Cortes* have assumed a preeminent role in the definition of the Spanish negotiating positions in the IGC, which has to be explained in terms of increased democratic control of EU policy and the search for greater legitimacy by the Government vis-à-vis increasingly harder negotiations at EU level. However, such parliamentary control has been practically absent precisely during the ratification process. One of the main EU-related problems yet to be solved within the Spanish politico-administrative system is the enactment of an effective coordination and representation mechanism for the interests and positions of the Autonomous Communities (Morata 1996; Arias Martín 1998; Comisión Mixta 1998). Taking into account the relevance and protagonism of the "nationalist" regional parties in the Spanish political arena, this issue may systematically tend to centre any public debate related to European integration in a somewhat sterile way.

Spain is increasingly becoming a difficult partner in EU negotiations; this is due not only to the coming to power of a political party (PP) with a less "integrationist" approach, but to the objective fact that Spain has naturally evolved from adapting its internal structures and interests to the EC/EU decision-making process to strengthening its negotiating positions with a view to a wider and stronger defence of its national interests (Barbé 1999, 170). A consequence of this new situation is the lack of clear and permanent alliances with other Member States, the abandonment of strict loyalties and the simultaneous participation in different negotiation *fora* within the EU system (Barbé 1999, 173).

In any case, Spain has been keen on playing a leading role in the fields of Home and Judicial Affairs, favouring all advances and proposing new initiatives in a systematic way; this has to be interpreted in terms of the relevance of such issues to domestic politics and its impact on the Spanish public opinion. Spain is particularly reluctant to major changes in issues related to the principle of "flexibility" for historic fears of losing the first-track group of Member States in the integration process, as well as with the transfer of certain policy areas to qualified majority voting. The defence of Spain's beneficial budgetary situation (Structural Funds, Cohesion Fund, agricultural and fisheries subsidies) and its special representation within the EU institutional structure remain the key guidelines of any future Spanish negotiating strategy. Their relevance vis-à-vis the negotiations ahead (IGC for institutional reform and enlargement to the CEECs) seems obvious.

In general terms, it could be concluded that domestic political constraints on the Spanish delegation were only felt in the 1996-97 IGC with regard to the "political asylum protocol" issue. The Spanish negotiation strategy, though effective in some issues, has increasingly become reactive and not anticipatory.[16] The Spanish negotiation positions are still very dependent on economic and geo-strategic factors; increased pragmatism can be also ascertained with regard to certain side issues and especially negotiation tactics and coalition formation; the lack of common interests – with the exception of some agricultural and cohesion dossiers – and a certain degree of rivalry with Italy do not allow for further effective functioning of the Southern European countries as a negotiating block. Finally, the previous dependence on the negotiating positions of the Franco-German axis has given way to a wider scope of looser bilateral alliances and transnational coalition opportunities for Spain.

---

[16] Recent joint initiatives of a clear proactive nature with the British Prime Minister with a view to the preparation of the Lisbon European Council may contradict this opinion.

Annex: Spanish Proposals For The 1996 IGC Negotiations

CONF/3903/96	Memorandum on the Common Fisheries Policy
CONF/3925/96	Justice and Home Affairs
CONF/3926/96	Codecision Process
CONF/3927/96	New Chapter on Employment
CONF/3928/96	Equal Treatment Men-Women
CONF/3929/96	Voluntary Services
CONF/3930/96	Modification of Art. ("Justiciability" of European Convention on Human Rights, Rome 1950)
CONF/3931/96	Sufficiency of Means
CONF/3932/96	Ultra-peripheric Regions
CONF/2501/96	Ultra-Peripheric Regions (together with France and Portugal)
CONF/3826/97	Political Asylum
CONF/3846/97	Legal Text of Principle of Equal Treatment Men-Women
CONF/3855/97	Amendments to Art. J.4 On Security and Defence + Protocol on Integration of W.E.U. Within The EU. (together with Belgium, France, Italy, Luxembourg and Germany)
CONF/3886/97	Response to British Memorandum on Common Fisheries Policy
CONF/3880/97	Protocol on Asylum
CONF/3890/97	Committee of the Regions
CONF/3908/97	C.F.S.P. – ARTS. J.2 & J.5 – Representation in International Organizations and United Nations' Security Council
CONF/3919/97	Political Asylum. Amendments to Protocol
CONF/3924/97	Declaration on the Family
CONF/3929/97	Internal Market. Modification of ART. 100A EC
SN/634/96	Obligatory Expenses of E.C. Budget
SN/513/97	Text of New Paragraph in Art. K.1C.2. National Treatment and Mutual Recognition of Judicial Decisions
SN/532/97	Public Health
SN/534/97	Religion and Religious Associations
SN/531/97	Legal Text on "Flexibility" (ADD.1 TO DOC. CONF/2500/96)
SN/537/97	Subsidiarity
SN/597/97	Public Health
SN/xxx/97	Modifications of Presidency Document SN/539/97 – Chapter 2: Creation of an Area of Freedom, Security and Justice

Spanish Complementary Proposals to the I.G.C. (Neither Numbered Nor Codified)

* Amendments to Conf/3835/97 on "flexibility"
* Amendments to Conf/3830/97 on Subsidiarity
* Island Regions
* Provisions to Be Included in Schengen Protocol
* Proposal of Modifications in Presidency's Chapter on Employment
* New Protocol on Art. 113 EC
* Letter to Mr. Patijn With Modifications to Draft Legal Text of Doc. SN/600/97 (Consolidated Version of Draft Treaty)
* Protocol on Integration of Schengen *Acquis* Within the EU Framework

Source: Vv.aa. (1998), *España y la negociación del Tratado de Amsterdam*, Biblioteca Nueva, Madrid, Ed. Política Exterior.

Bibliography

Almarcha Barbado, A. (ed.) (1993). *Spain and EC membership evaluated*, London: Pinter Publishers.

Alvarez-Miranda Navarro, B. (1994). "A Integración europea y sistema de partidos en el Sur de Europa: despolarización y convergencia," *Revista de Estudios Políticos*, Vol. 3, pp. 143-167.

Arias Martín, M.A. (1998). *Comunidades Autónomas y Elaboración del Derecho Comunitario Europeo*, Oñati, I.V.A.P.

Arias Salgado, R. (1995). "La política europea de España y la conferencia intergubernamental de 1996," *Política Exterior*, Vol. IX-47, pp. 38-46.

Baena del Alcazar, M. (1992). "Groupes de pression et Administration en Espagne," *Annuaire Européen d'Administration Publique*, pp. 137-151.

Barbé, E. (1997a). "De la ingenuidad al pragmatismo: diez años de participación española en la maquinaria diplomática europea," *Revista CIDOB d'Afers Internationals*, Vol. 34-35, pp. 9-30.

Barbé, E. (1997b). "Spain," pp. 169-174, in R. Hrbek. (ed.), *Die Reform der europäischen Union. Positionen und Perspektiven anlässlich der Regierungskonferenz*, Baden-Baden: Nomos Verlag.

Barbé, E. (1998). "The National Interests of Spain," pp. 70-81, in W. Wessels (ed.), *National vs. EU-Foreign Policy Interests. Mapping "important" national interests (Final Xollective Report)*, Köln/Brussels: TEPSA.

Barbé, E. (1999). *La política europea de España*, Barcelona: Ariel Practicum.

Basabe Lloréns, F. (forthcoming). "Spain: the Emergence of a New Major Actor in the European Arena?" in W. Wessels, A. Maurer & J. Mittag (eds.), *Fifteen into One?: The European Union and its Member States*, Manchester: Manchester University Press.

Boixareu Carrera, A. (1996). "Perspectivas de la Conferencia Intergubernamental de 1996. El Informe del Grupo de Reflexión," *Gaceta Jurídica de la CE*, D-25, pp. 3-12.

Bullaín, I. (1996). "Europa y la Conferencia Intergubernamental de 1996", *Revista de Instituciones Europeas*, Vol. 32-1, pp. 119-133.

Burgorgue-Larsen, L. (1995). *L'Espagne et la Communauté Européenne*, Etudes Européennes, Bruxelles: Université de Bruxelles.

Burgorgue-Larsen, L. (1997). "Espagne," pp. 135-184, in J. Rideau (ed.), *Les États Membres de l'Union Européenne. Adaptations – Mutations – Résistances*, Paris: L.G.D.J.

CEOE (1996). *Diez años de España en la Unión Europea (I y II), Informes y Estudios de CEOE 75*, Madrid: Publicaciones CEOE.

Cienfuegos Mateo, M. (1996). "El control de las Cortes generales sobre el Gobierno en asuntos relativos a las Comunidades Europeas durante la década 1986-1995," *Revista de las Cortes Generales*, Vol. 38, pp. 47-99.

Cienfuegos Mateo, M. (1997). "La Comisión Mixta para la Unión Europea: Análisis y balance de una década de actividad en el seguimiento de los asuntos comunitarios," *Gaceta Jurídica de la CE*, D-27, pp. 7-69.

Closa, C. (1996). "Spain: The Cortes and the EU – A Growing Together," pp. 136-150, in P. Norton (ed.), *National Parliaments and the European Union*, London: Frank Cass.

Dastis, A. (1995). "La Administración española ante la Unión Europea," *Revista de Estudios Europeos*, Vol. 90, pp. 223-250.

Donaire Villa, F.J. (1998). "El Tratado de Amsterdam y la Constitución," *Revista Española de Derecho Constitucional,* Vol. 54, pp. 119-167.

Elorza Cavengt, J. (1997a). "El Tratado de Amsterdam: valoración para España," *Meridiano CERI*, Vol. 16, pp. 4-7.

Elorza Cavengt, J. (1997b). "Reflexiones y balance de diez años de España en la Unión Europea," *Información Comercial Española*, Vol. 766, pp. 15-29.

European Parliament – Task-Force CIG 1996 (1995). *Relación de posiciones de los Estados miembros de la Unión Europea ante la Conferencia Intergubernamental de 1996*, PE 165.642 (JF/bo/178/95), Luxembourg, 8 December.

European Parliament – Task-Force CIG 1996 (1996). *Positions resumées des États membres et du Parlement Européen sur la Conference Intergouvernementale de 1996* (JF/bo/234/96), Brussels, 13 June.

European Parliament – Division "Relationships with National Parliaments" (1995). *État de la réflexion des Parlements nationaux sur la Conference Intergouvernementale de 1996*, Brussels, 20 March.

Fonseca Morillo, F. (1995). "Les travaux de préparation de la Conférence intergouvernementale," pp. 31-44, in *L'Union Européenne après Cannes*, Bruxelles: Institut d'Études Européennes, Université Libre de Bruxelles.

Fonseca Morillo, F. (1997). "Balance sobre el Tratado de Amsterdam," *Revista Europa Junta*, Vol. 62, July, pp. 5-15.

García, C. (1990). "Les groupes d'intérêt espagnols et la Communauté Européenne," pp. 115-163, in D. Sidjanski & U. Ayberk (eds.), *L'Europe du Sud dans la Communauté Européenne*, Paris: P.U.F.

García Santos, N. (1997). "El Consejo Europeo de Amsterdam: ocasión perdida para avanzar en la construcción europea," *Cuadernos de Información Económica*, Vol. 123, pp. 53-60.

Genieys, W. (1998). "Autonomous Communities and the State in Spain: the role of intermediary elites," pp. 166-180, in P. Le Galès & C. Lequesne (eds.), *Regions in Europe*, London: Routledge.

Gillespie, R., F. Rodrigo & J. Story (eds.) (1995). *Las relaciones exteriores de la España democrática*, Madrid: Alianza.

Gosalbo Bono, R. (1998). "Las disposiciones del Tratado de Amsterdam relativas a la cooperación policial y judicial en materia penal," *Revista General de Derecho*, A.54, Vol. 644, pp. 5863-5901.

Mangas Martín, A. & D.J. Liñán Nogueras (1999). *Instituciones y Derecho de la Unión Europea*, Madrid: McGraw Hill.

Mangas Martín, A. (1997). "Le droit constitutionnel national et l'intégration européenne: Espagne," pp. 206-230, in J. Schwarze (ed.), *XVII F.I.D.E. Kongress (Berlin, October 1996) – Ergebnisse und Perspektiven*, Baden-Baden: Nomos Verlag.

Martín, C. (1997). *España en la nueva Europa*, Madrid: Alianza.

Martínez Lage, S. (1997). "El Tratado de Amsterdam: algunos aspectos jurídicos," *Gaceta Jurídica de la CE y de la Competencia*, B-124, pp. 1-3.

Moderne, F. & P. Bon (eds.) (1993). *L'Espagne aujourd'hui. Dix années de gouvernement socialiste*, Paris: La Documentation Française.

Molina del Pozo, C.F. (ed.) (1996). *España en la Europa comunitaria: balance de diez años*, Madrid: CEURA.

Morata, F. (1996). "Fundamentals of Spain in EU Affairs," pp. 134-154, in W. Wessels & D. Rometsch (eds.), *The European Union and its Member States. Towards Institutional Fusion?*, Manchester: Manchester University Press.

Morata, F. (1998a). "Spain: Modernization through Integration," pp. 100-115, in K. Hanf & B. Soetendorp (eds.), *Adapting to European Integration. Small States and the European Union*, London: Longman.

Morata, F. (1998b). *La Unión Europea. Procesos, actores y políticas*, Barcelona: Ariel.

Moreno Juste, A. (1998). *España y el proceso de construcción europea*, Barcelona: Ariel Practicum.

Newton, M.T. & P.J. Donaghy (1997). *Institutions of modern Spain: A political and economic guide*, Cambridge: Cambridge University Press.

Ordoñez Solís, D. (1997). *Fondos estructurales europeos. Régimen jurídico y gestión administrativa*, Madrid: Marcial Pons.

Oreja Aguirre, M. (1996). "La revisión del Tratado de la Unión Europea: Los trabajos de la Conferencia Intergubernamental de 1996," *Revista Europa Junta*, Vol. 53, pp. 5-12.

Oreja Aguirre, M. (Dir.) & F. Fonseca Morillo (Coord.) (1998). *El Tratado de Amsterdam – Análisis y comentarios* (Vols. I y II), Madrid: McGraw Hill (especially, Chapter 3: Oreja Aguirre, M., *El desarrollo de la C.I.G.*, pp. 73-116).

Pérez Tremps, P. (1994). *Constitución Española y Comunidad Europea*, Madrid: Civitas.

Pueyo Losa, J. & M.T. Ponte Iglesias (eds.) (1997). *La actividad exterior y comunitaria de Galicia. La experiencia de otras Comunidades Autónomas*, Santiago de Compostela: Publics. Fundación Alfredo Brañas.

Ramírez Jiménez, M. (1996). *Europa en la conciencia española y otros estudios*, Madrid: Trotta.

Smith, E. (ed.) (1996). *National Parliaments as Cornerstones of European Integration*, London: Kluwer Law.

Spain, Ministerio de Asuntos Exteriores (Ministry of Foreign Affairs) (1995a). *La Conferencia Intergubernamental de 1996: Bases para una reflexión*, Madrid, 2 March.

Spain, Comité Organizador de la Presidencia Española del Consejo de la Unión Europea (1995). *Prioridades de la Presidencia española del Consejo de la Unión Europea*, Madrid: B.O.E.

Spain, Cortes Generales – Comisión Mixta Congreso-Senado para la Unión Europea (1995). "Dictamen de la Comisión Mixta para la Unión Europea en relación con el Informe elaborado por la Ponencia sobre consecuencias para España de la ampliación de la Unión Europea y reformas institucionales (Conferencia Intergubernamental, 1996)", 21 December 1995, *Boletín Oficial de las Cortes Generales*, Vol. 82 – Series 4 of 29 December, pp. 1-28.

Spain, Ministerio de Asuntos Exteriores (1995b). *Reflexiones sobre la Conferencia Intergubernamental 1996*, Madrid: Publicaciones del Ministerio de Asuntos Exteriores.

Spain, Ministerio para las Administraciones Públicas (Ministry of Public Administration) (1995). *La participación de las Comunidades Autónomas en los asuntos comunitarios europeos*, Madrid: Publicaciones del Ministerio para las Administraciones Públicas.

Spain, Ministerio del Interior (Ministry of Home Affairs) (1997). *El tercer pilar de la Unión Europea. La cooperación en asuntos de justicia e interior*, Madrid: Publicaciones del Ministerio del Interior.

Spain, Cortes Generales – Comisión Mixta para la Unión Europea (1998). "Proposición no de Ley sobre participación de las Comunidades Autónomas en la delegación del Estado en el Consejo de Ministros de la Unión Europea," *Boletín Oficial de las Cortes Generales*, Vol. 176, 10 March.

Spain, Ministerio de Asuntos Exteriores – Secretaría de Estado de Política Exterior y para la Unión Europea (1998). *Guía sobre el Tratado de Amsterdam*, Madrid: Publicaciones del Ministerio de Asuntos Exteriores.

Spain, Congreso de los Diputados – Secretaría General (1998). "Tratado de Amsterdam – Documentación preparada para la tramitación del Proyecto de Ley Orgánica por la que se autoriza la ratificación por España del Tratado de Amsterdam," *Boletín Oficial de las Cortes Generales*, Vol. 117-1/2 – Series A of 26 May.

Spain – B.O.E. (1998). "Ley Orgánica 9/1998, de 16 de diciembre, por la que se autoriza la ratificación por España del Tratado de Amsterdam...," *Boletín Oficial del Estado,* 17 December, pp. 42266.

Spain, Cortes Generales – Comisión Mixta para la Unión Europea (1999). *Informe sobre La ampliación de la Unión Europea*, Madrid: Publics. Secretaría General del Congreso de los Diputados.

VV.AA. (1992). *La izquierda y Europa. Una aproximación crítica al Tratado de Maastricht*, Madrid: Izquierda Unida/Los Libros de la Catarata.

VV.AA. (1994). *España y el Tratado de la Unión Europea*, Madrid: COLEX.

VV.AA. (1998). *España y la negociación del Tratado de Amsterdam*, Biblioteca Nueva, Madrid: Ed. Política Exterior.

15

Sweden: Constrained but Constructive?

Karl Magnus Johansson & Anna-Carin Svensson

This chapter analyses the negotiating positions and behaviour of Sweden during the Intergovernmental Conference (IGC) which led to the Amsterdam Treaty. Although the focus is on the positions of and processes within this particular Member State of the European Union (EU), our aim is also to make a contribution, however modest, to the literature on treaty-making "grand bargains" in connection to IGCs (see, for example, Lodge 1998; Moravcsik 1998). Despite the distinct features of the EU, we argue that these bargaining processes resemble multilateral negotiations more generally. Such multifaceted phenomena are conceived as a form and process of joint problem-solving and decision-making among three or more state governments, usually, but not necessarily, within international institutional arrangements (see, for example, Hampson with Hart 1995/1999; Zartman 1994). At the same time, bilateral alliances may emerge within this overall multilateral framework as well as transnational coalition opportunities (Mazzucelli 1997).

Membership of a complex organisation such as the EU, with its permanent search for compromise among its members and institutions, provides not only opportunities but also political constraints and risks. The metaphor of the "two-level game" applies in a situation where domestic constraints are imposed on the international negotiator (Evans *et al.* 1993; Putnam 1988). This perspective is thus useful in regard to participation in the EU, in so far as policymakers play two-level or even multi-level games in multiple arenas. Such participation and arena shifts provide another dimension to the tendency for political games to be "nested" one inside the other (Tsebelis 1990).

Analysing the complex interplay of the different levels of negotiation, it is thus important to take into account domestic factors and subprocesses. This applies to the entire time span, from the phase of prenegotiation up to ratification. At the ratifying stage, if not before, the agreed text and overall joint solution are scrutinised at the domestic level and in the national parliamentary arena. The primary task before us is to identify the preferences and positions of Sweden, thereby lifting the lid off the black box of domestic politics.

Sweden and European Integration

The matter of full EU membership rose to the top of the Swedish political agenda within a very short time. Although strongly associated with Western Europe, full membership had been ruled out with reference to the policy of neutrality and non-alignment in particular. However, the governing Social Democrats took a sudden step towards membership in October 1990, in the context of the management of an acute economic crisis (Gustavsson 1998). On December 12, 1990, the Riksdag voted in favour of applying for membership, by 289 votes to 28, with the reservation that it must be in a form compatible "with the retention of neutrality" (Miles 1997, 184). The application for membership was handed over to the Dutch presidency in The Hague on July 1, 1991.

The referendum on membership was held on November 13, 1994. As was expected, the outcome was tight, with a majority of 52.3% in favour and 46.8% against (Gilljam & Holmberg 1996). The referendum outcome can be explained by the massive economic imbalance in favour of the "yes" campaign and by persuasive opinion formers, notably the then Social Democrat leader Ingvar Carlsson. Nevertheless, the result clearly indicated that European issues would remain awkward for Swedish political leaders and parties.

The most salient questions during the referendum campaign concerned, in broad terms, foreign and security policy, democracy, the environment, and agriculture. And during the accession negotiations, the "devils" were in details such as regional aid for the scarcely populated northern parts of Sweden, "snus", or wet snuff tobacco, and alcohol. On politically salient issues such as the emerging Common Foreign and Security Policy (CFSP) of the EU, Swedish representatives were keen to stress the European dimension, and that Sweden would not hinder the further development of the Economic and Monetary Union (EMU) towards a single currency (Luif 1995, ch. 13; Miles 1997, ch. 8). Unlike Britain and Denmark, Sweden has no formal "opt-out" from the third stage of EMU. A decision would be taken by the Swedes in an election or in a referendum.

It is important to emphasise that much of the *acquis communautaire* was integrated into Swedish law through the European Economic Area (EEA). This made the accession negotiations easier and has contributed to Sweden's high degree of compliance with EC law and single market directives.

Although a consensual style prevailed during the negotiations for membership, and to a large extent also in the making of Swedish policies more broadly and towards the EU, the political priorities have very much been shaped by the Social Democrats. From the outset, a priority of theirs was to turn away the debate from institutional issues in particular. Since Sweden did not join the EU until January 1995, there was formally no possibility of influencing the contents of the Maastricht Treaty. Nevertheless, leading Social Democrats were critical of the focus on institutional reform and monetary union. They wanted to put other issues on the EU agenda, notably the environment and employment. At the same time, politicians across the political spectrum welcomed the insertion in the treaty of the subsidiarity principle, conveniently defining it in terms of "nearness," just as in Britain and Denmark. This served them well when objecting to EU intrusion into domestic matters. Thus, the inside-outside division is clearly present in Swedish attitudes towards European integration (Johansson 1999a).

The socioeconomic, or left-right, dimension has traditionally been the strongest in Sweden, but European integration constitutes a new kind of cleavage in Swedish politics. The pattern of party support and opposition to EU membership still reflects the positions in view of the referendum in November 1994. Accordingly, the Left Party and the Green Party are against, at least nominally, whereas the Social Democratic Party, the Liberal Party, the Moderate Party, the Christian Democratic Party, and the Centre Party remain principally in favour.

At the same time, however, there is opposition to supranational integration within all the basically pro-EU parties. Issues related to the EU have, more or less, disrupted the cohesion within the political parties represented in the *Riksdag*. Intra-party factionalism and conflicts are sometimes difficult to control for party managers. One strategy, most notably employed by the Social Democrats but also by other parties, is to contain intra-party divisions by avoiding clear-cut positions on different issues, such as EMU, and avoiding debate altogether. This strategy of party management, which can be interpreted as a lack of leadership, slows down, if not hinders, Europeanisation (Johansson & Raunio forthcoming). In effect, it is often difficult, not least for other EU governments, to identify the Swedish negotiation positions.

Sweden's approaches to EU affairs during the first years of membership can be characterised as largely reactive rather than proactive (Johansson 1999a). This situation has had negative effects for co-ordination, both horizontally among ministries and vertically between ministries and central administrative agencies. In addition, and perhaps most importantly, Sweden has been an unpredictable partner in the EU. There have probably been many missed opportunities for effective coalition-building, which is very much the name of the game in the EU. This situation has also diminished Sweden's overall influence in the EU.

Domestic Level of Negotiation

In terms of two-level games, it is important to identify the domestic constraints on the international negotiators. Such constraints are provided by interest groups and political parties and not least by public opinion and various opinion formers. As regards basic attitudes to the EU, Eurobarometer data have shown that the Swedes are the most reluctant of the EU citizens (see, for example, Lindahl 1999, 373). This results in restricted room of manoeuvre for Swedish decision-makers. At the same time, however, the Eurosceptical public is sometimes more of an asset than a liability in the context of the EU for Swedish negotiators and policymakers, playing two-level or even multi-level games (Miles 1998). That a Eurosceptical public opinion and thus a small "win-set" provides a safety-valve has, for example, been shown in connection to the accession negotiations and the Social Democratic government's justification for not joining the third stage of EMU initially. The same applies for IGC negotiations.

Public opinion, as well as party politics, reflects a basic anti-federalist and Eurosceptic sentiment. There is a deep-rooted "nation-state logic" behind the Swedish membership of the EU and a broad support for the welfare state and even feelings of uniqueness, some say "welfare chauvinism." In the light of such attitudes and feelings, and also that Sweden entered the EU at a time of economic recession, the EU has been seen by the public, especially by the young and by women, largely as a threat rather than as an opportunity (Ekengren & Sundelius 1998, 146). As for the IGC, *European Voice* (1995) pointed out that the report drawn up by the Swedish government and presented in December 1995 "reflects the scepticism which has grown rapidly since the country joined the EU..." This remark illuminates the constraining impact of public opinion.

To deal with Swedish scepticism, the government decided, in March 1995, to set up a Swedish Parliamentary IGC 96 Committee, with representatives from all political parties. The tasks of this committee was on the one hand, to produce reports on important issues likely to be on the IGC agenda, examine how Sweden could promote its goals in the focused issue areas and gather information on preparation in other Member States. On the other hand, it was also charged with encouraging debate on the main issues and inform the public by arranging seminars, hearings etc, and in this work take great care that both positive and negative views would be aired. The directives for the group especially pointed out the importance of examining "the balance between on the one hand intergovernmental co-operation and, on the other hand, the need for more co-ordinated decision-making procedures." Financial support – 11 million Skr – was granted to stimulate debate, information and opinion-making (Swedish Government 1995a).

In the end more than twenty reports were produced on a number of subjects related to the IGC, such as the CFSP, subsidiarity, enlargement, and the EU institutions, most of which "were unfortunately published very late and had only a marginal effect on the pre-IGC debate" (Lindahl 1996, 39). The reports remained of little importance throughout the IGC and were soon forgotten, as they were not really followed up. This is regrettable, since much research effort was invested in the reports overall. Curiously, and somewhat embarrassing for the Social Democrats, no report on employment was written, since apparently no single researcher was willing to take on this task (interview with Björn von Sydow, 6 June 1997).

Attention should also be drawn to the Advisory Committee on EU Affairs (or the EU Advisory Committee), that was created with the aim of scrutinising the government's handling of EU affairs (Hegeland 1999; Hegeland & Mattson 2000). It follows from its name that the committee is a forum for consultation with the government, which has to inform the *Riksdag* about all matters which are to be dealt with by the Council and has to confer about Sweden's positions on important matters more generally. Formally, the powers of the committee are limited since it is advisory only and therefore cannot bind a minister in regard to the Council negotiations. Nor can it submit issues under deliberation to the chamber for plenary debates.

Nevertheless, the committee exercises a real influence in so far as the committee's recommendations are taken into consideration. And if a minister does not follow the advice given by the committee, the matter could be scrutinised by the Committee on the Constitution and, theoretically, a no-confidence vote could be taken in the chamber. It is also interesting to note, given that IGCs formally are between governments, that the government consulted regularly with the committee during the IGC. The committee met several times at the final stage of the concluding IGC negotiations in Amsterdam in June 1997, having telephone conferences with the Minister for Foreign Affairs and negotiators (Hegeland 1999).

Swedish Positions in the IGC

Sweden's entry into the Union on January 1, 1995, meant that it was immediately thrown into the preparation of the IGC which, according to some debaters, would be a chance to deepen the co-operation and enhance the supranational character of the Union. This presented a problem for Sweden's governing Social Democrats, who did not want to extend the upsetting debate preceding the recent referendum. One could, therefore, at an early stage discern attempts to steer the debate away from institutional questions towards a focus on issues thought to be less controversial and of more direct relevance to the citizens.

Already in the autumn of 1994, the general goals to guide Swedish European policy were set out in the programme of the newly elected Social Democratic government: fighting against unemployment and environmental deterioration, building networks for information and communication, creating a European consumer policy, strengthening the regions, working for a restricted budget policy, for enhanced equality between men and women, for openness towards the rest of the world, for an all-encompassing peace and security arrangement, as well as a commitment to take decisions as close to the citizens as possible (Swedish Government 1994).

These goals also governed the selection and shaping of Swedish positions in the IGC, but it took until July 1995 for the government to present its IGC priorities, by way of a paper signed by the Prime Minister and the Minister for European Affairs. Translated into English, the title was "Swedish principal interests in view of the EU's Intergovernmental Conference of 1996" (Swedish Government 1995b). Whatever the audience this paper primarily aimed at, there was little substance in it, especially when compared to the memoranda presented by other governments in view of or during IGCs. It seemed that the paper was written in great haste, in the light of pressures from various sources, not least from the media.

Following a critical report from the Committee on the Constitution (Konstitutionsutskottet, KU) (Swedish Parliament 1994a), the government's IGC policy was therefore further elaborated and the official positions were presented to the parliament in December the same year (Swedish Government 1995c). The approach was, however, still quite broad and the proposals rather vague. The government essentially reaffirmed the foremost goals of promoting popular support and democratic legitimacy, clearing the way for further enlargement as well as promoting co-operation in the areas of employment and the environment (thus giving substance to the notion of citizen's Europe). The report stressed the issues of openness and transparency, subsidiarity, a new title for employment, and defence policy developed to include the Petersberg tasks. It also gave attention to free movement of people, strengthened co-operation in the justice and police areas, the need to reduce decision-making procedures, a more efficient CFSP, a safeguard of the institutional representation of small countries and, finally, showed a marked scepticism towards a Europe *à la carte*.

Presenting this position paper to the parliament, Mats Hellström, the Swedish Minister for European Affairs, pointed out that three priorities had guided the work: to give EU co-operation a stronger support from citizens, to prepare for enlargement, and to strengthen co-operation in areas considered to be important, especially employment and the environment (speech by Hellström, 7 December 1995).

Although the second priority, preparation for enlargement, figured a lot in the rhetoric, the opposition from the right claimed that the emphasis put on the other two rather worked against enlargement, and that the government in that way diverted much needed energy and attention from the institutional issues. "The government emphasises certain favourite questions on the national arena, for instance employment, youth issues and consumer policy, this might lead to a marginalisation of Swedish influence in the IGC," thundered Lars F. Tobisson, deputy chairman of the Moderate Party (*Dagens Nyheter*, 7 December 1995). The government was almost ridiculed for not having grasped what the whole IGC exercise was really about.

The criticism levelled from the left instead followed up on one of the themes from the referendum debate and concerned the government's alleged sell-out of Swedish national sovereignty and neutrality (*Dagens Nyheter*, 30 November and 2 December 1995). A speech by Foreign Minister Lena Hjelm-Wallén in the spring of 1995 stirred up strong feelings as she suggested considering giving up the national veto in some issues in the CFSP (speech by Hjelm-Wallén, 30 May 1995). The Green and the Left parties also took every opportunity to press for another referendum on the results of the new treaty (EU Advisory Committee).

The government finally decided upon Swedish positions after consultation with the Swedish Riksdag. The EU Advisory Committee was given information in advance and reports after negotiation meetings (Swedish Parliament 1994b), thus allowing the parliamentarians to follow the process closely and give continuous input on negotiation positions.

Most of the preparations of the more detailed positions were carried out in the EU-secretariat in the Ministry of Foreign Affairs, which in the IGC organisation was working directly under the government. The under-secretary of state, Gunnar Lund, was appointed as Swedish member in the Reflection Group and he also served as the government's representative in the IGC. It was mainly through Lund that the government consulted with the EU Advisory Committee.

The EU-secretariat also led an interdepartmental consultation group, which was composed of chairmen from 10 different working groups from varying ministries, dealing with questions as wide-ranging as consumer policy or foreign and security policy (IGC 96 Committee 1996).

The government's strategy in the actual IGC negotiation was to avoid biting off more than could be chewed, thus concentrating efforts on three to four issues. Employment, the environment and openness were singled out as the three main priorities (interview with Sven-Olof Petersson, 15 December 1997).

On employment, the Swedish government started early to lobby other Member States. First of all, a paper setting out Swedish ideas on the subject was presented in the Reflection Group. Secondly, governments showing some interest in the question were invited to Stockholm for a meeting in March 1996 to discuss how employment could be incorporated in the treaty (*Dagens Nyheter*, 14 March 1996; interview with Gunnar Lund, 11 September 1997). These governments included above all those of Austria, Belgium, Ireland, Denmark and Finland (see separate chapters in this volume). Thirdly, two position papers were presented which filled out the details (Swedish Government 1996a+b).

Essentially, besides specifying employment as a Union objective, the government wanted to create a new title for employment, with the view of co-ordinating the employment policy at Community level, develop common strategies to fight unemployment and also supervise their implementation. This meant that all Member States would be obliged to draw up employment programmes. These would be assessed annually by the Commission and the Council. Should it be that the objectives were not fulfilled, the Commission should be able to issue recommendations to the errant Member State. To facilitate such co-ordination and review of the work, it was also proposed to establish an Employment Committee (Swedish Government 1996a+b).

Concerning the issue of openness and transparency, the government also presented two papers to the IGC. The emphasis in the Swedish proposals lay on access to documents as a basic principle in the treaty. The reasoning behind this was that transparency could facilitate an understanding of and participation in the process, thus strengthening the democratic character of the Union and opening the way for a more efficient public administration. To fortify the general principle, Sweden wanted to lay down access to documents in a treaty article, and also to make a list of exceptions to the rule of access in the article, for instance to protect security of Member States, their economic interests, industrial secrets or relations to third countries, etc. (Swedish Government 1996c+d).

Backing up the Swedish papers on openness, civil servants from the Ministry of Justice made a tour of capitals to explain what was meant by the Swedish "offentlighetsprincipen" (the principle of public access to official documents) and the Swedish proposal. In addition, staffs from the governmental archives were invited to Stockholm to see for themselves how the system worked. The misconceptions were legio in the beginning of the process and Swedish proposals were treated with much scepticism (interview with Sven-Olof Petersson, 15 December 1997).

On the third core question, environment, the Swedish aim was to strengthen existing provisions, by more explicitly referring to environment and sustainable development among the objectives of the Union and also by integrating environmental aspects into other policy areas, such as agriculture and transport. Above all, Sweden proposed to change the treaty to allow Member States to set higher environmental standards, if justified with regard to environmental concerns and approved by the Commission as not constituting arbitrary discrimination or restrictions of trade (Swedish Government 1996e).

In addition to promoting these main priorities, the Swedish government was also active in other areas. For instance, it sought to incorporate the promotion of equal treatment and equal opportunities in the treaty, as well as to integrate consideration of equality in all issue areas, emphasising especially equal pay for equal work and the right to adopt measures to encourage and facilitate training and vocational activity for the underrepresented sex (Swedish Government 1996f). In addition to a position paper, an informal paper was handed to the Irish presidency. This apparently served as a basis for their draft articles on the subject. To lobby for such an inclusion, civil servants from the Ministry of Social Affairs paid visits to their colleagues in Dublin (interview with Sven-Olof Petersson, 15 December 1997), but also explained and clarified the Swedish position in several other capitals (Bergqvist & Jungar 1999,181).

As Sweden had high aims also concerning consumer policy, a paper on this had been prepared, but was never presented for fear of asking too much. Instead, the proposal was handed over to the Finnish delegation, which had not, up to that point, presented a paper (interview with Sven-Olof Petersson, 15 December 1997).

The close co-operation with Finland showed also in the joint initiative on an enhanced role for the EU in crisis and conflict management. This was proposed to be created through a revision of TEU/J.4 (1) by including humanitarian and rescue operations, peacekeeping and crisis management (the Petersberg tasks) into the CFSP as membership tasks. Moreover, operationalisation of EU competence in military crisis management would take place by the establishment of a reinforced institutional link between the Union and the WEU (thus revising TEU J.4 (2)). These proposals were first presented in a joint article, published on the same day in two leading national newspapers, by the Foreign Ministers Tarja Halonen and Lena Hjelm-Wallén (*Dagens Nyheter* 1996b). Later position papers filled in the details (Swedish and Finnish Governments 1996).

On other questions, such as institutional issues and flexibility, the Swedish government kept a rather low profile throughout the negotiation, reluctant to reopen any debate on national sovereignty and influence so soon after the referendum debate. *European Voice* (1995), for instance, commented that the report of the Swedish government "devotes little attention to the Reflection Group's preoccupation with maintaining the efficiency of the EU institutions."

Just as most other small- and middle-sized states, Sweden wanted to safeguard the institutional balance and the balance between the Member States. Consequently, the government said no to changes in the composition of the Commission. Concerning the reweighting of votes in the Council, the government first backed the proposal on double majority, but (after persuasion from the Finnish delegation) came to the conclusion that this would in the long run disadvantage smaller states. Instead, Sweden came to argue for finding a mathematical formula for allocating votes that could then be used to underpin the extrapolation of votes also in view of further enlargements. The point was to avoid going through the same upsetting discussion each time a new member would be accepted (EU Advisory Committee).

In the end, the Swedish government accepted the flexibility clause despite the fact that the notion of flexibility was seen as favourable for the larger Member States, eventually forming a hard core. However, it was stressed that flexibility would be of limited use given the right of veto and that it was done for reasons of solidarity among Member States accepted (EU Advisory Committee).

The Swedish government was also largely opposed to changes of the rules for qualified majority voting in the Council, except on environmental questions (Swedish Government 1995c) and co-operated in blocking further extension on for instance visas and border controls (Svensson 2000, 161).

At the outset, third pillar issues were not really prioritised by the Swedish government, but it came to be deeply involved in the discussion on the inclusion of the Schengen agreement in the treaty. This was subsequently accepted. However, a condition for this was that a solution to the matter of relations with the EEA countries Norway and Iceland could be found, in the light of the Nordic passport union (EU Advisory Committee).

Bilateral and Transnational Alliances

The Nordic countries certainly had similar interests in the IGC, all focusing efforts on the environment, employment, openness and the overall goal of preparing for enlargement (see Jonas Tallberg's contribution in this volume). However, there was no united "Nordic bloc," instead the governments opted for co-ordination in relevant issues.

The man behind this strategy was Niels Ersbøll, Denmark's experienced negotiator and former secretary-general of the Council (interview with Sven-Olof Petersson, 15 December 1997). His advice was that instead of talking with one voice all the time, several Nordic voices should be heard saying similar things, emphasising different details, but co-ordinating so that they would not thwart each other's interests. So even if both Denmark and Sweden gave openness high priority they went forward on separate fronts: Denmark's paper on openness focused mainly on making Council meetings official, whereas the Swedish paper concerned access to documents. The strategy was similar on the two countries' papers on employment.

Good personal relations between negotiation teams also meant that the Swedish and Finnish negotiators co-operated rather closely (interview with Heidi Kaila, 24 April 1998). Their joint proposal on the Petersberg tasks, the only exception to the rule of mere co-ordination, was well received in the other capitals, especially the fact that two non-aligned countries were prepared to rethink and re-evaluate an issue so crucial for them. This was seen to have set a good example, giving an important and constructive start to the discussion (Svensson 2000).

There was also co-operation with the aim of influencing the IGC negotiations among nongovernmental actors, including organised interests and political parties. There are longstanding cross-national networks of interaction between such actors in the Nordic area, where also regional and local authorities have established links across borders. In connection to the IGC, interest groups carried out influence strategies through organisations at the EU level, including the European Trade Union Confederation (ETUC), the Union of Industrial and Employers' Confederations of Europe (UNICE), and the Committee of Professional Agricultural Organisations in the European Community (COPA).

The Swedish political parties operated through Europarties. For the governing Social Democrats, the membership of the Party of European Socialists (PES) provided channels for access to other governing PES member parties. Specifically, there are the PES pre-meetings to European Council summits and the group of Sherpas, that is, the personal representatives of party leaders in government. These representatives prepare European Council summits and seek to co-ordinate EU policies more broadly. Such concerted efforts have, for example, been made in the issue area of employment, notably in the context of the IGC. As has been shown elsewhere, the employment title was to a large extent a result of a transnational policy contribution (Johansson 1999b). Those favouring such a title, and a strengthening of the co-ordination between Member States with regard to employment policies, constituted a transnational alliance, or an advocacy coalition. Among governments, the Swedish Social Democratic government was a driving force in that alliance, along with representatives of the EU institutions of the European Parliament and the European Commission, and of the ETUC and the PES. Although this transnational alliance was mobilised throughout the IGC, its impact was apparently greatest in the early agenda-setting stages and then even before the official opening of the IGC in late March 1996. From then on, and especially during the later stages, governments took a firmer grip on the process.

However, as "party governments" they suffered domestic constraints, as they were tied by electoral and party concerns, links to interest groups, and by public opinion.

Ratification of the Amsterdam Treaty

The Swedish government was very satisfied with the agreement reached in Amsterdam. Even if no solution had been found on the difficult institutional issues, the enlargement process was on track and, most importantly, the results on its three main issues of employment, the environment and openness were quite close to original Swedish positions. Above all, the Social Democrats claimed victory when the separate title on employment in the concluding treaty was a fact (Johansson 1999b).

To inform the public on the contents of the Amsterdam Treaty and stimulate a debate in view of the ratification, a large campaign was launched. The critics, however, argued that it seemed rather to concentrate on the putative success of the government's proposals than on actually reviewing and explaining the results.

The debate that followed was rather half-hearted. It focused above all on the incorporation of Schengen, the defence dimensions and issues of democracy and was conducted almost exclusively in the *Riksdag*, which ratified the Amsterdam Treaty on 29 April 1998. Since the treaty would entail a transfer of powers to the EU level, the Swedish constitution stipulated that a 3/4 majority was needed for ratification. This presented no problem. The treaty was adopted by 229 votes to 40, with 4 abstentions and 76 members absent. The Green party and the Left party were against ratification of the treaty (Swedish Parliament 1998).

Preparing for the IGC 2000

Whereas the government presented a rather long list of priorities for the Swedish presidency of the EU in the first half of the year 2001, a short agenda, including nothing more than the Amsterdam leftovers, was advocated for the IGC 2000 (see, for example, *Dagens Nyheter* 1999a). The report of the Three Wise Men, advocating a broader revision, was therefore not really welcomed (*Dagens Nyheter* 1999b). This stance was again motivated with a concern for the enlargement process, but to a large extent this no doubt had to do with the fact that likely issues on a wider agenda, not least defence, remain controversial in Swedish domestic politics and could affect the EMU debate. Moreover, the Social Democratic minority government had to take into account its informal coalition with the two anti-EU Green and Left parties.

Despite the basically anti-federalist stance one can nonetheless identify a growing awareness on the part of Swedish government ministers that supranationalism in the sense of strong EU institutions and decision-making procedures could be advantageous for the relatively small Member States, fearing the emergence of *directoires* among larger states. It follows that the Swedish government will defend the role of the Commission in particular. In general, positions on the questions of composition of the Commission, reweighting of votes in the Council and extension of qualified majority voting were essentially unaltered since the previous IGC.

Although Sweden has been an enthusiastic and unequivocal supporter of enlargement, the government has been cautious in questions related to institutional reforms and constitutional choice. Sweden has performed the role of an advocate especially for the Baltic states and a close relationship has also been established with Poland.

For the foreseeable future, the Swedish policy of non-participation in military alliances, with the aim of making it possible for the country to remain neutral in the event of a war in its vicinity, is likely to remain unchanged. However, the Social Democratic government has adopted a more pragmatic attitude towards existing alliances and joint operations. Some high-profile initiatives were prepared in regard to peacekeeping, crisis management and conflict prevention, which somewhat presumptuously is claimed to be a Swedish "trade mark." Anyway, it remains difficult for a Swedish government of whatever political colour to accept a common defence within the EU.

The Swedish Social Democratic government proclaims the employment title as a model for treaty changes in regard to other issue areas, such as consumer protection and equality between the sexes (Lindh 1999; Persson 1998). This implies that such matters would also be of common concern in the EU, but without binding supranational legislation and a supervisory role for the Court of Justice. Instead, "soft law" would apply in the form of guidelines and comparisons among the Member States, adopting national action plans and putting pressure on each other. This method has been called a "third way" between supranationalism and intergovernmentalism and even "offensive intergovernmentalism." However, in our view it is defensive rather in that it must be interpreted as an attempt to take the edge off the drive for further European integration along a federalist path.

In any event, the Social Democratic government is a victim of conflicting pressures arising from different constituencies, most notably from within the party itself and from EU partners. However, after the hesitancy characterising the first years of membership, the Swedish government would like to appear as a mainstream and constructive partner.

Bibliography

Bergqvist, Christina & Ann-Cathrine Jungar (1999). "Adaption or Diffusion of the Swedish Gender Model?," pp. 160-179, in Linda Hantrais (ed.), *Gendered Politics in Europe: Reconciling Employment and Family Life*, Basingstoke: Macmillan.

Dagens Nyheter (1995a). "Svensk öppenhet behövs i EU," 30 November.

Dagens Nyheter (1995b). "Ny omröstning om EU möjlig," 2 December.

Dagens Nyheter (1995c). "Sverige riskerar att marginaliseras," 7 December.

Dagens Nyheter (1996a). "Samling för jobb i EU," 14 March.

Dagens Nyheter (1996b). "Svensk-finsk WEU-aktion," 21 April.

Dagens Nyheter (1999a). "Ordföranden föreslås få mer makt," 19 october.

Dagens Nyheter (1999b). "Djärva förslag om EU reformer," 19 october.

Ekengren, Magnus & Bengt Sundelius (1998). "Sweden: The State Joins the European Union," pp. 131-148, in Kenneth Hanf & Ben Soetendorp (eds.), *Adapting to European Integration: Small States and the European Union*, London and New York: Longman.

European Voice (1995). "Nordics prepare IGC strategy," 7–13 December.

Evans, Peter B. et al. (1993). *Double-Edged Diplomacy: International Bargaining and Domestic Politics*, Berkeley: University of California Press.

Gilljam, Mikael & Sören Holmberg (eds.) (1996). *Ett knappt ja till EU: Väljarna och folkomröstningen 1994*, Stockholm: Norstedts.

Gustavsson, Jakob (1998). *The Politics of Foreign Policy Change: Explaining the Swedish Reorientation on EC Membership*, Lund: Lund University Press.

Hampson, Fen Osler with Michael Hart (1995/1999). *Multilateral Negotiations: Lessons from Arms Control, Trade, and the Environment*, Baltimore: The Johns Hopkins University Press.

Hegeland, Hans (1999). *Riksdagen, Europeiska Unionen och Demokratin: En studie av riksdagens arbete med EU-frågor*, Licentiate dissertation, Department of Political Science, Lund: Lund University.

Hegeland, Hans & Ingvar Mattson (2000). "Another Link in the Chain: The Effects of EU Membership on Delegation and Accountability in Sweden," *The Journal of Legislative Studies*, Vol. 6, No. 1, pp. 81-104.

IGC 1996 Committee (1996). *"EU:s regeringskonferens. Lägesrapport från EU 96 Kommittén,"* SOU, 1996:76.

Johansson, Karl Magnus (ed.) (1999a). *Sverige i EU*, Stockholm, SNS Förlag.

Johansson, Karl Magnus (1999b). "Tracing the employment title in the Amsterdam treaty: uncovering transnational coalitions," *Journal of European Public Policy*, Vol. 6, No.1, pp. 85-101.

Johansson, Karl Magnus & Tapio Raunio (forthcoming). "Partisan responses to Europe: comparing Finnish and Swedish political parties," Manuscript prepared for publication in *European Journal of Political Research*.

Lindahl, Rutger (1996). "The Swedish Debate," pp. 37-50, in Josef Janning et al., *The 1996 IGC–National Debates (2)*, London: The Royal Institute of International Affairs. Discussion Paper 67.

Lindahl, Rutger (1999). "Mångtydig EU-opinion," in Sören Holmberg & Lennart Weibull (eds.), *Den ljusnande framtid*, Gothenburg: University of Gothenburg. SOM-report, No. 22.

Lindh, Anna (1999). "Stoppa slöseriet i EU," *Dagens Nyheter*, 17 September.

Lodge, Juliet (1998). "Negotiations in the European Union: The 1996 Intergovernmental Conference, *International Negotiation*, Vol. 3, No. 3, pp. 345-362.

Luif, Paul (1995). *On the Road to Brussels: The Political Dimension of Austria's, Finland's and Sweden's Accession to the European Union*, Wien: Braumüller. Laxenburg Papers, No. 11.

Mazzucelli, Colette (1997). *France and Germany at Maastricht: Politics and Negotiations to Create the European Union*, New York and London: Garland Publishing.

Miles, Lee (1997). *Sweden and European Integration*, Aldershot: Ashgate.

Miles, Lee (1998). "Sweden and the Intergovernmental Conference: Testing the Membership Diamond," *Cooperation and Conflict*, Vol. 33, No. 4, pp. 339-366.

Moravcsik, Andrew (1998). *The Choice for Europe: Social Purpose and State Power from Messina to Maastricht*, Ithaca: Cornell University Press.

Persson, Göran (1998). "Följ vår jämställdhetsmodell!," *Dagens Nyheter*, 11 December.

Putnam, Robert (1988). "Diplomacy and domestic politics: The logic of two-level games," *International Organization*, Vol. 42, No. 3, pp. 427-460.

Svensson, Anna-Carin (2000). *In the Service of the European Union. The Role of the Presidency in Negotiating the Amsterdam Treaty 1995–97*, Uppsala: Acta Universitatis Upsaliensis.

Swedish Government (1994)."Regeringsförklaring," Prop. 1994/95: 4.

Swedish Government (1995a). "Kommittédirektiv. Utredning inför 96 års regeringskonferens med EUs medlemsstater för översyn av Fördraget om Europeiska Unionen," Dir. 1995:15.

Swedish Government (1995b). *Svenska principiella intressen inför EU:s regeringskonferens 1996*, Stockholm: Regeringskansliet.

Swedish Government (1995c). *EU:s regeringskonferens 1996*, Regeringens skrivelse 1995/96:30.

Swedish Government (1996a). "Employment," CONF/3859/1/96.

Swedish Government (1996b). "Proposals on Treaty Amendments on Employment," CONF/3921/96.

Swedish Government (1996c). "Transparency – Access to Documents," CONF/3853/96.

Swedish Government (1996d). "Transparency," CONF/3899/96.

Swedish Government (1996e). "Proposals on Treaty Amendments on Environment," CONF/3922/96.

Swedish Government (1996f). "Proposals on Treaty Amendments on Equality between Men and Women," CONF/3898/96.

Swedish and Finnish Governments (1996). "Note on Security and Defence," CONF/3946/46.

Swedish Parliament (1994a). "Konstitutionsutskottets betänkande," 1994/95:KU43.

Swedish Parliament (1994b). "Debatt om EUs regeringskonferens," Prot. 1994/95: 113

Swedish Parliament (1998). "Debatt om Amsterdamfördraget," Prot. 1997/98: 99.

Tsebelis, George (1990). *Nested Games: Rational Choice in Comparative Politics*, Berkeley: University of California Press.

Zartman, I. William (ed.) (1994). *International Multilateral Negotiation: Approaches to the Management of Complexity*, San Fransisco: Jossey-Bass.

Speeches
Speech by Mats Hellström to the Swedish Parliament, 7 December 1995.
Towards a New European Security Order – a Swedish view, speech by Lena Hjelm-Wallén, Brussels, 30 May 1995.

Archives
EU Advisory Committee in the Swedish Parliament. Shorthand records of deliberations from the Committee's meetings with Swedish negotiators 1995–97. Stockholm.

Interviews
Heidi Kaila, member of the Finnish IGC team, 24 April 1998.

Gunnar Lund, personal representative of the Swedish Foreign Minister in the Reflection Group and during the IGC, 11 September 1997.

Sven-Olof Petersson, Swedish deputy negotiator, 15 December 1997.

Björn von Sydow, Swedish Government Minister, Chairman of the Swedish Parliamentary IGC 96 Committee, 6 June 1997.

16

The United Kingdom: From Isolation Towards Influence?

Edward Best[1]

Introduction

The negotiations for the "1996" Intergovernmental Conference (IGC), understood as the time between the decision of the Corfu European Council in 1994 to set up a preparatory "Reflection Group" and the signature of the Amsterdam Treaty on 2 October 1997, coincided with – and are inseparable from – a period of transformation in British politics.

That period saw, internally, the collapse in support for a ruling Conservative Party which was tearing itself apart precisely over Europe, and the emergence of a "New" Labour Party, under the leadership of Tony Blair, which would win a landslide victory in the general elections of 1 May 1997. Externally, it was a point of inflection in the British political class's efforts to come to terms with a post-Cold War Europe in which the UK is looking for its place.

1996 saw a new low in British credibility as a European partner. May 1997 brought promises and expectations that this was the start of something New. There has undeniably been a remarkable change in attitudes and perceptions; yet is the difference more of content or of style? In the first paragraphs of the White Paper presented to the IGC 2000, Tony Blair himself stresses that, "unlike its predecessors," his Government is unwaveringly pro-European but that it will continue to defend British "national interests" (UK 2000). Did the "1996" negotiations and what followed in fact confirm that there are strong underlying continuities in British interests, and that the differences are more in negotiating style and strategy?

This contribution does not try to reconstruct in detail the British role in the 1996-97 IGC. It looks at the nature of the British interests pursued in the 1996-97 IGC; at how and why the UK was relatively isolated during most of the process; and at the prospects, following the change of government, for an effective UK strategy to build influence as a leading European player. Did the UK learn to negotiate in and as, rather than with, Europe?

---

[1] The author wishes to thank Mark Gray for his help, as well as Finn Laursen and Sophie Vanhoonacker for comments.

The Positions and Proposals of the Major Government

The Conservative Government's positions on the main issues of concern were outlined by Prime Minister John Major to the House of Commons on 1 March 1995.[2] The basic lines of the British approach to the IGC were then formulated in the UK's White Paper, "A Partnership of Nations," published in March 1996. These were expanded upon in the series of documents presented to the IGC as the negotiations developed (see Table 16.1).

Table 16.1: UK Positions at the 1996-97 IGC

General Approach		
White Paper, "A Partnership of Nations"	13.03.96	--
Constitutional/Institutional Issues		
Subsidiarity – proposed Protocol	30.08.96	CONF/3896/96
Subsidiarity – Non-Paper	14.10.96	CONF/3947/96
Quality of Legislation	24.07.96	CONF/3885/96
Role of National Parliaments	22.10.96	CONF/3961/96
National Parliaments	11.04.97	CONF/3871/97
Memorandum – Court of Justice	30.07.96	CONF/3883/96
Amendment of Arts. 100a (1) & 130s (2)	23.09.96	CONF/3919/96
Legal personality	05.06.97	--
Financial Management		
Court of Auditors and financial management	19.02.97	CONF/3825/97
Financial management, fraud and the Court of Auditors	23.05.97	--
Policies		
Common Fisheries Policy – Draft Protocol	22.07.96	CONF/3884/96
Quota-hopping	11.12.96	CONF/2502/96
Article 42. Competition rules for agriculture products	24.07.96	CONF/3886/96
Memorandum – Animal welfare	24.07.96	CONF/3887/96

---

[2] *Official Report*, 1 March 1995, cols. 1063-4.

Policies		
Suggested amendment to animal welfare protocol	05.06.97	--
Memorandum – TransEuropean Networks	24.07.96	CONF/3888/96
Working time	12.11.96	CONF/3978/96
Protocol on direct taxaation (UK/D)	27.05.97	CONF/3922/97
External economic relations	02.06.97	--
Common Foreign and Security Policy		
European Defence issues	01.03.95	--
Memorandum – Representative	30.07.96	CONF/3893/96
Memorandum – Planning Cell	30.07.96	CONF/3894/96
Defence	05.06.97	SN/560/97
Financing: suggested amendments to IIA and J.17	02.06.97	--
Justice and Home Affairs		
JHA – scope of application	23.09.96	CONF/3918/96
Other		
Statistics	14.04.97	--
Sugested declaration on the interests of disabled people	09.06.97	SN/602/97

The fundamental outlook remained that of the "awkward partner:" the UK would not accept "further European integration which is driven by ideology rather than the prospect of practical benefit." The common emphasis underlying the proposals was the stated desire in the White Paper that the UK Government wanted a Union "which concentrates single-mindedly only on what needs to be done at a European level, and doing it well."

Subsidiarity

In the March 1996 White Paper, the UK Government stated that it would seek inclusion in the Treaty of elements of the subsidiarity guidelines agreed at the 1992 Edinburgh European Council. This proposal was fleshed out in two subsequent documents. In August 1996, the UK presented a draft Protocol on the application of the principle of subsidiarity which goes somewhat further than the Edinburgh conclusions (and of the final text of the Protocol attached to the EC Treaty at Amsterdam) in its definition of the criteria which must be satisfied before the Community can act.³

National Parliaments
The White Paper also stressed that "National parliaments remain the primary focus of democratic legitimacy in the European Union." The UK would consider making the main elements of Maastricht Declaration 13 on national parliaments legally binding, including a minimum period for parliaments to scrutinise Community documents and notably draft legislation; as well as giving a greater role to national parliaments in the Justice and Home Affairs Pillar.

These proposals were further developed in the Memorandum of October 1996, which proposed inserting into the EC Treaty a provision stipulating a minimum period of four weeks for parliamentary scrutiny of legislative proposals; and into the Treaty on European Union a requirement for the elaboration of six-monthly written reports on Justice and Home Affairs and CFSP which the Member States could distribute to their national parliaments.

In April 1997, the UK delegation presented amendments in this sense to the protocol proposed in the Dublin II outline, and again insisted on inserting a new article into the TEU.

European Union and the Citizens
In contrast to the widespread view elsewhere that the European Union should incorporate new rights and adopt new policies in order to become closer to its citizens, the White Paper explicitly suggested that the EU was more likely to win popular support precisely by doing less – and better – rather than by trying to do more.

It was pointed out that *fundamental rights* were already more than sufficiently protected in Europe: making European rights and duties more extensive and explicit could create fears that the EU had a vocation to become a state. The UK did not support EU accession to the European Convention on Human Rights.

Whereas the White Paper argued that problems of discrimination are best dealt with through national legislation, the UK delegation ostensibly welcomed the introduction of a *non-discrimination* clause in the Irish draft treaty of December 1996, but wanted this not to have direct effect.

The Major Government stressed that *employment* continued to be a central preoccupation for the UK, but maintained its insistence on opting out from the

---

³ In October 1996, the British delegation produced an informal document comparing the draft Protocol elaborated by the Irish Presidency with the UK's own text and the Edinburgh conclusions.

Social Chapter, and opposed inclusion of a new chapter on employment in the Treaty. In November 1996 the UK presented a Memorandum mainly aimed at preventing qualified-majority voting being used, as a result of the legal base adopted, for questions of social policy which the UK considered should be dealt with in the framework of the 1992 Social Agreement signed between the other Member States at Maastricht.[4]

Fraud and Financial Management
On the other hand, the UK argued that public support could be increased if there were visible improvements in the fight against *fraud* and in *financial management* of the Community. This was not simple Brussels-bashing – the White Paper recognised that most "waste and mismanagement ... occurs at the level of the Member State rather than in the Community institutions." The UK presented specific proposals in a Memorandum of February 1997 aimed at strengthening the ability of the Court of Auditors to obtain information from all organisations and persons managing or receiving Community funds, including the power to take to the Court of Justice any Member State which refuses to comply, and to take action against persons, in cooperation with national authorities, in order to ensure compliance. This last power would require modifying Article 173 so that the Auditors' actions could be challenged before the Court of Justice. The UK also supported the Benelux proposal to give the Court of Auditors the right under Article 173 to protect its prerogatives.

Institutional questions
The Conservative Government was flatly opposed to any extension of *qualified-majority voting* – or of *co-decision*.[5]

The White Paper urged changes, preferably by *re-weighting of votes*, to the system of qualified-majority voting to ensure that "countries representing a significant percentage of the EU's population or the major net contributors as a group" could not be outvoted.

---

[4] The proposal was essentially to amend Articles 54, 57 and 118a to ensure that unanimity applied to working conditions, and to adopt a Protocol stating that the *Working Time Directive* (93/104/EC) had been adopted under the Social Agreement, excluding the UK.

[5] Moreover, in its September 1996 Memorandum on Articles 100a(2) and 130s(2), the UK argued that the wording of the provisions for decision-making by QMV in the internal market and environment respectively should be modified so as to make it absolutely clear that they were not intended to be used for fiscal matters, which remained subject to unanimity.

With regard to the *number of Commissioners*, the White Paper did not state an explicit preference, but the UK was reported in the discussions to be prepared to consider going beyond the principle of one Commissioner per Member State, and to be sympathetic to the French proposal for a Commission of 10-12 Members under a strong President.

The UK was not in favour of giving the European Union *legal personality*, and introduced a late proposal on 5 June 1997 suggesting that the Presidency might be mandated by the Council to sign agreements with one or more states or international organisations in the areas of CFSP and Justice and Home Affairs.

"Quality of Legislation"

Numerous proposals aimed at improving the "legislative process" were developed in the UK's July 1996 Note on the "quality of legislation":

- better *consultation*, including the obligatory distribution of Green Papers for all proposed legislation having a direct effect on persons or companies, a minimum period for scrutiny by national parliaments, and public access to expert analyses and fiches d'impact;
- greater control by the Council over implementing decisions adopted by the Commission, by allowing the Council to modify the legislation on "*Comitology*" without requiring a Commission proposal and to modify a Commission proposal by qualified majority with regard to the kind of comitology committee to be established, as well as by creating a single set of rules of procedure applicable to all committees;
- the possibility for the Council to consult the Court of Justice as to the *legal base* proposed by the Commission before an Act's adoption, as well as to challenge it afterwards;
- the automatic *withdrawal of Commission proposals* if not adopted before the end of each Commission's term;
- "*sunset clauses*" in Community legislation providing for expiry or automatic review after a fixed period;
- better *drafting;* and
- measures to improve *respect for Community law*, including clearer and more effective procedures for complaints, the obligation for the Commission to publish annual reports on its controlling activities, encouragement for the Commission to use Article 171 in ensuring compliance with Court rulings, increased resources for Commission controlling activities, reciprocal training programmes between the Member

States to spread best practice, administrative cooperation, and creation of an internal audit team in the Commission.

Court of Justice
While recognising the importance of a strong and independent Court, the White Paper drew attention to "judgments in recent years that have given cause for concern, particularly where they have imposed disproportionate costs on Governments or business, even when they have made every effort to meet their EC obligations. There is concern that the ECJ's interpretation of laws sometimes seems to go beyond what the participating Governments intended in framing these laws." Among the UK proposals, which were made in considerable detail in the Memorandum presented by the UK in July 1996, were "strengthening the ability of the Court to limit retrospective application of its judgments; introducing the principle that a Member State should only be liable for damages in cases of serious and manifest breach of its obligations;... streamlined procedures for the rapid amendment of EC legislation which has been interpreted in a way which was never intended by the Council." The possible options proposed to achieve this last point included the right for the Council to introduce corrective amendments with the normal participation of the European Parliament (according to the procedure specified in the Treaty Article in question) but without the need for a Commission proposal.

Common Foreign and Security Policy
The UK presented itself in the White Paper as a strong proponent of a "more active and effective" *CFSP*, but insisted on "maintaining its intergovernmental character." In no event would the UK accept "a commitment to be constrained by collective decisions which we do not support."

The Government also sought the development of *defence* cooperation as a means to strengthen the overall contribution which European countries could make to global and regional security. Yet the UK insisted that this should be on a purely intergovernmental basis, and that the Atlantic Alliance should remain the "bedrock" of European security. The UK Government recognised that European countries should also be able to act on their own when necessary, and saw the Western European Union (WEU) as the appropriate framework for such cooperation. The WEU, however, should be maintained as an autonomous organisation.

In the course of the negotiations the UK supported the inclusion of the "Petersberg tasks," but argued for only a very limited increase in the capacities of the EU institutions themselves in the area of CFSP. With regard to the tasks of a *Planning Unit* in the Council Secretariat, the UK proposed in its July 1996 Memorandum that the Unit should be incorporated in the existing

Directorate-General E; that five or six additional officials seconded from national foreign ministries plus liaison officers from the Commission and from the WEU would be quite sufficient; and that this supplementary capacity should be treated as a flexible resource. There would be no formal obligation for the Member States to transmit confidential information to the Council Secretariat. In another Memorandum of July 1996 the UK proposed that a *CFSP Representative* should be an official responsible to the Council, with the same rank as the Council Secretary-General.

Justice and Home Affairs
With regard to Justice and Home Affairs, the UK was adamant throughout the process about preserving the right to carry out border controls, and maintained a general insistence on intergovernmental approaches to cooperation based on unanimity.

The UK's September 1996 Memorandum on the objectives and scope of application of the Third Pillar proposed replacing the existing Article K by two new articles and to expand Article K.1. The new Article K would state the general objective of creating an area of freedom (including free movement of persons), security and justice. The new Article K *bis,* however, would introduce limiting conditions. Cooperative actions would only take place if they were to combat a serious threat to the citizens of the Union or if they required cross-border cooperation; or if, following the principle of subsidiarity, the objectives could not be achieved satisfactorily by the Member States acting individually.

The new Article K.1 would contain an expanded and modified list of fields of common interest. The reference to police cooperation would be rephrased to make it clear that Europol was no more than one of the aspects of police cooperation, and to provide explicitly for cooperation between police, customs and all other competent authorities (including, for example, financial controllers). The fight against terrorism, and the fight and against international corruption should be added.

Flexibility
Despite John Major's having himself contributed to this emerging debate in his Leiden speech of September 1994, the UK was generally reticent about flexibility, especially in the First Pillar, where there are British concerns as to practicability, with some lingering echoes of historical balance-of-power considerations: "a fear that the institutionalisation of flexibility would legitimise a hard core of member states which would drive the integration process forward against the will of the United Kingdom" (Stubb 1998, 203). In the first, rather confused, debates in May 1996, the UK seems to have argued for flexibility in the First Pillar on a case-by-case basis and not at all

in the Second and Third. The UK then "shifted from supporting case-by-case flexibility in the First Pillar to opposing any differentiation in Community matters" although in the Second Pillar the British Government could now envisage case-by-case flexibility" (Stubb 1998, 202). By early 1997 the British position was getting tougher, arguing that closer cooperation should not lead to a situation in which non-participants would be unable to join at a later stage; that no Member State should be forced to participate; that the cooperating Member States bear all the costs; that others should have observer status and have the right to voice their opinion in matters dealt with by the flexibility group (Stubb 1998, 226). UK IGC representative David Davis argued on 26 February 1997 that "Another UK condition for flexibility is that it must not presume there is a common goal in all areas. There must be room for permanent opt-outs, where necessary. Yet the Franco-German approach is predicated on a vision of a common destination ... Franco-German rhetoric assumes that all integration is good. We do not. And we will not accept any proposal that allows those who do not join to be penalized in any way." (*Agence Europe* 1 March 1997).

Other Issues
In July 1996, the UK presented a proposed Protocol concerning "*quota-hopping*," defined as the practice by which enterprises from one Member State register fishing vessels in another Member State in order to have access to the fish quotas of the latter, even if they have no real economic ties with that State or its fishing industries. The UK recognised that there was a certain tension between the original logic behind the setting of fish quotas (based on historical levels of catches, the granting of preferences to certain sensitive regions, and the reduction in the possibilities of deep-sea fishing) and certain provisions of the Treaties concerning free movement of goods and freedom of establishment. This problem could have been solved, argued the British Memorandum, had the Council adopted measures to protect coastal fishing communities. The Court of Justice had in several rulings prevented Member States from insisting that those registering vessels should be resident in the Member State in question, that the crew should be composed of that State's nationals, that the vessels should be based in a port on that State's territory, or that the catch should, to some extent, be landed in that State. One of the consequences of this for the UK was the *Factortame* saga (see below). The UK therefore proposed a Protocol to the EC Treaty to put an end to this practice. The Government of Spain, the Member State most involved in the problem with Britain, responded with a Memorandum of its own in September 1996, to which the UK came back in December 1996 with a detailed commentary disputing the Spanish position.

The UK also presented proposals aimed at:

- extending the application of *competition rules to all agricultural products*;
- making legally binding the Maastricht Declaration no. 24 on *animal welfare*;
- eliminating the reference to common projects "financed by the Member States" regarding *Trans-European Networks*, in order to open up this area of Community support to networks receiving private investment (a proposal with which the Commission agreed);
- adopting a Declaration to the effect that "in drawing up measures under Article 100s, the institutions of the Community shall take account of the *needs of disabled people*."

In the area of *external economic relations*, the UK opposed including services and intellectual property in Article 113.[6]

Change and Continuity in UK Positions, May-June 1997

The only issue reflecting any fundamental ideological difference between the parties in May 1997 was the immediate ending of the British opt-out on the Social Agreement, as well as the willingness to support inclusion of a chapter on employment. The Labour Government was more in favour than the Tories of enshrining basic human rights in the treaty. It was more willing to accept some extension of QMV in the First Pillar and some further increase in the powers of the European Parliament, both as a natural concomitant of QMV (i.e. extending co-decision) and in particular areas, such as anti-fraud and the environment.

Yet for the rest, there was much more continuity than change in substance. Labour shared the desire for a re-weighting of Council votes in favour of the larger States, the emphasis on subsidiarity and on the role of national parliaments. On 23 May, the Government presented new proposals on fraud and financial management very much in the spirit of the February Memorandum. There was no change on contentious issues such as quota-hopping.[7] Even in the sphere of social policy, moreover, there were

---

[6] In June 1997 the British delegation proposed a new Protocol on Article 113(5) TEC which would limit the scope of any such application.

[7] Shortly before the elections, Tony Blair made it clear that Labour will "take a very tough line" on fishing policy: "where Britain's interests are at stake, we are perfectly prepared to be isolated.... what we don't seek is a policy of perpetual isolation" (*Agence Europe* 14-15 April 1997). There was indeed a final episode at Amsterdam itself, to

continuities: as Moravcsik and Nicolaïdis (1999) point out: "Even the advent of a Labour government, while predictably reversing British opposition to membership of the social charter, did not lead to a major substantive shift in preferences on labour market policies."

The new Minister of State for Europe, Doug Henderson, himself pointed out in his maiden speech in the IGC framework on 5 May 1997 that there were three areas which remained controversial for the UK. These were all fundamentally shared between the main British political parties in regard to content.

The first was CFSP, on which the British position did not change.[8] Here, there has been a broad political consensus in the UK which reflects not only longstanding and generally-accepted "Atlanticist" feelings, but also a traditional pattern of UK influence in international organisations: the British have never felt themselves to be institutional architects of Europe and are not, by political culture, "constitutionalists" at all. Their most important contribution has always been to military alliances (Wallace 1996).

Second, on Justice and Home Affairs, Labour continued to insist on the UK's right as an island nation to maintain frontier controls, and obtained an opt-out in this sphere. Again there was cross-party consensus. This was not only because of sensitivity about national sovereignty and confidence in the efficacy of UK controls, but also because "the British believed themselves to have established a kind of equilibrium in their immigration and race relations policies, in sharp contrast to the increasing contention in continental Europe about immigration and asylum-seekers" (Wallace 1999, 106).

The third broad area was flexibility. Tony Blair openly saw more dangers than advantages in a flexibility clause: "If what you end up with is effectively an inner core ... that changes the whole nature of the arrangements within the European Union ... If that were to happen, Britain's influence in Europe would be hugely reduced." He was clear that a Labour Government would not hesitate in using the veto if need be: "If the rest of Europe wanted something that was wrong, we would be prepared to block it." (*Agence Europe* 17 January 1997). McDonagh points out that "No British government was likely to cede a right of veto over such enhanced cooperation – indeed, a new Labour Government, keen to bring Britain back into the mainstream of European developments, was likely if anything to take an even more jaundiced view of free-ranging flexibility. A change of government in London might, however, decrease the perceived need of some others for a circumnavigation mechanism

---

Spanish annoyance, involving an unpublicised exchange of letters between Blair and Jacques Santer on 18 June (Gowland & Turner 2000, 339).

[8] The series of amendments presented on 5 June thus continued the same line of caution as to EU defence capabilities and opposition to the integration of WEU.

around an immovable object, and might therefore defuse the issue somewhat." (McDonagh 1998, 149). Indeed at Amsterdam in June 1997, when the British Government was not perceived as the main target of flexibility, the issues were sorted out quickly. Supported by France, Blair demanded and obtained maintenance of the veto (the "emergency brake"), while the issue was somewhat communitarised by giving the Commission the final say in triggering flexibility in the first pillar, and the enabling clause in the Second Pillar was dropped in favour of "constructive abstention."

The Results of UK Negotiations in the IGC

Proposals and Perceptions
During most of the IGC negotiations the UK was in an isolated position, or at best seen as trying to "lead from the sidelines." Yet the concept of "isolation" requires some qualifications.

Various proposals were influential, especially where Britain found natural allies. This was the case, for example, of subsidiarity and the role of national parliaments. It was also clear from the beginning that the British position on non-integration of WEU would be shared by the neutral and non-aligned EU States (Austria, Finland, Ireland, Sweden). Proposals concerning fraud and financial management were put forward also by Benelux and Denmark, as well as the Court of Auditors.[9] In general, the UK was rarely alone in its minority positions in the 1996-97 IGC.

Nevertheless, from the start of the work of the Westendorp Reflection Group in 1995 on, Britain did usually prove to be the dissenting member so tactfully alluded to in the reports. "Its overall approach was certainly at one end of the spectrum of so-called "ambition for the Conference."" (McDonagh 1998, 72). This could all too easily become an image of complete isolation if the UK's different views were ever felt not to be offered in a constructive spirit – and/or if there were doubts as to whether the Major Government, with its minuscule majority by 1996, could actually carry through on what it said.

Second, although non-participation makes it extremely difficult to exert a positive influence over the definition of new agreements, isolation does not mean a lack of *impact* on the negotiating process as a whole. Quite the contrary, the debates in the UK and the increasingly precarious situation of the

---

[9] The proposed Declaration on the needs of disabled people became Declaration No. 21 attached to the TEC. The animal-welfare Protocol (that full regard should be paid to the welfare requirements of animals in agriculture, transport, internal market and research policies) was included, even if qualified with the clause: "while respecting the legislative or administrative provisions and customs of the Member States relating in particular to religious rites, cultural traditions and regional heritage."

Major Government – which all but gave up hope of winning the impending general elections half-way through the IGC – had significant consequences for how the negotiations were conducted. The rather distant deadline of June 1997 for conclusion of the IGC was fixed precisely because of the need to ensure that those elections would have taken place by then, even though this may have had some negative consequences for the conduct of the negotiations (Dorr 2000, 39). The Irish and Dutch Presidencies consciously postponed sensitive issues in order to avoid inflaming the situation and thus probably forcing any British Government into adopting a *less* constructive negotiating approach (McDonagh 1998, 98, 138). To some extent, moreover, frustration brought the UK's negotiating partners to raise again, however lightly, the threat of exclusion. From the British perspective, flexibility started as an apparently attractive option legitimising selective participation – the opt-out enshrined. Yet almost immediately, it was apparent that it would be seen by many continental integrationists, in one format or another, as a possible means to go ahead even without the awkward Brits (Philippart & Edwards 1999; Stubb 1998). The obstructionism in 1996, of course, only strengthened this feeling. Yet the frustrations appear almost always to have been accompanied by regret that the UK was not more in tune with the majority in view of its natural weight, especially in CFSP and defence matters.

The problem was only partly the substance of the British positions. Some UK positions were indeed considered unacceptable in the sense that they were felt to be anti-integrationist. The most notorious example was the UK's attitude to the Court of Justice (especially the critical remarks and more radical proposals made outside the IGC). This reflected not only the fairly widespread constitutional discomfort felt in Britain about the role of the Court, but also the feeling that, although the UK is one of the Member States with the best record of meeting its Community obligations, it was being harshly treated as a result of certain judgments which "have imposed disproportionate costs on Governments or business, even when they have made every effort to meet their EC obligations." The most prominent case at the time was the *Factortame* saga arising from the quota-hopping problem.[10] This had first brought a painful (and apparently surprising) demonstration of the supremacy of Community law over Westminster. In the second phase, the question of damages was to be dealt with. Timing was particularly unfortunate in this case. In March 1996, just before the start of the IGC, the Court of Justice issued a new ruling which meant that the UK would have to pay some 30 million pounds in compensation to Spanish fishing companies. With regard

---

[10] This began in July 1990, when the House of Lords acted on a preliminary ruling by the European Court of Justice to suspend new rules contained in the 1988 Merchant Shipping Act alleged to be in conflict with European law.

to the Court of Justice, the UK was isolated and its proposals were effectively dropped.[11]

Another example of going unacceptably against the Community grain was the British suggestion, in a series of proposals under the heading of "quality of legislation" (see above), which challenged one of the basic institutional principles of the Community, that Commission proposals can only be overruled by unanimity. It should be noted however, that the UK was not the only Member State which was felt to have tried this kind of thing. The Germans and the French also made their fair share of such proposals (Petite 1998).

Some other proposals failed, finally, because they were specific British problems for which others either had no specific sympathy (the Working Time Directive) or were the sources of specific conflict – notably the case of quota-hopping.

The Impact of the Domestic Conflicts over Europe

Yet the issue was not only the content of some proposals, so much as the spirit and atmosphere in which all were discussed. Between 1994 and 1996, the position of the British Government was strongly influenced by the Prime Minister's felt need to seek compromise between the conflicting factions in the Conservative Party. John Major's parliamentary majority was whittled away from 21 in 1992 to only one in April 1996. Party indiscipline was chronic, most famously resulting in the removal of the Conservative whip in November 1994 from eight Eurosceptic rebels. The Party was increasingly riven by the split into Eurosceptic pressure groups such as the Bruges Group, the No Turning Back Group, the Fresh Start Group, the '92 Group, the European Research Group and the European Foundation, and Europhile groups, such as the Action Centre for Europe, the One Nation Group, the Macleod Group and the Conservative Mainstream Group (see Gowland & Turner 2000, chapter 21).

In these circumstances, so long as it was not a matter of legislative responsibility,[12] Major treated the issue as one of party management, tending either to avoid commitments or, to pacify the Eurosceptics, to adopt extreme

---

[11] In McDonagh's words: "This particular hobby horse stayed up with the field around the first circuit of the course before falling into a ditch somewhere out of public view on the back straight." (McDonagh 1998, 153).

[12] For example, the 1994 European Communities (Finance) Bill implementing the Edinburgh agreement, when Major did do whatever was necessary to enact the Bill "whatever the difficulties we faced" (Major 1999, 599).

– and probably unsustainable – positions. It may be that he thus "missed the opportunity to lead it in a genuinely Euro-sceptical direction" (Holmes 1998, 134-5) which might have been the best course, in electoral terms, for the Conservatives.[13] In all events this contributed to the adoption of a series of negotiating positions over these years which were not to prove very effective, and which brought into question Britain's credibility as a European partner.

The first episode, in 1994, concerned the threshold for qualified-majority voting after the Eftan enlargement, in which Major first vetoed the proposal and then backed down (the Ioannina Compromise). Major himself recognises that this "most humiliating retreat" could have been avoided. The Cabinet would not step back once Germany and France had, in his account, changed their minds, since "compromise would have been a calamity within the Conservative Party" (Major 1999, 588-590). Foreign Secretary Douglas Hurd was worried but his negotiating hands were tied by the Cabinet subcommittee OPD(E), in which even pro-Europeans Michael Heseltine and Kenneth Clarke also wanted to stick to 23 votes as the blocking minority. On 16 March, Hurd told Major he felt that "Britain was becoming like a bank with a run on it; that it was using up valuable credit on an issue which it was not winning, just as a bank does when it customers demand their money" (Stuart 1998, 372-3).

In this respect, it is interesting to note the reaction of the House of Commons Select Committee on European Legislation to the initial Government position given in 1995. By staking prestige on preventing massive – but unlikely – constitutional changes as ending the veto and giving huge new powers to the European Parliament, the Committee wondered: "it is worth asking ... how strong a negotiating stance it is." (House of Commons 1995).

The most serious episode, that of "mad cows" (BSE), almost exactly coincided with the start of the IGC. On 20 May 1996, the Standing Veterinary Committee refused to lift the ban on UK beef exports which had been in place since the end of March – according to Major, because their governments had told them not to do so, in order to pacify their own public opinion. "I was as infuriated about this outcome as any Euro-sceptic. I had played by club rules, and the club had changed them. It persuaded me to take action which I disliked, and subsequently regretted, though with even pro-Europeans

---

[13] The study carried out by Evans (1998) suggests that "the optimal position on Europe for the Conservatives is as a united *Eurosceptic* party. This would be desirable not only because it would place the party nearer to more of the electorate, but it would also reduce (and probably remove) the negative relationship... between respondents' own attitudes and their perceptions of the party's position... opposition to integration is characteristic of the electorate in general and Conservative supporters in particular. Yet the cost of maintaining a distinctly Eurosceptic line is likely to be high in terms of intra-party strife..." (p. 589).

demanding retaliation, something of the sort was probably unavoidable." He consequently told the House of Commons on 21 May that Britain could not "continue business as usual within Europe." In his perception, moreover, "This was not the result of a uniquely British tantrum, but a variant of a tactic used previously by France, Italy and Spain" (Major 1999, 653-4). In the end, though, he backed down at Florence in June.

The episode of BSE and "non-cooperation" must indeed rank "as one of the most damaging British foreign policy episodes in recent history. The obstructive behaviour of the Major government was an important factor leading to calls for more flexibility in policy-making in the EU; the other Member States did not want future development of the EU held back by a negative, non-cooperative Britain" (Hughes & Smith 1998, 94). The effect on relations with Germany was particularly serious. It is notable that, at this point, the understanding that other Member States should accept the fact that internal politics exerted a certain influence over national negotiating positions, came to be matched by a feeling that internal British politics were an understandable concern of others, at least so far as common policies were concerned. "Apart from not being prepared to yield....most EU governments were determined not to make any concessions that might help Major to retain power." (Gowland & Turner 2000, 317-8).

Finally, in November 1996 John Major declared that he would refuse to sign any deal at the IGC unless it exempted UK from European job-protection measures under the Working Time Directive, as upheld by the European Court of Justice on 11 November. In the light of the Prime Minister's having on previous occasions marched to the top of the hill under a Eurosceptic banner only to back down, even the normally pro-Tory *Daily Mail* headlined the story "Does he mean it this time?" Tony Blair argued that the Government's strategy was to "talk tough, alienate everybody and then cave in" (*Financial Times* 13 November 1996). John Major himself was aware of the impression that Britain was giving. In his autobiography he admits that: "our EU partners began to believe that every European position we took was determined by our internal rows, not our objective judgements. This was not true but it appeared to be, and it weakened our case." (Major 1999, 593).

Towards a Strategy for Influence?

The change of government in May 1997 opened the possibility for a new UK strategy – not only for the immediate defence of particular interests in the IGC and elsewhere, but to establish a solid and durable base of influence within and *as* Europe. After so many years of semi-detached participation, this could not be achieved quickly. Moreover, it would be all the harder to do so without full participation in Economic and Monetary Union, which was (despite the hopes of some in the UK, for whom collapse of the project would have been a welcome face-saving device) already on the way to becoming the core of European Union.

The new Labour Foreign Secretary, Robin Cook, in May 1997 stated (*senza diplomazia*) that "We want to make sure that from now on there are three players in Europe, not just two" (Gowland & Turner 2000, 326). This appears to have developed into a medium-term strategy designed to give the UK, within five to ten years, the same kind of weight in Europe as France or Germany.

In late 1998, this strategy would become known as a Step Change initiative. In the Foreign and Commonwealth Office's *Public Service Agreement* for 1999-2002, the fifth aim listed is "to ensure the United Kingdom plays a strong role in a strong Europe, responsive to people's needs." The corresponding performance target, for achievement by March 2002, is "a step change in the UK's relations with the rest of Europe, with increasing public support for EU activities." The capitalised version – "a Step Change in our relations with all our EU partners and with the applicants from Central and Eastern Europe" – means, on the external front, a systematic effort to forge "new alliances, new links across the European Union"[14] by consciously strengthening "transgovernmental" contacts at all levels and on a day-to-day basis, as well as identifying common interests with individual countries and developing bilateral initiatives.[15] Equally important, the Foreign Office's approach had an internal dimension, a domestic campaign of "public diplomacy" to make the public more aware of the issues. Finally, of course, there was a sea change in the British position on security and defence in Europe in late 1998, which has significantly altered perceptions of what the UK is able – and now also willing – to offer.

Conclusions

In the process leading to Amsterdam, the Major Government lost credibility, and even goodwill, despite the Prime Minister's own intentions. Britain's image and influence with the rest of the European Union was weakened. Yet

---

[14] See, for example, the speech by the then FCO Minister of State Joyce Quin to the Franco-British Colloque in Paris on 14 January 1999.

[15] By January 1999, Ms Quin could already cite the UK-France initiative on defence, the Joint Initiative with Spain on promoting employment and labour market flexibility, the agreement with Sweden on promoting social inclusion and gender equality, and a Joint Statement with Germany on EU taxation.

in the end the UK succeeded in securing several key national objectives (and in a friendly atmosphere): the strengthening of CFSP but non-integration of WEU into the EU; the opt-out/in from the communitarised Schengen, albeit on terms (the requirement for unanimous approval by the existing Members) which could have been more favourable to the UK; a veto over flexibility arrangements; and so on.

Tony Blair was more willing and more able to find viable compromises. Yet he was also in a privileged position, able to benefit from the relief of the other Member States that there was now a solidly-based and constructively-oriented government in London, and from the fact that he could offer the end of the opt-out on the Social Protocol free of political charge; and, with a massive parliamentary majority, he was relatively free to act.[16]

However, there was much less change between Major and Blair in the substance of UK policy concerning Europe than may have appeared. There are clear "structural realities" shaping UK positions, most notably (and probably immutably, the Channel Tunnel notwithstanding) the "island logic" behind the UK's exceptionalism over border controls, as well as limits on governmental action arising from popular perceptions. Public opinion about Europe has not changed so radically regarding Europe. Although the British public does not appear ever to have cared about Europe as much as the Eurosceptics did (and continue to do), there remains a broad feeling of non-identification with the European project – and of opposition to British membership in the single currency – which will not change overnight.

The strategy is sound for weaving a web of shared interests and confidence with the other Member States, and for addressing domestic constraints caused by popular perceptions which continue to be shaped in an imbalanced way by the media. Yet British influence, to steal a phrase from Schuman, "will not be achieved all at once, or according to a single plan. It will be built through concrete achievements which first create a de facto solidarity." And that will certainly take time.

---

[16] In contrast to the agonies which John Major had gone through to ratify the Maastricht Treaty (see Best 1994) the Amsterdam Treaty was ratified with relative ease in the House of Commons. The Bill was submitted on 30 October 1997, and the third reading approved on 19 January 1998 by 370 in favour to 145 against. The only major problem arose in May when, during the final day of the Report stage in the House of Lords, an amendment was passed on quota-hopping, which then had to be overturned in the Commons. Royal Assent was given on 11 June 1998 and the instrument of ratification deposited on 15 June.

Bibliography

Best, Edward (1994). "The United Kingdom and the Ratification of the Maastricht Treaty," pp. 245-278, in Finn Laursen & Sophie Vanhoonacker, *The Ratification of the Maastricht Treaty*, Maastricht: EIPA.

Dorr, Noel (2000). "The IGC 2000 Agenda: An Irish Perspective," pp. 29-42, in Edward Best, Mark Gray & Alexander Stubb (eds.), *Rethinking the European Union: IGC 2000 and Beyond*, Maastricht: EIPA.

Evans, Geoffrey (1998). "Euroscepticism and Conservative Electoral Support: How an Asset Became a Liability," *British Journal of Political Science*, 28:4 (November), pp. 573-590.

Gowland, David & Arthur Turner (2000). *Reluctant Europeans. Britain and European Integration, 1945-1998*. Harlow: Pearson.

Holmes, Martin (1998). "The Conservative Party and Europe: From Major to Hague," *The Political Quarterly*, 69:2 (April-June), pp. 133-140.

House of Commons (1995). Select Committee on European Legislation, Twenty-fourth Report, *The 1996 Inter-Governmental Conference: The Agenda, Democracy and Efficiency, the Role of National Parliaments*, 17 July.

Hughes, Kirsty & Edward Smith (1998). "New Labour – New Europe," *International Affairs*, 74:1 pp. 93-104.

Major, John (1999). *John Major. The Autobiography*, London: Harper Collins.

McDonagh, Bobby (1998). *Original Sin in a Brave New World. An account of the negotiation of the Treaty of Amsterdam*, Dublin: Institute of European Affairs.

Moravcsik, Andrew & Kalypso Nicolaïdis (1999). "Explaining the Treaty of Amsterdam: Interests, Influence, Institutions," *Journal of Common Market Studies*, 37:1 (March), pp. 59-85.

Philippart, Eric & Geoffrey Edwards (1999). "The Provisions on Closer Co-operation in the Treaty of Amsterdam: The Politics of Flexibility in the European Union," *Journal of Common Market Studies*, 37:1 (March), pp. 87-108.

Stuart, Mark (1998). *Douglas Hurd. The Public Servant*, Edinburgh & London: Mainstream.

Stubb, Alexander (1998). *Flexible Integration and the Amsterdam Treaty: Negotiating Differentiation in the 1996-97 IGC*, Ph.D.-thesis, London: London School of Economics and Political Science.

UK, Secretary of State for Foreign and Commonwealth Affairs (2000). *IGC: Reform for Enlargement: The British Approach to the European Intergovernmental Conference 2000*, London, February.

Wallace, Helen (1996). "L'approche britannique de la CIG de 1996," *Politique étrangère*, (printemps) pp. 49-59.

Wallace, Helen (1999). "New Europe, New Labour: British European Policy Reconsidered," pp. 103-112, in John Milfull (ed.), *Britain in Europe. Prospects for Change,* Aldershot: Ashgate.

Young, Hugo (1999). *This Blessed Plot. Britain and Europe from Churchill to Blair*, Basingstoke: Macmillan.

Section 2:

Institutional Actors

17

The European Commission: Seeking the Highest Possible Realistic Line

Mark Gray[1]

Introduction

Nothing in an Intergovernmental Conference (IGC) negotiation is quite as it seems. Personal relationships cut across institutional boundaries, proposals are submitted on behalf of other delegations and the same meeting will produce eighteen different sets of minutes, which rarely correspond.[2] It is therefore extremely difficult to analyse the positions of each delegation, never mind how much influence they have on the final treaty text. This is borne out by the statement of one of the negotiators most closely involved who said, "There is a danger in trying to describe the Amsterdam Treaty from the point of view of a particular institution or a Member State: the danger to suggest winners and losers where there is simply process as a whole" (Petite 1998, 1).

This warning to those trying to analyse the Treaty of Amsterdam from one particular perspective is partly a reaction to the endless attempts to justify a particular theoretical interpretation of European integration by the results of a specific set of treaty negotiations and partly a reaction to the analysis of member state positions based on incorrect information.[3]

This chapter does not seek to justify a particular theory. Instead it looks at the role of the European Commission in the process of treaty reform, the internal structures to establish the Commission proposals and the proposals themselves. The chapter concludes with an overall assessment of how influential the Commission was during the process of drafting the Treaty of Amsterdam and whether its fingerprints can be found in the final treaty text.

---

[1] These are strictly personal views and do not represent the viewpoint of any institution or organisation.

[2] Each of the fifteen Member States, the European Commission, the Council Secretariat and the European Parliament (when invited) produce reports of the meetings. All of these are not available to the public.

[3] It is a justified argument that the IGC process should be more transparent. However, it is also true to say that a vast array of justifications have been based on analysis done by the European Parliament, and various think-tanks which is simply not correct. Member State positions cannot be depicted by those outside the negotiating room.

Placing the Commission Within the IGC Context

The timeframe and the mandate for the 1996 Intergovernmental Conference were outlined in the Treaty on European Union (Maastricht Treaty). Article N (2) TEU (now Article 48 TEU) stated that *"a conference of representatives of the governments of the Member States shall be convened in 1996 to examine those provisions of the Treaty for which revision is provided, in accordance with the objectives set out in Articles A and B."* This mandate was developed in the conclusions of the Corfu European Council on 24 and 25 June 1994 which called for the institutions of the Union to prepare a series of reports on the functioning of the Union and establish a Reflection Group to produce a report under the Spanish Presidency (July-December 1995).

The European Commission has no formal role in the Intergovernmental Conference itself. Article 48 TEU simply states that the Commission may be requested to give its opinion before the start of negotiations. The European Commission's presence is justified on the basis of its historical role, having been present at most of the previous treaty revisions; its traditional role as guardian of the treaties; and its ability to give its opinion before the opening of the Conference. The European Commission therefore has a seat (actually two) at the table. What still remains unclear is its actual role.

Petite (1998) has underlined this ambiguity by stating "Anyone taking part in the Maastricht and Amsterdam negotiations can witness that the very function of the Commission in an IGC is less than obvious." He concludes that the Commission does not have the role of honest broker (this task is performed by the Presidency), nor should it attempt to be the depositor of an ideal European construction or act as the 16th Member State. The role portrayed during the Treaty of Amsterdam negotiations was actually one of trying to propose the "highest possible realistic line." In effect, pushing upwards as much as possible the outcome of the Conference.

This may well have been the role of the Commission, but it must be recognised that each treaty reform is unique and it is not possible to look at only one set of negotiations in isolation. The reality is that the personalities and the dynamics involved are unique to the given time frame of the negotiations. During the negotiations for the Single European Act, the European Commission had a significant impact on the results of the negotiations on the institutional changes and development of policies. This was partly due to the crucial role the Commission played in the Dooge Committee preparing the Conference. On the other hand, the Commission was largely absent from the discussions on Political Co-operation. The same dynamic is true of the Maastricht negotiations where the Commission developed many of the main proposals for the first IGC on Economic and

Monetary Union while it so famously failed to make the same type of impact on the IGC developing Political Union.

As Dinan (1996) has underlined, IGCs present dangers as well as opportunities for the European Commission. The Commission has often gained from decisions taken in IGCs, but such meetings also provide Member States with the opportunity to roll-back specific aspects of legislation and attempt to undermine the role of the Commission itself. Indeed, in Maastricht and Amsterdam numerous attempts were made to weaken the role of the Commission.[4]

Before the preparation for the Conference began, the Commission had to consider what role it should play both in the public arena and behind the scenes during the Conference. Numerous factors had to be taken into account. The Commission had to consider what it wished to achieve from the negotiations, especially as the timing of the Conference was not particularly helpful. It also had to accept that it was perceived to have over-played its hand during the Maastricht negotiations. The Commission decided it would not seek new competences, would not present a complete draft treaty but would instead focus on specific proposals which would provide added value to the debate and work behind the scenes rather than through controversial political declarations.

Before looking at whether this strategic decision was successful, it is first necessary to consider how the Commission took these type of decisions.

The Internal Policy-Making Process in the Commission

The role of the College of Commissioners was crucial in setting the main political guidelines for the negotiators. The IGC featured on virtually every Commission meeting agenda for the best part of two years. An incredible amount of proposals and political guidelines were adopted by the College during that time (see annex 1). Unlike other IGC's, the Treaty of Amsterdam negotiations covered virtually every major policy area. This meant that individual Commissioners had a specific role to play. A number of Commissioners actively engaged in lobbying of the Presidency and specific Member States.

However, the dynamics of an IGC mean that it is impossible to consult the College on every major policy decision. A specially created Steering Group

---

[4] Specific proposals were made on an independent competition authority, common commercial policy, the right of initiative of the Commission and the length required to adopt Commission proposals (sunset clause) which would have weakened the present role of the Commission.

therefore gave the bulk of the political orientation on day to day issues.[5] The Steering Group played a particularly important role as it gave the political orientation for the vast majority of the speaking points that would be outlined by the Commission IGC negotiators. Before every meeting, a proposed briefing would be presented to the Steering Group, which was chaired by Commissioner Marcelino Oreja. This line was usually adopted, although changes were also not unusual.

One of the main advantages for the Commission in an IGC is that it has an institutional memory that can only be matched by the Council Secretariat. While the majority of Member States practice systematic rotation of staff, it is not unusual for Commission experts to have worked on two or three major treaty reform negotiations. The Commission is therefore equipped with vast experience and knowledge of all of the main proposals and options that have been presented in the past. This is invaluable when many of the proposals are a repeat of earlier negotiations. Although the Commission is not significantly involved in the ratification procedure following the signature of a treaty, a team is often maintained to oversee its entry into force and implementation. Following the eventual ratification of the Treaty on European Union this task was followed by the institutional unit (SGB.1) of the Secretariat General. This unit headed by Alain van Solinge was also the unit which had co-ordinated the negotiations of the Single European Act and the Treaty on European Union for the Commission. The Commission was therefore already well prepared before the formal preparation of 1996 began.

One of the final decisions of the Delors Commission was to break with tradition and create a special Task Force IGC 96, headed by Michel Petite, to co-ordinate the preparation and negotiations of the 1996 Conference. The Task Force reported directly to President Santer and the Commissioner for institutional affairs, Marcelino Oreja. Administratively the Task Force was located in the Secretariat General, which at that time was headed by David Williamson. The Task Force consisted of ten senior advisors and administrators from a mixture of nationalities with vast experience of institutional affairs.[6]

---

[5] The composition of the Steering Group tended to vary depending on the subject of the meeting. It mainly consisted of Commissioner Marcelino Oreja (Chairman), David Williamson, Carlo Trojan, Michel Petite, Jim Cloos, Daniel Calleja, Jean-Louis Dewost, Colette Flesch, Diane Schmitt and the member of the Task Force responsible for the issue of the meeting.

[6] Michel Petite (Cabinet of President Delors (F), Nigel Evans (Cabinet of Sir Leon Brittan (UK), Alain van Solinge (Secretariat General – SG B.1 (B), Andrea Pierucci (European Parliament (I), Franscisco Fonseca Morillo (Cellule de Prospective (E), Dominique Maidani (Legal Service (F), Paskavici Gilchrist (EL), Angela Bardenhewer (Legal Service (D), Veronique Warlop (Secretariat General – SG B.1 (B), Mark Gray

The first responsibility of the Task Force was to prepare the Commission report on the functioning of the European Union, which had been requested of all institutions by the Corfu European Council. Following numerous drafts and exhaustive consultation with the different departments in the Commission this report was adopted by the Commission on 10 May 1995.[7] The second task of the Task force was to prepare Commissioner Oreja for his work in the Reflection Group, which had also been created by the Corfu European Council. This Reflection Group started work in June 1995 and completed its final report in time for the Madrid European Council in December 1995.[8] Finally, the Task Force had the responsibility of preparing the briefings for the Intergovernmental Conference meetings and assisting the President and Commissioner where necessary.

The process of internal decision-making was focused on the Task Force, but not alone. Each major decision had to be co-ordinated with the relevant departments and a political orientation agreed with the Steering Group. Specific proposals were normally drafted in the Task Force together with the President's and Commissioner's Cabinet and then agreed by others depending on the nature of the proposal. Each Directorate General nominated a special IGC correspondent to liaise with the Task Force. The rhythm of negotiations often required immediate reaction to proposals from other delegations. The Commission also had to take into account the vast number of external contributions sent by other institutions, bodies and NGO's.

The agreed positions then had to be translated into a strong position within the negotiations. The main Commission negotiator was Commissioner Oreja, normally assisted by Carlo Trojan or Michel Petite. It is often remarked that the Commission did not have significant influence on the negotiations – this I believe is incorrect. That does not mean that the Commission was perfect in getting its message across. One criticism that can be made of the Commission is that it found it difficult to transmit a single coherent position to the other delegations. This is understandable, given that both the President and the Commissioner represented the Commission at the political level. However, at the representative's level the Commission was sometimes represented by the Commissioner, on other occasions by the Deputy Secretary General, Director of the IGC Task Force or by the Head of the Legal Service. This inevitably led to delegations perceiving different viewpoints in the Commission delegation.

(Secretariat General – SG B.1 (UK))

[7] Report of the Commission on the operation of the Treaty on European Union, 10 May 1995 (SEC (95) 731 final)

[8] Reflection Group Report and Other References for Documentary Purposes, General Secretariat of the Council of the European Union, Brussels, December 1995

The Proposals of the European Commission

The European Commission set out its position in a series of proposals throughout the negotiations. These can be divided into three main categories: general policy statements or papers adopted by the College, contributions on specific issues and proposals prepared and submitted by the services of the Commission.

Policy Statements and Papers Adopted by the College
The general starting point for an analysis of the Commission's position are the two general papers adopted by the Commission in 1995 and 1996.

The report on the operation of the Treaty on European Union, adopted by the Commission on 10 May 1995 was a detailed analysis of the strengths and weaknesses of the Maastricht Treaty. This report, which was the Commission's contribution to the Reflection Group, was the reference point for many of the later specific proposals. The report was divided into two main sections: the first dealt with democracy and transparency by looking at citizenship, the role of the institutions, decision-making and transparency; the second section concentrated on effectiveness and consistency of the Union's policies with specific focus on external political and economic relations and Justice and Home Affairs. This report was generally recognised as the most influential of all the institutional reports submitted to the Reflection Group. Indeed, many aspects of the analysis are outlined in the options presented in the final Reflection Group Report.

The formal opinion of the European Commission to the Intergovernmental Conference in accordance with Article N (now Article 48) of the Treaty was adopted on 28 February 1996 and was a more political statement of the Commission's priorities and intentions that would guide its representatives throughout the negotiations. Entitled "Reinforcing Political Union and preparing for enlargement," the opinion built on the earlier detailed report to the Reflection Group by prioritising the Commission's position. In a departure from the report to the Reflection Group, it placed "A People's Europe" as the main headline. This reflected a shift in emphasis, in part in a reaction to the issues that would be dealt with by the conference. The opinion was quite different to those produced by the Commission for the Single European Act and the Maastricht negotiations.

Throughout the course of the negotiations, the Commission held a number of seminars on specific issues. The first of these took place during the Reflection Group on the themes of Justice and Home Affairs and common foreign and security policy. Following a formal position on the final report of the Reflection Group, the College was routinely given information notes and presentations by Commissioner Oreja on the state of play of the negotiations themselves[9].

Specific Contributions Adopted by the Commission
The College of the Commission adopted five specific contributions to the Intergovernmental Conference. The first of these was a specific response to the mandate given to the Intergovernmental Conference by the Maastricht Treaty. The Commission adopted a report on civil protection, tourism and energy[10] in which it recommended that these issues should not be dealt with by the Intergovernmental Conference as Community competence should not be extended. This report is a good example of how the different and often differing positions within the individual Directorates General had to be coordinated into a single coherent document with a single message. It was also a crucial factor in the Conference deciding not to deal with this subject during the IGC.

The second specific contribution is seen as one of the most significant contributions of the Commission to the Conference. The report on the extension of the scope and the simplification of the codecision procedure[11] was a key priority for the Commission. The report commented on the historically ad hoc approach to the extension of codecision and set out for the first time a coherent set of principles for the extension of codecision. It has been suggested that the Commission did not achieve the extension proposed. This forgets the objective of the report. It sought to avoid a continuation of the case by case approach adopted in the past and it attempted to underline a certain set of principles.

The third specific contribution focused on services of general interest in Europe.[12] Although not specifically written for the Intergovernmental Conference this communication was later forwarded to the Intergovernmental Conference, and formed part of the discussion following the specific demands of the German Länder on possible amendment of Article 7 and the eventual Protocol on banking and public broadcasting.

---

[9] See for example the Communication of the state of play of the work of the Intergovernmental Conference, 25 November 1996, SEC(96) 2192.

[10] Report of the Commission to Council relating to civil protection, tourism and energy, 3 April 1996 (SEC (960 496 final – CONF/3838/96).

[11] Report on 189B (8) TEU: the scope of application of codecision – SEC (96) 1225 final – (CONF/3882/96), 3 July 1996.

[12] Communication of the Commission on services of general interest in Europe, COM(96)443 final – (CONF/3937/96), 11 September 1996.

The Commission also adopted a formal position on flexibility or as the Treaty references became known, closer cooperation. This document stemmed from a oral intervention of Commissioner Oreja at an IGC Representatives meeting in Luxembourg on 30 September 1996. The eventual orientation note that was distributed concentrated on the possible use of flexibility in the first pillar.[13] The main argument of the Commission was that it was extremely difficult to envisage any form of flexibility in the first pillar and any triggering mechanism should be based on qualified majority voting together with strict conditions. The Commission has been criticised for failing to make its position clear at an earlier stage in the negotiations (Stubb 1998). The demand by negotiators for a copy of the oral intervention of Commissioner Oreja perhaps underlines this point. However, the distributed orientation note was one factor in the final decision to set strict conditions on the possible use of flexibility in the first pillar.

The final specific communication adopted by the College itself dealt with the composition, organisation and functioning of the Commission.[14] Adopted on 6 March 1997 during the Dutch Presidency, the communication was the result of a specific debate in the College on the issue. The proposal was a compromise between the two well-known options of one Commissioner per Member State or a reduced Commission to 15-20 Commissioners. The proposal also made a number of recommendations on the internal organisation of the Commission. Some of these suggestions were taken up in the declaration attached to the Treaty on internal organisation.

Documents of the Services

The vast majority of the contributions of the Commission were directly submitted to the Representatives' Group of the Intergovernmental Conference without requiring formal adoption by the College. Nearly all of these were prepared by the IGC Task Force under the political authority of the President and Commissioner Oreja. These proposals took various forms: written contributions, draft articles, distributed speaking notes, meeting documents or oral amendments to Presidency texts.

Very early in the negotiations, the Commission submitted a meeting document on the weighting of votes[15] which was the culmination of extensive research on the different calculations used for voting in the Council. This

---

[13] Orientation Note on flexibility/closer cooperation, 22 January 1997 – (CONF/3805/97).

[14] Communication of the Commission on the composition, organisation and functioning of the Commission, 6 March 1997 – SEC(97) 451/2 – (CONF/3839/97).

[15] "Document de séance" on the weighting of votes in the Council presented by the Commission at the representatives meeting of the IGC, 2 May 1996 (SN 612/96).

proposal was accompanied by an internal study, which showed that based on three years of legislation, not one piece of legislation would have been affected by the different options being proposed. The study simply showed that the large Member States do not vote against the smaller Member States and vice versa.

A week later on 6 May 1996, the Commission distributed a second meeting document, this time concerning common foreign and security policy.[16] The proposal aimed to raise the possibility of a coherent approach between external economic policy and external foreign policy. The suggested format was a Presidency/Commission "tandem" to deal with these two areas rather than create a so-called "Mr CFSP." This suggestion was quickly rejected but it may have been a factor in the final alterations to the "troika" format.

Following the publication of the Presidency report at the Florence European Council in June 1996, the Commission services submitted suggested approaches on Article 113 and Article 228 concerning common commercial policy.[17] This was quickly followed by further suggested amendments to the Presidency approach on common foreign and security policy.

The start of the Irish Presidency led to a significant intensification of work and consequently an increased level of proposals submitted. In very quick succession in September and October, the Commission submitted papers on the areas of Justice and Home Affairs,[18] social policy,[19] flexibility,[20] legal personality[21] and Article 113.[22] A general communication was then issued on

---

[16] "Document de séance" on CFSP presented by the Commission at the representatives meeting of the IGC, 6 May 1996 (SN 613/96).

[17] Working document of the Commission presented to the representatives' group of the IGC on Article 228 bis and Article 113, 22 and 23 July 1996 (CONF 3890/96).

[18] Contribution of the Commission presented at the meeting of the representatives' group of the IGC on 16 and 17 September 1996 on the Justice and Home Affairs aspects of the EC Treaty, (CONF 3912/96).

[19] Contribution of the Commission on the Social Protocol presented at the representatives' group meeting on 23 and 24 September 1996 (CONF/3914/96).

[20] Intervention of Commissioner Oreja at the representatives' group meeting of the IGC on 30 September 1995 relating to flexibility.

[21] Intervention of the representative of the Commission at the meeting of the representatives' group of the IGC on 7 October 1996 concerning legal personality of the Union, 10 October 1996 (SN 611/96).

[22] Speaking brief for the meeting of the representatives' group of the IGC on 16 October 1996 concerning Article 113 TEC (SN 532/96).

10 December 1996 giving the Commission opinion on the general outline for a draft treaty that had just been issued by the Irish Presidency.

The start of 1997 led to increased reflection on qualified majority voting. Extensive consultation took place behind the scenes on a possible list of areas of decision-making that should move from unanimity to qualified majority voting. Outside the public glare, the Commission assisted the Presidency in this task and later put forward its views to the Conference on the specific areas of taxation, social policy and research and development.[23]

The shift of emphasis by the Dutch Presidency led to endless work on communitarisation of certain aspects of the third pillar, in particular asylum, immigration and related areas, the incorporation of the Schengen *acquis* and the strengthening of existing third pillar arrangements. During the spring of 1997, the Commission contributed a range of documents produced by the services which set out the Commission's preferred approach and treaty provisions. The Presidency presented a range of additions to the Irish outline draft treaty of December 1996. Each of these documents required detailed analysis and reaction to the Presidency both in the Conference itself and behind the scenes. The services of the Commission also presented specific proposals on comitology[24] and the Social Protocol.[25]

Unlike the Member States, the Commission did not use the last few weeks to bombard the Presidency with last-minute proposals. In fact, the final written contribution was submitted by the Commission on 20 May 1997 on financing of public broadcasting.[26] That of course did not mean that the Commission had stopped working. As the following section will demonstrate, Commission officials were significantly involved in the final negotiations of the Treaty.

The Influence of the European Commission

Given that treaty change is the most obvious example of intergovernmental co-operation, it would be surprising to find that the Commission has an

---

[23] Working document of the services of the Commission on the extension of qualified majority voting in the areas of social policy, taxation and research and development (CONF/3860/97), 4 April 1997.

[24] Non Paper presented by the Commission on comitology, 29 April 1997 (CONF/3900/97).

[25] Contribution of the Commission on the integration of the Social Protocol in the TEU, 5 May 1997 (CONF/3904/97).

[26] Non Paper presented by the Commission on the financing of public broadcasting, 20 May 1997 (CONF/3918/97).

influence on the proceedings. This type of view is presented by Moravcsik and Nicolaïdis (1999) who state, "We find, moreover, little evidence that either the Commission or Parliament provided either initiatives or compromise proposals that were unique and thereby altered the outcomes of the negotiations" and, "There appears to be no correlation between Commission support and the final outcome." They back this argument up by stating that the Commission failed to achieve its main priority (Article 113) and only achieved limited success on codecision.

So are there any Commission proposals that actually shaped or influenced the final decision?

Failing to achieve the final objective does not mean that a major initiative was not taken. Indeed the Commission proposal for a Presidency/Commission tandem for external affairs, the logic behind the lists produced on qualified majority voting and the codecision procedure are all examples of initiatives which were quite different to any of those produced by other delegations.

The belief that the Commission was not a key actor because it did not fully achieve its proposals on Article 113 or codecision must also be questioned. It is argued that the Commission proposal on codecision called for 23 areas to be changed of which only eight were accepted while 15 not mentioned by the Commission were designated by Member States and adopted. This misses the point. The Commission proposal had two main objectives: to simplify the procedure and to develop logical criteria for the choice of areas moving to codecision. Both of these objectives were achieved. The reason fifteen areas (e.g. employment, public health) were not included in the Commission list is that at that time the legal basis had not been created. These were only agreed at a later stage in the negotiations. Many Member States argued for consultation for these new areas, it was the Commission and the European Parliament together with key Member State allies that achieved these new legal bases and the qualified majority voting and codecision that went with them.

It is right to argue that the Commission did not achieve its main priority, namely the extension of qualified majority voting to services, investments and intellectual property aspects of Article 113 on common commercial policy. However, it is wrong to suggest that the Commission did not have an influence on proceedings. The final text is actually the result of a negative opinion of the Commission. Just before the Amsterdam Summit, the Commission decided that the proposals on the table were actually a step backwards. It therefore asked the Netherlands Presidency to withdraw the proposals and made it known that the Commission could not accept the changes being proposed by the Council Legal Service and various Member States. This was done by the Presidency and explains why only minor changes were made to the Maastricht Treaty.

One of the main problems is that the arguments put forward on each side of the debate are often mistakenly characterised by the definition of the Commission as a single actor. The reality is that Intergovernmental Conferences are shaped by different phases of negotiations and also by different levels of negotiations. The Commission also has a different impact depending on the topic that is being discussed.

The Commission's Influence at Different Stages of the Negotiations
An Intergovernmental Conference is essentially comprised of three different phases, preparation, negotiation and what have become known as the "end game." The preparation phase ran from the Corfu European Council in June 1994 until the end of the Italian Presidency in June 1996. The first real negotiations began during the Irish Presidency in the autumn of 1996 and the final "end game" started at the Noordwijk informal European Council in May 1997 and culminated at 04.00 a.m. on the morning of 17 June 1997.

i) Preparation
The Commission is generally considered to have produced the most influential report on the functioning of the Treaty on European Union during May 1995. This placed the Commission in an influential position at the start of the Reflection Group in June 1995. The discussions were a classic example of statement of positions without serious negotiations, but the report was important in that it set out the options on the table for each of the main topics. Following the first draft, which was presented to the Reflection Group on 1 September 1995, each delegation was able to present amendments. These short confidential papers which were produced in November 1995 gave a first indication of the positions that the Member States would take during the actual negotiations. The relationship between Commissioner Oreja and the Spanish Presidency was also a factor in helping the Commission shape the developments in the Reflection Group. A comparison between the chapters of the Commission report on the functioning of the Treaty in May 1995 and the Reflection Group of December 1995 bears this out. The order may have been different but the main components were the same. The Commission was therefore a key actor in this first stage of the preparation phase. This was not, however, to continue to the same extent during the first phase of the negotiations.

From the first IGC meeting on 2 April 1996 until the Florence European Council on 21-22 June 1996, the Italian Presidency struggled to start the negotiations. Many of the problems resulted from the fall of the Italian government and the vacuum this created. However, it is questionable that any Presidency would have been able to produce meaningful negotiations given the particular circumstances. Delegations were not prepared to move beyond traditional position-taking. The lack of involvement of the Commission by the

Presidency was noticeable. As the vacuum expanded, the Italian Presidency relied to an ever-increasing extent on the Council Secretariat for assistance. At this stage, a number of proposals appeared that were a direct attempt to undermine the powers of the Commission. These included a suggestion of giving the European Parliament a right of initiative even though the Parliament itself was no longer requesting this power. The Florence European Council did produce a report, but it was solely the responsibility of the Presidency and was largely written by the Secretariat – not something that could be said of the earlier Reflection Group report.

ii) Negotiation
The Irish Presidency inherited, rather reluctantly, the task of producing "an outline draft treaty" by the Dublin European Council in December 1996. As Bobby McDonagh states, "Lurking implicitly in that mandate was a tension. On the one hand, decisive progress was expected during the Irish Presidency. On the other hand, the IGC was to continue for six months beyond our Presidency. The Conference was not only expected not to conclude during our Presidency: it was instructed not to do so."[27] The Irish began to concentrate on certain themes rather than attempting to deal with the whole range of issues. The Presidency was conducted in three phases. From July - September a series of Introductory Notes were prepared on each major topic. In the second phase between October — November the Presidency tabled papers based on a Suggested Approach /based more on treaty language. The third phase from November – December was devoted to the preparation of the "outline draft treaty" for the Dublin European Council. Although the Irish have long been strong supporters of the role of the Commission, a small Member State often relies very heavily on the Council Secretariat during its Presidency. This was the case during the autumn of 1996 where much of the drafting was produced in Brussels even if Dublin kept a firm grip on the final outcome. The Commission played an important role without having the type of privileged access that had been given during previous negotiations.

The Netherlands' Presidency began with a significant amount of cooperation between the Presidency and the Commission, especially on the extension of qualified majority voting. This was to increase behind the scenes even if it was not so apparent in the public domain or even in the negotiating room. The focus on Justice and Home Affairs and the incorporation of the Schengen *acquis* helped to cement the close cooperation.

During the Netherlands' Presidency, the Commission was routinely invited to take part in meetings in the Hague or Brussels with the Presidency and the

---

[27] McDonagh, Bobby "Original Sin in a Brave New World: An account of the negotiation of the Treaty of Amsterdam," Institute of European Affairs, Dublin, page 70.

Council Secretariat. This cooperation together with close contacts with parts of the Council Secretariat were vital in cementing certain positions that the Commission had been defending. These sessions often involved a complete run-though of the texts or synthesis documents that the Dutch were due to propose to the Conference. It is therefore difficult to agree with Moravcsik and Nicolaïdis that the Commission only follows rather than shapes events.

iii) The "End Game"
The final couple of weeks of any negotiation help to concentrate the minds of negotiators. Priorities start to become clear and coalitions are readied for the final push for a deal.

The European Commission tends to play a traditional role of calling for ambition from the different actors. This perhaps reflects the reality that there is a limited amount that the Commission can do during those final weeks. The Commission does not have a vote and by that stage has already tabled its main proposals. The Commission is therefore left with a supporting role to the Presidency, which conducts a *tour des capitals* and plays the role of the honest broker.

It is true to say that the Commission failed to play a crucial role in the final Summit meetings. That does not mean that the Commission was not able to influence proceedings during the final weeks and in Amsterdam itself. The days preceding and following the distribution of the final draft treaty of the Netherlands Presidency on 12 June 1997 were crucial for every delegation. Many of the key decisions on issues such as Justice and Home Affairs decision-making were taken at this time. The Commission was regularly informed and asked to comment on changes being made to the draft treaty and played a key role together with the Council Secretariat at this time.

Commission Influence on Different Levels
An Intergovernmental Conference normally meets in four different formats: Heads of State and Government, Foreign Ministers, representatives of Foreign Ministers and Friends of the Presidency. Again the influence of the Commission varies depending on the level.

i) Heads of State and Government
The day to day running of a government or institution means that Heads of State and Government or the President of the Commission have very little time to concentrate on a specific set of negotiations like an Intergovernmental Conference.

The bi-lateral meetings with other Heads of State and Government and the formal or informal European Council meetings take on a crucial importance. A Presidency will often try to organise an informal summit a couple of months before the envisaged conclusion so that leaders can take the time to understand the dossier fully. In the case of Amsterdam, the negotiations were so drawn out that the Intergovernmental Conference or its preparation had been on the agenda of European Council meetings for over two years. Heads of State were only too well aware of the issues and options.

The President of the Commission is a full member of the European Council and can play a crucial role in its meetings. But, the ability of the Commission to influence a European Council depends on the status and influence of the President. President Santer was one of the most experienced politicians in Amsterdam and he had been involved in Maastricht and been a member of the European Council for most of the previous ten years. However, he had only been President of the Commission for eighteen months and he had not yet stamped his authority on the European Council. President Santer very rarely intervened during the formal meetings in Amsterdam, although the points made on simplifying the codecision procedure and on environment were crucial to the final compromises. The limited number of interventions does not mean that President Santer did not work behind the scenes in Noordwijk and Amsterdam. However, it is clear that President Santer did not have the type of influence that previous President's had been able to achieve.

ii) Foreign Ministers
Foreign Ministers are nominally responsible for the negotiations and met once a month (normally in the format of the General Affairs Council) to oversee the negotiations and provide the political orientation.

It quickly became apparent that the Ministerial level of the IGC was not producing substantive debates and political orientation. This became clear as the first meaningful negotiations began under the Irish Presidency. This reflects a problem that has also taken place during the Maastricht and Nice negotiations. The real difficulty seems to be that Foreign Ministers do not have a real ability to accept or reject proposals and at the same time they do not have a grasp of the detailed negotiations taking place at the level of personal representatives.

The Commission is normally represented by either the President or the Commissioner at Foreign Minister meetings. If only a small number of delegations are asked to intervene, the Commission can be virtually always guaranteed to be included. In the Amsterdam negotiations, Commissioner Oreja often addressed Foreign Ministers. The reality is that most delegations quickly realised that this aspect of the negotiations was often without added value and meetings were often a repeat of the positions expressed at the level of personal representatives.

iii) Personal Representatives
The personal representatives of Foreign Ministers undertook the bulk of the negotiations for the Treaty of Amsterdam and without doubt had the largest

impact on the final text adopted by the Conference. This was in part due to the vast array of issues with which Foreign Ministers did not have time to deal.

The representatives' group met nearly every two weeks for nearly eighteen months. The composition was a mixture of politicians, ambassadors and academics. This was different to Maastricht and Nice where the composition was mainly ambassadors. The Commission was represented by Commissioner Oreja. It is generally accepted that like the other politician figures on the group, the Commissioner found it difficult to adapt to the type of language used by Ambassadors. As outlined earlier, the Commission also presented too many different viewpoints to the Member States as different officials routinely replaced the Commissioner at meetings.

That said, the Commission probably had the most influence at this level. The different proposals of the Commission were a crucial part of the negotiations. Indeed on a number of occasions, different delegations specifically requested contributions from the Commission or indicated that their viewpoint would depend on the reaction of the Commission. The technical expertise of the Commission was a key factor in gaining the credibility of other delegations and this was utilised to the full by the Commission.

iv) Friends of the Presidency
The Friends of the Presidency Group more commonly known by its French name "Amis de la présidence" is a sub-group, normally comprised of lawyers who are tasked by the representatives' group to look at a specific issue or problem.

During the Nice negotiations, the group has examined the changes to the treaty and statute of the Court of Justice and the Court of First Instance. In Amsterdam, the group met to deal with the specific issue of the simplification and consolidation of the treaties. The group was also asked to meet during the final weeks of the negotiations to deal with a number of specific issues that the representatives' group did not have time to address such as Article 100a(4) TEC concerning the environment.

This group meets very infrequently so it is difficult to assess the specific influence of one delegation. In general, the Commission legal service which normally sends the Commission representative is well thought of by other delegations.

The Commission's Influence on Different Topics of the IGC
The 1996 Intergovernmental Conference dealt with a huge array of issues during the two years from preparation to completion of the Treaty. These ranged from hugely political issues like fundamental rights and common foreign and security policy to more practical issues like drug policy and animal welfare. The Conference essentially focused on five main headings: An

Area of Freedom, Security and Justice; the Union and the Citizen, An effective and coherent Foreign Policy; the Union's Institutions and finally Enhanced cooperation or flexibility. This distinction was kept until the end of the Netherlands Presidency. The amount of influence the Commission was able to exert often depended on the topic.

When the Commission put forward its meeting documents on Common Foreign and Security Policy and weighting of votes in the Council, it was more in hope than in expectation. The reality is that the Commission is unlikely to have significant influence over the final decisions in these areas. The distribution of votes in the Council is a question of power that Member States will decide while the lack of involvement of the Commission in foreign affairs seriously undermines any proposals it may come forward with.

Even the question of the number of Commissioners has proved difficult for the Commission to influence. This is because the Commission has been unable to take a clear position in any of the debates the College has had on the subject. This reflects the real divergence of views on the optimum number and the difficulty that each of the institutions has on presenting a clear position on issues relating to their own power.[28]

On other issues, the Commission is able to influence proceedings to a greater degree. The provisions adopted in Amsterdam on employment, social policy, environment, consumer protection, public health, Justice and Home Affairs and the codecision procedure all have aspects of Commission proposals. It is no coincidence that most of these areas are within the Community pillar. The Commission also tends to have a strong voice on decision-making procedures even if not on the role of institutions themselves.

The Commission focused on different issues depending on the timeframe of the negotiations. In its formal opinion, issues such as fundamental rights, employment and other "citizens issues" were to the forefront while Justice and Home Affairs and Article 113 were more prominent during the Dutch Presidency. The Commission made much of the phrase that it was not seeking new powers during these negotiations. Generally it can be said that the priorities were its efforts on extension of Article 113 (now 133 TEU) to include services, investments and intellectual property, communitarisation of Justice and Home Affairs and extension of the codecision procedure and qualified majority voting.

The Commission was certainly disappointed with the lack of progress on the number of Commissioners, weighting of votes in the Council, incorporation of Western European Union and extension of qualified majority

---

[28] The Commission has debated the issue during the Maastricht, Amsterdam and Nice negotiations without adopting a clear position. The European Parliament has adopted resolutions on its optimum number, but has been wary of trying to set out how this should be divided.

voting in general, and the inclusion of services, investments and intellectual property in Article 113 in particular. Except for the final issue, it is doubtful that the Commission can be seen as a key player in these areas and it is not surprising that the Commission proved to be disappointed. It is also true to say that on the number of Commissioners and the weighting of votes in the Council, the Commission felt their importance was over-played.

What is perhaps more surprising is that if the Commission opinion of 28 February 1996 is compared to the final outcome, there is a rather substantial correlation between the two documents. That does not prove that the Commission influenced those decisions, but it does show that the Commission position was broadly accepted on the majority of issues.

Conclusion

"IGC's are as much about people and circumstances than anything else." The most obvious example of this was the influence of the Dutch Foreign Minister, Michel Patijn on the debate on closer cooperation in the area of common foreign and security policy. The majority of actors are well known to each other, their influence often transcends traditional institutional boundaries.

The most notable difference to Maastricht was the concentration on quiet diplomacy rather than brash public posturing. The majority of the Commission's most effective work was done behind the scenes, often out of sight and mind of many of the delegations.

This type of approach relies heavily on working closely with the various Presidencies and the Council Secretariat. The Commission's ability to influence is based on its ability to understand the different positions of the Member States. Only the Presidency and the Council Secretariat has such an oversight. This influence is not however automatic – it depends on the level of the negotiations, the phase of negotiations and the subject matter.

Like in every negotiation, the Commission had success and failure. In the main, it negotiated well, but it also made some mistakes. This reflects the reality that the Commission is not a single actor, it relies on different personalities and negotiates at different levels and different phases while a treaty revision process is being undertaken.

Quite simply, while observers continue to state that the Commission does not have influence in an Intergovernmental Conference, the Commission will be happy to quietly go about its business.

Annex 1: Proposals of the European Commission during the Amsterdam Negotiations

Report of the Commission on the operation of the Treaty on European Union, 10 May 1995 (SEC (95) 731 final).

Seminar of the Commission on Common Foreign and Security Policy, 19 July 1995 (SEC 95) 1367), 24 July 1995.

Seminar of the Commission on Justice and Home Affairs, 13 September 1995 Information note of the President, Mr Oreja and Mrs Gradin, (SEC (95) 408).

Discussion on the interim report of the Reflection Group. Information note of the Heads of Cabinet of the President and Commissioner Oreja, 13 October 1995.

Meeting of the Heads of Cabinet, 17 November 1995 (SEC (95) 1993).

Commission position on the report of the Reflection Group, 6 December 1995.

Information note of Commissioner Oreja in association with the President, 5 December 1995 (SEC (95) 2146(2).

Opinion of the Commission "Reinforcing Political Union and preparing for enlargement," 28 February 1996.

Report of the Commission to the Council concerning civil protection, tourism and energy, 3 April 1996 (SEC (96) 496 final – CONF/3838).

"Meeting Document" on the weighting of votes in the Council presented by the Commission at the representatives meeting of the IGC, 2 May 1996 (SN 612/96).

"Meeting Document" on CFSP presented by the Commission at the representatives meeting of the IGC, 6 May 1996 (SN 613/96).

Report on Article 189b (8) TEU: scope of application of the codecision procedure, 3 July 1995 (SEC (96) 1225 final – CONF/2882.

Working document of the Commission presented to the representatives' group of the IGC on Article 228 bis and Article 113, 22 and 23 July 1996 (CONF 3890/96).

Comments of the Commission on document CONF 3846 at the representatives' group meeting of the IGC on 22 and 23 July 1996, 25 July 1996, (CONF 3889/96).

Communication of the Commission on the services of general interest in Europe, 11 September 1996 (COM (96) 443 final - CONF/3937/96).

Contribution of the Commission presented at the meeting of the representatives' group of the IGC on 16 and 17 September 1996 on the Justice and Home Affairs aspects of the EC Treaty, (CONF 3912/96).

Contribution of the Commission on the Social Protocol at the representatives' group meeting on 23 and 24 September 1996 (CONF/3914/96).

Intervention of Commissioner Oreja at the representatives' group meeting of the IGC on 30 September 1996 relating to flexibility.

Intervention of the representative of the Commission at the meeting of the representatives' group of the IGC on 7 October 1996 concerning legal personality of the Union, 10 October 1996 (SN 631/96).

Speaking brief for the meeting of the representatives' group of the IGC on 16 October 1996 concerning Article 113 TEC (SN 632/96).

"Exposé des motifs" for the draft presented on 18 September 1996 to the representatives of the governments of the Member States concerning the Justice and Home Affairs provisions of the EC treaty (SEC(96)2004 - CONF/3912/96), 29 October 1996.

Contribution of the Commission on a draft new Article 213 A and comments concerning statistics (CONF/3949/96), 13 November 1996.

Communication on the state of play of the work of the Intergovernmental Conference, (SEC(96) 2192), 25 November 1996.

Communication of Commissioner Oreja, in agreement with the President on the general outline for a draft treaty by the Irish Presidency, (SEC(96)2307/2), 10 December.

Orientation Note on flexibility/closer cooperation, (CONF/3805/97), 22 January 1997.

"Schéma d'approche" for the free circulation of persons / Justice and Home Affairs (CONF/3817/97), 7 February 1997.

Contribution of the Commission on the draft text concerning the new approach on Article 129, (CONF/3822/97), 18 February 1997.

Contribution of the Commission on the Justice and Home Affairs provisions on cross-border cooperation, (SN 515/97), 3 March 1997.

Communication of the Commission on the composition, organisation and functioning of the Commission, (SEC(97)451/2 - CONF/3839/97), 6 March 1997.

Comments of the Commission on the document of the Netherlands Presidency concerning CFSP, (CONF/3833/97), 11 March 1997.

Working document of the services of the Commission on the extension of qualified majority voting in the areas of social policy, taxation and research and development, (CONF/3860/97), 4 April 1997.

Non Paper presented by the Commission on comitology, (CONF/3900/97), 29 April 1997.

Contribution of the Commission on the integration of the Social Protocol in the TEU, (CONF/3904/97), 5 May 1997.

Non Paper presented by the Commission on the financing of public broadcasting, (CONF/3918/97), 20 May 1997.

Bibliography

Bulmer, Simon (1994). "The Governance of the European Union: A New Institutionalist Approach," *Journal of Public Policy*, 13, pp. 351-80.

Christiansen, Thomas & Knud Erik Jørgensen (1998). "Negotiating Treaty Reform in the European Union: The role of the European Commission," *International Negotiation*, Vol. 3, No 3.

Corbett, Richard (1992). "The Intergovernmental Conference on Political Union," *Journal of Common Market Studies*, Vol. 30, No. 2, pp. 271-298.

Delors, Jacques (1996). Public address at the Centre for European Studies, Harvard University.

Dinan, Desmond (1997). "The Commission and the Reform Process," pp. 188-211, in Geoffrey Edwards & Alfred Pijpers (eds.), *The Politics of European Treaty Reform: The 1994 Intergovernmental Conference and Beyond*, London: Pinter.

Dinan, Desmond (1998). "Reflections on the IGCs.," pp. 23-40, in Pierre-Henri Laurent & Marc Maresceau (eds.), *The state of the European Union Vol. 4: Deepening and Widening*, London: Lynne Rienner Publishers.

European Commission (1991). "Opinion of the Commission, 1990-1991," *Supplement 2/91 of the Bulletin of the European Union*.

European Commission (1995). "Report of the Commission on the operation of the Treaty on European Union," 10 May (SEC (95) 731 final).

European Commission (1996). "Reinforcing Political Union and preparing for enlargement," 28 February, ISBN 92-827-5857-5.

Hix, Simon (1998). "The Study of the European Union 11: the "new governance" agenda and its rival," *Journal of European Public Policy*, Vol. 5, No 1, pp. 38-65.

Kortenberg, Helmut (1997). "La négotiation du traité; Une vue cavalière," *Revue trimestrielle de droit européen*, Sommaire No. 4, pp. 709-721.

McDonagh, Bobby (1998). *Original Sin in a Brave New World. An account of the negotiation of the Treaty of Amsterdam*, Dublin: Institute of European Affairs.

Moravcsik, Andrew (1993). "Preferences and Power in the European Community: A Liberal Intergovernmentalist Approach," *Journal of Common Market Studies* 31, pp. 473-524.

Moravcsik, Andrew & Kalypso Nicolaïdis (1999). "Explaining the Treaty of Amsterdam: Interests, Influence, Institutions," *Journal of Common Market Studies*, Vol. 37, No. 1, pp. 59-85.

Oreja, Marcelino (1998). *El Tratado de Amsterdam: Analysis y commentaries*, Madrid: McGraw Hill.

Petite, Michel (1998). *The Commission and the Amsterdam Treaty*, Paper presented to the symposium on the Amsterdam Treaty, Harvard University, January 1998.

Puchala, Donald J. (1999). "Institutionalism, Intergovernmentalism and European Integration: A Review Article," *Journal of Common Market Studies*, Vol. 37, No. 2, pp. 317-331.

Reflection Group Report and Other References for Documentary Purposes, General Secretariat of the Council of the European Union, Brussels, December 1995.

Stubb, Alexander (1998). *Flexible Integration and the Amsterdam Treaty: Negotiating Differentiation in the 1996-97 IGC,* Ph.D.-thesis, London: London School of Economics and Political Science.

Treaty of Amsterdam amending the Treaty on European Union, the Treaties establishing the European Communities and certain related acts, signed on 2 October 1997 and entering into force on 1 May 1999 (OJ C 340, 10.11.97).

Wester, Robert (1992). "The European Commission and European Political Union," pp. 205-214, in Finn Laursen & Sophie Vanhoonacker (eds.), *The Intergovernmental Conference on Political Union, Institutional Reforms, New Policies and International Identity of the European Community*, Maastricht: EIPA.

Young, Hugo (1999). *This Blessed Plot. Britain and Europe from Churchill to Blair*, Basingstoke: Macmillan.

18

The European Parliament: Win-Sets of a Less Invited Guest[1]

Andreas Maurer

Introduction

With its evolving structure of a dynamic multi-level governance (for the concept see Marks 1993, 391-411; Bulmer 1994, 351-380; Kohler-Koch 1995), the EU is neither comparable with national constitutional systems nor with international organizations or associations. Its autonomous development depends on a process of a successive institutional, procedural and functional growth and differentiation which is not yet complete and might well not be in the near future. The nature of the EU is characterized by a continuous extension of its responsibilities and authorities which have enlarged the total range of policy fields community-wide. Simultaneously, more and more competencies have been partly transferred from the exclusive national to a supranational or intergovernmental level. To reconcile the management of growing responsibilities successfully with the demands for real and functional participation of the political actors involved, new institutions have been established and the already existing institutional framework has been altered (Wessels 1996, 57-69; 1997, 267-299). In this regard, the decision-making procedures, and especially the rules applied within and between the institutions of the EU which both the Maastricht and the Amsterdam Treaty have added to the Union's system, were often characterized as opaque and too complex. The complexity of the EU is a result of the huge number of its duties, legislative processes and implementation procedures and, at times, the unfathomable nature of the procedures and the roles of the actors involved. Above, the five principal procedures – simple Council procedure without EP participation, EP consultation, co-operation, co-decision and EP assent, the Treaties and other inter-institutional agreements offer further decision-making courses depending on the voting rules of the Council and the EP as well as on

---

[1] This paper develops further papers produced for ECSA-Pittsburgh (1999), the hearing on the "the EP 1994-1999" organised by the EP's DG II and DG IV, the DFG-project "Regieren in der EU nach Maastricht (GOVIUM)" and the European Parliament-National parliaments project (Maurer & Wessels 2001). It builds on earlier draft papers by the author for Monar/Wessels 2001 and on the publication "What next for the European Parliament," London 1999.

the participation of other institutions (Committee of the Regions, Economic and Social Committee, European Central Bank, EMU Committee, Employment Committee). The complex structure of the Community becomes visible in this variety of procedures. Decision-making methods differ both across the areas of application and across the institutions and bodies involved.[2] In addition, Maastricht introduced new institutions (Committee of the Regions, European Monetary Institute which was transformed into the European Central Bank with the beginning of the third phase to the EMU). This development – further enhanced in the Amsterdam Treaty by the creation of new institutions (Employment Committee, Mr./Mrs. CFSP, Policy Planning and Early Warning Unit) expresses the dynamic of growth and differentiation of European integration. New institutions are not established in order to swell even further the institutional structure of the EU, but because they are needed to deal with new – monetary or social policy – duties of the Union, to give the EU a single voice or interface for dealing with third countries and organizations, or – with regard to the Committee of the Regions – to become the EU's visible feedback towards the regional and local level of governance. New institutions do not operate in a political vacuum but in a closely connected system of power distribution in which the architects of the Treaty have implemented them. Whenever new institutions gain autonomy, they do not use it in isolation but in a framework of already established rules and bodies of political power. Concomitantly this process of institutional growth automatically attains a higher degree of complexity. This is obvious for the actors involved in decision-making processes, but for the citizens of the EU, it is not.

As a result of this incremental process of system change, the EU is widely perceived to suffer from an ever increasing complexity leading to a decline in responsiveness and democracy. And as the Intergovernmental Conferences (IGC) before, the Amsterdam process was not only due to reform the Union's policy agenda, but also to strengthen the democratic nature of its institutional basis. Giving this very task of the IGC, an outside observer with little knowledge about the special constitutional, institutional and political features of the EU system might perceive the European Parliament to be a "natural"

---

[2] For example, the EC Treaty chapters on EMU alone contain nine different decision-making procedures: assent of Parliament and unanimity of the Council: twice; co-operation procedure: four times; consultation of Parliament and unanimity of the Council: seven times; consultation of Parliament and qualified majority voting of the Council: seven times; information of Parliament and qualified majority voting of the Council: six times; information of Parliament and unanimity of the Council: twice; unanimity in the Council without any participation of Parliament: three times; qualified majority voting in the Council without Parliament's participation: nine times; two-thirds majority of weighted votes of the Council without Parliament's participation: once.

key player in any negotiation aimed at making the EU more democratic – especially when deliberations focus on institutional means of democracy. However, a brief examination of the Treaties will clarify such a positivist view and show the limited roles of the EP in participating in IGC's.

The notion of a democratic deficit (Hänsch 1986, 191-200; Reich 1991, 14-18; Williams 1991, 155-176; Neunreither 1994, 299-314; Pliakos 1995, 749-763; Birkinshaw & Ashiagbor 1996, 499-530; Follesdal 1998, 1-10) focuses mainly on the role of institutions designed to represent the different interests of the citizens and to establish different forms of linkage and interest mediation in and for a given polity. I refer to Jachtenfuchs' definition of democracy within the framework of EU governance: the "institutionalization of a set of procedures for the control of governance which guarantees the participation of those who are governed in the adoption of collectively binding decisions" (Jachtenfuchs 1998, 47). Of course, this definition does not automatically make democracy synonymous with parliamentary government. At least theoretically, there are many ways to secure participation of the citizenry in governing a given polity. However, if we turn to the evolution of the EU over the last decades, we observe a trend: the search to establish some kind of representative governance structures, in which institutions aggregate participation needs and try to fulfil their general functions as arenas and rules for making binding decisions, and for structuring the relationship between individuals in various units of the polity and economy (Hall 1986, 19). On this basis, I define the "democratic deficit" of the EU process as a gap between the institution-linked powers transferred to the EU level and the control of the European Parliament or the national parliaments over them: legislative competencies have constantly been shifted from a national parliamentary level towards the Council of Ministers without also including the European Parliament as an equal partner in the EC/EU legislative process.[3]

Of course, those stressing national interest as the decisive variable for understanding the EU's system development, and that national sovereignty may resist European integration, would argue that decision-making in the EU rests primarily upon the Member States and the Council of Ministers and, since Maastricht, on the European Council. Accordingly, this school of thought ascribes only a minor role to the European Parliament – both with regard to its role in IGCs and in the day-to-day process of Treaty implementation.[4] However, since the entry into force of the Single European

---

[3] For the original definition of the democratic deficit see the so-called Vedel-report of the European Commission (1972, 4) and the Toussaint Report by Michel Toussaint, PE DOC A 2276/87 of 1 February 1988.

[4] In this regard, the IGC blueprint of the old British Government is highly illustrative: Foreign and Commonwealth Office (1996) "A Partnership of Nations: The British

Act (SEA) and the introduction of the co-operation as well as the assent procedure, the real distribution of powers between the institutions goes far beyond this conceptualization of the Union. Within the sphere of the European Communities, the Treaty revisions from 1986 onwards reveal a tendency towards a multi-level polity where competencies are not only shared between the Members of the Council but also between the Council and the European Parliament. Nevertheless, even if the SEA and the Maastricht Treaty (TEU) opened new opportunities for an original kind of parliamentary democracy in the EC/EU, they left considerable gaps in parliamentary involvement and control in many policy areas which directly affect the way of living of the Union's citizens.

The EU's Legitimacy Crisis
While the legitimacy of democratic and representative policy-making is not fundamentally challenged within each of its Member States, the EU's institutions and their national counterparts face a multitude of questions as to how representative the system of multi-level governance is. In which way are the Union's quasi-executive branches, the Commission and the Council of Ministers, accountable to a directly legitimized body and how democratic are the decision-making procedures between the Union's legislative authorities? Moreover, and with regard to other than parliamentary or formal mechanisms of linkage between the political authority established by the Union and its citizenry, many scholars in integration studies highlight the fact that the EU lacks broad societal consent.

As Weiler (1992) pointed out, formal legitimacy requires that the evolving structure of power and authority is approved by democratically elected parliaments. In this sense, every stage of the integration process is legitimate when and insofar as it has been settled in a document of EU primary law and after "being ratified by all the Member States in accordance with their respective constitutional requirements" (Article 48 TEU). A political system which is entitled to limit national sovereignty and which has powers to make decisions directly binding the residents of its constituent Members without the prior and individual assent of each national government, requires more than the formal approval of its founding treaties and their subsequent amendments. In Weiler's terms, such a political system – like the European Union – needs social legitimacy: the willingness of minorities to accept the decisions of the majority within the boundaries of the EU's polity. In other words, social legitimacy supposes that decisions which are not made by unanimity at all levels of and at every stage in the policy cycle have to be based on a broad

---

Approach to the European Union Intergovernmental Conference 1996," Presented to Parliament, March 1996.

acceptance of the system. Even if the citizenry of the EU polity is not fully aware of or interested in the way binding decisions about their way of life are made, the system and the institutions laying down the laws must be aware of the risk that the public attitude towards them may shift from some kind of a "permissive consensus" or benevolent indifference to fundamental skepticism.

Thus, with regard to the 1996/1997 IGC, many if not all directly involved "collective actors"[5] argued for the need to enhance democracy in and the legitimacy of the EU. Although Member State governments, parliaments, parties and EU institutions recognized the need to achieve a higher degree of polity-acceptance by the Union's population, most of the proposals concentrated on reforming already existing forms and instruments of the EU's "input-legitimacy" (Scharpf 1975) and its observed deficiencies: decision-making procedures, institutions, and instruments.

The Amsterdam IGC attracted greater attention, interest and expectations in the parliaments of the EU Member States than any of the revisions of the Treaties establishing the EC carried out hitherto. Unlike the negotiations leading to the SEA and the Treaty on European Union (TEU), the Amsterdam deal was prepared and set in a relatively transparent space. Every institution produced its own document on the functioning of the Maastricht Treaty in order to fulfil the requirement of the then Article N TEU. In addition, every Member State government – with the exception of Germany where position papers were produced only in the format of "Franco-German" or "Italo-German" declarations or letters to the Presidency of the Union – published some kind of memorandum on institutional reform. Due to Swedish constitutional requirements, not only the papers circulating around the Reflection group but also those of the Member State delegations in the IGC were open to discussion for the interested citizenry. The European Parliament created a Task Force on the IGC which produced and updated systematic briefings summarizing the positions on every issue on the IGC's agenda. As the synoptic reports of the French National Assembly and the British House of Commons during the IGC, the European Parliament's briefings and summaries were open to the public and disseminated via the internet. Yet public opinion did not concentrate on institutional issues, such as the reweighting of votes in the Council, nor did it really focus on the extension of areas covered by majority voting and co-decision. In general, IGCs, as the Amsterdam process, are conceived by their political rather than institutional objectives.[6] Consequently, during the process of treaty reforms, new or

---

[5] For the use of the term see: Haftendorn (1990, 401-423).

[6] For public and published opinion, the Single European Act (SEA) has been the discovery of the internal market programme, the Maastricht Treaty has been about economic and monetary union and the introduction of a single currency. The

adjusted policy areas reveal higher interest and motivation than institutional or procedural questions. In turn, those actors who orient their argumentation towards mass media, public opinion and the electorate capture the issue of democracy and legitimacy in and of the EU, and its policy-making structure mainly by referring to its problem-solving capacity in specific policy areas. The EU has been seen as some kind of a regulatory regime (Majone 1994; Majone 1996) or a "special purpose organization" (Dehousse 1998, 1), which is less dependent on its parliamentary input legitimacy than on efficiently-oriented policies. In this perspective, the "output-legitimacy" of the Union "depends on its capacity to achieve the citizen's goals and solve their problems effectively and efficiently: The higher this capacity, the more legitimate the system" (Schimmelpfennig 1996, 19; Bogdandy 1993).

In contrast to this approach, elitist attention and interest with regard to the Amsterdam process were closely tied with the question of what institutional role both the European Parliament and the national parliaments will have to play in the future of the Union. Thus, parliamentary democracy within the institutional terrain of the EU became a central element of institutional reform. One may argue that Amsterdam – both the negotiations and the new Treaty itself – reflect a focal point of reference for a discussion on appropriate models of parliamentary and representative democracy in the European Union.

From Maastricht to Amsterdam

The Maastricht Treaty introduced several important changes concerning the role and position of the European Parliament. On the basis of the positive experiences gained from the co-operation procedure since the entry into force of the SEA, the TEU widened its scope of application and in addition created the so-called co-decision procedure, consisting of three readings, at most. In this way, the European Parliament gained the right to block a proposed legislative act without the Council having the right in the end to outvote the Parliament. With co-decision, the Parliament gained a nearly equal say at least in vetoing a legislative act. But unlike the Council, the European Parliament, however, was not able to bypass resistance in the Council against a specific legislative act and to subsequently adopt the act without the approval of the Council. Apart from co-decision, the TEU extended the assent procedure to a wider range of international agreements and other sectors of legislative nature.

Given the Maastricht provisions on the European Parliament's new opportunities to "co-govern" within the inter-institutional framework of the Union, it could be argued, that its position and role were considerably

---

Amsterdam Treaty was mainly considered a reform on employment and social policy, CFSP and the establishment of an area of freedom, security and justice.

strengthened. And indeed, many commentators underlined the importance of the upgraded Parliament with regard to its legislative, its control and its elective functions (Wallace 1996, 3-6; Maurer 1996, 15-38; Raworth 1994, 16-33). Some even concluded that the European Parliament "was perhaps the largest net beneficiary of the institutional changes in the TEU" (Wallace 1996, 63) and that "Maastricht marks the point in the Community's development at which the Parliament became the first chamber of a real legislature; and the Council is obliged to act from time to time like a second legislative chamber rather than a ministerial directorate" (Duff 1995, 253-254).

Despite these achievements, several structural deficits concerning the state, reached in the execution of democracy, remained and led to a controversial dispute about the pros and cons of Maastricht with regard to the European Parliament and the national parliaments in the EU Member States (Kohler-Koch 1998, 263-288; Nickel 1993, 117-135; Pliakos 1995, 749-763; Reich 1992, 287-292; Scully 1997; Smith 1996, 283-301). Whereas most of the early commentaries held that the European Parliament still lacks "true legislative capabilities" (Thomas 1992, 4) or that it could generally be "regarded as a somewhat ineffective institution" (Nugent 1994, 174), the German Constitutional Court's Maastricht ruling led to a more general critique of the EU's parliamentary model. The basic assumption of the Court and later on its protagonist commentators was that a polity presupposes a demos in ethno-national or ethno-cultural terms (the "Volk" instead of the "Gesellschaft" or "Gemeinschaft"), that without a single European people sharing heritage, language, culture and ethnic background, and that without a European public space of communication to shape the will and opinions of the population, no European statehood could be founded. Those who adopted this view (Kielmannsegg 1996, 47-72; Grimm 1993, 13-18), simply denied the pre-constitutional conditions for further integration and therefore concluded that in the absence of a demos there cannot be real democracy at the European level (for the critique on these interpretations see: Weiler 1995, 1651-1688; 1997, 249-287; Craig 1997, 105-130). Assuming a socio-political entity which is willing to produce democratic forms of governance simply cannot dictate structural prerequisites and pre-constitutional elements of the future polity, one could develop these arguments further to conclude that any attempt at institutional and procedural reform is senseless unless the different European Demoi are not identifying themselves as part of an emerging European Demos. Consequently, if one adopts this perspective, the European Parliament remains an artifact of elitist integration and cannot be considered a "Vollparlament" (Lübbe 1994, 147; Schröder 1994, 318 – a fully fledged or "real" parliament). Therefore, strengthening the European Parliament by means of institutional and procedural reforms would not lead to any kind of democratic system. Moving on to our general theme of actors driving the process of IGC's, one could conclude that the EP rests on an illegitimate body which should be excluded from any kind of – intergovernmental – authority to build the Union's foundations further.

Other commentators and involved actors criticized the Maastricht Treaty for moving in the right direction but not far enough. In this regard, criticism occurred because the co-decision procedure was only conceived for fifteen out of 162 EC and 11 EU articles containing procedural arrangements.[7] In approximately 140 possible cases these articles dealt with original, binding secondary legislation whereas the remaining provisions concern quasi-constitutional questions such as enlargement or Treaty reform. In other words, only 9.25 per cent of the EC Treaty arrangements were envisioned for co-decision and another 9.87 per cent for co-operation. By contrast, more than one third of the EC's procedural articles contained an opportunity for the Council to adopt binding secondary legislation without any participation of the European Parliament out of which 38 cases (22.43 per cent) were considered for simple or qualified majority vote (QMV).

Those policy areas where co-decision applied were considered to be rather limited (Gosalbo 1995, 22; Tsinisizelis & Chryssochoou 1996, 1-3). More specifically, it was argued, that "the granting of co-decision rights regarding internal market legislation is only of limited significance, given that such legislation should have been adopted by 1992 and that Articles 100a and 100b [TEC] would no longer serve a purpose after that date" (Corbett 1994, 209).

With regard to the impact of the European Parliament on the EU's legislative output, and therefore the potential of its "output-legitimacy," the co-decision procedure itself was interpreted as being (too) complex, lengthy, cumbersome and protracted (Earnshaw 1996, 109; Westlake 1998, 119; Nugent 1998, 119). Indeed, the procedure described in the then Article 189b TEC (now 251), could well be interpreted as symptomatic for the "general trade-off" between the efficiency of EU decision-making on the one hand and parliamentary involvement on the other. As Scharpf puts it: "Expanding the legislative (...) powers of the European Parliament could render European decision processes, already too complicated and time-consuming, even more cumbersome" (Scharpf 1994, 220; Wessels 1996, 58). Consequently, with regard to the Amsterdam IGC, one could propose either to make co-decision more efficient and to cut off those parts of the procedure which in practice were only rarely used, or to delimit co-decision to those policy-areas where inefficiency is less visible and therefore acceptable for those directly involved. However, it has to be noted, that unlike the above-mentioned fears, co-decision did not appear to have led to serious delays in the final adoption of

---

[7] For a general discussion on the legal aspects of the different decision-making procedures see: Kapteyn and VerLoren van Themaat (1998, 408-446); Schoo (1997).

EC legislation. Detailed analysis even indicates, that the average duration of co-decision fell dramatically from 769 days in 1994 to 344 days for proposals published in 1997 and adopted in 1997 or 1998. The average duration for all legislative acts adopted under the co-decision procedure until June 1999 was 710 days. This is less than the total average duration for all the acts hitherto adopted under the co-operation procedure, which is 734 days (Maurer 1999, 86).

Besides these innovations introduced in the framework of the TEC, the new fields of intergovernmental co-operation and co-ordination – Common Foreign and Security Policy (CFSP) and Co-operation in the fields of Justice and Home Affairs (CJHA) constituted what was probably the EU's most obvious parliamentary democratic deficit. The inadequacy of Parliament's powers of control was all the more serious, since many governments escaped any kind of parliamentary scrutiny at the national level. The scrutiny rights of Parliament were severely limited since its general participation in CFSP activities was specified neither in the Treaty provisions on common positions nor on the adoption of joint actions. In sum, the European Parliament's right to be consulted was restricted to the main aspects and basic choices of the CFSP, although the Council Presidency alone decided on the scale, content and timing of the information provided. Consequently, Parliament's active participation in shaping the substance of the CFSP depended entirely on the political will of the governments of the Member States. The Treaty provisions on the European Parliament's role in CJHA corresponded very largely to the CFSP. A positive factor for Parliament in this context was the fact that the Commission was at least given a right of initiative in the areas listed under the then Article K.1 (1) to (6) TEU, although it had to share this right with the Member States. Thus, there was a specific and effective opportunity for monitoring and censuring the Commission, but not the Council of Ministers.

The European Parliament's Roles at IGC's
As a dynamic political system, the EU faces a permanent process of institutional change. The very system is structured by process – an ongoing oscillation between para-constitutional Treaty amendments and Treaty implementation. According to Laursen, system change relates to the "extension to specific or general obligations that are beyond the boundaries of the original treaty commitments, either geographically or functionally. It typically entails a major change in the scope of the Community or in its institutions, that often requires *an entirely new constitutive bargaining process* among the Member States, entailing substantial goal redefinition among national political actors" (Laursen 1992, 242; see also: Genco 1980, 55-80).

It is therefore necessary to analyze the activities of the European Parliament in the transformation of institutional provisions and interinstitutional relations within the EU as well as in the intercourse of the relations between Member States and the EU. Due to the difficulty of quantifying informal contacts, it seems nearly impossible to measure the concrete influence of the EP in the institutional evolution of the European Union. How is the EP able to inject impetus into the process of system change? Does the EP's relative peripherality correspond to the empirical reality of the very process of system and para-constitutional change, which we observe when exploring the development of the Union during the last 50 years? Of course, if we concentrate our view on the shorter phases of IGCs as "big bargain decisions" (Moravcsik 1993, 473-524; Hurrell & Menon 1996, 386-402; Moravcsik & Nicolaidis 1999, 59-85), we could easily preclude that the direct impact of the EP on the final outcome is symbolic and indirect or at best entirely dependent on Member State behaviour. The EP would be identified as an actor able to steer political debates, to create tension on some parts of the agenda, to make issues public, but that it would never perform as a decisive player. Adopting this view, the influence of the EP appears at first sight to be rather restricted, although the EP has constantly been one of the most demanding actors for institutional changes and constitutional proposals. Even prior to the first European elections in 1979 there had been various resolutions to reform the system, such as the Pleven Report in 1961 or the Bertrand Report in 1975. The 1979 elections of the EP – "itself a major constitutional change in the community" (Jacobs, Corbett & Shackleton 1995, 299) – have further increased this role of the European Parliament. In 1984, the EP submitted a Draft Treaty on the European Union – the so-called Spinelli Draft –, which was one of its most important initiatives. Although the Spinelli Draft was not taken up as an actual constitution, it achieved a certain influence on debates at that time and inspired the proceedings leading to the conclusions of the Single European Act (Archer & Butler 1996, 49).

The puzzle emerges, that despite the modest role of the EP, three Intergovernmental Conferences (IGCs) – 1985, 1991 and 1996 – have shown a constant image of the system-development role of the European Parliament and the EP being granted with more and more powers transforming the EU's bilateral set up – Commission vs. Council and Member States – into a trilateral one.

Locating IGCs: Institutional Change Through Incrementalism
System and institutional change in the Union do not exclusively take place at IGCs. Relations between Treaty reform and Treaty implementation are not one-directional, but characterized by "mutual interdependencies between and within the many levels of governance within the EU" (Sverdrup 2000, 249). Treaty reforms do not come out of the blue as a "deus ex machina-" from some distant masters, but are reactions to prior trends. They "ratify" or

"rubberstamp" institutional evolutions which have taken place within or outside the existing treaty provisions. They try to address institutional and procedural weaknesses identified during the implementation of previous provisions or aim at adapting the Union to new – external and/or internal – contexts. Or, as Christiansen and Jørgensen put it:

> In so far as IGCs actually perform a function for national governments, this is rather ceremonial (states celebrating their status as states) and disciplinary (states exerting a slightly greater than usual degree of control over the agenda and time-scale of reform) than actually decisional. In the absence of a complete and final *Kompetenz-Kompetenz* in the EU, IGCs constitute the attempt by governments to assert their control of the expanding portfolio of EU competences. But the wave of IGCs during the 1990s, we believe, demonstrates conclusively the opposite: governments have lost command and control not just over every-day EU business, but even over something as "intergovernmental" as treaty reform (Christiansen & Jørgensen 1999, 1).

Treaty revisions are, thus, endemic parts of the very process of European integration; they are not just independent variables affecting the nature and the evolution of the system but they are themselves objects of the dynamism they might have shaped themselves. In other words, institutions and procedures are creations and creatures at the same time. In this perspective, the process of European integration is more than negotiated "grand bargains," "super-systemic" or "history-making decisions" (Peterson 1995; Pogge 1998, 161). Instead, integration needs to be conceived over the *longue durée*. Accordingly, it is insufficient to try to capture the dynamics of integration through snap-shot analyses of episodes of treaty reform.

The historical-institutionalist model of "path-dependency" of policy preferences, institutions and procedures, policy-outcomes and policy-instruments (Pierson 1998, 27-58) offers one important step to understand the ups and downs, pushes and pulls in institutional change. The approach suggests that in such an institutionalised arrangement like the EC/EU, "past lines of policy [will] condition subsequent policy by encouraging societal forces to organise along some lines rather than others, to adapt particular identities or to develop interests in policies that are costly to shift" (Hall & Taylor 1996, 941). Institutions, rules and procedural routines at both the national and the European levels of governance therefore "structure political situations and leave their own imprint on political outcomes" (Bulmer 1994, 356). In other words, institutional arrangements shape the realm for further developments insofar as they narrow down the areas for possible change and oblige Member

States to consider incremental revision of existing arrangements. Within these processes, national interests and preferences – as they are the articulated products of shared beliefs – "act as "focal points" around which the behaviour of actors converges" (Garrett & Weingast 1993, 176). This process presupposes interest aggregation by national governments (Putnam 1988, 427-460; Moravcsik 1993, 473-524; Skidmore & Hudson 1993). They are widely perceived as "unified actors" (Grieco 1988, 494) and remain key interlocutors for the EC/EU institutions and arenas. They perform as important addressees for non-governmental organisations and other functional "demoi" (Abromeit & Schmidt 1998, 301-303; Abromeit 1998). They provide essential resources for the system not only in respect to the financial basis of the Union, but also with regard to the effective functioning of the institutional setting. Hence, Member States second civil servants for the Council and the Commission, provide important intellectual and managerial resources for the Council Presidencies, and coercive resources for driving the Council to reach agreement (Metcalfe 1998, 413-434). However, like institutional and policy developments, national interest formation is "locked in": The preference aggregators and articulators of the EC/EU system (governments and parliaments) use the channels which they have offered themselves. Concomitantly, societal preference builders (political parties, non-governmental organisations, public opinion, mass media) also become involved in the process – some of them may be fully aware of these interaction mechanisms (parties and NGO's, because they are mirrored directly within the Brussels/Strasbourg arenas by similar and corresponding entities), others may only react to European policy and institutional outcomes (public opinion). In any case, the complex mechanism between institutions, interests and ideas needs to be taken into account. The EU institutions exert "pulls" on political actors, however, once engaged, these actors then exert a push in seeking to define the policy agenda.

Our alternative view to the – liberal – intergovernmentalist conceptualization of treaty reform takes the periods between IGC's more seriously. The "structurationalist" concept (Christiansen & Jørgensen 1999) of "summits and valleys" conceives constitutional and system development as a process – the "valley" – which culminates at IGCs – "the summits" and – most likely into the "peak" of a European Council adopting a new Treaty. In this view, system-development takes place through incrementalism in a valley of day-to-day politics where reform is not simply a matter of bargaining on preferences among states acting as unitary actors. Instead, incremental change suggests that treaty reform is subject to a wide range of actors (not only states) and to an unceasing process of discovering political preferences and "problem solving" in an unstable setting (Risse-Kappen 1996, 53-80). In this regard, Member States identify their preferences not simply as a fixed set of demands, but also during the process of Treaty implementation and Treaty reform. The EP can then be located as but an important actor able to influence the rolling agenda of the very process of system development.

As other treaties before and after it, the Maastricht Treaty left the EC institutions with a wide range of questions, particularly regarding their roles and powers in the European policy-making process. Interinstitutional agreements (IIA) concluded since October 1993 were a pragmatic answer to resolve frictions and conflicts between the European Parliament on the one hand and the Council and the Commission on the other (Monar 1994, 693-719). Some IIAs derive directly from Treaty provisions. In fact, Art. 195 TEC provides for an IIA on the regulations and general conditions governing the performance of the European Ombudsman, and Art. 193 assumes that the detailed rules governing the EP's new right of inquiry shall be determined by "common accord." Apart from these two IIA, the original "post-Maastricht-set" of IIAs included the general issue of democracy and transparency; the implementation of the subsidiarity principle; the operation of the Conciliation Committee under Art. 251 and the issue of budgetary discipline and budgetary procedures. Negotiations started in 1992 and were partly resumed under the Belgian Presidency in October 1993, when the Presidents of the three institutions signed the "budgetary" IIA in order to endorse the EC's 1993-1999 financial perspective. In January 1995, the three institutions also concluded an IIA on the official codification of EC legislation. However, given the restrictive position of the Council with respect to the powers of the temporary committees of inquiry, the relevant IIA negotiations continued until April 1995. Besides the successfully agreed IIAs, the proposals of the EP (submitted in December 1993) for three other IIAs on the implementation of CFSP, on the application of Title VI TEU (Cooperation in the fields of justice and home affairs) and on the implementation of EMU failed. In fact in February 1994, the Council informed the EP that it did not wish to enter into negotiations on the EP's draft IIAs (Monar 1994, 716-717; Maurer 1996, 26-28).

However, as regards the CFSP issue, the interinstitutional trialogue was reopened during the 1996/1997 IGC and the EP achieved an IIA on CFSP financing (replaced by the IIA on budgetary discipline of May 1999). This established a procedure for a formal consultation of Parliament about the main aspects involved in the CFSP. It required the Council to provide detailed financial plans of joint actions and the Commission to inform Parliament at least every four months about the implementation of CFSP action and to supply financial forecasts for the rest of the year.

In addition to these IIAs, the EP got the Council and the Commission to conclude an agreement on the question of Comitology with regard to legislative acts adopted under co-decision and cooperation – the so-called

Modus vivendi of 1995 (OJEC C043, 20.2.1995). This IIA provides Parliament with the power to monitor the implementing measures and enables it to be involved in the final decision in the event of disputes between the "Comitology Committee" and the Commission. Finally, under the pressure of the time-limits set by the conciliation procedure on the SOCRATES and YOUTH FOR EUROPE III programs, the institutions also set an IIA (in the form of a "joint declaration") on the incorporation of financial provisions into legislative acts. The EP accepted the inclusion of a financial framework in multi-annual programs. In exchange, the Council agreed that the budgetary authority (i.e. the EP and the Council) may depart therefrom. In adopting this IIA, the EP achieved a year-old objective, namely the "recognition of the primacy of the budgetary authority, as against the legislator, with regard to allocating the resources available" (EPDCC report, 1 March 1995, p. 11).[8]

During its last legislative plenary session in May 1999, Parliament finally approved the establishment of a new financial perspective for the years 2000-2006, the text of the IIA for the financial perspective for the years 2000-2006 and the new IIA on budgetary discipline and improvement of the budgetary procedure.[9] The IIA clarifies that policy initiation by budgetary politics is confined to a certain set of pilot schemes of an experimental nature, preparatory actions and specific actions listed in the IIA. Interestingly, the IIA deals with the applicability of Article 249 TEC in that it further defines the legislative character of the EC norms. Consequently, the IIA may therefore constitute a basis for revising Article 249 TEC in order to adapt the Treaty's classification of norms to the Union's empirical reality (existing distinction between legislative – action programs related – decisions and decisions in the original meaning of Article 249).

Even if IIAs cannot amend the Treaties (Monar 1994, 719), in practice, they can go far beyond what has been agreed under the Maastricht Treaty. IIAs have sown "the seeds of future Treaty amendments" (MEP Metten in: OJ Debates, 11 March 1993, 251). They have acknowledged and even increased the political role of the EP in the EC and, as the CFSP agreement shows, even in the EU's policy-making process.

In this regard, and contrary to Moravcsik and Nicolaidis (1999, 81) who argue, that the increase of Parliament's powers is explained mainly by ideological preferences of Member State governments, the European Parliament itself was able to set some important items on the agenda of the

---

[8] The IIA was replaced by the IIA of 6 May 1999 on budgetary discipline and improvement of the budgetary procedure, OJEC C 172 of 18 June 1999, Arts. 7 and 36-37.

[9] IIA of 6 May 1999 on budgetary discipline and improvement of the budgetary procedure, OJEC C 172 of 18 June 1999.

1996/1997 IGC – compare e.g., Parliament's blue prints which it discussed following the negotiations on Political Union for making co-decision more efficient and less complicated with the Amsterdam outcome or the Spinelli draft on subsidiarity with ex-Article 3b. Thus, IIAs are conditioning instruments for running the EU more efficiently, more transparently, and more democratically. In other words, IIAs are "important means of informal constitution building in the EU" (Dinan 1998, 298). Unlike in the IGC's on Treaty Reform, the European Parliament takes an active part in driving other institutions for new legal, organizational and budgetary arrangements. Thus, the European Parliament was able to set some important items on the agenda of the 1996/1997 IGC.

The Participation of the European Parliament in the Intergovernmental Conference 1996/1997
During the negotiations of the Intergovernmental Conference 1985, the involvement of the EP was limited. Although it monitored negotiations intensely and its then president Pierre Pflimlin and MEP Altiero Spinelli were invited to some ministerial meetings, their involvement in the end was only restricted which meant that the EP accepted the Single European Act with limited institutional proceedings for the Parliament. However, it was also the Parliament which pushed the governments to initiate a treaty revision.

In the 1991/1992 IGC, the European Parliament adopted several resolutions – based upon the Martin and Colombo reports – on the process of Treaty revision and stated its preferences for institutional reform. President Baron took part in all European Council meetings and in two meetings of the Foreign Affairs Ministers. Moreover, all members of the Council were expected to participate in various meetings with a delegation of the EP. While the pressure applied by Parliament was in no particular case decisive, the EP nevertheless accomplished some "major steps forward in the direction advocated by the European Parliament" (Jacobs, Corbett & Shackleton 1995, 304). It served as a supporting element to those governments and institutions pledging for substantial reforms. Neither the new policy areas, for example consumer protection, education and culture, nor the co-decision procedure would have come into force without the permanent pressure of the EP.

In a clear contrast to the proceedings in 1991, the preparation of the 1996 IGC revealed considerable progresses for the European Parliament.

In order to gain support and to succeed in system developing, the EP had at least four specific options. First, the EP could benefit from a partnership with national parliaments which evolved since 1989 under different formats (COSAC, Joint Committee Meetings, Joint Parliamentary Hearings etc.). Second, it could profit from alliances with certain national governments. Due to pressure from their national parliaments the Belgian as well as the Italian government connected their signature of the Treaty amendments to the vote of the EP. Both governments proclaimed that they would not accept the results of the IGC until the European Parliament had approved it. This proclamation put considerable pressure on the other European governments to take the view of the EP into account. A third option of the Parliament in order to gain support was to use its contacts with intermediary groups and, through its parliamentary groups and European parties, with national political parties. Finally, a fourth strategy of the EP resulted from linking important decisions and enacting a kind of package deal. In the 1996/1997 IGC, this last option had some influence. The European Parliament stated that if the results of the ongoing IGC were unsatisfactory, it would reject the future enlargement of the Union, which is a decisive right of the EP (Art. 49 TEU). As any future enlargement is subject to the assent procedure, Parliament's right embodies a tremendous potential.

In the 1996/97 IGC, the position of the EP was completely different from previous Intergovernmental Conferences. The Reflection Group was composed of personal representatives of the Foreign Ministers of the 15 Member States, a member of the European Commission and two members of the European Parliament. According to Dinan (1999, 8), the EP managed to exploit a crisis over qualified majority voting in 1994 for its own institutional interest. Dissatisfied with the 1994 Ioannina Compromise, it threatened to withhold its assent from the 1995 enlargement unless the Member States would involve it as fully as possible in the upcoming IGC. Even if one doubts that in the end, the EP would have blocked enlargement over the issue, it did give the parliamentarians some leverage over unsympathetic Member States (such as the United Kingdom and France). As a result, the EP was granted two representatives in the Reflection Group.

Due to a variety of factors, the two members of the European Parliament received praise from the other participants for their contribution to the work of the Reflection Group. First of all, Elmar Brok (a German Christian Democrat) and Elisabeth Gigou (a French socialist) supplemented each other very well, as a close collaborator of Brok observed. Not only did they originate from the two dominant parties in the European Parliament, but Gigou's "ENA-trained sharp intellect" complemented Brok, the "instinct politician" very well. In addition, the EP had learned from past mistakes. Marginalised at Maastricht by the Member States as a result of excessive demands, the two MEPs made certain that their demands and contributions to the Reflection Group always remained in the sphere of the realistic. On no occasion did the EP find itself in an isolated position in the Group, even when it demanded important progress e.g., on institutional reform or on employment policy, as on each point at least some Member States supported the EP's positions. Thus, the two MEPs "enjoyed a high degree of acceptance in the

Reflection Group. On no occasion were they considered as foreign bodies" (Interview with a Commission official).

As a result of the positive attitude of the Reflection group, the EP raised the question of its role in the IGC itself. Lodge (1998, 486) reports that the European Parliament demanded a place at the conference table on the grounds that the IGC was convened to prepare the Union for enlargement. Since an enlargement must be endorsed by the EP, the deputies argued, they could always withhold their assent unless they were granted a significant role in the IGC. In addition, the MEPs claimed that since they were the only directly elected EC institution, their participation in the IGC would lend the whole process of treaty reform an increased degree of legitimacy.

Apart from the fact that granting the EP a formal role at the IGC would have posed legal problems (the 1996/97 IGC was conducted under the terms of ex-Article N TEU which did not mention the European Parliament), France and the United Kingdom strongly resisted the demands of the EP and even vetoed suggestions by Benelux, Germany and Italy to allow the EP a status of permanent observer at the conference (Petite 1997, 23). In the end, the Foreign Ministers, meeting in Brussels on 25 March 1996, agreed on the following compromise (European Parliament 1995, 7):

- At the beginning of each ministerial session of the IGC, there would be an exchange of views with the EP President on the subjects on the agenda, in the presence of the representatives of the Parliament.
- Once a month and when the representatives of the Ministers considered it desirable, the Presidency of the Council would hold a working meeting on the occasion of the meetings of the IGC Representatives Group.
- The Presidency would keep the European Parliament informed, orally or in writing.

The reaction of the European Parliament was lukewarm. At a press conference, Klaus Hänsch, the President of the EP, stated that this compromise was "reasonable" even though not "formulated perfectly" (*Agence Europe* 1996). Nevertheless, these provisions were endorsed by the Heads of State and Government at the Turin European Council on 29 March 1996. This extraordinary summit further established the final mandate for the IGC and solemnly launched the 1996/97 intergovernmental conference (Presidency Conclusions 1996a).

As a letter from the EP President to the Council President of 12 March 1997 reveals, the implementation of the provisions concerning the EP's participation at the IGC was not satisfactory. In fact, the Turin European Council arrangements were undermined by "a minimalist interpretation, since the exchanges of views which are supposed to take place with the President of the European Parliament at the ministerial sessions of the IGC are, in practice, being restricted almost exclusively to a speech [...] without a proper ensuing debate" (CONF/3847/97, confirmed by: Speech of the Portuguese State Secretary for European Affairs, 11 November 1999).

The EP's Influence on the Outcome of the 1996/1997 IGC

The European Parliament was – as always – longing for a wide scope of powers and rights. The EP's main demands in the 1996/97 IGC referred, inter alia, to the decision-making process and the powers of the EP therein (CONF/3810/97; CONF/3891/97), the statute of MEPs (CONF/3881/97), employment policy (CONF/3891/96), and to CFSP reform (CONF/3885/97). The EP intended to be established as the co-player of the Council with equal rights. Therefore, it proposed a simplification of the various procedures by reducing them to three types: consultation, co-decision and assent. The second procedure – co-decision – should be the standard decision-making process of the Community, including qualified majority voting in the Council as a general rule.

The outcome of the 1996/1997 IGC for the EP was somewhat ambiguous (Nickel 1998, Nickel 1999). In particular, the parliamentary ambition of enlarging the co-decision procedure was not entirely successful, although 23 new cases were introduced. The budgetary division between obligatory and non-obligatory expenditures was not overthrown, as requested by Parliament. The EP did not receive any formal rights in changes of the TEU and – as other important examples – it did not obtain any specific titles in the common agricultural policy and in the second pillar. On the other hand, the simplification of the co-decision procedure was a major achievement according to the Parliament's demands. The new procedure for the investiture of the Commission, the incorporation of the social protocol into the TEC and the new title on employment policy were other examples – partly achieved due to the tension created by EP demands.

The Path to Amsterdam

Comparing the documents produced during the IGC process (Istituto Affari Internazionali 1994-1996; European Parliament 1996; Pijpers & Edwards 1997; Griller *et al.* 1996; Jopp & Schmuck 1996; Jopp, Maurer, & Schmuck 1996; Piepenschneider 1996), the proposals made under the headings of "democratization" can be classified as follows:

1. Democratization by reforming the decision-making procedures through an extension of the areas covered by the co-decision procedure according to the following four strategies:

(a) A systematic conjunction of the different types of decision-making procedures and the institutions to be involved in on the one hand, and the nature of the different legal acts at the EC/EU's disposal on the other. This approach – proposed by the EP from 1984 onwards – would have suggested some kind of a hierarchy of norms as if it might be derived from the legal definition of the Council acting as legislator (OJ L304/7 of 10th December 1993).[10] Originally, the joint declaration of the then German and Italian Foreign Affairs Ministers Kinkel and Agnelli was strongly in favour of classifying the decision-making system of the Union according to this approach. During the negotiations, the Commission, on 3rd July 1996, published a comprehensive report on the method of extending the coverage of co-decision based on the definition of EC legislation (European Commission 1996). The European Parliament, in its Bourlanges/De Giovanni report of 7th November 1996, largely welcomed this approach but suggested a more coherent way of separating "legislative" from "non-legislative" acts (European Parliament 1996). The main variable for identifying an area as subject to co-decision was the legal nature of legislation, its scope and its implications. However, apart from Germany, Greece and Italy, the Member States delegations did not develop further this approach.

(b) A systematic association of decision-making mechanisms in the Council of Ministers and decision-making procedures between the Council and the European Parliament. Protagonists of this approach suggested the introduction of co-decision in all cases where the Council decides by qualified majority. Consequently, the success of this strategy largely depended on the reform of the Council's own decision-making regime. The fact that after Maastricht the Council in the field of the EC's binding secondary legislation still had to decide unanimously in 57 TEC cases seemed to be characteristic for the incapability of acting as one Union of fifteen Member States. The unanimity requirement in the Council of Ministers proved to be a serious obstacle to efficient policy making.[11] However, negotiations on the reform of the Council's voting mechanisms and on the extension of the areas governed by the Damocles-sword of

---

[10] See: Rules of Procedure of the Council of Ministers, Annex.

[11] The refusal strategy of the British government in the "BSE/mad-cow disease conflict" in the preliminary stage of the Florence European Council highlighted this problem to a remarkable extent.

majority voting were not successful. The Member States discussed the possibility of an extension of qualified majority voting by referring to power (or status) oriented linkages between their personal representation in the EU institutions (namely with regard to the Commission), the representation of states by the weight of votes and the maintenance of Member State veto power with regard to the threshold for qualified majorities and blocking minorities. Since no compromise could be found between the large and the small Member States, the IGC postponed the whole issue of adjusting these representative aspects of institutional reform to the next enlargement round (McDonagh 1998; Duff 1997; Laffan 1997, 29-48). The "Protocol on the institutions with the prospect of enlargement of the European Union" concluded that by the next enlargement of the Union, Member States which actually nominate two Commissioners will have to give up one of these posting rights. However, this reform is conditioned by the need of a reorganization of the weighting of votes within the Council in order to compensate those states which stand to lose one of the two Commissioners to which they are entitled. Thus, the protocol reflects a strong cleavage between large and small Member States and admits the failure of Amsterdam in this respect. Consequently, in the absence of a solution to this cleavage, an extension of co-decision depending on the voting requirements in the Council was not achievable.

(c) The simple transfer of the existing co-operation procedures into co-decision procedures. Right from the beginning of the preparatory "reflection" phase on the IGC, Austria, Belgium, Germany, Italy, Luxembourg, the Netherlands and Portugal argued strongly in favour of replacing the co-operation procedure and its replacement with the co-decision procedure. During negotiations between the Member States delegations, this approach attracted the highest degree of sympathy. However, since an early agreement could be found not to reopen the Treaty provisions on EMU, it was very likely that four co-operation procedures would be retained.

(d) A policy oriented and single (national) interest guided re-ordering of decision-making procedures. Protagonists of such an approach looked at the European Parliament as a potential winning coalition partner in order to enforce or to block decision in specific policy areas. Given their general attitude of reforming the procedural set-up of the Union on a case-by-case basis, the governments of Finland, Ireland, Portugal and Sweden preferred this approach. Especially Sweden, where a majority of the political parties in government were reluctant vis-à-vis a general strengthening of the European Parliament, linked its "parliamentarisation" – suggestions to proposals on the improvement of policy areas such as environmental and social affairs.

2. The second path for democratization focused on the intergovernmental EU pillars (CFSP and CJHA). Proposals varied between (a) a full-scale or partial integration of one or both pillars into the EC Treaty and its procedural as well as institutional obligations, and (b) the introduction of more legally binding – similar to the EC Treaty – procedures and more participatory as well as control powers for the European Parliament and/or the national parliaments within the remaining EU pillars.

3. A third option for democratization of EC/EU decision-making procedures was discussed with regard to the roles of the national parliaments (Maurer/Wessels 2001). Proposals varied between those who opted for: (a) the introduction of direct participatory or control powers for national parliaments within the legal framework of the EC/EU, (b) the introduction of a provision within the EC/EU Treaty framework guaranteeing national parliaments some unilateral control mechanisms vis-à-vis their respective governments, and (c) the formal upgrading of existing multilateral scrutiny regimes bringing together members from both the European Parliament and the national parliaments. Several ideas had been suggested to institutionalize national parliaments in the European policy process. The French parliament considered that the establishment of a European Senate or an interparliamentary committee, made up of an equal number of representatives from each Member State, could represent the national parliaments in respect of the EU decision-making process. The vast majority of parliaments were against those ideas, arguing that the creation of new bodies leads to an overload of both the institutional framework of the Union and of the parliaments in the Member States. However, parliaments and governments in the United Kingdom and Denmark suggested to at least upgrade the Conference of European Affairs Committees (COSAC) in a pragmatic fashion in relation to the application of the principle of subsidiarity and the second and third pillars.

4. The fourth path for democratization of the EU concentrated on the structural prerequisites of the Union, and on how to provide opportunities for democratic and legitimate governance through the introduction or the reinforcement of new or more visible fundamental rights within the EC/EU Treaty set-up, of new information and deliberation rights for the citizenry or through the introduction of certain direct participation rights in the Treaties (Zürn 1996, 27-55; Abromeit 1998, 80-90).

The Result I – EP Powers

The Amsterdam Treaty widened the scope of application of the co-decision procedure extensively both with respect to those policy areas which it had just introduced into the EC sphere and with respect to policy areas already covered by the co-operation procedure. In future, the bulk of the EC's original secondary legislation will be adopted following the co-decision procedure. Apart from those areas where co-decision will apply right after the entry into force of the Amsterdam Treaty, it will automatically be extended to measures on the procedures and conditions for issuing visas by Member States as well as to rules on uniform visa formats after five years.

Table 18.1: Coverage of Co-decision after Amsterdam.

Treaty articles on co-decision between the European Parliament and the Council		Council decides by:	Comment:
Art. 12.2	Prohibition of discrimination	QM	Previously co-operation procedure
Art. 18.2	Citizens rights	U	Previously co-operation procedure
Art. 40	Free movement of workers	QM	Co-decision since Maastricht
Art. 42	Social Security for migrant workers	U	Previously co-operation procedure
Art. 44	Right of establishment	QM	Co-decision since Maastricht
Art. 46	Provisions concerning treatment of foreign nationals	QM	Co-decision since Maastricht
Art. 47.1	Mutual recognition of diplomas	QM	Co-decision since Maastricht
Art. 47.2	Provisions for the self-employed	U	Co-decision since Maastricht
Art. 55	Provisions of services	QM	Co-decision since Maastricht
Art. 62.2bii	Visa procedures and conditions	U→QM automatically	Co-decision five years after entry into force of Amsterdam

Treaty articles on co-decision between the European Parliament and the Council		Council decides by:	Comment:
Art. 62.2biv	Visa uniformity rules	U→QM automatically	Co-decision five years after entry into force of Amsterdam
Art. 71	Transport policy	QM	Previously co-operation procedure
Art. 80.2	Sea- and Air transport	QM	Previously co-operation procedure
Art. 95	Internal market – Harmonisation measures	QM	Co-decision since Maastricht
Ex.-Art. 100b	Internal market – Mutual recognition	Deleted	Co-decision since Maastricht, never applied
Art. 129	Incentive measures in the field of employment	QM	New
Art. 135	Customs co-operation	QM	New
Art. 137.2	Equal opportunities Women/Men	QM	Previously co-operation procedure
Art. 141.3	Equal treatment Women/Men	QM	New
Art. 148	European Social Fund – Operation	QM	Previously co-operation procedure
Art. 149	Education and Youth policy	QM	Co-decision since Maastricht
Art. 150	Vocational training policy	QM	Previously co-operation procedure
Art. 151	Cultural policy	U	Co-decision since Maastricht
Art. 152.4	Health policy	QM	Co-decision since Maastricht
Art. 152.4.a	Minimum requirements regarding quality and safety of organs	QM	New: previously treated under ex-Art. 43: Agricultural policy
Art. 152.4.b	Veterinary/phytosanitary health policy	QM	New: previously treated under ex-Art. 43: Agricultural policy

Treaty articles on co-decision between the European Parliament and the Council		Council decides by:	Comment:
Art. 153.4	Consumer protection	QM	Co-decision since Maastricht
Art. 156	Trans-European Networks – Guidelines	QM	Co-decision since Maastricht
Art. 156	Trans-European Networks – Actions	QM	Previously co-operation procedure
Art. 162	European Regional Funds – Operation	QM	Previously co-operation procedure
Art. 166	Research and Technology framework programme	QM	Co-decision since Maastricht; previously treated by unanimity in the Council
Art. 172.2	Joint undertakings in RTD	QM	Previously co-operation procedure
Art 175.1	Environment policy- Actions	QM	Previously co-operation procedure
Art. 175.3	Environment policy- Action programmes	QM	Co-decision since Maastricht
Art. 179	Development policy	QM	Previously co-operation procedure
Art. 255	Right of Access to EU documents	QM	New
Art. 280	Combating fraud	QM	New
Art. 185	Statistics	QM	New
Art. 286	Creation of Data protection unit	QM	New

The assent procedure was extended to the new TEU provision on sanctions in the event of a serious and persistent breach of fundamental rights by a Member State. Finally, the scope of application of the consultation procedure was expanded by nine treaty provisions. This procedure will cover an overall of 59 EC and 9 EU cases after the entry into force of the Amsterdam Treaty.

Table 18.2: European Parliament and Council decision making powers after the entry into force of the Amsterdam treaty.

Participation of the EP	Unanimity in Council		QMV in Council		Simple Majority in Council		Special majorities other than QMV		Sum	
	Nos.	%	Nos.	%	Nos.	%	Nos.	%	Nos.	%
Consultation	33 EC 4 EU	1.7e+07	23 EC 1 EU	1e+06	1 EC 1EU	5e+05	2 EC 1 EU	1e+05	59 EC 7 EU	3.1e+07
Co-operation	0 EC	0	4 EC	207	0 EC	0	0 EC	0	4 EC	207
Co-decision	5 EC	259	33 EC	1714	0 EC	0	0 EC	0	38 EC	1967
Assent	6 EC 2 EU	310689	2 EC	103	1 EC	518	2 EC	103	11 EC 2 EU	569689
Information	1 EC	518	8 EC	414	0 EC	0	0 EC	0	9 EC	466
Parliamentary exclusion	31 EC 9 EU	1.6e+07	31 EC 3 EU	2e+07	4 EC 3 EU	2e+06	6 EC 5 EU	3e+06	72 EC 20 EU	3.7e+07
Sum	76 EC 15 EU	3.9e+07	101 EC 4 EU	5e+07	6 EC 4 EU	3e+06	10 EC 6 EU	5e+06	193 EC 29 EU	1.0e+09

Own calculation; Source: Treaty of Amsterdam 1997.

As a result of the Amsterdam process, many core issues of European integration have been added to decision-making procedures providing the European Parliament with considerable powers vis-à-vis the Council of Ministers and the European Commission. However, the European Parliament continues to be excluded from dynamic and "costly" policy areas such as agriculture (Article 37 TEC), tax harmonization (Article 93 TEC) and trade policy (Article 133 TEC). Consequently, the effects of Amsterdam will be less visible, as the previous argument suggests.

Apart form the extension of co-decision, a position defended by the EP and several Member States during the IGC, and on the basis of the EP's own blueprint which dates back to the Maastricht IGC, the procedure itself has been considerably simplified in four ways:

First, it provides for the adoption of a legislative text at first reading phase if the European Parliament does not propose any amendment at first reading or if the Council agrees with all of the European Parliament's first reading amendments. The importance of this reform becomes clear when looking into the practice of co-decision and not simply at Member States' preferences at the IGC. Out of the 96 procedures concluded until mid-1997, 67 cases could have been closed after the first reading stage.[12]

Second, the phase whereby the European Parliament could vote on its intention to reject the Council's common position has been dropped – mainly on the basis of the EP's own attempts during the IGC. Consequently, the European Parliament can go straight to a vote of rejection and the draft proposal will fail. This part of the procedure's reform largely corresponds to the practice of co-decision.

Third, the so-called third reading whereby the Council could seek to impose the common position after a breakdown of conciliation, unless the European Parliament could overrule it by an absolute majority of its members, has been dropped, too. During the negotiations, some of the Member States opposed this abolition because it would appear to change the institutional balance between the institutions. Especially the Juppé-Government in France opposed any changes to the procedural set-up of the Union, that could change the institutional balance – particularly between the European Parliament and the Council (Assemblée Nationale 1996). Thus, the elimination of the third reading was the most controversial question. In the end, France accepted the new procedure for two reasons: First, the French proposals for strengthening the role of national parliaments in the Union were successful in that

---

[12] Either because the Council accepted all first reading amendments of the European Parliament, because Parliament accepted the common position of the Council, or because both Parliament and Council adopted the Commission's original proposals as final text (European Parliament Delegations to the Conciliation Committee 1997).

Amsterdam provides for a new, legal-binding protocol on the powers offered to these actors. Secondly, unlike its Gaullist predecessor, not only the French Socialist Party as such, but also the new Red-Green coalition lead by Lionel Jospin have a more positive attitude towards the European Parliament.

Fourth, as one of the most important achievements of Amsterdam, the new procedure now provides for the proposal to have failed in the absence of agreement in conciliation. This deletion of the third-reading phase finally puts Parliament on an equal footing with the Council in every stage of the procedure. Under the original co-decision procedure, the Council could obstruct Parliament with a "take-it-or-leave-it" offer after unsuccessful conciliation (Tsebilis 1994; Garrett 1995; Tsebelis & Garrett 1997). The "equalisation" of both legislative branches now implies a balanced set of veto powers. In more concrete terms, this provision will have important effects for how the Parliament is viewed by the outside world: Under the Maastricht rules, the Council could easily make the Parliament pay for the failure of a draft legislative act. With the entry into force of Amsterdam, both Council and Parliament will share the responsibility for the adoption as well as the failure of a proposed legislative act. Both institutions anticipated this reform in March 1998, when no agreement on the Comitology issue could be found within the conciliation committee on the draft directives 93/6/EEC and 93/22/EEC. Instead of revising the draft according to the Maastricht Treaty provisions, the two institutions declared the failure of the procedure after conciliation.[13]

Improvements in Amsterdam were also made with regard to the European Parliament's elective function (Article 214 TEC). The Maastricht Treaty already grants the European Parliament with the right to be consulted on the

---

[13] In addition, Article 251(4) TEC seeks to prevent too much flexibility in the consideration of European Parliament amendments in conciliation by stating "in fulfilling this task, the Conciliation Committee should address the common position on the basis of the amendments proposed by the European Parliament." This provision will certainly lead to more self-discipline in both the Council and the Parliament, because it leads to a higher degree of programming amendments before conciliation takes place. Finally, the new procedure also provides stricter time limits than at present. If – according to Article 251(3) TEC – the Council does not approve all of the European Parliament's amendments in the second reading, the meeting of the Conciliation Committee has to be convened within 6 weeks, extendable to 8 weeks if necessary. In close connection to this, the non-binding declaration No. 34 annexed to the Amsterdam Treaty states that "in no case should the actual period between the second reading by the European Parliament and the outcome of the Conciliation Committee exceed 9 months." These two provisions together with the broader application and the simplification of the procedure will certainly lead to (1) a new workload for some of the European Parliament's committees and the Commission's Directorates General, and (2) as a consequence, to new interinstitutional or even informal arrangements between the institutions.

Member State's choice of the President of the European Commission, to approve the European Commission, to be consulted on the President of the European Monetary Institute and, after the establishment of EMU, on the appointment of the President, Vice-presidents and the members of the Board of the European Central Bank. Appointments reflect a dynamic system of checks and balances or, in the language of the European Court of Justice, a system of loyal co-operation as envisioned in Article 10 TEC (OJ C246/81 1451). Given the EU's hybrid structure of indirect interest representation through its institutions, appointments create a relationship of accountability and responsiveness between the appointing and the appointed institution. The original right to nominate and to approve the Commission was held by the Member States alone. A new step in the direction of Parliament's elective function was taken with the introduction of the then Article 158 (2) TEC by the TEU. With the entry into force of the TEU, the Commission's mandate was aligned with the Parliament's mandate. Consequently, the right of approval could not only be perceived as a formal act, but also as a design for a genuine political decision. Accordingly, by amending its Rules of Procedure in September 1993, the European Parliament sent a clear signal that it insists on this right and regards it as an essential part of its competencies. Thus, the new mechanism became a very important element for the strengthening of the Commission's formal legitimacy and the European Parliament's visibility towards its electorate. The Amsterdam Treaty built this development further. Not only the Commission as a collegiate body, but also the President of the European Commission alone are subject to a vote of approval by the European Parliament. These innovations may have unexpected and far-reaching implications for the future style of governance in the Union. In their electoral campaigns for the European Parliament's elections, one can imagine the European political parties deciding to put up a top candidate for the Commission presidency. Consequently, the elections would become more alive and enriched through a kind of personalization of the Union's governing institutions. Moreover, provided that each of the European parties presents its contesting candidate for the post in question, not only the election campaign, but also the day-to-day life in Brussels and Strasbourg could induce politicizing and mobilizing effects for the Union's citizenry. In other words, there is a realistic chance that political parties at the European level will become a renewed source of legitimacy (Notre Europe – European Steering Committee 1998; Notre Europe – European Steering Committee & Padoa-Schioppa 1998; Padoa-Schioppa 1998; Hix 1995, 525-554).[14] However, assuming that the European parties would gain in autonomy by introducing

---

[14] The idea of creating a politicised linkage between the Commission and the Parliament is not as new as it seems; see: Jacqué (1989, 217-225).

such a mechanism, national parties will not automatically like the idea. Secondly, Member State governments may not admit the idea either, since the optional mechanism could restrict their autonomy in putting forward a candidate for the Commission's Presidency (Nickel 1997).

As far as the institutional-procedural democratization of CJHA is concerned, the Benelux countries, Italy, Germany and the EP itself succeeded for the first time in introducing the European Parliament as a consultative body within the new Title covering the "Area of Freedom, Security and Justice" (AFSJ). Yet with respect to Visa policy, co-decision is introduced for two fields formerly covered by the co-operation procedure (Articles 62.2.b.i and 62.2.b.iv). Moreover, Article 63 TEC stipulates a phasing of Parliament's involvement with regard to the Title IV in general. While until May 2004 the European Parliament will only be consulted, Article 63 allows the Council to introduce the co-decision procedure after the end of this transitional period. For the two areas which remain in the third pillar (police co-operation and judicial co-operation in criminal matters) the European Parliament shall be consulted when framework decisions, decisions and conventions are adopted.

Similar progress could not be achieved in the CFSP area. However, the Amsterdam Treaty introduced an inter-institutional agreement between the Parliament, the Council and the European Commission confirming that Parliament's role in scrutinizing CFSP expenditure will continue to be regarded as non-compulsory.

Serious deficits in the parliamentary dimension of the future European Union are as obvious as the achievements. As regards the assent procedure, the EP failed to extend it to cover all international agreements (Articles 133, 300 and 301 TEC), the decisions over the EC's own financial resources (Article 269 TEC), the extension of the authority of the institutions in pursuit of Treaty objectives (implied powers Article 308 TEC) and, finally, the amendment of the TEU itself (Art. 48 TEU). Moreover, the consultation mechanism in Article 39 TEU gives Parliament only a very limited power insofar as the Council may lay down a time-limit of at least three months. This in fact deprives the consultation procedure of its main impact for Parliament, namely to influence the Council's position by postponing its opinion. Furthermore, the provisions on the transfer of the Schengen *acquis* into the area of the EC/EU competencies do not foresee any involvement of either the European Parliament or the parliaments of the Member States. This in fact goes against every democratic principle, since the Schengen *acquis* contains not only the ratified Schengen Agreements but also a vast corpus of decisions exclusively adopted by the Schengen Executive Committee. Finally, the Council will decide to introduce closer co-operation between certain Member States by qualified majority. By virtue of Article 40 TEU, the request of the Member States concerned will be forwarded to the European Parliament. Yet neither the actual decision on closer co-operation nor the decision allowing a non-participating Member to opt in requires any parliamentary involvement. As far as the future CFSP is concerned, the European Parliament's role is maintained to be restricted to information. The revised CFSP Title emphasizes the predominant position of the European Council as a quasi-legislative body. As the common strategies of the European Council form the basis of joint actions and other measures to be decided by the Council of Ministers, the European Council will have a de facto right of initiative which is not open to censure. Thus, Parliament's active participation in shaping the substance of the CFSP rests entirely at the discretion of the Member States' governments.

The Result II – the EP and the National Parliaments

Supranational Democracy does not mean that democracy is secured exclusively by supranational institutions. The IGC led to the insertion of a "Protocol on the role of National Parliaments in the European Union" (PNP) into the Amsterdam Treaty, which addresses both the scope and the timing of parliamentary scrutiny. In its initial resolution on the report on the functioning of the Treaty on European Union, the European Parliament positioned itself on the role of the national parliaments and interparliamentary cooperation:

> "Democratic control of EU matters would be best achieved by partnership between the European Parliament and the national parliaments. The role of national parliaments should be reinforced in a number of ways, such as through strengthened cooperation between equivalent parliamentary committees of national parliaments and the European Parliament, and providing opportunities for specialist organs of national parliaments to discuss major European proposals with their ministers prior to Council meetings."[15]

The EP thus drew attention to the forms of multilateral cooperation preferred by a majority of its Members and to the unilateral rights of control over the Member States' governments to be granted to the national parliaments. In adopting the resolution, the EP amended the second sentence of the paragraph 23 proposed by Martin and Bourlanges, which read:

---

[15] European Parliament, Minutes of the sitting of 17 May 1995, A4-0102/95: Resolution on the functioning of the Treaty on European Union with a view to the 1996 Intergovernmental Conference – Implementation and development of the Union, OJ C 151, 19.6.1995, p. 56.

"The role of national parliaments should be reinforced in several ways by means of periodic meetings between their respective committees, through the strengthening of COSAC and through knowledge and prior study of the Commission's legislative program, always with due respect for the internal constitutional law of each Member State."[16]

The options proposed by the two Rapporteurs to the Committee on Institutional Affairs for authorizing the national parliaments to refer matters to the European Court of Justice when they believed the EU institutions had exceeded their authority (MARTIN option) or in order to ensure compliance with the subsidiarity principle (*Bourlanges* option) were not pursued further.[17]

The Initial Failure of the EP
At the first, and so far only, Conference of the Parliaments of the EC (Rome 27 to 30 November 1990) the French and Belgian delegations in particular called for the institutionalisation of the Assizes in the form of a senate of national parliaments.[18] The final declaration, adopted by 150 votes to 13, recommended a substantial increase in the European Parliament's law-making powers and – in contrast to the idea of a senate – the holding of further conferences of the Assizes type whenever a debate to determine the line to be taken in essential parliamentary questions seemed necessary. The Rome Assizes revealed that some national parliamentarians differed from MEPs in that they wanted greater institutionalisation of parliamentary conferences, while the MEPs preferred limited involvement of the national parliaments. In 1994, European Parliament President Hänsch called on the national parliaments to prepare and hold further Conference of Parliaments – the so-called Assizes.[19] However, only the Belgian Parliament supported these

---

[16] European Parliament (4 May 1995), Report on the functioning of the Treaty on European Union with a view to the 1996 Intergovernmental Conference – Implementation and development of the Union, rapporteurs: Jean-Louis Bourlanges and David Martin, A4-0102/95/Part I.A.

[17] European Parliament (12 April 1995), Draft report of the Committee on Institutional Affairs on the functioning of the Treaty on European Union with a view to the 1996 Intergovernmental Conference, rapporteurs: Jean-Louis Bourlanges and David Martin, PE 212.450/A.

[18] Agence Europe, No 5382, 1 December 1990, and No 5384, 5 December 1990.

[19] See the inaugural address by the President of the European Parliament, Dr Klaus Hänsch, on 20 July 1994. See also his statement at the meeting of the Committee on Institutional Affairs of 5/6 September 1994 and the speech of the former President of the European Parliament, Dr Egon Klepsch, to the European Council in Birmingham on 16 October 1992.

proposals (Assemblée nationale 30 mars 1995, 289-298). Proposals to revive the Assizes on the Rome model were guided by the rejection of this type of cooperation by the majority of the national parliaments. This rejection was mainly due to the impression wrongly gained by the public from the final declaration of the Rome Assizes that the national parliaments would freely relinquish further substantial powers without demanding additional rights of control over their governments (Judge 1995, 79-100).

The Initial Failure of the French Proposals
The former President of the French National Assembly, Séguin, proposed the establishment of a second chamber[20] where national parliaments together would play the role of a lower chamber and the European Parliament that of an upper chamber. Sir Leon Brittan's proposal for the establishment of a Council of the National Parliaments was similarly designed to involve national parliaments directly in the Community decision-making process. The "Council of the National Parliaments" should discuss the Commission's draft legislative program and directives at first reading (Brittan 1994, 227). The French Senate's Delegation for European Union Affairs also proposed the creation of a second chamber of national parliaments for the CFSP and Justice and Home Affairs policies. The report also advocated that this chamber should have competence in the areas of its own resource system in the Community budget, the enlargement of the Union, the association agreements and the monitoring of compliance with the subsidiarity principle (Sénat 15 février 1995; Sénat 2 décembre 1994). The French National Assembly's Delegation for European Union Affairs also called for the direct participation of national parliaments in the decision-making process before the Council takes its decisions. Therefore, it proposed the setting up of an interparliamentary committee composed of a limited, equal number of representatives of each Member State. At monthly meetings of limited duration, the proposed committee should approve or oppose certain texts without being able to amend them. Its terms of reference might extend to the European Union's major decisions – revision of the Treaties, international agreements, enlargements, budget, Justice and Home Affairs, monetary and defense questions and advance monitoring of compliance with the subsidiarity principle (Assemblée nationale 8 February 1995, 98-100).

Besides the EP, the other national parliaments were generally critical to negative in their attitude towards the creation of a chamber of national parliaments involved in the Community legislative process. Their argument held that the introduction of a body, in parallel with the Community institutions, representing (in theory and by derivation from Community law)

---

[20] See: Le Figaro, 7 December 1994.

the same, or broadly the same, interests as the Council would threaten not only the European Parliament's institutional interests but also the institutional balance required by the EC Treaty and the whole institutional structure of the Community. Thus, given the strong reluctance of the majority of the Member States and the EU institutions, the concept of institutionalizing the Assizes model seemed unlikely to perpetuate interparliamentary cooperation, mainly because this model would have had the contradictory effect of distorting the democratic foundations for the legitimization of parliamentary control and law-making activities in the Community.

The Compromise – the Limited Institutionalization of COSAC
In turn, proposals to institutionalise COSAC flourished in all EU Member States. In its "policy guidelines for the 1996 IGC," the Austrian Government took the view that "as regards cooperation between the national parliaments and the European Parliament, the Government advocates consolidating COSAC-type interparliamentary cooperation procedures. The Danish Folketing advocated increasing the influence of the national parliaments' European affairs committees by taking measures as conferment of powers similar to those of the Folketing's relevant committee; the appointment of an official to represent each parliament in Brussels; and closer cooperation within COSAC and closer multilateral cooperation between equivalent parliamentary committees in all the parliaments of the Union. The Danish Government put forward three further proposals: the incorporation of a specific reference to the national parliaments in the Treaty on European Union; and, during the preliminary legislative phase, granting national parliaments the opportunity to deliver an opinion, within a limited period to be determined, on Commission proposals before they are officially submitted by the Commission. The German Bundestag called for a stronger role of the EP and the national parliaments in intergovernmental activities, but strongly opposed any kind of formalization of COSAC. The Finnish Parliament pointed out that national parliaments should have access not only to Commission proposals but also to Commission preparatory working parties, whereas the Government (in a communication from the Finnish Council of Ministers to the Finnish Parliament on the aims and objectives of Finland regarding the 1996 IGC from the 27 January 1996), underlined making co-operation between the EP and national parliaments more efficient within the framework of declaration No. 13 of the annex in the TEU. The Finnish Parliament's Grand Commission, in its statement of 22 November 1995, stressed the importance of examining suggestions to assign national parliaments' rights or duties under the Treaties with great caution. The National Assembly's Catala report suggested to renew the powers (institutionalisation) of the COSAC by giving it, in principle, the possibility of stating a position – in a consultative capacity – on Community projects that are the subject of an exception from subsidiarity raised either by a

national parliament or the Committee of the Regions. Furthermore, the Delegation wanted COSAC to express its opinion on questions concerning the two intergovernmental pillars (CFSP and CJHA) and in the area of unanimous decision-making in the Council such as the application of Article 235 (own resources and fiscal affairs). For the Luxembourg Government, MEP Charles Goerens was appointed to suggest means for strengthening the national parliaments. Goerens considered a kind of "charter" of "minimum obligations which all governments would accept vis-à-vis their parliaments" with respect to parliamentary scrutiny of Community affairs. In his view, the best method would be to incorporate in the Treaty the "minimum obligations of governments vis-à-vis the national parliaments" and "to strengthen the Community institutions' obligations – already set out in the Treaty – vis-à-vis the European Parliament." In its resolution of 2 March 1995, the Portuguese Parliament called for greater involvement of the national parliaments and more effective scrutiny at national level, by attaching greater importance to COSAC and the continuity of its work. For the UK, the white paper on the Governments approach on the IGC of 12 March 1995, stressed that the Maastricht Declaration 13 should become legally binding through integrating it into the Treaty. A minimum period for national parliaments should be introduced in order to scrutinize Community documents and draft legislation. The two parliamentary committees concerned adopted their positions in July 1995. The Committee on Community Legislation proposed that the Treaty should provide for a minimum period of four weeks between the receipt of a document by a national parliament and the Council's decision. Moreover, it considered the possibility of giving the national parliaments a formal role in the legislative process.

Following these proposals which culminated in the first unanimously adopted resolution of the Dublin COSAC meeting of 16th October 1996, the PNP holds that national parliaments shall receive all Commission consultation documents as well as green and white papers or communications. However, the PNP implicitly excludes the following types of documents for the transmission of legislative proposals to national parliaments: all documents falling under the CFSP pillar, all documents concerning the entry into closer co-operation, all documents prepared by Member States for the European Council, and all documents falling under the procedure of the "Protocol on integration the Schengen *acquis* into the framework of the European Union." However, once the Schengen *acquis* is integrated into the first or third pillar, the appropriate legislative and scrutiny procedures for both the European Parliament and the national parliaments will apply. The PNP includes a commitment of timing addressed to the Commission and the Council. Firstly, the Commission shall ensure that the legislative proposal is "made available in good time." Second, a six-week-period has to elapse between issuing a "legislative proposal or a measure to be adopted under Title VI TEU and its discussion or adoption by the

Council. Of course, these provisions are geared to allow the governments to inform their parliaments on the proposal and leave parliaments time for discussion. However, the protocol does not commit the governments to really use the time provided by the Community institutions for informing their parliaments. Thus, it remains up to the parliaments and their governments to negotiate on the content and the procedures to be applied for the implementation of the PNP.

Besides the provisions on the improvement of national parliamentary scrutiny mechanisms, the PNP recognizes COSAC as a means to contribute to the improvement of parliamentary scrutiny in EC and EU Affairs on a multilateral basis. The PNP specifies three areas for deliberation within the COSAC framework: According to Articles 5 and 6 of the PNP, COSAC may examine "any legislative proposal or initiative in relation to the establishment of an area or freedom, security and justice," "legislative activities of the Union, notably in relation to the application of the principle of subsidiarity" and "questions regarding fundamental rights." Thus, the text leads to the question, whether COSAC is the appropriate body for these issues. The fact that the PNP focuses on areas of freedom, security and justice and on fundamental rights policies reflects the political and legal sensibility on this issue in both the European Parliament and the EU Member States.

Thus, we observe the introduction of a balanced kind of "three-level-scrutiny-mechanism" with regard to Justice and Home Affairs in the framework of the future EU. First, the EP will control, to a limited extent of course, the European level of decision-making in the first and the third pillar. Second, provided that they organize their scrutiny mechanism effectively, national parliaments may monitor unilaterally the stance of their governments on matters falling under this area. Third, COSAC will become able to deliberate these issues between the European Parliament and the national parliaments of the Member States.

Conclusion

System development appears to be the most laborious profile of the EP, considering that the Parliament has to improve both its situation within the institutional framework and advance the community's policies. System development proves to function "à longue durée." The EP still has to make use of its strategy of small steps and compromises with powerful partners. These compromises are, however, based on thin ice. A position of the EP, which is too inflexible and rigid, could obstruct further improvements. An attitude too weak, however, could prevent far-reaching solutions. To date, the European Parliament has not used this possibility against major reforms or constitutional decisions, but rather showed a constructive attitude (Wessels 1995, 893).

Assessing the overall development of the EU after Amsterdam with regard to its institutional and procedural democratization leads to an ambiguous picture. On the one hand, the European Parliament's potential for influence in the preparation, adoption, implementation and control of legislative binding acts has been considerably strengthened in the sphere of the EC. Amsterdam also marks a significant effort to strengthen the accountability of the executive with regard to the Commission. Moreover, Parliament's involvement in Justice and Home Affairs has been relatively increased. On the other hand, the fact that unanimity in the Council and consultation of the European Parliament still dominate the matters of Justice and Home Affairs falling under Title VI TEU and under the Title IV TEC reflects a strong reservation in the majority of the Member States against a wider recourse to genuinely supranational means of decision-making in these sensitive but – for the population living inside and outside the Union – important spheres.

The Amsterdam Treaty marks another step forward in the move of the EU from an economic problem-solving arena to an original polity. However, the institutional and procedural arrangements of the EU remain complex, fragmented and opaque. Amsterdam certainly provides new and important offers for strengthening parliamentary democracy in the Union. Seen from an institutionalist perspective, the process of "parliamentarisation" is impressive in its continuity (Dehousse 1998, 9). With regard to the formal revision as well as to the implementation of the subsequent reforms, the Parliament has developed considerably since the SEA, from a rather "decorative" to a fully-fledged legislative institution (Wallace 1996, 63). However, the question remains, whether these improvements will also provide new ground for enhancing the legitimacy and proximity of European governance towards the citizens of the Union. Hence, due to the exclusive nature of IGCs, active participation of the citizenry and the general acceptance of the Union can hardly be achieved.

Thus, it remains up to the implementation of the new Treaty, the "valley," and the actors then involved, to offer appropriate means for the involvement of the Union's Demoi in shaping the conditions for their way of living.

The extension of co-decision and the shift of co-operation into co-decision confirm the ongoing dynamics of organisational concentration and functional differentiation-specialisation within the European Parliament. The re-arrangement, decided in April 1999, of Parliament's Committee structure boosts these features to some extent. Concentration will remain within the family of former "legislative" Committees. Since the entry into force of the Maastricht Treaty, the shift towards legislative power and its effective execution results in a decrease in the number of non-legislative resolutions, own initiative reports (inviting the Commission to forward legislative initiatives) and resolutions after statements or urgencies. Own initiative and urgency resolutions reflect the individual and political awareness and interest of MEPs in making an issue public to the outside world – towards the Union's citizenry and electorate. MEPs and political groups use these instruments to give evidence of their general interests, their attention paid to a given issue or of their willingness to shape the policy agenda. For political groups, these resolutions are one of the core instruments, allowing them to present their original point of view on a given issue. In this respect, these instruments allow MEPs and political groups to demonstrate their collective – denationalized but transnationally politicized – interest in EU politics. In contrast to co-decision (or co-operation in EMU), where action against the Council (amendments to or rejection of its common position) requires the approval of an absolute majority (actually at least 314 votes), own initiative resolutions pass with a simple majority of votes cast. Accordingly, whereas co-decision condemns the EP's two major political groups to reach an agreement on parliamentary amendments which in consequence move the left-right cleavage away from the agenda, own initiatives and similar resolutions provide each political group with the opportunity to present its original socio-economic argument before the public. To accomplish its powers apportioned by the Amsterdam Treaty, the European Parliament will need more and more resources – time, staff and space – for legislation. Accordingly, it is easy to argue that the 1999-2004 Parliament faces the crucial question, in which respect the overall backbencher majority of MEPs can translate their position as representatives of the peoples, their constituency, their party interests and demands – into action enabling them to become re-elected. If the political groups want to develop further the "linkage between institutions and constituencies within the polity" (Gaffney 1996, 1-2; Hix & Lord 1997, 7-10), they must choose carefully between the different political and institutional capabilities at hand.

The greater involvement of the national parliaments in the Union's policy process may help render Governments more accountable for what they do in the Council of Ministers and its subordinated working mechanisms. However, one should also bear in mind that the simple formalization of COSAC within the realm of the new Treaty also renders the Union more complex and less understandable. Our citizens to whom we referred at the beginning, may again ask: If the (directly elected) European Parliament represents the peoples of the Union, the Council of Ministers, the Member States through (elected) governments, the European Economic and Social Committee some of the most important interest groups of the Union, and the Committee of the Regions the (elected) representatives of some of the Union's regional and local communities, what is the added value of a body bringing together some members of the European Parliament with some Members of the national parliaments?

Bibliography

Assemblée Nationale (1996). Déclaration du Gouvernement sur la préparation et les perspectives de la Conférence intergouvernementale, Assemblée Nationale, Compte rendu analytique officiel, 1ère Séance du 13 Mars.

Assemblée nationale (1994). Rapport d'Information déposé par la délégation de l'Assemblée nationale sur le role des Parlements nationaux dans la construction européenne, les enseignements de l'exemple danois, par Nicole Ameline, 28 juin.

Assemblée nationale (1995). Rapport d'information déposé par la délégation de l'Assemblée nationale pour l'Union européenne, sur les réformes institutionnelles de l'Union européenne, par Nicole Catala et Nicole Ameline, 8 février.

Communautés européennes (1972). Rapport du groupe ad hoc pour l'examen du problème de l'accroissement des compétences du Parlement européen, *Bull. C.E.,* No. 4.

Communautés européennes (1976). Rapport Tindemans, *Bull. C.E.,* No. suppl. 1.

Communautés européennes (1979). Rapport d'un groupe des personnalités indépendantes, *Bull. C.E.,* No. 9, pp. 16-25.

Communautés européennes (1984). Projet de traité instituant l'Union européenne, *Bull. C.E.*, No. 2, pp. 7-27.

Communautés européennes (1992). "Le principe de la subsidiarité," *Bull. C.E.* No. 10, p. 132.

European Commission (1996). Report on the co-decision procedure, *Doc. SEC* (96) 1225 fin. of 3 July.

Parlement européen (1988). Rapport fait au nom de la Commission institutionnelle sur le déficit démocratique des Communautés européennes, par Michel Toussaint, *PE DOC* A 2276/87 of 1 February.

European Parliament (1995). Opinion of the Committee on Foreign Affairs, Security and Defence Policy for the Committee on Institutional Affairs on the operation of the Treaty on European Union with a view to the Intergovernmental Conference in 1996, rapporteur: Enrique Barón Crespo, *PE* 211.022/fin., 21 February.

European Parliament (1996). Report on the report of the Commission, *SEC* (96) 1225 fin., Doc. A4-0361/96 of 7 November.

European Parliament (1997). Conciliation Stop Press, 9.

European Parliament (1997). Reply to Question No. 39/97 by Richard Corbett, *DOC PE* 259.385/BUR.

European Parliament (1998). Conciliation Procedures – Stop Press, 18 (March).

European Parliament, Delegations to the Conciliation Committee (1997). Progress report 1 August 1996 to 31 July 1997 on the Delegations to the Conciliation Committee, Annex 2, pp. 3-4.

European Parliament, Committee on Institutional Affairs (1995), Working Document on the CFSP process, Rapporteur: Raymonde Dury, *PE* 211.310.

European Parliament: Task Force "IGC 1996/1997" (1996). White Paper on the IGC, Vol. I to III, Luxembourg.

Parlement européen (1988). Résolution sur le déficit démocratique de la Communauté européenne; JOCE, C. 187/229, 18 July.

Parlement européen (Mai 1995). Les Commissions spécialisés dans les affaires européennes des parlements des Etats membres, DG II, Div. "Parlements des Etats membres" en collaboration avec la DG IV (Andreas Maurer).

Abromeit, H. (1998). "Ein Vorschlag zur Demokratisierung des europäischen Entscheidungssystems," *Politische Vierteljahresschrift*, No.1, pp. 80-90.

Abromeit, H. (1998). *Democracy in Europe – Legitimizing Politics in a Non-State Polity*, Oxford/New York: Bergahn.

Abromeit, H. & T. Schmidt (1998). Grenzprobleme der Demokratie: konzeptionelle Überlegungen, pp. 293-320, in Beate Kohler-Koch (ed.), *Regieren in entgrenzten Räumen*, Opladen: Westdeutscher Verlag.

Archer, C. & F. Butler (1996). *The European Union. Structure and Process*, 2nd edition, London: Pinter.

Birkinshaw, P. & D. Ashiagbor (1996). "National participation in Community affairs: Democracy, the UK Parliament and the EU," *Common Market Law Review*, No. 33, pp. 499-530.

Bogdandy, A. von. (1993). "Supranationale Union als neuer Herrschaftstypus: Entstaatlichung und Vergemeinschaftung aus staatstheoretischer Perspektive," *Integration*, No. 4, pp. 210-224.

Bulmer, S. (1994). "The Governance of the European Union. A New Institutionalist Approach," *Journal of Public Policy*, No. 4, pp. 351-380.

Christiansen, T. & K. Jørgensen (1999). "The Amsterdam Process: A Structurationist Perspective on EU Reform," *European Integration Online Papers*, No. 1.

Corbett, R. (1994). "Representing the People," pp. 207-228, in A. Duff, J. Pinder & R. Pryce (eds.), *Maastricht and Beyond: Building the European Union*, London: Routledge.

Craig, P. (1997). "Democracy and Rulemaking within the EC: An Empirical and Normative Assessment," *European Law Journal*, No. 3, pp. 105-130.

Dehousse, R. (1998). European Institutional Architecture after Amsterdam: Parliamentary System or Regulatory Structure? RSC No. 98/11, *EUI Working papers*, Florence.

Dinan, D. (ed.) (1998). *Encyclopedia of the European Union*, Boulder: Lynne Rienner Publishers.

Duff, A. (1995). "Building a Parliamentary Europe," pp. 253-254, in M. Télo (ed.), *Démocratie et Construction Européenne*, Bruxelles: Université de Bruxelles.

Duff, A. (1997). *The Treaty of Amsterdam, Text and Commentary*, London: Sweet and Maxwell.

Earnshaw, D. & D. Judge (1996). "From cooperation to codecision: The European Parliament's path to legislative power," pp. 96-126, in J. Richardson (ed.), *European Union: Power and Policy Making*, London: Routledge.

Fligstein, N. & J. McNichol (1998). "The Institutional Terrain of the European Union," pp. 59-91, in W. Sandholtz & A. Stone Sweet (eds.), *European Integration and Supranational Governance*, Oxford: Oxford University Press.

Follesdal, A. (1998). Democracy and the European Union: Challenges, pp. 1-10, in A. Follesdal & P. Koslowski (eds.), *Democracy and the European Union*, Berlin/New York/Tokyo: Springer.

Foreign and Commonwealth Office (1996). "A Partnership of Nations: The British Approach to the European Union Intergovernmental Conference 1996," Presented to Parliament, March 1996.

Gaffney, J. (1996). Introduction: Political parties and the European Union, pp. 1- 30, in J. Gaffney (ed.), *Political Parties and the European Union*, London, New York: Routledge Publisher.

Garrett, G. (1995). "From the Luxembourg Compromise to Co-decision: Decision Making in the European Union," *Electoral Studies*, No. 3, pp. 289-308.

Garrett, G. & G. Tsebelis (1996). "An institutional critique of intergovernmentalism," *International Organization*, No. 2, pp. 269-299.

Garrett, G. & B. Weingast (1993). "Ideas, Interests, and Institutions: Constructing the EC's Internal Market," pp. 173-206, in Judith Goldstein & Robert Keohane (eds.), *Ideas and Foreign Policy*, New York: Ithaca.

Genco, S.J. (1980). "Integration Theory and System Change in Western Europe: The Neglected Role of System Transformation Episodes," pp. 55-80, in Ole R. Holsti et al. (eds.), *Change in the International System*, Boulder: Westview.

Gosalbo Bono, R. (1995). "Co-decision: an Appraisal of the Experience of the European Parliament as Co-legislator," pp. 53-92, in *Yearbook of European Law*, Oxford: Clarendon Press.

Grieco, J. (1988). "Anarchy and the limits of co-operation: a realist critique to the newest liberal institutionalism," *International Organisation,* No. 3, pp. 485-507.

Griller et al. (1996). *Regierungskonferenz 1996: Ausgangspositionen*, Working paper No. 20, Vienna: Forschungsinstitut für Europafragen.

Grimm, D. (1993). "Mit einer Aufwertung des Europa-Parlaments ist es nicht getan - Das Demokratiedefizit der EG hat strukturelle Ursachen," pp. 13-18, in *Jahrbuch zur Staats- und Verwaltungswissenschaft 1992/93*, Baden-Baden: Nomos.

Haftendorn, H. (1990). "Zur Theorie außenpolitischer Entscheidungsprozesse," pp. 401-423, in V. Rittberger (ed.), Theorien der Internationalen Beziehungen. Bestandsaufnahme und Forschungsperspektiven, *Politische Vierteljahresschrift*, Sonderheft 21, Opladen: Westdeutscher Verlag.

Hall, P. & R. Taylor (1996). "Political Science and the Three New Institutionalisms," *Political Studies*, No. 5, pp. 936-957, XLIV.

Hall, P. (1986). *Governing the Economy: The Politics of State Intervention in Britain and France*, New York.

Hänsch, Klaus (1986). "Europäische Integration und parlamentarische Demokratie," *Europa-Archiv*, No. 7, pp. 191-200.

Hix, S. (1995). "Parties at the European Level as an Alternative Source of Legitimacy," *Journal of Common Market Studies*, 4, pp. 525-554.

Hix, S. & C. Lord (1996). "The Making of a President: The European Parliament and the Confirmation of Jacques Santer as President of the Commission," *Government and Opposition*, No. 31, pp. 62-76.

Hurell, A. & A. Menon (1996). "Politics Like Any Other? Comparative Politics, International Relations and the Study of the EU," *West European Politics*, Vol. 19-2, pp. 386-402.

Istituto Affari Internazionali, ed. Maastricht-Watch. Quarterly updates, Rome, 1994-1996.

Jachtenfuchs, M. (1998). "Democracy and Governance in the European Union, pp. 37-64, in A. Follesdal & P. Koslowski (eds.), *Democracy and the European Union*, Berlin/New York/Tokyo: Springer.

Jacqué, J. (1989). "Strategien für das Europäische Parlament: Abschied von nationalen Konfliktlinien," pp. 217-225, in O. Schmuck & W. Wessels (eds.), *Das Europäische Parlament im dynamischen Integrationsprozeß: Auf der Suche nach einem zeitgemäßen Leitbild*, Bonn: Europa Union Verlag.

Jopp, M. & O. Schmuck (eds.) (1996). *Die Reform der Europäischen Union. Analysen – Positionen – Dokumente zur Regierungskonferenz 1996/97*, Bonn: Europa Union Verlag.

Jopp, M., A. Maurer & O. Schmuck (eds.) (1998). *Die Europäische Union nach Amsterdam. Analysen und Stellungnahmen zum neuen EU-Vertrag*, Bonn: Europa Union Verlag.

Judge, David (1995). "The failure of national parliaments," *West European Politics*, No. 3, pp. 79-100.

Kapteyn, P.J.G. & P. VerLoren van Themaat (1998). "Introduction to the Law of the European Communities", 3rd and rev., L.W. Gormley (ed.), London: Kluwer.

Kielmansegg, P. Graf (1996). "Integration und Demokratie," pp. 47-72, in Markus Jachtenfuchs & Beate Kohler-Koch (eds.), *Europäische Integration*, Opladen: Leske + Budrich.

Kohler-Koch, B. (1995). *The Strength of Weakness. The Transformation of Governance in the EU*, AB III/No. 10, MZES Working Papers, Mannheim.

Kohler-Koch, B. (1998). "Die Europäisierung nationaler Demokratien: Verschleiß eines europäischen Kulturerbes?" pp. 263-288, in M. Greven (ed.), *Demokratie – eine Kultur des Westens?* 20. Wissenschaftlicher Kongreß der Deutschen Vereinigung für Politische Wissenschaft, Opladen: Leske + Budrich.

Laffan, B. (1997). "The Governance of the Union," pp. 29-48, in B. Tonra (ed.), *Amsterdam. What the Treaty means*, Dublin: IEA.

Laursen, F. (1992). "Explaining the Intergovernmental Conference," pp. 229-248, in Finn Laursen & S. Vanhoonacker (eds.), *The Intergovernmental Conference on Political Union*, Maastricht: European Institute of Public Administration.

Lodge, J. (1998). "Negotiations in the European Union: The 1996 Intergovernmental Conference," *International Negotiation* No. 3, pp. 481-505.

Lübbe, H. (1994). *Abschied vom Superstaat. Die Vereinigten Staaten von Europa wird es nicht geben*, Berlin: Siedler.

Majone, G. (1994). "The Rise of the Regulatory State in Europe," *West European Politics*, No. 3, pp. 78-102.

Majone, G. (1996). "European regulatory state?," pp. 263-277, in J. Richardson (ed.), *European Union. Power and Policy-Making*, London: Routledge.

Marks, G. (1993). "Structural Policy and Multilevel Governance in the EC," pp. 391-411, in A.W. Cafruny & G.G. Rosentahl (eds.), *The State of the European Community*, Vol. 2, Boulder: Lynne Rienner Publishers.

Maurer, A. (1996). "Die Demokratisierung der Europäischen Union: Perspektiven für das Europäische Parlament," pp. 15-38, in A. Maurer & B. Thiele, Hrsg., *Legitimationsprobleme und Demokratisierung der Europäischen Union*, Marburg: Schüren.

Maurer, A. (1999). *What next for the European Parliament*, London: Kogan Page.

Maurer, A. & Wessels, W. (2001). National Parliaments on their way to Europe. Losers or Latecomers?, Baden-Baden: Nomos.

McDonagh, B. (1998). *Original Sin in a Brave New World. An Account of the Negotiation of the Treaty of Amsterdam*, Dublin: IEA, pp. 151-164.

Metcalfe, D. (1998). "Leadership in European Union Negotiations: The Presidency of the Council," *International Negotiation*, No. 3, pp. 413-434.

Monar, Jörg (1994). "Interinstitutional Agreements: The phenomenon and its new dynamics after Maastricht," *Common Market Law Review*, 4, pp. 693-719.

Moravcsik, A. (1991). "Negotiating the Single European Act: National Interests and Conventional Statecraft in the European Community," *International Organization*, Vol. 45, No. 4, Winter, pp. 19-56.

Moravcsik, A. (1993). Preferences and Power in the European Community, A Liberal Intergovernmentalist Approach, *Journal of Common Market Studies*, Vol. 31, pp. 473-524.

Moravcsik, A. (1995). "Liberal Intergovernmentalism and Integration: A Rejoinder," *Journal of Common Market Studies*, Vol. 33, No. 4, December, pp. 611-628.

Moravcsik, A. (1997). "Taking Preferences Seriously: A Liberal Theory of International Politics," *International Organisation*, Vol. 51, No. 4, pp. 513-553.

Moravcsik, A. & K. Nicolaidis (1999). "Explaining the Treaty of Amsterdam: Interest, Influence, Institutions," *Journal of Common Market Studies*, No. 1, pp. 59-85.

Neunreither, K. (1994). "The democratic of the European Union: Towards closer cooperation between the European Parliament and the national Parliaments," *Government and Opposition*, No. 3, pp. 299-314.

Nickel, D. (1993). "Le Traité de Maastricht et le Parlement européen: Le nouveau paysage politique et la procédure de l'article 189b," pp. 117-125, in J. Monar, W. Ungerer & W. Wessels (eds.), *The Maastricht Treaty on European Union*, Brussels: European Interuniversity Press.

Nickel, D. (1997). *The Amsterdam Treaty – a shift in the balance between the institutions!?* Paper submitted for a lecture at Harvard Law School.

Nickel, D. (1999). *Beyond Treaty Revision: Shifts in the Institutional Balance?*, unpublished paper presented at the ECSA Sixth Biennial Conference, Pittsburgh, 2-6 June.

Notre Europe – European Steering Committee (1998). "Politicising the European Debate," *Agence Europe*, 2089, 27 May.

Notre Europe – European Steering Committee & A. Padoa-Schioppa (1998). "From the Single Currency to the Single Ballot-Box," *Agence Europe*, 2089, 27 May.

Nugent, N. (1994). *The Government and Politics of the European Union*, Durham, NC: Duke University Press.

Nugent, N. (1998). "Decision-making Procedures," pp. 117-121, in D. Dinan (ed.), *Encyclopedia of the European Union*, Boulder: Lynne Rienner Publishers.

Padoa-Schioppa, A. (1998). "The Institutional Reforms of the Amsterdam Treaty," *The Federalist*, No. 1, pp. 8-25.

Peterson, J. (1995). "Decision-making in the European Union," *Journal of European Public Policy*, No. 1, pp. 69-93.

Piepenschneider, M. (1996). *Regierungskonferenz 1996, Synopse der Reformvorschläge zur Europäischen Union, 2. Auflage*, Sankt Augustin.

Pierson, P. (1998). The Path to European Integration: A Historical Institutionalist Analysis, pp. 27-58, in Sandholtz & Stone Sweet (eds.), *European Integration and Supranational Governance*, Oxford: Oxford University Press.

Pijpers, A. & G. Edwards (eds.) (1997). *The Politics of European Treaty Reform. The 1996 Intergovernmental Conference and Beyond*, London: Pinter.

Pliakos, A. (1995). "L'Union européenne et le Parlement européen – y a-t-il vraiment un déficit démocratique?" *Révue du droit public et de la science politique en France et à l'Étranger*, No. 3, pp. 749-763.

Pogge, T. (1998). "How to create supra-national institutions democratically. Some reflections on the European Union's 'Democratic Deficit'," pp. 160-187, in A. Follesdal & P. Koslowski (eds.), *Democracy and the European Union*, Berlin/New York/Tokyo: Springer.

Putnam, R. (1988). "Diplomacy and Domestic Politics: The Logic of Two Level Games," *International Organisation*, No. 3, pp. 427-460.

Raworth, P. (1994). "A Timid Step Forwards: Maastricht and the Democratisation of the European Community," *European Law Review*, No.1, pp. 16-33.

Reich, Charles (1991). "Qu'est-ce que...le déficit démocratique?" *Révue du Marché Commun*, No. 343, pp. 14-18.

Reich, Charles (1992). "Le Traité sur l'Union européenne et le Parlement européen," *Revue du Marché Commun*, No. 357, pp. 287-292.

Risse-Kappen, Thomas (1996). "Exploring the Nature of the Beast: International Relations Theory and Comparative Policy Analysis Meet the European Union," *Jounal of Common Market Studies*, No. 1, pp. 53-80.

Scharpf, F.W. (1975). *Demokratie zwischen Utopie und Anpassung*, 2nd ed. Kronberg/Ts.

Scharpf, F.W. (1994). "Community and Autonomy: Multi-level Policy-Making in the European Union," *Journal of European Public Policy*, No.1, p. 2-20.

Schimmelpfennig, F. (1996). *Legitimate Rule in the European Union. The Academic Debate*, Tübinger Arbeitspapiere zur Internationalen Politik und Friedensforschung 27, Tübingen.

Schoo, J. (1997). "Kommentar zu Art. 189b-189c," in Groeben, Thiesing & Ehlermann, Hrsg., *Kommentar zum EU/EG-Vertrag*, Band 4 (Art. 137-209a EGV), Baden-Baden: Nomos.

Schröder, M. (1994). "Das Bundesverfassungsgericht als Hüter des Staates im Prozeß der europäischen Integration," *Deutsches Verwaltungsblatt*, No. 6, pp. 615-625.

Scully, R. (1997). *Institutional Change in the European Union: Maastricht and the European Parliament*, (unpublished paper) ECSA Fifth Biennial Conference, Seattle, May 29-June 1.

Shackleton, M. (1998). "Democratic Deficit," pp. 130-134, in D. Dinan (ed.), *Encyclopedia of the European Union*, Boulder: Lynne Rienner Publishers.

Skidmore, D. & V. Hudson (eds.) (1993). *The Limits of State Autonomy: Societal Groups and and Foreign Policy Formulation*, Boulder: Westview.

Smith, M. (1996). "Democratic Legitimacy in the European Union: Fulfilling the Institutional Logic," *Journal of Legislative Studies*, No. 4, pp. 283-301.

Sverdrup, U. (2000). "Precedents and Present Events in the European Union: An Institutional Perspective on Treaty Reform," pp. 241-265, in K.-H. Neunreither & A. Wiener (eds.), *European Integration after Amsterdam*, London: Routledge.

Thomas, S. (1992). "Assessing MEP's influence on British EC policy," *Government in Opposition*, No. 1, pp. 3-18.

Tsebelis, G. (1994). "The Power of the European Parliament as a Conditional Agenda-Setter," *American Political Science Review*, Vol. 88, No. 1 (March), pp. 128-142.

Tsebelis, G. & G. Garrett (1997). "Agenda Setting, Vetoes and the European Union's Co-Decision Procedure," *Journal of Legislative Studies*, No. 3, pp. 74-92.

Tsinisizelis, M. & D. Chryssochoou (1996). "From 'Gesellschaft' to 'Gemeinschaft'? Confederal Consociation and Democracy in the European Union," *Current Politics and Economics of Europe*, No. 4, pp. 1-33.

Wallace, H. (1996). "Politics and Policy in the EU: The Challenge of Governance," pp. 3-36, in H. Wallace & W. Wallace (eds.), *Policy-Making in the European Union*, 3rd ed., Oxford: Oxford University Press.

Weiler, J. (1992). "After Maastricht: Community Legitimacy in Post-1992 Europe," pp. 11-41, in W.J. Adams (ed.), *Singular Europe: Economy and Polity of the European Community after 1992*, Ann Arbor: University of Michigan Press.

Weiler, J. (1997). "Legitimacy and Democracy of Union Governance," pp. 249-287, in A. Pijpers & G. Edwards (eds.), *The Politics of European Treaty Reform. The 1996 Intergovernmental Conference and Beyond*, London: Pinter.

Weiler, J., U. Haltern & F. Mayer (1995). "European Democracy and Its Critique," *West European Politics*, No. 4, pp. 24-33.

Weiler, Joseph H.H. (1995). "The state 'über alles' - Demos, Telos and the German Maastricht Decision," pp. 1651-1688, in Ole Due, Marcus Lutter & Jürgen Schwarze (eds.), *Festschrift für Ulrich Everling*, Vol. II, Baden-Baden: Nomos.

Wessels, W. (1996). "The Modern West European State and the European Union: Democratic Erosion or a New Kind of Polity?," pp. 57-69, in S.S. Andersen & K.A. Eliassen (eds.), *The European Union: How democratic is it?*, London: Sage.

Wessels, W. (1997). "An Ever Closer Fusion? A Dynamic Macropolitical View on Integration Processes," *Journal of Common Market Studies*, No. 2, pp. 267-299.

Westlake, M. (1994). *A Modern Guide to the European Parliament*, London: Pinter.

Williams, S. (1991). Sovereignty and Accountability in the European Community, pp. 155-176, in R. Keohane & S. Hoffmann (eds.), *The New European Community*, Boulder: Westview Press.

Zürn, M. (1996). "Über den Staat und die Demokratie im europäischen Mehrebenensystem,"*Politische Vierteljahresschrift*, No. 1, 27-55.

Section 3:

Interstate Bargaining

19

First Pillar: The Domestic Politics of Treaty Reform in Environment and Employment[*]

Jonas Tallberg

Introduction

When the member governments of the EU specified in the 1991 Treaty on European Union (TEU) that an intergovernmental conference (IGC) were to be convened in 1996, for the purpose of preparing the EU institutions for enlargement, reform of the Union's core policies in the first pillar (e.g. the internal market, environment, social policy) was deliberately excluded from the mandate. To open up for a revision of existing policies, and the possible inclusion of new, would risk crowding the agenda and diverting the focus of the IGC from its key challenge. Yet when concluded in Amsterdam in June 1997, the new treaty contained a set of significant policy advances in the first pillar. Most notably, the Union's environmental policy had been further boosted, and an entirely new title on employment had been added to the Treaty establishing the European Community (EC Treaty).

These policy advances in the first pillar were all the more noteworthy, as they primarily had been promoted by the Nordic Member States. Despite being small states, and the fact that two of them had been thrown headlong into an IGC during their second year as members, Denmark, Sweden, and Finland succeeded in securing support for treaty reform in areas often associated with Nordic values and priorities. This outcome is puzzling in view of dominating analyses of intergovernmental bargaining in the EU and elsewhere, which tend to be "minilateral" in character, interpreting negotiation results as the product of bargaining among the most powerful Member States.

Indeed, in their analysis of the 1996-97 IGC, Andrew Moravcsik and Kalypso Nicolaïdis stress as one striking aspect of the distributional bargaining outcome that "some of the newer members – particularly the most recent accession countries – did unusually well in the negotiations" (1999, 75). Another observer takes the Nordic influence as evidence that a new and significant Member State grouping is emerging in the EU:

---

[*] For constructive comments on an earlier version of this chapter, I would like to thank the fellow contributors to this volume, as well as Christer Jönsson, Olav Schram Stokke, Arild Underdal, and Oran R. Young.

While the traditional subsystems failed to foster change, the new Scandinavian bloc did succeed in pushing its priorities for reform, thus leaving a clear Nordic trace in the Amsterdam Treaty. While reluctant to move on institutional dossiers and defence, the three social-democratic governments of Sweden, Finland and Denmark were successful in presenting their partners with a coherent message in favour of stronger Treaty language on employment, environment, fundamental rights and non-discrimination, equality between men and women, and transparency (Devuyst 1998, 622).

The reform of the first pillar in a "Nordic" direction thus poses a set of intriguing questions: Why did environment and employment become notable themes of the IGC, given that revision of first pillar policies deliberately was not included in the mandate? And how can we explain the alleged influence of the Nordic countries in the areas of environment and employment, given the limited structural power of these small states? The intention in this chapter is to address these questions.

Tracing the IGC negotiations on environment and employment from agenda-setting to bargaining outcome, I suggest that a consideration of domestic politics is imperative if we wish to understand this Nordic mark on the Amsterdam Treaty. Domestic politics, widely interpreted, determined the agenda-setting priorities of the Nordic Member States, shaped the form of institutional arrangements sought at the European level, and influenced other governments' willingness to accept proposals in these areas. The chapter is divided into three substantive parts, where the first introduces the theoretical logic of domestic-international interplay, the second analyses the negotiations on environment, and the third explores the bargaining surrounding the new employment title.

Domestic Politics and International Negotiations

In the last decade, a growing number of scholars have theorised about the interdependence between domestic politics and international negotiations, both in the study of the EU (e.g., Moravcsik 1993, 1998; Patterson 1997) and international relations generally (e.g., Putnam 1988; Evans, Jacobson & Putnam 1993; Milner 1997). While practitioners often have pointed to the importance of the internal side of international negotiations, political scientists have not been equally swift in integrating this insight into explicit theories of the interplay between internal and external negotiations. More often, explanations of interstate relations have tended to privilege either systemic forces or domestic politics.

In the new wave of research, Robert Putnam's (1988) conceptualisation of "two-level games" has become the preferred and dominant metaphor for negotiations at the nexus of domestic and international politics. "At the national level, domestic groups pursue their interests by pressuring the government to adopt favorable policies, and politicians seek power by constructing coalitions among those groups. At the international level, national governments seek to maximize their own ability to satisfy domestic pressures, while minimizing the adverse consequences of foreign developments. Neither of the two games can be ignored by central decision makers" (Putnam 1988, 434). In Putnam's metaphor, statesmen are strategically positioned between two tables, where one represents domestic politics and the other international negotiation. The strategies pursued by a national government are formed and constrained simultaneously by what domestic constituencies desire and what other states will accept. In the process of negotiation, the statesman must take both games into consideration, and any successful bargaining outcome is likely to reflect the necessities of reaching both an international agreement and securing domestic support.

Focusing on the domestic politics side of the equation, it is important to note that the two-level game metaphor rests on a liberal conception of the state, where political parties compete for the power of government and the definition of the national interest, while domestic societal groups exert pressure through legislatures, interest groups, elections, and public opinion. Putnam emphasises: "Unlike state-centric theories, the two-level approach recognizes the inevitability of domestic conflict about what the 'national interest' requires" (1988, 460). What counts domestically, then, is not the national costs and benefits of international agreements, but the costs and benefits to existing domestic constituencies. As Helen Milner notes in a powerful formulation: "All aspects of cooperation are affected by domestic considerations because cooperation is a continuation of domestic political struggles by other means" (1997, 10).

Turning specifically to European integration and the interaction between domestic politics and EU treaty reform, I will point to three aspects of the negotiation process where these forces are at play.[1] First, at the agenda-setting stage, domestic politics influences the political priorities of a particular government, while the likelihood of acceptance at the international level shapes the translation of these priorities into concrete proposals. Enjoying the privilege of formulating the national interest, each government is guided in its international actions by its own particular interpretation, coloured by ideology

---

[1] It should be recognised that there is no international political context where it is more difficult to draw a line between international and national than the EU. In this chapter, this distinction is used as an analytical tool to help sort out specific interaction effects.

and domestic political pressure. Recognising that the European-level realisation of these priorities through treaty change only can be achieved with the consent of other Member States, the individual government both seeks to influence other governments and formulates its proposals with a view to what these could accept, given their domestic constraints.

Second, in the negotiations about alternative rules and procedures at the European level, domestic politics influences the form of institutional arrangements sought by a government. Slightly simplified, governments will promote the form of institutional arrangements that facilitate the realisation of domestic political goals. This may take a variety of forms: attempting to export national models to the European level, seeking arrangements that will allow national rules to remain, pushing for binding commitments where the gains from ensuring the compliance of others are large, and promoting flexible arrangements where domestic constraints may require some room for manoeuver.

Third, at the stage of reaching a negotiation outcome, domestic politics in the Member States defines the "contract zone" or "settlement range," by determining each government's "resistance point." The only meaningful treaty change is the one that can be ratified by all Member States. Ratification is partly a question of formal acceptance in national parliaments, but should also be understood as sustained political support for the government on the domestic arena. An important implication is that national elections leading to shifts in government during the course of intergovernmental negotiations tend to either expand or shrink the contract zones pertaining to specific issues.

Negotiating the Treaty Changes in Environment at the 1996-97 IGC

Environmental policy was absent from the higher levels of the political agenda in the early days of European co-operation. Though, in the 1970s, the emergence of environmental concerns triggered a series of Community initiatives in this area, it was not until the entry into force in 1987 of the Single European Act (SEA) that environment was provided with a firm footing in the Treaty. Generally acknowledged as a turning point for environment as a policy domain, the SEA added a specific title on environment, thereby providing a legal basis and explicitly defining the objectives and guiding principles of Community action in this field.

The entry into force of the TEU in 1993 brought further progress on several fronts. The concept of "sustainable growth respecting the environment" was added to the Community's tasks, the "precautionary principle" was written into the EC Treaty, action in the environmental field was upgraded to the status of "policy" in its own right, and qualified majority voting (QMV) in the Council was extended. These advances notwithstanding, the TEU, too, was open to criticism. For instance, existing rules and procedures were accused of not being sufficiently clear in situations of potential conflict between the objectives of protecting the environment and safeguarding the Internal Market. Another charge levelled at the TEU was that it did not explicitly incorporate the commitment to sustainable development made at the 1992 Rio Conference.

Though not originally intended, environmental issues became a topic also of the 1996-97 IGC. On the one hand, a number of proposals concerning institutional reform were indirectly linked to EU environmental policy. However, more notably, Member States and EU institutions placed proposals for reform of the EU's environmental policy directly on the IGC agenda. "Where governments with particularly intense preferences felt the agenda was too narrow, they simply initiated proposals" (Moravcsik & Nicolaïdis 1999, 71).

Summarising the main points of negotiation at the 1996-97 IGC, these may be grouped in four categories. The first category pertains to environment as a horizontal concern in European policy-making. The second category concerns the decision-making procedures which apply to policy-making in the environmental field. The third category relates to the balance between environmental protection and the preservation of the Internal Market. The fourth and final category hosts a set of issues which concern the Union's general decision-making competence, and which are indirectly related to the environment.

The need to include environmental issues on the agenda became clear already in the work of the Reflection Group, charged with preparing the IGC. Stressing the pressure being brought by public opinion in this area, the Reflection Group canvassed a range of topics pertaining to the environment and sustainable development: integrating environment as a horizontal concern in all EU policies; incorporation of the sustainable development principle; extending Member States' possibilities of applying higher national standards than those specified in Community harmonisation; integrating environmental provisions in specific policy articles; extending QMV and the co-decision decision-making procedure, which allows for a more prominent role of the European Parliament (EP) in legislation; and the Euratom Treaty (Reflection Group, 1995).

Whereas there seemed to be broad agreement in the Group on the need to integrate the protection of the environment as a horizontal dimension in EU policy, the representatives disagreed as to what would be the best form. A majority of the representatives also seemed prepared to consider the extension of QMV in this area, while some stressed the need to preserve unanimity in environmental areas highly sensitive to national sovereignty and with potential financial implications (especially environmental taxes).

The Nordic Member States were particularly active in pushing for reforms in EU environmental policy, though other states, such as Austria, also played a prominent part (see Neuhold in this volume). As Moravcsik and Nicolaïdis note: "Nordic delegations designed and kept a constant eye on environmental proposals" (1999, 71). To a significant degree, the roots and causes of these campaigns are found in the domestic political context of, in particular, Sweden and Denmark.

In the Swedish case, the pressure for strengthening EU environmental policy must be viewed in relation to the referendum on EU membership in 1994 and the sharp division within the electorate. Environment policy was one of the most salient questions in the debate before the referendum, stressed by both protagonists and antagonists. Advocates of EU membership, including Prime Minister Ingvar Carlsson, pointed to the environment as an area where transboundary problems required co-operation on the European level. Critics, by contrast, pictured EU membership as a threat against the environment, since Sweden might be forced to lower its higher environmental standards in many areas. The prominent position of these claims in the debate is best explained by widespread environmental concerns in the electorate, regardless of stand on EU membership.

This domestic political situation moved the Swedish government to pursue a particular mix of strategies and issues at the 1996-97 IGC (e.g., IGC 1996c; European Parliament 1997a). On the one hand, the government wished to show that the EU could be used effectively to address problems of concern to Swedish citizens, and therefore advanced constructive proposals aimed at strengthening the provisions at the Community level (Swedish Government 1996). These proposals included fully replacing unanimity with QMV, and integrating environmental concerns in other issue areas. At a more general level, Sweden was concerned to act as "a good example" in EU environmental policy, thereby, possibly, pushing other Member States to agree to higher Community levels of environmental protection (Liefferink & Andersen 1998a). On the other hand, the government wished to defend domestic environmental arrangements, to the extent that these prescribed stricter protection than Community harmonisation within the specific area. To this effect, Sweden sought to boost Article 100a(4) EC, whereby Member States may be allowed to set and maintain higher environmental standards than specified by EC law – a treaty provision that in Denmark and Sweden often and slightly inaccurately is referred to as the "environmental guarantee." In a broader perspective, the Social Democratic government's focus on the environment as one of three prioritised issues at the IGC (the others being employment and openness), had the additional advantage of turning the domestic debate away from institutional issues, thereby preventing internal rifts over European policy from increasing (see Johansson and Svensson in this volume).

In many ways, Denmark's positions at the IGC were similar to Sweden's, but with their own history of domestic politics. In Denmark, too, the environment is a prominent concern in the population and an issue at the top of the political agenda, not least in relation to European integration. When the environment was developed as a Community competence in association with the SEA, this met with widespread fear of a loss of national control in Denmark. The introduction of QMV in this field was perceived as threatening high environmental standards in Denmark, since the state would now risk being outvoted in the Council. In this context, Denmark bargained hard for the introduction of the "environmental guarantee" of Article 100a(4), which would release Denmark from the obligation of accepting a relaxation of protection. At the time of the SEA negotiations, this was widely perceived as a concession to Denmark, for the sake of appeasing the Danish people and securing ratification. Later experience showed, however, that it was considerably more difficult to rely on this "guarantee" in practice (Liefferink & Andersen 1998a).

Denmark approached the 1996-97 IGC with a set of suggestions for strengthening co-operation in this area, though the high profile continued to be based partly on the wish to minimise the EU's impact on domestic policy, (Danish Government 1996a). Of four main areas of action, two were widely accepted: integrating the sustainable development objective of the Rio Conference, and integrating environmental considerations into other policy fields. The two remaining priorities – boosting Member States' possibilities of making use of the "environmental guarantee," and extending QMV to environmental taxes – were considerably more controversial. With respect to Article 100a(4), the Danish government called for the specification that "a Member State may apply national provisions where it deems a sufficiently high level of protection not to have been achieved at Community level" (Danish Government 1996a, 2). In a wider perspective, progress in revising the environmental section of the EC Treaty was seen by many as a necessary condition for having the new treaty accepted by the Danish people (Petersen 1997; Liefferink & Andersen 1998b).

The third Nordic Member State, Finland, largely espoused the proposals advanced by Sweden and Denmark, but was less aggressive in pushing them, focusing comparatively more of its energy on institutional reform. In a broader perspective, this conformed to a general pattern in Finland's, and some other Member States', way of approaching the domestic dimension of European environmental policy: "Austria and Finland, as well as the 'old' members Germany and the Netherlands, acknowledge the relevance of national experiences as examples of practicable, feasible policy alternatives during the negotiations about specific measures in Brussels. Contrary to Sweden, however, they hardly regard them as vehicles to instigate new policies at the EU level" (Liefferink & Skou Andersen 1998a, 259).

All in all, the Nordic Member States advanced, promoted, and defended the most far-reaching set of proposals on how to strengthen EU environmental policy at the 1996-97 IGC. While Sweden, Denmark, and Finland more or less pushed the same suggestions, their collective strategy very much conformed to that identified by Johansson and Svensson in this volume. Rather than appearing as a united bloc, several Nordic voices were heard saying essentially the same thing. For Denmark, the accession of its Nordic brethren provided it with an opportunity to supplement its more defensive approach with constructive calls for the further development of EU environmental policy.

While not conforming to the picture of these countries as sovereignty-protecting, the institutional rules and arrangements promoted by the Nordic countries are understandable in view of domestic political conditions in these countries. The widespread support in the electorates for firm environmental protection induced these governments to seek European institutional arrangements in a slightly paradoxical combination: on the one hand, more binding commitments through the extension of QMV, and on the other hand, amplified safeguards against insufficient European protection. Rather than a threat, the promotion of firmer European rules was considered a means for maintaining high national standards, and a way of reducing the competitive disadvantage of such standards for domestic industry.

The potential effects of this Nordic activism rested with the acceptability of these suggestions among the other Member States. Analysing the positions of national governments in February 1997, the EP noted that the first year of the IGC had not brought any radical changes of opinion as compared to the preliminary impression from the Reflection Group (European Parliament, 1997a). Broad agreement could be found with respect to the integration of the principle of sustainable development, and the horizontal inclusion of environmental protection in all EU policies. Questions, which at this point were deemed more controversial, included the "environmental guarantee," the extension of QMV, and the application of the co-decision procedure. Most controversial, and unlikely to be subject to agreement, were matters such as a new title on animal welfare, QMV and co-decision concerning economic instruments to promote environmental protection, and boosting the environmental dimension of the Euratom Treaty.

Often, the reasons for rejecting proposals aimed at strengthening EU environmental policy were found in the domestic politics of the particular Member States. Opposition to the extension of QMV to matters of environmental taxation and the use of land and water resources prevailed in a large number of Member States (e.g., Germany, Spain, Luxembourg, Ireland, the UK, the Netherlands), because of the implications for national sovereignty and fiscal control. Nowhere, however, were the objections as strong as in Spain and the UK (European Parliament, 1997a). Spain opposed binding institutional arrangements on the European level, since strengthened environmental protection was likely to involve substantial costs for the national economy, especially for countries such as Spain, where lower national environmental standards could function as a competitive advantage for industry. Consequently, Spain spoke against reinforcing the treaty provisions on environment, rejected the extension of QMV, and opposed the extension of the co-decision procedure. In the UK, John Major's Tory government opposed all proposals involving any form of further delegation of powers to the EU, in view of the national elections in May 1997. On this basis, the UK dismissed the broader application of QMV and co-decision.

In the run-up to the Amsterdam summit and the conclusion of the IGC, the most hotly disputed issue was the possible boosting of the "environmental guarantee" in Article 100a(4), which featured "heavy pressure from the Danes supported by a large majority of Member States" (Petite 1998, 13). Another essential development was the victory of the Labour party in the UK elections, which reduced the opposition to reinforced provisions on environment. In the end, the Amsterdam Treaty brought advances in EU environmental policy in three areas.

First, the horizontal profile of environment was strengthened considerably. The principle of sustainable development is now enshrined in the preamble and objectives of the TEU, as well as in Article 2 of the EC Treaty, which lays down the tasks of the Community. Through the new Article 6 of the EC Treaty, environmental protection requirements must be integrated into the definition and implementation of other EU policies. In addition, the IGC notes in a declaration annexed to the Amsterdam Treaty, that the Commission undertakes to prepare environmental assessment studies when making proposals which may have significant environmental implications.

Second, the "environmental guarantee" of Article 100a(4) was revised. While the new Article 95 retains the original principles, it significantly simplifies the procedure to the advantage of Member States, by altering the authorisation procedure. After a Community harmonisation measure has been adopted, Member States may either maintain existing national provisions to protect the environment, or introduce new national provisions for this purpose. In both cases, the Member State must notify the Commission and give its reasons, and in the second case, the national measures must be based on new scientific evidence. The Commission shall then approve or reject the request within six months, and in the absence of a Commission decision within this time, the request will be deemed approved.

Third, the Amsterdam Treaty simplifies the decision-making within the environmental field, without extending QMV. Whereas previously, several different procedures existed side by side, the new treaty replaces the co-operation procedure by the co-decision procedure, thus reducing the number of procedures to two and increasing the role of the EP. The general rule is now co-decision and QMV, with the important exception of measures concerning taxation, town and country planning, land and water use, and energy supply, where several Member States wished to retain the consultation procedure and unanimity.

Summing up, the negotiations on treaty reform in environment give evidence of pivotal Nordic agenda-setting, but also of an end result heavily influenced by the positions of recalcitrant governments. Intense concerns for the environment in Denmark and Sweden pushed these governments towards a particular mix of offensive and defensive strategies and propositions. Beyond promoting strengthened European-level rules, the Nordic Member States fought for a boosting of the "environmental guarantee" allowing them to keep higher national environmental standards. While leaving a clear mark on the new treaty, the Nordic campaign was limited in its effects by the positions of less enthusiastic governments, which managed to restrict the strengthening of treaty provisions in a number of particularly sensitive areas.

Negotiating the New Treaty Title on Employment at the 1996-97 IGC

Prior to the mid-1990s, employment had made few inroads into European-level policy-making. With the exception of scattered references to employment-related matters, such as equal pay and vocational training, the Treaty still lacked provisions for a European employment policy. The wish among EU governments to keep employment a national competence was evident, not least in the decision in the TEU to refrain from including employment among the convergence criteria to be met before participation in the single currency. However, as the economic situation in most European countries deteriorated in the early to mid-1990s, and unemployment rose to record-high levels, it became more difficult to dismiss the thought of joint initiatives at the EU level. The EU was heavily criticised for not addressing the issue of most concern to European citizens. Moreover, the strict convergence criteria of the EMU were sometimes viewed as contributing to the economic and social hardship.

The 1994 European Council in Essen became the first serious attempt to jointly approach the question of employment. At this summit, the heads of state and government adopted short and medium-term lines of action on employment and concluded that the reduction of unemployment must be an EU priority. The summit defined priorities for Member States' employment policies, and introduced an arrangement whereby these are implemented in multi-annual programs and the Commission each year evaluates employment trends and policies in the Member States in the light of these priorities. The commitment to fighting unemployment was later repeated at several European Council summits.

Like environment, employment was a policy domain that originally should not have been part of the agenda of the 1996-97 IGC. However, the extreme priority of this question at the domestic political arena in the Member States, and the new impetus at the European level, led several governments to push for the inclusion of this issue. Summarising the negotiations on employment at the IGC, these pertained to three principal sets of issues. First, member governments disputed whether or not to introduce a new chapter on employment in the EC Treaty. Second, they discussed the principles and objectives of a possible chapter. And third, Member States negotiated the institutional framework of a possible employment chapter.

It became clear already at the very first meeting of the Reflection Group that employment were to be one of the priorities of the IGC negotiations (Moravcsik & Nicolaïdis 1999). During the course of the Reflection Group's deliberations, several members proposed amendments to the EC Treaty for the purpose of raising the profile on employment. The Reflection Group was far from united, however, and in the final report of December 1995, disagreement was obvious along several dimensions (Reflection Group 1995). In unison, the Reflection Group stressed the urgent need to meet the challenge of job creation, in view of the pressing demands of Europe's citizens. Moreover, it was emphasised that competitiveness constituted the primary key to job creation, that employment was a national responsibility, but that the EU, nevertheless, would be able to co-ordinate efforts in a common direction. The representatives diverged, however, on the format of this "co-ordination." Some suggested that the goal of competitiveness should be given a more prominent position in the EC Treaty, while a large majority proposed that the objective of job creation be strengthened as a horizontal concern in the Union's policies. Several members wished to go further and supported the development of a new chapter on employment policy, whereas, from an opposite view, some members objected to such far-reaching steps on the basis that it would improve neither competitiveness nor job creation.

From the very beginning, the Nordic Member States constituted the chief advocates and drivers of a new chapter on employment in the Treaty.

Domestic political considerations featured prominently behind this stand. Like many other countries, the three Nordic Member States had experienced rising unemployment levels in the first half of the 1990s. In Sweden and Finland, the experience was particularly traumatic, since Sweden witnessed a near explosion of unemployment from almost full employment to nearly 15 per cent, and Finnish unemployment spiralled in the absence of immediate alternatives to the evaporating Soviet markets. In all three countries, unemployment was the most prominent concern of the electorate and probably the most prioritised issue on the political agenda.

For the Social Democratic governments in these countries, joint European action provided a way of mobilising all means available in their struggle to deliver what they had been elected for – reducing unemployment. From an ideological perspective, their joint action also offered an opportunity to steer the EU in a new direction, by supplementing its economic and market-oriented focus with a stronger social and political dimension. Again, it is essential to consider the visions and promises of, for instance, the Swedish Social Democrats, that EU membership should be actively utilised to address problems of concern to citizens and to balance the influence of the market.

Sweden was the first Member State to formally suggest the introduction of an employment chapter in the EC Treaty, in a proposal tabled by Gunnar Lund, the Swedish member of the Reflection Group, in September 1995 (Lund 1995). In this proposal, which opened up for the IGC debate on employment, Sweden suggested that the new title should set out common aims, common procedures, and a common commitment to certain principles of employment policy. The Social Democratic flavour was distinct: an employment title was necessary in order to compensate for the imbalance in ambitions resulting from the EMU, the means should involve an active labour market policy, and the goal should be "full employment." For the sake of avoiding negative reactions from other Member States, the reference to an "employment union," which had featured in a previous document on Sweden's principal interests at the IGC (Swedish Government 1995), was no longer included.

The Swedish proposal drew heavily on work conducted within the socialist and Social Democratic transnational party networks during the early 1990s (Johansson 1999). This co-operation had been instrumental in launching the 1994 Essen initiative and in shaping the co-ordination method then put into practice. In that perspective, Swedish and other proposals for an employment chapter outlined alternative arrangements for formally institutionalising a form of co-ordination that to some extent already existed.

Sweden remained a leading force on employment during the remainder of the IGC. In March 1996, the Swedish government arranged a high-level meeting in Stockholm on how to incorporate employment into the treaty, where representatives of all governments were invited, with the exception of the non-socialist governments of Britain, France, Germany, and Italy (Johansson 1999). Moreover, on two occasions during 1996, the Swedish government tabled position papers filling out the details of its proposal for an employment title (IGC 1996a, IGC 1996b).

Denmark and Finland endorsed the idea of an employment chapter in the Treaty. As in environmental matters, however, the Nordic Member States chose to proceed individually, saying essentially the same thing with many voices. In line with this philosophy, Denmark presented a proposal of its own in July 1996 (Danish Government 1996b). Following up on previously stated intentions to work for the incorporation of an employment title (Denmark 1995), the Danish government forwarded suggestions for objectives and principles, forms of co-ordination and surveillance, new instruments and procedures, and an employment committee.

The Nordic preference for a well-equipped institutional framework may seem puzzling in view of Denmark's and Sweden's traditional reluctance to delegate powers to the EU. For the Nordic governments, however, effective EU means to combat employment were appealing on ideological grounds and would indeed be compatible with, rather than opposed to, national policies within this area. The concept of an active employment policy which the Nordic countries traditionally had espoused and implemented on a national basis, could now be exported to the European level. Instead of fearing binding commitments and constraining institutional arrangements, the Nordic governments embraced them, and could even have considered more binding rules and objectives, had the preferences of the other Member States permitted this.

After the presentation of the Swedish proposal in the Reflection Group, the idea of an employment title became "a fixed item in the on-going negotiations" (Ladrech 1997, 29). Once the IGC was opened in March 1996, proposals were tabled, in chronological order, by the Swedish, Danish, Belgian, Swedish, Spanish, and Austrian governments (European Parliament 1997b). All tabled proposals subscribed to the idea of introducing an employment chapter, but the emphasis shifted on the objectives, principles, and procedures of the new title. While Austria and Belgium referred to "full employment" as the goal, both Sweden and Denmark now employed the term "high employment," which was an clear accommodation of the preferences of less enthusiastic governments. On the principles to guide common action, the proposals were quite eclectic in ideological terms, though, for instance, Austria put relatively more emphasis on productivity, competitiveness, and flexibility, where Sweden stressed an active employment policy. With regard to the co-ordination procedure, Sweden, Denmark, and Belgium proposed common principles and multilateral surveillance, with the possibility of issuing recommendations to governments falling out of line, whereas Spain envisaged a considerably weaker co-ordination mechanism.

The governments entirely opposed to a new title on employment did not submit any proposals in this area. Domestic political considerations played a prominent part in the reluctance of these states to agree to European-level co-ordination. In the UK, the Tory government firmly dismissed both the delegation of further powers to the EU and the strengthening of the Union's social dimension. There was considerable scepticism, or even outright opposition, on the part of the Gaullist government in France and the Christian Democrat government in Germany, though it was questionable whether any of them were ready to block an employment title (Johansson 1999). Likewise, the Dutch government, and to some extent the Spanish, had mixed feelings. Loosely united in ideological terms, all these governments tended to underline that greater competitiveness, a flexible economy, and reduced bureaucratic burdens held the key to higher employment; that a separate title on employment would be an intrusion into matters that should be dealt with at the national level; that there was an obvious risk of raising citizens' expectations in an area where little might be delivered; that common efforts would require financial resources which none of these states was ready to commit, and that such Keynesian spending could have negative consequences for the monetary union (Reflection Group 1995; McDonagh 1998; Petite 1998; Johansson 1999).

This opposition notwithstanding, broad consensus emerged in late 1996 on the main tenets of an employment chapter, "based on proposals that came largely from Sweden" (Petite 1998, 11). In its draft treaty of December 5 1996, the Irish Presidency proposed the incorporation of high employment among the Union's objectives and the introduction of a new title on employment. While obviously to the satisfaction of the new chapter's protagonists, this consensus was founded on a compromise, where the positions of the antagonists had been taken into account (Devuyst 1998; McDonagh 1998; Moravcsik & Nicolaïdis 1998). This accommodation, which was necessary in order to secure ratification by all Member States, had begun at an early stage, with the choice not to propose full EU competence and binding legislation in this area. During late 1996 and the spring of 1997, it continued with the softening of the title's objectives, the exclusion of sanctions and quantified criteria, the continued emphasis on employment as a national competence, and the avoidance of costly large-scale programs.

Following the broad consensus on the suggestions of the Irish draft treaty, few revisions of the text took place during the spring. Indeed, the area of employment experienced the same waiting exercise that characterised other negotiation items where the UK government formed somewhat of an outlier. As predicted, the Labour victory in the May elections brought an immediate shift in policy on many of the issues on the IGC agenda, employment included. Add the slightly more surprising ascent to power in France of Lionel Jospin's Socialist government, and the possibilities for securing final approval of the employment chapter had improved significantly. But whereas the new French government pressed hard for a strengthened legal basis for employment in the treaty, acting on the electorate's mandate to reduce unemployment, the new UK government combined its support for the new title with a continued British commitment to national prerogatives and flexibility in the employment field (Devuyst 1998; Johansson 1999). Even for a Labour government, flexible labour market arrangements constituted a prerequisite for British competitiveness. Though unable to bridge such internal divisions, the European family of socialist and Social Democratic parties could nevertheless steer the employment title towards adoption during the last month preceding the Amsterdam summit. The socialist dominance in European politics was epitomised by a strategic congress of the Party of European Socialists (PES) in Malmö, Sweden, just one week before the summit, where the European party could boast nine socialist prime ministers and socialist presence in another four governments.

In Amsterdam, EU governments agreed on the insertion of an employment title into the EC Treaty. In institutional terms, this title is a hybrid arrangement, since employment policy neither becomes a European competence nor remains strictly national. The new title specifies that employment should be considered a "common concern" for the Member States which shall work towards developing a "co-ordinated strategy" for employment, with the objective of achieving a "high level of employment." The Community's actions shall supplement those of the Member States and the objective of high employment shall be an integral part in the formulation and implementation of EU policies. At the core of the co-ordinated strategy is the procedure for implementing common guidelines, which has many traits in common with the practice established by the 1994 Essen European Council. In the implementation of its employment policy, each Member State must take into account common guidelines adopted by the Council on a proposal from the Commission. On the basis of annual reports submitted by the Member States on how these guidelines have been incorporated, the Council may then issue recommendations to Member States whose implementation is lacking in some respect. The new title also provides for the creation of an employment committee, whose task it is to promote co-ordination between the Member States, and "incentive measures" which may take the format of pilot projects on best practices, but must not include harmonisation of laws and regulations.

Summing up, the negotiations on a new employment title at the 1996-97 IGC constitute a case in which domestic political considerations were imperative in putting the issue on the agenda, in isolating the appropriate institutional arrangements, and in defining the scope for agreement. Acting on national political mandates to reduce unemployment, socialist and Social Democratic governments pushed jointly for a common European employment policy. The Nordic governments, especially the Swedish, were at the forefront of these efforts, which involved attempts to export an active employment policy to the European level. The diverging positions of certain non-socialist governments constrained the title's advocates and shaped the final outcome, by forcing accommodations as regards the objectives and institutional arrangements of the new employment title.

Conclusion

This chapter departed from two puzzles inherent in the treaty changes brought about by the Amsterdam Treaty. First, how can we explain significant advances in the domains of environment and employment, when the IGC initially was not supposed to revise first pillar policies? Second, how can we explain the success of the Nordic countries in promoting these changes, given the limited structural power of these Member States? This chapter suggests that a consideration of the interplay between domestic politics and international negotiations is imperative if we wish to understand this Nordic mark on the Amsterdam Treaty. Three forms of domestic-international interplay were prominent in both cases, and fundamentally shaped the final bargaining outcome.

First, domestic politics was essential in inducing Sweden and Denmark to table proposals on environment and employment, thus expanding the IGC's narrow agenda. In Sweden, the legacy of the EU referendum, the division within the Social Democrats, and electoral pressure for constructive efforts to protect the environment and combat unemployment, influenced the agenda-setting. In Denmark, progress in the environmental field was viewed as necessary to secure domestic ratification of the new treaty, and the fight against unemployment constituted a cause the Social Democratic government was not hard-pressed to join.

Secondly, domestic political considerations influenced the form of institutional arrangements promoted by the Nordic countries and other Member States. In the area of environment, both Denmark and Sweden espoused a paradoxical mix of binding European-level rules and safeguards permitting them to escape such rules, when these do not satisfy national environmental standards. By contrast, Member States which benefit from more lenient national environmental norms were less interested in constraining EU arrangements. The new employment title, for its part, offered a way of exporting national means for combating unemployment to the

European level – be they an active labour market policy or enhanced competition.

Finally, the bargaining outcomes, and thus the result of the Nordic agenda-setting, were heavily conditioned by the need to secure ratification in all Member States. As in any system of unanimity voting, the agreements were constrained by the most recalcitrant governments forcing the driving Member States to adapt their proposals either in anticipation of resistance or in reaction to dismissals. While the ascent to power of Labour in the UK in the eleventh hour of the IGC significantly expanded the zone of agreement, sufficient opposition still remained in some Member States to prevent agreement on the more radical suggestions forwarded by the Nordic countries. Whereas the agenda-setting influence of the Nordic states thus challenges a "minilateral" power perspective, the dynamic of the negotiations on environment and employment still lies comfortably within the general logic of inter-governmentalism.

Bibliography

Danish Government (1995). *Basis for Negotiations. Open Europe: The 1996 Intergovernmental Conference.*

Danish Government (1996a). *Intergovernmental Conference: The Environment*, 6 September.

Danish Government (1996b). *Intergovernmental Conference: Employment: Proposal for an Amendment to the Treaty Establishing the European Community*, July.

Devuyst, Youri (1998). "Treaty Reform in the European Union: The Amsterdam Process," *Journal of European Public Policy*, Vol. 5, No. 4, pp. 615-31.

European Parliament (1997a). *European Environmental Policy and the IGC*, IGC Briefing No. 32, 28 February.

European Parliament (1997b). *Employment and the IGC*, IGC Briefing No. 37, 2 April.

Evans, Peter B., Harold K. Jacobson & Robert D. Putnam (1993). *Double-Edged Diplomacy: International Bargaining and Domestic Politics*, Berkeley: University of California Press.

IGC (1996a). *Employment*, CONF/3859/96.

IGC (1996b). *Proposals on Treaty Amendments on Employment*, CONF/3921/96.

IGC (1996c). *Proposals on Treaty Amendments on Environment*, CONF/3922/96.

Johansson, Karl Magnus (1999). "Tracing the Employment Title in the Amsterdam Treaty: Uncovering Transnational Coalitions," *Journal of European Public Policy*, Vol. 6, No. 1, pp. 85-101.

Ladrech, Robert (1997). "Political Parties and the Problem of Legitimacy in the European Union," paper presented at the workshop on Legitimacy and the European Union, Georgetown University, 11-12 January.

Liefferink, Duncan & Mikael S. Andersen (1998a). "Strategies of the "Green" Member States in EU Environmental Policy-Making," *Journal of European Public Policy*, Vol. 5, No. 2, pp. 254-270.

Liefferink, Duncan & Mikael S. Andersen (1998b). "Greening the EU: National Positions in the Run-up to the Amsterdam Treaty," *Environmental Politics*, Vol. 7, No. 3, pp. 66-93.

Lund, Gunnar (1995). *Strengthening the Fight Against Unemployment – An Issue for the Intergovernmental Conference*, speech/paper delivered in the Reflection Group.

Milner, Helen V. (1997). *Interests, Institutions, and Information: Domestic Politics and International Relations*, Princeton: Princeton University Press.

Moravcsik, Andrew (1993). "Preferences and Power in the European Community: A Liberal Intergovernmentalist Approach," *Journal of Common Market Studies*, Vol. 31, No. 4, pp. 473-524.

Moravcsik, Andrew (1998). *The Choice for Europe: Social Purpose and State Power from Messina to Maastricht*, Ithaca: Cornell University Press.

Moravcsik, Andrew & Kalypso Nicolaïdis (1999). "Explaining the Treaty of Amsterdam: Interests, Influence, Institutions," *Journal of Common Market Studies*, Vol. 37, No. 1, pp. 59-85.

Patterson, Lee Ann (1997). "Agricultural policy reform in the European Community: A Three-level Game Analysis," *International Organization*, Vol. 51, No. 1, pp. 135-165.

Petersen, Nikolaj (1997). "The Nordic Trio and the Future of the EU," pp. 159-187, in Geoffrey Edwards & Alfred Pijpers (eds.), *The Politics of European Treaty Reform. The 1996 Intergovernmental Conference and Beyond*, London: Pinter.

Petite, Michel (1998). "The Treaty of Amsterdam," *Jean Monnet Papers,* No. 2, Harvard Law School, The Jean Monnet Chair.

Putnam, Robert D. (1988). "Diplomacy and Domestic Politics: The Logic of Two-level games," *International Organization*, Vol. 42, No. 3, pp. 427-460.

Reflection Group (1995). *Reflection Group's Report*, Brussels, 5 December.

Swedish Government (1995). *Sweden's Principal Interests in View of the 1996 EU Intergovernmental Conference*, The Cabinet Office, July.

Swedish Government (1996). *Statement of Government Policy Presented by the Prime Minister to the Parliament*, 22 March.

20

The Common Foreign and Security Policy: Significant but Modest Changes

Simon Duke

Introduction

The Maastricht Treaty marked a turning point since it incorporated the parallel European Political Cooperation (EPC) process, which began in 1970, into a new entity, the European Union. Although the idea of explicitly incorporating external relations, including security and defence, was by no means a new notion, the introduction of the Common Foreign and Security Policy (CFSP) into the Union ended the EPC's parallel process. Nevertheless, the cautious language used in Title V of the Treaty on European Union (TEU) made it evident that a number of significant differences had not been addressed and the intergovernmental nature of the second pillar also ensured that consensus would be difficult to achieve.

Since the TEU made provision for an Intergovernmental Conference in 1996, many of the more difficult issues pertaining to the CFSP were passed on.[1] Some of the issues were not specific to the second pillar but took the form of far more general questions concerning the actual form of European integration – deepening versus widening, *à la carte*, variable geometry, or some form of concentric circles with, by definition, a "core Europe" and others moving at a slower speed. Space does not permit an examination of these more general themes and the main aim of this chapter is twofold. First, to consider the nature of those security and defence issues that were passed on from the Maastricht IGC to Amsterdam. Second, to ask what progress was made during the IGC on second pillar related discussions. It will be argued that the changes introduced by the Amsterdam Treaty were significant but modest. Importance will be attached to identifying the unresolved issues since these shaped the agenda of the 2000 IGC.

By way of context, it is worth briefly noting that the unravelling of Federal Yugoslavia just before and during the 1991 IGC continued apace until the 1995 Dayton Accords and, even then, it was apparent that the more general

---

[1] Article N.2 of the TEU provides that, "A conference of representatives of the government of the Member States shall be convened in 1996 to examine those provisions of this Treaty for which revision is provided ..."

security of the region was parlous. Although the bloody struggle in Bosnia and the uneasy peace accord undoubtedly influenced the discussions in the 1996 IGC, there is little evidence to suggest that the Bosnian crisis had any major influence upon the determination of the EU Member States to work towards regional security and stability. A second crisis, this time in Albania, during the 1996 IGC also had little measurable impact upon the deliberations. Although it would be an exaggeration to claim that external events, in the Balkans and elsewhere, had no impact upon the IGC deliberations, it took the cumulative shocks of these crises plus Kosovo to profoundly reorient European security and defence. The purpose of the IGC, to consider and if necessary adopt changes to the Treaties founding the Communities and Union, also encourages a certain amount of insularity from which the 1996 IGC was certainly not exempt.

Moving Sands and Foundations

The European Council meeting in Corfu, on 24-5 June 1994, established a Reflection Group, chaired by Carlos Westendorp, and mandated that it focus on those areas of the TEU that were subject to revision. This included the Union's second pillar or CFSP. As far as the second pillar was concerned, two questions rose to the top of the agenda as the IGC approached. First, the development of a Common Defence Policy and Common Defence (CDP/CD) and second, the nature of the EU-WEU relationship. The Reflection Group had the unenviable task of finding consensus amongst (at least) France, Germany and the United Kingdom. France, with a Gaullist led government, was in favour of strengthening CFSP and developing the WEU as the defence component of the EU. Germany saw CFSP as "the core element of a future political union and insist[ed] that the development must correspond and keep pace with the evolution of European Monetary Union." The UK was broadly in favour of the *status quo* with any advances being accomplished through intensified intergovernmental co-operation (Emmanouilidis 1995, 1). However, prior to the unveiling of the Reflection Group's findings, a number of other proposals surfaced. In relation to the first issue, the 1994 *Reflections on European Policy* paper prepared by CDU/CSU Parliamentary leader Wolfgang Schäuble and foreign policy spokesman Karl Lammers, is worthy of note (*Agence Europe* 7 September 1994; Janning & Weidenfeld 1996, 521-36). With regard to the second issue, the WEU's 1995 *Contribution to the European Intergovernmental Conference of 1996* is important (WEU 14 November 1995).

The CDU/CSU *Reflections on European Policy* (henceforth "Reflections") aroused considerable controversy, not least from the French government.[2] The significance of the document lay in the fact that it shaped the CFSP-related debates of the IGC. The CDU/CSU's tactic of forwarding them in such a public and forceful manner meant that the issues could not easily be avoided nor would Germany's hands be tied.[3] In the Report's first section, in remarkably blunt language, the document warned that the Union risked becoming a "group of loosely knit grouping of states restricted to certain economic aspects and composed of various sub-groupings." Amongst the causes of instability in the Union mentioned were: the overextension of the EU's institutions dealing with the demands of Twelve members; the differentiation of interests due to varying levels of socio-economic development; the differentiation of perceptions of internal and, "above all, external priorities in a European Union stretching from the North cape to Gibraltar;" the evolution of profound structural economic change; the growth of "regressive nationalism;" the development of debilitating demands placed on national governments; and the emergence of questions of when and how the Central and East Europeans would be involved in the Union.

The second section of the report outlines Germany's interests, as perceived by the CDU/CSU. These interests were based on the underlying fact that, "Owing to its geographical location, its size and its history Germany has a special interest in preventing Europe from drifting apart." If Europe were to drift apart, the document argued, "Germany would once again find itself caught in the middle between East and West, a position which through its history has made it difficult for Germany to give a clear orientation to its internal order and to establish a stable and lasting balance in its external relations." A reference to the "military political and moral catastrophe of 1945" can also be viewed as a clear plea to EU colleagues to maintain the fundamentals of post-World War II European security.

The CDU/CSU attached the utmost importance to its relations with France since "no significant action in the foreign or EU policy fields should be taken without prior consultation between France and Germany." In order to bring about this essential fusion the report stated in no uncertain terms:

---

[2] See interview with Prime Minister, Edouard Balladur from *Le Figaro* reproduced in *Agence Europe* No. 1891, 3 September 1994.

[3] Since the document emanated from a parliamentary group (headed by Wolfgang Schäuble) it was not a document that necessarily expressed the position of the government or the Chancellor (although he was aware of its contents) and it therefore left Germany's position in the IGC relatively unconstrained.

If Germany puts forward clear and unequivocal proposals, then France must make equally clear and unequivocal decisions. It must rectify the impression that, although it allows no doubt as to its basic will to pursue European integration, it often hesitates taking concrete steps towards this objective – the notion of the unsurrenderable sovereignty of the "Etat nation" still carries weight, although this sovereignty has long since become an empty shell.

The *Reflections* use of the term "hard core", of "five or six countries,"[4] excluded the UK although it was hoped that "Great Britain will assume its role "in the heart of Europe" and thus in its core."

On the CFSP, the report observed that, "Action by the European Union in the field of [CFSP] must be based on a strategic concept which clearly defines common interests and objectives and stipulates the conditions and procedures as well as the political, economic and financial means." The *Reflections* recommend giving priority to:

– The stabilisation of central and eastern Europe;
– The development of a wide-ranging partnership with Russia;
– The development of a common policy in the Mediterranean;
– The advancement of a strategic partnership with Turkey;
– The reorientation of transatlantic relations.

In reference to the difficulties over Yugoslavia within the EU and between the U.S. and its allies, the *Reflections* suggested that the "creation of a common defence is a matter of much greater urgency than envisaged in the Maastricht Treaty." Movement towards a common defence would, it was argued, mean reorganising relations between the EU and the WEU in accordance with Article J.4(6) – in other words, the merging of the WEU and EU to the greatest extent possible. The recommendations also included realigning relations with NATO to allow the Europeans to "take independent action using NATO resources and parts of the NATO staffs."

The CDU/CSU *Reflections'* key problem was how to reconcile federalist versus national sovereignty issues in the particularly sensitive area of common defence. In grappling with this conundrum, the *Reflections* recognised that a "nation's awareness of its sovereignty determined not only its self-perception but also its relations with other nations." At the same time, the *Reflections* realised that the "common defence capability of this European community of states constitutes an indispensable factor in endowing the EU with an identity

---

[4] The "hard core" were assumed to be Belgium, France, Germany, the Netherlands and Luxembourg. Italy, notably, was not included in the "hard core."

of its own, an identity which, however, at the same time leaves room for the sense of identity of each individual state." Finally, with regard to enlargement of the EU towards the East, it urged that, "Poland, the Czech and Slovak Republics, Hungary (and Slovenia) should become Members of the European Union around the year 2000."

The second document, the WEU's *Contribution to the European Union Intergovernmental Conference of 1996*, was designed to encourage a structured debate on the question to what degree the WEU should be tied to the EU (WEU 14 November 1995). It was quite evident that the issue of the degree of intimacy that the WEU should enjoy with the EU, which had not been resolved at the Maastricht summit, would be one of the critical issues for the forthcoming IGC. Accordingly, the WEU Council of Ministers adopted the WEU's *Contribution* at their Madrid meeting on 14 November 1995. The document noted:

> Irrespective of the outcome of the institutional debate on European defence at the IGC, there is a broad consensus on the need to make available the operational capabilities necessary for European military action, particularly in the field of the new tasks defined at Petersberg. The mostly organizational measures agreed to this end at Maastricht have still to be fully implemented and additional efforts are needed to deliver appropriate military assets and capabilities that are both effective and credible.

The document also underscored the need to continue to strengthen ESDI and the Atlantic Alliance but more importantly, in view of the upcoming IGC, three options were outlined regarding WEU-EU relations. The first choice favoured the preservation of the WEU as an autonomous organisation based on the belief that "the principle of national sovereignty must continue to govern relations between European countries on defence matters, and that the intergovernmental nature of decision-making on defence matters must be preserved and this decision-making will be conducted on the basis of consensus" (WEU 14 November 1995, Paras. 50-9). This option did not envisage extensive changes in the institutional or legal framework of the organisation. The maintenance of the current relationship between the EU and the WEU could provide the "right framework."

The second option, encapsulating the "majority view;" also wanted to maximise the provisions bolstering the ESDI and to foster further collaboration between the WEU, EU and NATO. Unlike the first option however, the second advocated the "gradual integration" of the WEU into the EU with "the purpose of achieving greater coherence than at present of European action in the security and defence field." This objective could be met through a "flexible and juridically non-binding formula that would make the blocking of decisions politically more difficult" (WEU 14 November 1995, Paras. 59-75).

The third option posited integration of the WEU into the EU and, in a foreshadowing of the contemporary debate, the WEU noted that, "for this integration to provide further added value, the operational capabilities necessary for these kinds of actions should be made available, both through arrangements for the use of NATO assets and capabilities, including CJTF, and through the development of complementary EU capabilities" (WEU 14 November 1995, Paras. 76-98).

The *WEU Contribution* made it clear that all were in favour of "achieving greater coherence than at present of European action in the security and defence field." The principle of "reinforced partnership" was designed to achieve this but the question of how "reinforced" or integrated the WEU should be with the EU was subject to differing opinions. The language employed in the TEU suggested that the positions of the WEU members became polarised between the options but that there was a common understanding that more needed to be done for Europe's security and defence.

Two Franco-German statements also shaped the political agenda of the forthcoming IGC. The first was a letter of 6 December 1995 from the President of the French Republic, Jacques Chirac, and the Chancellor of the Federal Republic of Germany, Helmut Kohl. The second were common guidelines for the preparation of the 1996 IGC issued on the occasion of the Franco-German ministerial meeting held in Freiburg on 27 February 1996 between Klaus Kinkel and his French counterpart, Hervé de Charette. Both ministers took the view that the main objectives of the CFSP were to stabilise the Union's relations with its neighbours to the east and south, to consolidate the transatlantic relationship and to develop ties with Russia and Ukraine. With a view to improving the effectiveness of the CFSP, they proposed a number of practical improvements such as improvements to the decision-making process and the implementation procedures, with greater powers of control for the European Council. They also advocated that attempts should be made to overcome the rigidity inherent in unanimity; accordingly, consideration should be given to: reviewing the distinction between political decisions of principle and implementing decisions; invocation of the principle of constructive abstention on CFSP matters; and recourse to qualified majority voting for decisions at the implementation stage.

The text raises the question of greater solidarity, especially in the fields of security and defence. In this context, the foreign ministers proposed that the Treaty should include a "political solidarity clause" applying to all the Member States, with solidarity defined in such a way as to take account of individual Member States' legitimate interests. Additionally, the European

Council should lay down guidelines for security and defence on the basis of which the WEU could, at the request of the EU, undertake actions on the latter's behalf. This would include the WEU's 1992 "Petersberg missions", which should be incorporated in the TEU. The Union's role should also be strengthened as regards the definition of a common European defence policy. There should be a European capacity for action in all circumstances, even where certain partners do not take part in the military side of an operative action. In such cases, the non-participant Member States should express their solidarity through public support and, where necessary, financial aid. Both ministers expressly support the joint objective of incorporating the WEU into the EU, and consider that the IGC should produce clear and specific undertakings in this direction (European Parliament 1995).

The 1996 IGC and the Consolidated Treaty on European Union (CTEU)

The second IGC commenced on 29 March 1996 with a European Council meeting in Turin and culminated in the 16-17 June 1997 Amsterdam summit which covered, in order, the Presidencies of Italy, Ireland and the Netherlands. In the agenda prepared for the IGC by Westendorp's Reflection Group, which produced its report in December 1995, the necessity of giving the EU "greater capacity for external action" was one of three key areas highlighted.[5] The Group's deliberations were also notable for advocating greater "flexibility" in European integration if certain conditions were observed. The amount of "flexibility" varied according to the pillar. Thus, in the first pillar very little flexibility was anticipated while in the second pillar, bearing in mind the recent enlargement of the EU to include Austria, Finland and Sweden, a fair degree of flexibility was permissible.[6] The idea of "flexibility" (the interpretation of which depended critically upon the Member State in question) meant that the deliberations in the 1996 IGC were less about integration *per se* and more about various forms of "enhanced cooperation."

It would be almost impossible to sum up all of the papers, non-papers, letters and memoranda pertaining to CFSP that were forwarded to the IGC for consideration. Antonio Missiroli contends that during the conference some

---

[5] The other two were making the Union "more relevant to its citizens in the field of human rights, internal security, employment and the environment," and "improving the Union's efficiency and democracy."

[6] Flexible arrangements also applied to a certain extent to Justice and Home Affairs (the Third Pillar).

twenty-two documents were submitted on CFSP matters (Missiroli 2000, 8). If the pre-IGC positions are included, as well as the more informal communications, the number at least doubles. A few key documents, reflecting the views of the Presidency and the main actors, have therefore been selected in the hope that they will give an accurate impression of the IGC debates and the factors that shaped the Treaty of Amsterdam in the CFSP area.

The Turin European Council of 29 March 1996 established the mandate for the IGC and laid down its programme. In their final conclusions, the Heads of State and Government considered that the Conference should, in the light of the Reflection Group's report and without prejudice to any other matters which might be raised at it, concentrate on a number of key issues, including the reinforcement of the Union's capacity for external action. The European Council acknowledged that the international situation is increasing the Union's responsibilities and the need to strengthen its identity on the world stage with a view to working for peace and stability. It was also observed that the Union's political weight should be commensurate with its economic power. The coherence and unity of all aspects of its external action must be developed, on the basis of full respect for the role of the Commission. Finally, the difficulty of reaching agreement on the defence aspects of CFSP was acknowledged when the European Council spoke of "including a framework for the common defence policy which could, when the time is right, result in a common defence" (European Parliament 1995).

In the Italian Presidency's Progress Report on the IGC of June 1996, many of the key areas of agreement and disagreement had already been identified. Consensus had been established on the need for a stronger planning and warning system; the idea of appointing a High Representative had been forwarded; a revised Troika had already been suggested, as had the occasional need for special envoys. The procedures for decision-making were unsurprisingly not subject to consensus and, in the Presidency's view, the "general requirement of unanimity under the CFSP is often regarded as a factor causing rigidity and even paralysis in the decision-making process" (Italian Presidency June 1996 Section 2 (iii)). One of the options forwarded for overcoming rigidity was a constructive abstention clause. On security and defence, the Italian Presidency's Progress Report noted that the deliberations had been complicated by the North Atlantic Council meeting of 3 June which set out the objective of developing a European Security and Defence Identity (ESDI) within the Alliance, an important feature of which "is the possibility of operations including NATO resources but led by the WEU" (Italian Presidency June 1996 Section IV (1)). With regard to the "Petersberg tasks," "considerable interest" had been shown in their "explicit inclusion" in the Treaty. On the framing of a common defence it was evident that little progress would be made, beyond dropping the word "eventual" from Article J.4(1) TEU and replacing it with something suitably innocuous but more positive.[7]

Generally, the idea of flexibility was very much to the fore during the Irish Presidency. It was abundantly clear to the Presidency that the "development of the CFSP is a key task for the IGC" (CONF 3868/96 16 July:1). The Presidency also noted that "discussion to date has revealed a degree of convergence towards the view that the European Union should have an enhanced capacity to pursue objectives of the CFSP which may involve the use of military resources and capabilities, without the EU itself embarking on military operations, and in a manner which does not involve Article V clauses." There was also an emerging view, according to the Presidency, that "attention should be focused on the Petersberg tasks, and that this focus can and should be achieved without prejudice to such further development in the defence area as the European Union may be able to agree" (CONF 3869/96:1).

As a result of the views expressed by several delegations at a Representatives meeting, held on 22-23 July, the Presidency noted that it would be "preferable not to include some of the proposed changes to CFSP procedures in the Treaties since this might fix them too rigidly and make it more difficult to make further adaptations when necessary" (CONF 3935/96 30 September:1). The Presidency suggested that flexibility could be maintained by making certain (unspecified) changes by Treaty revision and others as declarations in the Final Act of the Conference.

The discussions of 22-23 July saw broad convergence on the idea of including the "Petersberg tasks," as formulated by the WEU in paragraph II.4 of its Petersberg Declaration of 19 June 1992, into the Treaty. Their inclusion however introduced a number of sub-issues such as, "the definition of tasks in question; the location of a reference to the tasks in the Treaty; and the decision-making and other rights which partners who are not full members of the WEU, but who wish to participate in Petersberg tasks, should enjoy in the WEU when the WEU acts to implement Petersberg tasks at the instigation of the European Union" (CONF 3936/96 30 September: 1). Although the formulation of the Petersberg tasks was included in the Treaty, the discussions of the drafts prepared under the Irish Presidency already indicated that the last of the tasks, "peacemaking," was a concept that was out of synch with the terminology employed by other principal security organisations such as the UN or OSCE. The Commission also raised the need for a distinction between humanitarian tasks that might arise under a revised Article J.4(1) and those arising under the Treaty establishing the European Community. The remaining issue, that of the form of association by those who are not full members of the

---

[7] For a detailed assessment of the Italian Presidency see the contribution by Laura Corrado in this volume.

WEU, was only partially addressed and this would continue to be a sensitive issue for the IGC 2000 where the various forms of WEU membership had risen to ten full members and eighteen in other categories of membership.

Aside from its Presidency role, the Irish case illustrated the profound difficulties of reaching common agreement on such sensitive matters as common defence. Prior to assuming the Presidency, the Irish government made it plain that, "To ensure that Ireland's traditional policy of military neutrality is unchanged ...the Irish Government's text recalls its undertaking to hold a referendum on any proposals emanating from the coming negotiations which could entail Irish participation in a common defence policy. The Irish Government will not propose that Ireland join NATO or the WEU or sign their mutual defence agreements" (White Paper 1996). As Patrick Keatinge notes, the Irish reservations on the introduction of the military instruments to the range of EC/EU policies "have generally been expressed with due deference to the overall rules of the game, on the grounds that it makes little sense to bite the hand that feeds you" (Keatinge 1996, 1). Although Fianna Fail and the Democratic Left had already signalled their acute sensitivity to security and defence issues in the context of the debate over membership of NATO's Partnership for Peace, Irish sensitivities were somewhat assuaged by the concentration on crisis management following the Finnish-Swedish proposals on the EU's role in crisis management which were tabled in April. Generally, the Irish Presidency had the task of reaching a difficult balance between being seen as effective, whilst preserving their neutrality, as well as avoiding the impression that Ireland was closely associated with the positions of the United Kingdom.[8] The Irish were, in the context of the 1996 IGC, less of a "special case" than they had been in the 1991 IGC since they could count on the support, or at least empathy, of the new neutral or non-aligned EU members.

One further document that does bear brief mention is a further Franco-German memorandum of 17 October 1996 forwarded by the respective foreign ministers, de Charette and Kinkel (CONF 3955/96 17 October). The basic argument, once again, was for the introduction of a general flexibility clause and a number of specific flexibility clauses based on two arguments. The first was that enlargement would call for more flexible arrangements. Second, flexibility clauses would allow awkward areas, such as CFSP, to progress within the EU framework (a lack of flexibility, it was argued, would merely encourage collaboration outside the EU). Although the idea of flexibility clauses was by no means new (it goes back at least to the Kohl-Chirac letter of December 1995 if not before) the Franco-German

---

[8] For more on this theme see the contribution of Ben Tonra in this volume.

memorandum at least served to keep flexibility at the forefront of the IGC proceedings for all pillars.

The conclusions of the European Council meeting in Dublin on 13-14 December 1996 saw the reaffirmation of the aim that the European Council had set in Florence of developing the external action of the Union (European Council, Dublin 1996). The conclusions stated that the "Union must enhance its capacity to ensure that its external action is coherent and effective in all its aspects, and it must improve its decision-making procedures, if it is to play a role in the world commensurate with its responsibilities and its potential." The European Council noted the approaches that the Irish Presidency identified in CFSP-relevant areas, including the option of establishing a new function to enhance the visibility of the CFSP and the strengthening of links with the WEU. On the need for flexibility generally, the European Council observed that, "the Presidency document, responding to a view of many delegations that certain issues can be settled definitively only at a later stage in the Conference, does not include texts in Treaty form on the issue of flexibility and on certain sensitive institutional questions, although it offers an analysis of the issues and identifies options" (European Council, Dublin 1996). However, in spite of the fact that "Dublin II's" focus was very much upon EMU, the "General Outline for a Draft Revision of the Treaties" did include a draft text for "constructive abstention" for CFSP (CONF 2500/96 of 5 December). The Irish Presidency concluded in this regard that, "Some delegations consider that the unanimity requirement does not constitute a significant constraint on decision-making and oppose any extension of qualified majority voting." While other delegations could accept that "even joint actions be adopted by qualified majority within general guidelines laid down by the European Council. To the extent that qualified majority voting were to apply, accompanied by a right of veto, it has been suggested that a qualified majority could nevertheless decide to proceed to a vote on the matter in question" (CONF 2500/96 5 December: 82-3). If we assume that "General Outline" accurately reflects the state of play at the end of the Irish Presidency, it is notable that much of what became the final text was already on the table in draft form including the "constructive abstention" clause, the Secretary-General of the Council (later High Representative), the Policy Planning and Early Warning Unit (PPEWU) and the "Petersberg tasks." Amongst the major items still missing were common strategies and the budgetary stipulations.

The incoming Dutch presidency had to take on the difficult task of reaching an agreement by the Amsterdam summit in June 1997, as had been agreed upon at the conclusion of the Irish Presidency. A number of writers have noted the "flexibility" issue assumed centre stage in the first few months of the Dutch Presidency and the number of meetings on flexibility doubled in comparison to the previous Presidency (see Stubb 1998, 211). Specifically with regard to the second pillar, the role of the IGC Chairman of the Dutch Presidency, Michiel Patijn, was critical. Alexander Stubb goes as far as to argue that, "Without Patijn's personal vision of an Atlanticist security structure it could have been possible that the member governments would have been able to agree on an enabling clause in the second pillar, which might have led to flexible defence arrangements within the treaty framework" (Stubb 1998, 212). Missiroli also observes that the Dutch Presidency voiced doubts "as to the necessity of an enabling clause in the second pillar, and in any case the final draft prepared for the Amsterdam summit envisaged unanimity as the necessary trigger mechanisms, whereas QMV was deemed sufficient for the first and third pillars" (Missiroli, 9).

The Italians helped keep the flexibility issue on the table for the first few weeks of the Dutch Presidency with the submission of a document arguing strongly for flexibility in the second pillar (CONF 3801/97 quoted in Stubb 1998, 222-3). The document proposed that some areas should be subject to QMV while those that remained should be subject to unanimity but also allowing for "constructive abstention." The thinking behind the document was to permit the efficient functioning of the foreign policy aspects of CFSP, where flexibility was seen as not necessary, as well as security and defence, where flexibility was seen as desirable. The Commission, in a paper on flexibility of 23 January, also supported the notion of flexibility for those areas of greatest need (the second and third pillars were highlighted) (CONF 3805/97). The Dutch Presidency steered the debate on flexibility in the first six weeks of their Presidency towards the first and third pillars. In mid February, the Dutch Presidency introduced a section addressing an "enabling clause" for the second pillar. The Dutch proposal observed that the existing Article J.4(4-5) provides for some flexibility in defence cooperation, while the Dublin II draft provided for "constructive abstention" in the context of CFSP. The two, as Patijn argued, should provide for sufficient flexibility in the second pillar (CONF 3813/97).

Drawing heavily on the Dublin II outlines, the Dutch Presidency (CONF 3833/97:1-2) invited the delegates to embark upon an article by article examination of the draft treaty with particular attention being paid to:

- The appointment of a prominent figure to enhance the effectiveness, continuity and profile of the CFSP, and whether such an appointment should be established by developing the role of the Secretary-General of the Council, or the creation of a new function of CFSP High Representative.
- Discussion of Dublin II's innovations in CFSP decision-making: "constructive abstention" where unanimity would apply and an extension of QMV coupled with a "safety mechanism" for all other decisions.
- Whether a specific reference should be made to the binding character of joint actions and common positions on some or all of the institutions of the Union.

– The question of the development of the relationship between the EU and WEU including whether gradual integration of the latter into the former is envisaged.

The difficult question of the extent to which the WEU should be associated or merged with the EU was forced to the fore following proposed amendments to Article J.4 of the TEU by six Member States in March 1997. After a year's deliberation, the six (Belgium, France, Germany, Italy, Luxembourg and Spain) proposed that the EU should aim to "integrate the WEU progressively into the European Union." Furthermore, they proposed that integration would be achieved in three phases to be defined in greater detail in a Protocol attached to the Treaty (CONF 3855/97 24 March). The proposal drew less than enthusiastic support (only Greece and Portugal seemed somewhat supportive) and, as a consequence, an enabling clause was eventually adopted that left it to the European Council to decide on the feasibility and desirability of any eventual merger of the WEU into the EU. The lacklustre response can be accounted for by the lack of convincing consensus amongst the six themselves, alongside the fact that a Finnish-Swedish proposal the previous year for the incorporation of the "Petersberg tasks" into the CFSP had removed much of the wind from the sails of the six.

It should also be noted that political developments in several EU members took a decisive hand in shaping the IGC negotiations. In the earlier part of the IGC under the Italian and Irish Presidencies Britain adopted, on the whole, an antagonistic stance against the EU following the imposition of a general ban on all British beef imports in an effort to stop the spread of BSE ("Mad Cow Disease"). Britain's attitude altered perceptibly following the election of Tony Blair to office in May 1997. Meanwhile, fractious Franco-German relations, prompted by a unilateral French defence review, were smoothed over by Kohl and the newly elected French President, Jacques Chirac, at the Franco-German Nuremberg summit of 9 December 1996, where their *Common Concept on Security and Defence* was unveiled. Volker Rühe's decision, in his capacity as Germany's Defence Minister, to publicly make clear that he was not informed of the details of Chirac's defence restructuring plan prior to its announcement was extraordinary given the "overriding importance attached to the Franco-German relationship by Chancellor Kohl" (*Financial Times* 5 March 1996, 5). If the restructuring of the French forces cast into doubt the intimacy of Franco-German defence relations, the French decision of the previous year to resume nuclear testing emphasised the differences between France and its other European allies.

Kohl's and Chirac's relations grew less cordial with both leaders' weakening of power. In France, Chirac's disastrously mistimed call for early parliamentary elections witnessed the defeat of Alain Juppé's right-wing government and the election of Lionel Jospin's left-wing coalition. Jospin's election significantly impaired Chirac's ability to take any further initiatives. Within Germany, Kohl's position was weakened by the Bavarain Premier of the CSU, Edmund Stoiber – a well-known Eurosceptic who had been calling for the "controlled delay" of EMU. Kohl's governing coalition depended upon the support of the Bavarian CSU. In order to keep the coalition together, Kohl was forced to depart significantly from the *Reflections* document and the *Common Concept* and to adopt a strict line on EMU, which provoked the ire of Jospin. The battle over EMU threatened at several points during the IGC to sideline the deliberations on CFSP, which is all the more surprising since EMU should not even have been on the agenda since the parameters of the meeting had already been established in Maastricht (Lenzi 1997, 6).

In retrospect, the differences between the major players during the IGC had a twofold effect. First, it encouraged Germany to look to Britain and the U.S. for support and, by so doing, induced Britain and others to play a more active role in shaping the second pillar of the Union. Second, although the weakening of the strong Franco-German engine inspired others to become more active, their increased activity came at the expense of formulating a CFSP that was likely to be innovative or flexible. During the IGC negotiations, the German position (and, to an extent, that of France) shifted on the earlier designs to move towards a "core Europe" through the use of flexibility clauses. Germany was nevertheless vilified in the sense that flexibility had been included in the draft Amsterdam treaty of June 12, even if not to the extent originally desired (CONF 4000/97). It became increasingly obvious under the Dutch EU Presidency that flexible practices and voting (Qualified Majority Voting) could be applied in the first pillar and, to an extent the third, but that the specific nature of the second pillar made excessive flexibility undesirable when discussing, literally, life and death issues. Britain's unequivocal position on this issue was outlined during a press conference by the Foreign Secretary, Robin Cook. He stated, "we are anxious to make sure that Britain retains its veto over matters relating to foreign and security policy and it looks as if, on the basis of the current text, we have a real possibility that we will be able to achieve that negotiating goal at Amsterdam." In a remark, obviously aimed towards Washington, Cook added:

> We want to make it plain that the defence of Europe will remain through the North Atlantic Treaty Organisation, not through the European Union. For that reason we will be resisting a complete merger of the Western European Union with the European Union, and again I am hopeful that that is a negotiating objective we can secure at Amsterdam (Cook 1997).

France supported the UK on the decision-making mechanisms for flexibility. It was eventually the UK, supported by Austria and Greece, who successfully advocated that the enabling clause for CFSP should be dropped in favour of constructive abstention (Stubb 1998, 254). Throughout the IGC, the question of an enabling clause in the second pillar had been extremely contentious and, when faced with the reservations of the Dutch Presidency from February on, it was evident that constructive abstention would win through. Enabling clauses were however adopted in the first and third pillars.

The results – Amsterdam and CFSP

The IGC terminated with the Amsterdam Summit and the end of the Dutch Presidency in June 1997. After several months of tidying up and translating, the *Treaty of Amsterdam amending the Treaty on European Union, the Treaties establishing the European Communities and certain related acts* was signed on 2 October 1997 (Amsterdam Treaty 1997). In the Consolidated Version of the Treaty on European Union Title V, which incorporates the Treaty of Amsterdam, the Provisions on the CFSP eventually appeared in Articles 11-29. Title V's title, *Provisions on a Common Foreign and Security Policy*, was retained. For the sake of brevity the Consolidated Version of the TEU will be referred to as CTEU. In order to assist the reader, new or modified text will be indicated in *italics* and, where appropriate, the original wording from the TEU will be included for comparative purposes.

Broadly speaking, the debates about flexibility in the 1996 IGC resulted in three forms of flexibility: enabling clauses, case-by-case flexibility and pre-defined flexibility (Stubb, 69-91 and *verbatim* in Missiroli, 10). Of these the second applies exclusively to CFSP. According to Stubb, case-by-case flexibility is the mode of flexible integration which allows a Member State the possibility of abstaining from voting on a decision and formally declaring that it will not apply the decision in question whilst at the same time accepting that a decision commits the Union. This device specifically applied to the second pillar in the so-called "constructive abstention" mechanism (Article 23 CTEU) whereby, "Abstentions by members present in person or represented shall not prevent the adoption of ... decisions." Although the abstaining Member State is not bound it shall nevertheless accept that "the decision commits the Union." The constructive abstention clause is the nearest the actual treaty comes to a specific flexibility clause. This will be discussed in greater detail in due course.

Title I of the CTEU, on "Common Provisions," lays out the broad goals and objectives of the Union. The provisions include the stipulation that, "The Union shall be served by a single institutional framework which shall ensure the consistency and the continuity of the activities carried out in order to attain its objectives while respecting and building upon the *acquis* communautaire." Article 3 continues:

488 *Simon Duke*

> The Union shall in particular ensure the consistency of its external activities as a whole in the context of its external relations, security, economic and development policies. The Council and the Commission shall be responsible for ensuring such consistency *and shall cooperate to this end*. They shall ensure the implementation of these policies, each in accordance with its respective powers (CTEU Article 3).

The idea of ensuring consistency or *"cohérence"* is one that originally arose out of the incorporation of the EPC into the second pillar of the Union.[9] As in the Maastricht Treaty, specific reference is not made to either foreign policy or defence – instead the CTEU refers to the more vague notions of "external relations" and "security." The addition of wording to emphasise the importance of cooperation between the Commission and the Council on consistency is symbolic but does little to illuminate how the respective bodies actually ensure consistency.

Overall the most "substantive amendments," to use the CTEU's terminology, in the second pillar are to be found in the following areas:

– Redefinition of security and defence responsibilities;
– Decision-making;
– Institutional modifications;
– Voting procedures regarding unanimity and qualified majority voting (QMV);
– Relations with the WEU and other international organisations;

These will be analysed according to the sub-headings suggested above.

Redefinition of Security and Defence Responsibilities
The CTEU's attempt to specify how the CFSP should progress towards a common defence policy and common defence (CDP/CD) encountered many of the same fundamental disagreements as in the 1991-2 IGC and again reflected little specificity (CTEU Article 17.1). Article 17 of the CTEU reads:

> The common foreign and security policy shall include all questions relating to the security of the Union, including the *progressive* framing of

---

[9] Christian Tietje notes that the English language version of the TEU refers to "consistency" while the French and German versions refer to "cohérence" and "Kohärenz" respectively. He noted that "one of the first tasks of the Review Conference in 1996 should be to clarify the language of the English version of the treaty." As is indicated in the main text, this was not done. See Christian Tietje, "The Concept of Coherence in the Treaty on European Union and the Common Foreign and Security Policy," *European Foreign Affairs Review*, No. 2, 1997, pp. 211-233.

a common defence policy, in accordance with the second subparagraph, which might lead to a common defence, *should the European Council so decide. It shall in that case recommend the adoption of such a decision in accordance with their respective constitutional requirements.*

Unlike the TEU, the CTEU was a little more specific about what "questions" may be appropriate for the CFSP; these shall *"include humanitarian and rescue tasks, peace-keeping tasks and tasks of combat forces in crisis management, including peace-making"* (CTEU Article 17.2). The scope of the CFSP therefore reflected those outlined in the WEU's 1992 Petersberg Declaration. The CTEU though did not restrict the CFSP to these tasks; it merely includes them – a qualification that is easy to miss. Other than this condition, placing the onus on the European Council makes little practical difference, while the wording regarding "constitutional requirements" indicates not only the sensitivities of Ireland but also the three newer EU members (Austria, Finland and Sweden) as well as Denmark with its defence "opt-out." As a more general safeguard to possible constitutional clashes with agreements adopted through CFSP procedures, the CTEU clearly stated that, *"No agreement shall be binding on a Member State whose representative in the Council states that it has to comply with the requirements of its own constitutional procedure"* (CTEU Article 24).

Although the CTEU did not explicitly confine the Common Defence to Petersberg tasks, the implication was that NATO would assume primary responsibility for collective defence. However, the reference to the Petersberg tasks and in particular "peace-keeping" and "peace-making," introduced an element of confusion. In June 1992 the UN Secretary General, Boutros Boutros-Ghali, outlined his *Agenda for Peace.* In it he foresaw many different variants of peace-keeping including peace-enforcement which was presented as a more muscular form of peace-keeping involving, if need be, the use of force of the type employed in Somalia (Boutros Boutros-Ghali 1992). The CTEU did not specifically mention "peace enforcement" (or, for that matter, conflict prevention) but it did include "peacemaking."[10] As is observed below, this rather curious term was out of synch with the terminology preferred by the United Nations (UN) or the Organisation for Security and Cooperation in Europe (OSCE). The term does however indicate the apprehensions of some, like the neutral or non-aligned EU members, towards peace-enforcement – especially in light of the UN Security Council's post-cold war willingness to sanction intervention with broad mandates for those involved in peacekeeping operations.

It has already been observed that defence marked one of the most sensitive areas of the IGC deliberations. The CTEU modified Article B of the TEU in a

---

[10] The term "peace enforcement" was included in the treaty negotiations but was dropped at a late stage.

slight, but significant, manner. Under the CTEU the Union set itself the following goal:

> ... to assert its identity on the international scene; in particular through the implementation of a common foreign and security policy including the *progressive* framing of a common defence policy, which might lead to a common defence, *in accordance with the provisions of Article J.7* (Art. 17 CTEU).

The word "progressive" took the place of "eventual" in the Maastricht Treaty, thus implying slightly more determination to work towards that end but, again, with no firm timetable in mind. The significant qualifier is that under the CTEU any common defence will be framed according to the provisions of Article 17 CTEU which clearly states that the WEU, which is an "integral part of the Union" providing the Union with access to an *"operational capability,"* also supports the Union in framing the "defence aspects" of the CFSP. The provisions of Article 17 CTEU also include specific reference to the WEU providing an operational capability *"notably in the context"* of the Petersberg tasks. This is an important further qualification since the WEU's membership does not include all EU members and those outside the WEU (Austria, Finland, Ireland, Sweden and, as a special case, Denmark) will have fewer difficulties collaborating in Petersberg (i.e. peacekeeping and humanitarian tasks) than in defence-related roles. For the ten WEU members the possibility of a common defence policy and common defence capability is left open, particularly since the operational capability applies notably, but not exclusively, to the Petersberg tasks.[11] The qualifying phrase also supports Article 17(3) whereby the Union "will *avail itself* of the WEU to elaborate and implement decisions and actions of the Union which have defence implications." In this eventuality *"all Member States of the Union shall be entitled to participate fully in the tasks in question."* This was an important mechanism to allow the non-WEU EU members to participate fully in Petersberg tasks but the issue of association of Associate Members and Observers of the WEU and, in time, the Associate Partners, would become increasingly difficult.

---

[11] A further facet to this argument is that it is the WEU that provides access to NATO assets for "Europe only" operations under NATO's 1994 Combined Joint Task Force (CJTF) concept. Although some of the "operational capability" would come from indigenous multinational European forces (coming under the collective heading of Forces Answerable to the WEU or FAWEU), it was assumed that particular assets would be provided through the CJTF concept. Hence it was important to keep open the door, via the WEU, to NATO while at the same time appeasing the concerns of the neutral and non-aligned EU members.

The WEU's access to "an operational capability" for Petersberg-type tasks could refer to indigenous capacities but in may also refer to NATO's 1994 Combined Joint Task Force Concept (CJTF) whereby "separable but not separate" assets can be made available to the WEU for "Europe only" operations.[12] The concept was further elaborated upon at the North Atlantic Council's June 1996 meeting in Berlin. Again, the problem of asymmetrical membership between the WEU, NATO and EU was to become an increasingly complex problem. The wider institutional aspects of the CTEU are considered in more detail below.

Decision-Making
Article 17 (2) of the CTEU introduces a new instrument of decision-making – common strategies. The device was included in the IGC at a late stage in an attempt to address the differences between primarily France, with its devotion to consensual decision-making, and Germany with its preference for majority voting. Common strategies are to be decided on, presumably unanimously, by the European Council and Council shall then implement them by QMV. Common strategies are to be decided upon by the European Council "in areas where the Member States have important interests in common." They should set out the "objectives, duration and the means to be made available by the Union and the Member States."

The introduction of common strategies has, in retrospect, been a mixed blessing. The two common strategies that exist thus far, on Russia and the Ukraine, are positive in the sense that it is the only decision-making mechanism that spans the three pillars. As such, it can only be a positive influence upon consistency in external relations. It is not though a tool for rapid reaction, since the European Council only meets twice per annum. The amount of detail involved (objectives, duration and means) also ensured that these common strategies will be few and far between. Common strategies also run the risk of pushing decision-making upward, by providing a mechanism for those committed to consensus.

Institutional Modifications
One of the objections raised to the TEU and the CFSP was that it lacked a strong identity or persona. A suggested French solution to this was to appoint the equivalent of a Secretary-General or a "Monsieur PESC." The holder of this office would be a senior figure who would ensure the "continuity, visibility and

---

[12] This is referred to in *Treaty of Amsterdam*, Declarations adopted by the Conference, *Declaration of Western European Union on the Role of Western European Union with the European Union and with the Atlantic Alliance*, Part C. "WEU's Operational Role in the Development of ESDI," Para.13.

efficacy" of the Union's external actions and represent the Union in its negotiations with third countries. According to the French design, the holder of this office would be an independent personality outside the existing structures. Those hoping for such an appointment were frustrated by the objection that such an office would detract from the intergovernmental nature of the CFSP process and the role of the Presidency. The British, following the May 1997 election, suggested that rather than a "Baroness CFSP" a "Comrade CFSP" might be more appropriate, but one that would be within the existing structures (McDonagh 1998, 116). During the Dutch Presidency, a consensus emerged that the office should be located within existing structures and that it should, at least, strengthen the role of the Council Secretary General. A compromise however was reached whereby the Presidency "shall represent the Union in matters coming within the [CFSP]" (CTEU Article 18.1-5), and shall be assisted by a "High Representative for the common foreign and security policy" who is the Secretary-General of the Council of Ministers (CTEU Article 18.3). The High Representative's duties are laid out in Article 26 of the CTEU. The High Representative also assists in the implementation of *"common strategies,"* an idea which first appeared in the CTEU, which is designed to enable specific foreign policy actions to be taken by a majority vote, based on a unanimously agreed general strategy.

The CTEU's stipulations on the role of the High Representative left open considerable room for latitude depending, in particular, upon the identity of the High Representative and the willingness of the Presidency to use the office. In retrospect the appointment of Javier Solana as the first High Representative for the CFSP (as well as Secretary-General of the WEU) was an inspired choice. However, having such a prominent and well-known figure as High Representative has created its own problems as well as opportunities. It is not always apparent who, amongst the myriad of Commissioners (including the President of the Commission), the Presidency or the High Representative, actually speaks for the EU in its external relations.

A further problematic aspect with the High Representative's position is that the intended functions of the High Representative, who is also Secretary General of the Council (as well as WEU Secretary General now), were framed in CFSP terms. The role of the then current Secretary-General was, in effect, handed to the Deputy Secretary-General (DSG) who is responsibly for running the Council Secretariat. As Simon Nuttall has noted, the effect may well be that the DSG finds himself unable to carry out his important "political and mediatory role… because the existence of a hierarchical superior will impair his authority." Nuttall also observes that a further result may be that the impression may be given that the Union "perceives itself as essentially a foreign policy actor, which in view of the modicity of the means available might be thought overweening" (Nuttall 1997, 2).

Some of the other criticisms of the High Representative's position are related to a further innovation. Under Article 18 of the CTEU, the new "Troika" shall be composed of the Presidency, the Secretary General of the Council, the Commission (who is fully associated) and, if need be, the next Member State to hold the Presidency (making a Troika of four!). It was feared that the Secretary-General would be under the shadow of the President of the Council while the Commission representative, who also has an inside line to the Policy Planning and Early Warning Unit (see below), would operate quasi-autonomously. Hence, rather than give CFSP the flexibility and "face" it requires, it may only have enhanced the role of the Commission, thus defeating much of the purpose of having a High Representative. The subsequent appointment of Javier Solana has done much to undermine these fears and, if anything, the opposite is true. Solana is not easily overshadowed by the Presidency, there have been no noticeable detrimental effects on the Council Secretariat and relations between the Commission (especially the Commissioner for External Relations) have not been unduly fractious. Whether the EU will be so fortunate in attracting highly visible and respected figures for future High Representatives remains to be seen.

The High Representative's post also saw the creation of a new subordinate unit – the Policy Planning and Early Warning Unit (PPEWU).[13] A declaration attached to the CTEU by the IGC refers to the establishment of PPEWU in the General-Secretariat of the Council under the responsibility of the Secretary-General. The unit is to be comprised of personnel drawn from the General Secretariat, the Member States, the Commission and the WEU. The responsibilities of the new unit should include:

- Monitoring and analysing developments in areas relevant to the CFSP;
- Providing assessment of the Union's foreign and security policy interests and identifying areas where the CFSP should focus in future;
- Providing timely assessments and early warning of events or situations which may have significant repercussions for the Union's CFSP, including potential political crises;
- Producing, at the request of either the Council or the Presidency or on its own initiative, argued policy papers to be presented under the responsibility of the Presidency as a contribution to policy formulation in the Council, and which may contain analyses, recommendations and strategies for the CFSP.

In the aftermath of the IGC, the precise composition of the unit remained unclear following the rejection of proposals forwarded by Jürgen Trumpf, Secretary General of the Council of Ministers. According to one report, "Paris wanted the

---

[13] *Treaty of Amsterdam*, Declarations adopted by the Conference, Declaration 6 on the establishment of a policy planning and early warning unit, 2 October 1997.

unit to go considerably further than Trumpf's paper indicated, while other countries claimed it went too far" (Turner 1998, 6). The issues to be decided, as mentioned above, included its composition, its rules of operation, its relations with the Council Secretariat and to whom it reports. The procedure for the adoption of answers to these issues is also unclear – should majority or consensus take them? Most members preferred that the PPEWU be a separate unit within the Directorate-General of the Council Secretariat responsible for external relations (thus separate but integrated within the Directorate-General). A minority though, alongside the Commission, wanted to see the PPEWU as autonomous within the General Secretariat, under the direct line and management of the High Representative (*Agence Europe* 6-7 July 1998, 4). Although the respective powers of the High Representative, the PPEWU, the Council and the Presidency are all defined in the CTEU, the relations between the constituents were ill defined.

On a practical level no guidance was given to the PPEWU as to how they were supposed to procure information that was likely to be of assistance in the "early warning" role (presumably much of this would be classified). The provision of any assessment of the Union's foreign and security interests assumes that these interests are transparent to the PPEWU as well as other relevant bodies. It certainly should not be the job of the PPEWU to define them. Furthermore, if the unit is to function as a situation centre, providing the Presidency and High Representative with a rapid assessment capability to address crises and current developments, it would be "essential to effect a considerable improvement in the flow and the quality of information available to the General Secretariat."[14] A balanced input can be assured only if the Member States recognise their responsibility, as laid out in the CTEU, to support the policy planning process by providing, "to the fullest extent possible", relevant information which may include confidential information.

The Commission's role was also enhanced in the CFSP area by the secondment of a number (unspecified) of Commission officials to the unit. This implies not only a more active role for the Commission in policy options but also involvement of Commission officials in any task forces established by the High Representative. Success of the PPEWU and, more generally CFSP, became far more dependent on close cooperation between the High Representative and the Commission Vice-Presidents with external relations mandates (and this could conceivably include many). Although the PPEWU appears to be a slight and relatively uncontroversial addition to the CFSP machinery, it may have subtly altered the institutional balance within external relations more towards the Commission.

---

[14] *Report from the Secretary-General of the Council to the Council*, "Setting up the CFSP policy planning and early warning unit," Brussels, 6 November 1996, Para. 9 (a).

The Council's role remained largely unchanged in the CTEU (with the significant exception of alterations in voting rules addressed separately below). Three slight modifications were, however, made to the Council to accommodate the High Representative's position. The TEU's Article 151.2 was replaced with the following:

> *The Council shall be assisted by a General Secretariat, under the responsibility of a Secretary-General seconded by a Deputy Secretary-General who shall be responsible for the running of the General Secretariat. The Secretary-General and the Deputy Secretary-General shall be appointed by the Council acting unanimously.*

A further retooling of the Council's role stated that it may "request the Commission to submit to it any appropriate proposals" relating to the CFSP to "ensure the implementation of a joint action"(CTEU Article 14.4). The Council may also, "whenever it deems it necessary, appoint a special representative with a mandate in relation to particular policy issues" (CTEU Article 18.5). This they have done on no less than seven occasions.[15] Arguably, this provision has given the EU tremendous flexibility and representation in its external relations.

The readjustment of the "Troika" to include the Commission "who shall be fully associated" and the inclusion of Commission officials in the PPEWU may

---

[15] *Miguel Angel Moratinos* was appointed EU Special Envoy for the Middle East peace process on 25 November 1996 (Joint Action, OJ L 315, 4.12.1996). *Aldo Ajello* was appointed EU Special Envoy for the African Great Lakes Region on 25 March 1996 (Joint Action, OJ L 87, 4.4.1996). *Nils Eriksson* was appointed EU Adviser on 29 April 1997 (Joint Action 97/289/CFSP, OJ L 120, 12.5.1997, p. 2) to oversee the implementation of the European Union assistance programme to support the Palestinian Authority in its efforts to counter terrorist activities emanating from the territories under its control, and to contribute to the Middle East Peace Process. *Bodo Hombach* was appointed EU Special Representative on 29 July 1999 (Joint Action 1999/523/CFSP, OJ L 201, 31.7.1999, p. 2) to carry out the tasks defined in the Stability Pact for South Eastern Europe of 10 June 1999 to help the countries concerned develop a joint strategy for ensuring the stability and growth of the region. *Panagiotis Roumeliotis* was appointed EU Special Representative on 31 May 1999 (Council Decision 1999/361/CFSP, OJ L141, 4.6.1999, p. 1) to support his role as Coordinator of the process of stability and good neighbourliness in South-East Europe (Royaumont Process). On 8 June 1998 the Council appointed *Felipe González* EU Special Representative for the Federal Republic of Yugoslavia (Joint Action 98/375/CFSP, OJ L 165, 10.6.1998). Mr González's mandate ended on 11 October 1999 (Council Decision, OJ L 264, 12.10.1999). *Wolfgang Petritsch* was appointed EU Special Envoy for Kosovo on 30 March 1999 (Joint Action 1999/239/CFSP, OJ L 89, 1.4.1999). In the light of developments in the region, in particular the deployment of the United Nations Mission in Kosovo, Mr Petritsch's mandate terminated on 29 July 1999 (OJ L 201, 31.7.1999).

have enhanced the role of the Commission. Certainly the reorganised Troika will enhance the role of the Commission in CFSP, but the presence of an "inside line" to the PPEWU may turn out to be less important than some have argued due to the limited size and resources of the PPEWU. Aside from this, the role of the Commission remained largely unchanged except for the stipulation that the Council and Commission shall not only ensure consistency in the EU's external relations, security, economic and development policies, but shall also "*cooperate to this end.*" Since no enforcement or any other mechanisms are referred to, it remains unclear how the Commission and Council are supposed to ensure consistency.

The role of the European Parliament remains unchanged with the verbatim reproduction of the TEU's Article J.7 as the CTEU's Article 21. The fact that there was absolutely no change in the role of the European Parliament vis-à-vis the CFSP indicates willingness on the part of the Member States to retain as much executive control as possible. It is though worth noting that the CTEU's provisions on the financing of CFSP activities may give the European Parliament increased oversight since CFSP activities charged to the budget of the Communities are subject to the scrutiny and oversight of the parliament. An Interinstitutional Agreement between the Parliament, Council and Commission confirmed Parliament's role in scrutinising CFSP expenditure that is regarded as non-compulsory (see below). The abolition of the reserve, which had enabled Parliament to exert some pressure on the Council, was replaced by a line for "urgent actions" which may then give "Parliament a similar margin for manoeuvre" (European Parliament 1997, Para. 6).

Voting Procedures Regarding Unanimity and Qualified Majority Voting (QMV)
The question of QMV was one of the most politically sensitive since it went right to the fundamentals of CFSP's supranational or intergovernmental nature. The concerns with the existing stipulations on QMV, laid out in Article J. 3 of the TEU, centred on the vagaries of how the Council, "when adopting a joint action and at any stage in its development," shall define "those matters on which decisions are to be taken by a qualified majority." The TEU was also unclear about the scope of QMV voting and implications of the accession of new members (German reunification had already necessitated a revision of the weighted voting procedures).

Underlying the IGC's debates on QMV was the tension between protecting vital national interests by observing the unanimity principle and avoiding paralysis by constant use of the veto. In order to avoid the CFSP being paralysed by the need for unanimity, the aforementioned "constructive abstention" (or "destructive abstention" as some have called it) clause was built into the CTEU. Under Article 23, CTEU decisions falling under Title V (CFSP) are to be taken unanimously, with the exception of those mentioned above, and "*abstentions by members present in person or represented shall not prevent the adoption of such decisions.*" When abstaining from a vote, any member of the Council "*may qualify its abstention by making a formal declaration....*" The abstaining member "*shall not be obliged to apply the decision, but shall accept that the decision commits the Union,*" and "*the Member State concerned shall refrain from any action likely to conflict with or impede the Union based on that decision and the other Member States shall respect its position.*" If the amount of abstentions numbers more than a third of the weighted votes, the decision shall not be adopted.

By "derogation" from the above stipulations, the Council shall take votes by qualified majority (QMV) when:

– Adopting joint actions, common positions or taking any other decisions on the basis of a common strategy;
– Adopting any decision implementing a joint action or a common position.

This means in practical terms that a decision must have an affirmative of 62 votes, cast by at least ten members, except when the vote is on a proposal from the Commission, in which case there must be simply 62 votes in favour.[16] However, if a member of the Council declares that, "*for important and stated reasons of national policy, it intends to oppose the adoption of a decision to be taken by qualified majority, a vote shall not be taken. The Council may, acting by a qualified majority, request that the matter be referred to the European Council for decision by unanimity.*" It should be noted, as an important qualification, that QMV shall *not* apply to decisions having military or defence implications.

Since the decisions that can be taken by QMV include common positions, it is unclear how (or whether) the provisions of Article 23 CTEU correspond with the commitment in Article 15.[17] This is a significant point since common positions, much more than joint actions, depend for their credibility on the extent to which they are seen to enjoy support. Any objection based upon a formal declaration or a stated reason based on national policy, can only impair the credibility of CFSP and its policy instruments. On the inclusion of a veto possibility due to a Member State pleading for national interest into the Treaty,

---

[16] See Article 205 (ex Article 148.2 of the Treaty Establishing the European Community) of the *Consolidated Version of the Treaty Establishing the European Community*, for vote weighting.

[17] Article 15 states, "The Council shall adopt common positions. Common positions shall define the approach of the Union to a particular matter of a geographical or thematic nature. Member States shall ensure that their national policies conform to the common position."

the European Parliament's Committee on Institutional Affairs, commented that "it must be deplored on principle. It might be justified if in practice it would only be applied as an "emergence brake"" (European Parliament 1997, Para. 6). The provision for such a matter to be referred to the European Council will hopefully make the veto application an exceptional practice.

Although the "constructive abstention" mechanism opened up the possibility of an *à la carte* approach to CFSP it also sits uncomfortably with Article 11 of the CTEU which reminds Member States to support the Union's external and security policy actively and unreservedly "in a spirit of loyalty and mutual solidarity." The impression of solidarity (or lack thereof) given to third parties will inevitably depend partly upon the issue at stake but also upon who is abstaining. Put rather bluntly, it may not be noticed if Austria abstained but the impression of "mutual solidarity" might be strained if it is France or Germany. Even if the abstaining member represents a smaller EU member it is difficult to imagine a decision being made in the face of a "formal declaration." Since the declaration is voluntary, not compulsory, any such declaration would carry considerable weight.

The largely theoretical, but nonetheless worrying, question of the "constructive abstention" mechanism being used for "free riding" was also raised. It is certainly conceivable that abstention may be exercised upon the grounds of cost considerations (perhaps even more so with evidence of "mission creep" in contemporary Kosovo) in which case, presumably, the abstaining member would decide not to make "a formal declaration." A more salient shortcoming of the "constructive abstention" decision-making form is that it may encourage bifurcation of security concerns so that they are no longer "common." The slide of Albania into unruliness following the collapse of a government-backed pyramid investment scheme in March 1997 hints at the type of "not in my back yard" reaction that may be evoked. It is worth a brief note that the EU Council was unable to agree upon a peacekeeping operation for Albania at its Apeldoorn and Rome meetings. A handful of EU Member States offered to contribute troops to a "coalition of the willing." Security may, in other words, be the responsibility of those nearest and most directly affected. Significantly in the Albanian case, the EU passed the buck to the WEU, who proved to be too weak to address the crisis, and it was the OSCE who eventually took the lead.[18]

On balance, it is far from clear that the IGC succeeded in both of its aims; namely, to create a more flexible decision-making mechanism for CFSP while at the same time maintaining a façade of mutual solidarity. There is also the risk that if a decision is adopted in the face of an abstention accompanied by a formal

---

[18] An Italian led force did eventually intervene on 11 April and 6,000 troops followed subsequently. By this time, the Albanian authorities had regained partial control but not before many had been killed and arsenals looted.

declaration, the member(s) abstaining may be encouraged to work outside the CFSP in future. Similarly, if there are grounds to expect abstention and a formal declaration, Member States may find it desirable to keep certain issues out of the CFSP remit.

Relations with the WEU and Other International Organisations
The question of the extent to which the WEU should be integrated with the Union was the subject of fierce debate. Britain and the four neutrals or non-aligned members (Austria, Finland, Ireland and Sweden) were adamantly opposed to full integration of the WEU with the EU. Britain wished to protect NATO's position as Europe's central defence organisation while the others objected to the possibility that the move would militarise the EU. For their part, Belgium, France, Germany, Italy, Luxembourg and Spain proposed a protocol that set out a timetable for the full integration of the WEU and EU. In spite of clear differences regarding the extent of association between the WEU and the EU, the wording pertaining to the WEU in the CTEU changed significantly from the TEU and reflected a stronger association between the WEU and EU. The European Council was also given new competency with regard to the possible integration of the WEU and EU:

> The Western European Union (WEU) is an integral part of the development of the Union *providing the Union with access to an operational capability notably in the context of [Petersberg Tasks]. It supports the Union in framing the defence aspects of the common foreign and security policy as set out in this article. The Union shall accordingly foster closer institutional relations with the WEU with a view to the possibility of integration of the WEU into the Union, should the European Council so decide. It shall in that case recommend to the Member States the adoption of such a decision in accordance with their respective constitutional requirement* (CTEU Article 17.1).

The reservations of the neutral and non-aligned Member States and those of Britain were addressed in the same article with the following statement:

> The policy of the Union in accordance with this Article shall not prejudice the specific character of the security and defence policy of certain Member States and shall respect the obligations of certain Member States, *which see their common defence realised in NATO*, under the North Atlantic Treaty and be compatible with the common security and defence policy established within that framework (CTEU Article 17.1).

The onus therefore appears to once again be placed on the European Council to set the pace, or the brake, on integration of the WEU and EU. In a potentially interesting development it also appears to be up to the Member States themselves, based on their constitutional stipulations, to decide on whether to adopt a recommendation from the European Council in favour of integration. This presumably allows certain states, such as the neutral or non-aligned ones, to opt out. But it also exacerbates the problems of differing membership in institutions and overlapping tasks of the pillars of the Union. Even if the possibility of the integration of the WEU into the EU is mentioned as a possibility, it still remained implausible that any such decision would be reached by unanimity given the openly expressed concerns of the UK, Finland, Sweden and Denmark.[19]

The operational relationship between the EU and WEU changed from the TEU to CTEU in some significant ways. Under the CTEU the EU will *"avail itself of the WEU* to elaborate and implement decisions and actions of the Union which have defence implications" (CTEU Article 17.3). The difference between the somewhat awkward word "avail" and the word, "request," which appear in the TEU, is the result of a compromise reached by the Dutch Presidency between those who wished to keep the original wording and those who wished to emphasise the authority of the EU over the WEU (by proposing that the Union should *"instruct"* the WEU) (McDonagh, 119). If the EU does avail itself of the WEU, the European Council shall *"establish guidelines"* and thereafter

> *...all Member States of the Union shall be entitled to participate fully in the tasks in question. The Council, in agreement with the institutions of the WEU, shall adopt the necessary practical arrangements to allow all Member States contributing to the tasks in question to participate fully and on an equal footing in planning and decision-taking in the WEU* (CTEU Article 17.3).

The above text apparently allows the five non-WEU states in the EU to associate fully with the WEU. Since they are for the most part neutral or non-aligned states and the tasks they are likely to be involved in are Petersberg tasks, "association" permits them to participate without the political costs of full membership of the WEU. However, such a status might create problems in terms of whether a non WEU member could "participate fully" and on an "equal footing" without representation or even voting rights in an organisation of which it is not a member. Further objections to those "contributing to the tasks in

---

[19] The later proposals to merge the WEU with the EU in the June 1999 Cologne European Council summit only included those elements of the Alliance relevant to the Petersberg tasks.

question" being guaranteed an equal footing may be voiced by the major powers who are likely in most cases to be contributing (and risking) more.

More generally, it was agreed that the WEU and EU should, within a year of the IGC, draw up arrangements for enhanced co-operation. The provisions of Article 17.3 of the CTEU were noted by the WEU as was the need to develop the role of the observer members, so that they may participate "fully and on an equal footing" in planning and decision-making in the WEU. In its subsequent relations with the EU, the WEU adopted a number of measures designed to lead to enhanced collaboration, such as improving consultation and decision-making processes, holding joint meetings, harmonising the sequence of Presidencies of the WEU and EU, and emphasising close co-ordination between the staff of the Secretariat-General of the WEU and the General Secretariat of the Council of the EU.

The IGC also noted the existence of a declaration adopted by the Council of Ministers of the WEU on 22 July 1997 (see Treaty of Amsterdam, 125-131). The declaration reaffirmed the importance of strengthening efforts towards the creation of a genuine ESDI and reminded the EU that the WEU was "an integral part of the development of the EU providing the Union with access to an operational capability" (a phrase which appeared verbatim in the CTEU) and that it also was an "essential element of the development of the ESDI within the Atlantic Alliance." In the context of the WEU's role in developing an ESDI within the Alliance, it was acknowledged that the Alliance "continues to be *the basis of collective defence* under the North Atlantic Treaty" and that, "it remains the essential forum for consultation among Allies and the framework in which they agree on policies bearing on their security and defence commitments under the Washington Treaty." (Treaty of Amsterdam, 129). For its part, the WEU was portrayed as "an essential element of the development of the European Security and Defence Identity within the Atlantic Alliance..." Cooperation between the WEU and NATO would, according to the declaration, be enhanced by:

– Crisis consultation mechanisms;
– The WEU's active involvement in the NATO defence planning process;
– Operational links between the WEU and NATO for the planning, preparation, and conduct of operations using NATO assets and capabilities under the political control and strategic direction of the WEU;
– Military planning, and exercises conducted by NATO in co-ordination with the WEU;
– Agreement on the transfer, monitoring and return of NATO assets and capabilities;
– Liaison between the WEU and NATO in the context of European command arrangements.

In its ESDI guise, the WEU would "develop its role as the European politico-military body for crisis management." But amongst the many facets which require further attention are the "definition of principles on the use of armed forces of the WEU States for WEU Petersberg operations;" the "organisation of operational means for Petersberg tasks;" "strategic mobility…" and "defence intelligence."[20]

In the CFSP's relations with the UN, special responsibility (and trust) was accorded to France and Britain who, as UN Security Council members, should ensure that "in the execution of their functions [they] will ensure the defence of the positions and interests of the Union, without prejudice to their responsibilities under the provisions of the United Nations Charter" (CTEU Article 19.2). This point, originally made in Article J 2.3 of the TEU with somewhat looser wording, has become increasingly important given the considerable number of UN mandated operations involving contributions by EU member states. The obligation to ensure the defence of the interests of the Union extends implicitly to the possible exercise of the veto. Although there are few recent instances of Anglo-French differences on the use of the veto in the Security Council, there is nevertheless the possibility that differences will arise between the two countries. For example, differences might arise over the question of lending support to U.S. operations. This is especially the case in the Middle East where significant differences of opinion exist between the EU and Britain.

Budgetary Questions
Progress was also made towards addressing the budgetary arrangements for the CFSP and those activities with defence implications. The TEU had established a basic intergovernmental procedure for the adoption of joint action but the Community procedures (which need the Parliament's consent) applied to the financing of the measures. "Administrative expenditure" is charged to the budget of the Communities while "operational expenditure" leaves the Council the possibility of either charging expenditure to the Community by unanimous decision or it may determine that the costs should be borne by the Member States themselves (TEU Articles 199 & J.11). If the Council chose to use the former, the European Parliament has the final say on all non-compulsory expenditure (according to Article 203 TEU). This therefore opened up the possibility of a clash between the European Council and the Council, who bear responsibility for initiating and adopting joint actions, and the MEPs who have the ability to grant or deny the financial means for the action. Although in cases

---

[20] All of these factors were to reappear in a more visible form in the WEU's *Audit of Assets and Capabilities*, conducted at twenty-one, at the Luxembourg Ministerial, 23 November 1999.

such as the provision of humanitarian aid in Bosnia-Herzegovina, where the total amount was split between the Community and the Member States, the problem proved to be with the Member States not the Parliament. The first eighteen months of CFSP showed, as Thomas Hagleitner has argued, that the CFSP was "unable to provide an efficient "intergovernmental" way of financing CFSP." He also claimed that the Parliament's medium term strategy "is to use its budgetary powers as a tool in order to get a say on the political substance of CFSP" (Hagleitner 1995, 7).

Under the CTEU, administrative expenditure would continue to be charged to the budget of the European Communities. "Operational expenditure" would be charged to the budget of the European Communities, "except for such expenditure arising from operations having military or defence implications, and cases where the Council acting unanimously decides otherwise" (CTEU Article 28.3). Again, subject to the Council's unanimous decision, in those cases where expenditure is not charged to the European Communities, it shall be charged to the Member States on a weighted GNP scale. Expenditure arising from activities having military or defence implications was not assessed for those states who made a formal declaration of non-participation and thus are not obliged to contribute" (CTEU Article 28.3).

Under an Institutional Agreement, signed on 16 July 1997, between the Commission and the Council on the financing of the CFSP, it was agreed that operational expenditure should be charged to the budget of the European Communities but that the costs of military action should be borne by the Member States themselves. The European Parliament and the Council annually secure agreement on the amount of the operational CFSP expenditure to be charged to the Communities' budget as well as the allocation of the total amount to the CFSP budget. In the absence of agreement, the amount designated for the previous fiscal year shall be allocated, unless the Commission lowers it. The amount allocated to the CFSP budget shall "cover the real predictable needs and a reasonable margin for unforeseen actions" (*Bulletin EU* 1997). It was suggested that within the budget, the estimated expenses could be entered under the following headings:

– Observation and organisation of elections/participation in democratic transition processes;
– EU envoys;
– Prevention of conflicts/peace and security processes;
– Financial assistance to the disarmament process;
– Contributions to international conferences;
– Urgent actions.

The European Parliament, the Council and the Commission agreed that the amounts for the actions entered under the "urgent actions" sub-heading cannot exceed 20% of the global amount of the CFSP budget. Broadly speaking, the general terms of reference suggested in the Interinstitutional Agreement were applied in the CTEU. The agreement is of interest not only because of the budgetary aspects of the CFSP, but also because it is an indication of the Commission's and the Council's perception of the parameters of the CFSP.

In general, the budgetary procedures in the CTEU do not overcome David Allen's "horns of a dilemma":

> Anxious to preserve their independence and to give both the European Parliament and the Commission as little control of their CFSP activities as possible, the Member States have a principled interest in paying for the CFSP themselves. However most diplomatic services have a natural resistance to multilateral calls on their often tightly restricted budgets and so have a pragmatic interest in "losing" such expenditure in the overall Community budget (Allen 1997, 298).

Although not strictly budgetary, but certainly with potential budgetary implications, Article 17.1 of the CTEU states that:

> *The progressive framing of a common defence policy will be supported, as Member States consider appropriate, by cooperation between them in the field of armaments.*

Although the extent to which co-operation occurs is very much up to the individual Member States, there is nevertheless the implicit recognition that the construction of a CDP/CD will not only be difficult but divisive unless some thought is given to collaborative armaments development and procurement. A slightly cynical interpretation of this clause is that it was inserted not so much as an underpinning for a CDP but as a reaction to a series of mergers in the American defence industry. It is also unclear what effect, if any, the addition has since Article 223 of the TEC remains unchanged and, at the time, there were no provisions on arms exports.[21] It is also notable that the idea of a European Armaments Agency was not retained (although it has since reappeared).

---

[21] The European Parliament had demanded the amendment of Article 223, to no avail.

Conclusions

As far as CFSP was concerned the text which emanated from the IGC presented a few changes over its previous version. Where there were changes or modifications on critical issues, such as defence and the role of the WEU, the phrasing left sufficient latitude for interpretation to keep all happy – but also guaranteed the issue would remain on future agendas. By incorporating sufficient latitude for interpretation the text was also ambiguous. It was, as Simon Nuttall has suggested an "exercise in collusive ambiguity" where the negotiations were conducted on "the Alice in Wonderland principles of the caucus race: you have all won, and you shall all have prizes" (Nuttall, 1). Official reactions were mixed. One of the most critical was the European Parliament's Committee of Foreign Affairs, Security and Defence Policy who deplored the fact that "CFSP will continue to be the result of the lowest common denominator between Member States, thus largely depending on the political will of each." But, at the same time the Amsterdam Treaty was seen as containing "the potential for a European performance that is more than purely intergovernmental bargaining" (European Parliament 1997, Para. 11).

On a slightly more optimistic tone, Guido Lenzi notes that although the achievements may have been modest, compared to the great expectations, the establishment of "common strategies," the creation of a High Representative for CFSP and the PPEWU, "constitute the initial "sensors" and mechanisms through which a CFSP activity will emerge and manifest itself more visibly" (Lenzi, 6). It is also worth noting, on the positive side, that the incorporation of the "Petersberg tasks" into the CTEU substantially diminished concerns about whether the presence of neutral and non-aligned EU Member States was compatible with a vigorous CFSP. The possibility, even though slim, of cooperation between the Member States in the field of armaments was also introduced into the treaty for the first time.

Perhaps a more worrying aspect of the IGC, again with CFSP in mind, is how little external security events seemed to intrude into the conference. The overall impression is very much one of an internal game with bargaining and trade-offs between the intergovernmentalists and integrationists, the transatlanticists and Europeanists, with little regard to the Europe around them for which they were supposed to be designing an effective security and defence. The lessons of Bosnia and the Dayton Process appear rather little in the deliberations. Similarly, the collapse of Albania towards the end of the negotiations also seemed to have little "real world" effect on the bargaining and outcome.

In retrospect the 1996 IGC and resultant Treaty of Amsterdam had some positive effects that were not evident at the time. Compared to the Treaty of Maastricht, it is undeniable that some progress was made: the creation of the High Representative for CFSP's post and the PPEWU has proved innovative and helpful; at least on paper, the introduction of "constructive abstention" has provided sufficient flexibility to avoid the risk of constant paralysis of the CFSP; the appointment of seven Special Envoys since the Treaty of Amsterdam also enhanced the visibility and effectiveness of the EU on the international level. An additional, unintended, effect of the Amsterdam Treaty (as well as the EU's poor performance in the Albanian crisis) was that it must have been reassuring to Washington that the Europeans were unable, or even unwilling, to organise a credible indigenous defence capability.[22]

In spite of the positive developments, the Treaty of Amsterdam is notable for its caution in the notoriously sensitive second pillar area. A number of fundamental questions were grappled with, but not answered. For instance, the development of a common defence policy and common defence was not addressed head-on, nor was the issue of whether the WEU should be merged with the EU. Both were postponed indefinitely, subject to the pleasure of the European Council. With the benefit of hindsight it is obvious that the adjustments made at the 1996 IGC have been far outpaced by the realities of European security. Kosovo, in particular, made it clear that the next IGC would have to address these and other issues in a forthright manner.

The conclusion of one IGC normally sets the agenda for the next. Arguably the agenda for the current 2000 IGC has been shaped primarily by events in the Balkans and, most notably, the crisis in Kosovo which once again faced the EU with evidence of its impotence when it came to ability to match economic clout with political and military leverage. The year 1999, which may in time be seen as CFSP's *annus mirabilis*, changed CFSP almost beyond recognition, introduced new concepts such as the Common European Security and Defence Policy, and undid Gordian knots, such as those surrounding the merger of the WEU and EU, with apparent ease.

---

[22] John Peterson has commented on this point that, "From an American perspective, the problem of the CFSP has been one of raised expectations. US officials often argue that if it had been "sold" as a marginal advance on the EPC, then the EU's subsequent disunity on Macedonia, Rwanda and Bosnia would have caused less indignation in Washington. The Americans cannot be blamed for believing that the EU's rhetoric about its common purpose in foreign policy actually means something," "Europe, America & the CFSP: "While the Europeans, literally, sleep through the night?", *CFSP Forum*, (1) 1996.

Bibliography

Agence Europe (1994). "Reflections on European Policy," No.1895/6, 7 Sept.

Agence Europe (1998). No. 7257, 6/7 July.

Allen, David (1997). "The European Rescue of National Foreign Policy," pp. 288-304, in Christopher Hill (ed.), *The Actors in Europe's Foreign Policy*, London: Routledge.

Amsterdam Treaty (1997). *Treaty amending the Treaty on European Union, the Treaties establishing the European Communities and certain related acts,* Luxembourg: Office for Official Publications of the European Communities.

Boutros Boutros-Ghali (1992). *An Agenda for Peace: Preventive diplomacy, peacemaking and peace-keeping*, 17 June UN Doc, A/47/277.

Bulletin EU (1997). "Interinstitutional Agreement on the financing of the common foreign and security policy," 7/8.

Cook, Robin (1997). Press Conference by the Foreign Secretary, Luxembourg, 2 June at http://britain-info.org/bis/fordom/eu/97602fs.htm.

CTEU (1997). Consolidated Version of the Treaty on European Union and The Treaty Establishing the European Community, Luxembourg: Office for Official Publications of the European Communities.

Emmanouilidis, Janis A. (1995). "Reflections on Revising the CFSP," *CFSP Forum*, 2, p. 1.

European Council Dublin (1996). 96/382 *Conclusions of the European Council meeting in Dublin*, 13-14 December.

European Parliament (1995). *White Paper on the 1996 Intergovernmental Conference*, Volume II, "Summary of Positions of Member States of the European Union with a View to the 1996 Intergovernmental Conference," European Parliament, Intergovernmental Conference Task Force.

European Parliament (1997). Opinion for the Committee on Institutional Affairs of the Treaty of Amsterdam, Chapter III Provisions on the Common Foreign and Security Policy (CFSP), Committee on Foreign Affairs, 29 October 1997, PE 224.338/DEF.

Hagleitner, Thomas (1995). "Financing the Common Foreign and Security Policy," *CFSP Forum*, 2.

Italian Presidency (June 1996). *Progress Report on the Intergovernmental Conference*, Chapter III, "A Strengthened capacity for external action."

Janning, Josef & Werner Weidenfeld (1996). "La Nouvelle Europe: stratégies d'integration différenciée," *Politique Etrangère*, 3, pp. 521-36.

Keatinge, Patrick (1996). "Ireland Presides – is small beautiful?", *CFSP Forum*, 3 & 4.

Lenzi, Guido (1997). "European Security after Amsterdam," *CFSP Forum*, 3.

McDonagh, Bobby (1998). *Original Sin in a Brave New World: An Account of the Negotiation of The Treaty of Amsterdam*, Dublin: Institute of European Affairs.

Missiroli, Antonio (2000). "CFSP, Defence and Flexibility," *Chaillot Papers,* 38, February.

Nuttall, Simon (1997). "The CFSP Provisions of the Amsterdam Treaty: An Exercise in Collusive Ambiguity," *CFSP Forum*, 3.

Stubb, Alexander (1998). *Flexible Integration and the Amsterdam Treaty: Negotiating Differentiation in the 1996-7 IGC*, Ph.D.-dissertation, London: London School of Economics and Political Science, December.

Turner, Mark (1998). "CFSP Gets New Marching Orders," *European Voice*, 5-11 February.

WEU (14 November 1995). *WEU's Contribution to the European Union Intergovernmental Conference of 1996*, WEU Council of Ministers, Brussels: Press and Information Service.

White Paper (1996). Irish Government White Paper on Foreign Policy, *External challenges and opportunities*, 26 March.

21

A New Area of Freedom, Security and Justice: The Shaping of a Hybrid Compromise

Monica den Boer

Introduction

The Maastricht Treaty on European Union heralded a special Title on Justice and Home Affairs Cooperation. On the one hand, it seemed a progressive step forward to institutionalise a new field of cooperation and embed it within a Treaty, on the other hand, this progress was rather cautious as it was characterised by intergovernmental decision-making, which implied the unanimity requirement for the adoption of legal instruments by the Council, no (or a shared) right of initiative for the European Commission, a very limited role for the European Parliament and the European Court of Justice, a limited potency of the relevant legal instruments, and a haphazard working structure dictated by a strong influence of the national administrations of the EU Member States.

Although the Maastricht Treaty had been in force for only about two years when the first deliberations for the 1996-IGC started, the EU Member States, the EU institutions and the relevant Presidencies had already brought up their guns against the infamous "Third Pillar." Almost all actors in the IGC-game agreed that Title VI had to undergo a more or less intensive revision. The Reflection Group summarised the existing critique as the lack of an institutional driving mechanism, the overlapping of themes and objectives between the different pillars, and the lack of a structured co-operation with other bodies, such as the Council of Europe.[1]

Hence, the 1996 Intergovernmental Conference provided an excellent opportunity for reformists to table their proposals. As we will see below, the papers and proposals that were submitted covered a wide array of different views, methods and instruments. From the very beginning – even back in 1994 and 1995 – several different objectives were discussed relating to Title VI. This multiple agenda covered matters of substance as well as matters related to form and procedure. The discussion relating to matters of substance evolved

---

[1] See SN 520/95 (REFLEX 21), *Reflection Group's Report*, Messina 2nd June 1995, Brussels 5th December 1995.

from a perceived need to improve the operability and efficacy of Title VI,[2] as well as a broadening of its thematic coverage. The discussion relating to form and procedure centered around a number of different scenarios, oscillating between two extremes, namely complete communitarisation of Title VI on the one hand, and the preservation of status quo on the other. These scenarios were extended by a third avenue, namely the incorporation of the Schengen *acquis* into the Treaty on European Union, a proposal that could be justified for institutional, legal and political reasons. The background tune to the various scenarios was provided by discussions about the application of flexibility or reinforced cooperation.

This chapter seeks to examine the creation of an 'Area of Freedom, Security and Justice' (AFSJ) by carving out the positions of the various actors who were involved in the IGC-process, which included the Member States, several EU-Presidencies, and the EU-institutions. To unravel this multi-actor and multi-level process, a historical reconstruction of the evolution of the ASFJ is presented, based on a sequential analysis of numerous views that can be traced in Council documents, national parliamentary debates, political speeches and other relevant documents. The narrative of this chapter unfolds in four different parts. In the first part, we will take stock of the national and institutional positions concerning JHA-matters and the reform of Title VI throughout the IGC-process. In the second part, four successive Presidencies enter the stage and an analysis will be drawn up of their priorities and negotiation styles concerning JHA-matters. In the third part, we will (blessed with the advantage of retrospective wisdom!) reduce the complexity of the IGC-negotiations in this field, and distill a number of prevailing scenarios and intermediate options. In the fourth and final part, we will focus on the application of flexibility on JHA-matters in the Amsterdam Treaty on European Union, and try to demonstrate that some of the original safeguards could not be maintained when the negotiations were terminated.

National Positions: A Fuzzy Logic

Not long after the 1996 Intergovernmental Conference had been announced, the Member States and the EU-institutions started to mobilise their forces. Most of them came out with more or less explicit statements about their ambitions with regard to Title VI on Justice and Home Affairs Cooperation. A simple inventory reveals a rich tapestry of styles and positions, but also that some national positions shifted from one end to the other in the course of only

---

[2] E.g. the 1997 High Level Group Action Plan on organised crime, which was adopted under the Dutch Presidency.

one year. In a more abstract sense, the following opposite views and styles emerged:

- Defensive versus offensive views:[3] these were sometimes ventilated particularly strongly on the (limits to the) application of flexibility, but also on the maintenance of voting by unanimity;
- General versus refined views: some delegations had no specific views on the reform of Title VI per se, but felt that their proposals on voting procedures and institutional reform would also embrace JHA-cooperation;
- Substantive versus procedural views: some Member States seemed to have strong views on new areas of activity that should be added to the mandate of the Third Pillar, others were more adamant about the reform of decision-making structures and legal instruments (some Member States of course had views on both);
- Introvert versus extrovert views: some Member States looked at the protection of their national interests only and seemed less keen to conjure up reflections on behalf of the Union; extroverted views also seemed to take more account of other Member States' positions, which might facilitate the process of coalition-building.

The national and institutional positions concerning JHA-matters throughout the IGC are occasionally hard to qualify. Spain, for instance, demonstrated reticence against the abolition of the unanimity rule and eventual communitarisation, but took a very integrationist stance and supported the idea of an area of freedom, security and justice. Similarly puzzling is Spain's style of negotiation in JHA-matters: on the one hand a clear desire can be detected of wanting to play a leading role in this field by favouring all advances and proposing new initiatives in a systematic way, on the other hand its tough claims with regard to terrorism and external border controls – which are understandably propelled by domestic circumstances – often make Spain a very defensive negotiator.

The styles and preferences of other Member States concerning JHA-matters can roughly be described as follows:

Austria

Negotiating style: Offensive, extrovert, refined, substance and procedure in balance.

---

[3] Defensive views are negatives or exclusions of certain options, whereas offensive views are of a constructive nature and often compromise-brokering.

JHA-substance: Internationalisation of organised crime, human rights, overlapping of competences in the field of JHA within the three pillars to be clarified and the possibility of the incorporation of the Schengen agreement were to be goals for the IGC.
JHA-procedure: Enforced communitarisation of some 3rd pillar issues, especially in the fields of visa policy, asylum- and immigration policy, control of external borders and customs co-operation; criminal law should remain third pillar; possibility of QMV was to be introduced step by step especially when it came to organised crime (!); stronger role for the institutions in JHA policy field (Commission as "motor" of integration and obligatory integration of ECJ into the third pillar).

Belgium

Negotiating style: Offensive, extroverted, refined, mostly procedural/institutional.
JHA-procedure: Total communitarisation and abolition of the Third Pillar, as distinction between pillars is artificial; working procedures should be more transparent (e.g., Dehousse & van den Hende, 1996, 714-718).

Denmark

Negotiating style: Defensive, general, introverted, more emphasis on procedure.
JHA-substance: Fight against fraud.
JHA-procedure: Preservation of intergovernmentalism; in favour of enlargement and therefore institutional adaptation. Tabled proposal on the improvement of the role of national parliaments in JHA-matters (subsidiarity) (CONF 3915/97).

Finland

Negotiating style: Offensive, extroverted, refined, substance and procedure in balance.
JHA-substance: Committed to advance the idea of accession of the Community to the ECHR; strengthening the civil protection of individuals in the Third Pillar (CONF 3923/97).
JHA-procedure: Initially in favour of increasing the influence of the Commission in the Third Pillar. Council of Ministers should however remain

the central decision-making body; however, in favour of expansion of QMV; sympathetic to the idea that the ECJ competence should be considered in the Third Pillar, but opposed its extension in the Second; at the end of the negotiations, Finland's position was less intergovernmentalist than at the start.

France

Negotiating style: Defensive, introverted, refined, procedural.
JHA-procedure: Maintenance of the rule of unanimity for the adoption of Title VI instruments. The Guéna report, for instance, which was presented on 19 February 1995 on behalf of the delegation of the French Senate for the European Union by Senator Guéna, stated that the character of intergovernmentalism should be reinforced and that new, efficient institutions should be set up (such as separate Secretariats-General for each of the pillars and a European Senate of representatives of national parliaments). A later report, was submitted at the end of December 1996 by deputies Fanton and De Roux, and was entitled "l'Europe de la liberté et de la sécurité." The report proposes conservation of the Pillar structure, a shared right of initiative between Commission and Member States, a reiteration of the proposal to create new Secretariat(s) General, the possibility of enhanced cooperation, "rolling ratification" to encourage early implementation of Title VI conventions, a list of issues to which QMV could apply, and a consultative role for national parliaments (Agence *Europe*, No. 6883, 30/31 December 1996). Tabling of document on 18 February 1997 with detailed comments to Dublin II drafts (CONF 3824/97).

Germany

Negotiating style: Offensive, but defensive in the end about communitarisation of asylum matters, extrovert, general/specialist, procedural/substantive.
JHA-procedure: Tabling of a proposal on the communitarisation of customs cooperation (CONF 3938/96).

Greece

Negotiating style: Defensive, introvert, specialist, procedural.
JHA-procedure: In favour of elevation of EP's role in the field of migration and asylum and not too much divergence between political and legal level;

insistence on maintaining unanimity for decisions affecting the vital national interests of a country (Agence *Europe*, No. 6690, 18-19 March 1996).

Ireland

Negotiating style: Defensive, general, extrovert, more emphasis on procedure than substance.
JHA-substance: Fight against drugs important priority.
JHA-procedure: Stick with existing institutional structure; incremental change; strong role for the European Commission as being at the heart of integration; no support for extension of QMV in JHA areas.

Italy

Negotiating style: Offensive, extrovert, refined, balance between substantive and procedural proposals.
JHA-substance: JHA = key issue for Italy; anti-corruption and an approximation of police and justice systems; convergence between national and European interest.
JHA-procedure: Italy wanted complete communitarisation for issues such as migration, asylum, external border controls and a joint strategy against organised crime; an exclusive right of initiative for the Commission, full competence ECJ and automatic application of co-decision after 5 yrs; police and judicial co-operation in criminal matters: similar to those proposed for CFSP: Council would adopt pluri-annual working programmes unanimously, and on that basis, it would adopt single pieces of legislation by qualified majority; every Member State would nevertheless maintain the possibility of applying national provisions "on grounds of public policy or the protection of the principles of its legal order and as far as necessary;" simplification of decision-making process; the Amsterdam outcome was certainly not the treaty Italy would have liked, but the outcome of the Third Pillar and partial communitarisation including incorporation of Schengen was more satisfactory.

Luxembourg

Negotiating style: Mildly offensive, extroverted, general, procedural.
JHA-procedure: Reconsideration of the ways in which Title VI functions and the associated legal procedures.

The Netherlands

Negotiating style: Offensive, extrovert, refined, more procedure than substance.
JHA-substance: More effective fight against organised crime, multidisciplinarity.
JHA-procedure: Transitional period of gradual communitarisation; reduction of democratic deficit, limited role of the ECJ and limited access to documents and information; difference between extreme options and intermediary options (e.g. adaptation of objectives, of working structure, reinforcement of Commission's right of initiative, simplification of decision-making structure, clarification of legal status, clarification of financing structure, reinforcement of European Parliament and national parliaments, and reinforcement of European Court of Justice).[4]

Portugal

Negotiating style: Offensive, extroverted, general, balance between procedural and substantive.
JHA-substance: Seeks total achievement of measures in the area of migration and asylum.
JHA-procedure: No specific views in early stages of IGC (1995).

Spain

Negotiating style: Offensive/defensive, rather refined, extroverted style, both substance and procedure.
JHA-substance: Leading role in the field of JHA, favouring all advances and proposing new initiatives in a systematic way; migratory movements, terrorism, external border control – link with domestic circumstances; reinforcement of Europol and judicial co-operation at a European scale and the prohibition of the admissibility of political asylum requests by EU nationals.

---

[4] See e.g. *Fiche thématique sur la communautarisation de troisième piller (CAIJ) du traité sur l'Union Européenne*, Task-force "Conference Intergouvernementale", Groupe de Travail du Secretariat General, Parlement européen, Luxembourg, 27 juillet 1995 (JF/bo/141/95), p. 11.

JHA-procedure: reservations about abolition of unanimity rule and eventual communitarisation, but integrationism; support of the creation of an area of freedom, security and justice.

Sweden

Negotiating style: Mildly offensive; difficult to characterise.
JHA-substance: International fraud and discrimination (racism and xenophobia).
JHA-procedure: Improved democratic control in early stages of IGC (1995), also in intergovernmental fields of cooperation.

United Kingdom

Negotiating style: Mostly defensive, introvert, refined proposals, more emphasis on procedure.
JHA-substance: Fight against fraud and the financial management of the Community; one-sided preservation of the right to carry out border controls; reference to police cooperation would be rephrased to make it clear that Europol was no more than one of the aspects of police cooperation, and to provide explicitly for cooperation between police, customs and all other competent authorities (...); the fight against terrorism and international corruption should be added to Title VI.
JHA-procedure: Insistence on intergovernmental approaches to cooperation based on unanimity;[5] proposal to replace existing Article K by two new articles and to expand Article K.1;[6] new article K would state the general objective of creating an area of freedom (including free movement of persons), security and justice and the new Article K *bis* would introduce limiting conditions (subsidiarity); new article K.1 would contain an expanded and modified list of fields of common interest; emphasis on revision Title VI working structures (reconsideration of position Steering Groups).

The above listing demonstrates how widely varied the positions of the Member States concerning JHA-matters during the 1996 IGC were. The multitude of proposals range from a maintenance of intergovernmentalism

---

[5] Speech by Foreign Secretary Douglas Hurd on 12 January 1995.

[6] UK September 1996 memorandum on objectives and scope of application of the Third Pillar.

(United Kingdom) to a complete swing to supranationalism (Belgium).[7] Looking ahead at the end result of the Amsterdam negotiations, it is hard to avoid the impression that all Member States got at least a bit of what they wanted. The result is a win-win-situation, which was carefully plotted in the initial stages, but which was dominated by garbage-can-decisionmaking during the final session in Amsterdam.

Pride, Prejudice and Presidency

A sequential analysis of successive Presidencies may shed a structured perspective on the switches, turns and transformations during the IGC-negotiations concerning JHA. For this purpose, the content analysis below focuses on four EU-Presidencies, starting with Italy, followed by Ireland, the Netherlands, and Luxembourg. The identification of their agenda-setting behaviour and the main dossiers that were under discussion, assists us in analysing the evolution of the drafting process. Similar to the Member State actors, the question is whether different Presidential styles can be distilled, and whether presidential priorities are clearly discernible throughout the process.

Italian Presidency 1/1/96 – 30/6/96
The Italian Presidency tabled reinforcement of the Third Pillar (Title VI) during the IGC, especially in view of the enlargement process. The most important document tabled on 8 May 1996 was CONF 3848/96, in which three papers about a Union close to its citizens were presented. Concerning JHA-cooperation, the Italian Presidency established that there was a need to clarify the objectives in the Treaty; that the achievement of such objectives could be covered by multiannual programmes; that the list of matters of common interest could be extended to include approximation of policies to combat crime, approximation of rules on conflict of laws, and action to combat corruption on an international scale. The methods of action proposed included the principle of transferring some areas to the Community sphere (visas, asylum and immigration), which had found support from a large proportion of representatives. This could be facilitated, in the view of some, by retaining certain particular procedures and by a phased implementation timetable. In other areas, the Presidency established that many had advocated stepping up cooperation on the basis of Community methods (a non-exclusive

---

[7] For an excellent overview of Member States' positions regarding a whole range of proposals, see Hix and Niessen (1996).

right of initiative for the Commission, greater involvement of the European Parliament, etc.).

The Italian Presidency seemed slightly more explicit on issues of substance than on issues of procedure or institutional reform, although a revision of the competence of the European Parliament in relation to Third Pillar matters was mentioned. Substantive issues which were placed on its ongoing Presidency-agenda included: repatriation, police co-operation, ratification of the Europol Convention, related jurisdiction of the European Court of Justice, the exchange of information between Europol and third countries, the fight against terrorism and some other sectoral themes. The achievements of the Italian Presidency in the field of Justice and Home Affairs included the ironing out of final differences in extradition convention, and the agreement that the European Court of Justice may give preliminary ruling on the interpretation of the Europol Convention.

On 17 June 1996, the Italian Presidency issued a Progress Report on the IGC (CONF 3860/1/96), in which it was established that there was a broad acceptance that Union action on Justice and Home Affairs ought to be made more effective. Two complementary avenues might be explored more thoroughly, namely the clarification of objectives assigned to JHA, and the extension of scope by adding new areas to the list of common matters of interest. Without formulating different scenarios, the Presidency outlined several methods of action, such as partial incorporation into the Community sphere (visas, asylum and immigration), the use of certain Community methods and mechanisms (e.g., non-exclusive right for the Commission, majority voting, closer involvement of the institutions), and strengthening cooperation arrangements in Title VI. Moreover, cautious suggestions were made concerning the improvement of the decision-making system, a revision of legal instruments and a strengthening of the role of national parliaments.

Irish Presidency 1/7/96 – 31/12/96
The Irish Presidency took a strong lead in tabling procedural IGC-issues, but was not too keen on driving the discussion on flexibility forward. In its Presidency introductory note (CONF 3866, 6 July 1996), the two main issues for consideration were which of the Title VI matters should be transferred to the TEC, and the means for improving the effectiveness of action for those areas remaining under Title VI. The note provided texts on the scope and institutional set-up in the context of communitarisation, details on Title VI cooperation and common objectives. At their meeting on 17 July, the Representatives found it difficult to consider meaningfully the question of what topics might be transferred to the First Pillar without more precise details about the matters covered in each area concerned. It was decided, therefore, to discuss communitarisation again on the basis of a paper from the

Conference Secretariat which would provide the necessary clarification (CONF 3908/96, 18 September 1996).

One of the main efforts of the Irish Presidency concerned the translation of the various proposals into draft articles, which were in part submitted by the negotiating partners. The Commission tabled a proposal on 18 September 1996 concerning a possible location of Justice and Home Affairs in the EC Treaty (CONF/3912/96). This proposal already bears the traces which are still visible in the text of the Amsterdam Treaty, as it lays down a new treaty title, named "an Area of Freedom, Security and Justice." In terms of width, the proposals concerning communitarisation were ambitious, as they also included an integrated anti-drugs policy and the fight against economic and financial crime. A consensus could not be reached among all delegations; some of them proposed integrating some communitarian elements into the Third Pillar without contemplating a further total transfer.[8] Also coalitions began to take shape. The Belgians, known as the most fervent integrationists, tabled a joint proposal with their fellow Benelux partners Luxembourg and the Netherlands about a special Treaty article concerning the communitarisation of external border controls, immigration and asylum, within certain parameters (CONF/3909/96, 13 November 1996).

The Presidency carefully reformulated the discussion by the Representatives to: there was a "measure of agreement on the use of Community methods and procedures to deal with some of the matters which until now have been dealt with by Title VI of the TEU" (CONF/3976/96, 11 November 1996). On the basis of "a measure of agreement," it submitted a draft text for a new Title in the TEC – entitled "an Area of Freedom, Security and Justice" – and invited the Representatives to focus on specific areas at their meeting on 18/19 November 1996, in particular on specific areas and topics where Community methods and procedures could apply, decision-making procedures, voting procedures, instruments, the role of the European Parliaments and the national parliaments. At this meeting, the Presidency also tabled the possibility of a gradual approach, involving a pre-determined timetable for the introduction of Community methods and procedures.

The most important substantive issues that the Irish Presidency placed on its agenda were the fight against drugs and the fight against organised crime and trafficking of persons. The efforts on the issue of drug trafficking seemed triggered by domestic events, particularly by the killing of journalist Veronica Guerin by a Dublin drugs mafia gang. More generally, it seems typical for Presidencies to let their agenda-setting behaviour be inspired by issues which are high on the domestic political agenda, or by contextual crisis-events, such as the arrival of Albanian and Iraqi refugees at the Italian coast or the

---

[8] Tweede kamer, vergaderjaar 1996-1997, 24 609, nr. 12 (22 October 1996).

attempted escape by Dutroux in Belgium. These "crisis" events often have the potential to provide a momentum which facilitates sluggish decision-making, or to constitute a disrupture in a more continuous process.

The main substantive achievements of the Irish Presidency included preliminary reflections on the creation of a European FBI, a range of concrete measures against drug trafficking, and in the field of anti-organised crime the creation of a high-level group responsible for establishing an action programme "with a tight schedule."

Dutch Presidency 1/1/97 – 30/6/97
During early Dutch parliamentary debates prior to the IGC in 1995 (which were orientated on the deliberations of the Reflection Group), inventories were already drawn up of the positions of the Member States concerning procedural and institutional changes in the field of Justice and Home Affairs cooperation. At that time, most Member States (minus the United Kingdom) seemed prepared to extend the Commission's right of initiative to the whole area of JHA. However, no Member State seemed prepared to relinquish the unanimity requirement in the Third Pillar; all Member States wanted revision of the layered working structure in JHA matters. It was expected that the role of the European Parliament would not be greatly enhanced, but that the role of the national parliaments would increase. Since 1995, it was known that 14 of the 15 Member States wanted incorporation of Schengen, primarily under the Third Pillar.

The Dutch Presidency still had the pre-Maastricht experience fresh in mind – i.e. the rejection of its ambitious federalist proposals for a Treaty on European Union – when it entered the negotiations that prepared the ground for the Amsterdam Treaty. This time round, the Dutch Presidency took a more cautious approach as the delegations were invited to an article-by-article discussion of texts (drawing heavily on the Dublin II lines).[9]

Concerning JHA-elements of the IGC, the Dutch Presidency started out by revising the text of Article K of Title VI (CONF 3803/97). The philosophy being that the Area of Freedom, Security and Justice should be linked up with intergovernmental JHA-cooperation. In a non-paper, issued by the Dutch Presidency in February 1997, delegations were invited to take certain texts as the basis for discussion by Representatives on the strengthening of the Treaty provisions on free movements of persons, asylum and immigration. As the Dublin II outline had stressed, the starting point for an examination of Treaty changes in this area should be an identification of the objectives to be achieved, followed by an examination of the instruments to achieve those objectives and, possibly, a timetable for their implementation. The Presidency

---

[9] See Duke's chapter elsewhere in this book.

was of the opinion that the issue of where any agreed provisions should be located in the Treaties should be left for a later stage. Moreover, comments were invited on the issues of the role of institutions and decision-making procedure, and on the suggested setting-up of an overall target date to complete the progressive establishment of an area of freedom, security and justice.

On the basis of discussions on 19 February 1997 (CONF 3823/97), the Presidency established a common ground concerning the following issues: the political importance of the issues involved in achieving free movement of persons and combating international crime, to be regarded as a priority; the objective to be pursued: the progressive establishment of the European Union as an area of freedom, security and justice; the link between free movement of persons and a number of directly related flanking measures concerning the crossing of external borders and the impact on the security of individuals of abolishing checks at internal borders; the need to envisage a measure of differentiation for the procedural and institutional handling of these questions, given their political sensitivity; and the desirability of providing for possibilities for enhanced cooperation in this area. An interesting aspect of this Presidency note is the very open questioning attitude of the Presidency vis-à-vis the delegations. In CONF 3828/97, the Dutch Presidency made an inventory of agreements on several of its proposals, such as the introduction of flanking measures and the gradual introduction of the exclusive right of initiative for the Commission and QMV in the AFSJ.

The substantive issues that were placed on the agenda by the Dutch Presidency were internal security (fight against international crime and illegal drugs trade) and the fight against racism.[10] Its actual achievements were, except for concluding the negotiations on the Amsterdam Treaty, the adoption of the High Level Group Action Plan against organised crime, the Joint action on the early warning system of synthetic drugs, the Protocol on privileges and immunities for Europol officials, the signing of Convention on the significance and notification in Member States of legal and extra-judiciary actions in civil or trade matters and the related protocol on the role of the European Court of Justice, the signing of an anti-corruption convention, and the achievement of political agreement on the second protocol to the convention on the protection of the European Communities' Financial Interests.

---

[10] Tweede kamer, vergaderjaar 1996-1997, 25 110, 19 November 1996; Tweede kamer, vergaderhar 1996-1997, 25 110, nr. 12, 14 January 1997.

Luxembourg Presidency 1/7/97 – 31/12/97
Early June 1997 – just after the "Consolidated Texts of the Draft Treaty" were distributed by the Dutch Presidency – the Luxemburgers discreetly announced a number of backup European Councils, if Amsterdam was unable to reach an agreement (Edwards and Philippart, 1997). Even though a political agreement had been reached before the Dutch Presidency ended, negotiations continued during the Luxembourg Presidency about the exact legal wording of Title IV, Title VI and the interpretation of the Schengen Protocol until the signing of the Amsterdam Treaty on 1 October 1997. The Presidency acted progressively and pragmatically, created two Schengen Working Parties which were to prepare the "ventilation" of the Schengen *acquis* and the Schengen association agreements with Norway and Iceland. Its actual achievements included the signature of Naples II (convention on customs co-operation), political agreement on "Brussels II," and the adoption of the first concrete measures for putting the Action Plan on organised crime into effect.

Scenario-Building: Realist Options and Counterfactuals

Throughout the IGC-negotiations, the options for revising Title VI gradually began to take shape and subsequently crystallised in the form of different scenarios. Numerous documents were produced by virtually all actors involved. In this sequence of textual production, new meanings were added to already existing scenarios revealing a complex – not always rational – moulding process. The semantic mutations can be analysed by comparing the initial terms of reference of the Reflection Group with the documents that were produced by the institutional actors (Council, European Parliament, European Commission, European Court of Justice and European Court of Auditors), and with the relevant parts of the final draft of the Amsterdam Treaty. This textual analysis may help us verify whether there was a growing convergence of views and whether we can detect traces of a defensive bargaining process, in which Member States insisted on the maintenance of sovereignty.

For the purpose of this analysis, we shall draw a distinction between four phases, namely 1) the publication of the report authored by the Reflection Group directed by Carlos Westendorp, 2) the release of statements by all actors involved (Member States[11] and the institutions[12]), 3) the Dublin II draft, 4) the Amsterdam Treaty on European Union.

---

[11] Already summarised in the previous chapter, see *infra*.

[12] See *infra*, below.

The Report of the Reflection Group

The deliberations of the Reflection Group concerning Justice and Home Affairs cooperation start by identifying a number of deficits,[13] such as the lack of efficiency and efficacy, the lack of an institutional driving mechanism, inadequate Title VI provisions, a complex decision-making structure, the overlapping of themes and objectives between the different pillars, and the lack of a structured cooperation with bodies other than the EU, such as the Council of Europe:

> "The Union is an area of free movement for people, goods, capital and services. Yet people's security is not sufficiently protected on a European scale: while protection remains essentially a national matter, crime is effectively organized on an international scale. Experience of the implementation of the Maastricht Treaty over the last few years shows that opportunities for effective European action are still very limited. Hence, the urgency for a common response at European level, following a pragmatic approach. We all agree that the Conference should strengthen the Union's capacity to protect its citizens against terrorism, drug trafficking, money laundering, exploitation of illegal immigration and other forms of internationally organized crime. This protection (...) must not diminish individual safeguards."

Without taking precise stock of the positions of the Member States, the Reflection Group established that many of its members took the view that, in order to act more efficiently, matters concerning third country nationals, such as immigration, asylum and visa policy, as well as common rules for external border controls, needed to be put fully under Community competence. A minority wanted expansion of Community competence to combating drug addiction and fraud on an international scale, and to customs cooperation. Hence, one of the early scenarios under discussion concerned partial communitarisation of issues that were thought to be the least sovereignty-sensitive ones. All of the issues mentioned had already been subject to the passerelle-clause (Article K.9) of Title VI of the Maastricht Treaty, but this clause had never been applied. Whilst rejecting an *à la carte Europe*, various members of the Reflection Group were in favour of incorporating the Schengen Agreements.[14]

---

[13] For critical assessments of the functioning of the Third Pillar by academics, see e.g. Monar (1996) Dehousse (*Les enjeux*), Benyon (1996), Nentwich and Faulkner (1996) and Den Boer (1998).

[14] See *infra*, chapter on flexibility clauses.

Statements Issued by the EU-Institutions

Of the EU-Institutions, the European Parliament and the European Commission expressed their opinions most clearly and comprehensibly.

The European Parliament issued various statements, among which a very helpful document by an IGC Working Group of the Secretariat General.[15] On procedural and institutional issues, the European Parliament wanted to introduce more efficacy into JHA co-operation, and pleaded in favour of a more flexible application of the *passerelle*, the adoption of a qualified majority in the Council, no restriction on right of initiative for the Commission, reinforcement in several areas of the role of the European Court of Justice, Court of Auditors and the European Parliament.[16][17] With regard to a gradual integration of the Third Pillar, the European Parliament wanted a progressive integration of the Schengen agreement into the politics of the Union.

The European Parliament envisaged a "path of democratisation," which was focused on the two intergovernmental pillars. Its proposals varied between the full-scale or partial integration of one of both pillars into the EC Treaty and its procedural as well as institutional obligations. Another, not incommensurable option would be the introduction of more legally binding procedures (similar to the EC Treaty, such as directives and regulations) and more participatory as well as control powers for the European parliament and/or the national parliaments within the intergovernmental pillars.

The European Commission launched progressive and clearly delineated proposals that implied farreaching communitarisation of Third Pillar issues, a consolidation of the mandate of the EU-institutions in the field of JHA, and

---

[15] See e.g., *Fiche thématique sur la communautarisation de troisième piller (CAIJ) du traité sur l'Union Européenne*, Task-force "Conference Intergouvernementale," Groupe de Travail du Secretariat General, Parlement européen, Luxembourg, 27 juillet 1995 (JF/bo/141/95), p. 13.

[16] For the consideration of revised competences of the European Parliament, e.g., its involvement as a consultative body in the new Title of Freedom, Security and Justice, see Maurer elsewhere in this volume. Path of democratisation focused on intergovernmental pillars: proposals varied between the full-scale or partial integration of one of both pillars into the EC Treaty and its procedural as well as institutional obligations; and b) the introduction of more legally binding procedures – similar to the EC Treaty – and more participatory as well as control powers for the European parliament and/or the national parliaments within the remaining two pillars.

[17] See document /PE 197.390, Resolution on Parliament's opinion on the convening of the Intergovernmental Conference; and evaluation of the work of the Reflection Group and definition of the political priorities of the European Parliament with a view to the Intergovernmental Conference, for a selection of subjects that could be dealt with by means of Community procedures and institutions.

an improvement of legal instruments. More particularly, the Commission proposed the creation of an Area of freedom and security, remedying the shortcomings of Title VI. "Substantial modifications" were proposed, notably the transfer of the Third Pillar to the Community framework in the majority of areas. In accordance with this philosophy, instruments and methods had to be improved, such as QMV, closer involvement of the European Parliament, an extension of the Commission's power of initiative in all fields concerned. Moreover, the Commission wanted more effective instruments than the common position, the joint action and international agreements, that decisions would be subject to review by the European Court of Justice, the Council's present working structures would be simplified, that JHA would be transferred to the Community (with the exception of judicial cooperation in criminal matters and police cooperation), and incorporation of the Schengen Agreement in the Treaty.[18]

On substantive issues, the Commission's objectives included the establishment of common rules on entry, residence and status of nationals from non-member countries in the Union, the effective mutual recognition of judgements by national courts, the adoption of measures to combat all forms of crime and fraud, and stimulation of effective cooperation between public administrations of the Member States.[19]

The Council took a far more conservative point of view and rejected QMV for Third Pillar matters. On the other hand, however, it clearly favoured revision of the heavy JHA-working structure (5 layers), a reappreciation of the functions of senior civil servants groups, and a reconsideration of Article K.3 par. 2 and K.4 art. 2 which give the Commission a possibility of playing an important role in the realisation of Title VI.

The Court of Justice and the Court of Auditors took a more restricted view on the reforms of the Third Pillar and mainly translated it in terms of their own institutional tasks. The Court of Justice was defensive and did not want a shattered Treaty which would risk incoherence in the application and interpretation of Title VI instruments. Meanwhile, the Court of Auditors desired competence in the control of expenditure related to the Second and the Third Pillar, and also concerning expenditure which is partitioned between the Member States. Moreover, the Court of Auditors was in favour of supervision of programmes which are paid directly from the Member State's budgets and which are subject to control by separate national bodies.

---

[18] See also Commission Opinion, "*Reinforcing Political Union and Preparing for Enlargement,*" Europe, No 1978, 8 March 1996.

[19] President Santer (28/02/96), giving the Commission's opinion on the IGC.

A first stocktaking exercise of the various scenarios at hand[20] had been relatively straightforward. Roughly, four scenarios presented themselves, which could be summarised as follows:

- *Scenario I*: Total communitarisation or an encompassing transfer of all Third Pillar matters to the First Pillar.
- *Scenario II*: Partial communitarisation of certain Third Pillar matters (likely candidates: asylum, immigration, external borders and visa policy; less likely but mentioned in early stages: fraud, drugs and judicial cooperation in civil matters).
- *Scenario III*: No communitarisation, preservation of the status quo (intergovernmentalism, unanimity rule).
- *Scenario IV*: Application or modification of the passerelle (Article K.9) and abandonment of unanimity voting in the Council.

"Sub-scenarios" were created around middle-of-the-road options which were less radical in nature and which could always be introduced in a more piecemeal fashion. Proposals in this range included new legal instruments, an adaptation of the JHA working structure, reinforcement of the role of the European Commission, simplification of the decision-making structure, clarification of legal status, clarification of financing structure, reinforcement of the role of the national parliaments and/or the European Parliament, and a reinforcement of the European Court of Justice.[21]

Dublin II
"Dublin II" – the draft revision of the Treaty for the second Dublin European Council in December 1996 – proposed the creation of a new Title "Free movement of persons, asylum and immigration." In the words of the human rights organisation Justice – this was "an interesting and logical solution to the current division of competence in the field between the first and third pillars."[22] According to a memorandum of the Irish Presidency, the text would

---

[20] See e.g. *Fiche thématique sur la communautarisation de troisième piller (CAIJ) du traité sur l'Union Européenne*, Task-force "Conference Intergouvernementale", Groupe de Travail du Secretariat General, Parlement européen, Luxembourg, 27 juillet 1995 (JF/bo/141/95).

[21] See e.g. *Fiche thématique sur la communautarisation de troisième piller (CAIJ) du traité sur l'Union Européenne*, Task-force "Conference Intergouvernementale", Groupe de Travail du Secretariat General, Parlement européen, Luxembourg, 27 juillet 1995 (JF/bo/141/95), p. 11.

[22] JUSTICE's response to the Dublin II Outline document for a Draft Revision of the EU Treaties, London, February 1997.

define objectives, set target dates, establish provisions for common rules for visas and free movement of third country nationals, provisions on asylum and immigration which must be tackled in common, and coherent action in relation to certain aspects of illegal drugs (the latter was not included in the Amsterdam Treaty). The European Parliament showed itself not so content with the Dublin II text as it found that some Member States were not genuinely prepared to forge a profound reform and, hence, that the proposals could not be considered as more than a halfway house.[23]

Notwithstanding institutional criticism, the Dutch Presidency decided to draw heavily on Dublin II lines. A meeting of the personal representatives of the Foreign Affairs Ministers on 11 February 1997 was devoted solely to the consolidation of an area of freedom, security and justice. Chief negotiator Patijn admitted after the meeting that there were still serious reservations to substantial amendments to the Treaty (*Agence Europe*, No. 6912, 12 February 1997). One of the stumbling blocks was a request from Spain to block the right of asylum in the EU for EU nationals. In the Amsterdam Treaty, a protocol to this extent was included but Belgium revolted with a special exception clause.

An inventory during the second month of the Dutch Presidency[24] shows:

- Strong support for the application of flexibility in the Third Pillar
- A clear majority in favour of the transfer of visa, asylum and immigration policy to the First Pillar[25]
- Many Member States want intensification of cooperation against crime, terrorism and drugs or to (partially) communitarise these fields
- Strong support for the expansion of Europol's mandate
- Most Member States are prepared to expand the competence of the European Court of Justice in the Third Pillar (prejudicial competence is sensitive, however)
- Wide support for the incorporation of the Schengen *acquis*, but opinions differ on the method
- Large support for gradual approach towards exclusive right for the Commission

---

[23] OJ C 33, 9 February 1997, Resolution B4-0040/97.

[24] Tweede kamer, vergaderjaar 1996-1997, 24 609, 20 February 1997.

[25] However, minutes of the Council meeting of 27 and 28 January 1997 reveal that one representative opposes any transfer of areas to the first pillar: http://www.xs4all.nl/~nelvdijk/minutes1.html.

- Support for linkage between free movement of persons and internal security[26]

The Dutch Addendum to Dublin II, presented in March 1997,[27] presented a three-part structure, which was received positively, as well as the suggested need for a timetable for measures to be implemented to attain the overall objective and the link established between the free movement of persons and accompanying measures aimed at guaranteeing the security of individuals (*Agence Europe*, No. 6927, 5 March 1997).

Around that time, European Commission President Jacques Santer emphasised that an acceptable outcome of the IGC concluded the realisation of the goal shared by all, namely the creation of an area of freedom, security and justice. However, the Commission was of the view that the Dutch draft could still be improved on the role of the European Parliament and European Court of Justice, and action on customs cooperation and the fight against drugs. Klaus Kinkel, then Germany's Foreign Minister, thought the Dutch draft formed a good basis for future work, but the French delegation pointed out that the freedom of movement and security should progress by setting a time limit of perhaps 5 years, which would give time for an assessment of accomplishments (*Agence Europe*, No. 6921, 24/25 February 1997).

An interesting political event about halfway during the Dutch Presidency was the emergence of a German-Italian coalition, which included the adoption of a common position about various matters, such as the extension of Europol's mandate with operational powers, the introduction of Community methods for immigration, visas, terrorism, drugs and so on, the insertion of a general flexibility clause and the transfer of the Schengen system to the EU institutions (*Agence Europe*, No. 6925, 1 March 1997).

The Outcome at Amsterdam
After having combed through all the national and institutional proposals, it cannot come as a big surprise that the actual result achieved at Amsterdam is a virtually impenetrable hybrid product, at least when it concerns Justice and Home Affairs cooperation. The debate at Amsterdam concerning the establishment of an area of freedom, security and justice was reported as tough, and even terms as "hectic" and "horse-trading" have been used to qualify the negotiating climate in June 1997. This can be explained partly

---

[26] This support was established at a later meeting, namely the IGC-session of 3 and 4 March 1997. Source: Tweede Kamer, vergaderjaar 1996-1997, 24 609, nr. 16.

[27] Addendum to Dublin II – General outline for a draft revision of the Treaties, Conference of the Representatives of the Governments of the Member States, Brussels, 20 march 1997. CONF 2500/96 Add.1.

because account had to be taken of the exceptional positions of the United Kingdom and Ireland in view of their Common Travel Area, and because of Denmark's constitutional reservations. Bilateral contacts apparently benefited the conclusion of an agreement with the British Government on the inclusion of two protocols, one that would remove the obligation from the UK and Ireland to abolish their border controls, and one that would make it possible for the UK and Ireland to participate in immigration, asylum and visa matters if they so wished (*Agence Europe*, No. 6925, 1 March 1997).

In summary, the three main surgical operations that took place at Amsterdam were (Den Boer 1997a and b, 1999):

- Creation of a new Title IV of the EC Treaty, covering issues on the free movement of persons, which were formerly part of the intergovernmental Third Pillar. Significant for the new Title IV is the application of a temporal clause for the progressive establishment of measures, after which it has to be decided by unanimity whether or not QMV shall apply in the future; the Commission shall however automatically gain the exclusive right of initiative after these five years have lapsed. Moreover, opt-outs apply to the United Kingdom, Ireland and Denmark.
- Re-boosting Title VI of the EU Treaty, which was virtually depleted after various issues had been transferred to the First Pillar, but which was now blessed with the opportunity of a renewed programmatic focus on police and judicial cooperation in criminal matters. Significant are the new legal instruments (joint positions, decisions, framework decisions and conventions), "rolling ratification," a facultative agreement for the role of the Court of Justice, an enhanced role for the European Parliament, a shared right of initiative between Commission and Member States, and a provision on reinforced cooperation.
- The incorporation of the Schengen *acquis* into the TEU, paving the way for political, legal and institutional absorption of Schengen on the basis of a definition and allocation process. Exceptional opt-out arrangements were made for the United Kingdom and Ireland, providing that they could join (parts of) the Schengen cooperation, but that allowing these would have to be decided by unanimity in the Council.[28]

---

[28] Under the Portuguese Presidency, the Council decided to approve the request of the UK and Ireland to participate in some provisions of the Schengen *acquis* (OJ L 131/43, 1.6.2000).

Flexibility Clauses: A Panacea for Progress?

In the meantime, numerous contributions have been written by academics and practitioners about the application of flexibility in the European Union. What is for sure, is that "flexibility" has been applied abundantly in the TEU's Area of Freedom, Security and Justice. The reservations of chief negotiator Michiel Patijn about its use in the CFSP-domain[29] did not seem to prevail in the JHA-domain. In the context of this contribution, a rather wide definition is used which refers to the term as a means for the European Union to encourage progress in certain areas by allowing two or more Member States to pursue a form of reinforced cooperation. The discussion above has already revealed that it was semi-impossible to achieve progress on the basis of consensus within the Council. Hence, "flexibility" became the miracle recipe to overcome stalemates during the negotiations. The table below shows the various opinions of the negotiating actors (Member States, institutions and Presidencies) about the application of flexibility in the field of Justice and Home Affairs cooperation.[30]

Table 21.1: Actor opinions on flexibility in JHA.

Actor	Flexibility
Austria	From the Austrian perspective, the development of modalities of participation within the field of JHA for non-EU states such as Switzerland was welcomed. Some reservations on flexibility but ready to compromise.
Belgium	Pro-flexibility.
Denmark	More at risk were the Danish exemptions in respect to (defence policy) and JHA cooperation – these were central issues on the IGC agenda. The Danish exemption in respect to JHA co-operation turned out to be the greatest problem for Denmark. As the determination of the dominant actors to move major parts of the third pillar to the first pillar became clear, Denmark had to seek a special protocol to retain the Danish exemption. Integration of the Schengen *acquis* into the treaty made things even more complicated (Protocol on the position of Denmark).
Finland	Generally pro-flexibility, but under certain conditions. Flexibility was seen in two ways: flexible in institutional matters although the strategy was initially cautious; no strong opinions were presented in the early stages of the negotiations.

---

[29] See Duke elsewhere in this volume.

[30] This figure only shows the positions that are known to the author.

Actor	Flexibility
United Kingdom	Under Blair[31] general reticence about flexibility, especially in the first pillar. First no argument for flexibility in the Third Pillar, then a toughening on (case-by-case) flexibility. There had to be room for permanent opt-outs, where necessary. Already in 1995, it was known that the UK would not object incorporation but it wished to maintain its internal border controls: the possibility of an opt-out was mentioned by the Dutch Foreign Affairs Minister.[32] In Amsterdam, Blair demanded and obtained maintenance of the veto (the 'emergency brake') over flexibility arrangements. Threat of exclusion vs. flexibility as an attractive option legitimising selective participation. In the end, UK secured a national objective by opt-out/in from the communitarised Schengen, albeit on terms (the requirement for unanimous approval by the existing Members) which could have been more favourable to the UK.
Italian Presidency	Proposal of 1) enabling clause; 2) incorporation of the Schengen system (CONF 3860/1/96.).
Irish Presidency	Not too keen to deal with flexibility, but left discussion to representatives. On 20 November 1996 not yet much progress in this area; opinions are becoming more and more differentiated. Franco-German contribution, submitted in October 1996, was welcome.
Dutch Presidency	Regarded flexibility as one of the main end-trajectories of the IGC.[33] Application of flexibility in third pillar within certain parameters. Acknowledgement that flexibility in first pillar is very difficult. In favour of flexibility; Michiel Patijn sought incorporation of Schengen *acquis*. Throughout the negotiations, in April/May 1997, it had become clear that the enabling clauses would not be sufficient in third pillar matters, or in matters relating to the incorporation of the Schengen Agreement and the new Community provisions on visas, asylum and immigration. Consequently, the UK, Ireland and Denmark would have to be dealt with in the traditional way, that is, through pre-defined opt-outs. Meeting on Schengen incorporation (*Agence Europe* 12 Feb. 97): at that point in time substantial divergence. Discussion about two scenarios, namely a) integration based on a general flexibility clause in the first and third pillar, and b) adoption of a special protocol with an exemption clause for countries that do not want to give up their internal border controls. One week later, disussion about Dutch presidency proposal on flexibility with clauses specific to the third pillar (authorisation of closer cooperation) (*Agence Europe*, No. 6917, 19 February 1997).

---

[31] As opposed to his predecessor Major, who favoured an *à la carte* Europe.

[32] Tweede kamer, vergaderjaar 1995-1996, 24 167, No. 3, p. 7 (verslag van een algemeen overleg, vastgesteld 2 november 1995, "Europese samenwerking op het gebied van Justitie en van Binnenlandse Zaken").

[33] Tweede kamer, vergaderjaar 1996-1997, 24 609, 20 November 1996.

Actor	Flexibility
Reflection Group[34]	Various members of the Group propose the incorporation of Schengen into the EU by means of flexible arrangements. Rejection of *à la carte* Europe, but some JHA matters enable a higher degree of flexibility.
Commission	Acceptance of flexibility under certain conditions and guarantee that institutional unity of the Union would be retained as well as the Commission's central role as guardian of the treaties and final say in triggering flexibility in the first pillar.
European Parliament	Not involved in decision about provisions on the transfer of the Schengen *acquis* into the area of the EC/EU competencies. The Council would decide to introduce closer cooperation between certain member states by QMV – but no decision of EP would be involved.
Council Legal Service	Drafted all of the early flexibility articles! Negotiations about flexibility continued after the Amsterdam summit. The question of what had actually been decided on the decision-making mechanism for incorporating the Schengen agreement into the treaty proved problematic.[35]

The flexibility arrangements in the field of Justice and Home Affairs cooperation strongly veer towards the model of an *à la carte* Europe, especially as Member States had negotiated an opt-out from co-operation in Title IV (Article 69 TEC).[36] Two Member States had negotiated an opt-in for co-operation within the Schengen framework,[37] and one Member State negotiated an exemption protocol on the basis of constitutional reservations.[38]

The possibility of closer cooperation (which might even herald a Schengen *bis*!) is laid down in Article 40 (ex Article K.12) of Title VI: Member States may establish closer cooperation between themselves, provided the powers of the European Community will be respected and provided the closer cooperation has the aim of enabling the Union to develop more rapidly into an Area of Freedom, Security and Justice.

---

[34] Reflection Group Report and Other References for Information Purposes, 1996 Intergovernmental Conference, General Secretariat of the European Union, Brussels, December 1995.

[35] See contribution Stubb elsewhere in this volume.

[36] "Protocol on the application of certain aspects of Article 7a of the Treaty establishing the European Community to the United Kingdom and to Ireland."

[37] "Protocol on the position of the United Kingdom and Ireland."

[38] Although Denmark signed the Schengen Agreement in December 1996, Article 3 of the Schengen Protocol and the "Protocol on the position of Denmark" provide that it will not take part in the adoption of the *acquis* in this section of the First Pillar.

Member States have various ways to maintain national sovereignty, to be exempted from certain forms of cooperation, or to pursue more intensive integration. Examples include:

- Progressive establishment of measures within a period of five years after entry into force of the TEU (Title IV, Article 61 (a)) after which the Council will decide by unanimity (Title IV, Article 67 (2, 2nd par.) to subject Title IV areas to Community procedures. This means effectively that the Member States can use their veto against the extension of QMV in these areas of cooperation.
- Internal security clause (Title IV, Article 64), which can be regarded as an escape clause for Member States if they want to preserve their national sovereignty;[39]
- Internal security clause (Title VI, Article 33), which states the prevalence of national responsibilities for the maintenance of law and order;
- "Rolling ratification" of conventions (Title VI, Article 34 (2(d, 2nd par))), which makes it possible for conventions to enter into force, once adopted by at least half of the Member States, to enter into force for those Member States;
- Facultative declaration concerning the competence of the European Court of Justice concerning framework decisions, decisions and conventions (Title VI, Article 35 (2));
- Maintenance of the *passerelle* (Title VI, Article 42), which provides that the Council (…) may decide that action referred to in Article 29 shall fall under Title IV of the TEC.

Concluding Remarks: What Will Nice Bring Us?

When looking at the Amsterdam Treaty one cannot avoid the impression that all Member States got at least a bit of what they wanted. The greatest losers were perhaps the small states that opposed flexibility, but they received compensation by means of procedural and substantive revisions. In retrospect, it seems that the rationally planned stocktaking exercise of the Reflection Group changed into a rhetorical game where IGC-options underwent semantic massages to make them acceptable for reluctant Member States.

Notwithstanding the legal and institutional complexity of the new Area of Freedom, Security and Justice, substantial progress has been made in the field of Justice and Home Affairs cooperation. However, more than one year after the entry into force of the Treaty of Amsterdam it seems too early to judge

---

[39] Compare with Article 2a of the Schengen Implementing Convention (1990).

whether the innovations of Amsterdam have improved the efficiency and efficacy of the cooperation in this policy arena. Confidential sources in Brussels admit that the JHA-working structure has become very complex: as a result of the incorporation of Schengen, various constellations have had to be created, such as a Mixed Committee with Norway and Iceland as members.

A Treaty of Nice, which will be concluded under the French Presidency, heralds no significant revisions for JHA-cooperation. This can be considered as fortunate, as all actors are still trying to recover from the Amsterdam shell-shock.

Bibliography

Benyon, John (1996). "The Politics of Police Cooperation in the European Union," *International Journal of the Sociology of Law*, Vol. 24, pp. 353-379.

Dehousse, Franklin (1996). *Les enjeux de la conference intergouvernementale de 1996*, Politique europeenne, 14 High European Reference Access.

Dehousse, Franklin & Lode van den Hende (1996). "Plaidoyer pour la réforme du troisième piller," *Revu du Marché Commun et de l'Union européenne*, No. 403, December, pp. 714-718.

Den Boer, Monica (1997a). "Hollen of Stilstaan? Justitie en Binnenlandse Zaken in het Nieuwe Verdrag van Amsterdam," *Nederlands Juristenblad*, 3 October, Issue 35, pp. 1625-1630.

Den Boer, Monica (1997b). "Justice and Home Affairs Cooperation in the Treaty on European Union: More Complexity Despite Communitarization," *Maastricht Journal of European and Comparative Law*, 1997, Vol. 4, No. 3, pp. 310-316.

Den Boer, Monica (1998). *Taming the Third Pillar. Improving the Management of Justice and Home Affairs Cooperation in the EU*, Current European Issues, Maastricht: European Institute of Public Administration.

Den Boer, Monica (1999). "An Area of Freedom, Security and Justice: Bogged Down by Compromise," pp. 303-321, in David O'Keeffe and Patrick Twomey (eds.), *Legal Issues of the Amsterdam Treaty*, Oxford: Hart.

Edwards, Geoffrey & Eric Philippart (1997). *Flexibility and the Treaty of Amsterdam: Europe's New Byzantium?* CELS Occasional Paper, No. 3, November, Cambridge: University of Cambridge, Centre for European Legal Studies.

Hix, S. & J. Niessen (1996). *Reconsidering European Migration Policies. The 1996 IGC on the reform of the Maastricht Treaty*, Brussels: MPG, CCRE, SLG.

Monar, Jörg (1996). "Der Dritte Pfeiler der Europäischen Union zu Beginn der Regierungskonferenz: Bilanz und Reformbedarf," *Integration*, Vol. 19, No. 2, (April), pp. 93-101.

Nentwich, Michael & Gerda Faulkner (1996). "Intergovernmental Conference 1996: Which Constitution for the Union?" *European Law Journal*, Vol. 2, No. 1 (March), pp. 83-102.

22

Negotiating Flexible Integration[1]

Alexander Stubb[2]

In the early hours of 18 June 1997, the Amsterdam European Council concluded the 1996-7 Intergovernmental Conference (IGC) of the European Union (EU). This chapter will focus on the negotiations which led to the institutionalization of closer cooperation or flexible integration,[3] that is, the possibility for a number of Member States to cooperate more closely in specific areas using the institutional framework of the Union. Although it might not be used in the short term, flexibility is an important legal and political issue, influencing all aspects of Union activity in the long term. The notion of flexibility is not new to the Union, but the Amsterdam Treaty provides the first institutionalization of this concept as a basic principle in the Treaties. This chapter tries to determine how the subject was approached in the negotiations. It is divided into four parts: first, a description of the flexibility clauses in the treaty; second, the agenda-setting stage, which lasted

---

[1] This chapter has been previously published in K. Neunreither and Antje Wiener (eds.), *European Integration After Amsterdam: Institutional Dynamics and Prospects for Democracy* (Oxford: Oxford University Press, 2000). The chapter contains parts of the author's Ph.D. thesis, "Flexible Integration and the Amsterdam Treaty: Negotiating Differentiation in the European Union," at the International Relations Department of the London School of Economics and Political Science under the supervision of Professor William Wallace.

[2] The views presented in this paper are strictly personal, and do not necessarily reflect those of the Finnish Ministry for Foreign Affairs, by whom the author was employed before and during the IGC. The assessment is based on public documentation of the Conference. References to the negotiations were obtained from a number of anonymous interviews with other participants in the IGC. The author was a member of the Finnish negotiating team during the negotiations.

[3] It is interesting to note the evolution of the general terminology of differentiation between 1994 and 1997. When the IGC debate was launched in 1994, Schäuble and Lamers, among others, referred to a "hard core" of Member States, and the academic community began talking about "differentiated integration." Next, the Reflection Group preparing the agenda for the IGC talked about "flexible integration," and finally, the Amsterdam Treaty institutionalized the most politically correct and least ideologically-charged term of "closer cooperation." This chapter will use "flexibility" as the over-arching term, because it is the broadest one signifying all forms of differentiation. Closer cooperation only covers what can be called "enabling clauses."

from June 1994 to June 1996; third, the drafting stage, which ran from July 1996 to December 1996; and finally, the negotiating stage, which lasted from January 1997 to October 1997.

Both internal and external factors influenced the end result of the IGC negotiations on flexibility. Internally, the negotiations were difficult because flexibility meant different things to different people. For Germany and France, for instance, flexibility was a means by which to deepen the integration process, whereas for the United Kingdom (UK) it was a way of opting-out from further integration. From the publication of the Schäuble and Lamers paper in 1994 to the final stages of the negotiations, there seemed to be an unusually high level of confusion and, on occasion, ignorance about the subject being negotiated. For this reason, the new treaty provides a rather random set of rules for the management of flexibility.

Externally, there were three hidden agendas in the negotiations, each of which was addressed before the end of the IGC. First, there was the aim of driving the integration process forward without the awkward, unwilling Member States. This problem partially solved itself through the British elections on 1 May 1997, when a more pro-European Labour government was elected. Second, there was the prospect of enlargement to over 25 Member States. This challenge was met by the Commission's "Agenda 2000" document, and a consensus among the Member States that the enlargement negotiations would begin with 5+1 applicant countries. Third, there was the prospect of a small Economic and Monetary Union (EMU). When the IGC began, it appeared that the convergence criteria would be met by only a limited number of Member States, and that EMU would therefore go ahead with only a few countries. By the time the IGC negotiations drew to a close, it had become clear that a total of 11 Member States would be likely to join the third stage of EMU, with the result that the need for institutionalized flexibility seemed less acute.

This chapter is the story of the flexibility negotiations as seen through the eyes of a practitioner. The analysis is heavily actor-based but, for the sake of streamlining the analysis, Member States are presented as unitary actors.

The Flexibility Clauses in the Amsterdam Treaty

The new treaty provides for three basic forms of flexibility: enabling clauses, case-by-case flexibility and pre-defined flexibility.

Table 22.1: Main forms of flexibility in the Amsterdam Treaty.

Form of Flexibility	Definition	Example
Enabling clauses	Enables willing and able Member States to pursue further integration (subject to certain conditions set out in the treaties) in a number of policy areas within the institutional framework of the Union.	• general flexibility clause (Articles 43-45 TEU) • clauses specific to the first pillar (Article 11 TEC) • clauses specific to the third pillar (Article 40 TEU)
Case-by-case flexibility	Allows a Member State to abstain from voting on, and to formally declare that it will not apply, a decision which will nonetheless commit the Union.	• constructive or declaratory abstention (Article 23 TEU)
Predefined flexibility	Covers a specific field, is pre-defined in all its elements including its objectives and scope, and is applicable as soon as the Treaty enters into force.	• Protocol No. 2 integrating the Schengen *acquis* into the framework of the EU. • Protocol No. 3 on the application of certain aspects of Article 14 TEC to the UK and Ireland. • Protocol No. 4 on the position of the UK and Ireland in the new Title IV of the TEC. • Protocol No. 5 on the position of Denmark in Schengen.

Enabling Clauses

The enabling clauses are the main flexibility innovation of the Amsterdam Treaty. They enable the willing and able Member States to pursue further integration in a number of policy areas within the institutional framework of the Union, subject to certain conditions set out in the Treaties. Examples include a general flexibility clause and clauses specific to the first and third pillars.

A general flexibility clause to be inserted as a new Title VII into the Treaty on European Union (TEU) (Articles 43-45 [K.15 – K.17]), sets out the general conditions and institutional arrangements for the enabling clauses. The aim is to preserve the basic principles of the Treaties, and to safeguard the interests of any Member State which is outside the framework of closer cooperation. Eight conditions are laid down, which set the framework for closer cooperation.

Flexibility must:

- further integration,
- maintain the single institutional framework,
- constitute a measure of last resort,
- involve the majority of the Member States,
- preserve the *acquis communautaire*,
- protect outsiders,
- be open to all, and
- comply with the additional criteria laid down in the pillar-specific enabling clauses.

The clauses applicable to the first and third pillars (Articles 11 [5a] TEC (Treaty of the European Community) and Article 40 [K.12] TEU) set out the specific conditions and decision-making mechanisms in each of those areas. In the first pillar, flexibility is restricted by a so-called "negative list," which states that flexibility can be established so long as the proposed cooperation:

- does not concern areas which fall within the exclusive competence of the Community;
- does not affect Community policies, actions or programmes;
- does not concern the citizenship of the Union, or discriminate between nationals of Member States;
- does not go beyond the limits of the powers conferred upon the Community by the treaty; and
- does not constitute a discrimination or a restriction of trade between Member States, or distort the conditions of competition between them.

The decision triggering flexibility in the first pillar is taken by a qualified majority vote (QMV) in the Council. If, however, a Member State declares that, for important and stated reasons of national policy, it opposes the granting of the authorization of a flexible measure, the matter is referred to the European Council for decision by unanimity (the so-called "emergency brake"). The initiative for a flexible solution originates in a request to the Commission from the Member States concerned. The Commission then submits a proposal, and has the final say as to whether or not a particular flexible solution will be pursued. The possibility of joining a flexible solution is also dependent on a decision by the Commission.

In the third pillar, two conditions apply for flexibility. The cooperation proposed should respect the powers of the European Community and the objectives laid down in the third pillar, and must have the aim of enabling the Union to develop more rapidly into an area of freedom, security and justice. These conditions are in line with the more specific conditions set out in areas covered by pre-defined flexibility (see below). The trigger mechanism is the same as in the first pillar (QMV and the "emergency brake"). The difference from the first pillar is that, instead of a binding proposal, the Commission gives only a non-binding opinion on the initiative put forward by the Member States. In addition, instead of the Commission's approval being required, it is the participating Member States who decide whether a non-participating Member State may join the flexible solution.

Case-by-Case Flexibility
Case-by-case flexibility allows a Member State to abstain from voting on, and to formally declare that it will not apply, a decision which will nonetheless commit the Union. This so-called "constructive" or "declaratory" is a cross between a decision-making mechanism and flexibility, and is provided for in the second pillar (Article 23 [J.13]).

Constructive abstention is not new to the Treaties. Article 205(3) [148(3)] TEC states that: "Abstentions by members present in person or represented shall not prevent the adoption by the Council of acts which require unanimity." Article 23 [J.13] now contains almost exactly the same wording: "Abstentions by members in person or represented shall not prevent the adoption of ... decisions." The difference between the two forms of declaratory abstention is that, in the first pillar the decision binds the Union as a whole, including the abstaining Member States, whereas in the second pillar, the decision does not bind the abstaining member state. Nevertheless, Article 23 of the Amsterdam Treaty includes a mutual solidarity clause similar to that of Declaration 27 of the TEU. Article 23 states that: "In a spirit of mutual solidarity, the Member States concerned shall refrain from any action likely to conflict with or impede the Union action...."

Pre-Defined Flexibility
Pre-defined flexibility covers a specific field, is pre-defined in all its elements (including its objectives and scope), and is applicable as soon as the treaty enters into force. In the Amsterdam Treaty, pre-defined flexibility is primarily laid down in the protocols and declarations. Examples include:

- Protocol No. 2 integrating the Schengen *acquis* into the framework of the European Union;
- Protocol No. 3 on the application of certain aspects of Article 14 of the TEC to the UK and to Ireland;
- Protocol No. 4 on the position of the UK and Ireland in the new Title IV on visas, asylum, immigration and other policies related to the free movement of persons; and
- Protocol No. 5 on the position of Denmark in Schengen.

The most obvious previous examples of pre-defined flexibility are the British opt-outs from the Social Protocol and EMU, and the Danish opt-outs from EMU, defence, citizenship and police cooperation.

The Agenda Setting Stage: June 1994 to June 1996

The first stage in the negotiations which resulted in the institutionalization of closer cooperation was the agenda-setting stage, when the agenda for the 1996 IGC was established and some of the most important questions on flexibility were raised. It began with the Corfu European Council in June 1994, included the opening of the IGC at the informal Turin European Council on 29 March 1996, and ended with the Florence European Council in June 1996. It can be further divided into four sub-phases.

From Corfu (June 1994) to Rome (June 1995)
The Corfu European Council established "a Reflection Group to prepare for the 1996 Intergovernmental Conference" to be headed by Carlos Westendorp of Spain, and asked it to begin its work during the Italian Presidency (European Council 1994a: 15). The heads of state and government further invited the institutions of the Union to submit reports on the functioning of the Maastricht Treaty by the spring of 1995, which they duly did (Council 1995; European Parliament 1995b; Commission 1995a; European Court of Justice 1995; Court of First Instance 1995; Court of Auditors 1995; Economic and Social Committee 1995; Committee of the Regions 1995). The mandate for the Reflection Group did not make a direct reference to the examination of flexibility. Nevertheless, the Group was urged to examine measures "deemed necessary to facilitate the work of the institutions and guarantee their effective operation in the perspective of enlargement" (European Council 1994a: 16).

Although there had been extensive debate on the issue of flexibility since the publication of the Schäuble-Lamers paper on 1 September 1994, only two of the eight reports submitted to the Reflection Group contained specific references to the notion of flexible integration. The Commission's report suggested that further enlargement would force the Union "to look more closely at the possibility of different speeds of integration" (Commission 1995a: 6). The Commission was anxious to ensure that the single institutional framework be preserved, and that any form of flexibility would aim to achieve the Community's common objectives. The report made it clear that the Commission was "utterly opposed" to any form of *à la carte* integration which would allow the Member States to pick and choose areas of policy preference.

The European Parliament (EP) had clarified its thinking on flexibility since its somewhat contradictory "Resolution on a multi-speed Europe" of 28

September 1994. In its report to the Reflection Group, the Parliament noted that the increase in diversity might well require flexible arrangements in the future. Following the same general line as the Commission, the EP said that flexibility should not lead to a Europe *à la carte,* and should not undermine the principle of equality of all states and citizens of the Union. In specifying the first strict conditions of flexibility, the EP emphasized that flexibility "should not undermine the single institutional framework, the *acquis communautaire* or the principles of solidarity and social cohesion throughout the European Union" (European Parliament 1995a: 8).

At first sight, it seems somewhat surprising that the Council's report made no mention of flexible integration. After all, at a later stage it was the Council Secretariat which provided the impetus for the institutionalization of flexibility as a treaty principle (see below). The reason is that the Council's report differed from those of the Commission and the EP in as much as it had no political preface. It focused, as requested, on the experiences relating to the implementation of the Maastricht Treaty, whereas the other reports were policy papers with a clear political agenda and vision, which sought to influence the debate in the Reflection Group.

The Dutch government released an important early contribution to the flexibility debate in 1994, in which it argued that flexibility should be temporary. This Dutch intervention was important in that it provided the first set of conditions for flexibility introduced by a Member State. On 2 March 1995, the Spanish government elaborated on these conditions in a white paper dealing with the IGC. This document introduced the idea of non-exclusion in relation to flexibility, by stating that no Member State should be excluded from closer cooperation. More importantly, it provided a second set of conditions on flexibility to be introduced by a Member State. These conditions were later to be found, virtually unchanged, in the report of the Reflection Group, which was chaired by Carlos Westendorp of Spain, who was involved in the drafting of both the Spanish white paper and the report of the Reflection Group. The language of the document clearly shows that Spain was on the defensive about flexibility, believing that decisions should be made by unanimity, and cohesion should be safeguarded.

From Rome (June 1995) to Madrid (December 1995)
The Reflection Group was set up in Messina on 2 June 1995. It was composed of the personal representatives of the Foreign Ministers of each of the Member States, a representative of the Commission and two representatives of the EP. The group met 14 times between June and December 1995, and the discussions revolved around five separate topics: challenges, principles and objectives; the institutional system; the citizen and the Union; the Union's external and security policy; and the instruments at the Union's disposal. The

meetings were usually structured around a set of questions which had been sent out to members of the group in advance. The notion of flexible integration was discussed nine times, not as a separate topic but mostly under the heading of challenges, principles and objectives. It was to become a separate topic only when the IGC began.

The Reflection Group submitted its final report to the Madrid European Council in December 1995. After the publication of the report, it became clear that the institutionalization of flexibility would be a permanent part of the IGC's agenda, with the result that the EU capitals began considering the issue more carefully. Many Member States advocated limits and restrictions on flexibility, and stressed the importance of cohesiveness. The notion of restricted flexibility had its roots in the reactions of the Member States to the proposal, set out in the Schäuble-Lamers paper of 1994, of the creation of a core of Member States which would drive the integration process forward, namely Germany, France and the Benelux. This put many of the other members on the defensive, since they were afraid of being excluded. It is also important to note that the Reflection Group rejected flexibility in the first pillar, and only saw it as a viable option in the second and third pillars. This shows a certain bias and prejudice on the part of some members of the group, who viewed the new Member States as prospective trouble-makers in the second pillar. Flexibility could overcome this problem, they thought. It was also clear that the UK, Ireland and Denmark would have problems adopting new provisions relating to the third pillar in general, and the Schengen agreement in particular, and it was thought that flexible solutions could solve this problem too. The first pillar, however, was considered sacrosanct, a notion which was emphasized by the Commission in particular.

By December 1995, the debate on flexibility had come a long way. In enabling the ideas of Schäuble and Lamers to find their way into the Conference documentation, the Reflection Group had performed an essential role in setting the agenda for the flexibility debate in the IGC.

From Madrid (December 1995) to Turin (March 1996)
During the time between the end of the work of the Reflection Group, and the beginning of the IGC on 29 March 1996, the member governments worked on their positions for the IGC. The political impulse for the flexibility debate was established in two Franco-German documents which were published before the IGC. The first was a letter produced by Chancellor Helmut Kohl and President Jacques Chirac on 7 December 1995, born out of a Franco-German summit in Baden-Baden. The underlying idea on flexibility was that willing and able Member States should not be prevented from closer cooperation so long as that cooperation remained within the established institutional framework, and was open to all members of the Union. The second document

was also a joint Franco-German paper, published by Foreign Ministers Klaus Kinkel and Hervé de Charette, and stemming from a seminar held in Freiburg on 27 February 1996. This document referred to the Kohl-Chirac letter, and added that a possibility for opt-outs should be linked to the new proposed flexibility clause, so as to prevent any Member State being forced into a particular area of cooperation.

The Member States and the EU institutions set out their positions on flexibility in a number of papers on the eve of the IGC. Most of the Member States' reports outlined their general IGC positions, and gave a brief overview of the issues pertaining to flexibility. Without going into detail about the individual reports, Table 22.2 outlines some general observations about their content.

Table 22.2: Content of the Member States' and institutions' IGC reports.

Issue	Member State/Institution
Mentions flexibility	Commission 1995c, 1996, Belgium 1995, Benelux 1996, Denmark 1995a, European Parliament 1995c, Germany 1996b, Greece 1995, 1996, Spain 1995, 1996, France 1996, Ireland 1996, Italy 1995a, 1995b, 1996, Luxembourg 1995, the Netherlands 1994, 1995a, 1995c, 1996, 1995, Austria 1995, 1996, Portugal 1996, Finland 1995, 1996, Sweden 1995a, 1995b, UK 1995, 1996
Does not mention flexibility	European Parliament 1996b, Denmark 1995b, the Netherlands 1995b
Is generally progressive about flexibility	Commission 1996, Belgium 1995, Benelux 1996, Germany 1996, Spain 1995, 1996, France 1996, Ireland 1996, Italy 1995, 1996, Luxembourg 1995, the Netherlands 1994, 1995a, 1995c, 1994, Austria 1995, Austria 1996, Finland 1995, 1996
Is generally open about flexibility	Sweden 1995a, 1995a, UK 1995, 1996
Is generally hesitant about flexibility	Denmark 1995a, Greece 1995a, 1995b, 1996, Portugal 1996
Pegs flexibility to enlargement	Commission 1996, Spain 1995, 1996, Italy 1995, the Netherlands 1994, 1995c, Austria 1995, Finland 1996
Pegs flexibility to the slowest Member State	Commission 1996, Belgium 1995, Spain 1995, Austria 1996

Issue	Member State/Institution
Rejects *à la carte* as a viable option	Commission 1996, Belgium 1995, Benelux 1996, Spain 1996, Luxembourg 1995, the Netherlands 1994, 1995c, Finland 1996, Sweden 1995a, 1995b
Supports *à la carte*	No-one
Mentions constructive abstention	Luxembourg 1995, Netherlands 1994, 1995a
Mentions the willing and the able	Commission 1996, France 1996
Lists conditions and principles	Commission 1996, Belgium 1995, Benelux 1996, Spain 1995, 1996, Italy 1995, 1996, the Netherlands 1994, Austria 1995, 1996, Finland 1996, Sweden 1995a, 1995b, UK 1996
Does not list conditions and principles	Denmark 1995a, Germany 1996, France 1996, Ireland 1996, the Netherlands 1995c, 1996, Finland 1995, Sweden 1995, UK 1995

It is equally useful to outline what the Member States and the institutions said about the conditions for flexibility; these observations are outlined in Table 22.3.

Table 22.3: An outline of the conditions for flexible integration.

Condition	Member State/institution
Flexibility as the last resort	Commission 1996, Belgium 1995, Benelux 1996, Spain 1995, Spain 1996, Austria 1995, Austria 1996, Finland 1996
Maintaining the single institutional framework	Commission 1996, Benelux 1996, Spain 1996, Italy 1995, Italy 1996, Austria 1995, Finland 1996, Sweden 1995a, Sweden 1995b
Compatibility with the objectives of the treaty	Benelux 1996, Netherlands 1994, Finland 1996
Open to all Member States	Commission 1996, Belgium 1995, Benelux 1996, Spain 1995, Spain 1996, Italy 1995, Italy 1996, the Netherlands 1994, Austria 1995, Austria 1996, Finland 1996, UK 1996
Safeguarding the single market	Commission 1996, Belgium 1995, Benelux 1996, Spain 1995, Spain 1996, Italy 1996, the Netherlands 1994
Safeguarding the *acquis communautaire*	Benelux 1996, Spain 1995, Spain 1996, Italy 1995, Italy 1996, the Netherlands 1994, Finland 1996

Condition	Member State/institution
Control of the European Court of Justice	Commission 1996
Trigger by other than unanimity	Belgium 1995, the Netherlands 1994
Key role for the Commission	Belgium 1995, Benelux 1996
Supporting measures for outsiders	Spain 1995, Spain 1996, Finland 1996
Flexibility should be temporary	Spain 1996, Austria 1996, Finland 1996
Flexibility judged on a case-by-case basis	Spain 1996
Flexibility should not distort competition	Austria 1995

The following observations can be extrapolated from these reports. First, by the end of March 1996 (just before the opening of the IGC), it had become clear that flexibility would be on the agenda. Each of the Member States mentioned the subject in their reports. Second, all the Member States and the institutions seemed to reject the notion of an *à la carte* Union – or at least no Member State advocated a pick-and-choose form of flexibility. Third, a group of hesitant Member States began to emerge; it included Sweden and the UK (both of whom were open to flexibility but did not advocate it), Greece, Denmark and Portugal. Somewhat surprisingly, Spain saw itself as a core country, and seemed to support some institutionalization of flexibility. Fourth, it is also interesting to note that, while many Member States seemed to support the notion of flexibility, almost all of them suggested tight straitjackets for its application. This was a clear indication of the general feeling that, although flexibility was desirable, it should be managed in such a way that it would not get out of hand.

From Turin (March 1996) to Florence (June 1996)
The Turin European Council of 29 March 1996 provided the mandate for examining flexibility in the IGC by asking it:

> to examine whether and how to introduce rules either of a general nature or in specific areas in order to enable a certain number of Member States to develop strengthened cooperation, open to all, compatible with the Union's objectives, while preserving the *acquis communautaire*, avoiding discrimination and distortions of competition and respecting the single institutional framework (European Council 1996a: 5).

From the start of the negotiations, it was clear that flexibility would be one of the most difficult and sensitive areas of discussion. Between the European Councils of Turin and Florence in March and June 1996 respectively, the

Member States began discussing their general positions on flexibility. During that time, the Italian presidency submitted two background documents on flexibility (CONF 3821 1996 and CONF 3860 1996) which were, by nature, rather general, in that they asked questions rather than provided answers. Among other things, the Member States were asked whether they would prefer a general flexibility clause or flexibility on a case-by-case basis. At this stage, an interesting coalition of willing and able Member States emerged: The six founding countries and the three newest Member States preferred a general flexibility clause, whereas the rest suggested that a case-by-case approach would be sufficient. The reason for these preferences was grounded in the assumptions, current at the time, about which countries would be eligible to participate in the third stage of EMU. The oldest and newest Member States believed they would form the core, whereas the remainder assumed they would be left out on the periphery. As will be shown, these attitudes changed as the IGC progressed.

The German and French delegations were the first to speak on flexibility in the first meeting where the subject was discussed. Both delegations alluded to the Kohl-Chirac and Kinkel-de Charette letters, and explained that they had been working together on the subject. In spite of this, the parameters for the application of flexibility came from the so-called "Ten Commandments of Flexibile Integration," a non-paper presented by the Finnish government on 30 May 1996. These commandments comprised a number of rules intended to help govern the application of flexibility, such as the single institutional framework. The creation of these commandments constituted a milestone for the new articles on flexibility in the Amsterdam Treaty since, in one way or another, each of them played a part in the new treaty provisions.

The Florence European Council on 21-22 June 1996 asked the IGC to continue to examine the notion of flexibility. By this stage it had become clear that all the Member States wanted strict rules regulating flexibility. Nevertheless, flexibility was discussed on a rather general level, and few delegations wanted to reveal their true position. Indeed, none of the Member States seemed to have a clear set of answers to all the questions posed by the presidency documents. This was hardly surprising, since the position papers issued by the Member States before the IGC began had been abstract, not only because the Member States did not want to reveal their positions, but also because they were not sure what their actual positions were. (This supports the idea that IGC negotiations are a learning process.) Despite the vagueness of the positions of the Member States, however, the agenda for flexibility had been set, and issues of decision-making, form and control had been raised. It then became the task of the Irish presidency to draw up the first, concrete draft article on flexibility.

The Drafting Stage: July 1996 to December 1996

The Irish followed the advice of the Florence European Council, and put flexibility on the agenda at an informal meeting of the representatives of the Foreign Ministers in Cork on 5-7 July 1996. The discussions were based on a non-paper questionnaire circulated by the presidency, which dealt with the arguments for and against flexibility, the conditions and principles of flexibility and the methods and instruments of flexibility. The debate was not conclusive at this stage, but it was nevertheless helpful in mapping out the more concrete positions of the various Member States.

On 25 September 1996, the first draft article on flexibility was introduced by the Irish presidency (CONF 3914 1996). A general flexibility clause (without specific conditions) was accompanied by three specific flexibility clauses which set out the conditions for flexibility in each pillar. The first trigger mechanism for flexibility was outlined. In the first pillar, the decision to seek a flexible solution was to be made by QMV, whereas in the second and third pillars unanimity would be required. The debate on the draft article at the level of the representatives on 30 September demonstrated that flexibility had become one of the most difficult issues under negotiation. Most delegations thought that the flexibility issue would be solved in the final stages of the negotiations. A feeling of indecisiveness reigned, along with a belief that there were far more questions than answers. At this stage, a majority of the Member States were of the opinion that flexibility was more suitable for the second and third pillars than the first, an assumption which was to be overturned later by the Dutch presidency. It should be noted that the article was not drafted by Irish civil servants, but rather by the Legal Service of the Council, whose influence in IGCs is a much neglected issue in the literature on European integration. Given the fact that it provided over 90% of the draft articles which were used as the basis for negotiation in the 1996-7 IGC, its role should not be underestimated.

After the informal Dublin European Council in early October 1996, the general positions on flexibility began to change. By the spring of 1996, nine Member States had advocated a general flexibility clause, and six Member States had supported a case-by-case approach to flexibility. By October 1996, flexibility was being seen as a necessity, everyone accepted that both general and specific flexibility clauses would be inserted into the new treaty, and the remaining differences in opinion concerned how, rather than whether, these clauses would be incorporated.

The political impulse for flexibility was further strengthened by a third Franco-German memorandum, presented on 17 October 1996 (CONF 3955 1996). The document supported a general flexibility clause for the first pillar, so long as the institutions retained their regular role and the *acquis communautaire* was preserved. This was the first time that flexibility in the first pillar emerged as a viable option. The document was diplomatic about the trigger mechanism for flexibility, suggesting that no Member State should have the right of veto on this point. It is interesting to note that the subject of the document was defined as "closer cooperation with a view to increased European integration," a clear indication that, throughout the IGC, France and Germany viewed flexibility as a way forward towards deeper integration.

Flexibility was discussed at ministerial level on 25 November 1996. The discussions were not based on a draft article; instead, ministers were asked to discuss a set of questions (CONF 3985 1996). This highlights the self-evident: drafting is seldom done at ministerial level, at least not in the early stages of the negotiations. Most ministers stressed the importance of keeping flexibility within the treaty framework, both before and after the next enlargement. Many emphasized the importance of safeguarding the objectives, the *acquis communautaire* and the institutional framework of the Union. However, the ministers were not willing to discuss specifics, such as the decision-making mechanisms of flexibility. At this ministerial meeting, Portugal announced that it would submit a draft article on flexibility, but when it appeared it was defensive in character, and was never really discussed at ministerial or representative level (CONF 3999 1996). The main aim of the document was to ensure that any decisions on flexible arrangements would require unanimity.

The legacy of the Irish presidency was a Draft Treaty, published in December 1996 (CONF 2500 1996). It did not propose a draft article on flexibility, but rather outlined a number of issues where a degree of common agreement seemed to have emerged: for example, flexibility should not be regarded as an alternative to the normal decision-making process, it should only be used subject to precisely defined conditions, it should be open to all Member States, and the rights of non-participating Member States should be respected. Nevertheless, the Irish presidency had done very important groundwork for the final stage of the negotiations. The parameters and models of flexibility had been defined in earlier draft articles at the level of the representatives. With hindsight, it could be argued that flexibility was a less sensitive issue to negotiate than many had been led to believe. When looking at the articles on flexibility being discussed before the Irish Draft Treaty, it is clear that they do not differ much from those which were negotiated in the final stages of the IGC. The rather timid approach of the participants can, however, be explained by the fact that none of the three "hidden agendas" of the flexibility negotiations – awkward Member States, EMU and enlargement – had been resolved by the time of the Dublin European Council of 13-14 December 1996.

The Negotiating Stage: January 1997 to October 1997

The first draft article on flexibility proposed by the Dutch presidency was released on 11 February 1997, following a discussion about flexibility at ministerial level on 20 January 1997. The Dutch document was influenced by five other documents which had been released in the previous weeks. The first of these was a non-paper (SN 639 1996), distributed on 20 December 1996 before the end of the Irish presidency. It contained a general flexibility clause, supported by three specific flexibility clauses. The second document was a questionnaire released on 8 January 1997 (Non-Paper SN 500 C1 1997) and again on 16 January 1997 (CONF 3802 1997), which asked the Member States to indicate their positions on flexibility, ranging from enabling clauses to pre-defined flexibility. The third document was a draft article on flexibility, circulated by the Italian delegation on 15 January (CONF 3801 1997). The fourth was a paper distributed by the Commission on 23 January (CONF 3805 1997), and the fifth one, dealing with the incorporation of Schengen, was released on 4 February by the presidency. These documents, and the ministerial debate on flexibility held on 20 January 1997, were important in moulding the Dutch presidency's thinking on flexibility. The Commission document was particularly important, in that it gave a "green light" to the idea of an enabling clause, provided that it was accompanied by safeguards.

The first Dutch draft article (CONF 3813 1997), mentioned above, had an important impact on the final version of the flexibility clauses included in the Amsterdam Treaty. It was based on the premise that a general flexibility clause and three specific clauses could be incorporated into the new treaty. The need for a flexibility clause in the second pillar was questioned by the presidency, however, which suggested that constructive or declaratory abstention combined with the "old" Articles J.4(4) and J.4(5) would provide sufficient flexibility for Common Foreign and Security Policy (CFSP) matters. The reason for this stems from the fact that the president of the group of representatives, Michiel Patijn, was personally very sceptical about any form of flexibility in the second pillar. He believed that questions with defence implications would be better taken care of by the North Atlantic Treaty Organization (NATO) than by any flexible arrangement which might eventually lead to the incorporation of Article 5 of the Treaty of West European Union (WEU) into the EU. Patijn's influence on flexibility in relation to the Schengen agreement was equally important.

The representatives' meeting of 17-18 February 1997 witnessed the first, detailed discussions on flexibility, indicating that the real negotiations had finally begun. The Member States began to reveal their positions on questions relating to decision-making mechanisms, the budget, the number of participants and the involvement of the institutions, and a new set of coalitions began to emerge. At this stage of the negotiations, the Member States could be grouped as follows:

- the *progressive* Member States: those able and willing to pursue closer cooperation (Germany, France, Italy, Belgium, Luxembourg, the Netherlands, Austria, Ireland and Finland);
- the *hesitant* Member States: those able but not necessarily willing (the UK, Sweden and Denmark); and
- the *reluctant* Member States: those not able but willing (Portugal, Spain and Greece).

The reluctant Member States were aiming to limit flexibility, because they knew they would have difficulty in participating in every flexibility measure proposed. The hesitant Member States, on the other hand, wanted to put the brakes on flexibility, because they knew they did not want to participate in all the proposed areas of closer cooperation. Perhaps most surprisingly, it was not the big Member States (that is, Germany, France and the UK) who were leading the movement for the institutionalization of flexibility. Even though the political impulse had come from the Franco-German axis, it was the progressive quintet of Italy, Ireland, Finland, the Netherlands and Belgium which was orchestrating the process.

By this stage, the three different forms of flexibility – enabling clauses, case-by-case flexibility and pre-defined flexibility – had been clarified. In the very early stages of the IGC, in April 1996, the governments had been asked to choose between three different models of flexibility. The first was a multi-speed model, which corresponds to transitional clauses, for example in relation to enlargement. The second was a variable geometry model, which corresponds to enabling clauses, and the third was an *à-la-carte* model, which corresponds to both case-by-case flexibility and pre-defined flexibility, where a Member State can pick and choose in which policy area it wants to participate. The more ideologically-charged terminology had gradually given way to more practical and concrete examples of various possible forms of flexibility. As a result, only the enabling clauses, case-by-case and pre-defined flexibility were left on the agenda at this stage; transitional clauses were no longer being considered by the IGC. Interestingly, there was a slight contradiction in terms in the position of those Member States which rejected the *à-la-carte* model, but supported case-by-case and pre-defined flexibility, since they are essentially the same thing. Nevertheless, by February 1997, the negotiators finally had a clearer picture of what was meant by flexibility.

At the end of March, the Dutch presidency circulated a revised draft of some of the issues in the Irish Draft Treaty (CONF 2500 ADD1 1997), in which a draft article on flexibility was also proposed. The trigger mechanism (that is, unanimity or qualified majority) in the first pillar was left in square brackets, indicating that agreement had not as yet been reached on this issue; pillar two required unanimity; and flexibility in pillar three could, interestingly enough, be triggered by qualified majority voting. The document drew on suggestions from a revised version of the first Dutch draft article on flexibility (CONF 3835 1997), two Irish non-papers – one on the third pillar (3-4 March 1997) and the other on the first pillar (7 March 1997) – and a presidency progress report on the state of play of the Conference on March 19 (CONF 3848 1997). In the ministerial meeting held on 25 March, commemorating the 40th anniversary of the signing of the Treaties of Rome, the presidency's draft article was generally well-received. Nevertheless the UK, Greece and Portugal were still sceptical about the enabling clauses, and noted that, if they were incorporated into the new treaty, any decision based on them should require unanimity. Ireland and Austria, on the other hand, were sceptical about an enabling clause in the second pillar, and suggested that constructive abstention would be sufficient for CFSP matters. On the eve of the ministerial meeting, the Greek delegation had submitted a proposal on flexibility which, much like Portugal's suggestion in 1996, was defensive in character (CONF 3866 1997).

By the time the representatives met on 14-15 April, the negotiations had moved to the stage of drafting articles. The comments from delegations were detailed and technical in nature, confined to proposing changes to the draft article. The delegations were happy by and large with the general enabling clause, and the enabling clause relating to the third pillar. However, there were two specific problems in the first pillar flexibility clause: the first concerned the decision-making mechanism, and the second related to the number of participants in any given flexible arrangement. The hesitant and reluctant Member States wanted decisions to be taken by unanimity, while having at least three quarters of the Member States participating at any given time. The progressive Member States, on the other hand, sought a QMV mechanism, and argued that half of the Member States were enough for any given flexible arrangement. In the second pillar, the debate revolved around whether an enabling clause was necessary for CFSP matters. Here, the reluctant and hesitant Member States were joined by Ireland and Austria in supporting constructive abstention in place of an enabling clause. Finland was the odd-man-out among the ex-neutral countries, because it did not object to a general flexibility clause in the second pillar. Spain, on the other hand, did not support constructive abstention. Interestingly, all the Member States who supported an enabling clause in the second pillar suggested that the trigger should be QMV.

The mid-April meeting of representatives preceded the final stage of the negotiations. Three more documents were submitted before the Amsterdam Treaty was concluded. The first was a non-paper (SN 2555 1997), called a

"Compilation of texts under discussion" rather than a draft treaty, because the presidency wanted to keep the debate as objective as possible. The document was discussed in a ministerial conclave on 20 May, at an informal European Council on 23 May and at the level of representatives on 26-28 May. The second document, a "Consolidated Draft Treaty" (Non-Paper SN 600 1997), amended as agreed in the preceding meetings, was not very different from the first. It had two options for negative lists (that is, areas which would not be suitable for flexibility) in the first pillar, one more specific than the other. The document was discussed by the Foreign Ministers on 2-3 June, and by their representatives on 5-6 and 9-10 June. The third document, the Draft Treaty published on 12 June 1997 (CONF 4000 1997), was drafted on the basis of these discussions; it included a more restrictive negative list, and the trigger mechanism for pillars I and III was qualified majority, while pillar II required unanimity.

Throughout May and early June, negotiations on flexibility appeared to lose the heat of the previous months, and a mood of indifference prevailed. As mentioned earlier, this was mainly due to the election of a pro-European government in the UK, and the fact that the EMU and enlargement questions had been implicitly agreed. There no longer seemed to be a pressing need for enabling clauses. This was the explicit message from the Franco-German grouping, which seemed to have little passion for enabling clauses, particularly when compared to their positions in the early stages of the negotiations. Also, the fact that the principle would in any event be included in the new treaty was enough for the progressive Member States, who must have implicitly believed that the instruments of flexibility could be perfected in future IGCs. In addition, it had become clear that the enabling clauses would not be sufficient in third pillar matters, or in matters relating to the incorporation of the Schengen Agreement and the new Community provisions on visas, asylum and immigration. Consequently, the UK, Ireland and Denmark would have to be dealt with in the traditional way, that is, through pre-defined opt-outs.

On the eve of the Amsterdam European Council, only three open questions concerning the flexibility provisions remained: First, what should be the trigger for flexibility? Second, who should have the final say in initiating flexibility in the first pillar? And third, should there be an enabling clause in the second pillar? The debate about flexibility at the Amsterdam summit took less than ten minutes. First, France and the UK suggested that the trigger mechanism for flexibility should be qualified majority, with a so-called emergency brake similar to the Luxembourg Compromise. This idea had been discussed in relation to the second pillar in earlier representatives' meetings, but had not received much support. At the European Council in Amsterdam, however, no-one objected to the idea, and the institutionalization of the

Luxembourg Compromise in relation to flexibility became a reality. Second, Portugal, supported by Italy, Greece, Belgium and Austria, suggested that the Commission, in its role as the guardian of the treaties, should have the final say in triggering flexibility in the first pillar. The change was accepted, and the Commission retained its central role in first pillar flexibility. Finally, the UK, Greece and Austria suggested that the enabling clause in the second pillar be dropped in favour of constructive abstention. The presidency agreed, and the enabling clause was dropped without any objections from other Member States.

For those who had been involved in the flexibility negotiations, it all seemed rather anti-climactic. Over thirty months of preparations and negotiations were concluded in less than ten minutes. In retrospect, however, this rather suggests that the subject had been well prepared. Only a few issues were left open before Amsterdam, and the heads of state or government were able to come to an agreement about the new provisions on flexibility relatively easily.

Conclusions

The IGC discussions on flexibility took place at two levels: an abstract political level (prominent during the agenda-setting stage), and a concrete legal one (during the drafting and negotiating stages). As with all IGCs, the focus was on legal detail, rather than political reality. During the Conference, the debate focused mostly on the institutional as opposed to the political implications of flexibility; no-one asked what flexibility was really needed for, whom it would benefit or in which areas it should be employed.[4] So it is no surprise that, while the Reflection Group suggested that flexibility be applied in the second and third pillars but not the first, the end result was that the new treaty institutionalized flexibility in the first and third pillars, but not the second. Nor is it surprising that, although all the Member States had rejected the *à la carte* model at the beginning of the negotiations, it became the central plank of flexibility as institutionalized in the Amsterdam Treaty, in the form of case-by-case and pre-defined flexibility.

The documentation clearly shows that the evolution of flexibility was typical of any new concept developed in an IGC. First, the idea was launched; second, the concept was defined; third, a draft article was provided; and finally, the draft article became subject to interpretation and negotiation. No-one, however, expected that the flexibility negotiations would continue after

---

[4] Admittedly, the Dutch presidency circulated a so-called "positive list" of areas in which flexibility would be applied, but this list was considered too restrictive.

the Amsterdam Summit, up until the signing of the new treaty on 2 October 1997 (see below). For an illustration of the evolutionary stages of the debate on flexibility, see Table 22.4.

Table 22.4: Evolutionary stages of the flexibility negotiations.

Stage	Evolution
Preparatory stage – June 1994 to June 1996	• political impulse from Franco-German letters • conditional outline by the Reflection Group • mandate from the Turin European Council • definitions and forms of flexibility outlined • conditions for flexibility established • enabling clauses introduced • Florence European Council announces that flexible provisions will be included in the new treaty
Drafting stage – July 1996 to December 1996	• first draft article on flexibility introduced by the Irish presidency • first trigger mechanism introduced • political impulse strengthened by Franco-German initiative on flexibility • Irish Draft Treaty does not provide a draft article
Negotiating stage – January 1997 October 1997	• Italian draft article focuses the debate • Commission's outline of flexibility in the Community pillar • doubts on enabling clause in the second pillar cast by Dutch presidency • enabling clause in the second pillar dropped at Amsterdam European Council • flexibility institutionalized in the new treaty

Much of the flexibility debate revolved around "what should not" as opposed to "what should be done." This approach was evident throughout the IGC, from the agenda-setting stage with the Reflection Group's conditions and Finland's Ten Commandments, to the European Council in Amsterdam. Flexibility was not about allowing, it was about disallowing. The reason for this "defensive" approach to flexibility was that the Schäuble-Lamers paper of September 1994 suggested that a hard core of five Member States (Germany, France and the Benelux) would drive the integration process forward. A majority of Member States saw flexibility as a means of exclusion. In addition a plethora of terms (multi-speed, variable geometry, *à la carte*, and so on) emerged to exacerbate the confused debate (Stubb 1996: 283). The flexibility debate could have been very different if the Dutch government paper of November 1994 had been published earlier. This paper focused mainly on multi-speed integration, and established conditions on the basis of which it could be pursued. However, the stir caused by the Schäuble-Lamers paper ensured that not much attention was given to the Dutch document.

It was during the drafting stage, which occurred under the Irish presidency in the latter half of 1996, that the debate began to gain focus. The presidency, pushed by the Council Legal Service, introduced the first draft article, which was mostly discussed at the level of representatives. In fact, the Irish were not too keen to deal with flexibility and procrastinated for some time. Despite its hesitancy, the Irish presidency should be given credit for the way in which it conducted the flexibility debate. It was wise to make the ministers debate the principles, and to leave the discussion of the draft articles to the representatives. It was equally wise to insist that much of the outcome of the flexibility clauses in the new treaty should depend on how much progress had been made in the IGC in general. This approach maintained the pressure for reform in other areas. It is also important to note that all of the early flexibility articles were drafted by the Council Legal Service, which serves as a reminder of the multitude of players which influence an IGC process: Member States, EU institutions and the presidency. However, although some scholars have argued that interest groups also influence an IGC process (Mazey & Richardson 1997), from personal experience I must disagree. Their influence is more apparent than real, especially in institutional matters. The opposite, of course, is true in the day-to-day business of the Community.

The negotiating stage – from January 1997 to October 1997 – was not as exciting as had been expected. The Dutch presidency had prepared the issue well, and by the time of the Amsterdam European Council, it was clear that flexibility would not take centre-stage at the summit meeting. Other issues, such as the re-weighting of votes in the Council and the number of Commissioners, were competing for that privilege.

But perhaps the most interesting negotiations on flexibility took place after the Amsterdam summit. The question of what had actually been decided on the decision-making mechanism for incorporating the Schengen agreement into the treaty proved problematic. The post-Amsterdam version of the treaty (CONF 4004 1997) stated that unanimity was required, whereas the pre-Amsterdam Draft Treaty (CONF 4002 1997) suggested that QMV would be sufficient for deciding whether an outsider could adopt legislation which was based on the Schengen *acquis*. The Irish, Danish and British governments claimed that the original formulation (QMV) had not been changed at Amsterdam, but the Spanish disagreed. After a review of the informal notes and the tapes from the Amsterdam meeting, it was concluded that a change *had* been agreed. Consequently, a unanimous decision will be required of the

Schengen members if the UK, for example, wants to adopt Schengen legislation.[5]

During the course of the IGC, a clear difference emerged between the Member States' policy papers and their actions in the negotiations. This was inevitable, since the initial policy papers needed to be sufficiently vague in order to provide the necessary room for manoeuvre and for error during the course of the negotiations. Consequently, the Member States' positions changed throughout the IGC, following the mood of the negotiations. Sweden, for example, started with a positive view of enabling clauses, but ended up as one of the most fierce advocates of unanimity as the trigger for flexibility. Positions in IGCs swing for many reasons, but rational choice and calculation are rarely among them. IGC negotiations are a messy and often confusing learning process, where the basic positions of the Member States show some continuity, but the specific positions of the negotiators fluctuate in line with the dynamics of the negotiations.

This chapter categorized the positions of the Member States as progressive, hesitant or reluctant, but EU negotiations are too complex and fluid to fit neatly into boxes; these simplified categorizations should therefore be treated with caution. The position of a Member State is not that of a unitary actor; it is adopted by the government in power, and mediated through ministers or representatives. The ministries in a particular Member State can differ more over the national position than the actors at ministerial or representative level in Brussels. During the Dutch presidency, for example, cleavages emerged in the positions on flexibility advocated by the Foreign Ministry and the Ministries of Finance and Social Affairs & Employment in The Hague. Nevertheless, these simple categories do help to shed light on the complex policy developments which took place during the IGC.

The new treaty provisions do not correspond to the form of flexibility advocated by Schäuble and Lamers in 1994 because, in the end, there was no need to push flexibility to the extreme. The most awkward Member State had a new pro-European government, the EMU countries had implicitly been chosen and the enlargement question had been solved. By the late spring of 1997, it was clear that flexibility would not be an issue over the next 10-15 years, or at least not before the applicant countries' long transitional periods run out. This should not, however, hamper long-term research on flexibility, and indeed some studies of post-Amsterdam flexibility have already emerged (Shaw 1998c; de La Serre & Wallace 1997; Ehlermann 1997; Edwards & Philippart 1997; Philippart & Edwards 1999; Stubb 1997, 1998 and 1999).

---

[5] The background to the tension relates to the on-going debate between Spain and the UK over the status of Gibraltar.

Expansion leads to diversity, and the greater the diversity, the more the issue of flexibility comes to the fore. The institutionalization of flexibility marks a new phase in the process of European integration. Up until the Amsterdam Treaty, common objectives were sought in unison; now a mechanism for permanent differentiation has been established. In the end, the effects of flexible integration will depend on the desire and the ability of the member governments to apply the policies and the objectives established in the treaties.

Bibliography

Austria (1995). *Guidelines of the Austrian Government on the subjects likely to be dealt with at the 1996 IGC*, June 1995.

Austria (1996). *Austria's Positions of Principle on the Intergovernmental Conference*, 26 March.

Belgium (1995). *Government Policy Paper Addressed to the Belgian Parliament on the 1996 IGC*.

Benelux (1996). *Memorandum of March 1996 of Belgium, the Netherlands and Luxembourg for the IGC*, 7 March.

Commission (1995a). *Report of 10 May 1995 on the operation of the Treaty on European Union*.

Commission (1995b). *Position of 6 December 1995 on the Reflection Group Report*.

Commission (1996). *Opinion of 28 February 1996 on reinforcing political union and preparing for enlargement*.

Committee of the Regions (1995). *Opinion of 20 April 1995 on the revision of the Treaty on European Union*.

CONF 3821 (1996). *Enhanced Co-operation – Flexibility*, 16 April.

CONF 3860 (1996). *Progress Report on the Intergovernmental Conference*, June 17.

CONF 3914 (1996). *Flexibility*, 24 September.

CONF 3955 (1996). *Closer co-operation with a view to increased European integration, France and Germany*, 18 October.

CONF 3985 (1996). *IGC Ministerial meeting on 25 November*, 19 November.

CONF 3999 (1996). *Flexibility - Draft general clause on enhanced co-operation*, Portugal, 29 November.

CONF 2500 (1996). *Draft Treaty*, Irish Presidency, 13-14 December.

CONF 3801 (1997). *Flexibility*, Italy, 15 January.

CONF 3802 (1997). *Enhanced co-operation – Flexibility*, 16 January.

CONF 3805 (1997). *Flexibility*, Commission, 23 January.

CONF 3806 (1997). *Schengen and the European Union*, 4 February.

CONF 3813 (1997). *Flexibility – enabling clauses approach*, 11 February.

CONF 3835 (1997). *Closer Co-operation/Flexibility*, March 4.

CONF 2500 ADD1 (1997). *Addendum to Irish Draft Treaty*, 20 March.

CONF 3848 (1997). *Presidency progress report on the state of play of the Conference*, 19 March.

CONF 3866 (1997). *Enhanced co-operation*, Greece, 8 April.

CONF 4000 (1997). *Draft Treaty of Amsterdam*, Dutch Presidency, 12 July.

CONF 4007 (1997). *Treaty of Amsterdam*, 2 October.

Council (1995). *Report of 6 April 1995 on the functioning of the Treaty on European Union* (5082/95).

Court of Auditors (1995). *Report of May 1995 to the Reflection Group on the operation of the Treaty on European Union.*

Court of First Instance (1995). *Contribution of 17 May 1995 by the Court of First Instance on the operation of the Treaty on European Union.*

Court of Justice (1995). *Report of May 1995 on certain aspects of the implementation of the Treaty on European Union.*

de la Serre, F. & H. Wallace (1997). "Flexibility and Enhanced Co-operation in the European Union: Placebo rather than Panacea?," Paris: Groupement d'études et de Recherches "Notre Europe," *Research and Policy Papers*, No. 2.

Denmark (1995a). *Dagsorden for Europa: Regeringskonference 1996*, Report of the Danish Foreign Ministry, June.

Denmark (1995b). *Bases for Negotiations: an Open Europe – The 1996 IGC*, Memorandum of the Danish Government, 11 December.

Economic and Social Committee (1995). *Opinion of 22 November 1995 on the 1996 Intergovernmental Conference and the role of the Economic and Social Committee.*

Edwards, G. & E. Philippart (1997). "Flexibility and the Treaty of Amsterdam: Europe's New Byzantium?," Cambridge: *CELS Occasional Paper*, No. 3.

Ehlermann, C-D. (1997). "Differentiation, Flexibility, Closer Co-operation: The New Provisions of the Amsterdam Treaty," Florence: EUI.

European Council (1994). *Presidency Conclusions, Corfu European Council*, SN 100/94, 24-25 June.

European Council (1995). *Presidency Conclusions, Madrid European Council*, SN 400/95, 15-16 December.

European Council (1996a). *Presidency Conclusions, Turin European Council*, SN 100/96, 29 March.

European Council (1996b). *Presidency Conclusions, Florence European Council*, SN 300/96, 21-22 June.

European Parliament (1994). *Resolution on a multi-speed Europe*, 28 September.

European Parliament (1995a). *Draft working document on variable integration: principles and fields of application* (PE 211.102/rev.).

European Parliament (1995b). *Resolution of May 17 1995 on the operation of the Treaty on European Union with a view to the 1996 Intergovernmental Conference* (PE 190.441).

European Parliament (1995c). *Resolution of 14 December 1995 on the Agenda for the 1996 Intergovernmental Conference* (PE 195.289).

European Parliament (1996a). *Briefing on differentiated integration* (PE 165.802).

European Parliament (1996b). *White Paper on the 1996 Intergovernmental Conference, Volumes I and II*.

European Union (1995). *European Union: Selected Instruments Taken from the Treaties*, Book I, Volume I.

Finland (1995). *Memorandum concerning Finnish points of view with regard to the 1996 Intergovernmental Conference of the European Union*, September.

Finland (1996). *Finland's points of departure and objectives in the 1996 Intergovernmental Conference*, 27 February.

Finland (1996). *The Ten Commandments of Flexible Integration*, non-paper, 30 May.

France (1996). Memorandum on France's guidelines for the 1996 IGC, *Le Figaro*, 20 February.

Germany (1995c). Letter by Kohl and Chirac to the European Council 15-16 December of Madrid, Bonn/Paris 5 December.

Germany (1996a). *Common Foreign and Security Policy: Guidelines Adopted by the German and French Foreign Ministers at Freiburg*, 27 February.

Germany (1996b). *Germany's Objectives for the Intergovernmental Conference*, 26 March.

Greece (1995). *Conclusions of the interministerial committee of the Greek Government*, 7 June.

Greece (1996). *For a Democratical European Union with Political and Social Content: Greece's Contribution to the 1996 Intergovernmental Conference* (sic.), 24 January.

Ireland (1996). *White Paper on Foreign Policy: External Challenges and Opportunities*, 26 March.

Italy (1995a). *Italian Government statement on foreign policy guidelines*, 23 February.

Italy (1995b). *Italian Government Statement on the Intergovernmental Conference to review the Maastricht Treaty*, 23 May.

Italy (1996). *Position of the Italian Government on the IGC for the Revision of the Treaties*, 18 March.

Luxembourg (1995). *Luxembourg Government Memorandum on the 1996 IGC*, 30 June.

Mazey, S. & Richardson, J. (1997). "Policy-Framing: Interest Groups and the lead up to the 1996 Inter-Governmental Conference, *West European Politics*, Vol. 20, No. 3, July.

Netherlands (1994). *The Enlargement of the European Union: Opportunities and Obstacles*, 14 November.

Netherlands (1995a). *European Foreign Policy, Security and Defence: Moving Towards a More Decisive External Action by the European Union*, 30 March.

Netherlands (1995b). *European Co-operation in the Fields of Justice and Home Affairs*, 23 May.

Netherlands (1995c). *Institutional Reform of the European Union*, 12 July.

Netherlands (1996). *Between Madrid and Turin: Dutch priorities on the eve of the 1996 IGC*, March.

Non-paper (1996). *Non-paper on Flexibility*, Irish Presidency, 5 July.

Non-paper (1996). *Enhanced co-operation – flexibility*, SN 639, 20 December.

Non-paper (1997). *Enhanced co-operation – flexibility*, SN 500, 8 January.

Non-paper (1997). *JHA Matters*, Ireland, 3-4 March.

Non-paper (1997). *Flexibility under the first pillar*, Ireland, 7 March.

Non-paper (1997). *Closer Co-operation/Flexibility under the first pillar*, Ireland, 18 April.

Non-paper (1997). *Compilation of texts under discussion*, SN 2555, 14 May.

Non-paper (1997). *Consolidated draft treaty texts*, SN 600, 30 May.

Philippart, E. & G. Edwards (1999). "The Provisions on Closer Cooperation in the Treaty on European Union: Politics of a Multi-faceted System," *Journal of Common Market Studies*, Vol. 37, No. 1, pp. 87-108.

Portugal (1996). *Portugal and the IGC for the Revision of the Treaty on European Union*, March.

Reflection Group (1995b). *Reflection Group's Report of 5 December 1995* (SN 520/95 REFLEX 21).

Schäuble, W. & Lamers, K. (1994). "Reflections on European Foreign Policy," document by the CDU/CSU Group in the German Bundestag, 1 September.

Shaw, J. (1998). "Flexibility and Legitimacy in the Domain of the Treaty Establishing the European Community," *European Law Journal*, 4, pp. 63-86.

Spain (1995). *The 1996 Intergovernmental Conference: Starting Points for a Discussion*, 2 March.

Spain (1996). *Elements for a Spanish Position at the 1996 Intergovernmental Conference*, 28 March.

Stubb, A. C-G. (1996). "A Categorisation of Differentiated Integration," *Journal of Common Market Studies*, Vol. 34, No. 2, June, pp. 283-95.

Stubb, A. C-G. (1997). "The Amsterdam Treaty and Flexible Integration: A Preliminary Assessment," paper presented at the IPSA World Conference in Seoul, 17-21 August.

Stubb, A. C-G. (1998). "Flexible Integration and the Amsterdam Treaty," Pittsburgh: *ECSA Newsletter*, Spring, pp. 1-4.

Stubb, A. C-G. (1999). "Flexible Integration and the Amsterdam Treaty: Negotiating Differentiation in the European Union," Ph.D. thesis, London: London School of Economics.

Sweden (1995a). *Sweden's Fundamental Interests with a view to the 1996 IGC*, July.

Sweden (1995b). *Svenska regeringens skrivelse: EU:s regeringskonferens 1996*, November.

Treaty of Amsterdam (1997). *European Union: Consolidated Versions of the Treaty on European Union and the Treaty Establishing the European Community*, Luxembourg: Office for Official Publications of the European Communities.

United Kingdom (1995). *Memorandum on the treatment of European defence issues at the 1996 IGC*, 2 March.

United Kingdom (1996). *A Partnership of Nations: The British Approach to the European Union Intergovernmental Conference 1996*.

23

Institutions and Procedures: The Limited Reforms

Finn Laursen

Introduction[1]

The Intergovernmental Conference (IGC) which negotiated the Amsterdam Treaty was called under Article N(2) of the Maastricht Treaty. Article B in that Treaty referred to the IGC as a possible forum for considering whether the policies and forms of cooperation, which were introduced by the treaty, should be revised to ensure the effectiveness of the mechanisms and institutions of the Community. More specifically, Article 189B(8) mentioned the scope of co-decision as an item for the agenda of the IGC. The Treaty further mentioned Common Foreign and Security Policy (CFSP) (Art. J 10) and the role of the Western European Union (WEU) (Art. J 4(6)) as agenda items for the IGC. This, of course, included institutional issues, especially the question of whether the role of the Commission in the second pillar should be increased.

The European Council meeting in Brussels 10-11 December 1993 was more specific: the IGC should look at the role of the European Parliament, the number of members of the Commission, the weights of member states' votes in the Council and the efficiency of the institutions (*EC-Bulletin* 12-1993, point I.17). Thus, it was a clear idea from the outset that the role, composition and functions of EU institutions would be central items on the agenda.

The Context

Part of the context of the IGC was the upcoming eastern enlargement of the Union. Soon after the entry into force of the Maastricht Treaty, the EU went through its 4th enlargement. The end of the Cold War made it possible for three (formerly?) neutral countries, Austria, Sweden and Finland, to join the

---

[1] This chapter is a revised version of a paper presented on July 30 – August 1, 2000, at ECSA-Canada Conference, Quebec City, and on 21 September 2000 at the Annual Conference of the Danish Association of European Studies, Copenhagen. The author would like to thank participants in those two conferences for comments on earlier versions of the paper, including Wolfgang Wessels in Quebec City and Susana Borrás in Copenhagen.

EU from 1 January 1995. This enlargement took place on the basis of the Maastricht Treaty. It was, however, agreed that further enlargements should await the next IGC, where the institutions should be adapted to allow for enlargement without weakening the EU institutionally (Laursen, 2001).

Over the years, the EU had been enlarged from the original six to now 15 members without radical change in the institutions. 10 Central and Eastern European Countries (CEECs) had applied for membership. So had Cyprus, Malta and Turkey. This opened the prospect of an EU with nearly twice as many members. How could such a Union be ensured of an adequate capacity to make and implement decisions?

Council Voting and the Presidency

The fourth enlargement, as mentioned, took place on the basis of the Maastricht Treaty. However, at each enlargement it has to be decided how many votes the new Member States get in the Council and what implications this will have for a qualified majority vote (QMV) and, by implication, how many votes will constitute a blocking minority. In this connection, a conflict broke out in the spring of 1994 about the redefinition of the QMV in the enlarged EU. Among the Twelve, a QMV was set at 54 out of a total of 76 votes. This meant that 23 votes constituted a blocking minority. With the existing weighting of votes this meant that two big Member States plus one small Member State (except Luxembourg) could form a blocking minority. During the negotiations with the four applicants (the three mentioned plus Norway which eventually did not join) it was decided to give Sweden and Austria four votes and Finland and Norway three votes each. This would have taken the total of votes to 90. On the basis of an extrapolation, it was suggested to set the new blocking minority at 27. The United Kingdom and Spain went against this. These two countries wanted to maintain the blocking minority of 23.

Eventually a compromise was found at the foreign ministers meeting in Ioannina, Greece, 26-27 March 1994 (*EC-Bulletin* 3-1994, points 1.3.27 and 28). The blocking minority was set at 27 on the condition that the Council would endeavour to reach a satisfactory solution in case there was a minority of between 23 and 26 votes against a proposal.

Since Norway did not join, the current EU has 15 members with a total of 87 votes in the Council. A QMV was defined as 62, implying a blocking minority of 26 votes, i.e. more than two big and one small state (see table 23.1).

Table 23.1: Council Voting.

	Number	Population (millions)	Citizens per vote (million)
Germany	10	81.7	8.2
United Kingdom	10	58.6	5.9
France	10	58.1	5.8
Italy	10	57.7	5.8
Spain	8	39.1	4.9
Netherlands	5	15.5	3.1
Greece	5	10.5	2.1
Belgium	5	10.2	2.0
Portugal	5	9.9	2.0
Sweden	4	8.9	2.2
Austria	4	8.1	2.0
Denmark	3	5.2	1.7
Finland	3	5.1	1.7
Irland	3	3.6	0.9
Luxembourg	2	0.4	0.2
Total	87	371.6	
Qualified majority	62		
Blocking minority	26		

Source: Simon Hix, *The Political System of the European Union*. New York: St. Martin's Press, 1999, p. 70.

The table shows that the existing weighting of votes is far from proportional. The big states are relatively underrepresented, especially Germany. The small states are relatively overrepresented, especially Luxembourg. Future membership of smaller countries like Cyprus, Malta, Slovenia and the Baltic countries would make this situation more visible. Thus, there was a need for changes in the weighting of votes in the Council.

Table 23.2 shows the votes the new members would get if the current system were to be applied. In a Union of 27 members a blocking minority would be 39, a number of votes which could be reached by the 10 Central and Eastern European countries (CEECs).

Another problem in connection with the Council was also discussed prior to the start of the IGC, viz. the Presidency. It was argued that the rotating Presidency caused problems for continuity and in view of the future enlargements, the question was asked whether all future small members would have the capacity to handle the Presidency. Some were less worried, pointing to the fact that Luxembourg had been able to handle the job quite well. In respect to CFSP, the so-called troika had been created to represent the Union externally. The order of rotation was further changed at the meeting of the European Council in Brussels in December 1993 to make sure that the troika always includes one of the bigger members, considered especially important for CFSP (*EC-Bulletin* 12-1993).

Table 23.2: Extrapolation of the Current Voting System to a Union of 27 Members.

	Population (in millions)	*Votes*
Union of 15 members	371.0	87
Poland	38.5	8
Romania	22.8	6
Czech Republic	10.3	5
Hungary	10.3	5
Bulgaria	8.5	4
Slovakia	5.3	3
Lithuania	3.7	3
Latvia	2.6	2
Slovenia	2.0	2
Estonia	1.5	2
Cyprus	0.7	2
Malta	0.4	2
Union of 27 members	477.6	131
Qualified majority		93 (70.99%)
Blocking minority		39 (29.77%)

Source: Commission Doc SN 612/96 (C 4)

Composition and Role of Commission

The composition of the Commission was also on the agenda. Already in the 1970s it was argued that the Commission was getting too big for the existing portfolios. After the fourth enlargement in 1995 the Commission had 20 members, two from the big Member States, Germany, France, UK, Italy and Spain, and one from each of the remaining Member States. Should each future member, even very small ones like Cyprus, Malta and the Baltic states, have a Commissioner? Might the big Member States accept having only one Commissioner? Or was it time to stop thinking in national terms? After all, once appointed the Commissioners are supposed to represent the European interest and not take instructions from their home countries. Could one imagine the European Parliament appointing the Commission from a more political than national perspective? Or could one imagine groups of states sharing a Commissioner? Or should one move towards some kind of rotation?

The question of right of initiative was also discussed prior to the IGC. Could the first pillar's rule of exclusive right of initiative of the Commission be extended to the second and third pillars, where the Commission shared the right of initiative with the Member States? What about the European Parliament, should it also have a right of initiative? After all, such a right is normal in national parliaments.

The European Parliament

In relation to the European Parliament we also have the issue of the relative representation of the Member States (see table 23.2). How big should the Parliament be allowed to become? What is a just division of the seats?

A mini-reform took place in connection with the Brussels summit in December 1993 (*EC Bulletin* 12-1993)). The united Germany got an additional 18 seats, while Italy, United Kingdom, France and the Netherlands got extra six, Spain four, Portugal, Greece and Belgium one each. Ireland, Denmark and Luxembourg did not get additional seats. Maybe the most important development was that the principle of equal representation of the four largest members was broken, a principle so far especially emphasised by France. It was French insistence on the principle that had made a reform impossible at the time of the Maastricht negotiations.

The discrepancy between the representation of the big and small Member States, however, remains large. It takes 66,000 votes to get elected to the European Parliament from Luxembourg, while it takes 805,000 votes in Germany. This does not seem very just, and enlargement with many relatively small states would make this problem more visible.

The 1993 reform increased the total number of members of the European Parliament to 567. The enlargement in 1995 added 22 seats to Sweden, 21 to Austria and 16 to Finland, taking the total to 626 members of the European Parliament (MEPs).

Another question in connection with the European Parliament was the many legislative procedures that involved the Parliament in various ways. For some questions, the Parliament is only consulted, for other questions, the so-called cooperation procedure applies which involves two readings in the Parliament, but not a real veto for the Parliament. The Maastricht Treaty introduced the so-called co-decision procedure (art. 189b) which gave the Parliament a veto on some legislation. There is also the assent procedure requiring the Parliament to accept certain decisions, especially enlargement and association agreements. For the budget there are separate procedures. It has all become very complicated and wishes for simplification were expressed from various sides.

The whole issue of democracy in the Union affects the role of the European Parliament in various ways. Should for instance the Parliament's influence on the nomination of the Commission be increased?

Table 23.3: European Parliament.

Member state	Number of seats	Population (millions)	Citizens per EP seat
Germany	99	81.7	826,000
France	87	58.1	670,000
Italy	87	57.7	659,000
United Kingdom	87	58.0	675,000
Spain	64	39.1	613,000
Belgium	25	10.2	404,000
Greece	25	10.5	420,000
Netherlands	31	15.5	500,000
Portugal	25	9.9	396,000
Sweden	22	8.9	400,000
Austria	21	8.1	386,000
Finland	16	5.1	319,000
Denmark	16	5.2	331,000
Ireland	15	3.6	240,000
Luxembourg	6	0.4	67,000
Total	626	371.1	

Source: Based on Simon Hix, *The Political System of the European Union.* New York: St. Martin's Press, 1999, p. 77.

The Pillar Structure

Questions relating to the pillar structure of the Union have institutional implications. Within the first pillar the so-called Community method is used. The Commission has an exclusive right of initiative, majority voting is possible in a number of cases and it is binding "legislation" which is adopted (regulations and directives). The European Court of Justice (ECJ) plays the role of a real court that makes binding judgements. Pillar two and three, on the other hand, have remained more traditional intergovernmental cooperation. The Commission plays a less important role. Decisions normally require unanimity. It is not "legislation" that is adopted and the ECJ normally does not get involved.

Those who would like to strengthen CFSP or Cooperation in Justice and Home Affairs (JHA) want to varying degrees to use the Community method for CFSP and/or JHA.

Report of the Reflection Group

According to the Reflection Group, which prepared the IGC, institutional changes should increase the citizens' confidence in the European institutions. Reform should "improve the efficiency, democracy, and transparency of the Union" (Reflection Group, 1995b, 4).

More concrete proposals were often drafted in very careful language. Concerning the European Parliament "it seems appropriate to fix a maximum number of seats. A majority accept a maximum of 700 in an an enlarged Union" (ibid., p. 30). In respect to procedures a large majority was in favour of simplification, reducing them to the following three: consultation, co-decision and assent. It would also be appropriate to simplify the co-decision procedure.

Concerning QMV: "In the case of Community legislation, a large majority in the Group is prepared to consider making qualified majority voting the general rule, on grounds of efficiency, since it will facilitate decision-making" (ibid., p. 33).

Concerning the weighting of votes, the Reflection Group was clearly split: "Several members point to a gradual deterioration in popular representation in the weighting of qualified majority voting as a result of the underrepresentation of the people of the more populous States and the growing number of less populous States in the Union" (ibid., p. 34) "In the view of some the answer is a new weighting of votes that takes greater account of population. On the other hand, a system of double majority of votes and population has been suggested. Other members, however, did not endorse that analysis. They referred to the principle of the sovereign equality of states, suggesting that the population factor was adequately represented in the representation of the European Parliament. They also found the problem false." There was no systematic pattern of small-population countries forming coalitions against the large-population countries.

The Reflection Group was in favour of maintaining the Commission's monopoly of legislative initiative. Concerning the composition of the Commission, the Reflection Group basically mentioned two options: (1)

Maintaining a system involving Commissioners from all Member States, which would promote a feeling of belonging on the part of citizens or (2) "fewer than the number of Member States." The number of really necessary portfolios should determine the size of the Commission. Pros and cons of the two options were presented.

It clearly was not decision time yet!

The IGC Agenda

When the IGC started in connection with the meeting of the European Council in Turin in the spring of 1996, the agenda was grouped in three main points: (1) a Union close to the citizens, (2) institutions in a more democratic and efficient Union, and (3) strengthened capacity for the Union's external action (*EC Bulletin* 3-1996, point I.5). Questions relating to the Third pillar were included in the first group.

Among institutional issues the following were mentioned:

- Extent of majority voting, weighting of votes, threshold for QMV
- Commission efficiency and composition
- Role of ECJ and Court of Auditors
- Rules to "enable a certain number of Member States to develop a strengthened cooperation."

The latter point became known as flexibility.

The various institutional issues during the IGC were dominated by four themes:

1. The wish to simplify and make the decision-making process more efficient.
2. The wish to strengthen the democratic basis of the Union. This led to various negotiations concerning the role of the European Parliament as well as national parliaments.
3. The wish of some countries to change the balance between the big and small Member States. Two issues were central: the composition of the Commission and the weighting of votes in the Council.
4. The wish to clarify and limit the role of the European Court of Justice especially pursued by the UK which, however, did not lead to any changes (Isaksen, Toft & Bødtcher-Hansen, 1998: 120).

Actor Positions

As the IGC got started, the Belmont European Centre in Brussels started following the positions of the actors. The results of questions addressed by Belmont to the actors are given in tables 23.3, 23.4 and 23.5.[2] They illustrate the situation in the spring of 1996. A quick consultation of the tables will show that much convergence of positions was needed before agreement could be reached on the institutional issues.

Table 23.4: Actor Positions Concerning Role of Commission.

Removal of sole right of initiative:
  Yes: None
  No: A, B, FIN, D, GR, IRL, I, LUX, NL, P, E, S, UK, Commission, EP
  Don't know: DK, F
Reduce Commissioners to one per Member State:
  Yes: A, F, FIN, D, GR, I, UK, Commission
  No: B, DK, IRL, LUX. NL, P, E
  Don't know: S
Change nomination of President:
  Yes: F, GR, P, EP
  No: A, FIN,
  Don't know: B, DK, D, IRL, I, LUX, NL, E, S, UK, Commission
Change nomination of Commissioners
  Yes: F, GR, Commission, EP
  No: A, FIN, UK
  Don't know: B, DK, D, IRL, I, LUX, NL, P, E
Change dismissal of Commissioners:
  Yes: A, LUX, NL, Commission, EP
  No: FIN
  Don't know: B, DK, F, D, GR, IRL, I, P, E, S, UK
Reduce powers:
  Yes: UK
  No: A, B, DK, F, FIN, D, GR, IRL, I, Lux, NL, P, E, S, Commission, EP
  Don't know: None

Source: Belmont European Policy Centre, *Challenge 96*, Issue 8, May/June 1996.

---

[2] One has of course to be aware of the limitation of these data. As pointed out by Andrew Moravcsik in a communication to the author: "(1) What is reported in the Challenge data are public positions. These may be strategic. (2) "Don't know" reports that the government has not determined preferences." In the latter case it may be that the government has not consulted civil society and figured out what the preferences are.

In respect to the Commission we note that none of the actors except the UK stated that it wanted to reduce its powers. No one wanted to abolish the exclusive right of initiative of the Commission. So on these points change should not be expected. Eight actors wanted to reduce the number of Commissioner to one per Member State, but seven were against. On nomination and dismissal of Commissioners, most actors answered "Don't know."

Table 23.5: Actor Positions concerning the European Parliament.

Increase powers:
  Yes: B, D, GR, I, Lux, NL, P
  No: None
  Don't know: A, DK, F, FIN, IRL, E, S, UK Commission, EP
Decrease powers:
  Yes: None
  No: A, B, D, GR, IRL, I, LUX, NL, P, EP
  Don't know: DK, F, FIN, E, S, UK, Commission
Increase involvement of national parliaments:
  Yes: A, B, DK, F, FIN, GR, IRL, I, LUX, NL, P, UK, Commission
  No: None
  Don't know: D, E, S

Source: Belmont European Policy Centre, *Challenge 96*, Issue 8, May/June 1996.

Although seven actors were in favour of increasing the powers of the European Parliament and none were against there were still ten who answered "Don't know." Overall, however, it was not unlikely that the European Parliament might end up being one of the institutional winners from the IGC. The idea of increasing the involvement of national parliaments was supported by a large majority.

Concerning the Council there was a large majority in favour of increased use of QMV. The linkage to future enlargements probably had an effect here. Ten actors answered "yes" to the question of introducing population-weighted voting, but seven small states answered "no." Since the question is very general, it might include a reweighting of votes, as well as the possibility of a double majority which would require a majority of the population in the EU as well. The idea of public legislative meetings was supported by 11 actors and opposed by none. All the talk about greater openness seemed to have had its effects, although there may have been more hidden opposition than the answers showed. Nine actors supported change in the Presidency system but their answers do not indicate what kind of changes.

Table 23.6: Actor Positions concerning the Council.

Increase qualified majority voting:
  Yes: A, B, DK, F, FIN, D, GR, IRL, I, LUX, NL, P, E, Commission, EP
  No: UK
  Don't know: S
Introduce super-qualified majority:
  Yes: A, P, EP
  No: FIN, IRL
  Don't know: B, DK, F, D, GR, I, LUX, NL, E, S, UK, Commission
Introduce population-weighted voting:
  Yes: B, DK, F, D, I, LUX, NL, E, UK, Commission
  No: A, FIN, GR, IRL, P, S
  Don't know: EP
Make public legislative meetings:
  Yes: B, DK, FIN, GR, IRL, LUX, NL, P, S, Commission, EP
  No: None
  Don't know: A, F, D, I, E, UK
Change in Presidency system:
  Yes: B, DK, F, I, LUX, NL, P, S, UK
  No: A, FIN, IRL,
  Don't know: D, GR, E, Commission, EP

Source: Belmont European Policy Centre, *Challenge 96*, Issue 8, May/June 1996.

Early agreements

More than 75 official documents submitted to the IGC dealt with institutional issues. Certain institutional issues were solved relatively early during the IGC. This included the idea of an increased use of the co-decision procedure and a reduction in the number of decision procedures by eliminating the co-operation procedure (except for EMU not dealt with by the IGC). There was also early support for the idea of simplifying the co-decision procedure. Finally, all Member States agreed to limit the number of seats in the European Parliament to 700. These early agreements were reflected in the draft treaty proposal presented by the Irish Presidency in December 1996 (Isaksen, Toft & Bødtcher-Hansen 1998, 120).

The Irish draft also included a draft protocol on the role of national parliaments which, with minor changes, went into the final treaty. It was especially France, the UK and Denmark which had wanted to strengthen the role of national parliaments (Isaksen, Toft &- Bødtcher-Hansen 1998, 121.)

Small Versus Big: The Difficult Issues

When the Dutch Presidency took over in January 1997, the more sensitive issues remained and these were the issues which largely confronted the big and the small countries. The last months of the negotiations concentrated on three main issues:

1. The future size and composition of the Commission.
2. Changes in the weights of votes in the Council and threshold of QMV.
3. Expansion of the scope of QMV in the First Pillar (Isaksen, Toft & Bødtcher-Hansen 1998, 121).

The three issues were linked, and it was thus a question whether a package solution could be found.

In respect to the Commission, a number of big Member States wanted to set a ceiling on the number of Commissioners. Especially France was pressing the issue, suggesting a ceiling as low as 10 Commissioners. This reduction would be combined with a system of rotation. Most small Member States, however, insisted on retaining a Commissioner from their country.

Concerning weighting of votes it was especially the UK, France, Italy and Spain that wanted a reweighting in favour of big states. Germany suggested a system of double majority, where the current system is combined with the requirement that a majority should include a majority of the citizens of the Union. The smaller Member States took a rather sceptical position on changing the voting weights.

On 11 February 1997, the Dutch Presidency presented a Non Paper on Reweighting of votes and the threshold in the Council decision-making process (CONF/3815/97). This document included two tables showing the evolution of the qualified majority and the blocking minority in terms of minimum of population (see tables 23.7 and 23.8).

Table 23.7: The evolution of qualified majority in terms of minimum of population.[3]

	12 Member States	15 Member States	26 Member States
Total of votes in the Council	76	87	132
Qualified majority expressed in number of votes	*54*	*62*	*94*
Qualified majority expressed in % of the total of votes in the Council	71.05	71.26	71.21
Qualified majority expressed in minimum of population necessary to achieve it (millions of inhabitants)	203.73	216.3	240.308
Minimum coalition of Member States	France, United Kingdom, Belgium, Greece, the Netherlands, Portugal, Spain, Denmark, Ireland	France, Italy, Spain, Belgium, Greece, Portugal, Austria, Sweden, Denmark, Ireland, Finland, Luxembourg	Italy, Poland, Rumania, the Netherlands, Greece, Czech Republic, Belgium, Hungary, Portugal, Sweden, Bulgaria, Austria, Slovakia, Denmark, Finland, Lithuania, Ireland, Latvia, Estonia, Cyprus, Luxembourg
Qualified majority expressed in % of the total population of the Union	*63.21*	*58.3*	*50.29*

Source: CONF/3815/97 of 11 February 1997

---

[3] Maintaining and extrapolating the current weighting system to a twenty-six Member State Union.

Table 23.8: The evolution of blocking minority in terms of population.[4]

	12 Member States	15 Member States	26 Member States
Total of votes in the Council	76	87	132
Blocking minority expressed in votes	23	26	39
Blocking minority expressed in % of the total of votes in the Council	30.26	29.88	29.54
Blocking minority expressed in minimum of population necessary to achieve it (millions of inhabitants)	39.015	45.9	54.888
Minimum coalition of Member States	Belgium, Greece, Portugal, Denmark, Ireland, Luxembourg	Portugal, Sweden, Austria, Ireland, Belgium, Finland, Luxembourg	Portugal, Sweden, Bulgaria, Austria, Finland, Lithuania, Ireland, Latvia, Slovenia, Estonia, Cyprus, Luxembourg
Blocking minority expressed in % of the total population of the Union	12.1	12.28	11.48

Source: CONF/3815/97 of 11 February 1997.

[4] Maintaining and extrapolating the current weighting system to a twenty-six Member State Union.

The tables show that moving from 12 to 15 member states a QMV declines from 63.21 percent of the total population to 58.3 percent. In a Union of 26 it would fall to 50.29 percent if the current weighting system was extrapolated. Interestingly enough the blocking minority did not change so much. It had represented 12.1 percent in the Union of 12, 12.28 percent in the Union of 15 and would be 11.48 percent in a Union of 26.

The non-paper in January was analytical. Only towards the end of the negotiations did the Dutch Presidency issue a note (CONF/3888/97 of 24 April 1997) which in two annexes included two variants of possible reweighting of votes in a Union of 15 and a Union of 26 respectively (see tables 23.9 and 23.10).

Table 23.9: Variants of a possible reweighting of votes in a 15 Member State Union.

Member States	Variant I EU 15	Variant II EU 15
D	25	12
UK	25	12
FR	25	12
I	25	12
SP	20	9
NL	12	6
GR	10	5
B	10	5
PORT	10	5
SW	8	4
A	8	4
DK	6	3
FIN	6	3
IRL	6	3
LUX	3	2
Total	199	97
QMV	142	69
Block. min.	58	30
QMV % pop.	61%	60%

Source: CONF/3888/97 of 24 April 1997

Table 23.10: Variants of a possible reweighting of votes in a 26 Member State Union based on the linear extrapolation of the figures contained in Table 23.7.

Countries	Population (Million of Inhabitants)[5]	Variant I EU 26	Variant II EU 26
D	81.538	25	12
UK	58.503	25	12
FR	58.020	25	12
I	57.268	25	12
SP	39.177	20	9
PO	38.390	20	9
RO	22.840	12	6
NL	15.424	12	6
GR	10.442	10	5
CZ	10.300	10	5
B	10.130	10	5
H	10.110	10	5
PORT	9.912	10	5
SW	8.816	8	4
BUL	8.770	8	4
A	8.039	8	4
SLK	5.350	6	3
DK	5.215	6	3
FIN	5.098	6	3
LITH	3.700	6	3
IRL	3.579	6	3
LAT	2.560	3	2
SLOV	1.950	3	2
EST	1.530	3	2
CYP	0.742	3	2
LUX	0.406	3	2
Total	477.809	283	140
QMV		201	100
Block. min.		83	41
QMV % pop.		56.7%	57.6%

Source: CONF/3888/97 of 24 April 1997.

---

[5] The population figures for the 15 Member States in this column have been produced by EUROSTAT. The population figures for the prospective new accessions are derived from the most recent, available population census.

The suggested reweighting of votes was established by allocating votes to Member States in a decreasing scale subject to size of population. Both variants would result in a minimum level of support of +/- 60% of the total Union population and respect the current level of the threshold for the qualified majority (71.2%).

The proposals were discussed by the foreign ministers on April 29-30 without any agreement (*Agence Europe* 1 May, 1997). The Dutch chief negotiator during the IGC, Michiel Patijn, later told the press that the issue of reweighting had "raised a confrontation between small and large Member States without precedent in the Community's history" (*Agence Europe* 16 May, 1997).

The question was left to the Amsterdam summit. None of the variants were accepted. The Belgians did not like suddenly having fewer votes than the Dutch. They referred to the equal treatment of Germany and France, which was maintained in the variants. The Belgian prime minister Jean-Luc Dehaene got quite angry with his Dutch counterpart Wim Kok and is said to have threatened to leave the meeting of the European Council (Kerremans, contribution to this volume). There was also the Spanish problem: The Spanish claimed extra compensation for losing a Commissioner since they had accepted fewer votes than the other big Member States in exchange for two Commissioners when they joined (Duff 1997, 133).

According to one account, France and Spain had been the countries pressing most for a reweighting of the votes (Svensson 2000, 165). The solution of double majorities was also discussed in Amsterdam, but France and the UK were against this solution which would have been to Germany's advantage. President Chirac called the solution "dangerous" (*Agence Europe* 19 June, 1997).[6]

Concerning the extended use of QMV, all states, with the exception of the UK, agreed to the idea, but disagreement on which areas to include remained until the final decision on this in Amsterdam. In the end, the extension was not as large as expected since Germany at the last moment decided in favour of a shorter list.

But the main failure of Amsterdam was the fact that no agreement was reached on the two most central issues of the composition of the Commission and the voting system in the Council. The Treaty included a *protocol on the institutions with the prospect of enlargement of the European Union* which stipulated that "At the date of entry into force of the first enlargement of the Union ... the Commission shall comprise one national of each of the Member States, provided that, by that date, the weighting of the votes in the Council has been modified, whether by reweighting of the votes or by dual majority,

---

[6] There is an inconsistency here in comparison with the Belmont data.

in a manner acceptable to all Member States, taking into account all relevant elements, notably compensating those Member States which give up the possibility of nominating a second member of the Commission." Article 2 of the protocol further stipulated: "At least one year before the membership of the European Union exceeds twenty, a conference of representatives of the governments of Member States shall be convened in order to carry out a comprehensive review of the provisions of the treaties on the composition and functioning of the institutions."

There was also a declaration relating to this protocol which said: "Until the entry into force of the first enlargement it is agreed that the decision of the Council of 29 March 1994 ("the Ioannina Compromise") will be extended and, by that date, a solution for the special case of Spain will be found" (quoted from Duff 1997, 129). The reference to the Spanish problem afterwards was to be at the core of the Spanish ratification debate (Basabe Lloréns, contribution to this volume).

The protocol on institutions committed the EU to a new IGC to solve the unsolved institutional issues.

Summary of Institutional Changes

The widened scope of the co-decision procedure makes the European Parliament the big winner of Amsterdam. Most of the areas covered by the cooperation procedure were transferred to co-decision.

The *co-decision procedure* now applied to the following provisions:

New Treaty Provisions
Article (5)	Employment - Incentive measures
Article 119	Social policy - Equal opportunities and treatment
Article 129	Public health (former basis Article 43 - consultation)
	- minimum requirements regarding quality and safety of organs
	- veterinary and phytosanitary measures with the direct objective of protecting public health
Article 191a	General principles of transparency
Article 209a	Countering fraud affecting the financial interests of the Community
New Article	Customs cooperation
Article 213a	Statistics
Article 213b	Establishment of independent advisory authority on data protection

Existing Treaty Provisions[7]

Article 6	Rules to prohibit discrimination on grounds of nationality (cooperation)
Article 8a(2)[8]	Provisions for facilitating the exercise of citizens' right to move and reside freely within the territory of the Member States (assent)
Article 51(2)[9]	Internal market (consultation) – rules on social security for Community immigrant workers
Article 56(2)[10]	Coordination of provisions laid down by law, regulation or administrative action for special treatment for foreign nationals (right of establishment)
Article 57(2)[11]	Coordination of the provisions laid down by law, regulation or administrative action in Member States concerning the taking up and pursuit of activities as self-employed persons (consultation) Amendment of existing principles laid down by law governing the professions with respect to training and conditions of access for natural persons (consultation)
Article 75(1)	Transport policy (cooperation) – common rules applicable to international transport to or from the territory of a Member State or passing across the territory of one or more Member States; – the conditions under which non-resident carriers may operate transport services within a Member State; – measures to improve transport safety.
Article 84	Transport policy (cooperation) – sea and air transport
Social policy	Articles resulting from the transposition into the Treaty of the agreement on social policy (Article 2(2)), except for aspects of that Agreement which are currently subject to unanimity (Article 2(3)) (see Chapter 4 - Social provisions)(cooperation)

---

[7] The procedure applicable before Amsterdam is indicated between brackets after the content of each Article.

[8] The Council shall act unanimously.

[9] The Council shall act unanimously.

[10] As simplified (see CONF/4152/97)

[11] The Council shall act unanimously.

Article 125	Implementing decisions relating to the European Social Fund (cooperation)
Article 127(4)	Vocational training (cooperation) - Measures to contribute to the achievement of the objectives of Article 127
Article 129d	Other measures (TENs) (cooperation) 3rd subpara.
Article 130e	ERDF implementing decisions (cooperation)
Article 130o	Adoption of measures referred in Articles 130k and 1 - 2nd subpara. research (cooperation)
Article 130s(1)	Environment (cooperation) - action by the Community in order to achieve the objectives of Article 130r
Article 130w	Development cooperation (cooperation).

QMV was extended to the following areas:

New Treaty Provisions

Article 4	new Title on Employment	- Employment guidelines
Article 5	new Title on Employment	- Incentive measures
Article 118(2)	- Social exclusion	
Article 119(3)	- Equality of opportunity and treatment of men and women	
Article 129(4)	- Public health	
Article 191a	- Transparency	
Article 209a	- Countering fraud	
Article 213a	- Statistics	
Article 213b	- Establishment of independent advisory authority on data protection	
Article 227(2)	- Outermost regions	
New Article	- Customs cooperation	

Existing Treaty Provisions

Article 45(3)	- Compensatory aid for imports of raw materials
Article 56(2)	- Coordination of provisions laid down by law, regulation or administrative action for special treatment for foreign nationals (right of establishment)
Article 130i(1)	- Adoption of the research framework programme
Article 130i(2)	- Adapting or supplementing the research framework programme
Article 130o	- Setting up of joint undertakings in R&T development

Andrew Duff commented: "It may be regretted that the modest but respectable extension of the co-decision procedure was not accompanied at Amsterdam by the equivalent wider use of qualified majority voting in the Council. Indeed the mixture of co-decision and unanimity is bizarre ... (Duff 1997, 149).

The co-decision procedure was simplified *inter alia* by abolishing the third reading phase. If the Conciliation Committee fails to agree on a joint text, the proposal is dropped.

Amsterdam did agree on the 700 seats maximum for the European Parliament, one of the proposals that should prepare the EU for enlargement.

Explaining the Limited Results

Andrew Duff wrote:

> The biggest surprise at Amsterdam was that Helmut Kohl pulled back from traditional German positions on QMV. Led by Bavaria, the Länder governments, which compose the SPD-led Bundesrat, were anxious to protect their prerogatives over areas of domestic legislation, particularly concerning the environment and immigration (Duff 1997, 155).

He went on to talk about bureaucratic politics in Bonn in the form of "turf battles about European policy, notably between the FDP-led foreign ministry and the CSU-led finance ministry" and continued:

> The Chancellor himself was said to be preoccupied with the single currency project and unable to forge either a coherent or progressive German policy on institutional questions.

To that he further added:

> Lastly, the shock election of a socialist-communist government in France on 1 June scuppered the usual Franco-German joint formulation of positions before meetings of the European Council (Duff 1997, 155).

According to this interpretation, a combination of domestic politics and lack of leadership explains the failure of Amsterdam in respect to institutions. Franklin Dehousse also mentions the special Belgian-Dutch problem:

> ... the Dutch presidency presented a reweighting that was favourable for the big Member States, but with some aspects which led to specific problems, amongst others in the Benelux countries (Dehousse 1999, 61).

Another participant observer, Bobby McDonagh, describes the final deadlock in this way:

> Most delegations had a preference for the introduction of a dual majority system in the Council (to ensure that a qualified majority of votes in the Council would require also the support of Governments representing a specified percentage of the Union's population). A significant minority, however, preferred an actual reweighing of votes. Some on either side of this particular argument indicated that they were unable to compromise (McDonagh 1998, 193).

McDonagh went on to say that it was the view of some, himself included, that "a settlement there and then on these sensitive institutional questions was not beyond the reach of the Conference." He does not, however, offer an explanation of why it did not happen.

In the end, the most important explanation was probably timing. The issue was simply not sufficiently urgent to be solved quickly Tuesday night in Amsterdam when the heads of state and government finally got to that point on the agenda. Enlargement was still a few years ahead.

Concluding Remarks

Amsterdam thus finished without deciding on the reweighting of votes in the Council or the composition of the Commission, and there were some who felt that the increased use of QMV decided in Amsterdam was too limited. The unsolved issues became known as the Amsterdam "left-overs."

They all were related in various ways to issues of efficiency and legitimacy. The question of more QMV was first of all a question of efficiency. According to Andrew Moravcsik QMV can be seen as a "pooling of sovereignty" to create "credible commitments." The second aspect of institutional choice to create credible commitment according to Moravcsik, viz. delegation of authority to supranational institutions like the Commission and ECJ, was much less at stake at Amsterdam, although of course the move of important parts of JHA cooperation from the third to the first pillar implies further delegation in those areas. So Amsterdam included both some pooling and some delegation of authority (for the concepts, see especially Moravcsik, 1998).

The question of weighting of votes turned out to be a real battle between the small and big Member States. It was of course a battle for influence. It took on the nature of a zero-sum game, which made it impossible to find a solution in Amsterdam in June 1997. In this connection legitimacy was at stake. For many Member States the underrepresentation of the big Member States would become too great a problem of legitimacy in a future enlarged Union. The issue was postponed, but most actors agreed that it had to be solved prior to or in connection with future enlargements in order for the Union not to lose too much legitimacy.[12]

---

[12] Eventually the issues were solved at the Nice summit in December 2000.

Bibliography

Belmont European Policy Centre, *Challenge*, various issues.

CEPR (1995). *Flexible Integration*, London: Centre for Economic Policy Research.

Club de Florence (1996). *Europe: L'Impossible statu quo*, Paris: Éditions Stock.

Commissariat Géneral du Plan (1999). *L'Union européenne en quête d'institutions légitimes et efficacies. Rapport du groupe de réflexion sur la réforme des institutions europénnes*, Paris: La Documentation française.

Dehousse, Franklin (1998). "Les changements institutionnels," pp. 33-51, in Franklin Dehousse, Jacques Vandamme & Louis le Hardy de Beaulieu (eds.), *Union Européenne: Quels défis pour l'an 2000?*, Brussels: Presses Inter-universitaires Européennes.

Dehousse, Franklin (1999). *Amsterdam: The Making of a Treaty*, London: Kogan Page.

Denmark, Foreign Ministry, Nordgruppen (1995). *Regeringskonferencen i 1996: Institutionernes Rapporter om Traktaten om Den Europæiske Union*, København.

Devuyst, Youri (1998). "Treaty reform in the European Union: the Amsterdam process," *Journal of European Public Policy*, Vol. 5, No. 4 (December), pp. 615-31.

Duff, Andrew (1997). *The Treaty of Amsterdam: Text and Commentary*, London: Federal Trust.

European Commission (1995). *Report on the Operation of the Treaty on European Union*, SEC(95) final, Brussels, 10th May.

European Union, Council (1995). *Report of the Council on the functioning of the Treaty on European Union*, Luxembourg: Office for Official Publications of the European Communities.

Federal Trust (1996). *Enlarging the Union: The Intergovernmental Conference of the European Union 1996*, London: Federal Trust for Education and Research.

Gaudissart, Marc-André (1999). "Le traité d'Amsterdam et l'avenir de l'Europe élargie," pp. 11-34, in Marianne Dony (ed.), *L'Union européenne et le monde après Amsterdam*, Brussels: Editions de l'Université de Bruxelles.

Griller, Droutsas, Falkner, Forgó, Klatzer, Mayer & Nentwich (1996). "Regierungskonferenz 1996. Ausgangspositionen," *Forschungsbericht der Julius Raab-Stiftung Nr. 2, IEF Working Paper* No. 20 (July). Vienna: Forschungsinstitut für Europafragen.

Isaksen, Susanne, Ole Toft & Jens Bødtcher-Hansen (1998). *En traktat bliver til. Amsterdam-traktaten. Forberedelse, forhandling og resultat*, Copenhagen: J.H. Schultz Information A/S.

Laffan, Brigid (1997). "The IGC and Institutional Reform of the Union," pp. 288-305, in Geoffrey Edwards & Alfred Pijpers (eds.), *The Politics of European Treaty Reform: The 1996 Intergovernmental Conference and Beyond*, London: Pinter.

Laursen, Finn (1994). "The Not-So-Permissive Consensus: Thoughts on the Maastricht Treaty and the Future of European Integration," pp. 295-317, in Finn Laursen & Sophie Vanhoonacker (eds.), *The Ratification of the Maastricht Treaty*, Dordrecht: Nijhoff.

Laursen, Finn (1995). "The Role of the Commission," pp. 119-141, in Svein S. Andersen & Kjell A. Eliassen (eds.), *European Union - How Democratic is it?*, London: SAGE Publications.

Laursen, Finn (1996). "Regeringskonferencen '96: Institutionernes rolle," *Samfundsøkonomen*, No. 5, September, pp. 35-41.

Laursen, Finn (1997). "The Lessons of Maastricht," pp. 59-73, in Geoffrey Edwards & Alfred Pijpers (eds.), *The European Union: 1996 and beyond*, London: Collins/Pinter.

Laursen, Finn (2001). "EU Enlargement: Interests, Issues and the Need for Institutional Reform," pp. 206-228, in Kjell A. Eliassen & Svein S. Andersen (eds.), *Making Policy in Europe*, 2nd edition, London: SAGE.

Ludlow, Peter, et al. (1994). *Preparing for 1996 and a Larger European Union: Principles and Priorities*. CEPS Special Report No. 6, Brussels: Centre for European Policy Studies.

McDonagh, Bobby (1998). *Original Sin in a Brave New World: An Account of the Negotiation of the Treaty of Amsterdam*, Dublin: Institute of European Affairs.

Maurer, Andreas (1998). "Die institutionellen Reformen: Entscheidungseffizienz und Demokratie," pp. 41-81, in Mathias Jopp, Andreas Maurer & Otto Schmuck (eds.), *Die Europäische Union nach Amsterdam: Analysen und Stellungnahmen zum neuen EU-Vertrag*, Bonn: Europa Union Verlag.

Moravcsik, Andrew (1998). *The Choice for Europe*, Ithaca, NY: Cornell University Press.

Moravcsik, Andrew & Kalypso Nicolaïdis (1998). "Keynote Article: Federal Ideals and Constitutional Realities in the Treaty of Amsterdam," *Journal of Common Market Studies*, Vol. 36, Annual Review (September), pp. 13-38.

Moravcsik, Andrew & Kalypso Nicolaïdes (1999). "Explaining the Treaty of Amsterdam: Interests, Influence, Institutions," *Journal of Common Market Studies*, Vol. 37, No. 1 (March), pp. 59-85.

Neunreither, Karlheinz & Antje Wiener (eds.) (2000). *European Integration After Amsterdam: Institutional Dynamics and Prospects for Democracy*, Oxford: Oxford University Press.

Reflection Group (1995a). "Progress Report from the Chairman of the Reflection Group on the 1996 Intergovernmental Conference," *SN 509/95* (REFLEX 10), Madrid, 24 August.

Reflection Group (1995b). "Reflection Group's Report. Messina 2nd June 1995. Brussels 5th December 1995. Downloaded from http://europa.eu.int/en/agenda/igc-home/eu-doc/reflect/final.html

"La Reforme institutionelle de 1996: Les enjeux," (1995). *Revue des affaires européennes*, No. 1.

Svensson, Anna-Carin (2000). *In the Service of the European Union: The Role of the Presidency in Negotiating the Amsterdam Treaty 1995-97*, Acta Universitatis Upsaliensis, Uppsala: Statsvetenskapliga föreningen.

Section 4:

Conclusions

24

Negotiating the Amsterdam Treaty: When Theory Meets Reality

Derek Beach

Introduction

While there are a plethora of social science theories that attempt to explain the constitutive decisions in European integration,[1] looking at the "input" of demands for integration, and the "output" of Treaty revision, there is a scarcity of theoretical literature on the actual *process* of the negotiation of intergovernmental conferences (IGCs).[2] This lack of literature on IGC negotiations is particularly surprising when one considers the importance of the negotiation process in determining the final outcome of the IGC, the increasing frequency with which IGCs to undertake major Treaty revision have been called since 1985, and the almost nightmarish prospects of a whole series of minor and major IGCs during the next decade as the Central and Eastern European countries accede to the EU.

If the initial national preferences of Member States were the sole determinant of the outcome of an IGC on EU Treaty reform, there would of course be no need to investigate the actual negotiation process. In relation to this research programme, we would have been able to stop at the first stage, where we investigated national preferences, for us to determine the outcome of the 1996-97 IGC.

However there are many indications that negotiations matter in translating national preferences into final Treaty revisions. If we look at the initial preferences of the Member States in the 1996-97 IGC, there was a decisive coalition of Member States that wanted to introduce a form of "hard core" flexibility into the Treaty framework. However, as observed by Stubb (1998), after this issue had been negotiated for twenty months the Franco-German idea of a "hard core" had been transmogrified into a "complicated flexibility formula...unlikely to be of much use to those wishing to establish a hard core" (Stubb 1998, 282). This is not an instance of initial preferences solely determining the outcome!

---

[1] Major EU Treaty reform.

[2] This situation has improved recently with several works, e.g. Moravcsik's 1998 *The Choice for Europe* and Stubb's 1998 *Flexible Integration in the Amsterdam Treaty*.

This chapter has two primary goals. The empirical goal is an investigation of some of the dynamics in selected key issue-areas of the negotiations of the Amsterdam Treaty. Turning towards theory, existing *competing* theories will be tested vis-à-vis the empirical record, and then tentative steps will be taken towards developing a next generation of theory on IGC negotiation that focuses more explicitly on actual bargaining processes than existing theory.

Research Design

This chapter will investigate the key factors in the 1996-97 IGC bargaining process that determined how Member State preferences were translated into the final outcome (Treaty reform). A single case study is used in the following, but in a longer survey it would be appropriate to adopt a comparative, multi-case approach in order to create a more robust research design.

However even though this chapter looks at only one IGC, an accurate empirical description of the negotiation of the Amsterdam Treaty far exceeds the space constraints of a single chapter. I will therefore structure my analysis around two central theoretical debates, testing competing theories vis-à-vis the empirical record in strategically selected issues-areas. Explicit competing hypotheses will be developed from each theory, creating a more rigorous empirical analysis which removes some of the bias inherent in a single theory design, where there is often a tendency towards only selecting data that confirms the chosen theory.

This research design is inspired by Moravcsik's well-argued 1998 book *The Choice for Europe*. In his study Moravcsik however only looks at one theoretical dimension of interstate bargaining: i.e. whether IGC negotiations are intergovernmental, being based upon asymmetric interdependence, or whether outcomes are significantly influenced by supranational actors. The problem with this single dimension is that Moravcsik actually conflates *two* different theoretical debates. The first debate contained in his question is whether *supranational actors* play any significant role in IGC negotiations? The second debate revolves around what factors determine *actor power*, where Moravcsik assumes that if supranational actors do not play a significant role, then governmental power is based upon asymmetric interdependence. But it can be argued using a *realist* approach that governmental power can be based upon the *distribution* of *capabilities* and *resources*, and not actor dependence upon agreement. Using a realist approach, we would then expect that the outcomes of IGCs closely follow the preferences of the most powerful actors, primarily the Franco-German "core," and not patterns of asymmetric interdependence among Member States.

This chapter will be structured around these two theoretical questions, which should enable us to shed light on the key determinants of the IGC bargaining process that determined how Member State preferences were translated into the final outcome (Treaty reform).

Theory – The Two Questions

The Sources of Actor Power?

Looking first at actor power, international negotiation theories agree that actor power determines a large part of the outcome of a negotiation. In mainstream IR theory there are two primary competing positions as to what factors determine actor power.[3] *Realist theories* hold that actor power is determined by the relatively static *distribution of power resources or capabilities* among actors, traditionally defined as strategic resources, but when looking at the EU, many theorists also include economic strength in measures of actor power. The outcome of a negotiation will therefore reflect the preferences of the strongest actors, most often the Franco-German core, with the result that the history of the EC/EU is viewed by realists as a series of "grand bargains" between France and Germany (e.g. Simonian 1985; McCarthy 1993; Pedersen 1998).

The other main position can be termed the *asymmetric interdependence approach*, viewing power primarily as based upon actor *dependence upon agreement* (Keohane & Nye 1989; Habeeb 1988; Sebenius 1992; Moravcsik 1998; Zartmann 1991, 69). Following this approach, the strongest actor on paper is not necessarily the strongest actor in practice. European integration since 1945 can therefore be interpreted as showing that Germany, despite its economic strength, is often very dependent upon securing EU-level agreements due to both historical factors and the need for market access for its exporters, with its relative "weakness" reflected for example in Germany's disproportionately large contribution to the EU budget.

---

[3] Ideational power approaches will not be investigated here. It must be pointed out that the power of ideas and information underlies the second question to be investigated; i.e. for supranational actors to be significant, the possession of ideas and information must provide some form of power resources to the actor.

Hypotheses – actor strength
Realist approach
– outcomes reflect the national preferences of the most powerful actors, particularly the Franco-German core. – small Member States have little influence over the outcome of an IGC except in peripheral issues.
Asymmetric interdependence approach
– outcomes reflect patterns of preferences and actor dependence upon agreement – outcomes are skewed towards the preferences of reluctant governments given the need for unanimity in an IGC. – Member States that are most dependent upon agreement will have incentives to offer compromises and side-payments to less-dependent actors. Threats of exit and exclusion will also be used when credible.

The Role of Supranational Actors?
The second category of independent variable is the *importance of supranational actors* in IGC negotiations. While the Commission and other supranational actors play little if any *formal* role in an IGC, there is an extensive debate in the literature about whether supranational actors play a causally significant *informal* role, by shaping the agenda of an IGC, and/or upgrading the common interest through brokering and mediation.

Proponents of *supranational entrepreneur theory* such as Sandholtz and Zysman (1989), Pollack (1997, 1999), and Christiansen and Jørgensen (1998) argue that the Commission for example is able to act as *informal* agenda-setter or "policy-entrepreneur" in the run-up to an IGC by identifying problems and proposing solutions, mobilising support for certain policy proposals, and mediating compromises between Member States. Commission agenda-setting can increase the "efficiency" of agreements and/or lead to outcomes that are closer to the pro-integration preferences of the Commission. The theory assumes that Member States possess imperfect information both as regards their own and other Member States' preferences, while supranational entrepreneurs are perceived as possessing privileged access to information. This enables the Commission to exploit "*policy windows*," where the Commission submits acceptable solutions to common problems at strategic points in the negotiations (Pollack 1999, 5-6). Another way in which supranational actors can influence an IGC is by providing "*focal points*," such as ECJ rulings, around which the behaviour of actors converges, making policy choices restricted and particular outcomes more likely (Garrett & Weingast 1993; Mazey & Richardson 1997).

Intergovernmentalists such as Moravcsik (1998, 1999) counter that the outcome of an IGC is the result of the *demand* for integration from national actors, and not the *supply* of information from supranational "entrepreneurs." National governments are able to act as effective policy entrepreneurs, as information is both readily available and evenly distributed among Member States (low transaction costs) (Moravcsik 1998, 55). The outcomes of interstate negotiations are usually "efficient," meaning no joint gains are left on the table, as all actors are fully informed about the nature and intensity of their own and others' preferences, and the negotiation process itself does not pose impediments to the ability of actors to achieve joint gains.

Hypotheses – the role of supranational actors?
Supranational entrepreneur approach
– Member States have imperfect information and unclear preferences, while the Commission has privileged access to information, allowing the Commission to exploit "policy windows." – The Commission and other supranational actors are able to provide "focal points," shifting agendas and outcomes of the IGC towards their own preferences.
Intergovernmental approach
– Information and ideas are widely and evenly distributed among Member States. – Negotiation outcomes are "efficient" without supranational entrepreneurship.

Analysis of the 1996-1997 IGC

Introduction
There are significant methodological problems in attempting to investigate the two theoretical questions described above. What happens inside IGC negotiations is confidential, and there are many indications that there is bias in the secondary reports of the IGC negotiations. Press accounts of the IGC are naturally biased, given that journalists often do not (or cannot) empirically verify the validity of public statements from politicians and civil servants. There are several accounts of the negotiations of the Amsterdam Treaty from national civil servants, but again there are bias problems, given that these officials have incentives to stress the "rational," state-based character of the negotiations. In addition, it can also be argued that Commission officials in public statements also had incentives in *downplaying* their role in the negotiations. It had become very evident by the mid-1990s that the high profile role of the *Delors* Commission had been in many instances counterproductive. We should therefore expect that the Commission as a strategic institution would change to a lower-profile public relations strategy, but that it as a rational, "utility-maximising" institution would also attempt to

maintain its actual, behind-the-scenes influence.[4] The *Santer* Commission did follow a lower-profile strategy in its public relations in the IGC,[5] but whether the Commission also played a lesser role in the 1996-97 IGC is a matter for further investigation, of which public statements and interviews from Commission officials are probably not the most reliable sources.[6]

The Sources of Actor Power
The concepts of power and influence, while being central to political science, raise difficult empirical problems. First, any but the simplest definition of power is difficult to measure in practice. Second, as power is in essence a relational possession, it is not enough to show that actor A possesses objective power resources. It must be *proven* that actor A's intended actions had a real effect upon actor B. However, this raises further methodological problems. Actor B can also have acted in *advance* of actor A's actions, *anticipating* these actions and reacting to them before the event, making it almost impossible for an analyst to measure power relationships empirically. With these caveats in mind, two theoretical approaches to actor power will be tested vis-à-vis the 1996-97 IGC.

A Franco-German Core?

Following the hypotheses above, did the outcome of the IGC reflect the preferences of the most powerful actors, e.g. the Franco-German core? Were France and Germany able to act as a regional core, or the "motor" of integration, effectively shaping and controlling the negotiation agenda, pushing proposals in key issue-areas that led to an outcome reflecting Franco-German preferences? We should also expect that small Member States had little influence upon the final outcome. The test of this argumentation will proceed in three steps. The basic preferences of France and Germany will first briefly be canvassed together with the more specific positions taken during the IGC. The next step will be to investigate whether France and Germany did in

---

[4] The European Court of Justice has pursued a similar strategy in the 1990s, toning down public statements while still maintaining its actual level of influence through many pro-integration rulings (see Beach (2001)).

[5] See Petite 1998; Dinan 1997.

[6] In an interview, one Commission official has hinted that the Commission used this strategy in the IGC, talking down in public its role while still playing an influential part in the IGC behind-the-scenes (in Pollack 1999, 14).

fact shape and control the agenda and the negotiations of the IGC. Finally, did the outcome reflect Franco-German preferences and positions?

Preferences and Positions of France and Germany
France's articulated preferences for the IGC were: introduction of some form of flexibility; extensive institutional reforms; no increase in Commission competences in external economic relations; an enhancement of the role of national parliaments; a strengthened *intergovernmental* CFSP which also incorporated the WEU into the EU; and limited reforms of JHA in the field of internal security (European Parliament 1996; European Policy Centre, various issues; Stubb 1998; Le Figaro 20.02.96; Isaksen 1998, 22; Deloche-Gaudez, contribution to this volume).

During the IGC France put forward 29 proposals,[7] with the most central being: a joint Franco-German proposal on flexibility; a "High Representative" for the CFSP; an extensive reduction in the size of the Commission; enhanced security measures in JHA; no extension of Commission competences in external economic relations; the protection of public services; and a "Court-bashing" proposal with specific amendments to the Treaty articles on the ECJ relatively late in the IGC, echoing an earlier British proposal.

Germany's preferences overlapped with the French in some areas, such as flexibility and institutional reforms, but whereas French visions of flexible cooperation tended towards non-exclusive, overlapping, concentric circles, Germany saw some form of "hard core" centred on the Franco-German axis[8] (European Parliament 1996; Stubb 1998). In addition, when it came to specific positions, while France was able to contemplate a drastically reduced Commission potentially *without* a French Commissioner, Germany categorically ruled out a Commission without a German member. Other German preferences dealt with: an increase in EP co-decision and QMV in the Council; giving the Commission increased competences in external economic relations coupled with tighter control mechanisms; a strengthened *supranational* CFSP incorporating the WEU into the EU; and communitarisation of sections of the 3rd pillar, including a "balance of efforts" among Member States regarding receiving refugees and restricting ECJ jurisdiction in JHA (European Parliament 1996; European Policy Centre, various issues; Isaksen 1998, 26; Beuter, contribution to this volume; Beach, 2001).

---

[7] For a partial list and the numbering of the proposals see appendix 1.

[8] These views evolved during the IGC, with France towards the end arguing for a core centred on EMU, whereas German views shifted towards advocating a more open core encompassing all of the willing and able Member States (Stubb 1998, 148).

Germany put forward 39 proposals during the IGC,[9] but upon closer examination most were in peripheral issue-areas such as sport or statistics. The more important German proposals were: the joint Franco-German proposal on flexibility; two proposals on defence co-operation, including plans to integrate the WEU into the EU; and a limited increase in Commission competences in external economic relations together with a long list of exceptions of areas not to be transferred.

The Agenda-Setting Phase – Franco-German Influence?
Both France and Germany wanted the agenda for the IGC to concentrate on a relatively limited number of topics, but were unable to limit the agenda as it developed in the Reflection Group, or the final mandate given to the IGC by the European Council Summit in Turin in March 1996 (Isaksen *et al.* 1998, 22, 26).

The agenda of the IGC, as articulated in the Reflection Group report, dealt with three broad topics: bringing the Union closer to its citizens; institutional reform preparing for enlargement (including flexibility); and strengthening and enlarging the scope of CFSP (Reflection Group 1995). The topic on the "citizen and the Union" contained both discussions on employment, the environment, and JHA issues.

Certain issues such as institutional reform, and the revision of the 2nd and 3rd pillars of the TEU were *automatically* on the agenda due to Articles A, B, and N(2) of the TEU. There were also numerous issues that were put on the agenda by *other Member States* in the agenda-setting phase, such as the environment, employment, fundamental rights, and the British demands for reducing the ECJ's powers.

Turning to the issue of flexibility, the issue had been discussed extensively since the September 1994 Lammers/Schäuble paper, but first came onto the official agenda during the work of the Reflection Group (Stubb 1998). The agenda was further influenced by the broad ideas proposed in the joint Franco-German letter to the Madrid Summit in December 1995, at which time the Reflection Group report was accepted as the basis for the negotiations. However if we look at the *form* of flexibility contained in the Reflection Group report, the Spanish Presidency in the second half of 1995 together with the Council Secretariat was able to influence the form of flexibility discussed, removing the issue of first pillar flexibility temporarily from the agenda, and leading to a report that more closely echoed Spanish positions of strictly limited flexible integration than Franco-German ideas of a form of hard core "motor" of integration (Stubb, contribution to this volume; Dehousse 1999, 8).

---

[9] For a partial list and the numbering of the proposals see appendix 2.

Concluding, there is little evidence that France and Germany effectively controlled either the number of topics on the agenda, or which issues were on the agenda at this stage of the IGC, a point corroborated by participants in the IGC (McDonagh 1998, 37; Stubb 1998,145; Isaksen *et al.* 1998).

The IGC Negotiations – Franco-German Control?
France and Germany attempted to give the impression in public that the Franco-German *entente* was effective during the 1996-97 IGC, providing political leadership to the IGC negotiation process. France and Germany held joint summits prior to European Council meetings, and the French and German foreign ministers held several joint seminars during the IGC. France and Germany presented a joint proposal on flexibility in October 1996 accompanied by a letter from Chirac and Kohl. Prior to the Dublin II Summit in December 1996, Chirac and Kohl also submitted a joint letter, attempting to set the agenda on the reform of the CFSP and JHA, and institutional reforms. What effect did this co-ordination have? Was there a Franco-German core that was able to control the negotiation process and the final outcome of the IGC?

Looking at progress in key issue areas for France and Germany, there were many instances where they were unable to control developments in the negotiations. In central issue-areas it was often small Member States that ended up setting the substantive agenda during the negotiations. While *defence issues* were central to both France and Germany, it was the Swedish/Finnish proposal on the incorporation of the "Petersberg tasks" into the CFSP that effectively set the agenda and the final outcome as regards defence.[10] Franco-German proposals on the incorporation of the WEU into the EU, echoed by many other delegations, stayed on the agenda until the Amsterdam Summit, where it was agreed to disagree, with the decision put off until a future date.[11] Specific proposals dealing with *employment* were put on the table by among others Sweden, Denmark, Belgium, Spain and Austria (see chapters in this volume). Germany was opposed to the issue due to concerns of the financial implications, but only managed to reduce the scope of the provisions in the final Treaty, while also ensuring that references to employment were linked with competitiveness (European Policy Centre, September/October 1996, 11; Petite 1998; Dehousse 1999, 37-38; Duff 1997, 63). France was opposed to the proposed amendments dealing with employment until after the change of government in June 1997.

---

[10] CONF/3832/96.

[11] Article 17 TEU (ex Article J.7).

In the *flexibility* debates, while France and Germany provided political leadership throughout the IGC, they were unable to translate their broad positions into concrete legal texts, leaving this job to the Netherlands' Presidency and the Council Secretariat (see below) (Stubb 1998; Isaksen 1998, 133-146).

The Outcome – the Amsterdam Treaty as the Product of Franco-German Interests?

Comparing the outcome to initial French and German preferences and positions, a general *flexibility* clause was included in the final Treaty, together with specific provisions in the 1st and 3rd pillars (see appendix 3). However in key aspects of the flexibility provisions the Netherlands' Presidency and the Council Secretariat was more influential in shaping the final outcome than France or Germany (Stubb 1998, 212). The Netherlands succeeded in both removing a flexibility clause from the 2nd pillar, and creating a form of flexible integration in the 1st pillar by incorporating the Schengen agreement (ibid.). The Council Secretariat (CS) drafted the conditions that would apply for the use of flexibility (Stubb 1998, 217-219), effectively removing the possibility of a liberal use of flexibility, which was seen by CS officials as a potential threat to the *acquis communautaire* (interview with member of Danish IGC delegation).

In *institutional reforms*, proposals by the Commission were closer to the final outcome than French/German proposals.[12] The decision to put off reforms of the size of the Commission until there are twenty Commissioners was proposed by the Commission in March 1997,[13] and formed the basis for further discussions on the issue (*Agence Europe* 07.04.97, 26.05.97). In contrast, both France and Germany had strongly pushed for a revision of the size of the Commission in the Amsterdam Treaty. If we look at the extension of co-decision, while France was lukewarm/negative towards the extension of EP co-decision, Germany strongly advocated increased co-decision (appendix 3). However, the final outcome on the extension of EP co-decision more closely reflects the proposals from the Commission on the issue[14] (Petite 1998), with the notable exception that certain sensitive areas were excluded due to national demands, for example CAP due to French pressure. Both

---

[12] It must be emphasised here that I am not arguing that this *activity* by the Commission *equals* influence over outcomes, but simply that the final outcome was not a close reflection of Franco/German preferences and positions. The role of the Commission will be further investigated.

[13] CONF/3839/97.

[14] CONF/3882/96.

France and Germany had argued for some extension of QMV in the EC pillar, which did occur. In addition, both succeeded in preventing the extension of QMV to areas that they viewed as "sensitive," such as the CAP for France and employment and taxation for Germany (*Agence Europe* 23.06.97; *Financial Times* 19.06.97, 2; Moravcsik & Nicolaïdis 1999).

Looking at the *CFSP*, QMV was extended, and the Commission was given a minor role (German preferences). French ideas of an independent "High Representative" for CFSP were not adopted in the final Treaty. While a form of flexibility was introduced (constructive abstention), the power of veto was also preserved.[15] In *JHA* a partial communitarisation was achieved (German preferences), with one key indicator of the fulfilment of German demands the restrictions in the jurisdiction of the ECJ in JHA and a "balance of efforts" regarding refugees being envisioned. French proposals on JHA were partially fulfilled regarding the strengthening of the policies remaining in the third pillar, but France was unable to prevent the inclusion of a reference to a "balance of efforts" as regards refugees (see below on the Franco-German "compromise" on JHA).

Neither France nor Germany fared well with their other specific proposals to the IGC (see appendixes 1 and 2). France was successful in proposing certain clarifications to EC competition and state aid rules for public services in the Amsterdam Treaty,[16] and together with Spain and Portugal was able to strengthen policies regarding overseas departments and outermost regions.[17] Other proposals such as the French "Court-bashing" proposal were never even seriously discussed in the IGC. Germany fared even worse viewed in relation to its proposals in the IGC, with central German proposals on defence and external economic relations not ending in the final Treaty (see appendixes 2 and 3).

Conclusion – a Franco-German Core?

There are elements in the Amsterdam Treaty that reflect Franco-German interests, with the Treaty outcome on the whole closer to German preferences than to French. There is little evidence though that the overall outcome of the IGC reflected the preferences of the Franco-German "core," and there are

---

[15] This reflected a Franco-German compromise, in that while Germany favoured QMV, France wanted to preserve some form of "Luxembourg compromise" in CFSP (Nuttall 1997).

[16] Article 16 (Art. 7 D, AT) and Declaration no. 13 (on Article 7 D) (see Dehousse 1999, 41-42. For a contrasting view see Duff 1997, 84-85).

[17] Article 299.2 EC (new subsection of ex Article 227 EC) and Declaration no. 36 (on overseas territories).

many issue-areas where the final outcome diverged significantly from initial Franco-German preferences. Indeed, in many issue-areas such as employment, the environment, and the CFSP, the final Treaty was closer to the preferences of smaller Member States such as Austria, Denmark, Finland, and Sweden (see Tallberg, contribution to this volume). Finally, specific Franco-German proposals to the IGC faired poorly in the IGC.

A realist would argue that the reason for the lack of explanatory power of the theory is that the *issues* under negotiation in the Amsterdam Treaty IGC were *"second order,"* while more important issues such as EMU were not under negotiation within the IGC forum.[18] However contrary to the conventional wisdom, I contend that questions such as the institutional balance between small and large Member States, flexibility, and defence issues should be classified as *"first order"* issues. The question of the institutional balance between small and large Member States is a fundamental problem that plagues most federal-type systems, and for instance in the American Constitutional Convention of 1787 the question of institutional balance almost proved to be the death knell for the fledgling Union. Likewise, in the EU today this question has profound implications for the balance of power between large and small states, and for the effectiveness and legitimacy of the Union. Turning to the other two issues, flexibility can have potentially revolutionary long-term effects upon European integration (if it is ever used), while discussions on EU defence policy strike at the very heart of national sovereignty. While it may not be surprising that little progress was made on such difficult issues in the 1996-97 IGC, the lack of a Franco-German core influencing the debates and outcomes in such key issue-areas is a significant problem for realist theory.

Another problem deals with *negotiation tactics*. There are difficulties in measuring which actor "won" in a negotiation by comparing opening and final positions, thus posing significant problems for realist theories when looking at an IGC negotiation. While one delegation might put forward proposals that are very close to their "real" preferences, other delegations might prefer the more "bombastic" tactic of putting forward "blue sky" proposals that are very far from what it would accept in the final agreement in order to push the outcome closer to their "real" preferences (posturing). We could therefore argue that France put forward proposals and articulated positions that it knew never would be accepted, but that could possibly nudge the agenda closer towards France's "real," more modest positions.

---

[18] Moravcsik and Nicolaïdis echo this position, but argue that their liberal intergovernmentalist theory is still able to explain some of the outcome despite the IGC dealing with many "second order" issues.

Based on realist logic, one interpretation of the lack of French influence over the Amsterdam Treaty IGC outcome could be to argue that the relative power resources of France vis-à-vis Germany had shifted since German reunification, leading to an outcome in the IGC skewed towards German preferences. The discrepancy in power can also have led to the problems in co-ordinating the French and German positions during the IGC, as France as the weaker party would always be wary of being dominated by Germany. This interpretation can potentially explain the decline in French influence that Moravcsik and Nicolaïdis flag as a topic for further scholarly attention (1999, 75). However more idiosyncratic factors specific to the 1996-97 IGC can also explain the lack of Franco-German influence, such as the election of the Socialist government in France on June 1, 1997, and the general contradictory positions of the French during the IGC (Deloche-Gaudez, contribution to this volume).

Finally, there is a substantial methodological problem with the realist approach, in that basing measurements of actor power solely upon outcomes creates in essence a tautological model of power!

Asymmetric Interdependence?
Moravcsik and Nicolaïdis argue that the major bargains in the 1996-97 IGC reflect patterns of Member State preferences and asymmetric interdependence, with agreements constrained by the positions of recalcitrant governments (1999, 73-5). While it is a banal point that the outcome of a negotiation reflects patterns of actor preferences, the theoretically more interesting question is to what degree outcomes reflect patterns of issue-specific dependence. These two questions will be tested in the following vis-à-vis the negotiations of the Amsterdam Treaty.

Relational power is based upon actor dependence upon an agreement. Actor dependence can be defined as the availability to an actor of *alternatives* to agreement, the level of actor *commitment* or *interests* in an agreement, and the level of *control* of the actor's ability to unilaterally achieve its preferred outcome (Habeeb 1988, 19-23). We should therefore expect that actors who have strong interests in a certain issue-area will have strong incentives to offer side payments and issue-linkage to other actors, also using threats of exit and exclusion when credible to decrease the control of other actor's over an outcome. We should also expect that recalcitrant governments are able to skew the outcome towards their preferences, given their high level of issue-specific power due to the unanimity requirement in IGCs. These hypotheses will be tested on two cases. First, did reluctant/recalcitrant governments have significant power during the 1996-97 IGC? Second, did governments that had strong interests and little control of an issue-area achieve their preferences? If so, how was this achieved?

Patterns of Member State Preferences

If we glance at the charts published by the European Policy Centre during the IGC on the preferences of all 15 Member States on a wide variety of issues,[19] the tables show that in the end-game (May 1997) there was near unanimity on issues such as flexibility, increased QMV in the EC pillar, and an increase in the powers of the EP – all issues that made their way into the final Treaty.

Other issues such as restricting the powers of the ECJ in the existing EC Treaty were "no fliers," given that there was a coalition of Member States against any reduction in the ECJ's powers (Beach 2001 – however see below). In contrast, when discussing whether the ECJ would be given unrestricted jurisdiction over the new EC Treaty title on the free movement of persons, a coalition led by Germany was able to restrict the ECJ's jurisdiction, with the pattern of preferences showing that only a few small Member States wanted to give the Court jurisdiction without restrictions in the third pillar (Pijpers & Vanhoonacker 1997, 134-35; Isaksen *et al.* 1998; Beach 2001).

French preferences during the IGC also illustrate the effects of patterns of preferences, in that France despite having strong interests in certain issues, was unable to influence the outcome in these issues as its positions were often too isolated, for example on the reform of the Commission (see McDonagh 1998, 159).

The Power of Reluctant Governments – the United Kingdom and Denmark

Investigating first the most "recalcitrant" government in the IGC,[20] the *United Kingdom* was very influential in several key issue-areas; for example the discussions on WEU integration into the EU. Expressed in theoretical terms, the UK had little interest in the issue, and the UK had a credible and preferred alternative in close NATO co-operation. The UK possessed extensive control over outcomes given the unanimity requirement for Treaty revision, whereas given the lack of consensus among the other Member States due to resistance on the part of the neutral Member States, the advocates of WEU incorporation were unable to use the threat of exclusion against the UK (low level of control). This leads us to expect that the UK would possess extensive relational "power" in the WEU debate, clearly evidenced in the final outcome by the lack of WEU integration into the final Treaty despite the intensive

---

[19] This simple categorisation leaves much to be desired, as it reduces complicated issues such as flexibility to a yes/no answer, preventing us from analysing the more interesting question of what specific *forms* of integration were supported and by whom? To the European Policy Centre's defence, a more detailed chart with a nuanced categorisation would be of a level of complexity approaching the Tower of Babel.

[20] McDonagh uses diplomatic language when he describes the British position in the IGC as "distinctive" (1998, 37).

pressure in the end-game of the IGC from both the Commission and a coalition of Member States including Belgium, France, Germany, Italy, and Spain for an incorporation.

Denmark presents a similar picture in several issue areas, in that the Danish government had few interests in a new Treaty almost immediately after the problematic ratification of the Maastricht Treaty (status quo was valued highly).[21] The Danish government entered the IGC with its hands effectively tied by domestic factors, allowing the Danish government to play a *two-level game*, credibly arguing that unless Danish positions in key areas were fulfilled, Denmark would be unable to ratify the Treaty in the coming referendum (i.e. risk of involuntary defection). The Danish government needed issues that could be used to "sell" the Treaty domestically in the upcoming referendum, and chose to focus on measures combating *unemployment*, strengthening the *environmental* provisions of the Treaty, and on provisions strengthening *transparency* and combating fraud (Laursen, forthcoming; interview with member of Danish IGC delegation).

This Danish "control" over the final outcome, and thereby also power, can be seen in relation to the negotiations of the environmental "guarantee" in Article 95 EC (ex Article 100A). The Danish delegation presented a proposal in September 1996 on the issue, but it gained little interest, as most Member States were uninterested in opening the delicate balance contained in the article (see Irish Presidency paper of 22 October 1996, CONF/3958/96). The Danish delegation was able to resuscitate the proposal in the final weeks of the IGC, playing on the fact that Denmark needed to have "selling" points in order to ratify the final outcome (high level of Danish control) (Isaksen 1998, 69-70; McDonagh 1998, 88-89; Petite 1998). After being debated in the Amsterdam Summit the proposal was included in the final Treaty. In this and the other mentioned issue-areas, Denmark was able to achieve outcomes that were disproportionate to its size due to its possession of relational power.

However playing difficult only works to a certain point, as indicated by the extensive *opt-outs* given to the UK and Denmark. In issue-areas such as the communitarisation of the free movement of persons, a coalition of Member States was unwilling to allow the "laggards" to control progress on the issue, and opted to use exclusion in order to lower British and Danish control over progress in the issue. McDonagh attributes British acceptance of the opt-out instead of vetoing the transferral due to British reluctance to spoil the negotiating environment, making it impossible for the British to achieve satisfactory outcomes in other issue-areas (1998, 178). Provisions for flexible integration should also be seen in this light, although the veto power contained in the provisions dilutes its effect to some extent, precisely as intended by the

---

[21] See Laursen in this volume.

British delegation (Moravcsik & Nicolaïdis 1999, 80; interview with member of Danish IGC delegation). Theoretically, if one is unable to unilaterally control one's ability to achieve preferred outcomes, then one can change the structure of the game by lowering the ability of *other* actors to control outcomes in the issue in question.

Interestingly, it can be claimed that *exclusion* was actually *in Danish (elite) interests*, as exclusion can lead to *negative policy externalities* for Denmark. This paradox can be explained by the difficulties of ratifying new integration measures in Denmark due to the Euro-sceptical Danish population. If Denmark had chosen to opt-in to the agreement on the communitarisation of the free movement of persons, this would have required that the Danish "exception" on supranational JHA co-operation from Edinburgh would have to be overturned in a public referendum, most likely coupled with the referendum on the Amsterdam Treaty. This linkage would have been very risky for the government, with a "no" the probable result of the referendum![22] In contrast, by being excluded from the supranational new JHA policies there will almost certainly be negative policy externalities for Denmark over time.[23] These negative externalities can then be used by the government domestically to convince voters over time that it would be best for Denmark to get rid of its exemption on supranational JHA policies – a classic *two-level game* logic.[24]

Strong Member State Interests – JHA Communitarisation and Flexibility
Turning to cases where Member States were very dependent upon agreement in an issue-area, one obvious example is Germany and the communitarisation of immigration and asylum policies. Germany had very strong interests in the issue[25] and few alternatives to agreement, leading us to expect low German power in the issue-area. We should expect that Germany would give side-

---

[22] The Danish government had promised before the IGC that the Edinburgh exceptions would remain in place "before, during, and after the IGC." Opinion polls since 1993 have shown a majority in favour of preserving the JHA exception (Heurlin *et al.* 1999).

[23] Either real quantifiable effects, or even more likely as perceived by politicians and governmental officials who have incentives to "overstate" the impact of the negative policy externalities for Denmark.

[24] A similar strategy was used to attempt to convince Danish voters to vote "yes" to joining the third stage of EMU in the referendum held on September 28, 2000, arguing that by opting-out, the Danes lost "influence" in the EU.

[25] German interests in a "balance of efforts" as regards refugees are clearly indicated by the large share of refugees that it receives in comparison to other EU states. The figures for 1995 were: Germany = 128,000 refugees, France = 20,000, UK = 55,000, the Netherlands = 29,000, and Denmark = 5,000 (Eurostat 1997, 84).

payments and issue-linkages in this issue, and use threats of exclusion and exit where credible.

A majority of Member States supported the communitarisation of parts of the 3rd pillar, including Germany, Italy, the Netherlands, and Spain (European Policy Centre, May/June 1997, 10-11; McDonagh 1998, 168; European Parliament 1996). Once it became clear that the "laggards" would accept exclusion (UK, Ireland and Denmark), the discussions focused on whether the new EC Treaty title should be fully or only partially communitarised (McDonagh 1998, 178). France argued against full communitarisation, envisioning a strengthening of JHA but with exceptions from normal EC co-operation such as the right of initiative for Member States (pillar 1bis solution) (Isaksen *et al.* 1998, 104).

While there are indications that France opposed the communitarisation of the free movement of persons,[26] it also appears that the issue was of lesser importance to France,[27] with the only French "sticking points" being preventing a strong role for supranational institutions in the new Treaty title (Menon 1996, 231; European Policy Centre, March/April 1996, 17-18; *Agence Europe* 16.06.97). France therefore indicated that it would be satisfied with issue-linkage and side-payments in return for accepting a form of communitarisation.

Regarding issue-linkage, France created a *linkage* between communitarisation and a strengthening of the existing measures in the third pillar regarding the fight against crime, arguing even for a formal linkage of the two issues in the Treaty (*Agence Europe*, 01.02.97, 07.02.97, 03.03.97, 16.06.97). Chirac at the Amsterdam Summit while discussing communitarisation of certain JHA issues explicitly indicated the "price" of the *side-payment* for French acceptance by publicly "recalling" the importance to France of two points: the seat of the EP in Strasbourg, and the recognition of the "specific nature of our Overseas Territories" (*Agence Europe* 16.06.97). In the Amsterdam Treaty a protocol was included guaranteeing EP meetings in Strasbourg together with a strengthening of measures dealing with overseas territories (especially amendments to Article 299 EC (ex Article 227)).

It must be pointed out in connection with the above that Germany proved not to be a unitary actor in the JHA issue. In the end-game of the IGC, under domestic pressure from the *Länder* governments, the German position became more cautious regarding communitarisation, with Kohl arguing for communitarisation but with unanimous voting in all areas except visas (*Agence Europe* 16.06.97, 18.06.97; Petite 1998; Dehousse 1999, 30-31).

---

[26] See European Policy Centre, "The IGC State of Play," and *Agence Europe*, 16.02.97.

[27] Substantiating Moravcsik's point that governments concede only where they have little at stake.

The negotiations of flexibility can also be partially explained using asymmetric interdependence theory. Both Germany and France had a high level of power in this issue, given that they possessed credible alternatives,[28] as they could simply take Franco-German co-operation outside of the Treaty framework, a fact which they stated publicly (*Agence Europe* 01.02.97). Given their overall structural power when working together, and the credibility of the threat of exit, the two delegations possessed a high level of control regarding flexibility. Not surprisingly, flexibility made its way into the Treaty. But as also predicted by asymmetric interdependence theory, reluctant governments were able to control outcomes to some extent given the need for unanimous agreement. The UK proposed the inclusion of veto power, while the Netherlands' Presidency removed flexibility from the 2nd pillar (Stubb 1998, 268; Dehousse 1999, 5-6). However, in contrast to asymmetric interdependence theory, it is questionable whether these two governments would have been able to partially "control" the outcome if the French and Germans had managed to submit a detailed draft text proposal to the IGC.

Conclusion – Patterns of Preferences and Asymmetric Interdependence?
Evidence seems to corroborate significant elements of the asymmetric interdependence thesis, but there are several empirical puzzles that are more difficult to explain using the theory. There were several instances where outcomes do not only reflect patterns of preferences and relative power, but also reflect idiosyncratic bargaining dynamics.

In contrast to many accounts of the negotiations on Commission competences in external economic relations (Article 133 EC (ex Article 113)), it can be argued that France's acceptance *in principle* in the Amsterdam Treaty that the Commission could be given negotiation competences in services and intellectual property is a paradox. The ECJ ruling in Opinion 1/94 on Commission competences clearly supported the French position that the Commission does not have implicit negotiating competences in most policy-areas of services and intellectual property (see Emiliou 1996; Bourgeois 1995). This clear legal precedent can be interpreted as giving France a very strong "alternative" to further integration in the issue-area. France also had strong ideological interests in preventing the extension of Commission competences (Meunier & Nicolaïdis 1998, 10). In addition, France was backed by a coalition of Member States, including the UK, Denmark, and partially by

---

[28] The importance of credibility is underlined by the failure of the Spanish delegation to use the threat of exit in the end-game of the IGC. The Spanish stated that unless an immediate reweighting of Council votes was included in the final Treaty text, they would not sign the Treaty (*Agence Europe* 07.04.97). These threats were ignored by other Member States.

Germany[29] (Meunier & Nicolaïdis 1999, 494). Given what can be interpreted as a very high level of French power in the issue, why did France accept even *in principle* that the Commission's competences could be extended to services and intellectual property? Sources within the Council Secretariat point out that the issue was extensively debated in the end-game of the IGC, and that on the last day bargaining fatigue set in, leading the French to "give in" to other delegations, and accept the transferral of competences in principle (Article 133(5) EC (ex Article 113 as amended by the AT)). Deloche-Gaudez attributes the slight change in the French stance to the change of government in June 1997, removing Alain Juppé, who had strongly opposed Commission powers given his experience with the Uruguay Round (contribution to this volume).

The relative decline in French influence in the IGC can also potentially be explained by looking more closely at bargaining dynamics instead of exclusively focusing on relative power and patterns of preferences. It can be argued that France used poor negotiating tactics during the IGC, with the French delegation often split, proposing contradictory positions on several issues (Dehousse 1999, 27, 37; *Financial Times* 16.12.96, 15). For example in JHA reforms France argued against a role for the Commission, while at the same time advocating majority voting (Petite 1998; Menon 1996, 231).

There were also differences in negotiation dynamics depending upon whether the issue was perceived as a "legitimate" subject for reform or not. The proposals by the UK and France to "curb" the Court were never seriously discussed despite tacit support from several core Member States, something that cannot *fully* be explained based upon the presence of a small blocking coalition of pro-integration Member States. It can be argued that the lack of debate on the ECJ was also due to two additional factors.

First, it is evident that politicians do not always "understand" legal politics in the same way that they understand more political questions such as battles for competences between the Council and Commission (interviews with Danish and British civil servants).

Second, and more importantly, curbing the powers of the Court is widely perceived to be "improper" and even "illegitimate," going against notions of the "rule of law." It is of course perfectly legitimate for a legislature or constitutional assembly to amend either primary or secondary legislation to "reverse" unwanted rulings, but to actually curb the *powers* of a court is widely perceived as illegitimate and improper (Alter 1996; Beach 2001). Over time a normative "hard legal core" has developed in the EU that protects the

---

[29] Germany, while supporting some extension of Commission competences, was also interested in preventing a universal extension of Commission competences to a long list of perceived sensitive sectors (see CONF/3912/97).

ECJ from attempts by the Member States to curb its powers (Shaw 2000, 297). During the IGC Spain's Personal Representative to the IGC, Javier Elorza, for example characterised the Court-bashing proposals as "dangerous" (*Agence Europe* 27.02.97). The political "incorrectness" of anti-Court sentiments is also reflected in national position papers published prior to the IGC, where only the UK came out strongly for curbing the Court (see for example European Policy Centre, "The IGC State of Play," various issues).

The Role of Supranational Actors?
How can the influence of supranational actors in IGC negotiations be measured given their lack of formal powers in an IGC?[30] As argued by Pollack, *activity* does not equal *influence* (1999). It is therefore necessary to prove that supranational actors had a significant causal impact on the negotiations, performing functions that would otherwise not have been performed, thereby changing outcomes.

A test of the two competing sets of hypotheses will be undertaken in three steps. First, a key assumption of supranational entrepreneur theory is that Member States possess imperfect information and are unclear about their own preferences. Was this the case in the 1996-97 IGC? Second, were supranational actors able to exploit "policy windows," identifying key problems, brokering compromises between Member States, and putting forward "unique" proposals? Finally, did supranational actors provide "focal points" either during the agenda-setting phase, or during the IGC itself, around which the behaviour of Member States converged? In the following the role of the Commission will be investigated as regards exploiting policy windows, whereas the role of the ECJ will be investigated regarding focal points.

There are many methodological problems involved in assessing the influence of the Commission in proposing solutions and mediating compromises. First, the Commission has "friends" among the (smaller) Member States, and often uses other delegations to put forward proposals and suggestions, making it difficult to discern the actual influence of the Commission. In addition, there is also the subtle but potentially very important role played by the Commission in assisting Presidencies, especially in drafting

---

[30] The only formal roles given to supranational institutions under Article 48 TEU (ex Article N TEU) are: the ability of the Commission to suggest that an IGC be called (must be accepted by the Council); the Commission is entitled to submit opinions before and during an IGC; and the EP must be heard before the start of the IGC. Additionally, supranational authorities do not have assent power over the decision to start an IGC or over the final outcome (Treaty revision), and their opinions are not binding upon Member States prior to or during the IGC.

Treaty texts.[31] Unfortunately, these subtle effects are very difficult if not impossible to measure empirically.

The Role of Information During the 1996-97 IGC
Most accounts agree that the 1996-97 IGC was conducted in a very information-rich environment (McDonagh 1998; Pollack 1999; Moravcsik & Nicolaïdis 1999). Work in the Reflection Group forced Member States to formulate positions on issues that were not solved by the Maastricht Treaty (McDonagh 1998, 48). During the negotiations there was "no shortage of proposals and papers from national delegations" (Ibid. 206). The basic preferences of the Member States also appear to have been relatively stable during the IGC (Moravcsik & Nicolaïdis 1999), although there were significant exceptions to this in policy areas such as flexibility (Stubb 1998, 172-173, 202-203, 208, 224). These factors led Pollack to conclude that "...the opportunities for entrepreneurial agenda-setting by supranational organizations were correspondingly weak." (Pollack 1999, 13). However if we lower the level of aggregation of the analysis and look beyond general positions towards the actual drafting of texts at the technical level of the negotiations, there are indications that at this level the possession of detailed information was skewed towards the Commission and the Council Secretariat (see Stubb, contribution to this volume; Christiansen & Jørgensen 1998, 445). In addition, both Ireland and the Netherlands as small states did not possess the analytical apparatus that a large Member State has. During their Presidencies they were therefore more dependent upon the technical expertise of both the Commission and the Council Secretariat.[32] Finally, contrary to the predictions of liberal intergovernmentalism, during the IGC Member States often did not have *detailed* positions on the myriad of issues in the IGC (on flexibility, see Stubb, contribution to this volume; 1998, 208).

Was the Commission Able to Exploit "Policy Windows" During the IGC?
Despite the relatively information-rich environment, was the Commission able to perform a unique function of identifying problems (demand for integration) and proposing solutions (supply of integration) that enabled it to influence the

---

[31] Christiansen and Jørgensen argue that during the Dutch Presidency, the Commission was able to assist in the demanding task of preparing a draft Treaty, influencing "disproportionately" the final shape of the Treaty (1998, 449). However in their otherwise well-argued article they do not go into details about where the Commission's fingerprints can be seen, leaving us with a plausible claim without any substantive empirical evidence.

[32] On Ireland, see McDonagh 1998. On the Netherlands' Presidency see Christiansen & Jørgensen 1998, 449.

outcome of the IGC? Was the Commission able to mediate compromises between Member States, skewing outcomes towards Commission preferences?

The decision to call the 1996-97 IGC was based of the terms of the TEU, which called for a revision of the provisions of the Treaty in 1996. In contrast, previous IGCs had been called because of the "demand" for integration. In addition, as the agenda was partially set by the TEU the pre-IGC phase was not a fluid situation where there were many unidentified problems and only vague conceptions of what solutions were appropriate. This had been the case prior to the TEU IGC, giving supranational entrepreneurship opportunities to identify problems and propose solutions.

The impact of the Commission on the agenda-setting work of the Group of Representatives is difficult to discern. McDonagh argues that in the Group the Commission played an important role in "highlighting the broader picture and the common interest" (1998, 39). The appointment of the Spanish Commissioner Oreja to represent the Commission in the Reflection Group should not be discounted either, as there are indications that he was able to influence the Spanish Presidency in the second half of 1995 during the final agenda-setting phase prior to the submission of the Reflection Group Report to the Madrid Summit in December 1995 (Dinan 1997, 209).

The Commission's Opinion prior to the start of the IGC does not appear to have highlighted any significant "problems" that were not already raised in the Reflection Group Report or the national position papers prior to the start of the IGC (Commission 1996). The Opinion did however propose "solutions" to certain problems that were able to gain the support of a winning coalition of Member States. Examples include the Commission's proposal regarding the scope of co-decision, reforms of the Commission, and voting weights in the Council. However while it can be argued that these proposals shifted outcomes, it can also be submitted that the Commission had merely canvassed the views of the Member States during the working of the Reflection Group, and in the Opinion presented proposals that were in the median of the distribution of Member State preferences – classic anticipatory behaviour (Pollack 1999, 14).

If we turn to the Commission's strategy during the IGC, the Commission had "learned" from its mistakes in the TEU IGC, and played a more low-profile, pragmatic role in the 1996-97 IGC (Dinan 1997, 193; Christiansen & Jørgensen 1998, 443-444). As argued above, this does not however mean that the Commission necessarily was less interested in shaping the outcome of the IGC; simply that the Commission as a strategic institution attempted to choose a strategy that best allowed it to achieve its goal. In the following we will investigate three issue-areas that were central to the Commission during the IGC negotiations: JHA, institutional reforms, and an increase in Commission competences under Article 133 EC (ex Article 113).

The Commission concentrated much of its efforts on the communitarisation of selected areas of *JHA* (Petite 1998). However comparing the outcome with both the Commission's Opinion from February 1996 and the Commission proposals on JHA[33] shows significant differences, such as the scope of the communitarisation of JHA, the decision-making mechanisms to be used within the new EC Title, and the role of the Commission. There are also few indications that the Commission in JHA was able to propose significant solutions to problems or broker compromises (for one minor example see Moravcsik & Nicolaïdis 1999, 72). However the Commission's positions on a partial "communitarisation" of the 3rd pillar did end up in the final Treaty (Christiansen & Jørgensen 1998, 449).

Turning to *institutional reforms*, it was argued above that certain outcomes were close to the proposals by the Commission.[34] The Commission proposal on the size of the Commission[35] formed the basis for further discussions on the issue, leading to the decision to postpone the debate on the size of the Commission until there are over twenty Commissioners (*Agence Europe* 07.04.97, 26.05.97; Isaksen *et al.* 1998, 123).[36] Similarly, the formula for deciding which types of EC acts are legislative, and therefore should be adopted by EP co-decision, closely reflects the proposals from the Commission.[37] There are indications that the debate in the Personal Representatives' Group, together with the texts produced by the Netherlands' Presidency on co-decision, centred on the Commission's proposal.

Moravcsik and Nicolaïdis question the Commission's influence as regards the extension of co-decision. They point out that the policy-areas that the Commission had selected in its proposal for co-decision and the final Treaty text were negatively "correlated" (1999, 70-71). While it cannot be denied that in the end-game many Member States removed certain sensitive issue-areas such as CAP and taxation from the list, this misses the point. The argument

---

[33] See CONF/3912/96 and CONF/3817/97. The latter also suggests that Schengen be incorporated into the 1st pillar.

[34] In other areas of institutional reforms, such as the extension of QMV, Commission proposals fared very poorly (see CONF/3860/97).

[35] CONF/3839/97.

[36] Prior to the Dublin I Summit in October 1996, Chancellor Kohl suggested the possibility of a Maastricht III IGC to settle institutional issues not solved by "Maastricht II," but at the actual Dublin Summit Kohl pointed out that he had been discussing institutional issues *not* on the current IGC agenda (*Agence Europe* 04.10.96; European Policy Centre, September/October 1996, 15).

[37] CONF/3882/96.

here is that the Commission's formula supplied the winning *solution* to the problem of determining a formula for which issue-areas should come under co-decision. Whether the Member States would have been able to find a similar formula without Commission intervention is of course speculative, but given the Commission's role both as "guardian" of the Treaties and as an "honest broker" during the negotiations, it seems plausible that a similar proposal from a national delegation would not have been treated in the same manner, i.e. the Commission supplied a "unique" solution to the problem.

Finally, regarding *external economic relations*, the Commission put the issue on the agenda following the ECJ ruling in Opinion 1/94 (see below), submitting a "solution" to the perceived problem of the lack of effectiveness of the EC in international trade negotiations. The Commission's solution was a draft Treaty article which would give the Commission exclusive competences in services and intellectual property negotiations,[38] later echoed in the proposed draft Treaty articles by the Dutch Presidency.[39] During the IGC the Commission supported by the Irish and Dutch Presidencies kept the issue on the negotiating agenda (McDonagh 1998, 120-122). In the end the final outcome did not follow the Commission proposal, but the final amendments to Article 133 EC (ex Article 113) in the Amsterdam Treaty are not what many observers make them out to be (e.g., Meunier & Nicolaïdis 1998, 1999) (see above). While the Commission might have lost the battle regarding negotiating competences, and pulled back its support for the German position of a transferral of competences together with an extensive list of exceptions (see Gray, contribution to this volume), the Commission may have won the long-term war, as the Member States accepted in Amsterdam that the Commission has *in principle* negotiating competence in services and intellectual property. This principle acceptance by the Member States then influenced the debates in the 2000 IGC, with the result that Commission negotiating competences have been significantly extended in the Nice Treaty to trade in services and intellectual property with certain restrictions.

Conclusion – Role of the Commission
The conditions for supranational entrepreneurship were relatively poor in the 1996-97 IGC, given that: much of the agenda was already set by the TEU, there was a relatively information-rich environment, and the external environment was not as labile as in the 1990-91 IGC. Despite this, there is some evidence showing that the Commission did have some impact on the

---

[38] CONF/3890/96.

[39] CONF/3834/97.

agenda-setting phase of the IGC, influencing the content of the debates in certain issue-areas.

The negotiation of three issues in the IGC were then looked at, where it was found that the Commission did provide "solutions" (proposals) to several problems faced by Member States, and that these were "unique" and "successful" in issues such as the formula for which issues should come under the co-decision procedure. In other issues such as the reweighting of Council voting and the reduction in the size of the Commission, the Commission proposals formed the debates, leading to the eventual postponement of the issue.[40] However there were also many areas where Commission proposals fared poorly, such as in JHA.[41]

If we lower the level of analysis and investigate the often overlooked technical level, there are indications that the Commission (together with the Council Secretariat) possessed detailed knowledge that especially the Irish and Dutch Presidencies were dependent upon, enabling the Commission and the Council Secretariat to influence debates over issues such as flexibility (Stubb, contribution to this volume).

Did Supranational Actors Provide "Focal Points" Before or During the IGC?
Did the ECJ provide "*focal points*" prior to the IGC around which the behaviour of actors converged, making policy choices restricted and particular outcomes more likely? While the ECJ played no formal role in the IGC, and while the ECJ's report to the IGC was never seriously discussed,[42] the Court, through its judgements, did influence the IGC agenda and outcome in several significant policy areas. Rulings influence IGCs either positively by forming a basis for future interaction, or negatively by spurring Member States to try to reverse the perceived negative effects of a ruling.[43]

The best example of the effects of ECJ rulings is provided by the *Kalanke* ruling (C-450/93). Briefly, the case involved a reference from a German court

---

[40] The Commission was also able to influence the debates on flexibility, ensuring with the backing of several small Member States that the Commission was entrusted with a key role in initiating flexible co-operation (interview with Danish IGC participant).

[41] The lack of overall influence of the Commission in the IGC is corroborated by Dehousse (1999, 9).

[42] In the Reflection Group Report it is diplomatically put that "The Group has not been able to deepen the valuable ideas put forward by the Court in its report." (Reflection Group 1995, 38) (European Court of Justice 1995).

[43] It must be emphasised that in contrast to Garrett and Weingast, I do not argue that the rulings of the ECJ necessarily follow the preferences of a majority (or even minority) of Member States – a point clearly indicated by the *Kalanke* ruling.

618 *Derek Beach*

on whether certain provisions for positive action on the behalf of women in a Bremen law were legal under EC law. The ECJ held in October 1995 that the Bremen positive action system was not permissible under EC law. However the sparse reasoning of the judgement raised the question of whether *any* form of positive action programmes was legal under existing EC law, provoking a severe political response from the European Parliament, the Commission, several Member States, and key lobby groups.

There were two major effects of the *Kalanke* ruling. First, it fed into German views about the ECJ, increasing its resistance to applying the preliminary ruling procedure within JHA. Second, the ruling led to demands from the Commission and the European Parliament, supported by several Member States together with interest groups,[44] to amend the Treaty in order to make is easier for Member States to adopt measures providing for "specific advantages" for the underrepresented sex (*Agence Europe* 13.01.96, 18.10.96, 18.04.97, 06.06.97; European Parliament 1996). Sweden submitted a proposal to the IGC in September 1996 for an amendment to the Treaty articles on equality,[45] which served as the basis for further negotiations, ending in the introduction of a new paragraph to Article 141 EC (ex Article 119 EC) specifically allowing Member States to introduce measures providing for specific advantages for the underrepresented sex.

This is a clear example of the ECJ providing a "negative" focal point, where Member State preferences converged on an issue in reaction to an unwanted and unanticipated ECJ ruling. This led to an amendment of the EC Treaty that otherwise most likely would not have been undertaken, in that prior to the *Kalanke* ruling, there were few indications that positive discrimination would be an issue in the 1996-97 IGC. There are also other examples of negative focal points provided by the ECJ prior to the 1996-97 IGC, such as in public broadcasting, where unintended ECJ rulings led Belgium to put forward successful proposals on public service broadcasting (see Dehousse 1999, 40-43; Petite 1998).

While it can be argued that issue-areas such as positive discrimination and public services were relatively peripheral to the IGC negotiations, Commission competences in external economic relations were certainly not. The question of EC contra Member State competences deals with one of the fundamental questions in European integration; namely the division of powers between the EC and the Member States.

---

[44] The European Women's Lobby in its March 1996 position paper on the IGC called for a revision of Article 141 EC (ex Article 119) to reverse the effects of *Kalanke* (European Women's Lobby 1996).

[45] CONF/3898/96. Other similar proposals came from Austria, Belgium and Finland (CONF/3843/97, CONF/3998/97, and CONF/3907/97).

The Commission after the dramatic end-game of the WTO negotiations had referred a question to the ECJ on whether the Commission had exclusive negotiating competences under Article 133 EC (ex Article 113) in services and intellectual property. The ECJ ruled in the *WTO case* (Opinion 1/94) that the Member States retained competences within these policy-areas, with the exceptions of sectors where a harmonised internal EC policy had already been adopted.

The ECJ ruling provided a focal point for the subsequent behaviour of both the Commission and several Member States during the IGC, effectively setting the negotiating agenda as regards external economic relations. The Commission regarded that it was necessary to amend the Treaty to change the ruling in order for the EC to be able to act effectively in international trade negotiations, whereas "sovereignty protecting" Member States such as France and the UK sought to preserve the effects of the ECJ's ruling by resisting revision of Article 133 EC (ex Article 113) (see above). Whether the issue would have arisen without the ECJ ruling can be debated, but had the Commission not raised the case before the ECJ it is probable that the bargaining dynamics of the issue in the IGC would have been different. It is too speculative to comment on what the outcome of the negotiations might have been without the ECJ ruling.

Conclusion – Focal Points
ECJ rulings do not automatically place issues on the agenda, nor do they determine the final outcome of a negotiation. However ECJ rulings did provide focal points around which actor demands converged, leading to a shift in outcomes that demonstrates the autonomous effects of supranational actors upon the negotiation process. This was evident as regards both the *Kalanke* ruling, the series of ECJ rulings in the early 1990s that questioned the protection of public services, and in the *WTO* case (Opinion 1/94).

Conclusion

The negotiation process mattered in translating national preferences into the final Treaty revisions in the Amsterdam Treaty IGC. Two theoretical questions were investigated regarding the IGC negotiations in an attempt to discern more precisely some of the key independent variables that determined how preferences were translated into outcomes in the negotiations. First, what determined actor power during the IGC? Second, did supranational actors play any role in the negotiations?

Actor Power – Asymmetric Interdependence with Anomalies?
There was little evidence of a Franco-German core that was able to shape the agenda and control the final outcome of the IGC. French and German proposals fared poorly in the IGC, and overall the final outcome did not reflect a convergence of Franco-German preferences. In many respects, both the agenda and the final outcome more closely reflected the preferences of smaller Member States such as Denmark in key issue-areas. The Franco-German proposal on flexibility was incorporated in the final Amsterdam Treaty, but in a form that did not fully reflect Franco-German preferences.

Hypotheses on asymmetric interdependence provided a better explanation in the issue-areas in which it was tested. Reluctant Member States such as Denmark and the United Kingdom were able to skew outcomes towards their preferences in several issue-areas. At the same time, the use of extensive opt-outs and the introduction of flexibility also substantiated the hypothesis that other governments will attempt to exclude reluctant Member States in order to lower the ability of reluctant governments to "control" outcomes. It was also found, somewhat paradoxically, that the "threat" of exclusion can be both negative and positive, in that governments can in selected circumstances actually have incentives to be excluded, allowing them to use the negative policy externalities of exclusion domestically to further their own interests.

However there were also anomalies that were more difficult to explain. Why did France accept even in principle that the Commission could be given negotiating competences in services and intellectual property? To explain this we have to delve down into the actual bargaining situation, as it is difficult to explain by only looking at patterns of preferences and relative power (see above). In addition, the theory cannot explain why certain issues never even were seriously discussed, such as curbing the powers of the ECJ. There was a large coalition of Member States interested in reducing the powers of the Court, especially as regards the retroactivity of judgements and financial liability (Tallberg 2000, 112-115). However these demands were never seriously on the negotiating agenda, an omission that is difficult to explain by looking exclusively at patterns of preferences and relative power.

The Role of Supranational Actors – Behind-the-Scenes Influence and Focal Points?
The question of the significance of supranational actors was investigated by looking at the role of the Commission prior to and during the IGC, and the effects of the ECJ's rulings prior to the IGC.

Looking at the Commission, the evidence shows that the "conditions" for supranational entrepreneurship were relatively poor in the run-up to the IGC. There is though some evidence showing that the Commission did have some impact on the agenda-setting phase of the IGC, influencing the content of the debates in certain issue-areas. During the IGC itself, the Commission played a low-profile but not necessarily less influential role. Several of its proposals proved to be in the median of Member State preferences, but it is difficult to discern whether Member State preferences converged on the Commission proposals or vice versa. There is little evidence substantiating whether the Commission was able to play a key brokering or mediating role in major policy-areas except in a few isolated cases. Where the Commission was more important, but where it is also more difficult to measure, is the subtle influence gained from technical assistance to Presidencies in drafting of Treaty texts (see e.g. McDonagh 1998, 77, 209; Stubb 1998). Available evidence however seems to point towards the Council Secretariat playing a larger role than the Commission as a form of supranational entrepreneur due to the possession of technical knowledge in selected issue-areas.[46]

The role of the ECJ was easier to discern, with several ECJ rulings clearly acting as focal points around which the behaviour of both Member State and EC institutions converged. Both the *Kalanke* ruling and the *WTO* opinion spurred Treaty revision, and it can be plausibly argued in both cases that the outcome would not have been the same had there not been an ECJ ruling (focal point) prior to the IGC.

Some Tentative Thoughts on How to Move Theory Forwards
Where do we stand? In the above analysis it is evident that while Moravcsik's asymmetric interdependence model of integration[47] can explain many aspects of the 1996-97 IGC, reality is not as simple as his rational, state-centred theory leads us to believe.

Supranational actors do play a role, bargaining dynamics make a difference, and not all issues have the same logic. Non-governmental actors such as the ECJ, the Commission and the Council Secretariat played an important, if arguably secondary role in determining outcomes. Bargaining factors such as the coherence and timing of proposals play an important role in their success. The effects of bargaining dynamics were clearly seen in the significance of the lack of concrete proposals from France and Germany on flexibility, giving other delegations increased influence over the outcome. In addition, given the unique bargaining dynamics of every negotiation, we should *not* expect that if an IGC is "rerun" that the same outcomes will be achieved in the myriad of different issues under negotiation. Finally, some issues are more "legitimate" than others, as was seen in the example of the demands for "curbing" the powers of the ECJ.

---

[46] For examples in flexibility – see Stubb, 1998, 155, 192-193, 209, 217-218.

[47] Liberal intergovernmentalism.

How can we incorporate these factors into a model where integration is still viewed as demand-driven, and where outcomes are primarily determined by relative power? One method would be to simply *loosen the assumption of governmental rationality*, arguing that governments are not "always" in charge in an IGC. While governments dominate in settings such as European Council Summits, there are many indications that when we look closer at details, other actors such as the Council Secretariat and the Commission are very influential at the technical level. One does not have to agree with Stubb's view that 95% of the decisions in an IGC are taken at this level to see that this is a very important source of leverage for non-governmental actors (Stubb 1998, 17).[48]

By loosening the assumption of rationality and near-perfect information, we can partially account for the role of the Commission, ECJ, and Council Secretariat in the negotiations. Non-governmental actors are able to influence the agenda by for example providing technical knowledge and focal points, and in certain situations are also able to put forward unique, successful proposals to an IGC (e.g. the Commission's 1985 White Paper on the Internal Market). For example, Commission officials often possess a higher level of information about the day-to-day functioning of Treaty articles and the potential consequences of amendments than many of the national officials negotiating in an IGC, especially those from small Member States. This technical knowledge can be translated into influence over outcomes if used skilfully by the Commission to subtly push the debate towards their preferred outcomes (interview with member of Danish IGC delegation).

There is however still very little in-depth empirical material available on the *actual* negotiation process of IGCs. This scarcity of data is especially glaring as regards the role of the Council Secretariat in IGCs. There are many indications that the Council Secretariat can be very influential during an IGC, but there are many unanswered questions such as *how influential* it is, under *what conditions*, and even the basic question of *whose interests* the Council Secretariat promotes in an IGC?[49]

Bargaining dynamics should be more thoroughly incorporated into a model of IGC negotiation, creating a model that does not a priori assume "efficient" outcomes. The actual drafting process of the Treaty text is important, with one example the dilemma of whether it is best to submit specific or general proposals, and at what time in the negotiations. While a specific text submitted either too early or late to an IGC risks being ignored, a general text allows

---

[48] See also on this McDonagh 1998, 206-210.

[49] While the Council Secretariat's official function is to service the Council and Presidencies, it is not self-evident whether the Secretariat serves: the interests of large or small Member States; what it *perceives* as the "general interest" of the Member States; and/or its own institutional interests (see e.g. Stubb 1998, 217-218).

other actors to tailor the contents to their own preferences, sometimes transmogrifying the proposal into something that was not intended (as happened in flexibility). In a recent book on the 1996-97 IGC, several Danish civil servants have pointed out that a very well-prepared specific text submitted shortly before a draft Treaty text from a Presidency is prepared has a good chance of "success" (Isaksen *et al.* 1998, 57-58). Personalities obviously also matter in negotiations, as was clearly seen in the partial breakdown of the Franco-German axis following the election of Chirac in 1995. The level of preparedness and coherence of delegation positions should not be underestimated either, with one prominent cause of the relative weakness of the French during the 1996-97 IGC the incoherent and ill-prepared positions of the French delegation. The role of brokering and mediation by the Presidency and/or the Commission should not be ruled out either.

The truth is that those of us who have not actually sat around an IGC negotiating table do not know that much about the *internal* dynamics of IGC negotiations. In research for this chapter I only found one cursory, non-empirical study by Lodge (1998) on the subject. None of the "kiss-and-tell" reports about the 1996-97 IGC *detail* the bargaining dynamics of the IGC.[50] On questions such as whether there are wide discrepancies between *stated* and *real* national positions during IGCs, the answer is that there is little data available on the subject, and no systematic investigations have been undertaken. While it can be plausibly argued that the credibility of submitting "blue sky" proposals is lower in a setting such as an IGC, given its iterated nature, where the participants know each other well both through contacts in general EU business and through repeated participation in IGCs, the answer to the question is that we just do not know.

A final modification to existing theory should be the creation of a *more inclusive definition of state interests and preferences*, including *ideology* and the *role of norms*. Moravcsik's theory focuses on instrumental state interests, but he acknowledges that there are sometimes exceptions where governments also have ideological-based preferences (but only in "second-order" issues!) (1998, 1999 with Nicolaïdis). One example was French resistance to the role of the Commission in the free movement of persons, which is difficult to explain based upon instrumental French interests, as the French also argued simultaneously for an *increase* in the effectiveness in JHA including an increase in QMV voting! Turning to the role of norms, there is evidence that over time national actors begin to perceive EC law and the EC legal system as a form of law analogous to domestic law. This provides the EC legal system

---

[50] Stubb's excellent 1998 dissertation is perhaps a notable exception, but unfortunately he only describes the bargaining dynamics within the issue of flexibility. Whether these can be generalised to the whole IGC is an open question.

with a normative dimension, where concerns such as the "rule of law" make behavioural claims upon actors. Corresponding to what would happen in a similar situation in a domestic legal system, attempts by the political authorities to sanction the ECJ due to unwanted jurisprudence were viewed by many actors in the 1996-97 IGC as "illegitimate" and against the "rule of law."

Moravcsik has shown the way forward with *The Choice for Europe*, but as I have indicated in this chapter, Moravcsik has not closed the book on what factors determine the outcome of an IGC. What we now need is a further fresh infusion of data to move theory forward, looking in detail at the actual bargaining dynamics of an IGC, and the influence of non-governmental actors such as the Council Secretariat and the Commission at the technical level. This research should enable us to give more qualified answers to questions such as who "wins" in an IGC negotiation and why.

Appendix 1 – Major French Proposals to the 1996-97 IGC.

Conf. nr.	Subject matter	Included in Amsterdam Treaty?
2501/96	Outermost Regions – including fisheries policy	(+)
3863/96	High Representative of CFSP	(-)
3911/96	Public Services	(+)
3955/96	Flexibility (together with D)	(+)
3964/96	Overseas departments	+
3990/96	Subsidiarity	(-)
3824/97	Third Pillar	(-)
3852/97	Commission	-
3853/97	Court of Justice	-
3854/97	Enhancement of the Social Agreement before its integration into the Treaty	-
3855/97	Article J.4 Co-operation (together with B, D, ES, I, LUX)	-
3882/97	External Economic Relations	(+)
3902/97	Seat of the EP	+
SN nr.		
614, 619/96	Security and Defence	(-)
618/96	Role of National Parliaments	(-)
629, 630/96	Article D and Article J.4	(-)
526/97	Rules of accompaniment	-
527/97	Harmonisation of criminal justice co-operation	(+)
528/97	Civil and criminal justice co-operation	(+)

Key : + = fully incorporated   (-) = only partially incorporated
      (+) = significant sections incorporated   - = no inclusion

Appendix 2 – Major German Proposals to the 1996-97 IGC.

CONF nr.	Subject matter	Included in Amsterdam Treaty?
3855/96	Creation of a Restrictive Practices Office	-
3897/96	Subsidiarity	(+)
3938/96	Customs Co-operation	(+)
3939/96	Statistics	+
3952/96	Fundamental Rights	-
3953/96	Subsidiarity	(+)
3955/96	Flexibility	(+)
3960/96	Direct elections to EP	+
3962/96	Transferring preliminary ruling proceedings to the Court of First Instance	-
3966/96	Environment	(+)
3967/96	Local self-government	-
3971/96	Solidarity Clause	-
3972/96	Defence Co-operation (new version of Article J.4.)	(-)
3983/96	Animal Protection	-
3984/96	Consultation of Committee of Regions	+
3807/97	Customs Co-operation	-
3844/97	Court of Auditors	(+)
3851/97	Subsidiarity Protocol	(+)
3855/97	Article J.4 Co-operation (together with B, ES, F, I, LUX)	-
3906/97	Statute of officials and other servants of the EC	+
3909/97	Subsidiarity	(+)
3910/97	Police Co-operation	(+)
3911/97	Town & Country Planning	-
3912/97	External Economic Relations	-

CONF nr.	Subject matter	Included in Amsterdam Treaty?
3922/97	Protocol on Direct Taxation (toghether with UK)	-
3926/97	Property Ownership, public credit institutions	(+)
3927/97	Sport	+
SN nr.		
580/97	Health insurance and the regulation of labour markets	(+)
n/a	Communitarisation of judicial co-operation in criminal matters	-
n/a	Equality of men and women (proposed amendment to CONF/3883/97) (21 April, 1997)	(-)

Key : + = fully incorporated (-) = only partially incorporated
       (+) = significant sections incorporated - = no inclusion

Appendix 3 – Comparison of Initial F/D Preferences and Positions with the Final Outcome.

Germany	*France*	*Amsterdam Treaty*
Flexibility in EC pillar		
•Franco-German proposal for a general clause (CONF/3955/96). •non-exclusive clause. •maintain institutional structures and the *acquis communautaire*. •no veto. •Commission assent necessary. •operational costs born by participating Member States.	•Franco-German proposal for a general clause (CONF/3955/96). •Conditions: non-exclusive clause; maintain institutional structures and the *acquis communautaire*. •no veto. •Commission assent necessary. •operational costs born by participating Member States.	•introduced in 1st pillar. •no positive or negative list of areas. •no co-operation in areas of exclusive EC competence. •Conditions reflect Franco-German proposals (but also Commission's position (see CONF/3805/97)). •flexibility initiated by QMV, with veto power. •Commission submits proposal only when deemed within strict criteria, EP consulted. •operational costs born by participating MS.
Fewer Commissioners		
•number of Commissioners limited to fewer members than Member States (Joint Franco-German letter 12.96).	•proposal for a reduction of number to 10, 12 if the number of Member States exceeds 20 (CONF/3852/97).	•Protocol on the Institutions: at least one year before membership of EU exceeds twenty, a new IGC will be convened to undertake a review of the composition and organisation of the Commission.
Increased QMV		
•extend QMV to almost all voting in Council. •cautious in many financial areas and employment policy (Moravcsik & Nicolaïdis 1999, 77).	•limited increase in QMV in social and employment policies, in exchange for better weighting of Council votes.	•limited increase in QMV in social and employment policies, public health, openness, equal opportunities, research framework programme, and customs co-operation.

Germany	France	Amsterdam Treaty
Reweight Council votes		
•reweight votes to ensure "representative balance" (joint Franco-German letter 12.96). •Introduce double majority including population (Hoyer, in European Policy Centre 1996e, 11).	•reweighting of votes to take into account population, budget contributions (Le Figaro 20.02.96).	•Protocol on the Institutions: at least one year before membership of EU exceeds twenty, a new IGC will be convened to undertake a review of the provisions of the Treaties on the weighting of votes in the Council.
Increased co-decision		
•use in all areas where Council votes by qualified majority (position paper 03.96).	•opposition to increase in EP powers (French memorandum on 1996 IGC – Le Figaro 20.02.96).	•extension of co-decision to most legislative measures in Treaty (16 existing and 8 new article), with the exception of agriculture, tax harmonisation, and trade policy.
External Economic Relations		
•favours limited transfer of competences to Commission in services and intellectual property with list of exceptions for sensitive sectors (CONF/3912/97).	•strengthened Council role in the Comitology procedure *(CONF/3882/97)*. •against transfer of competences to Commission in services and intellectual property *(CONF/3882/97)*.	•existing measures maintained, with the possibility of transferring negotiation competences in services and intellectual property by a unanimous Council vote.

Germany	France	Amsterdam Treaty
CFSP		
•extension of QMV, but with unanimity kept in certain areas (Position paper 03.96; joint Franco-German letter 12.96).
•introduce constructive abstention (joint Franco-German letter 02.96).
•proposed flexibility clause in 2nd pillar, especially in defence co-operation (Art. J.4) (CONF/3955/96).
•COM involvement in proposals and implementation of CFSP (joint Franco-German letter 12.96).
•incorporate Petersberg tasks into TEU (joint Franco-German letter 02.96; Position paper, 03.96).
•gradual incorporation of WEU into EU (Position paper 03.96; CONF/3855/97).
•long-term: common defence (EPC 1996e:10).
•political "solidarity" clause (joint Franco-German letter 02.96; CONF/3971/96).	•limited extension of QMV to implementation phase (joint Franco-German letter 12.96).
•introduce constructive abstention (joint Franco-German letter 02.96; Le Figaro, 20.02.96).
•proposed flexibility clause in 2nd pillar, especially in defence co-operation (Art. J.4) (CONF/3955/96).
•COM involvement in proposals and implementation of CFSP (joint Franco-German letter 12.96).
•incorporate Petersberg tasks into TEU (joint Franco-German letter 02.96).
•gradual incorporation of WEU into EU (EP, 1996,5; CONF/3855/97).
•proposes powerful and independent "High Representative" for CFSP (CONF/3863/96).
•political "solidarity" clause (joint Franco-German letter 02.96).	•QMV in joint actions and common positions, with veto for "important and stated reasons of national policy." Council can then decide by QMV to refer question to European Council for decision by unanimity.
•Unanimity for all other decisions.
•Constructive abstention introduced.
•no specific flexibility clause introduced.
•Commission involved in CFSP.
•Petersberg tasks incorporated.
•closer institutional co-operation between EU and WEU, with a view towards the possible incorporation of WEU into the EU should the European Council so decide.
•Strengthened Council Secretary General, who shall act as CFSP "High Representative."

Germany	France	Amsterdam Treaty
JHA		
•common policy on internal borders, visas, immigration, asylum, customs introduced in stages (joint Franco-German letter 12.96). •proposed communitarisation of judicial co-operation in criminal matters (letter from German Delegation 03.03.97). •balance of efforts in receiving refugees (EPC 1996e, 11). •flexibility clause applicable to all areas of Title (CONF/3955/96).	•common policy on internal borders, visas, immigration, asylum, customs introduced step-wise over 5-year period (joint Franco-German letter 12.96; CONF/3824/97). •introduce measures to combat organized crime, terrorism, drug addiction and drug trafficking (CONF/3824/97). •opposed to balance of effort in receiving refugees (CONF/3824/97). •preserve public policy/national security proviso (CONF/3824/97). •use flexibility (CONF/3955/96; 3824/97).	•communitarisation over a 5-year period of visas, asylum, immigration and other policies related to the free movement of persons. •all policies except visas decided by consultation w/ unanimity, with CM decision after 5 years on co-decision. •introduce measures to combat organized crime, terrorism, drug addiction and drug trafficking. •Schengen *acquis* incorporated into TEU. •ECJ has limited jurisdiction w/in remaining 3rd pillar. •measures to promote a balance of efforts in receiving refugees. •flexibility introduced.

Bibliography

Agence Europe. *Europe Daily Bulletins*, various issues.

Alter, Karen J. (1996). "The European Court's Political Power," *West European Politics*, Vol. 19, No. 3, July, pp. 458-487.

Alter, Karen J. (1998). "Who Are the "Masters of the Treaty"?: European Governments and the European Court of Justice," *International Organization*, Vol. 52, Number 1, Winter 1988, pp. 121-147.

Bachrach, P. & M.S. Baratz (1962). "The two faces of power," *American Political Science Review*, Vol. 56, No. 4, pp. 942-952.

Beach, Derek (1998). "The Negotiation of the Europe Agreements with Poland, Hungary, and Czechoslovakia: A Three-Level Game," *TKI Working Papers on European Integration and Regime Formation*, No. 31, Esbjerg: South Jutland University Press.

Beach, Derek (2001). *Between Law and Politics: the relationship between the European Court of Justice of the European Communities and the Member States*, Copenhagen: DJØF Publishing.

Bourgeois, Jacques H.J. (1995). "The EC in the WTO and Advisory Opinion 1/94: An Echternach Procession," *Common Market Law Review*, Vol. 32, No. 3, June, pp. 763-787.

Christiansen, Thomas & Knud Erik Jørgensen (1998). "Negotiating Treaty Reform in the European Union: The Role of the European Commission," *International Negotiation*, Vol. 3, No. 3, pp. 435-452.

Christiansen, Thomas & Knud Erik Jørgensen (1999). "The Amsterdam Process: A Structurationist Perspective on EU Treaty Reform," *European Integration online Papers* (EIoP), Vol. 3, No. 1, Published on Internet site http://eiop.or.at/eiop/texte/1999-001a.htm.

Dahl, Robert A. (1957). "The Concept of Power," *Behavioural Science*, Vol. 2, No. 3, pp. 201-215.

Dahl, Robert A. (1961). *Who Governs? Democracy and Power in an American City*, New Haven, Connecticut: Yale University Press.

Dehousse, Franklin (1999). *Amsterdam: The Making of a Treaty*, London: London European Research Centre.

Digeser, Peter (1992). "The Fourth Face of Power," *Journal of Politics*, Vol. 54, November, pp. 977-1007.

Dinan, Desmond (1997). "The Commission and the Reform Process," pp. 188-211, in Geoffrey Edwards & Alfred Pijpers (eds.), *The Politics of Treaty reform – the 1996 Intergovernmental Conference and Beyond*, London: Pinter.

Devuyst, Youri (1998). "Treaty reform in the European Union: the Amsterdam Process," *Journal of European Public Policy*, Vol. 5, No. 4, December, pp. 615-631.

Duff, Andrew (1997). *The Treaty of Amsterdam: Text and Commentary*, London: Federal Trust.

Edwards, Geoffrey & Alfred Pijpers (eds.) (1997). *The Politics of European Treaty Reform: The 1996 Intergovernmental Conference and Beyond*, London: Pinter.

Emiliou, Nicholas (1996). "The Death of Exclusive Competence?," *European Law Review*, Vol. 21, August, pp. 294-311.

European Policy Centre (Belmont European Policy Centre / European Policy Centre) (1996-1997). *Challenge 96. / Challenge Europe*, Brussels: IGC Intelligence Service, European Policy Centre.

European Commission (1996). *Reinforcing Political Union and Preparing for Enlargement*, Commission Opinion of 28 February 1996, COM (96) 90 Final. 28.2.96.

European Court of Justice (1995). *Report of the Court of Justice on certain aspects of the application of the Treaty on European Union*, Luxembourg: Office for Official Publications of the European Communities, May.

European Parliament (1995a). *Denmark's position with respect to the 1996 IGC: Note on the positions of the Member States of the European Union with respect to the 1996 IGC*, Luxembourg: European Parliament, 8 December.

European Parliament (1995b). *Netherland's position with respect to the 1996 IGC: Note on the positions of the Member States of the European Union with respect to the 1996 IGC*, Luxembourg: European Parliament, 8 December.

European Parliament (1995c). *Spain's position with respect to the 1996 IGC: Note on the positions of the Member States of the European Union with respect to the 1996 IGC*, Luxembourg: European Parliament, 8 December.

European Parliament (1995d). *The United Kingdom's position with respect to the 1996 IGC: Note on the positions of the Member States of the European Union with respect to the 1996 IGC*, Luxembourg: European Parliament, 8 December.

European Parliament (1996). *White Paper on the 1996 Intergovernmental Conference–Volume II: Summary of Positions of the Member States of the European Union with a view to the 1996 Intergovernmental Conference*. Brussels: European Parliament Intergovernmental Conference Task Force.

European Parliament (1997a). *European Environmental Policy and the IGC*. Intergovernmental Conference Briefing Number 32, First update, 28 February.

European Parliament (1997b). *The Court of Justice*. Intergovernmental Conference Briefing Number 1, Sixth update, 3 March.

European Parliament (1997c). *Differentiated Integration.* Intergovernmental Conference Briefing Number, No. 4, Fourth update, 19 March.

European Parliament (1997d). *Common Foreign and Security Policy.* Intergovernmental Conference Briefing Number, No. 5, Fourth update, 21 March.

European Women's Lobby (1996). Position Paper on the Intergovernmental Conference 1996, Brussels, 4 March.

Eurostat (1997). *Eurostat Årbog 1997: 1986-1996 Statistisk set,* Luxembourg: Statistical Office of the European Communities.

Evans, Peter B., Harold K. Jacobson, & Robert Putnam (eds.) (1993). *Double-Edged Diplomacy: International Bargaining and Domestic Politics,* Berkeley: University of California Press.

Federal Trust (1996). "Dividing the Union? Britain and the IGC," Background paper, Federal Trust Conference, London, 22 May.

Financial Times (various issues).

Garrett, Geoffrey (1992). "International cooperation and institutional choice: the European Community's internal market," *International Organization,* Vol. 46, No. 2, Spring, pp. 533-560.

Garrett, Geoffrey & Barry. R. Weingast (1993). "Ideas, Interests, and Institutions: Constructing the European Community's Internal Market," pp. 173-206, in Judith Goldstein & Robert O. Keohane (eds.), *Ideas and Foreign Policy: Beliefs, Institutions, and Political Change,* Ithaca: Cornell University Press.

George, Stephen (1996). "The approach of the British government to the 1996 Intergovernmental Conference of the European Union," *Journal of European Public Policy,* Vol. 3, No. 1, pp. 45-62.

Gordon, Philip (1995). *France, Germany, and the Western Alliance,* Boulder: Westview Press.

Habeeb, William Mark (1988). *Power and Tactics in International Negotiation,* Baltimore: Johns Hopkins University Press.

Heurlin, Bertil & Hans Mouritzen (eds.) (1999). *Danish Foreign Policy Yearbook 1999,* Copenhagen: DUPI.

Isaksen, Susanne, Ole Toft & Jens Bødtcher-Hansen (1998). *En traktat bliver til: Amsterdam-traktaten: forberedelse, forhandling og resultat,* Albertslund: Schultz.

Keohane, Robert O. & Joseph S. Nye Jr. (1989). *Power and Interdependence: World Politics in Transition,* 2nd Edition, Boston: Little, Brown & Co.

Lang, John Temple (1997). "The Duties of National Courts under Community Constitutional Law," *European Law Review*, Vol. 22, February, pp. 3-18.

Laursen, Finn (forthcoming). "Denmark: In Pursuit of Influence and Legitimacy," in Wolfgang Wessels, Andreas Maurer & J. Mittag (eds.) *Fifteen into One? The European Union and Member States*, Manchester: Manchester University Press.

Le Figaro (1996). "Les orientations de la France pour la Conférence Intergouvernementale de 1996," 20 February.

Lodge, Juliet (1998). "Negotiations in the European Union: The 1996 Intergovernmental Conference," *International Negotiation*, Vol. 3, No. 3, pp. 481-505.

Lukes, Steven (1974). *Power: A Radical View*, Houndmills: Macmillan.

Mazey, Sonia & Jeremy Richardson (1997). "Agenda Setting, Lobbying and the 1996 IGC," pp. 226-248, in Geoffrey Edwards & Alfred Pijpers (eds.), *The Politics of Treaty reform – the 1996 Intergovernmental Conference and Beyond*, London: Pinter.

McCarthy, Patrick (ed.) (1993). *France-Germany, 1983-1993: The Struggle to Cooperate*, Houndmills: Macmillan Press Ltd.

McDonagh, Bobby (1998). *Original Sin in a Brave New World: An Account of the Negotiation of the Treaty of Amsterdam*, Dublin: Institute of European Affairs.

Menon, Anand (1998). "France and the IGC of 1996," *Journal of European Public Policy*, Vol. 3, No. 2, pp. 231-252.

Meunier, Sophie & Kalypso Nicolaïdis (1998). "Who Speaks for Europe? The Delegation of Trade Authority in the European Union," *Working Paper Series in Politics*, Cambridge, MA: Kennedy School of Government.

Meunier, Sophie & Kalypso Nicolaïdis (1999). "Who Speaks for Europe? The Delegation of Trade Authority in the European Union," *Journal of Common Market Studies*, Vol. 37, No. 3, September, pp. 477-501.

Middlemas, Keith (1995). *Orchestrating Europe: The Informal Politics of European Union 1973-1995*, London: Fontana Press.

Moravcsik, Andrew (1993). "Preferences and Power in the European Community: A Liberal Intergovernmentalist Approach," *Journal of Common Market Studies*, Vol. 31, No. 4, December, pp. 473-524.

Moravcsik, Andrew (1995). "Liberal Intergovernmentalism and Integration: A Rejoinder," *Journal of Common Market Studies*, Vol. 33, No. 4, December, pp. 611-628.

Moravcsik, Andrew (1997). "Taking Preferences Seriously: A Liberal Theory of International Politics," *International Organization*, Vol. 51, No. 4, Autumn, pp. 513-553.

Moravcsik, Andrew (1998). *The Choice for Europe: Social Purpose and State Power from Messina to Maastricht*, Ithaca: Cornell University Press.

Moravcsik, Andrew (1999). "A new statecraft? Supranational entrepreneurs and international cooperation," *International Organization*, Vol. 53, No. 2, Spring, pp. 267-306.

Moravcsik, Andrew & Kalypso Nicolaïdis (1999). "Explaining the Treaty of Amsterdam: Interests, Influence, Institutions," *Journal of Common Market Studies*, Vol. 37, No. 1, March, pp. 59-85.

Nehring, Niels-Jørgen (1996). *Regeringskonference '96*, Copenhagen: Dansk Udenrigspolitisk Institut.

Nugent, Neill (1999). *The Government and Politics of the European Union. Fourth Edition*, Houndmills: MacMillan Press Ltd.

Nuttall, Simon (1997). Presentation on CFSP given at Federal Trust conference on "Britain's Agenda in Europe: The British Presidency of the Council of the European Union," London School of Economics, 22 November.

Pedersen, Thomas (1998). *Germany, France and the integration of Europe: a realist interpretation*, Pinter: London.

Petersen, Nikolaj & Finn Laursen (1998). *Amsterdam Traktaten: Baggrund, kommentarer og perspektiver*, København: Den Danske Europabevægelse.

Petersen, Nikolaj (1999). "The Danish Referendum on the Treaty of Amsterdam," pp. 101-121, in Bertil Heurlin & Hans Mouritzen (eds.), *Danish Foreign Policy Yearbook 1999*, Copenhagen: DUPI.

Petite, Michel (1998). "The Treaty of Amsterdam," *Harvard Law School – Jean Monnet Chair Working Paper*, No. 2.

Pijpers, Alfred & Sophie Vanhoonacker (1997). "The Position of the Benelux Countries," pp. 119-142, in Geoffrey Edwards and Alfred Pijpers (eds.), *The Politics of Treaty reform – the 1996 Intergovernmental Conference and Beyond*, London: Pinter.

Pollack, Mark A. (1997). "Delegation, Agency, and Agenda Setting in the European Community," *International Organization*, Vol. 51, No. 1, Winter, pp. 99-134.

Pollack, Mark A. (1999). "Delegation, Agency and Agenda Setting in the Treaty of Amsterdam," *European Integration online Papers* (EIoP), Vol. 3, No. 6, published at Internet site: http://eiop.or.at/eiop/texte/1999-006a.htm.

Putnam, Robert D. (1988). "Diplomacy and domestic politics: the logic of two-level games," *International Organization*, Vol. 42, No. 3, Summer, p. 427-60.

Reflection Group (1995). Reflection Group's Report of 5 December 1995, SN 520/95 REFLEX 21, Brussels.

Rosamond, Ben (2000). *Theories of European Integration*, Houndmills: MacMillan Press Ltd.

Sandholtz, Wayne & J. Zysman (1989). "1992: Recasting the European Bargain," *World Politics*, Vol. 41, No. 1, pp. 95-128.

Sebenius, James K. (1992). "Challenging conventional explanations of international cooperation: negotiation analysis and the case of epistemic communities," *International Organization*, Vol. 46, No. 1, Winter, pp. 323-365.

Shaw, Jo (2000). "Constitutional Settlements and the Citizen after the Treaty of Amsterdam," pp. 290-317, in Karlheinz Neunreither & Antje Wiener (eds.), *European Integration after Amsterdam: Institutional Dynamics and Prospects for Democracy*, Oxford: Oxford University Press.

Simonian, Haig (1985). *The Privileged Partnership: Franco-German Relations in the European Community, 1969-1984*, Oxford: Clarendon Press.

Stone Sweet, Alec (1998). "Chapter 11 – Constitutional Dialogues in the European Community," pp. 305-330, in Anne-Marie Slaughter et al. (eds.), *The European Court and National Courts – Doctrine and Jurisprudence: Legal Change in its Social Context*, Oxford: Hart Publishing.

Stone Sweet, Alec & Wayne Sandholtz (1998). *European Integration and Supranational Governance*, Oxford: Oxford University Press.

Stubb, Alexander Cai-Göran (1998). *Flexible Integration and the Amsterdam Treaty: Negotiating Differentiation in the 1996-97 IGC*, dissertation submitted for the degree of Doctor of Philosophy. London: London School of Economics and Political Science.

Tallberg, Jonas (2000). "Supranational influence in EU enforcement: the ECJ and the principle of state liability," *Journal of European Public Policy*, Volume 7, Number 1, pp. 104-121.

Underdal, Arild (1991). "The Outcomes of Negotiation," pp. 100-115, in Victor A. Kremenyuk (ed.), *International Negotiation: Analysis, Approaches, Issues*, San Francisco: Jossey-Bass Publishers,

Wincott, Daniel (1995). "Institutional Interaction and European Integration: Towards an Everyday Critique of Liberal Intergovernmentalism," *Journal of Common Market Studies*, Vol. 33, No. 4, December, pp. 597-609.

Zartmann, William I. (1991). "The Structure of Negotiation," pp. 65-77, in Victor A. Kremenyuk (ed.), *International Negotiation: Analysis, Approaches, Issues*, San Francisco: Jossey-Bass Publishers.

25

Explaining and Evaluating the Amsterdam Treaty: Some Concluding Remarks

Finn Laursen

Introduction

The Amsterdam Treaty was yet another treaty in the history of European integration. It was not normal politics; it was constitutive politics (Pedersen 1998, 56). It was yet another big bargain among the EU's Member States, setting some new rules for their cooperation. If we use the categories suggested by John Peterson, the type of decision finalized in Amsterdam in June 1997 was "history-making" and it took place at the super-systemic level. It was not policy-setting or policy-shaping, the more normal day-to-day decisions that take place at the systemic and sub-systemic levels. In the case of a history-making decision, the dominant actors would be the national governments in an Intergovernmental Conference (IGC) and the Heads of State and Government in the European Council. The kind of rationality, according to Peterson, would be political and legalistic, not the kind of technocratic, administrative rationality found at lover levels of decision-making (Peterson 1995).

In this final chapter the editor will suggest some conclusions from the chapters included in this volume and move beyond questions of explanation to briefly discuss how we can evaluate the Treaty of Amsterdam. How significant was it?

Explaining the Amsterdam Results

Andrew Moravcsik has developed a model for studying the major decisions in European integration. He calls it "liberal intergovernmentalism." When he first developed his approach, he suggested a two-step analysis: first national preference formation and then interstate bargaining (Moravcsik 1993). Later he added a third step, institutional choice (Moravcsik 1998a). The framework is summarized in table 25.1.

The first stage is to try to explain national preferences. The central question asked by Moravcsik here is whether economic or geopolitical interests dominate when Member States form their preferences. The answer based on major decisions in the European integration process was that economic interests have been the most important. Geopolitics and ideas play a secondary role (see also Moravcsik 1998b).

Table 25.1: International cooperation: A rationalist framework.

Stages of Negotiation	National Preference Formation	Interstate Bargaining	Institutional Choice
Alternative independent variables underlying each stage	What is the source of underlying national preferences?	Given national preferences, what explains the efficiency and distributional outcomes of interstate bargaining?	Given substantive agreement, what explains the transfer of sovereignty to international Institutions?
	Economic interests or Geopolitical interests? ↓	Asymmetrical interdependence or Supranational entrepreneurship? ↓	Federalist ideology or Centralized technocratic management or More credible commitment? ↓
Observed outcomes at each stage	Underlying national preferences ⟶	Agreements on substance ⟶	Choice to delegate or pool decision-making in international institutions

Source: Moravcsik (1998a), p. 24.

The second stage, interstate bargaining, seeks to explain the efficiency and distributional outcomes from EU negotiations. Here two possible explanations of agreements on substance are contrasted: asymmetrical interdependence or supranational entrepreneurship. Moravcsik arrives at the answer that asymmetrical interdependence has the greatest explanatory power. Some Member States have more at stake than others and will work harder to influence outcomes. The role of the Commission or other Community actors is not considered very important. According to Moravcsik three factors are likely to determine the outcomes of interstate bargaining:

1. The value of unilateral policy alternatives, relative to the status quo which underlies credible threats to veto,
2. The value of alternative coalitions which underlies credible threats to exclude, and
3. The opportunities for issue linkage or side-payments which underlie "package deals" (Moravcsik 1998a, 63).

Summarizing the discussion of the first point, Moravcsik says: "those who more intensely desire the benefits of cooperation will concede more to get them." Summarizing the discussion of the second point he says: "the credible threat of exclusion is likely to generate an even more powerful pressure on recalcitrant states than does the threat of nonagreement." In respect to linkage strategies, Moravcsik observes that the major constraint lies in their domestic distributional implications. Concessions often create domestic losers. This will limit the use of package deals (Moravcsik 1998a, 63-67).

The third stage explores the reasons why states choose to delegate or pool decision-making in international institutions. Delegation in the EU refers to the powers given to the European Commission and the European Court of Justice (ECJ). Pooling of sovereignty refers to the application of majority decisions, in practice mostly qualified majority voting (QMV). To explain institutional choice, Moravcsik contrasts three possible explanations: Federalist ideology, centralized technocratic management or more credible commitment. The answer he gives is that states delegate and pool sovereignty to get more credible commitment. Pooling and delegation is a rational strategy adopted by the Member States to pre-commit governments to future decisions, to encourage future cooperation and to improve future implementation of agreements (Moravcsik 1998a, 73).

The brief overview given here cannot do justice to the richness of the analysis of European integration in *The Choice for Europe*. Using theories of decision-making, negotiations and international political economy in general in an elegant combination has allowed Moravcsik to construct a parsimonious framework for the study of international cooperation including international integration.

The question could be asked: Could we use liberal intergovernmentalism to explain Amsterdam? Moravcsik did so together with Nicolaïdis (Moravcsik & Nicolaïdis 1999). The answer they gave was affirmative.

Although the Moravcsik scheme was mentioned during our discussions, we did not impose it on the contributors. We can therefore in no way claim to have tested it. But some comments can be made.

Preference Formation

Concerning preferences, the question can be asked whether the primacy of economic factors still holds for the process of European integration after the end of the Cold War. As long as we analyse the original European Economic Community (EEC), the Common Agricultural Policy (CAP), the European Monetary System (EMS), the Internal Market or Economic and Monetary Union (EMU) as the most important part of the Maastricht Treaty, it should not come as a surprise that economic factors were rather decisive. Also, European integration during the Cold War took place under the security overlay of bipolarity, and NATO largely handled Western European security and defence issues. However, matters started changing after the end of the Cold War, and Maastricht was more than EMU. It included the second pillar on Common Foreign and Security Policy (CFSP) and the third pillar on Justice and Home Affairs (JHA) cooperation (Laursen & Vanhoonacker 1992). Thus, the new Union was explicitly concerned with external and internal security issues, including emerging ethnic conflicts in the new "near abroad," new migration flows, international crime, etc.

Amsterdam was also about giving the EU a more human face, bringing it closer to its citizens as well as making improvements in the second pillar and in JHA. Looking at the first pillar some of the changes took place as especially Social-Democrat-led governments wanted a more "progressive" EU in respect to employment (which has, of course, very much to do with economic conditions), environment and social policy (which are also partly economic policy areas). However, second and third pillar issues were about security in a broad sense. Although second pillar changes were not radical they were not insignificant and JHA changes were rather important, with the creation of the new Area of Freedom, Security and Justice (AFSJ) under the first pillar, and the incorporation of the Schengen *acquis* into the Treaty. The latter constituted some of the most important changes brought about by Amsterdam. These changes suggest that a deepening of integration is taking place at least partly for security reasons.

We do, of course, note the point made by Simon Duke in his contribution on CFSP to this volume, namely that external events, from the Dayton Accords in 1995 to the Albania crisis during the IGC, "had little measurable impact upon the deliberations." On the other hand, Monica den Boer mentions "contextual crisis events, such as the arrival of Albanian and Iraqi refugees at the Italian coast" as events providing a momentum which facilitated sluggish decision-making. So the jury may still be out on this question, but it could also be that decision makers perceived internal security issues as more important than external security issues.

If demands for integration, according to liberal intergovernmentalism, are expected to come mainly from economic and business circles it is not clear how important such demands were in the case of Amsterdam. Alexander Stubb, in his contribution on flexibility, explicitly disagrees with scholars emphasizing the role of interests groups in the IGC process. However, this does not rule out the possibility that interest groups influenced the process of preference formation in the Member States. Karl Magnus Johansson and Anna-Carin Svensson, for instance, in their contribution on Sweden, emphasise the two-level bargaining process, with demands and expectations from interest groups and civil society. No doubt, similar mechanisms played an important role in other Member States, probably more so during the agenda-setting phase than during later stages of the negotiations, and more so in some countries than in others. Esko Antola says about the Finnish case: "A very comprehensive organisation was set up involving not only different ministries and interest groups but also the civil society and the Parliament. In the end, however, the drafting of the national positions was in the hands of a very small group of diplomats and civil servants."

Talking about Sweden and Finland – and we could add Austria here – it was of course the geopolitical changes in and after 1989 that had made it possible for these former EFTA members to join the EU in 1995. But, apart from the Finnish-Swedish proposal to integrate the Petersberg tasks into the EU's defence policy, these new Member States put the greatest emphasis on employment, environment, openness, etc. The older Member State Denmark also belonged to this group of states concentrating on low politics issues, issues expected to provide the EU with more legitimacy.

The Benelux countries had concerns about environment and employment, too. But they were much more explicit in their concerns about institutional changes prior to enlargement, and thus issues of efficiency. Being among the original EC members they had a stronger attachment to the Community method, even to federalist ideology, although we learn about a certain amount of pragmatism sneaking into Benelux policies, especially in the case of the Netherlands. The need to confront the geopolitics of the New Europe was strong, but the costs of reform made these countries look closely at the specifics. The question of re-weighting of votes in the Council in the end led to a major conflict between the Dutch and the Belgians. According to Kerremans' contribution to this volume, there was an element of misunderstanding between the two traditional EU partners. The Belgians misread the Dutch steps as tactical, whereas the Dutch sincerely felt they should have more votes than the Belgians, given the larger Dutch population.

If we look at the preferences of some of the big Member States, Rita Beuter mentions the changing geopolitical situation after the end of the Cold War and German unification. "For Germany enlargement to the East was top priority, whereas France was concerned about the EU's balance of power tilting to the North and East." She goes on to say that Germany was preoccupied with EMU and stability, "whereas France was haunted by having to cope with unemployment." On the latter point, which of course concerns economic interests, we could add that there was an internal split in France with the Gaullists being more geopolitical – and even ideological – in their approach to the issues, and the Socialists being more concerned about economic aspects of the situation. The election of the Jospin government on 1 June therefore contributed to a situation where France occasionally spoke with two voices in Amsterdam. In a wider sense, according to Florence Deloche-Gaudez's contribution: "The French seemed to be torn between, on the one hand, the desire to promote a continuation of the European construction and, on the other hand, their determination to preserve the "sovereignty" of France."

In the British case, despite the differences in the approach of the Major government during most of the IGC 96-97 and the Blair government during the end game, Edward Best concludes that "There are clear "structural realities" shaping UK positions, most notably (and probably immutably, the Channel Tunnel notwithstanding) the "island logic" behind the UK's exceptionalism over border controls, as well as limits on governmental action arising from popular perceptions." In connection with the latter point, Best talks about "a broad feeling of non-identification with the European project." So, a mix of geopolitics and questions of identity need to be considered if we want to understand the British position.

The so-called cohesion states, Greece, Spain, Portugal and Ireland, had an economic interest connected with enlargement. Would less money be available for them through structural and regional policies after enlargement? The Mediterranean cohesion states also had a geopolitical orientation towards North Africa and the Middle East, including concerns about instability and migratory flows from a southern "near abroad." Italy, of course, had a similar concern. Clearly, this added up to a mix of economic and security issues that affected the positions of these countries.

In the Irish case there was an element of geopolitics in its relationship with the UK. According to Ben Tonra, "a key function of the Irish Presidency was to ensure that Britain was kept on board." Even if the Irish wanted "to maintain a position at the core of the integrative project" they were, because of the Common Travel Area with the UK, forced to accept an opt-out when it was decided to incorporate the Schengen *acquis* into the Treaty. Historical relations with the UK also continue to affect the Irish position on defence policy. Interestingly enough, in this area, the Irish "were more than happy to sail in the wake of British objections to an EU/WEU merger."

As a relatively big EU Member State Spain had, as we have seen in Felipe Basabe's contribution, special problems with institutional changes, and financial repercussions affected its attitude towards enlargement. "The access of Spanish economic actors to [the new CEEC] markets is limited and unlikely to result in greater expansion, and historical and cultural links with [these] countries are not very close either." On the other hand, Spain's cultural and historic ties with Latin America and the Islamic countries influenced Spanish positions in Second and Third Pillar issues. Spain's geographic situation made the country both a "bridge" and a "gatekeeper" with regard to migratory movements from Northern Africa and Latin America.

Concerning Italy, Laura Corrado wrote: "It is obvious that a country like Italy, with its 8,000 kilometres of maritime frontiers, and thus highly exposed to illegal immigration, tended to favour a common European approach and responsibility on [JHA] issues."

In the case of Greece, security considerations, both traditional ones and the newer ones of post-Cold War Europe, played a rather decisive role. Papadopoulos said in his contribution: "At the most macroscopic level, Greece's positions were, and are, influenced by its geostrategic position in southern Europe. In this sense, Greece occupies a unique position among the Union's fifteen Member States, being not only the sole Member State without a common border with any other Member State, but also located in the most turbulent corner of the continent." Greece has become "a frequent destination of illegal immigrants." As regards the new Area of Freedom, Security and Justice, Greece therefore "has a strong vested interest in an effective coordination of policies at the EU-level." Partly because of the conflict with Turkey, Greece also wanted to include territorial defence commitments in the EU's defence policy, not just the Petersberg tasks which were incorporated in the CFSP.

The argument then is that we cannot fully explain Amsterdam without reference to geopolitical factors. This does not mean that economic interest were unimportant. Even special interest groups had an impact, especially during the last part of the negotiations. It was special interests which produced what has been called the "Christmas tree" effect, with a number of protocols and declarations attached to the Treaty, concerning public broadcasting, public services, overseas territories, animal welfare, etc. (Dehousse 1999, 17).

It appears from this overview that a mix of different factors affected the preferences, interests and positions of the Member States during the 1996-97 IGC. Clearly, security questions in a wide sense were not unimportant. For some countries they seem to have been very important. The economic contents of the Amsterdam Treaty were more limited to some improvements in the first pillar. The most important economic issue during the years of the Amsterdam Treaty reform process, EMU, was not a direct part of the 1996-97 IGC. But it conditioned positions of many Member States, with some being very concerned about meeting the convergence criteria for participation in the third phase of EMU, the creation of the single currency, the euro. Needless to say, economic interdependence in a wider sense was still an important parameter of the whole process. It is this factor that makes the costs of exit so high that exit is not really a rational option for the Member States. In that sense, economic factors remain the glue of the Union. It helps us understand that the threat of marginalisation remains an important factor in the EU. It entered into the Member States thinking on "flexibility" and explains the strict conditions put on future use of the Treaty's enabling clauses. No one wants to become a second-class member.

What the Amsterdam preferences also suggest is an increased importance of questions of legitimacy. This problem clearly emerged with the Maastricht Treaty because of the Danish "no" in June 1992 and *le petit oui* in France in September the same year (Laursen 1994). The lesson drawn was the need of a Union closer to its citizens (Laursen 1997). Many of the preferences with which the Member States went into the 1996-97 IGC fit in with this preoccupation.

Interstate Bargaining
If we look at the bargaining process during the IGC an important question is whether liberal intergovernmentalism makes the process appear neater that it was. Monica den Boer, for instance, talks about "garbage-can-decisionmaking during the final session in Amsterdam." Alexander Stubb had this to say about the process:

> Positions in IGCs swing for many reasons, but rational choice and calculation are rarely among them. IGC negotiations are a messy and often confusing learning process, where the basic positions of the Member States show some continuity, but the specific positions of the negotiators fluctuate in line with the dynamics of the negotiations.

So a messy learning process is one possible verdict. Several contributors to this volume mentioned the changing positions of the actors during the conference. "Some national positions shifted from one end to the other in the course of only one year," said Monica den Boer. Others see a certain amount of continuity in national preferences during the negotiations.

The question of the relationship between preferences and positions in the actual negotiations is a tricky one. Declared positions are not necessarily the real ones. There is a tactical dimension involved here. States may send trial balloons and be hesitant to reveal their bottom lines in negotiations. This creates uncertainty and the negotiation process may not always be as information-rich as liberal intergovernmentalism claims.

Another question concerning the negotiation process concerns the relative roles of the big versus small Member States. In his studies Andrew Moravcsik mainly studied the bigger member states, Germany, France and the UK (see also Moravcsik 1991). However, it emerges from Jonas Tallberg's contribution on the first pillar that the small states, in particular the Nordic ones, were rather successful in leaving imprints in the Treaty of Amsterdam. Even in the second pillar, the Swedish-Finnish proposal on integrating the Petersberg tasks into the treaty was rather important.

We should, of course, remember in this connection that Moravcsik looks at asymmetrical interdependence when he explains influence. This concept does allow for the influence of small Member States because of the unanimity requirement of IGCs (see also Derek Beach's contribution to this volume).

Looking at the Franco-German duo, it seems that the traditional close cooperation between France and Germany worked less well in the Amsterdam negotiations. Simon Duke said:

> Kohl's and Chirac's relations grew less cordial with both leaders' weakening of power. In France, Chirac's disastrously mistimed call for early parliamentary elections witnessed the defeat of Alain Juppé's right-wing government and the election of Lionel Jospin's left-wing government. Jospin's election significantly impaired Chirac's ability to take any further initiatives. Within Germany, Kohl's position was weakened by the Bavarian Premier of the CSU, Edmund Stoiber – a well-known Eurosceptic who had been calling for the "controlled delay" of EMU. Kohl's governing coalition depended upon the support of the Bavarian CSU.

These factors seem to have weakened the influence of these traditionally very influential actors.

A third question concerns the role of the Community actors. We included chapters on the European Commission and the European Parliament in this study. As mentioned earlier liberal intergovernmentalism does not attribute a great role to these Community actors. However, some of the contributors to this volume were clearly not convinced. Alexander Stubb said : "It is ... important to note that all of the early flexibility articles were drafted by the Council Legal Service, which serves as a reminder of the multitude of players which influence an IGC process: Member States, EU institutions and the presidency." Monica den Boer mentions the Commission proposal on JHA of 18 September 1996 as evidence of Commission influence. "This proposal already bears the traces which are still visible in the text of the Amsterdam Treaty."

Similarly Mark Gray, in his contribution on the Commission, disagrees with the liberal intergovernmentalist position. After looking at some of the evidence he said that it is "difficult to agree with Moravcsik and Nicolaïdis that the Commission only follows rather than shapes events." One of the points made was that "if the Commission opinion of 28 February 1996 is compared to the final outcome, there is a rather substantial correlation between the two documents." He goes on to say, however, that this does not prove influence, but at least it shows "that the Commission position was broadly accepted on the majority of issues."

Also Andreas Maurer in his contribution on the European Parliament disagrees with liberal intergovernmentalism. But he too makes an important methodological point: "... it seems nearly impossible to measure the concrete influence of the EP in the institutional evolution of the European Union." As an alternative to liberal instergovernmentalism he suggests a historical institutionalist approach (see for instance Pierson 1996). According to this view, governments are no longer in full control of the integration process, not even in IGCs. Yesterday's decisions condition tomorrow's decisions. Things happen between IGCs that contribute to institutional change, for instance inter-institutional agreements (IIAs). It was through such an IIA that the Parliament gained more influence on budget issues related to CFSP. However, Maurer goes beyond that point, arguing for instance "Neither the new policy areas, for example consumer protection, education and culture, nor the co-decision procedure would have come into force without the permanent pressure of the EP."

What then could explain such influence? Contrary to the Commission that took part in the IGC, the EP only took part in the preceding Reflection Group. But the Parliament could use a linkage strategy, threatening to veto enlargement, where the treaty gives it the right of assent. Further, the Belgian and Italian Parliaments had stated that they would not authorize the ratification of the new treaty if the European Parliament did not accept the treaty. Thus indirectly the Parliament did have a credible threat of non-agreement. The governments, therefore, could not ignore its views.

Related questions concern the role of the presidency and the Council secretariat. Although not explored in specific chapters, some of the contributors mention the roles played by the Presidency and the Council secretariat. The Dutch presidency, it seems, played an important role in not including a specific flexibility clause in the second pillar. The Dutch were also influential in getting the Schengen *acquis* incorporated into the Treaty. The Dutch president of the group of representatives, Michiel Patijn, is mentioned a number of times as being especially influential.

Concerning the Legal Service of the Council, Alexander Stubb says that its "influence in IGCs is a much neglected issue in the literature on European integration. Given the fact that it provided over 90% of the draft articles which were used as the basis for negotiation in the 1996-7 IGC, its role should not be underestimated."

Derek Beach's theoretical contribution to this volume explores these aspects of the interstate bargaining further. On the basis of Moravcsik's contribution, he mainly looks at two questions: the factors determining actor power and the roles played by supranational actors. After discussing the relative influence of the Franco-German core and the reluctant states, the UK and Denmark, he found a certain amount of support for interpretations based on asymmetric inter-dependence, but he also found "several instances where outcomes not only reflect patterns of preferences and relative power, but also reflect bargaining dynamics." In his discussion of the role of supranational actors, he looks at the Commission and the ECJ. On the role of the Commission his conclusion is carefully drafted:

> The conditions for supranational entrepreneurship were relatively poor in the 1996-97 IGC given that: much of the agenda was already set by the TEU [Maastricht Treaty], there was a relatively information-rich environment, and the external environment was not as labile as in the 1990-91 IGC. Despite this, there is some evidence that the Commission did have some impact on the agenda-setting phase of the IGC, influencing the content of the debates in certain issue-areas.

During the negotiations "the Commission did provide "solutions" (proposals) to several problems faced by Member States." Some of these were "unique" and "successful." Others fared poorly. Concerning the ECJ, Derek Beach argues that certain rulings of the Court provided "focal points" for the IGC, such as rulings on public broadcasting, the WTO case and the *Kalanke* ruling. So, without playing a formal role in the IGC, the ECJ did play an autonomous role influencing the IGC deliberations.

Institutional Choice
Institutional choice in the Moravcsik scheme refers to pooling and delegation of sovereignty, i.e. introduction of QMV and delegation of authority to Community institutions, especially the European Commission and the ECJ.

Amsterdam involved some pooling of sovereignty by transferring certain policies under the first pillar from unanimity to QMV. However, as we saw in the chapter on Institutions and Procedures, the final list adopted was shorter than expected, partly because of the German pullback in Amsterdam. In the end, QMV was extended to 11 new treaty provisions, including employment, and five existing treaty provisions, including research framework programmes. It did not include any very heavy areas. This issue, extended use of QMV, therefore went into the IGC 2000 as one of the so-called Amsterdam "leftovers."

The decision to transfer some issues from the third pillar to the first pillar involves both pooling and delegation of sovereignty – with some delays because of the five-year transition period. Further, the introduction of QMV after the transition period will only take place after a unanimous vote. So it is with some hesitation that this "communitarization" took or takes place. But, eventually we should expect a full use of the Community method in the new Area of Freedom, Security and Justice. This will also increase the roles of the Commission and the ECJ. Further, the role of the ECJ is increased somewhat in the remaining third pillar, Police and Judicial Cooperation in Criminal Matters, in the Amsterdam Treaty.

In the second pillar we saw the introduction of Common Strategies coupled with the idea that Joint Actions and Common Positions can be adopted by a special QMV. This chance, however, was even more half-hearted, because of the two safeguards of unanimity in the European Council and the possibility of constructive abstention. The need for QMV is felt, but the issues remain too sensitive for a full-blown pooling of sovereignty.

How do we explain these institutional changes? We recall that Moravcsik contrasted three possible explanations: Federalist ideology, centralized technocratic management or more credible commitment.

It seems that "more credible commitment" survives the studies in this volume as a very plausible explanation. Due to migratory and other pressures, the Member States concluded that improved cooperation in matters of JHA was needed; thus, the introduction of a "communitarized" Area of Freedom, Security and Justice.

In the case of the first pillar, the IGC discussions took place because of the enlargement perspective, but when it was concluded that re-weighting of votes in the Council and the final decision about the composition of the Commission could be postponed, this created two other Amsterdam "left-overs" for the IGC 2000.

It is probably fair to say that federalist ideology did not play a major role (see also Sverdrup 2000). There is still federalist rhetoric in some of the original EC Member States, especially the Benelux countries, Germany and Italy. However, according to some of the contributions to this volume, we also note a certain movement towards pragmatism in some of these countries, especially the Netherlands. On the other hand, there seems to be a certain strengthening and consolidation of pro-integration attitudes in some Member States, such as Finland, Greece and Portugal. All in all the Community method seems to have wide support, even if the Member States remain unwilling to extend it to CFSP. Nothing came of efforts to weaken the Commission during the Amsterdam process.

It is a little unclear how the European Parliament fits into the Moravcsik scheme. But we should note that the role of the EP was once again increased in this treaty reform. The increased use of co-decision made the EP an institutional winner in the process. Co-decision was chosen for eight new treaty provisions, including employment and new provisions relating to social policy and public health. Co-decision was introduced in fifteen existing treaty provisions (replacing consultation or co-operation procedures, and in one case the assent procedure). Co-decision now includes transport policy, aspects of social policy and environment as well as development cooperation. With all the talk about legitimacy – and democratic deficit – these increases in the use of the co-decision procedure come as no surprise to us.

Evaluating Amsterdam

Did it all matter? This, of course, calls for political judgements which depend on value premises. On such value premises scholars can and do of course disagree.

The Amsterdam debate was cast in terms of efficiency and legitimacy. If we accept the premises that the EU needs to increase both efficiency and legitimacy, especially because of future enlargements, what can we say about Amsterdam?

Institutions and procedures are of course important for efficiency. QMV should be more efficient than unanimity. Community institutions like the Commission should also be able to advance decisions by exercising supranational leadership. At least that is a point advanced by some authors (e.g. Lindberg & Scheingold 1970; Sandholtz & Zysman 1989; Laursen 1990). The most important decision from the point of view of efficiency may therefore turn out to be the transfer of asylum, immigration and external border control from the Third Pillar to the First Pillar. This area has even been compared with the role played by the internal market during the latter part of the 1980s (Wallace & Den Boer 2000).

The concept of legitimacy may be more difficult. Andreas Maurer mentions, with references to some German literature, that there is both input and output legitimacy. Input legitimacy has to do with the way decisions are made. Moves towards greater transparency can be seen as a factor which may potentially increase the EU's legitimacy. For some, the increased role of the European Parliament in the form of more co-decision may also lead to more legitimate policies and decisions. To the extent that the weights of votes in the Council became an issue during the Amsterdam (and later Nice), process it had to do with a feeling in the big Member States that their relative underrepresentation was getting too big a problem in connection with successive enlargements.

The question of output legitimacy has to do with what is actually decided. Do EU policies and decisions meet the needs of EU citizens and groups, including farmers, industrialists, workers, consumers, etc.? The efforts in Amsterdam to strengthen the EU's role in respect to employment, environment, consumer protection and other policy areas can be seen as a potential contribution to the EU's output legitimacy.

Looking back on Amsterdam, the verdict will have to be mixed. From the perspectives of increasing efficiency and legitimacy there was some "progress." But the mood in 1997 was not for giant steps. But small steps, as long as they are in the "right" direction, can also be important.

So, Amsterdam was not a huge reform, but it was yet another reform on a trajectory that, with ups and downs, has taken the EC/EU towards both a deepening and a widening of integration in Europe since the process started in 1950. It was yet another step in what can be seen as a federalizing process (Laursen 1992b; Sbragia 1992), even if the word has bad press and a lot of actors are busy distancing themselves from it. During the post-Amsterdam period, prior to the agreement on the next treaty reform in Nice in December 2000, Europe started a new "constitutional" debate, with especially the German political leaders not hesitating to talk about a federal core in the future European institutional system (Laursen 2001b). On the agenda of the next IGC in 2004 are topics such as the incorporation of fundamental rights in a "constitutional" treaty and the working out of a catalogue of competences. These kinds of issues are well known to students of federal systems.

No one can make safe predictions about the future of European integration. But, if explaining the past helps us predict the future, we should not rule out further deepening and widening of the process. But too much widening can still produce system overload and thus contribute to disintegration (Wessels 1996). Finding the right balance between deepening and widening remains the challenge for our political leaders.

Bibliography

Den Boer, Monica & William Wallace (2000). "Justice and Home Affairs: Integration through Incrementalism?" pp. 493-519, in Helen Wallace & William Wallace (eds.), *Policy-Making in the European Union*, Fourth Edition, Oxford: Oxford University Press.

Dehousse, Franklin (1999). *Amsterdam: The Making of a Treaty*, London: Kogan Page.

Duff, Andrew (ed.) (1997). *The Treaty of Amsterdam: Text and Commentary,* London: Federal Trust.

Isaksen, Susanne, Ole Toft & Jens Bødtcher-Hansen (1998). *En traktat bliver til. Amsterdam-traktaten: Forberedelse, forhandling og resultat*, Copenhagen: Schultz Information.

Laursen, Finn (1990). "Explaining the EC's New Momentum," pp. 33-52, in Finn Laursen (ed.), *EFTA and the EC: Implications of 1992*, Maastricht: European Institute of Public Administration.

Laursen, Finn (1992a). "Explaining the Intergovernmental Conference on Political Union," pp. 229-248, in Finn Laursen & Sophie Vanhoonacker (eds.), *The Intergovernmental Con-ference on Political Union,* Maastricht: EIPA.

Laursen, Finn (1992b). "The Maastricht Treaty: A Critical Evaluation," pp. 249-265, in ibid.

Laursen, Finn (1994). "The Not-So-Permissive Consensus: Thoughts of the Maastricht Treaty and the Future of European Integration," pp. 295-317, in Finn Laursen & Sophie Vanhoonacker (eds.), *The Ratification of the Maastricht Treaty: Issues, Debates and Future Implications*, Dordrecht: Nijhoff.

Laursen, Finn (1997). "The Lessons of Maastricht," pp. 59-73, in Geoffrey Edwards & Alfred Pijpers (eds.), *The Politics of European Treaty Reform: The 1996 Intergovernmental Con-ference and Beyond*, London: Pinter.

Laursen, Finn (2001a). "EU Enlargement: Interests, Issues and the Need for Institutional Reform," pp. 206-228, in Svein S. Andersen & Kjell A. Eliassen (eds.), *Making Policy in Europe*, 2nd edition, London: SAGE.

Laursen, Finn (2001b). *Guide til Nice-traktaten: Baggrund, kommentarer og perspektiver*, Copenhagen: The Danish European Movement.

Laursen, Finn & Sophie Vanhoonacker (eds.) (1992). *The Intergovernmental Conference on Political Union: Institutional Reforms, New Policies and International Identity of the European Community*, Maastricht: European Institute of Public Administration.

Laursen, Finn & Sophie Vanhoonacker (eds.) (1994). *The Ratification of the Maastricht Treaty: Issues, Debates and Future Implications*, Dordrecht: Martinus Nijhoff.

Lindberg, Leon N. & Stuart A. Scheingold (1970). *Europe's Would-Be Polity: Patterns of Change in the European Community*, Englewood Cliffs, NJ: Prentice-Hall, Inc.

McDonagh, Bobby (1998). *Original Sin in a Brave New World: An Account of the Negotiation of the treaty of Amsterdam*, Dublin: Institute of European Affairs.

Moravcsik, Andrew (1991). "Negotiating the Single European Act: National Interests and Conventional Statecraft in the European Community," *International Organization*, Vol. 45, No. 1 (Winter), pp. 19-56.

Moravcsik, Andrew (1993). "Preferences and Power in the European Community: A Liberal Intergovernmentalist Approach," *Journal of Common Market Studies*, Vol. 31, No. 4 (December), pp. 473-524.

Moravcsik, Andrew (1998a). *The Choice for Europe,* Ithaca, NY: Cornell University Press.

Moravcsik, Andrew (1998b). "Europe's Integration at Century's End," pp. 1-58, in Andrew Moravcsik (ed.), *Centralization or Fragmentation? Europe Facing the Challenges of Deep-ening, Diversity and Democracy*, New York: Council on Foreign Relations.

Moravcsik, Andrew & Kalypso Nicolaïdis (1999). "Explaining the Treaty of Amsterdam: Interests, Influence, Institutions," *Journal of Common Market Studies*, Vol. 37, No. 1 (March), pp. 59-85.

Pedersen, Thomas (1998). *Germany, France and the Integration of Europe: A Realist Inter-pretation*, London: Pinter.

Peterson, John (1995). "Decision-making in the European Union: towards a framework for analysis," *Journal of European Public Policy*, Vol. 2, No. 1 (March), pp. 69-93.

Pierson, Paul (1996). "The Path to European Integration: A Historical Institutionalist Analysis," *Comparative Political Studies*, Vol. 29, No. 2, pp. 123-63.

Sandholtz, Wayne & John Zysman (1989). "1992: Recasting the European Bargain," *World Politics*, Vol. 41, No. 1, pp. 95-128.

Sbragia, Alberta (1992). "Thinking about the European Future: The Uses of Comparison," pp. 257-291, in Alberta M. Sbragia (ed.), *Euro-Politics: Institutions and Policymaking in the "New" European Community*, Washington: The Brookings Institution.

Sverdrup, Ulf (2000). "Precedents and Present Events in the European Union: An Institutional Perspective on Treaty Reform," pp. 241-265, in Karlheinz Neunreither & Antje Wiener (eds.), *European Integration after Amsterdam: Institutional Dynamics and Prospects for Democracy*, Oxford: Oxford University Press.

Wessels, Wolfgang (1996). "Evolution possibles de l'Union européenne. Scénarios et strate-gies pour sortir d'un cercle vicieux," *Politique Étrangère*, No. 1, pp. 139-150.

Wessels, Wolfgang (2001). "The Amsterdam Treaty in Theoretical Perspectives: Which Dynamics at Work?" pp. 70-84, in Jörg Monar & Wolfgang Wessels (eds.), *The European Union after the Treaty of Amsterdam*, London: Continuum.